Lecture Notes in Computer Science 3968

Commenced Publication in 1973
Founding and Former Series Editors:
Gerhard Goos, Juris Hartmanis, and Jan van Leeuwen

Editorial Board

Kenneth P. Fishkin   Bernt Schiele
Paddy Nixon   Aaron Quigley (Eds.)

Pervasive Computing

4th International Conference, PERVASIVE 2006
Dublin, Ireland, May 7-10, 2006
Proceedings

 Springer

Volume Editors

Kenneth P. Fishkin
Google, Inc.
Kirkland, WA 98033, USA
E-mail: fishkin@acm.org

Bernt Schiele
University of Technology
Computer Science Department
Darmstadt, Germany
E-mail: schiele@informatik.tu-darmstadt.de

Paddy Nixon
Aaron Quigley
University College Dublin, UCD
School of Computer Science and Informatics
Belfield, Dublin 4, Ireland
E-mail: {Paddy.Nixon,Aaron.Quigley}@ucd.ie

Library of Congress Control Number: 2006924368

CR Subject Classification (1998): C.2.4, C.3, C.5.3, D.4, H.3-5, K.4, K.6.5, J.7

LNCS Sublibrary: SL 3 – Information Systems and Application, incl. Internet/Web and HCI

ISSN   0302-9743
ISBN-10   3-540-33894-2 Springer Berlin Heidelberg New York
ISBN-13   978-3-540-33894-9 Springer Berlin Heidelberg New York

Springer is a part of Springer Science+Business Media

springer.com

© Springer-Verlag Berlin Heidelberg 2006
Printed in Germany

Typesetting: Camera-ready by author, data conversion by Scientific Publishing Services, Chennai, India
Printed on acid-free paper   SPIN: 11748625   06/3142   5 4 3 2 1 0

Preface

Welcome to the proceedings of the Fourth International Conference on Pervasive Computing. We are honored to serve as chairs in this conference series, founded in 2002, which has emerged as one of the most respected venues for publication of research in pervasive and ubiquitous computing.

This year's conference demonstrated the increasing breadth and depth of worldwide research on pervasive and ubiquitous computing, with a record number of submissions (178) from a record number of countries (26). From among these high quality submissions, the Technical Program Committee accepted 24 papers. These papers were chosen solely on quality, using a double-blind review process.

There was also a striking breadth of submissions. The submissions covered 29 topics, ranging from health care applications to embedded systems programming, from sensor networking to ethnography, from novel user interface techniques to power harvesting hardware. This year the most popular topics were programming environments, location-aware computing, and cell-phone interaction techniques.

Our first thanks goes to all the 541 authors who submitted full papers to this conference. Presenting research work in a paper requires a great deal of effort. We hope that these authors were rewarded with insightful reviews and an enjoyable conference program.

Any conference is only as strong as its reviewers and Program Committee. This is particularly true for this conference, which placed a very heavy load on its Program Committee. We were fortunate to have an outstanding and hardworking Program Committee: each Program Committee member was responsible for personally reading and reviewing at least 15 papers, and each paper discussed at the Program Committee meeting had been read by at least 3 Program Committee members.

To handle this breadth and depth, we were fortunate to have a talented reviewer pool with the multi-disciplinary expertise required. The 148 reviewers, from 57 different institutions, wrote over 1.5 million words of reviews – we thank them again for their selfless constructive criticisms.

In addition to the technical sessions, we were delighted to have two keynote speakers. David Tennehouse, CEO of A9.com, discussed "Proactive Computing" and Joe Marks, Research Director, MERL, presented "Pervasive Computing: Off the Beaten Path". Following the tradition of earlier Pervasive conferences, Pervasive 2006 also provided a number of other participation categories, including a doctoral colloquium, workshops on topics of special interest, a poster session for presentation of late-breaking results, and videos and demonstrations as interactive contributions.

Several organizations provided financial and logistical assistance, and we are grateful for their support. Special thanks go to the local organizers from several institutions in Ireland. We also thank Karen Dickey and Boston MERL for graciously hosting our Program Committee meeting.

Final thanks goes to all the authors who entrusted their work to Pervasive 2006 and everyone who attended the conference. None of this would have been possible, or worthwhile, if it were not for your research in pervasive computing. Your continued contribution and support of this conference is most gratifying.

March 2006   Ken Fishkin, Bernt Schiele
                                                Paddy Nixon, Aaron Quigley

Organization

Conference Committee

General Chair:	Paddy Nixon, UCD, Ireland
Conference Chair:	Aaron Quigley, UCD, Ireland
Program Co-chairs:	Ken Fishkin, Google Research, USA Bernt Schiele, TU Darmstadt, Germany
Late Breaking Results:	Tom Pfeifer, Waterford, Ireland Albrecht Schmidt, LMU Munich, Germany Woontack Woo, KJIST, S. Korea
Workshops:	Vinny Cahill, Trinity College Dublin, Ireland Thomas Strang, DLR and U Innsbruck, Austria
Videos:	Gavin Doherty, Trinity College Dublin, Ireland Frederic Vernier, U Paris-Sud, France
Demonstrations:	Kieran Delaney, Cork, Ireland Bill Yerazunis, MERL, USA
Doctoral Colloquium:	Matthew Chalmers, U of Glasgow, UK Joe Kiniry, UCD, Ireland
Volunteers:	Lorcan Coyle, UCD, Ireland Steve Neely, UCD, Ireland
Publicity:	Simon Dobson, UCD, Ireland Rene Mayrhofer, Lancaster U, UK
Webmaster:	Graeme Stevenson, UCD, Ireland

Program Committee

Gregory Abowd, Georgia Tech, USA
Michael Beigl, University of Karlsruhe, Germany
Matthew Chalmers, University of Glasgow, UK
Nigel Davies, Lancaster University, UK
Anind Dey, CMU, USA
Hans Gellersen, Lancaster University, UK
Ken Hinckley, Microsoft Research, USA
Hideki Koike, University of Electro-Communications, Japan
Antonio Krueger, University of Münster, Germany
John Krumm, Microsoft Research, USA
Anthony LaMarca, Intel Research, USA
Marc Langheinrich, ETH Zurich, Switzerland
Paul Lukowicz, UMIT, Austria
Chandra Narayanaswami, IBM Research, USA
Brian Noble, University of Michigan, USA
Donald J. Patterson, UC Irvine, USA
Dan Russell, Google Research, USA
Albrecht Schmidt, Ludwig-Maximilians-Universität München, Germany
Paris Smaragdis, Mitsubishi Electric Research Laboratories, USA
Thomas Strang, DLR, Germany and University of Innsbruck, Austria
Joshua Smith, Intel Research, USA
Mirjana Spasojevic, Yahoo, USA
Yoshito Tobe, Tokyo Denki University, Japan
Khai Truong, University of Toronto, Canada

Reviewers

Tim Adlam, University of Bath, UK
Fahd Al-Bin-Ali, University of Arizona, USA
Jakob Bardram, University of Aarhus, Denmark
Louise Barkhuus, University of Glasgow, UK
Sumit Basu, Microsoft Research, USA
Patrick Baudisch, Microsoft Research, USA
Christian Becker, Universität Stuttgart, Germany
James Begole, PARC, USA
Hrvoje Benko, Columbia University, USA
Alastair Beresford, University of Cambridge, UK
Aggelos Bletsas, Massachusetts Institute of Technology, USA
Gaetano Borriello, University of Washington, USA
Barry Brown, University of Glasgow, UK
Andreas Butz, University of Munich, Germany
Dipanjan Chakraborty, IBM Research, India
Han Chen, IBM Watson Research Center, USA

Keith Cheverst, Lancaster University, UK
Luca Chittaro, University of Udine, Italy
Tanzeem Choudhury, Intel Research Seattle, USA
Elizabeth Churchill, PARC, USA
Sunny Consolvo, Intel Research Seattle, USA
Vlad Coroama, ETH Zurich, Switzerland
Landon Cox, Duke University, USA
Andy Crabtree, University of Nottingham, UK
Paul Dietz, MERL, USA
Danyel Fisher, Microsoft Research, USA
George Fitzmaurice, Alias, Canada
Morten Fjeld, Chalmers University of Technology, Sweden
Rich Fletcher, Tagsense, USA
Christian Floerkemeier, ETH Zurich, Switzerland
James Fogarty, Carnegie Mellon University, USA
Adrian Friday, Lancaster University, UK
Kaori Fujinami, Waseda University, Japan
Krzysztof Gajos, University of Washington, USA
William Griswold, UC San Diego, USA
Jonna Hakkila, Nokia Group, Finland
Beverly Harrison, Intel Research Seattle, USA
Gillian Hayes, Georgia Institute of Technology, USA
Mike Hazas, Lancaster University, UK
Ernst Heinz, UMIT, Austria
Jeffrey Hightower, Intel Research Seattle, USA
Jason Hong, Carnegie Mellon University, USA
Eric Horvitz, Microsoft Research, USA
Stephen Intille, Massachusetts Institute of Technology, USA
Susumu Ishihara, Shizuoka University, Japan
Anthony Jameson, DFKI, Germany
Rui Jose, University of Minho, Portugal
Holger Junker, ETH Zurich, Switzerland
Karrie Karahalios, MIT, USA
Henry Kautz, University of Washington, USA
Yoshihiro Kawahara, University of Tokyo, Japan
Nicky Kern, TU Darmstadt, Germany
Tim Kindberg, Hewlett-Packard Laboratories, UK
Gerd Kortuem, Lancaster University, UK
Noboru Koshizuka, University of Tokyo, Japan
Gabriele Kotsis, Johannes Kepler University Linz, Austria
Albert Krohn, University of Karlsruhe, Germany
Yang Li, University of Washington, USA
Cristina Lopes, University of California, Irvine, USA
Natalia Marmasse, IBM Research, Israel
Thomas Martin, Virginia Tech, USA

Yasuo Tan, JAIST, Japan
Peter Tandler, Fraunhofer IPSI, Germany
Andreas Timm-Giel, University of Bremen, Germany
Quan Tran, Georgia Institute of Technology, USA
George Tzanetakis, University of Victoria, Canada
Theo Ungerer, University of Augsburg, Germany
Harald Vogt, ETH Zurich, Switzerland
Matthias Wagner, DoCoMo Communications Labs Europe, Germany
Jamie Ward, ETH Zurich, Switzerland
Rainer Wasinger, DFKI GmbH, Germany
Andy Wilson, Microsoft Research, USA
Daniel Wilson, Carnegie Mellon University, USA
Woontack Woo, GIST, Korea
Allison Woodruff, PARC, USA
Daqing Zhang, Institute for Infocomm Research, Singapore
DaQing Zhang, I2R, Singapore
Hui Zhang, Carnegie Mellon University, USA
Thomas Zimmerman, IBM Research, USA

Sponsors

Science Foundation Ireland (SFI)
Intel Ireland
Intel Research
University College Dublin (UCD)
Irish Software Engineering Research Centre (Lero)
Mitsubishi Electric Research Laboratories (MERL)
Ubisense, The Smart Space Company
Telecommunications Software & Systems Group (TSSG), Waterford Institute of
Technology (WIT)
Microsoft Research
Fáilte Ireland
Irish Computer Society
Adaptive Information Cluster (AIC)

Table of Contents

A Practical Approach to Recognizing Physical Activities

Jonathan Lester[1], Tanzeem Choudhury[2], and Gaetano Borriello[2,3]

[1] Department of Electrical Engineering, University of Washington, Seattle, WA 98195, USA
[2] Intel Research Seattle, Seattle, WA 98105, USA
[3] Department of Computer Science, University of Washington, Seattle, WA 98195, USA

Abstract. We are developing a personal activity recognition system that is practical, reliable, and can be incorporated into a variety of health-care related applications ranging from personal fitness to elder care. To make our system appealing and useful, we require it to have the following properties: (i) data only from a single body location needed, and it is not required to be from the same point for every user; (ii) should work out of the box across individuals, with personalization only enhancing its recognition abilities; and (iii) should be effective even with a cost-sensitive subset of the sensors and data features. In this paper, we present an approach to building a system that exhibits these properties and provide evidence based on data for 8 different activities collected from 12 different subjects. Our results indicate that the system has an accuracy rate of approximately 90% while meeting our requirements. We are now developing a fully embedded version of our system based on a cell-phone platform augmented with a Bluetooth-connected sensor board.

1 Introduction

The task of recognizing human activities from body worn sensors has received increasing attention in recent years. With a growing demand for activity recognition systems in the health care domain, especially in elder care support, long-term health/fitness monitoring, and assisting those with cognitive disorders [1, 2, 3]. For an automatic activity recognition system to be useable in these domains it is important for it to be practical as well as accurate.

Current methods for tracking activities in the healthcare field are time and resource consuming manual tasks, relying on either paid observer (i.e. a job coach who periodically monitors a cognitively disabled person performing their job or a nurse monitoring an elderly patient) or on self-reporting, namely, having patients complete an activity report at the end of the day. However, these methods have significant deficiencies in cost, accuracy, scope, coverage, and obtrusiveness. Paid observers like job coaches and nurses must typically split their time among several patients at different locations, or the patients must be clustered together. Self-reporting is often inaccurate and of limited usefulness due to patient forgetfulness and both unintentional and intentional misreporting, such as a patient reporting more fitness activities than they actually completed.

An automatic activity recognition system would not only help reduce the errors that arise from self-reporting and sparse observational sampling, but hopefully also improve the quality of care for patients as caregivers spend less of their time

K.P. Fishkin et al. (Eds.): PERVASIVE 2006, LNCS 3968, pp. 1 – 16, 2006.
© Springer-Verlag Berlin Heidelberg 2006

performing bookkeeping duties. In addition, unobtrusive monitoring enables people to go about their daily lives in an unimpeded manner while providing their caregivers with a more accurate assessment of their real life activities rather than a small sample. While the full extent to which patients would benefit from such a device is not currently known, an accurate automated system does have a clear benefit over existing methods such as surveys in providing a continuous activity log along with times and durations for a wide range of activities.

Moreover, if monitoring can be accomplished using a personal device that looks like any other common consumer device (rather than a device with many wires to all the limbs, for example) then there is less resistance to wearing it as it does not cause a social stigma that would identify a person's ailment to others. Acceptability is further enhanced by the embodiment in a personal device over which the user has complete control, and may choose to share (or choose not to share) their data with health care professionals or choose to not wear the device (or turn it off) for some occasions.

1.1 Related Work

A majority of the research using wearable sensors for activity recognition has so far focused on using a single sensor modality, typically accelerometers, placed in two or more (up to 12) locations on the body [4, 5, 16]. Placing sensors in multiple pre-defined locations or even a single, fixed, location every time can be quite cumbersome when one has to collect data on a daily and continuous basis. Work by [5] has showed that placing an accelerometer at only two locations (either the hip and wrist or thigh and wrist) did not affect activity recognition scores significantly (less than 5%) when compared to a system with five sensors; whereas the use of a single sensor reduced their average accuracy by 35%. In our recent work [7], we showed that we could compensate for the accuracy lost using a single sensing location by using a single sensing location with multiple sensor modalities (in this case 7 different sensor types).

This is a promising line of investigation as it is much more comfortable for the user to wear a single device at only one location. Moreover, because we only need a single sensing location these sensors could be incorporated into existing mobile platforms, such as cell phones or wristwatches. Integrating sensors into devices people already carry is likely to be more appealing to users and garner greater user acceptance as these consumer devices do not make them look "different". Greater user acceptance would hopefully also mean that users would be more inclined to wear the device more often and for a larger part of the day, allowing it to capture a greater range of activities than a device worn only sparingly.

1.2 Our Hypotheses

In this paper, we investigate several practical aspects of creating an automatic, personal activity recognition system. More specifically, there are three aspects we want to understand in more detail: location sensitivity, variations across users, and the required sensor modalities. Through our experiments, we seek to answer the following questions:

- Does it matter where on their person the user carries the device? If we have training examples that contain data from multiple body locations, will the recognition algorithm generalize such that we do not have to learn location specific models?
- How much variation is there across users? Does the device need to be customized to each individual for reliable accuracy or can it be trained more generally so that it works "out-of-the-box"?
- How many sensors are really needed to recognize a significant set of basic activities? Are 7 really necessary or can a cheaper, lower-power system be built from fewer sensors but still have similar recognition accuracy?

The remainder of the paper presents answers to these questions by providing evidence based on data collected from 12 different individuals performing 8 different activities over several days, carrying a collection of sensors worn in three different locations on the body. The activities include: sitting, standing, walking, walking up/down stairs, riding elevator up/down, and brushing teeth. These activities were selected because they correspond to basic and common human movements and will be useful for elder care and personal fitness applications. These physical tasks are also similar to the tasks previous activity recognition systems have attempted to recognize.

The three locations where volunteers wore the sensors correspond to locations where people already carry devices – (i) wrist (e.g., wristwatch), (ii) waist (e.g., cell phone or pager clip), and (iii) shoulder (e.g., cell phone pouch on a bag's strap). Data was collected from these three locations simultaneously by using a wired set of three sensor boards, one at each location. However, we currently have a wireless implementation that sends data from a single sensing unit via Bluetooth to any commodity Bluetooth device, like a cell phone. In the future, we expect that the sensors will be part of the cell phone itself and the challenge lies in implementing all of our classification algorithms on that platform. Wristwatch type platforms (e.g. Microsoft SPOT) are also becoming more capable but are likely to only provide a glanceable user interface rather than a capable computational resource in the short to medium-term future.

To accurately track various activities using a single wearable unit, we use the activity classification algorithm we developed in [7]. This algorithm employs an ensemble of very simple static classifiers to select the most useful features and then uses those features to recognize a set of basic human movements (walking, sitting, going down stairs, etc.). Each simple static classifier in the ensemble operates on a single feature, giving the system the flexibility to use a varying number of features. A second layer of hidden Markov models (HMMs) combines the outputs of the classifiers into an estimate of the most likely activity while providing temporal smoothing.

The results presented in this paper show that the classification algorithms are robust to the realistic variations that appear in the data. Furthermore, they are well behaved with respect to different locations, different people, and a smaller set of sensors. Of course, further testing across a larger population is still needed to fully understand the limits of this approach. This paper makes the case that the approach is worth investigating further and meets many of the practicality requirements of the real world.

In the following sections we will describe in more detail the multi-modal sensor platform we use, the machine learning algorithms for robustly inferring activities, and our experimental methodology and results. We will conclude with a summary of our contributions and directions for future work.

2   Experimental Methodology

To gather data simultaneously from a large set of sensors and to better understand the usefulness of different sensor modalities in inferring human activities, we used the multi-modal sensor board (MSB) (shown in Figure 1). The MSB is designed to attach to the Intel Mote (iMote, also shown in Figure 1), a Bluetooth/32-bit ARM7-based wireless sensor node, but can also communicate with handheld, desktop computers, and cell phones via Bluetooth, serial, or USB. The iMote allows us to send the MSB's sensing data to any commodity Bluetooth device like a cell phone[1] and our other interfaces allow us to connect to handhelds, laptops, and other devices.

Fig. 1. The multimodal sensor board *(top)*, a Bluetooth iMote *(lower left)*, and USB rechargeable battery board *(lower right)*. A Nokia 6600 series phone with a sensor board on the back for scale *(middle image)*. The data collection setup consisted of three sensor boards and a small Vaio Notebook for data logging (inside the pouch on the user's right side).

The sensor board contains seven different sensors and is capable of sampling them all simultaneously at fairly high sampling rates (see Table 1). The sensors on the MSB were selected for their general usefulness (as evidenced by related work in activity inference [6, 8, 9]), small footprint, low power consumption, and availability of digital interfaces. Sensors such as those used on the MSB are already being incorporated into cell phones and similarly equipped wristwatches are likely to follow soon [10].

The MSB is small and light enough (9.2g) to wear comfortably for long periods of time. Even with an iMote (5.7g) and battery board (9.6g including a 200mAh battery), it only weighs 25g. While streaming data to the cell phone the iMote+MSB can run

---

[1] Due to the limitations of Bluetooth and cell phones we can only transmit audio data at 8kHz all other sensor can function at their normal rates.

Table 1. Sensors on the multi-sensor board and the sampling rates used for the experiments in this paper

Manufacturer	Part No.	Description	Sampling Rate
Panasonic	WM-61A	Electric Microphone	~ 16000 Hz
Osram	SFH-3410	Visible Light Phototransistor	~ 550 Hz
STMicro	LIS3L02DS	3-Axis Digital Accelerometer	~ 550 Hz
Honeywell	HMC6352	2-Axis Digital Compass	30 Hz
Intersema	MS5534AP	Digital Barometer / Temperature	15 Hz
TAOS	TSL2550	Digital Ambient (IR and Visible+IR) Light	5 Hz
Sensirion	SHT15	Digtial Humidity / Temperature	2 Hz

for approximately 4 hours on a single 200mAh Li-Polymer battery. The battery board can also use one or two 1800mAh Li-Ion batteries allowing for a runtime of more than 36 hours (72 hours with two batteries).

2.1   Data Collection from Multiple MSBs

As the basis for this and future research we have created a multi-person dataset from 12 individuals (two female ten male) containing 8 basic physical activities. Eight of the volunteers in the study were graduate students in their mid 20s and four were older in their 30s. Two-thirds of the data was collected from a computer science building and the other third was collected in an office building. Volunteers collected data wearing three MSBs: one on a shoulder strap, one on the side of their waist, and one on their right wrist. The volunteers were given a sequence of activities to perform, like sitting on a couch for a few minutes before walking upstairs to brush their teeth. A miniature notebook (a Sony Vaio U750 measuring 16.8cm×6.6cm ×2.5cm and weighing 560g) was carried in a small pouch to collect the data from the three MSBs and an observer annotated the data in real time by using a simple annotation program on an iPAQ. The observer also provided cues to the volunteers about the sequence of activities they should be performing. Figure 1 shows a picture of the setup the volunteers wore while collecting their data. And Table 2 lists the activities collected from this experiment along with the amount of data recorded and the number of times a label appeared in our annotations.

Table 2. Data collected for the second data set, consisting of 8 basic activities collected by 12 volunteers. A total of 12 hours of data was recorded, 7 hours of which was labeled as corresponding to any one of our set of 8 activities.

		Duration		Instances
	Sitting		56 mins	22
	Standing	1 hr	13 mins	135
	Walking	1 hr	43 mins	215
Labeled Activities	Walking up stairs		19 mins	34
	Walking down stairs		14 mins	30
	Riding elevator down		16 mins	42
	Riding elevator up		15 mins	39
	Brushing Teeth		20 mins	12

Average Duration:		40 mins
Total Labeled Data:	6 hrs	55 mins

Table 3. An example subset of some of the features calculated with descriptions. Note, that a single feature type, such as frequency bands, can have multiple outputs in the feature vector, i.e. one feature per band.

Feature	Description
Cepstral Coefficients	The FFT of the log FFT spectrum, that is FFT(log(FFT(x)))
Log FFT Frequency Bands	Real valued FFT values grouped into logarithmic bands
Spectral Entropy	Measure of the distribution of frequency components
Energy	The sum of the real FFT spectrum
Mean	The average value of the time series
Variance	The square of the standard deviation
Linear FFT Frequency Bands	Real valued FFT values grouped into linear bands from 100Hz - 2kHz
Correlation Coeffs	Correlation between axis pair, XY, XZ, YZ
Integration	Integration of the timer series over a window

2.2   Ground Truth

For our data set, ground truth was obtained while the experiments were being carried out. An observer carrying an iPaq marked the start and end points of the activities as the volunteer performed them by clicking on a set of labels on the iPaq. This on-line ground truth collection eliminated the need for the volunteers to annotate their data after they had completed the experiment and helped to reduce timing and annotation errors. If the user was performing an activity that wasn't in our list of activity classes the segment was automatically marked as null/do-not care and was ignored when we trained and tested our classifiers.

2.3   Classification Features

As we collect approximately 18,000 samples of data per second we do not use the samples directly for classification, but instead we compute features to summarize the data, reduce the dimensionality of our data, and to bring out important details from the data. We currently compute a total of 651 features; which include linear and log-scale FFT frequency coefficients, cepstral coefficients, spectral entropy, band-pass filter coefficients, correlations, integrals, means, and variances. Table 3 gives a description of the various types of features used – note that a feature type (e.g., linear FFT bands is based on FFT magnitudes grouped in linear bands) can account for multiple features in the feature vector. Also, we do not compute every type of feature for every sensor, e.g., an FFT is only computed for the audio, accelerometer and high frequency light sensors, as it does not make sense to compute it for the other sensors. We combine the features from various sensors to produce a 651 dimensional feature vector at 4Hz. Due to the fact that we have sensors with different sampling rates; there are multiple instances of some features within each 0.25 second window. Furthermore, when calculating some features (e.g., the integral features) we incorporate a longer time window that varies from several seconds to as long as a minute. For those features, we restrict the time windows to only use data from the past, so that our system functions without a time lag.

It might be intuitively clear which features our algorithms should use for some activities (e.g., FFT coefficients of acceleration will likely capture walking gait); while for others it might not be as clear (e.g., for riding an elevator). Using all 651 features might solve the feature selection problem; however, the disadvantage of this approach is that we might not have enough data to reliably learn all the parameters of our models and some features might even confuse the classification algorithms rather than help discriminate between the various activity classes. In section 3, we briefly describe the algorithm developed in [7] that automatically picks the most useful features and learns classifiers from these.

2.3 Classification

To train our classifiers we needed to separate our data into training and testing sections. To do this we divided up our data set into a 4-folded test and training set by segments, or continuous blocks of data that were classified as the same activity. We randomly selected segments from our available data and placed them into our folds until we had about the same number of segments in each fold. We then train our static and HMM classifiers using 3 of the 4 folds and then test on the remaining fold (75% for training and 25% for testing), performing this same training/testing operation four times, using the different combinations of our 4 folds. Note that all the feature extraction, classification, and data analysis presented in this paper was performed offline.

The static decision stumps classifiers we learned were all trained using our 651 features computed at 4Hz. To prevent our classifier from over fitting to properties of the locations where our data was collected, we did not allow it to use the temperature or humidity sensors. These sensors should have very little to do with the actual recognition of the physical activities and could potentially cause the classifier to report results that were good classifications; but, were influenced by the locations where the data was collected and not the actual activities. For example, if you collected a lot of data of a person sitting in a cool air conditioned room and then standing in a warm heated room. During the training phase the classifier would see temperature as being the most telling feature in determining whether you were sitting or standing, even though temperature clearly has no direct bearing on whether one is sitting or standing. Of course, in the real data similar effects may be more subtle, nonetheless to avoid any obvious problems temperature and humidity are not used as sensor inputs for our activity recognition.

The HMM classifier was trained using the margin output of the decision stumps classifier (calculated at 4Hz) and uses a 15 second sliding classification window with a 5 second overlap between windows (a 10 second window advancement).

3 Learning Activity Models

The two principal approaches used for classification in machine learning are: (i) generative techniques that model the underlying distributions of the data classes and (ii) discriminative techniques that only focus on learning the class boundaries [11]. Both of these approaches have been used extensively in the vision and wearable-sensing communities for recognizing various human behavior and activities. In [7], we developed a hybrid approach that combines the two techniques and demonstrated it to be quite effective. We only provide a brief summary of the techniques here, readers are referred to [7] for more details.

First, a modified version of AdaBoost proposed by [12], was used to automatically select the best features and rank them based on their classification performance. Given the maximum number of features the activity recognition system can use, the system automatically chooses the most discriminative sub-set of features and uses them to learn an ensemble of discriminative static classifiers for the activities that need to be recognized. As the features are selected incrementally based on their usefulness, desirable classifier performance was achieved while using less than 10% of the possible features (i.e., the top 50 features). Including additional features beyond the top 50 had very little impact on the classification performance. On average using classifiers with 600 features improves training error by less than 1% compared to classifiers with 50 features.

Second, the class probabilities estimated from the static classifiers are used as inputs into hidden Markov models (HMMs). The discriminative classifiers are tuned to make different activities more distinguishable from each other, while the HMM layer on top of the static classification stage ensures temporal smoothness and allows for continuous tracking of the activities. Using HMMs to recognize activities in continuous time chunks has the following advantages: (i) the classification output will incorporate history information to smooth out much of the sporadic errors that occur during the static classification step and (ii) we can learn how people transition between activities and thereby more about people's composite activity routines.

4 Location Sensitivity

In [7], we colleted a large data set of about 30 hours[2] of data from two volunteers wearing a MSB on their shoulder performing various activities. From this data set, features and classifiers were developed that could robustly detect 10 activities with greater than 90% accuracy: sitting, standing, walking, jogging, walking up/down stairs, riding a bicycle, driving a car, and riding an elevator up/down. This larger dataset served to verify that the algorithms would work on a variety of data using a single multi-modal sensor placement trained with a large amount of data. In this paper we build on this result. It should be noted that even though the results in this paper are slightly lower than those in [7], we would expect that with more training data from each individual we would approach the results in [7].

Previous methods have shown that by using sensors placed on different parts of the body one can classify activities fairly well. However, the problem with multiple sensor placements is of course that they can be quite obtrusive; but, similarly a single sensor placement can also be obtrusive (although to a lesser extent) if the user is required to carry it in the same location all of the time. Ideally, we would like the classification algorithms to work accurately with data from different locations on the body. This would allow the user to carry the device in a location that is the most convenient for a given context. For example, although a majority of men do not object to wearing devices on their waist belts, it is not always practical to do so; and women often do not wear a belt.

To determine the role sensor placement in recognition accuracy, we trained four sets of classifiers using data from the three locations (i) trained using data from all three locations, (ii) trained using data from the shoulder, (iii) trained with data from the waist, and (iv) trained with data from the wrist.

---

[2] We collected approximately 30 hours of data; however, due to memory limitations we could only train our classifiers using approximately 12 hours of this dataset.

Note that the first classifier (using data from all three locations) does not combine all the locations together and require the user to simultaneously wear three sensors. Instead it treats each location as a separate input; so that when a user wears a single sensing device, they may wear this device at any of the three locations and use this classifier to classify that data. Table 4, shows the confusion matrix for this more location-independent first classifier and Table 5 lists the overall precision and recall[3] for each of our four classifiers (note that since the HMM uses the output of the static classifier as input, it is the final classification and the static classifier is only an intermediate stage – we show both to highlight the effect of the combining the two methods).

As we can see from Tables 4 and 5 the more generic classifier trained on data from all three locations does quite well over all. The classifiers trained for specific locations achieve slightly higher overall precision and recall scores. As mentioned in section 3, the algorithm uses the training data to select the most discriminative subset of features. So the first classifier (which uses training data from all three locations) succeeds in finding features that are common to the data from all three locations and builds classifiers that work reliably on data from all three locations.

These results show that it is possible to train a generalized classifier that can recognize our 8 activities when worn in any of the three locations and that if we train for a specific location we can achieve slightly higher classification results. In addition it is also possible for us to train several classifiers (i.e., a generic one and more location-specific ones) and determine the most appropriate classifier to use at runtime. There are some existing techniques that have shown promise in determining where a device is being carried on the body [6] and using the output from these techniques we could select location specific classifiers to boost our accuracy when the device is carried in a well-characterized location.

While the locations here do not represent all the possible locations where one could carry the sensing device they do cover the most common ones where people carry existing devices. It is also unlikely that subtle variations in the actual locations will change the classification significantly. Intuitively, there should be much larger differences between the waist and the wrist than there would be between the waist and a pocket. When we take our location specific classifiers and test them on data from another location (for example when classifiers are trained on the shoulder and tested on data from the waist), we suffer a 20% reduction in precision/recall. And when trained on data from the shoulder and waist and tested on data from the wrist there is about a 10-15% reduction in precision/recall.

---

[3] Overall precision and recall are calculating by normalizing the confusion matrix so that each labeled class has the same number of examples (i.e. all rows sum to 1).
  Precision is defined as the proportion of the data labeled as activity N that actually was from data labeled as activity N in the ground truth:
        True Positive / (True Positive + False Positive)
  While recall is defined as the proportion of the data originally labeled as activity N that was correctly classified as activity N:
        True Positive / (True Positive + False Negative)
  Overall accuracy is defined as:
        True Positive + True Negative / Total Number of Examples
        Where the True Negative and False Positive counts are normalized by dividing by the (number of classes − 1)

Table 4. Confusion matrix for the static and HMM classifier trained using a single stream of sensor data from all three locations on the body

Static Classifier Confusion Matrix		Recognized Activity							
		Sitting	Standing	Walking	Walking up stairs	Walking down stairs	Riding elevator down	Riding elevator up	Brushing Teeth
Labeled Activities	Sitting	19245	17941	501	82	39	30	34	267
	Standing	6118	37602	3154	245	87	520	331	747
	Walking	998	7280	57658	1965	1907	771	666	1004
	Walking up stairs	1	297	1481	11277	35	23	188	39
	Walking down stairs	7	139	1422	59	7959	294	1	28
	Riding elevator down	68	2326	328	9	451	8023	214	11
	Riding elevator up	24	1936	332	267	4	332	7817	31
	Brushing Teeth	231	5252	1052	65	50	20	21	7859

Static+HMM Classifier Confusion Matrix		Recognized Activity							
		Sitting	Standing	Walking	Walking up stairs	Walking down stairs	Riding elevator down	Riding elevator up	Brushing Teeth
Labeled Activities	Sitting	28526	9173	404	0	0	0	0	36
	Standing	14308	26956	2791	261	204	2106	1241	937
	Walking	2933	4719	57278	2195	2770	941	766	647
	Walking up stairs	0	71	467	12632	10	29	132	0
	Walking down stairs	20	110	728	42	8821	188	0	0
	Riding elevator down	0	189	156	0	936	9992	157	0
	Riding elevator up	0	194	221	648	0	295	9385	0
	Brushing Teeth	252	1523	399	0	0	0	65	12311

Table 5. Overall precision/recall for the static and HMM classifiers trained/tested on all locations *(top row)* and a single location *(bottom rows)*. The classifier trained on all three locations does not combine all three sensing positions to perform its classification; rather it is a generalized classifier, using a single sensor placement, which works at all three locations. The overall accuracies for all cases were approximately 90%.

	Static Classifier		HMM Classifier	
	Overall Precision	Overall Recall	Overall Precision	Overall Recall
Trained on Location 1,2,3 *(all locations)* Tested on Location 1,2,3 *(all locations)*	79.18%	71.14%	82.07%	81.55%
Trained on Location 1 *(shoulder)* Tested on Location 1 *(shoulder)*	79.37%	71.26%	83.84%	82.64%
Trained on Location 2 *(waist)* Tested on Location 2 *(waist)*	81.83%	77.05%	85.87%	84.85%
Trained on Location 3 *(wrist)* Tested on Location 3 *(wrist)*	81.01%	68.66%	87.18%	87.05%
Single Location Average:	80.74%	72.32%	85.63%	84.85%

5 Variation Across Users

An important practical issue with any device based on statistical inference is whether it can be useful immediately to the end user or whether it has to go through a training period. Clearly most users will want any device to work immediately upon purchase. If it gets better over time, that is a plus, but it must perform reasonably out of the box. Ideally, we would want to collect a lot of training data from a large diverse group of individuals to train a generic classifier, and then apply this classifier to classify a new individual's data without having to collect any new training data or retrain the classifier.

To test how well our classifiers could handle the variations that exist across different users we created several combinations of the 12 individuals' data on which to train. These combinations were created by randomly selecting N individuals' data for training, where we varied N = 1 (training data from one individual) to N = 12 (training data from all of our 12 test subjects). For each combination we performed four folded cross validation where we used 75% of our data to train with and 25% to test. The data used for this experiment uses data from the shoulder location only, so we would expect similar results to those we saw in row two of Table 5.

We measured the performance of our classifiers under two test conditions: (i) in the first case we tested on data from all 12 individuals but trained on data from [1, ... ,N] individuals (ii) in the second case we tested on data from individuals who had not been in the training set, i.e. if we trained on individuals [1,...,N] we would test on data from individuals [N+1, ... , 12].

The objective of the first test case was to determine if training on an increasingly larger subset would improve recognition accuracy. We would expect that each additional individual we add to our training data would improve our recognition accuracy. The objective of the second test case is to ensure that any improvement in recognition accuracy comes solely from the classifier being more "generalized" and not because data from an increased fraction of individuals is used during training as in the first test case.

Figure 2 shows the overall precision and recall for the first test where we add in more and more people into the training set while always testing on all the test data from

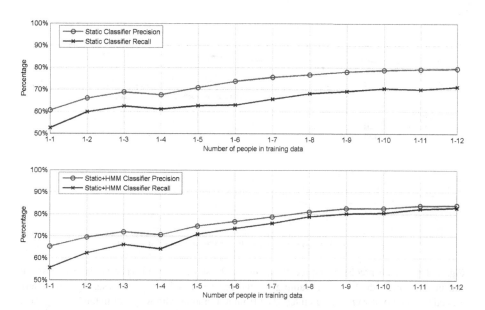

Fig. 2. The overall precision and recall graphs for the static and static+HMM classifier. As we add in more individuals to our training set the precision and recall increase. The classifiers trained at each point were tested on test data from all 12 volunteers. E.g. data point [1-10] corresponds to training on 10 individuals and testing on the test data from all 12. The overall accuracy for this test case reaches approximately 95%.

the 12 individuals. As we can see from Figure 2 the overall precision and recall increase as we add more and more individuals into our training set, eventually reaching about 84%. The [1-12] data point Figure 2 also corresponds very closely to the results we saw in row two of Table 5 as they both represent very similar tests.

Figure 3 shows the overall precision and recall for the second test case where we again add more and more people into the training set but test using test data from people who were not in our training set. And again we see an increase in overall precision and recall, eventually reaching around 80%. As figures 2 and 3 indicate, the more people we include in our training data the better our classifiers perform and that they are able to operate on a diverse set of individuals. In practice, manufacturers of an activity recognition system should be able to pre-train a set of classifiers so the device will work well for most users right away.

As you may have noticed in [7] we achieved ~90% accuracy for our classifiers and here we're only obtaining about 80-84%. The reason for this difference is that the data used in [7] contains a large amount of data (~30 hours) from two individuals over a period of six weeks, whereas the data set here contains a total of 6 hours of data from 12 individuals. We would expect that with more data these results would approach those in [7].

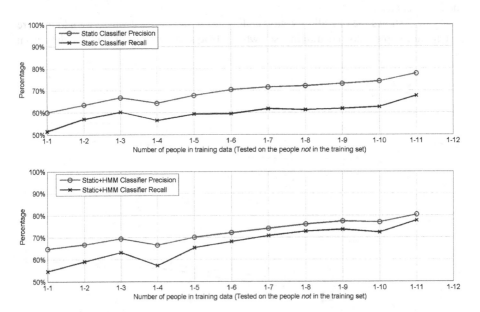

Fig. 3. The overall precision and recall graphs for the static and static+HMM classifier. As we add in more individuals to our training set the precision and recall increase. The classifiers trained at each point were tested on test data from individuals who were not in the training data. E.g. data point [1-10] corresponds to training on 10 individuals and testing on the test data from the other two (of our 12) individuals who were not in the training dataset. The overall accuracy reaches approximately 87%.

6 Sensors Necessary for Classification

While all the sensors on the MSB platform are interesting and provide some useful information, we do not necessarily need all the sensors to perform accurate classification. In fact, the results presented here and in [7] discarded information from the temperature and humidity sensors, simply because the classifiers would often incorrectly choose them as being indicators of when a physical activity was performed (sitting and standing shouldn't be strongly correlated to the temperature).

In addition, sensors such as light can often be obscured because the device is being carried in a pocket or obscured by clothing. By examining the features selected by the classifier we can see that the three most important sensors for the classifiers are the accelerometer, audio, and barometric pressure sensors. These correspond to basic motion of the user (acceleration) and the changing properties of their environment (sound profile and altitude). Table 6 contains the results of re-training the four classifiers (as described in section 4) using only the accelerometer. As we can see, using a single modality, even though it is the most important one, causes a rather large decline in precision/recall for all the different locations. However, if we include accelerometer, audio, and barometric pressure sensors (as in Table 7) we obtain precision/recall numbers that are very comparable to the results using more of the sensors shown in Figures 2 and 3.

Reducing the number of sensors not only makes the system less susceptible to environmental changes but also enables us to make more practical devices. As we add more and more sensors to our device the system complexity, computational/power requirements, and cost increase. Reducing the number of sensors also reduces the size requirements for incorporating these sensors into a mobile platform, such as a cell phone. Many cell phone manufacturers are starting to add accelerometers to their devices to enable games, interfaces, and basic pedometer functionality, and they already contain an audio sensor. The barometric pressure sensor is typically found in GPS units, where it is used to adjust altitude calculations. However, given the usefulness in localization tasks, they could easily become a common feature of cell phones.

Table 6. Summary statistics for the static and HMM classifiers trained/tested on all locations *(top row)* and a single location *(bottom rows)*. The classifiers trained here only used a single sensor, the accelerometer. The overall accuracies here were all approximately 65%.

	Static Classifier		HMM Classifier	
	Overall Precision	Overall Recall	Overall Precision	Overall Recall
Trained on Location 1,2,3 *(all locations)* Tested on Location 1,2,3 *(all locations)*	40.49%	32.63%	41.15%	38.96%
Trained on Location 1 *(shoulder)* Tested on Location 1 *(shoulder)*	41.12%	36.15%	45.78%	42.46%
Trained on Location 2 *(waist)* Tested on Location 2 *(waist)*	39.61%	33.67%	38.67%	38.30%
Trained on Location 3 *(wrist)* Tested on Location 3 *(wrist)*	39.58%	34.41%	45.81%	45.10%
Single Location Average:	40.10%	34.74%	43.42%	41.95%

Table 7. Summary statistics for the static and HMM classifiers trained/tested on all locations *(top row)* and a single location *(bottom rows)*. The classifiers trained here use three sensors: the accelerometer, audio, and barometric pressure. The overall accuracies here were all approximately 90%.

	Static Classifier		HMM Classifier	
	Overall Precision	Overall Recall	Overall Precision	Overall Recall
Trained on Location 1,2,3 *(all locations)* Tested on Location 1,2,3 *(all locations)*	75.53%	68.45%	81.97%	81.38%
Trained on Location 1 *(shoulder)* Tested on Location 1 *(shoulder)*	76.26%	69.48%	83.52%	82.49%
Trained on Location 2 *(waist)* Tested on Location 2 *(waist)*	78.29%	73.88%	85.50%	84.60%
Trained on Location 3 *(wrist)* Tested on Location 3 *(wrist)*	76.44%	56.33%	85.94%	85.76%
Single Location Average:	77.00%	66.56%	84.99%	84.28%

7   Conclusion

The work presented here further demonstrates that accurate recognition of a range of physical activities can be achieved by a light-weight and unobtrusive multi-modal wearable device. The experimental results presented in sections 4, 5, and 6 demonstrate the promise of this approach. Specifically, our contribution is that the activity recognition approach is accurate even under practical considerations such as where the device is worn, that it can be pre-trained by other individuals, and that we can use fewer and cheaper sensors. We have answered the three questions we posed in the beginning:

(i)   Our single-board activity recognition system generalizes well and we do not need to learn location-specific activity models. As long as we have training data from the different locations we expect to carry the sensing device, the algorithm can pick the right subset of discriminatory features that will work for all those locations (as in [6]).

(ii)   For our dataset, we do not require customization to specific individuals and the system works reliably when tested on data from a novel individual. However, we need activities collected over longer periods of time and over people of differing ages, body types, and in more varied settings to get a better understanding of how broadly this result will hold.

(iii) Although our sensor-board was equipped with seven different modalities, we found that three modalities in particular yielded the most discriminative information for our activities: the audio, barometric pressure, and accelerometer sensors. These three modalities provide complementary information about the environment and the wearer. The audio captures the sounds produced during the various activities, whereas the accelerometers data is sensitive to the movement of the body, and the barometric pressure provides important movement queues, such as detecting the activity of riding in an elevator or moving up and down stairs.

Some important things to keep in mind about the results are that the 12 individuals in this paper were all young healthy individuals, so while the results can generalize to wider populations they do not necessarily cover all possible groups, like elderly patients or people with health impairments. In addition, of the 12 hours of data we collected, only 7 hours of it was labeled as belonging to our 8 classes; which raises an interesting problem of how to handle activities that don't quite fall into our labeled activities. We could add an 'other' class to handle these activities; however, to handle ambiguities associated with compound activities like 'sitting' and 'driving a car' we would need to create a hierarchy of activities. This would allow us to recognize an activity like 'driving a car' as both 'driving a car' and 'sitting' and more gracefully handle unrecognized activities.

The fact that a small, single sensor device can classify activities reliably opens the doors to several lines of further exploration. We are currently working on an embedded version of our system that incorporates the sensing and the feature processing on a cell-phone like platform. Embedding the device in such widespread consumer electronics would make such computing truly ubiquitous. We believe the most promising potential applications of such activity recognition systems are in health-care and health maintenance. For many years, a successful and often life-saving device for the elderly has been a simple "help button" that can be used to initiate a phone call after a disabling fall. For health maintenance and personal fitness, commercially available devices like pedometers are also gaining popularity, but they often lack the subtlety or range of activities performed throughout the day. For example, a pedometer displays the same step count for steps taken on a flat surface as it does for steps walked up the stairs, despite the fact that walking upstairs takes much more effort. The fact that such a simple devices can still be beneficial gives a glimpse of the potentially vast health-care benefits that wireless, unobtrusive activity-recognizing sensors could bring about.

Acknowledgements

The authors would like to thank our 12 volunteers for their time and effort in helping us collect out data. We would also like to thank Yaw Anokwa and Adrienne Andrew for administering the data collection efforts.

References

1. Morris, M., Lundell, J., Dishman, E., Needham, B.: New Perspectives on Ubiquitous Computing from Ethnographic Study of Elders with Cognitive Decline. In: Proc. Ubicomp (2003)
2. Lawton, M. P.: Aging and Performance of Home Tasks. Human Factors (1990)
3. Consolvo, S., Roessler, P., Shelton, B., LaMarcha, A., Schilit, B., Bly, S.: Technology for Care Networks of Elders. In: Proc. IEEE Pervasive Computing Mobile and Ubiquitous Systems: Successful Aging (2004)
4. Kern, N., Schiele, B., Schmidt, A.: Multi-Sensor Activity Context Detection for Wearable Computing. In: Proc. Proc. EUSAI, LNCS (2003) 220-232
5. Bao, L., Intille, S.: Activity Recognition from User-Annotated Acceleration Data. In: Proc. Proc. Pervasive (2004) 1-17

6. Lukowicz, P., Junker, H., Stäger, M., T. von, B., Tröster, G.: WearNET: A Distributed Multi-sensor System for Context Aware Wearables. In: Proceedings of the 4th international conference on Ubiquitous Computing. Springer-Verlag (2002) 361-370
7. Choudhury, T., Lester, J., Kern, N., Borriello, G., Hannaford, B.. A Hybrid Discriminative/Generative Approach for Modeling Human Activities. 19th International Joint Conference on Artificial Intelligence (IJCAI), Edinburgh, Scotland. (2005)
8. Park, S., Locher, I., Savvides, A., Srivastava, M., Chen, A., Muntz, R., Yuen, S.: Design of a Wearable Sensor Badge for Smart Kindergarten. In: Proc. 6th International Symposium on Wearable Computers (2002) 231-238
9. Mainwaring, A., Polastre, J., Szewczyk, R., Culler, D., Anderson, J.: Wireless Sensor Networks for Habitat Monitoring. In: Proc. Proceedings of the 1st ACM International Workshop on Wireless Sensor Networks and Applications (2002) 88-97
10. Smailagic, A., Currens, B., Maurer, U., Rowe, A.: eWatch.[Online]. Available: http://flat-earth.ece.cmu.edu/~eWatch/
11. Rubinstein, Y. D., Hastie, T.: Discriminative vs. informative learning. In: Proc. In the Proceedings of Knowledge Discovery and Data Mining (1997) 49-53
12. Viola, P., Jones, M.: Rapid Object Detection using a Boosted Cascade of Simple Features. In: Proc. Computer Vision and Pattern Recognition (2001)
13. Schapire, R. E., Freund, Y., Bartlett, P., Lee, W. S.: Boosting the margin: a new explanation for the effectiveness of voting methods. In: Proc. (1997) 322--330
14. Oliver, N., Horvitz, E.: Selective Perception Policies for Limiting Computation in Multimodal Systems: A Comparative Analysis. In: Proc. Proceedings of Int. Conf. on Multimodal Interfaces (2003)
15. Jaakkola, T., Haussler: Exploiting generative models in discriminative classifiers. In: Proc. In Advances in Neural Information Processing Systems (1999)
16. Zhang, F., Pi-Sunyer, F. X., Boozer, C. N.: Improving Energy Expenditure Estimation for Physical Activity. In: Medicine and Science in Sports and Exercise (2004) 883-889.

Building Reliable Activity Models Using Hierarchical Shrinkage and Mined Ontology

Emmanuel Munguia Tapia[1], Tanzeem Choudhury[2], and Matthai Philipose[2]

[1] Massachusetts Institute of Technology,
1 Cambridge Center 4FL,
Cambridge, MA, 02142, USA
emunguia@mit.edu
[2]Intel Research Seattle,
1100 NE 45th St., 6th Floor,
Seattle, WA, 98105, USA
{tanzeem.choudhury, matthai.philipose}@intel.com

Abstract. Activity inference based on object use has received considerable recent attention. Such inference requires statistical models that map activities to the objects used in performing them. Proposed techniques for constructing these models (hand definition, learning from data, and web extraction) all share the problem of *model incompleteness*: it is difficult to either manually or automatically identify all the possible objects that may be used to perform an activity, or to accurately calculate the probability with which they will be used. In this paper, we show how to use auxiliary information, called an ontology, about the functional similarities between objects to mitigate the problem of model incompleteness. We show how to extract a large, relevant ontology automatically from WordNet, an online lexical reference system for the English language. We adapt a statistical smoothing technique, called shrinkage, to apply this similarity information to counter the incompleteness of our models. Our results highlight two advantages of performing shrinkage. First, overall activity recognition accuracy improves by 15.11% by including the ontology to re-estimate the parameters of models that are automatically mined from the web. Shrinkage can therefore serve as a technique for making web-mined activity models more attractive. Second, smoothing yields an increased recognition accuracy when objects not present in the incomplete models are used while performing an activity. When we replace 100% of the objects with other objects that are functionally similar, we get an accuracy drop of only 33% when using shrinkage as opposed to 91.66% (equivalent to random guessing) without shrinkage. If training data is available, shrinkage further improves classification accuracy.

1 Introduction

Automated reasoning about human activity is central to a variety of pervasive computing usage models and applications. Usage models include activity-aware actuation, proactive reminding, automated activities-of-daily-living (ADL) monitoring and prompting, embedded health assessment, computer supported coordinated care giving, and task monitoring and prompting in the workplace. Specific applications that have been proposed include the automated control of HVAC and home entertainment

K.P. Fishkin et al. (Eds.): PERVASIVE 2006, LNCS 3968, pp. 17–32, 2006.
© Springer-Verlag Berlin Heidelberg 2006

systems based on current user activity, automated filling of medical forms about activities of elderly users, delivery of information about care recipients' behavior via shared scheduling tools, and the semi-automated evaluation of student performances of standard medical procedures. For these applications to be practical, the underlying activity recognition module often needs to detect a wide variety of activities (people may routinely perform dozens to hundreds of relevant activities a day, for instance) performed in many different ways, under many different environmental conditions; the particular aspects of the activity that are of interest (e.g. user motion, task progress, object usage or space usage) also vary widely across applications. Such robust recognition across a variety of activities and their variations has proved to be difficult to engineer.

A central challenge underlying activity recognition is that of bridging the gap between conventional sensors and informative high-level features such as objects used, body motion and words spoken. The most common approach is to use a few (typically one per room or user) very rich sensors such as cameras and microphones which can record very large quantities of data about the user and their environment. Although in principle the data captured by these sensors should be as useful as that captured by the key human senses of sight and hearing, in practice the task of extracting features from rich low-level representations such as images has proved to be challenging in unstructured environments. A popular alternate approach is to use specialized sensors (of the order of one per user) such as accelerometers and location beacons to get precise information about a particular small set of features related to the user, such as limb-movement and user location. The simplicity, however, comes at a price: by ignoring the environment of the user, these sensors limit the number of activities they can discriminate between. The inability to distinguish between opening a dishwasher and opening a washing machine can be a deciding factor in discriminating between the corresponding activities.

Recent years have seen the emergence of a third approach to sensing that may be termed *dense* sensing. Exploiting advances in miniaturization and wireless communication, this approach attaches sensors directly to many objects of interest. The sensors are either battery-free wireless stickers called Radio Frequency Identification (RFID) tags[1-3] or small wireless sensor nodes powered by batteries[4, 5]. The sensors transmit to ambient readers the usage of the objects they are attached to by detecting either motion or hand-proximity to the object. Further, since each sensor has a unique identifier, information about the object that does not change (such as its color, weight or even ownership), which would conventionally have to be discerned by sensors, can be associated in a directly machine readable way with the object. The reliable sensing of detailed object use enabled by dense sensing has a few advantages. First, for very many day-to-day activities, the objects used serve as a good indicator as to which activity is being performed. Second, the objects used remain fairly invariant across different ways of performing these activities. Third, since the sensors detect the features quite well regardless of most environmental conditions, activity recognition can be robust to changes in these conditions. Finally, objects used can serve as a powerful cue as to other aspects of interest: if a hammer or a knife is known to be in use, the space of possible user motions is highly constrained.

Systems based on dense sensors model activities in terms of the sequence of objects used, typically using generative Bayesian representations such as Hidden

Markov Models (HMM's)[6-8] or Naïve Bayesian models[9]. Models for individual activities in these representations are generated in one of three ways. The simplest, and least scalable, approach is to construct the model by hand: an application designer can simply list the objects expected to be used in an activity of interest, along with the probability of use. A conventional alternative is to learn the model by performing the activity in a variety of exemplary ways, labeling traces of objects used during the performances with the corresponding activities, and using supervised machine learning techniques to learn the corresponding model. A final approach is to note that the model is essentially a probabilistic translation between the activity name and the names of objects used, and to mine large text corpora such as the web to obtain these translations. The approaches are not mutually exclusive. For instance, both hand-made and web-mined models can be used as priors which are further customized using observed data.

All three approaches to constructing models suffer from what may be termed the *model incompleteness* problem: the models they produce have objects that are either missing or that have inappropriate probabilities. Incomplete models can, of course, result in faulty inference. Humans who hand-write models typically do not have the patience (and often the judgment) to list all objects that may be used in an activity, especially when alternate or obscure objects need to be considered: the model for "making tea" may mention neither "coffee cup" nor "honey". Further, the probability of use ascribed to unfamiliar objects may be quite skewed. Similarly, given the inconvenience of generating labeled examples of all (or most) possible ways to execute an activity, it is likely that uncommon objects will be missing or under-represented. Finally, when models are mined from the web, the vagaries of the web may result in certain objects (e.g. "cup") being ascribed vastly higher probabilities than others (e.g. "teacup").

The use of objects as the underlying features being modeled suggests a simple approach to countering incompleteness. Intuitively, we can exploit common sense information on which objects are functionally similar. If the model ascribes very different probabilities to two very similar objects, we can "smooth" these probabilities into more similar values. As a degenerate case, if the model omits an object while incorporating very similar ones, we can postulate that the omitted object is likely to be observed in the model. We show below how to realize this idea in a completely unsupervised way and provide evidence that the idea is quite effective. Earlier work [7, 10] has used manually extracted hierarchy to incorporate the notion of object similarity into activity models. In this paper, we show how to extract relevant information on the functional similarity of objects automatically from WordNet, an online lexical reference system for the English language. The similarity information is represented in a hierarchical form known as an ontology. Given the similarity measure provided by the ontology, we formalize the above intuitive notion of smoothing by adapting from statistics a technique called *shrinkage*. Shrinkage is a well established technique for estimating parameters in the presence of limited or missing training data and has been successfully used in classifying text documents [11, 12], in modeling the behavior of web site users [13], and in service-oriented context-aware middleware applications [14]. We use a mixture of real-world data and synthetic data to evaluate our system. Our results show that our techniques have three benefits. First, mined models that are smoothed recognize activities with significantly higher accuracy than those that are not. Second, models that are learned from data can make do with significantly less training data when smoothing is applied versus when it is not. Third, when faced with test data that contains objects not seen in training data, but that are similar to those in the model, smoothing yields substantially better recognition rates.

This paper begins by describing the procedure for automatically extracting the ontology of objects from WordNet in Section 2. Then, Section 3 covers the algorithm used for performing shrinkage over the ontology of objects. Section 4 shows the results of running simulated experiments over a large ontology of objects, and Section 5 of experiments ran over real sensor data. Finally, Section 6 summarizes the main results and conclusions drawn from this work.

2   Automatic Ontology Extraction from WordNet

WordNet [15] is a hierarchically organized lexical system motivated by current psycholinguistic theories of human lexical memory. WordNet resembles a thesaurus more than a dictionary since it organizes lexical information in terms of word meanings (or senses), rather than word forms. In WordNet, nouns, verbs, adjectives and adverbs are organized into synonym sets called synsets, each representing one underlying lexical concept. For example the noun *couch* in WordNet has three senses or word meanings, and the synset corresponding to the first sense {*couch#1*} defined as '*an upholstered seat for more than one person*' is {*sofa, couch, lounge*}. The sense number in WordNet indicates the frequency of use, where 1 corresponds to the most commonly used.

The real power and value of WordNet relies on the way different semantic relations link the synonym sets (or word senses). Currently, WordNet comprises the following kinds of semantic relations between word meanings: (1) hypernyms, (2) hyponyms, (3) meronyms, and (4) holonyms. Two of these semantic relations are especially important for their usefulness in extracting a semantic hierarchy or an ontology of objects: hyponyms, and hypernyms. Hypernyms are *is-a* relationships were the meaning of a word is a superset of another. For example, {*cooking utensil#1*} is a superset or hypernym of {*pan#1*}. On the contrary, hyponyms are *inverse-is-a* relationships were the meaning of a word is a subset of the meaning of another. Figure 1 shows examples of the hypernyms tree for three everyday objects.

Hypernyms of coffeepot	Hypernyms of eyeliner	Hypernyms of cheese
0:coffeepot	0:eyeliner	0:cheese
1:pot	1:makeup	1:dairy_product
2:cooking_utensil	2:cosmetic	2:foodstuff
3:kitchen_utensil	3:toiletry	3:food
4:utensil	4:instrumentality	4:substance
5:implement	5:artifact	5:entity
6:instrumentality	6:object	1:food
7:artifact	7:entity	2:solid
8:object	6:whole	3:substance
9:entity	7:object	4:entity
1:food	8:entity	
2:solid		
8:whole		
9:object		
10:entity		

Fig. 1. Hypernyms tree for three objects: Coffeepot, eyeliner, and cheese

WordNet organizes nouns into a set of 25 semantic primes or unique beginners of separate hierarchies. Five of these unique beginners are particularly important because they encompass all possible natural and man made objects {*non-living things, objects*}, and living organisms commonly used in meal preparation {*living thing, organism*}. These five semantic primes are: {*natural object*}, {*artifact*}, {*substance*}, {*food*}, and {*plant, flora*}. All these unique beginners are hyponyms or subsets of the more abstract concept {*entity*}.

Since all the physical objects of interest found in everyday environments are subsets or hyponyms of {*entity*}, a tree-like ontology of objects can be automatically extracted. This follows from the lexical tree (free of circular loops) design imposed over the nouns by the creators of WordNet.

As of September 2005, WordNet 2.1 contains approximately 117,097 noun word forms organized into approximately 81,426 word meanings (synsets) that make WordNet a unique and rich semantic database for recovering complete ontology of objects automatically.

2.2   Ontology Extraction Algorithm

The generation of the ontology or hierarchy of objects can be divided in two steps (1) the generation of the ontology skeleton, and (2) the expansion of the ontology. In order to generate the ontology skeleton, an initial list of objects of interest is required. In the context of our work, this initial list of objects is the list of all objects that appear in the mined activity models (or activity recipes) plus all the objects (RFIDs object labels) found in the sensor traces. The ontology skeleton generation algorithm proceeds as follows: (i) since everyday tangible objects correspond to nouns in natural language, we proceed to search the objects or words of interest in the noun files of WordNet, and (ii) once the noun has been found, we proceed to automatically select the sense of the word by looping through all the senses of the word until finding the first sense that is a hypernym or subset of {*entity*}. As discussed in the previous section, the node {*entity*} includes as subsets all possible natural and man made objects and living organisms commonly used in meal preparation. This guarantees that the selected sense will be the most commonly used sense that is also a physical object.

After the appropriate word sense has been selected, we proceed to find the hypernym tree or superset (parent) nodes of the selected sense of the word (or object). It is important to notice that some words may have multiple parents (who are descendants of *entity*) at the same level of the hypernyms tree, since in the previous step, we only ensured that the leaf node has a unique sense that is a descendant of the {*entity*} node. Figure 1 shows an example of such case for the object *cheese*. In situations when multiple parents are found at the same level in the hypernyms tree, only the first one is considered for being the most common, and the other ones are discarded. In practice we have found that this does not represent a major problem in extracting the hierarchy of objects. When the ontology is generated, a synonyms file is also generated so that any synonym of a word can be used while performing search operations in the ontology. For example, the synset for the object *cleaner* is {*cleansing_agent, cleanser, cleaner*}.

It is important to note that in order to perform shrinkage, the ontology must not have any loops. Our algorithm generates a tree structured ontology by only selecting

```
//GENERATION OF ONTOLOGY SKELETON
For i:=1 to objectList.length(){
    object = objectList(i);
    word = find_word_in_wordnet_noun_file(object);
    If(!empty(word)){
    For j:=1 to word.getSenses.length(){
        wordsense = word.getSense(j);
        If(wordsense.ishypernym("entity")) break;
    }
    hypernyms = getHypernymsTree(wordsense);
    ontologytree.addNodes(hypernyms);
}

//ONTOLOGY EXPANSION
For i:=1 to ontologytree.getLeafNodes().length(){
    Node = ontologytree.getLeafNode(i);
    ancestors = getHypernymsTree(Node, MaxParentLevel);
    For j:=1 to ancestors.length{
        Hyponyms = getHyponymsTree(ancestors(j), MaxChildLevel);
        ontologytree.addNodes(hyponyms);
    }
}
```

Fig. 2. Simplified version of the pseudo-code for automatically extracting the ontology of objects from WordNet

word senses that are hyponyms or subsets of the concept node *{entity}* and by ensuring each node has a unique parent. Thus, the node *{entity}* having the single sense: *'that which is perceived or known or inferred to have its own distinct existence (living or nonliving)'* correspond to the root node, and the highest abstraction level of the ontology. Also note that the leaf nodes or most specific terms in the ontology will correspond to the objects provided in the original list.

Once the ontology skeleton has been generated, it is useful to expand the ontology to accommodate for possible objects that might be used while performing an activity, but were not provided in the original list of objects. The expansion of the ontology consists of finding all the ancestor (parents) nodes for all the ontology leaf nodes up to a specified level *MaxParentLevel*. Then, we proceed to find all the hyponyms (children nodes) of those ancestor nodes up to a maximum depth level *MaxChildLevel*. By performing this procedure, we create sibling nodes for the leaf nodes of our original ontology that might appear in sensor traces in the future. Figure 2 shows a simplified version of the pseudo-code for extracting the ontology from WordNet.

3 Shrinkage over the Hierarchy of Objects

Shrinkage [16] is a well established statistical technique for improving parameters values estimated for a given model, when they can not be computed reliably from training data alone. By exploiting the similarity between nodes in a hierarchy, shrinkage estimates new parameter values for child nodes by linearly interpolating the values from the child node to the root node [11]. This represents a trade-off between specificity and reliability. The child node estimate is the most specific (low bias), but high variance (less reliable), and the root node is the most reliable (low variance), but general (high bias). By combining these estimates we can end up with a better and more reliable model.

In this work, we use shrinkage to create improved probability estimates of the leaf nodes of the ontology. Our assumption is that the leaf nodes in our ontology represent $P(o_i | a_j)$, the probability estimates of observing an object $o_i \in O$ during the performance of an activity $a \in A$, and that the hierarchy structure characterizes the functional similarity between objects. We denote $\tilde{P}(o_i | a_j)$ the new probability estimates of observing an object given an activity class, and we compute them as follows:

$$\tilde{P}(o_i | a_j) = \lambda^0 P^0(o_i | a_j) + ... + \lambda^k P^k(o_i | c_j) = \sum_{l=0}^{k} \lambda^l P^l(o_i | a_j) \tag{1}$$

$P^l(o_i | a_j)$ denotes the maximum likelihood (ML) probability estimate of a node at level l in the leaf ($l = 0$) to root ($l = k$) path. The interpolation coefficients (weights) are denoted $\{\lambda^1, \lambda^2, ... \lambda^k\}$ where $\sum_{l=0}^{k} \lambda^l = 1$. j denotes the activity class number, and i the object used. The ML probability estimates at each node are computed using the following equation:

$$P(o_i | a_j) = \frac{N(o_i, a)}{\sum_{s=1}^{|O|} N(o_s, a)} \tag{2}$$

where $N(o_i, a)$ is the number of times object o_i occurs in activity a, and $|O|$ denotes the set of all possible objects.

3.1   Determining Mixture Weights

The weights $\{\lambda^1, \lambda^2, ... \lambda^k\}$ used during shrinkage balances the influence of the nodes containing specific information but little training data, with those nodes containing more generic information but larger amounts of training data. The mixture of weights can be computed in one of the following ways: (1) uniformly where all the weights are equal (2) by applying the Expectation-Maximization algorithm (EM) as in [11] to find the weights that maximize the likelihood of the data or (3) using heuristics schemes that are a function of the rank (level) of the node in the ontology [13].

Since the goal of this work is to have a completely unsupervised approach to activity recognition where no sensor traces are available, we decided to estimate the weights using the following heuristics: (1) $\lambda^{level} = 1 / c^{level}$, and (2) $\lambda^{level} = e^{-c \cdot level}$, where c is a constant. These heuristics correspond to exponentially decaying functions that will assign large weights to nodes in the neighborhood of the leaf node, and low weights to the generic nodes found in the upper levels of the ontology.

The use of shrinkage over the ontology of objects in our unsupervised approach provides two main benefits: (1) it improves the probability estimates in the leaf nodes by taking advantage of the functional relationship of objects represented by the ontology. The effect of this improvement is a reduction in the number of training examples required to achieve a desired accuracy. If the number of training examples is kept constant, an increased accuracy will be observed by performing shrinkage; (2) shrinkage provides robustness when objects not present in the activity models are used while performing an activity. This effect is achieved by creating object observation probability estimates for those objects not present in the models by shrinking them

```
//ASSIGNING COUNTS TO LEAF NODE IN ONTOLOGY
ontology.setLeafNodeCounts(modelsObjectProbs*Factor);
//COMPUTE MAXIMUM LIKELIHOOD COUNTS FOR INTERNAL NODES
 internalNodes = ontology.getInternalNodes();
 For node:=1 to internalNodes.length(){
    inode = internalNodes(node);
    childrenLeaves = getChildrenLeafNodes(inode);
    inode.setMLCount(getCountsSum(childrenLeaves));
 }

//OBTAIN LEAF NODES SMOOTHED COUNTS BY SHRINKAGE
leaves = ontology.getLeafNodes();
For leaf:=1 to leaves.length(){
    lnode = leaves(leaf);
    nodes = getNodes2RootNode(lnode);
    For l:=0 to nodesPath.length()-1{
        lambda = ComputeHeuristics(level);
        If(level==0) //if leaf node
            SmoothCount = lambda*lnode.getCounts();
        Else{ //if internal node
            //substract node counts to reduce dependency
            counts = nodes(l).getCounts()-nodes(l-1).getCounts();
            smoothCount = smoothCount + lambda*counts;
        }
    }
    lnode.setCounts(smoothCounts);
}
```

Fig. 3. Pseudo-code for performing shrinkage over the ontology of objects

towards the objects present in the models using the ontology. This means that we are able to compute educated probability estimates for unseen objects when it was not previously possible.

The pseudo-code for performing shrinkage over the ontology of objects is shown in Figure 3, and consists on the following steps: (1) set the object observations (counts) for each leaf node by converting object probabilities to counts by multiplying them by a factor (2) compute the maximum likelihood counts for all the internal (non-leaf) nodes and (3) compute the smoothed count (shrinkage) for all the leaf nodes using equation 1. The counts are converted back to probabilities by normalizing them.

4   Experimental Results: Effect of Limited or Missing Data

In this experiment, we test the effectiveness of shrinkage over a large ontology of objects when we have limited training data or missing objects. We use Hidden Markov Models (HMMs) to parameterize the activities and assume that the objects used during an activity appear on the leaf nodes of the ontology. This assumption is plausible since usually one interacts with a specific instance of an object during an activity and not the broader abstract category. HMMs are a particular type of dynamic Bayesian Networks (DBNs) consisting of three parameters: (1) prior probabilities for each state π, (2) a state transition probability matrix T, and (3) the observation probabilities for each state B. The observation matrix represents the object observation probabilities for a given activity. Our experimental results show that shrinkage over the HMM object emission probabilities helps not only in reducing the number of training examples required to achieve a given accuracy, but also in providing robustness when objects not present in the activity models are used.

The ontology used in this experiment was generated from a list of 815 objects used in performing household activities. The list was obtained from objects appearing in the mined activity models, and sensor traces used in [1]. The ontology consists of 4188 nodes, 815 leaf nodes, and has a maximum depth of 14. The results presented in this section are based on simulated sensor traces (i.e. sampled from a true model that we create and not from actual observations from people). However, the ontology contains representative information about objects used during performing everyday activities. In the next section we will present results on using shrinkage in real sensor traces obtained from multiple individuals.

The experiment proceeds as follows: We first create a true activity model *model#0* represented by a 3 state HMM (3 subtasks in activity) with random prior, transition, and observation matrices. Next, we generate training data by sampling n number of sequences from *model#0*. We learn the model parameters from the training data in two ways: (i) by computing the maximum likelihood estimate of the prior (π), transition (T), and observation (B) matrices *(model#1)* and (ii) by re-estimating the observation matrix (B) using shrinkage *(model#2)* and $\lambda^l = e^{-3.5 \cdot l}$. We measure the closeness of the learned models *(model#1, model#2)* to the true model *model#0* by computing the Kullback-Leibler (KL) divergence between the observation matrices of *model#0*, and *model#1*, and *model#2*, respectively. The KL divergence $D(p \parallel q)$ is a measure of the similarity between two probability distributions p and q. The smaller the KL divergence, the more similar the compared distributions are. Finally, we compute the log-likelihood for models *#1* and *#2* on a test dataset sampled from the true model *#0*.

4.1 Reducing the Number of Training Examples by Shrinkage

The plots in Figure 4 were generated by iteratively increasing n, the number of training sequences, to learn parameters for *models #1* and *#2*. Figure 4a shows the log-likelihood computed over the test sequences (50 of length 13) using the learned models. The higher the log-likelihood, the better the model explains the test dataset, which in turn leads to higher accuracy. By inspection of Figure 4a, we note that 70 training examples are required by *model#1* to achieve the same log-likelihood that *model#2*

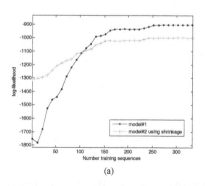
(a)

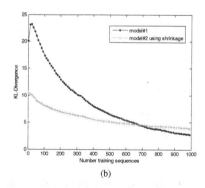
(b)

Fig. 4. (a) Log-likelihood, and (b) KL-Divergence between the baseline HMM model, learned model, and learned model using shrinkage over the ontology

achieves using a single training sequence. This is an important result because it shows that shrinkage can dramatically reduced the number of training examples required to achieve a specific log-likelihood. When n is greater than 100, the log-likelihood of *model#1* is higher than *model#2* for the specific test dataset. However, Figure 4b shows that the KL divergence is lower for *model#2* up to when $n = 675$. This signifies that shrinkage *model#2* is a closer match to the true *model#0* and will explain new test data more often, when trained on less than 675 example sequences. When we have enough representatives training examples the maximum likelihood (ML) solution will converge to the true model and shrinkage will not improve the parameter estimates anymore. Although, depending on the complexity of the model the number of training data required to have a reliable ML solution may be huge.

4.2 Robustness to Unseen Objects by Shrinkage

Often it might be the case that the initial model specifies the use of an object during an activity (e.g. use of *teacup* while *making tea*) which is later substituted by a functionally similar object (e.g. *mug*). If the activity model does not incorporate the similarity between a *teacup* and a *mug* then the model won't be able to correctly identify the activity *making tea* when a mug is used. In this experiment, we simulate the use of objects not present in the activity models by modifying the observations in the sequences sampled from *model#0* in the previous experiment. The modification consists of replacing $m\%$ of observations by observations of one of their randomly selected sibling nodes in the ontology.

This simulates the effect of having observed the sibling nodes (objects) in the sequences rather than the original leaf nodes. Once the replacements have been performed, we proceed to learn the transition, and observation matrices from the training sequences for models *#1* and *#2*. Figure 5 shows the resulting plots for the likelihood over the test sequences and the KL divergence when the percentage of replaced observations is modified from 0% to 100%. The fact that the likelihood is always greater, and the KL divergence smaller for *model#2* than for *model#1* corroborates the usefulness of shrinkage when unseen objects in our models are used.

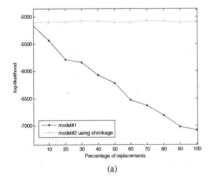 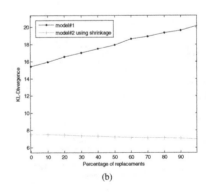

Fig. 5. (a) Log-likelihood, and (b) KL-Divergence between the baseline HMM model, learned model, and learned model using shrinkage over the ontology

5   Experimental Results: Performance on Data Collected from Multiple Individuals

In this section, we show the benefit of incorporating high level information into activity models using shrinkage over an ontology and measure the performance in real sensor traces. To get the initial models, we adopt the procedure followed in [6] to mine activity models from the web, compute object observation probabilities, and to perform inference using hidden Markov models. We extend the work done in [6] by showing how to improve the quality of the mined models without requiring additional training data and how to deal with novel unseen objects.

5.1   Data Collection

The sensor data used in this experiment has already been used in [1, 6], thus, allowing us to compare our results against this work. In this data collection, over one hundred everyday objects in a real home were instrumented with passive RFID tags. Objects tagged include silverware, cooking utensils, hygienic products, and furniture among others. Over a period of six weeks, nine non-researcher subjects spent a single 20-40 min session to collect data by carrying out 14 activities of their choice out of a provided list of 65 activities of daily living (ADLs) while wearing a glove equipped with an RFID reader. In practice, the subjects selected to perform only the 26 activities shown in Figure 7.

5.2   Mining Activity Models from the Web

Given a set of activities A, the authors of [4] mine the list of objects O used for each activity a, and their corresponding usage probabilities $P(o \in O \mid a \in A)$ from the web. The primary assumption underlying the mining process is that textual description of activities on the web reflects the performance of activities in everyday life. The mining process mainly consists in the following steps: (1) First, find instructional or "how to" web pages $\tilde{P}$ that contain a detailed description on how to perform each activity in A. (2) Second, extract the set of objects mentioned in each page by identifying nouns phrases (using a part of speech tagger), these nouns will be hypernyms or subsets of {object} or {substance} in WordNet. For each extracted object, the probability that the extraction denotes a physical object is computed as $w_{i,p} = p(object \mid noun)p(noun)$. In this equation, $p(noun)$ is the probability that the last word of the noun phrase is a noun as assigned by the POS tagger, and $p(object \mid noun)$ is computed by dividing number of occurrences of noun senses that are hypernyms of {object} or {substance} by the total number of occurrences of all noun senses. It is possible for a single object to have multiple weights by appearing several times in a single page, the final weight used is the average weight $\hat{w}_{i,p}$. Finally, the object probabilities $p(o_i \mid a)$ are computed as the fraction of pages in which the object o_i appeared weighted by its average extraction score on each page, i.e.:

$$p(o_i \mid a) = \frac{1}{|\tilde{P}|} \sum_p \hat{w}_{i,p}$$

The common sense information mined (activity recipes, and object observation probabilities) is compiled into an HMM for the task of activity inference. Each activity A is represented as one internal state in the HMM, and the object usage probabilities mined are used as the set of observations for each state $B_{ji} = P(o_i \mid a_j)$. For the transition matrix T, an expected activity duration $\gamma = 5$ is assumed, thus, all self-transition probabilities are set to $T_{jj} = 1 - 1/\gamma$. The remaining probability mass is uniformly distributed over the transitions to all other states. Finally, the prior state probabilities π are set to the uniform distribution over all activities. Using this representation, the classification task simply consists of inferring the most likely sequence of internal states by running the Viterbi algorithm over the sequences of observations. For more details about mining models from the web please see [4].

5.3 Improving Object Probabilities by Shrinkage

This experiment demonstrates the usefulness of shrinkage in improving the classification accuracy. First, we proceeded to generate the ontology from the list of 68 objects in the mined models and the sensor traces in [6]. Then, we construct two HMM models, *model#1* as described in Section 5.2, and *model#2* by performing shrinkage over the observation matrix of *model#1*. Finally, we search over the values of c to find the optimal value for the two heuristic functions (H1) $\lambda^{level} = e^{-c \cdot level}$, and (H2) $\lambda^{level} = 1/c^{level}$.

The plots in Figure 6a show the results for various values of c. In these plots, we observe that the maximum accuracy obtained is 48.35%, located at $c = [16,18]$ for heuristics (H2). This accuracy represents an improvement of 15.11% over the accuracy obtained using *model#1* (42%). This is an important result, because in [6] the authors also describe a procedure to learn from the sensor traces. Based on the segmentation obtained using mined models, new model parameters are learned using 126 sensor traces, which improve the accuracy of *model#1* by 19.2%. Here we have shown that just performing shrinkage and without using sensor data whatsoever, we achieve an improved accuracy of 15.11%. Consequently, we believe learning for sensor traces

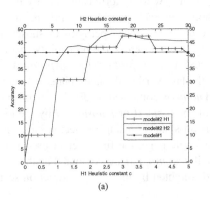
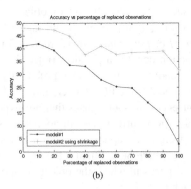

(a)   (b)

Fig. 6. (a) Accuracy results after performing shrinkage using different constant values c in the heuristics, (H1) $\lambda^{level} = e^{-c \cdot level}$, and (H2) $\lambda^{level} = 1/c^{level}$ and (b) Accuracy vs. percentage of replaced observations using *model#1* and *model#2*

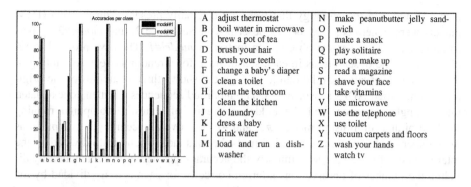

A	adjust thermostat	N	make peanutbutter jelly sandwich
B	boil water in microwave	O	
C	brew a pot of tea	P	make a snack
D	brush your hair	Q	play solitaire
E	brush your teeth	R	put on make up
F	change a baby's diaper	S	read a magazine
G	clean a toilet	T	shave your face
H	clean the bathroom	U	take vitamins
I	clean the kitchen	V	use microwave
J	do laundry	W	use the telephone
K	dress a baby	X	use toilet
L	drink water	Y	vacuum carpets and floors
M	load and run a dishwasher	Z	wash your hands
			watch tv

Fig. 7. List of the 26 ADLs activities collected and accuracy per activity results before and after performing shrinkage using the best heuristic and c value found

Table 1. Confusion matrix for the classification of the 26 ADLs using the shrinkage model (*model#2*). The letters are the same as the ones used in Figure 7. Rows indicate the hand-labeled class and columns indicate the predicted class label.

	a	b	c	d	e	f	g	h	i	j	k	l	m	n	o	p	q	r	s	t	u	v	w	x	y	z
a	8	0	0	0	0	0	0	0	0	0	0	0	1	0	0	0	0	0	0	0	0	0	0	0	0	0
b	0	5	0	0	0	0	3	2	0	0	0	0	0	0	0	0	0	0	0	0	0	0	0	0	0	0
c	1	8	1	0	0	0	0	4	0	0	0	0	0	0	0	0	0	0	0	0	0	0	0	0	0	0
d	0	0	0	8	0	8	0	0	0	1	0	2	0	0	2	0	0	0	0	0	0	2	0	0	0	0
e	12	0	0	0	16	2	3	12	0	0	0	0	4	0	0	0	4	0	0	0	4	5	0	0	0	0
f	1	0	0	0	0	40	0	0	0	0	8	0	0	0	0	0	0	0	0	0	1	0	0	0	0	0
g	2	0	0	0	0	0	0	0	0	0	0	0	7	0	0	0	0	0	0	0	0	0	0	0	0	0
h	0	0	0	0	0	0	15	0	0	0	0	0	0	0	0	0	0	0	0	0	0	0	0	0	0	0
i	0	0	0	0	0	0	0	9	4	0	0	0	0	0	0	0	0	0	0	3	0	0	0	0	2	0
j	0	0	0	0	0	0	8	0	0	1	0	0	14	0	0	0	0	0	0	0	0	6	0	0	0	0
k	0	0	0	0	0	0	3	0	0	0	19	0	0	0	0	0	0	0	0	0	1	0	0	0	0	0
l	0	3	0	0	0	0	13	3	0	0	1	0	0	0	0	0	0	0	0	0	0	0	0	0	0	0
m	0	0	0	0	0	0	0	0	0	0	0	16	0	0	0	0	0	0	0	0	0	0	0	0	0	0
n	1	0	0	0	0	0	1	0	4	0	0	2	11	31	2	0	0	0	0	8	0	0	0	2	0	0
o	0	0	0	0	0	0	3	4	8	0	0	0	0	3	2	0	0	0	0	0	0	0	0	0	0	0
p	0	0	0	0	0	0	0	0	0	0	0	0	0	0	0	4	0	0	0	0	0	0	0	0	0	0
q	0	0	0	7	0	0	1	0	0	0	0	0	0	0	0	0	0	0	0	0	2	0	0	0	0	0
r	0	0	0	0	0	0	2	0	0	0	0	0	0	0	0	0	0	0	0	0	0	0	0	0	0	0
s	1	0	0	0	0	0	0	1	0	0	0	0	0	0	0	0	0	0	20	0	0	0	0	1	0	
t	0	0	0	0	0	0	0	0	0	0	19	0	0	0	0	0	0	0	6	1	0	0	0	0	0	0
u	0	4	0	0	0	0	0	0	0	0	0	1	0	0	0	0	0	0	4	0	0	0	0	0	0	0
v	1	0	0	0	0	0	19	0	1	0	0	0	0	0	0	0	0	0	0	0	15	3	0	0	0	0
w	12	0	0	0	0	0	4	0	0	2	0	0	0	0	0	0	0	0	0	0	0	26	0	0	0	0
x	2	0	0	0	0	0	0	0	0	0	0	1	0	0	0	0	0	0	0	0	0	0	9	0	0	0
y	5	0	0	1	0	0	0	0	0	0	0	0	5	0	0	3	0	0	0	0	0	5	0	0	0	0
z	0	0	0	0	0	0	0	0	0	0	0	0	0	0	0	0	0	0	0	0	0	0	0	0	0	35

will further improve the accuracy. Figure 7 presents the accuracy per class results before and after performing shrinkage. Table 1 presents the confusion matrix as computed over the 65 segmented examples of the 26 ADLs.

5.4   Robustness to Unseen Observations by Shrinkage

In this section, we provide experimental results showing that shrinkage improves model robustness when objects not found in the activity models are present in the sensor traces.

The experiment is performed as follows: first, the ontology generated in the previous experiment was expanded to *MaxParentLevel*=1, and *MaxChildLevel* =1 as described in Section 2.1. This guarantees that sibling nodes will exist for each leaf node in the ontology tree. Secondly, the observation matrix is extended to include all the new leaf nodes in the ontology that were not originally present. Thirdly, two HMM models were generated, *model#1* as described in Section 5.2, and *model#2* by performing shrinkage over the observation matrix of *model#1*. Then we proceed to replace *m%* of the observations in each sensor trace for a randomly selected sibling of the original observation in the ontology. Figure 8 shows three examples of the original, and modified ADLs sensor traces. The modified sequences are then concatenated into a single sequence, and the hidden sequence of states is computed running the Viterbi algorithm using models *#1*, and *#2*. The overall accuracy is computed as the number of observations whose inferred label matched ground truth divided by the total number of observations. Similarly the accuracy per activity is calculated by dividing the number of observations inferred correctly for each activity divided by the total number of observations for each activity.

Activity	Original and Replaced Traces
Brushing teeth	Original: light toothpaste floss light Replaced: light tooth_powder floss lamp
Watching TV	Original: remote magazine remote magazine Replaced: remote newspaper remote newspaper
Watching TV BAD EXAMPLE	Original: television couch remote couch Replaced: television sofa water_cooler lawn_chair

Fig. 8. Example sequences where 50% of the observations were replaced

Figure 6b shows a plot comparing the overall accuracy versus the percentage of replaced observations for the two models. From this plot we can observe that (1) the accuracy of *model#2* is always greater than that of *model#1*, and (2) when 100% of the observations are replaced, the accuracy of *model#2* drops only 33% (from 48% to 32%) when the accuracy for *model#1* drops 91.66% (from 42% to 3.8%, which is equivalent to random guessing).

6 Conclusions

In this paper, we have presented a completely unsupervised approach to activity recognition that uses activity models automatically mined from the web in combination with shrinkage over an object ontology extracted from WordNet. The novelty of this approach relies on the fact that high level information is incorporated using shrinkage which provides the following benefits: (1) an improved accuracy by re-estimating the object observation probabilities of the mined models. We achieve an improvement of 15.11% in the overall accuracy in Section 5.3. (2) An approach to activity classification that requires no real sensor traces or training data, however, if training sequences are available, shrinkage can further improve accuracy. This is shown in Section 4.1 by simulation, where shrinkage reduces the number of training examples required to achieve a particular log-likelihood value from 70 to 1. Model parameters learned using shrinkage are closer to the true model as measured by the KL divergence between the true model, and the learned model. (3) And finally, the ability to reason about objects that are not present in the mined activity models but are used while performing an activity. This is achieved by estimating observation probability for theobjects not present in the models by shrinking them towards the objects found in the models using the ontology. This is exemplified by showing that when 100% of the observations in real sensor traces are replaced, accuracy drops 91.66% for a model not using shrinkage, and only 33%, when shrinkage is used.

References

[1] M. Perkowitz, M. Philipose, D. J. Patterson, and K. Fishkin, "Mining Models of Human Activities from the Web," in *Proceedings of The Thirteenth International World Wide Web Conference (WWW '04)*. New York, USA, 2004.

[2] K. Fishkin, M. Philipose, and A. Rea, "Hands-On RFID: Wireless Wearables for Detecting use of Objects," in *Proceedings of the Ninth Annual IEEE International Symposium on Wearable Computers (ISWC '05)*. Osaka, Japan.

[3] A. Feldman, E. Munguia-Tapia, S. Sadi, P. Maes, and C. Schmandt, "ReachMedia: On-the-move Interaction with Everyday Objects," in *Proceedings of the Ninth Annual IEEE International Simposium on Wereable Computers (ISWC '05)*. Osaka, Japan, 2005.

[4] E. Munguia-Tapia, S. S. Intille, L. Lopez, and K. Larson, "The Design of a Portable Kit of Wireless Sensors for Naturalistic Data Collection," in *Proceedings of the 4th International Conference on Pervasive Computing (PERVASIVE '06).*, Dublin, Ireland: Springer-Verlag, 2006., to appear

[5] E. Munguia-Tapia, N. Marmasse, S. S. Intille, and K. Larson, "MITes: Wireless Portable Sensors for Studying Behavior," in *Proceedings of Extended Abstracts Ubicomp 2004: Ubiquitous Computing*. Vienna, Austria, 2004.

[6] D. Wyatt, M. Philipose, and T. Choudhury, "Unsupervised Activity Recognition Using Automatically Mined Common Sense," in *The Twentieth National Conference on Artificial Intelligence (AAAI 05')*. Pittsburgh, Pennsylvania, 2005.

[7] E. Munguia-Tapia, T. Choudhury, M. Philipose, and D. Wyatt, *Using Automatically Mined Object Relationships and Common Sense for Unsupervised Activity Recognition*, Technical Report IRS-TR-05-014, Intel Research Seattle, Seattle, WA, May 2005.

[8] J. Lester, T. Choudhury, N. Kern, G. Borriello, and B. Hannaford, "A Hybrid Discriminative/Generative Approach for Modeling Human Activities," in *Proceedings of the International Joint Conference on Artificial Intelligence (IJCAI '05)*, 2005.

[9] E. Munguia-Tapia, S. S. Intille, and K. Larson, "Activity Recognition in the Home Setting Using Simple and Ubiquitous Sensors," in *Proceedings of PERVASIVE 2004*, vol. LNCS 300, B. Heidelberg, Ed.: Springer-Verlag, 2004, pp. 158-175.

[10] D. Patterson, D. Fox, H. Kautz, and M. Philipose, "Fine-Grained Activity Recognition by Aggregating Abstract Object Usage," in *Proceedings of The Ninth Annual IEEE International Symposium on Wearable Computers (ISWC '05)*. Osaka, Japan, 2005.

[11] A. McCallum, R. Rosenfeld, T. Mitchell, and A. Ng, "Improving Text Classification by Shrinkage in a Hierarchy of Classes," in *Proceedings of the 15th International Conference on Machine Learning (ICML-98)*, J. W. Shavlik, Ed.: Morgan Kaufmann Publishers, San Francisco, US, 1998, pp. 359-367.

[12] D. Freitag and A. K. McCallum, "Information Extraction with HMMs and Shrinkage," in *Proceedings of the AAAI '99 Workshop on Machine Learning for Information Extraction*, 1999.

[13] C. R. Anderson, P. Domingos, and D. Weld, "Relational Markov Models and their Application to Adaptive Web Navigation," in *In Proceedings of the 8th ACM SIGKDD International Conference on Knowledge Discovery and Data Mining*, 2002, pp. 143-152.

[14] T. Gu, H. K. Pung, and D. Q. Zhang, "A Service-oriented Middleware for Building Context-aware Services," *Journal of Network and Computer Applications (JNCA '05)*, vol. 28, pp. 1-18, 2005.

[15] G. A. Miller, R. Beckwith, C. Fellbaum, D. Gross, and K. Miller, *Introduction to WordNet: An On-line Lexical Database*, 1993.

[16] C. Stein, "Inadmissibility of the Usual Estimator for the Mean of a Multivariate Normal Distribution.," in *Proceedings of the Third Berkeley Symposium on Mathematical Statistics and Probability.*: University of California Press, 1955, pp. 197-206.

"Need to Know": Examining Information Need in Location Discourse

Derek Reilly[1], David Dearman[1], Vicki Ha[1],
Ian Smith[2], and Kori Inkpen[1]

[1] EDGE Lab, Dalhousie Faculty of Computer Science, 6050 University Avenue,
Halifax, Nova Scotia, B3H 1W5, Canada
{reilly, dearman, vha, inkpen}@cs.dal.ca
http://www.edgelab.ca/
[2] Intel Research Seattle, 1100 NE 45th Street, 6th Floor,
Seattle, Washington, 98105, USA
ian.e.smith@intel.com

Abstract. Location discourse involves the active or passive sharing of location information between individuals. Related applications include mobile friend locators, and location-dependent messaging. Privacy issues pertaining to location disclosure have been considered in research and relevant design guidelines are emerging, however what location information a user actually "needs to know" has received little systematic analysis to date. In this paper we present results from a questionnaire study and a diary study considering location information need. We provide a classification of location discourse and the factors which impact location need, showing that seemingly small changes in a scenario can yield drastically different location information needs. Finally, we summarize trends that are of interest to designers of location discourse applications.

1 Introduction

Location discourse, or sharing location-related information, is part of our daily lives. We often need to know where others are or will be in order to coordinate our own activities. People commonly establish one another's location during mobile phone conversations [19], in human centric terms [20]. Sharing location information often leads to an action (e.g. meeting up) or decision making (e.g. asking a favor), but can also simply provide contextual information that helps to frame a conversation. Increasingly, applications to support location discourse of one type or another are being designed and evaluated in research labs and in industry.

In this paper we define a *location discourse application* to be any application in which location plays a direct communicative role, whether it is purposeful or incidental in nature. This communication may be synchronous (live), or asynchronous (messaging), or even indirect (via an established protocol to automatically disclose location information). Such an application might facilitate organizing groups of people without requiring individual phone calls, give an indication of a contact's availability before one decides to call, or simply augment a phone conversation with

K.P. Fishkin et al. (Eds.): PERVASIVE 2006, LNCS 3968, pp. 33–49, 2006.
© Springer-Verlag Berlin Heidelberg 2006

photo sharing. There exists a significant body of work examining various styles of location discourse application, including [6, 8, 10, 17]. Privacy issues, in particular, have been a central concern for location-awareness applications, examining issues such as what a person is willing to disclose about their location [8].

Despite the large amount of research on location discourse applications, there has not been a systematic analysis of *information need* (i.e. "what a person actually needs to know about another's location"). Information need (or desire) is an obvious counterpart to information disclosure. As shown in previous work, a person's perception of another's information need is an important determinant of what they will disclose [2]. This phenomenon—assessing what information the receiver in a conversation needs—is known in conversation analytic terms as "recipient design" of an utterance [2]. Establishing information need can assist individuals when making decisions about disclosure, and can assist designers when developing applications that involve sharing of location information. If we understand location discourse from the perspectives of both the requester and discloser, we will be in a better position to develop applications that provide real value without imposing undesirable demands on either user. Consider the following mismatched example:

> *Eve's husband only needs to determine whether she has left work to pick him up. Providing him with a detailed map of her office building showing the exact room she is in is irrelevant and will make it difficult for him to quickly answer his question. In addition, if Eve's husband sees that she is no longer in her office building (when she is actually at a meeting elsewhere), he may assume that she has left to pick him up. In this instance, the system led to misinterpretation and a very frustrated spouse.*

As with other applications that provide location information (such as navigation systems and tour guides), information need in location discourse is influenced by such factors as someone's prior knowledge of an area, and their activity. The social element of location discourse adds further complexity, introducing expectations and interactions that can greatly influence need. For example, when checking on Alice's availability to discuss some current work, does Frank really care to know where she is precisely located in the city, or that she is grocery shopping? If Bob is upset because Alice is late for a dinner he prepared, does he want the same or a different kind of location detail than when he's lost during a family canoe trip?

Users may be willing to accept location information that is not explicitly tailored to their current situation, if that information is *appropriate* to the task they are trying to accomplish. One motivation for the work presented here is to understand when too little, too much, or inappropriate location information impedes our ability to accomplish tasks and support our relationships. In the study presented in this paper, we examine information need in location discourse using a questionnaire that presents contextual *moments* of location exchange. By varying aspects of context concerning *activity, location, relationship,* and *emotional state*, we begin to identify how various facets of these broad contextual dimensions can impact location information need.

1.1 Contribution

This paper presents a systematic, in-depth examination of what location information is needed (and preferred) by a requestor, depending on the context of the request. Context is examined in terms of *activity, location, relationship,* and *emotional state.*

The results of this study clearly demonstrate that these dimensions, while interrelated, can be used to help focus an analysis of location information need. Further, our results have yielded several key observations that can help reduce the complexity of this problem space and that are relevant to designers of location discourse applications. The results also show that the design issues presented by location information need are not always the same as those presented by location information disclosure.

2 Background

A variety of location-based services have been considered by the pervasive computing research community. These have been designed to support a range of needs, including facilitating interaction within our environment [1], our social communications [3, 8, 10], and our community [6], or benefiting people with disabilities [12]. These services provide contextual information that *context consumers* (i.e. friends, tourists, workers) use to assist decision making. Typically, the focus of context-aware computing has been on location because of its usefulness in a social context [6, 8]. Beyond physical location, activity at a location (e.g. in a meeting) has been shown to be useful for determining availability and providing awareness [8]. However, location is sensitive information [11]. Previous research [2, 7] has shown that there are numerous considerations that influence location disclosure, the most significant being the relationship [2, 11, 15] between the sender and receiver. Consolvo et al. [2] have shown that beyond relationship, location disclosure is additionally dependent on what information the user perceives as useful to the location requestor. Our research reveals a similar concern for the information discloser on the part of the location requestor.

The dominant methodological approach for examining social location discourse applications has been the user study [8, 9, 12, 14-17]. The majority of location applications are designed to fulfill a presumed location need given a specific context such as rendezvousing, or benefiting social interactions. Location applications such as WatchMe [14], often run pilot studies to explore the design features that should be incorporated within their system. Additionally, projects like Guide Me [12] use experience prototypes to refine the information presentation to their users. There have been a number of niche popular commercial location applications [4, 13] used to facilitate social interaction. Applications like Dodgeball [4] provide a tailored service benefiting a specific task, but are limited as a robust general purpose social location system. Information discourse between users is limited not only by the system itself, but by their prevalent medium, mobile phones.

It is important in the design of location discourse applications to consider information need not only from the perspective of the location discloser [2] but also that of the location requestor. Designers explore the usability of their systems [8, 9, 12, 14-17], but often make assumptions concerning information importance [14], which should be a significant part of the system design itself [12].

3   Classifying *Information Need* in Location Discourse

We can characterize all location discourse simply as finding out something about a person's location, and then possibly acting on that information. Interest in another's location can vary from incidental (e.g. "just curious") to purposeful (e.g. "do I have time to grab a bite to eat before they arrive?"). The term *location discourse* is used loosely here to describe an exchange of location information, involving synchronous, asynchronous, one-way, two-way, or n-way communication.

Location discourse can involve discussion about a specific location (e.g. "where is the mall?"), about someone's location (e.g. "is Sue still at the mall?"), and about someone's relationship to a location (e.g. "what is Sue doing at the mall?"). In every-day life, location discourse can contain combinations of these elements, such as want-ing to know if Bob is still at the bowling alley (person), and if so, are there lanes open (location), and if not, is he available for a friendly match in an hour (relationship).

Because information need in location discourse is fluid and varied, we cannot eas-ily discuss "social location discourse" as a distinct genre of location application. We therefore include in our definition applications that are directly social (e.g. rendez-vous, dating), indirectly social (e.g. community annotation, mob-logging), and even applications where the social component is unknown (e.g. a taxi locator). While we are most interested in direct social location discourse, we consider the broader defini-tion—encompassing all three elements above—to better understand the parameters influencing location information need in general.

3.1   Categories of Location Discourse Needs

Based on a review of related literature, we tentatively defined several broad categories of information need in location discourse. Throughout our work, we continued to refine our categories, and ultimately settled on the following set:

Inquiry. Determining the whereabouts or status[1] of others. Examples are checking availability (is now a good time to call?), and estimated time of arrival (ETA).

Coordination. Coordinating location with others. Examples are rendezvous (e.g. meeting up after work for a drink) and dispatching (e.g. hailing the nearest taxi).

Sharing. Sharing in the environment or experiences of others. Examples are shar-ing experiences (a rock concert) or places (a new house), or incidental social ex-change (sharing contextual information to augment conversation).

Assistance. Receiving or providing assistance relevant to one's own or someone else's location. Examples are roadside assistance (e.g. OnStar), location memos (e.g. DeDe [10]), and location-based messaging (e.g. Place-Its [18]).

While these categories have provided a useful means of organizing *moments* of loca-tion discourse need, needs can be fluid during location discourse. For example, Bob might want to know where Alice is (Inquiry), and finding that she's at a festival downtown want to know what it's like (Sharing), and then decide to meet (Coordination).

---

[1] As explored in other research [e.g. 8], whereabouts, status and activity are highly interrelated aspects of location discourse. Therefore we consider all such inquiry under a large category.

3.2 Dimensions Impacting Location Need

In addition to categorizing information need in location discourse, we outlined general dimensions of context that could influence need. We first identified specific aspects of context that might impact need, by examining applications explored in previous work and implemented in industry. We accomplished this by asking ourselves "What would change a person's relationship to this application? When would this application cease to be useful? When is it useful?" The set of 'facets' we derived is necessarily incomplete, but can be classified under four broader, interrelated dimensions:

Activity. The activities being performed by all parties. Facets include how easy it is to describe an activity, and the cognitive and physical demands of an activity.

Location. The location pertaining to which information is exchanged. Facets include spatial knowledge/awareness, associations and impressions, relation to the requestor's location, and mobility.

Relationship. The relationship between parties. We can consider relationship from a functional perspective (by applying Fiske's framework of social relations [5]), or consider archetypal relationships (immediate family, close friend, colleague).

Emotional State. The emotional state of the parties. Emotional state is often influenced by the other dimensions. Facets include the emotion and its cause.

In real life, facets influencing information need in location discourse are tightly interwoven in ways that can span more than one dimension. For example, a university student may be angry at their roommate for not being at the grocery store buying food for the party they are having. This involves facets of emotional state, location, relationship and activity in ways that are not easily distinguished. It is therefore neither straightforward nor always desirable to vary 'facets' in isolation to understand their impact on location discourse. The facets must be reasonable to vary under a given context, and any impact of varying a facet must be considered in the context under which it was varied. This was an important consideration when designing the questionnaire study presented in section 5.

4 Diary Study

We conducted a diary study to collect concrete location discourse scenarios for a subsequent questionnaire study, and to explore how needs are impacted by context.

Ten diarists participated in this week-long study, all researchers affiliated with the EDGE Lab at Dalhousie University. After an open discussion of what constitutes location discourse, diarists were asked to record any opportunities for location discourse that arose naturally throughout the week. To tease out the impact of context, the diary entry format included sections for general description, the current location and activity of themselves and others involved, and their relationship with others involved in the scenario. Diarists were also given an opportunity to describe an application that they felt would appropriately address their need.

4.1 Results

Over the course of the week, respondents logged a total of 52 diary entries (max 10, min 3, median 4). Some of the scenarios captured were quite straightforward, such as "is my colleague at the lab?". Others were more complex, as shown in Figure 1.

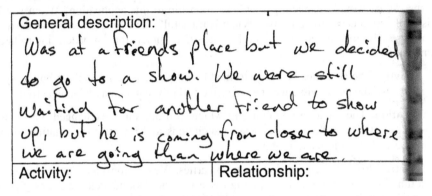

Fig. 1. Portion of a diary entry from Diarist #1 concerning a complex rendezvous need

We grouped diary entries according to the categories of need presented in section 3.1. Complex diary entries such as the one presented above were more difficult to categorize under a single location discourse need, and were sometimes placed under more than one category. After applying a weight according to the number of entries a respondent provided, 8% of responses were classified as *Assistance*, 15% as *Sharing*, and 20% as *Coordination*. As expected, *Inquiry* was the largest category, with 58% of diary entries. Within this category the specific need expressed was split between wanting to know *where* someone was, *what* someone was doing, *when* someone would arrive (ETA), and someone's *availability* (usually for a conversation). The reasons for the need varied from "just wanting to know" to specific planning purposes.

The scenarios collected in the diary study varied widely across each of the contextual dimensions identified in section 3.2. The information needs and envisioned technological support were correspondingly varied, but differences in information need arose even with subtle differences in context. For example, diarist #10 described eight "inquiry" scenarios. In each scenario, she was at home, and interested in knowing either someone's progress on a task or errand, or an estimated time of arrival. Despite this superficial similarity, the type of information desired differed with the specific errand, or the person they were inquiring about. The diarist alternately wanted to interpret a location on a map, get an ETA, place a call, or view status info. The variety of contexts described by the diarists and the variety of needs expressed influenced the design of the questionnaire study, described below.

5 Questionnaire Study

In order to begin examining location information need, we designed a questionnaire study encompassing a wide variety of possible scenarios. The goal of this study was to investigate how the context dimensions of activity, location, relationship, and emotional state impact information need, and whether commonalities exist within these dimensions to help design effective location discourse systems.

5.1 Design

Methodology. Respondents first completed a demographic and personalization questionnaire, followed by a location discourse needs analysis questionnaire. This questionnaire presented fifteen scenarios, each describing a potential need for location information, and several options to address that need. Respondents rated each option according to its usefulness for the scenario, provided a freeform explanation for their rating, and selected one option as their favorite.

Using questionnaires and surveys for assessing need in mobile or ubiquitous applications is problematic in part because such methods rely on the imagination of the respondents; however this can be mitigated by taking their experiences into consideration when designing questions. A full discussion of the challenges and benefits of the questionnaire format as a means of evaluation in pervasive computing is beyond the scope of this paper; however the measures we have taken to ensure an effective questionnaire are detailed in the following sections.

Population Sample. Fifty respondents were recruited through a variety of channels, including university and industry notice boards, special interest listservs, company email, and flyers in public locations. Our sample was correspondingly varied, with 25 male and 25 female, of which 23 were students, 26 employed, and one retired. Respondents were predominantly in the 20-34 (29) age range, with two 13-19, twelve 35-49, six 50-65 and one over 65.

A technology expertise score was assigned according to respondents' frequency of use of various technologies such as cell phones, SMS messaging, mobile internet, and GPS devices. Respondents were then sorted into three groups: limited technological experience (16 respondents), moderate (26 respondents), and expert (8 respondents).

Our sample was drawn from residents of Halifax, Canada. A city with less than 500,000 inhabitants, it is broadly representative of North American life. Obviously, this is not a universally representative sample; for example, residents of Tokyo deal with entirely different population densities, transit patterns, technology adoption rates, street numbering schemes, and cultural norms. This is important when interpreting the results of this and other studies examining mobile technology use.

Scenarios. Based on an analysis of previous work and the results from our diary study, we collected over forty concrete scenarios to consider in the questionnaire. From these we selected and revised fifteen, according to the following criteria:

- The scenarios permitted exploration of several facets across the context dimensions (*activity, location, relationship, emotional state*).
- The categories of location discourse (*inquiry, coordination, sharing, assistance*) were represented in the same proportions as in the diary study and related work[2].
- The scenarios were applicable to our population sample.
- The scenarios include a mix of "standard" (similar to scenarios in previous literature), and non-standard or creative scenarios.

---

[2] We selected five "coordination" questions due to our own interest in this domain.

Each scenario constituted a single 'question'. For each scenario, respondents were presented with four to six technology options. Options were briefly described in terms of how they would be used in the scenario, and most had accompanying images (see Figure 1). Respondents were told that the images presented were just approximations, and that they were to assign ratings based primarily on the textual description.

The technology options provided for each scenario were determined by interpreting interface descriptions provided by our diary study participants, based on implementations in research and industry, and by explicitly designing solutions in response to a particular scenario. Generally each option was within current or emerging technological capability, however technical details (such as update frequencies and location precision) were not normally specified. At least one "current standard" option was provided to counter new technology (e.g. check the Departures screen at the airport).

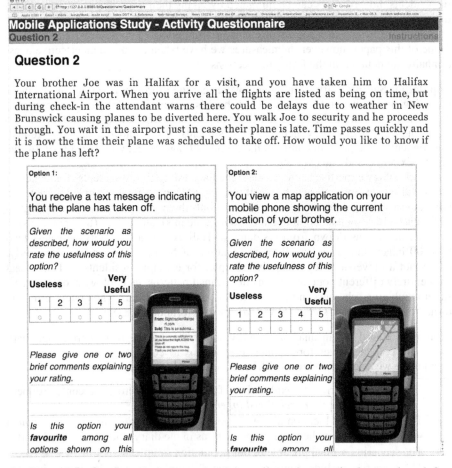

Fig. 2. Questionnaire page displaying a sample question and two technology options (other technology options are not shown here). Text is personalized using details about a family member. Variants of this question had the respondent driving home from the airport, or at home.

Question Variants. In order to more closely examine the dimensions of *activity*, *location, relationship*, and *emotional state*, between two and four versions of each question were created. For example, for the scenario presented in Figure 1, we varied the respondent's location (at the airport, driving home, at home). Although the impact of the facet is very much tied to the scenario in the specific question, we also varied certain facets (such as familiarity with a location) in several different scenarios to get a better sense of overall impact. Options were consistent across scenario variants, except where a specific variant warranted a modified or different option (e.g. checking the Departures screen was only possible if the respondent was at the airport. While driving a community service radio station listing delayed departures was provided as an option, and when home, the airport's website on a home computer). Respondents were assigned question variants so that the "limited", "moderate" and "expert" levels of technology expertise were balanced across variants.

Personalization. A key challenge was to provide questions that had a high degree of realism for our respondents. Using data from the background questionnaire, we personalized scenarios where feasible and appropriate. For example, instead of "your friend calls to see if you want to go out later", we personalize the scenario so that for example "Steve calls to see if you are available for a game of racquetball".

In order to accomplish this, we had to ask respondents to answer a set of personalization questions as part of the preliminary questionnaire. This included some quite specific questions such as "name a leisure activity you are likely to enjoy with a friend". The effect is an increase in realism for the respondent: by incorporating their experience we provide real examples, and they are more able to envision how they would likely respond to the situation given the options provided. They are less apt to answer questions indifferently or to consider the question in abstract terms. Personalization was instrumental to the success of our questionnaire, as made evident by the evocative, engaged nature of the comments entered by many respondents.

Implementation and Procedure. As outlined previously, respondents began by completing an online background and personalization questionnaire. This included basic demographic data, questions measuring experience with a suite of relevant technologies, and questions collecting data to enable scenarios to be personalized. Respondents were given the option of leaving questions blank if they were uncomfortable answering, or if they felt the question did not apply to them. Virtually all respondents answered all questions. Respondents were then assigned scenario variants, maintaining roughly even numbers[3] for each variant and balancing technology expertise.

Personalized questionnaires were dynamically generated for each respondent. XSL Stylesheets were used to personalize the scenario description, the description of each option, and to select appropriate images to illustrate the options. Thorough piloting and exhaustive validation was performed prior to running respondents.

Once a personalized questionnaire was created, the respondent was notified to complete the second part of the questionnaire. An instruction page described the procedure, the intent of the questionnaire scenarios, and the question format. For each question, respondents rated the usefulness of options on a five-point scale, and provided a freeform explanation for their rating. In addition, respondents were required

---

[3] Some variants required that certain choices be made in the personalization questionnaire, so it was not possible to always get the same number of respondents in each question variant.

to select one option as their favorite among those presented. Question ordering was randomized across respondents, as was the ordering of options on each question page.

The questionnaires took 50-90 minutes to complete. Respondents received $10.

5.2 Results

In this section we present results for thirteen questions[4], organized by the categories of information need described in section 3.1. For each question we focus on the technology options that were chosen by many respondents as highly appropriate and/or a favourite option for the scenario. We compare results across similar questions in each category, and within variants of the same question, to illustrate the impact of context on technology option choices.

Table 1. Sharing questions

Question	Contextual dimensions varied
Holiday. Friends are at a holiday destination that interests you.	Location (landmark or visual event), during or after visit.
Showing off. A friend calls from a place they are excited about.	Relationship and location (friend at new cottage or colleague at new workplace).
Touching base. A colleague/friend calls you at work.	Activity (busy or free), relationship (manager or friend).

Sharing. *Sharing* applications emphasize the exchange of location-related information because of its intrinsic value, or incidentally in a spirit of openness. The *Holiday* and *Showing off* questions share location information that is intrinsically interesting. *Touching base* considers sharing location information incidentally.

In *Holiday* and *Showing off*, video was chosen as a favourite option by 18/50 and 24/50 respondents, respectively, and photo slideshows by 20/50 and 23/50 respondents, respectively. Video was the favourite option only when there was some possibility of sharing the visit in real time in *Holiday* (U=193, p=.003). This was particularly true when the holiday's intent was to visit landmarks (ancient Rome, immigration history in NYC). For other holidays (safari or rodeo), some felt that video distracted from conversation. Receptivity to video was mixed in the workplace variant of *Showing off*. 3/25 respondents expressed that video might be inappropriate in the new workplace, and 9/25 expressed that video provides the wrong kind of information:

> *"... I am more interested in their experience than the exact details of what their new workplace looks like."* - Respondent #54.

In both questions, slideshows were appreciated for the ability to editorialize and share asynchronously. Slideshows fared well across all question variants. Augmenting slideshows with a map was not seen as useful, however some weren't sure how the map would relate to the slideshow. Those who were positive toward the map imagined some direct utility (e.g. to get to their friend's cottage, or to track friends on their trip).

---

[4] The remaining two questions involved personal location information only. They are not presented in this section but are considered alongside the other questions in the discussion.

For the *Touching base* question, no respondent expressed that it was just "nice to know" where their friend or manager was. Instead, many respondents envisioned using location information in ways not mentioned in the question description. Some felt knowing where their manager was would let them decide how to respond to a call when still working on a project. Others said that knowing where their friend was would help in planning for the night's activities, especially when they were too busy to take the call. However, the mean usefulness rating for options providing location (3.2/5) in *Touching Base* is lower than similar options in questions where there was a more explicit need for location information (grand mean 3.7). 34/50 respondents cited some kind of location indicator as their favourite option. Of these, 14 preferred textual descriptions, due to their simplicity and because they felt familiar with the routines of their friend or their manager. The remaining 20 preferred maps, as they provided a more detailed, visual reference. Four respondents expressed concern about the privacy of location information. In each case this was in relation to a friend, and when the variant suggested they could take the call anyway. Basic contact info (without location data) was preferred by a majority of respondents only in the variant where the manager calls to ask about a project they have just finished. At that point they have no immediate use for location information.

Table 2. Assistance questions

Question	Contextual dimensions varied
Remote guide. Friends in another city need help navigating.	Location/activity (navigating a city or an attraction), familiarity with the city or attraction.

Assistance. *Assistance* applications emphasize the exchange of location information to help the requestor or discloser. In *Remote guide*, location and activity are tightly intertwined – either friends are trying to find a hotel (and driving) in a city, or they are trying to find an exhibit (and walking) at an attraction. Guiding remotely without a map was not perceived as useful in the attraction setting, even when familiar with the attraction – most respondents did not think they would be able to recall detail useful for navigation. By contrast, while nobody's favourite option in the city setting, many respondents felt it a reasonable approach if the city was familiar. Guiding remotely using a map tracking their friends' location was evaluated positively by 23/25 respondents regardless of their familiarity with the city, but was a favourite of just 7/25. The same option was seen as problematic in the attraction setting, however, with 9/25 respondents positive or luke-warm toward the option, and a favourite of 1/25. A number of respondents cited issues with using a stylized attraction map as a navigation tool, others difficulty communicating, and others issues of time and convenience:

"This is ok, but then they have to go right there. I also have to tell them how to get there." – Respondent #27.

When unfamiliar with the attraction, many respondents felt it reasonable to have their friends ask for help from staff; in the city setting, third party directions were said to be unreliable. Respondents were happy to identify the destination on a map application used by their friends, allowing them to navigate on their own. This was true regardless of the respondent's own knowledge of the city or attraction. Despite concern

Table 3. Inquiry questions

Question	Contextual dimensions varied
Airport arrival. A family member is arriving.	Activity (preparing a surprise reception or a casual dinner).
Plane left. Know that a family member has made their flight.	Location (at airport, driving home, at home).
Carpool. Determine the ETA of your ride to work.	Relationship (carpool or public transit).
Meeting. Determine whether someone will make a meeting.	Activity (formal pitch or casual meeting), relationship (business partner or potential investor).

that their friends be comfortable navigating, this was the favourite option of 36/50 respondents.

Inquiry. *Inquiry* applications emphasize an exchange of location information to determine whereabouts or status.

Airport arrival and *Carpool* are ETA-type questions. In *Airport arrival*, a simple phone call to see if their relative had arrived was the favourite option of more respondents (12/23) than any other option when there was no need for secrecy. Many respondents felt the phone call was the richest information source, while others worried about getting accurate ETA information and engaging in a possibly lengthy conversation:

"Not bad, but the ... alerts are less time consuming, I wouldn't have to talk to me [sic] sister. She can be chatty..." – Respondent #94.

When preparing a surprise reception, 18/27 respondents preferred an alarm notification when their relative has left the airport, and again when they are within a specified distance from the house. Some respondents were skeptical that the family member driving to the airport would remember to set the notifications, however. A similar preference is seen in *Carpool*, where an ETA display was the favourite option of 24/50. Respondents who didn't rate the ETA display highly were skeptical of its accuracy. Were traffic conditions taken into account? What if the carpool route changes or they stop for coffee? Is it as unreliable as the existing bus schedule? In both questions, many respondents cited that these options were simple but effective, and that they could get on with their activities without needing to monitor the screen.

Tracking location using a map was an option in both *Airport arrival* and *Carpool*. In *Airport arrival*, the option was the favourite of 9/50 respondents, who liked its unobtrusiveness and precision. Other respondents felt that it required too much monitoring, and provided no clear indication of the situation (e.g. did your brother-in-law actually arrive, or is your spouse driving home because the flight was cancelled?). In *Carpool*, the option was the favourite of 20/50 respondents, citing that it was an accurate visual representation, allowing them to calculate their own ETA. Several respondents wanted additional information, such as an ETA, who was driving, or the route, while others felt the map gave too much information and required frequent views.

Meeting and *Plane left* involve checking whereabouts or status. In the *Meeting* question, option evaluations varied with meeting formality, and the person being inquired about. In most variants calling was seen as reasonable and direct, and was the favourite option of 19/48 respondents. However many saw a phone call as pushy when checking the status of a potential investor for a formal 'pitch'. Others worried that the person might not respond, or that it may disrupt the meeting. Phone calls were not provided as an option in *Plane left*.

Tracking location with a map was again an option in both *Meeting* and *Plane left*. This was the favourite option of 21/48 respondents in the *Meeting* question, and had the highest mean usefulness rating (3.4/5) in the formal pitch/investor variant. Five respondents explicitly mention privacy concerns when tracking a potential investor, while no respondents mention this in relation to a business partner. In the formal meeting variants, many felt that this was a discreet, unobtrusive solution and were comfortable actively interpreting the position data, while others were concerned that it did not conclusively mean the person was on their way. For an informal meeting many respondents felt this technology was overkill. A similar option was the favourite of 16/50 respondents in the *Plane left* question. Most respondents preferred to track the individual rather than the plane, to be certain that the person made the flight. When at the airport, several respondents cited that they could actively track and even contact the person if it looks like they might miss their boarding call, whereas while driving or at home several respondents indicated that they were not familiar enough with the airport to make such interpretations. An alarm-based notification of departure was preferred by 21/50 respondents, regardless of their location. The remaining 13/50 preferred to access departure information on public screens or via mobile phone.

Table 4. Coordination questions

Question	Contextual dimensions varied
Project. Meet a colleague when they are at a particular location.	Location (communal space on campus or office in same building), urgency.
Interception. Meet a friend mid-activity.	Activity (walking, jogging, or cycling).
Shopping. Arrange to meet after splitting up to shop.	Location (mall or shopping district), relationship (family or tour group).
Returning item. Return an item you have borrowed.	Location/activity (conference or resort), urgency/familiarity (first day, last day).
Get a lift. Arrange transportation.	Location (home or unfamiliar city), relationship (friends or taxi company).

Coordination. *Coordination* applications emphasize actively using location information to arrange meetings. *Project* and *Returning item* involve meeting up with others without their prior knowledge. When the need was urgent, a majority (15/24) of respondents preferred calling to arrange a meeting in the *Project* question. Otherwise opinion was mixed, with some respondents concerned about interrupting the person to just check their location. When the need was not urgent, a triggered notification when the individual is in the particular location was a popular option for the office, but not on campus. Respondents doubted that the person would visit the specified campus building at a good time, while the office worker could be expected to return to their office. A proximity trigger was also an option in the *Returning Item* question; it received reasonably positive reviews when in the structured (and physically enclosed) conference, but not in the open resort setting. A phone call was the favourite option for 24/51 respondents in *Returning item*, again as a direct way to arrange and guarantee a meeting. However, it was preferred in the resort setting (18/28) more than in the conference (6/22), where many respondents were concerned about causing an interruption. A map-based tracking application was the favourite of 7/48 respondents in *Project*. Many respondents felt that location tracking gave either too much or the wrong kind of information for the scenario:

> *"Can I get in touch with them there? How long will they be there? I would want these questions answered"* – Respondent #41.

In *Returning item*, a similar application was the favourite of 16/50 respondents. It was selected as a favourite option more often in the conference setting, with 11/22 votes, than in the resort setting (5/28).

The *Interception* and *Shopping* questions involve planned meetings, similar to *Meeting* except that steps are taken to ensure that the meeting takes place. Additionally, some options permitted dynamically establishing a meeting point, while some rely on a predetermined place and possibly time. In *Interception*, arranging a time and place beforehand was the favourite of 6/16 walkers, but was more problematic for runners and cyclers, who preferred setting a meeting place dynamically (the scenario involved meeting mid-activity). Arranging by phone was the favourite of 5/17 cyclers and was evaluated positively by most walkers, but phones were too cumbersome when running, and no runners favoured this option; instead 13/16 runners favoured map-based tracking applications, as did 10/17 cyclers and 8/16 walkers. Despite the strong numbers for tracking applications, most evaluations also expressed concerns about map legibility, having to refer frequently to it, and safety issues especially if cycling. The *Shopping* question involved rounding up a group of people. In the results we found that a city shopping district was considered in much the same way as a mall. We also found relatively little impact of relationship, except for a common concern about being respectful and democratic with family, versus a general awareness of the responsibilities of a tour group chaperone. 27/49 respondents preferred arranging a meeting place and time beforehand, tracking locations with a map application, and calling stragglers individually. The same setup minus the tracking application was also highly rated, however, and was the favourite of 8/49 respondents. Setting a meeting place dynamically using a tracking application had high ratings for usefulness and was the favourite of 12/49 respondents, however many were critical of the unilateral nature of the option described, especially in the family variants.

Get a lift is a question that includes aspects of Assistance or Inquiry, but ultimately involves Coordination. Variants involved one of two diverse settings (at home, or in a possibly dangerous part of an unfamiliar city). This impacted the priorities expressed by respondents, however the usefulness ratings of the options were similar between settings. An option to broadcast your location to one or more cab companies was the favourite option for 8/12 respondents in the unfamiliar city, and given 5/5 as a usefulness rating by all eight. However this option was also the favourite of 6/12 respondents calling cabs from home, albeit with a lower mean usefulness rating. When arranging a ride with friends, 4/25 respondents preferred to just call, while 12/25 preferred viewing the locations and availability of their friends on a map prior to calling. When at home, some commented that this was more applicable to emergency situations, while in the city some felt this would be useful only if you were familiar with the city. Another 8/25 respondents preferred the broadcast option here, because it lets their friends decide whether to respond or not; however others felt that it was not guaranteed to work in the city setting, or an awkward approach when at home:

"...*too impersonal a way to ask someone to do you a favour*" – Respondent #1.

6 Discussion

In this section we characterize the broad trends observed in our questionnaire results that have direct implications for application designers.

Incorporate the requestor's concern for others. Throughout the responses respondents were very aware of the social ramifications of using technology in discourse. While many respondents were concerned for the privacy of the location information discloser, this was usually part of a larger concern for *what is appropriate*. Some expressed discomfort with tracking someone else's movements, while others felt it would be ok if the discloser gave permission. Many options were only considered useful if there was a good chance the other person would have their mobile phone, knew how to use the application correctly, and when it was safe for them to use it. Many respondents were excited by the prospect of using live video or pictures to get a sense of immersion in another's experience, however there was concern that this might be disruptive or disallowed in a colleague's new workplace, for example. Being able to unilaterally set a meeting time and place was only useful if the respondent had been given clear authority to do so. Even with immediate family this was usually not the case. More generally, respondents were uneasy with interfaces that managed requests (for meeting up, etc.) that might be more gracefully handled by a voice conversation.

Verbal communication is often best. Verbal communication was often cited as the most preferred means of obtaining both location and status information. Many respondents felt that they could negotiate their needs more effectively with a phone call than by checking status messages or tracking locations on a map. This was especially true when they had a pressing need or knew someone was available to talk. Often, talking was considered best when augmented with contextual cues like maps or pictures. In cases where a phone call might be intrusive, more surreptitious methods including tracking were considered, as were less intrusive messaging options. When the focus of their need was precise location or ETA, many respondents did not trust the ability of the information discloser to be accurate. In such cases more automated tracking was considered useful. Finally, while voice was favoured less when the *Shopping* scenario required communicating with several people at once, it was considered effective in rounding up a few lost or late individuals.

Interaction should be minimized. Respondents often made it clear that they do not want to be fiddling with technology in their daily lives. The most common complaint about tracking applications (far more common than concerns about privacy) was the need to monitor. Small maps and images, grainy video, slow text entry and needing to carry a mobile phone around were cited as weaknesses of the technologies provided in the questionnaire. Alarm-based notification was embraced by many respondents because it was unobtrusive and to the point; sending out an automatic dispatch for a cab in a strange city was viewed as a comfort and a time saver.

Location requestors want targeted information. The perceived usefulness of a location discourse technology often hinges on the possibility of inaccuracy and misinterpretation. This includes status messages that could be left unchanged, or that are too vague to be useful in the context (e.g. "in transit" is not enough information if you need to be sure someone is on their way to meet *you*).

Too much detail (e.g the tracked locations of all nearby available taxis) can overwhelm. The suitability of information presentation is highly context-dependent: an address list of people's current locations is useful as a directory or to provide passive status information, but useless when trying to determine where they are unless already familiar with the region. Maps assist in navigation and planning but are less useful as generic context.

7 Conclusion

We have presented results from a structured analysis of information need in location discourse. Our results illustrate that an analysis of need based on contextual dimensions can shed light on key design concerns. At the same time, the results support the idea that information need is rarely determinable by location, activity, relationship or emotional state in isolation. Instead a change in need is most often brought about by a combination of factors (e.g. my friend calls me at work *and* I am busy *and* we are planning to go out after work). When context clearly influenced technology choices in the questionnaire, it was often because a question variant emphasized a concern for propriety (e.g. capturing video in an office building vs. a cottage), or changed what was known and unknown (e.g. routes are more volatile for a carpool than for public transit). A need for convenience or safety can also impact choices (e.g. an alarm notification is appropriate while driving), however as can be expected many respondents chose the most convenient or unobtrusive option regardless of the situation.

Our analysis highlights the importance of considering information need in location discourse. First, relationship alone was not a strong determinant of need. This contrasts with findings pertaining to information disclosure [2, 11, 15]. Second, the requestor's and the location discloser's activity were equally important when determining how needs will be negotiated, again stressing the importance of considering the perspective of the information requestor. Third, precise visual location was often considered to be more trustworthy and useful than text descriptions of activity or location, although providing both might help prevent misinterpretation. Again, this may be at odds with design advice derived solely from an analysis of location disclosure.

The questionnaire study, despite considerable efforts to achieve realism, relies on self-reported evaluation of technology options described by a short paragraph and an image. In future work we will further explore and validate the findings presented in this paper in realistic contexts, and with interactive technology.

References

1. Abowd, G.D., et al., *Cyberguide: a mobile context-aware tour guide*. Wireless Networks, 1997. **3**(5): p. 421-433.
2. Consolvo, S., et al. *Location disclosure to social relations: why, when, & what people want to share*. in *CHI 2005*. 2005. Portland, Oregon, USA: ACM Press.
3. Dearman, D., K. Hawkey, and K.M. Inkpen, *Rendezvousing with location-aware devices: Enhancing social coordination*. Interacting with Computers, 2005. **17**(5): p. 542-566.
4. Dodgeball, *Dodgeball*. 2005.
5. Fiske, A.P., *Structures of Social Life: The Four Elementry forms of Human Relations*. 1991, New York: Free Press.
6. Griswold, W.G., et al., *ActiveCampus: Experiments in Community-Oriented Ubiquitous Computing*. Computer, 2004. **37**(10): p. 73-81.
7. Hong, J.I., et al. *Privacy risk models for designing privacy-sensitive ubiquitous computing systems*. in *DIS 2004*. 2004. Cambridge, MA, USA: ACM Press.
8. Iachello, G., et al. *Control, Deception, and Communication: Evaluating the Deployment of a Location-Enhanced Messaging Service*. in *UbiComp 2005*. 2005. Tokyo, Japan: Springer.
9. Iachello, G., et al. *Developing privacy guidelines for social location disclosure applications and services*. in *SOUPS 2005*. 2005.
10. Jung, Y., P. Persson, and J. Blom. *DeDe: Design and Evaluation of a Context-Enhanced Mobile Messaging System*. in *CHI 2006*. 2005. Portland, Oregon, USA: ACM Press.
11. Lederer, S., J. Mankoff, and A.K. Dey, *Who wants to know what when? Privacy preference determinants in ubiquitous computing*, in *Ext. Abstracts CHI 2003*. 2003, ACM Press: Ft. Lauderdale, Florida, USA. p. 724-725.
12. Loh, J., et al. *Technology applied to address difficulties of alzheimer patients and their partners*. in *the conference on Dutch directions in HCI*. 2004.
13. MamJam, *MamJam*. 2005.
14. Marmasse, N., C. Schmandt, and D. Spectre. *WatchMe: communication and awareness between members of a closely-knit group*. in *UbiComp 2004*. 2004: Springer.
15. Patil, S. and J. Lai. *Who gets to know what when: configuring privacy permissions in an awareness application*. in *CHI 2005*. 2005. Portland, Oregon, USA: ACM Press.
16. Persson, P., J. Blom, and Y. Jung. *DigiDress: A Field Trail of an Expressive Social Proximity Application*. in *UbiComp 2005*. 2005. Tokyo, Japan: Springer.
17. Smith, I., et al. *Social Disclosure of Place: From Location Technology to Communication Practices*. in *Pervasive 2005*. 2005. Munich, Germany: Springer.
18. Sohn, T., et al. *Place-Its: A Study of Location-Based Reminders on Mobile Phones*. in *UbiComp 2005*. 2005: Springer.
19. Weilenmann, A., *"I can't talk now, I'm in a fitting room": Formulating availability and location in mobile phone conversations*. Environment and Planning, 2003. **35**(9): p. 1589 - 1605.
20. Weilenmann, A.H. and P. Leuchovious. *"I'm waiting where we met last time": Exploring everyday positioning practices to inform design*. in *NordiCHI 2004*. 2004. Tampere, Finland: ACM Press.

Collaborative Localization: Enhancing WiFi-Based Position Estimation with Neighborhood Links in Clusters

Li-wei Chan, Ji-rung Chiang, Yi-chao Chen, Chia-nan Ke, Jane Hsu,
and Hao-hua Chu

Graduate Institute of Networking and Multimedia,
Department of Computer Science and Information Engineering,
National Taiwan University
{yjhsu, hchu}@csie.ntu.edu.tw

Abstract. Location-aware services can benefit from accurate and reliable indoor location tracking. The widespread adoption of 802.11x wireless LAN as the network infrastructure creates the opportunity to deploy WiFi-based location services with few additional hardware costs. While recent research has demonstrated adequate performance, localization error increases significantly in crowded and dynamic situations due to electromagnetic interferences. This paper proposes *collaborative localization* as an approach to enhance position estimation by leveraging more accurate location information from nearby neighbors within the same cluster. The current implementation utilizes ZigBee radio as the neighbor-detection sensor. This paper introduces the basic model and algorithm for collaborative localization. We also report experiments to evaluate its performance under a variety of clustering scenarios. Our results have shown 28.2-56% accuracy improvement over the baseline system Ekahau, a commercial WiFi localization system.

1 Introduction

Technologies for indoor location tracking are important for deploying *location-aware services* in public buildings like museums, transit stations, or hospitals. For example, visitors can receive background information about the exhibit they are viewing, passengers can obtain real-time status update on their next connections, and emergency medical personnel can locate critical patients or equipments. Given accurate and reliable location information, an intelligent museum guide can provide museum visitors with relevant information and timely services. In contrast, location errors may result in undesirable deliveries of the wrong information to the wrong people at the wrong place.

The widespread adoption of 802.11x wireless LAN as a common network infrastructure enables WiFi-based localization with few additional hardware costs. Microsoft Research proposed an RF-based indoor location tracking system by processing signal strength information at multiple base stations [1]. Since then, much research has focused on improving WiFi-based localization from noisy signals, and has achieved position estimation with up to 90% accuracy within an error of 1 meter. While such performance is sufficient for most indoor pervasive computing

K.P. Fishkin et al. (Eds.): PERVASIVE 2006, LNCS 3968, pp. 50–66, 2006.

applications, the results are somewhat misleading since they are usually measured in static, ideal situations with minimal signal interference. Our previous work [12] demonstrated the impact on position estimation with people moving around a target mobile device. Not only does the estimated position become unstable, but the error also rises twofold due to electromagnetic interferences by the human body.

People cluster naturally in typical social settings. Based on observing museum visits, people often browse through the exhibits with their family or friends, forming relatively *stable moving clusters*. Visitors also tend to gather in front of popular exhibits, instantly creating *temporary static clusters*. Figure 1, two random snapshots taken at the National Museum of Natural Science, illustrates that most visitors are in the midst of small crowds. In addition, clusters are dynamic. First, they may move as a group with varying speeds. Second, they may assemble and disassemble over time. Similar scenarios happen frequently in other public places, such as passengers departing or arriving in transit stations.

Fig. 1. Visitors at the National Museum of Natural Science in Taiwan

This research investigates the problem of WiFi-based localization in clustering scenarios. This paper starts by analyzing the effects on positioning errors due to human clusters of varying sizes. We then propose *collaborative localization* as an approach to improving position estimation accuracy by leveraging potentially more accurate position information from nearby neighbors. Section 3 introduces the basic idea and models supporting collaborative localization. Section 4 presents the experimental results showing the advantages of the proposed approach. Section 5 provides pointers to related research, followed by the conclusion and future work in Section 6.

2   Clustering

A traditional WiFi-based location system utilizes wireless signal strength to estimate locations in two phases. First, the offline training phase collects Received Signal Strength Indicator (RSSI) from multiple access points (APs) at each sampled location. The results are saved in a radio map. Second, the online estimation phase matches the RSSI from a target mobile device to each sampled location on the radio map. The coordinates of the target location can be estimated deterministically or probabilistically. To understand the impact of human clusters on location accuracy, we have conducted preliminary experiments described in our previous work [12]. Results of these experiments have shown that human clustering can create strong interferences with surrounding signals, leading to significant degradation in location accuracy. In a case of six people walking around a user carrying the target mobile device, the position estimated by the Ekahau location system [4] becomes unstable, leading to doubling of the average positioning error.

Several recent localization systems [11][12] have worked on the challenge of providing stable position estimation under different environmental dynamics, including change of floor layout, change in relative humidity, and moving people. Since major floor layout changes occur less frequently, they can be managed by rebuilding a selective part of a radio map. To adapt to different relative humidity levels, a separate radio map can also be constructed for each humidity level. However, coping with moving people is more challenging, because it is infeasible to model and enumerate all possible cases of human clustering formations, human orientations and moving speeds, and further, to construct corresponding radio maps. To our knowledge, we have not found any satisfactory solution that can address the challenge of people dynamics.

To measure quantitatively the impact of people clustering on the amount of degradation in positioning accuracy, we have conducted experiments, again using Ekahau as an example. For each test, users stand at pre-specified positions to form clusters of sizes 1, 3, and 7 person(s). Each user carries a Notebook PC equipped with a wireless network card to collect RSSIs from APs. The same WiFi cards are used to minimize errors due to different signal strength interpretations by different WiFi card drivers. The results are plotted in Figure 2, showing that the positioning accuracy degrades significantly with an increasing cluster size. In a single person case (no clustering), Ekahau can achieve a high positioning accuracy of approximately 80% within an error of 2 meters. In comparison, Ekahau's positioning accuracy degrades to 60% in the case of 3-person clusters, and further degrades to less than 30% in the case of 7-person clusters. The general trend is that increasing cluster size leads to rapidly decreasing average positioning accuracy and precision.

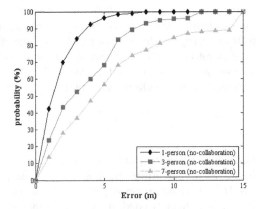

Fig. 2. CDF of the cluster's average positioning errors

To investigate how clustering influences the positioning estimation accuracy for each individual in a cluster, we have plotted *cumulative density functions* (CDFs) of average positioning errors experienced by each individual in Figure 3. It shows a 7-person clustering case where each colored curve represents the positioning accuracy experienced by one person in a cluster. The relative position of each person in a cluster is shown in a small diagram at the bottom. Although clustering degrades average positioning accuracy of a cluster (shown in Figure 2), the amount of degradation experienced by people varies within the same cluster. In the 7-person clustering case shown in Figure 3, *user-7*'s accuracy is almost unaffected, whereas *user-3*'s accuracy is significantly reduced.

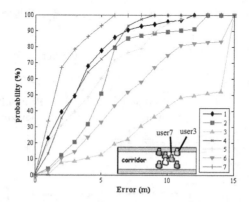

Fig. 3. CDFs of each node's average positioning error within a 7-person cluster

The next question is what causes such large variance in positioning accuracy among individuals within the same cluster? We have found several possible direct and indirect causes, such as people's relative position within a cluster, their orientation, the way (e.g., the height) they hold the device, the geometry of the environment, etc. Rather than considering clustering as a hindrance to improving accuracy in localization systems, we turn them into an advantage by exploiting *collaboration* among neighbor nodes.

3 Design and Implementation

We propose *collaborative localization* to leverage the variance in location accuracy among nodes within a cluster. Intuitively, nodes in the same cluster may help localize each other so as to enhance the overall average positioning accuracy of the cluster. By identifying nodes with high location accuracy, we can use their location estimations to help better localize neighbor nodes with lower location accuracy. The design for collaborative localization is shown in Figure 4. It consists of the following three modules: *Neighborhood Detection*, *Confidence Estimation*, and *Collaborative Error Correction*. The general work flow of the system is summarized as follows.

1. Neighborhood Detection identifies nearby neighbor nodes as possible candidates for collaborative localization;
2. Confidence Estimation computes and attaches a *confidence score* to the position estimation returned by a given localization system (e.g., Ekahau). *Confidence* measures the probability of a location estimation being accurate, and it will be formally defined in Section 3.2.
3. Collaborative Error Correction adjusts the estimated location of the target node using the estimated locations of neighboring nodes with higher confidence scores. This way, the error in location estimation of the target node can be reduced.

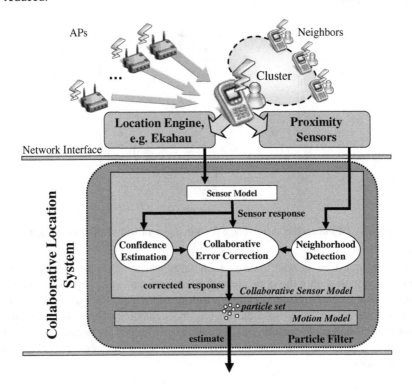

Fig. 4. Design of collaborative location system

3.1 Neighborhood Detection

For each target node, the Neighborhood Detection finds its neighbor nodes within a certain proximity radius (e.g., 2 meters). Each node periodically probes its neighborhood through a proximity sensor, and the system continues to track the neighboring relationships among all target nodes.

We experimented with a number of proximity sensors, including Bluetooth, Zig-Bee, infrared, and ultra-sound, and have chosen ZigBee in our implementation. Zig-Bee offers the following advantages: (1) ZigBee's signal strength decays quickly over a relatively short distance, so its signal strength signatures can be mapped accurately to proximity distances within a range of 1 ~ 2 meters; (2) The simplicity of ZigBee protocol supports instantaneous connection, which facilitates proximity detection based on signal strength; (3) ZigBee does not suffer from the line-of-sight problem as with infrared sensors, so users can carry their WiFi nodes in their pockets; and (4) ZigBee radio has relatively low power consumption.

In our current implementation, the neighborhood detection is defined in terms of the actual distance calculated from the ground truths of the target nodes. A neighbor node is defined as having a proximity distance of less than 2 meters to the target node.

3.2 Confidence Estimation

Confidence Estimation measures the probability of the location estimation, obtained from an underlying localization engine, being close to its true location. In other words, a high (low) confidence score implies that the location estimation has a high (low) probability of being the true location. *Confidence* in location estimation correlates highly to *positioning stability* of a target node computed over time from a particle filter. Location estimation is based on the *sensor model* generated by the Ekahau localization engine, which is used in conjunction with a *motion model* to constrain location estimation within a reasonable variation consistent with human movement. That is, given the current location of a target, there is a limited range of possible locations that a human may reach. As a result, the difference between the location estimated from a sensor response S and the bounded estimation P returned from a particle filter implies the uncertainty in location estimation. If the position of a target node changes beyond what's prescribed by the motion model, a low confidence score is assigned.

The confidence estimation can be derived by accumulating successive uncertainties over a specified time window. Specifically, we define the confidence at time t according to the following equation:

$$Conf(t) = e^{\dfrac{-\left[\sum\limits_{i=0}^{s} w(i) \cdot uc(t-i)\right]^2}{k}} . \tag{1}$$

Here, t is the current time stamp, i is an accumulation index, and s is the length of the time window. Let $w(i)$ be the weight to accumulate uncertainties at different times within the window, and $uc(t-i)$ measure the *uncertainty* of a sensor response, i.e. the difference between the location estimation from the sensor response and the bounded estimation returned from a particle filter at time $(t-i)$. Equation (1) computes the weighted sum of uncertainties over an accumulation window s, normalizing it to a value between $[0, 1]$. The value k is a constant that adjusts the speed of decline in a logarithmic curve - a higher k value means that the curve will decline more slowly. A high confidence score, e.g., 0.95, means that a particle filter has found little uncertainty over the time window, indicating high accuracy in location estimation. In the current implementation, s is defined as the 3 most recent samples, constant k is 300, and the weight $w(i)$ is equal for the three samples.

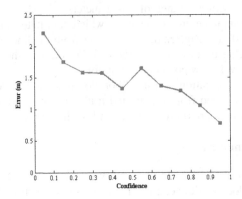

Fig. 5. Confidence scores and location estimation errors

In order to validate how well Equation (1) models the relationship between *confidence* and *accuracy* of position estimations, we have conducted an experiment by collecting 1179 location estimation samples. These samples' confidence scores are computed from Equation (1) and then plotted against their estimation errors from their true locations. Results in Figure 5 show a good inverse relationship between confidence and error.

Other applications can be created using the framework illustrated in Figure 4. Since a confidence estimation is independent of sensor models, a different localization algorithm (e.g., a simple nearest neighbor algorithm) can be used in a sensor model. At the same time, a different confidence function that is more accurate than the one described in Equator (1) can be used.

3.3 Collaborative Error Correction

Collaboration Error Correction (CEC) enhances location estimation from particles of a target node by removing estimation that has a lower confidence score, from estimations of its neighbor nodes that have higher confidence scores. In order to produce this enhancement, the collaborative error correction step requires the following information: (1) a set of neighbor nodes within proximity of a target node $N_s = \{N_1, N_2, .. N_s\}$ detected from the neighborhood detection, and (2) a set of pairs of their location estimations and confidence scores $\{<N_1^{pos}, N_1^{conf}>, <N_2^{pos}, N_2^{conf}>, .. <N_s^{pos}, N_s^{conf}>\}$.

Collaborative enhancement is based on the concept of attraction from magnetic interactions in nature. A high confidence node N_x, whose location estimation is at N_x^{pos}, is assigned a stronger magnetic charge N_x^{conf}. On the other hand, a low confidence neighbor node N_y, whose location estimation is at N_y^{pos}, is assigned a weaker magnetic charge N_y^{conf}. Based on natural magnetic interactions, a low confidence node, acting as a nail, will be pulled from its original position at N_y^{pos} toward the position of a high confidence node at N_x^{pos}. The magnitude of this attraction force (refer to as the *neighboring force*) is proportional to the ratio N_x^{conf} / N_y^{conf}.

The actual mechanism can be described as follows. In step 1, for each node N, we collect its proximity nodes and *<estimated location, confidence score>* pairs. In step 2, the neighboring force F_b between a target node N and one of its neighbor node N_b, is computed as follows:

$$F_b = \frac{N_b^{Conf}}{N^{Conf} + N_b^{Conf}} \times \left| D(N^{pos}, N_b^{pos}) - r \times (1 + \varepsilon) \right| \times u(N^{pos} - N_b^{pos})$$ (2)

Here, r measures the proximity distance between the node pairs, ε is a constant measuring the amount of error ratio in a neighbor proximity measurement, D is the Euclidean distance between two coordinates N^{pos} (a target node's position) and N_b^{pos} (a neighbor node's position), and the unit vector $u(N_b^{pos} - N^{pos})$ gives the direction of this neighboring force. In step 3, since a target node can have multiple neighbor nodes, individual attraction forces contributed from each of its neighbor nodes are summed into an *aggregate neighboring force F*, which is defined in equation (3). Note that F is computed as a weighted sum of neighboring forces, with the weight equal to the normalized confidence level of each of its contributing neighbor nodes.

$$F = \sum_{b=1}^{s} \frac{N_b^{Conf}}{\sum_{i=1}^{s} N_i^{Conf}} \times F_b.$$ (3)

In the last step, we apply F to correct the location estimation of a target node. This corrected location estimation is then used to assign probabilities of particles. Finally, the particle with the highest probability is chosen as location estimation.

4 Experimental Results

The following experiments were performed on the corridors of the 3rd floor of the Computer Science Department building in our university as shown in Figure 6. The baseline WiFi positioning engine is a commercial product Ekahau [4]. All users brought mobile devices equipped with the same brand IEEE 802.11g WLAN card.

4.1 Neighborhood Sensing

In the real environments, errors caused by neighborhood sensing technology will reduce benefit generated by the proposed algorithm. The error model of the neighborhood detection is derived from ZigBee radio, which is the chosen sensor. In neighborhood detection, each radio periodically transmits and receives signals from neighbor radios. From the received signals, their RSSI values are measured. Figure 7(a) shows that RSSI decays rapidly when distance between two radios increases from 1 to 3 meters, which is an ideal range for neighbor proximity detection. We adapt a simple method to detect neighbors within 2 meters proximity. First of all, the average received signal strength corresponding to the 2 meters distance mark is chosen as a threshold. When received signal strength is greater than the threshold, two radios are recognized as neighbors. Figure 7 (b) shows the probability that two radios are detected as neighbors at different distances. For nodes that are more than 2 meters apart, there is still a small 20% probability that they will be incorrectly detected as neighbor nodes. When two radios are less than 2 meters, there will be 71.6% probability that they are correctly detected as neighbors.

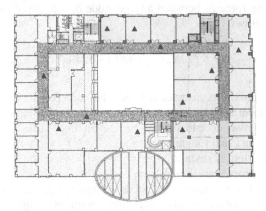

Fig. 6. Floor layout for the experiments. The red triangles are locations of IEEE 802.11 AP and the rectangular area is the corridors of the floor.

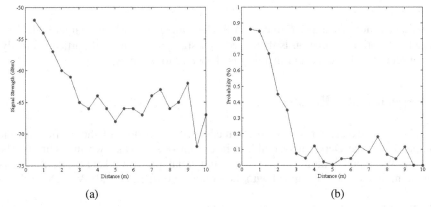

(a)   (b)

Fig. 7. Distance and the error model: (a) The relationship between distance of two ZigBee radios and the received signal strength, and (b) the relationship between distance of two ZigBee radios and the probability that they will be detected as neighbors.

We have found several sources of errors in the ZigBee-based neighborhood detection. The first source of error occurs when two nearby persons standing back-to-back, their neighboring links will not be detected, because ZigBee radio signal does not penetrate human bodies well. The second source of error occurs when a third person comes between two persons standing face-to-face, again their neighboring links will also be broken due to human body interference from the third person.

4.2 Performance Evaluation

To evaluate performance of our collaborative localization, we have designed two scenarios for experiments. The first scenario consists of stationary people forming *stationary clusters*. Locations of stationary clusters are pre-arranged shown in Figure 3. We then observe how well our collaborative localization can improve positioning accuracy over a baseline WiFi positioning engine. The second scenario consists of mobile people forming *mobile clusters*. Movements of people are modeled after an ordinary group visit shown in Figures 12 and 15. In addition, two persons standing at two fixed locations on a corridor act as stationary passers. We then observe collaborative localization on how well stationary passers can help improving positioning accuracy of mobile clusters.

In the experiments, we simulate the error induced from ZigBee. The error is then appended to the ground truth to evaluate our collaborative location system. This is the preliminary study of deploying ZigBee as proximity sensor.

4.3 Stationary Clusters (Scenario I)

Scenario I consists of two cases of 3-person and 7-person stationary clusters with a cluster radius fixed to either 0.5 meter (called a *dense cluster*) or 1 meter (called a *sparse cluster*). Figure 8 plots cumulative distribution functions (CDF) of average positioning errors for 3-person dense and sparse clusters. Curves labeled "*no-collaboration*" show results when collaboration is not applied to location estimations, whereas curves labeled "*collaboration*" show results when collaboration is applied to location estimations. In addition, the curve labeled "*3-person non-clustering*" shows results when 3 stationary persons are standing apart without forming any cluster. This is used as a reference line for comparing with clustering cases. In the 3-person sparse cluster case, collaboration produces 37.2% accuracy improvement from 3.38 meters (no-collaboration) to 2.12 meters at 75% precision. Moreover, the average error is reduced by 34% from 2.41 meters to 1.59 meters. In the 3-person dense cluster case, collaboration produces 38% accuracy improvement from 5.38 meters (no-collaboration) to 3.34 meters at 75% precision. Moreover, the average error is reduced by 28.2% from 3.33 meters to 2.39 meters.

Figure 9 shows a positive relationship between the amount of accuracy improvement received by a target node, after applying collaboration, and $\triangle Confidence$, which is the difference in confidence scores between a target node and its neighbor node, in a 3-person dense cluster case. The plot shows that when $\triangle Confidence$ is positive (i.e., a neighbor node has a higher confidence score than a target node), collaboration can help improving positioning accuracy of a target node. More importantly, a larger $\triangle Confidence$ results in a higher accuracy improvement, because a target node can benefit more from a neighbor node whose location estimation has a better accuracy than its location estimation. On the other hand, when $\triangle Confidence$ is negative (i.e., a neighbor node has a lower confidence score than a target node), collaboration is disabled because a neighbor node is likely to have worse positioning accuracy than a target node.

Figure 10 plots cumulative distribution functions (CDF) of average positioning errors for 7-person dense and sparse clusters. Results show that the amount of accuracy improvement in 7-person clusters is greater than that of 3-person clusters. In the 7-person sparse cluster, collaboration produces 54.7% accuracy improvement from 6.26 meters (no-collaboration) to 2.83 meters at 75% precision. Moreover, the average error is reduced by 49% from 4.20 meters to 2.14 meters. In the 7-person

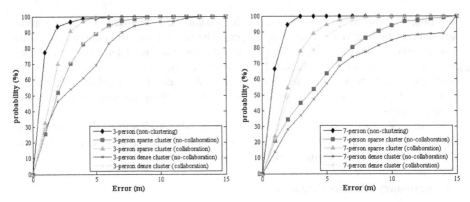

Fig. 8. CDF of average positioning errors in the 3-person cluster scenario

Fig. 10. CDF of average positioning errors in the 7-person cluster scenario

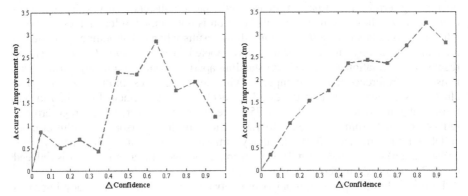

Fig. 9. The amount of accuracy improvement versus the neighborhood confidence difference in the 3-person dense cluster

Fig. 11. The amount of accuracy improvement versus the neighborhood confidence difference in the 7-person dense cluster

dense cluster, collaboration produces 49.2% accuracy improvement from 7.25 meters (no-reduced by 56.3% from 5.95 meters to 2.60 meters. Similar to the 3-person case, Figure 11 shows a positive relationship between the amount of accuracy improvement and the confidence difference with a neighbor node.

4.4 Mobile Clusters (Scenario II)

Scenario II consists of two cases of 4-person and 5-person mobile clusters with a cluster radius fixed to 0.5 meter. In addition, one more person in a 4-person case and two more persons in a 5-person case stand at fixed locations on a corridor as stationary passers. These settings are shown in Figure 12 and Figure 15. The total distance of the corridor is about 30 meters. Figure 13 plots cumulative distribution functions (CDF) of positioning errors for the stationary passer and average errors of the

Fig. 12. 4 clustered persons walking by a stationary passer

Fig. 15. 5 clustered persons walking by 2 stationary passers

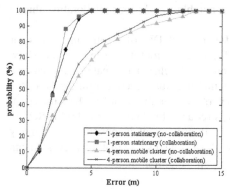

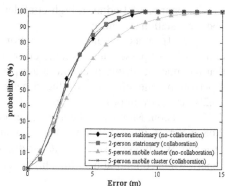

Fig. 13. CDF of average positioning errors in the 4-person mobile cluster case

Fig. 16. CDF of average positioning errors in the 5-person mobile cluster case

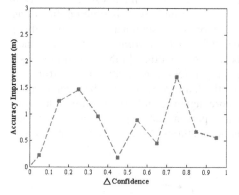

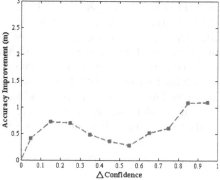

Fig. 14. Average of accuracy improvement in the 4-person mobile cluster case

Fig. 17. Average of accuracy improvement in the 5-person mobile cluster case

4-person mobile cluster. The curve labeled "*1-person stationary*" shows positioning error of the stationary passer, and the curve labeled "*4-person mobile cluster*" shows average positioning error of a 4-person mobile cluster. In addition, curves labeled "*no-collaboration*" show results when collaboration is not applied to location estimations, whereas the curves labeled "*collaboration*" show results when collaboration is applied to location estimations. For the 4-person mobile cluster, the collaborative localization produces 16% accuracy improvement from 5.67 meters (no-collaboration) to 4.76 meters at 75% precision. Moreover, the average error is reduced by 17.5% from 4.57 meters to 3.77 meters. Figure 14 shows the relationship between

the amount of improvement in positioning accuracy received by a target node and
$\triangle Confidence$. Results show a target node can benefit when collaborating with a
higher confident neighbor node. However, we have found that accuracy improvement
in mobile clusters is smaller than accuracy improvement in stationary clusters. The
reason is that mobile nodes in general receive less accurate location estimations from
a localization engine than stationary nodes; therefore, a node in a mobile cluster has a
smaller chance of finding a high confidence neighbor node for collaboration than a
node in a stationary cluster.

Figure 16 plots cumulative distribution functions (CDF) of positioning errors for
two stationary passers and average errors of a 5-person mobile cluster. Results show
that the amount of improvement in a 5-person mobile cluster is greater than that of a
4-person mobile cluster. For the 5-person mobile cluster, collaboration produces
26.2% accuracy improvement from 5.58 meters (no-collaboration) to 4.12 meters at
75% precision. Moreover, the average error is reduced by 33.5% from 4.03 meters to
2.68 meters. Figure 17 shows the amount of improvement in positioning accuracy
received by a target node and $\triangle Confidence$. Results also show that a target node can
benefit when collaborating with a higher confident neighbor node.

4.5 Evaluation of Confidence Estimator

We compare the accuracy improvement between our confidence estimation method,
calculated from Equation (1), and two alterative estimation methods called uniform
and random. Results, shown in Figure 18, plot cumulative distribution functions
(CDF) of average positioning errors for a 7-person dense stationary cluster over three
confidence estimation methods. Curves labeled "*no-collaboration*" shows a reference
line when collaboration is not applied to location estimations. In the uniform method,
every node receives equal confidence scores regardless of estimation errors from the
underlying location engine. In the random method, a random number between 0 and 1
is assigned to each node as its confidence score, again regardless of estimation errors
from the underlying location engine. In a 7-person stationary dense cluster, our
method outperforms both uniform and random methods. Note that both random and

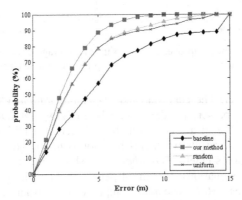

Fig. 18. Comparison of three confidence estimation methods (our current method, uniform, and
random) in a 7-person, stationary, dense cluster

uniform methods can still benefit from collaboration. The reason is that positioning errors from the underlying Ekahau location engine in general follow a *symmetric distribution*. Symmetric distribution means that while some location estimations of nodes are off in one direction, some location estimations of nodes in the same cluster are off in an opposite direction. Therefore, applying collaboration has a beneficial effect of error cancellation within a cluster of nodes.

5   Related Work

There has been extensive research on indoor localization. WiFi-based location systems can be either deterministic [5-8] or probabilistic [1-4] in matching RSSI from-mobile devices to a radio map. The best systems claim 90% accuracy with an error of less than 1~2 meters. Some of these systems achieve better accuracy by combining different localization methods. That is, a hybrid system can benefit under situations where one method works poorly while another still works well. For example, Graumann et al. [9] aim at designing a universal location framework by using GPS in an outdoor environment, WiFi for an indoor environment, and Motes for proximity detection. Gwon et al. [10] proposed algorithms combining WiFi and Bluetooth sensors as information sources and selectively weighting them such that error contribution from each sensor can be minimized to improve the positioning accuracy. However, these systems do not address the human clustering problem.

Dynamic environmental factors can incur location estimation errors in traditional Wi-Fi location systems. Some proposed methods have attempted to address this issue. The temporal prediction approach in [11] can observe and learn how a radio map changes over time by employing emitters and sniffers to observe Wi-Fi RSSI variations. By applying regression analysis, the temporal prediction approach can learn the temporal predictive relationship between RSSI values received by sniffers and those received by target mobile devices. However, the temporal prediction approach assumes that changes in the environmental factors follow some predictable temporal patterns. However, in the people clustering case, such assumption does not hold given that people clustering is highly dynamic with individual node experiencing large variations of degradation. Reference points and regression model would not be able to capture such dynamic variations. Chen et al. [12] also addressed the challenge of providing stable position estimation under different environmental dynamics, including change of floor layout, change in relative humidity, and moving people. Since major floor layout changes occur less frequently, they can be managed by rebuilding a selective part of a radio map. To adapt to different relative humidity levels, a separate radio map can also be constructed for each humidity level. However, coping with moving people is more challenging, because it is infeasible to model and enumerate all possible cases of human clustering formations; furthermore, to construct different radio maps.

The idea of utilizing neighbor information to help localization is also used in sensor network localization and network coordination. DOLPHIN [13] deployed fixed nodes with ultrasonic and RF sensors in an environment. Nodes with known location coordinates are called master nodes. Non-master nodes can compute their relative locations to multiple master nodes by exchanging ultrasonic and RF signals. After performing iterative triangulation, nodes can get their absolute coordinates and become master nodes. He *et al.* [17] proposed a cost-effective, range-based localization approach called APIT for large scale sensor networks. Like the DOLPHIN system, the sensor network contains anchor devices that can obtain their locations through GPS receivers. Anchor nodes first broadcast their locations to non-anchor nodes. A non-anchor node then iteratively chooses different combination of 3 received anchor nodes and performs a Point-In-Triangulation (PIT) Test, which is used to determine whether a non-anchor node is inside a triangular region formed by 3 anchor nodes. If a non-anchor node resides in that triangular region, that region is marked as a possible location of the non-anchor node. After all combinations are exhausted, the center of intersections from all possible regions is calculated to estimate a non-anchor node's location. AFL [18] is a fully decentralized, anchor-free approach, utilizing the idea of fold-freedom to build a topology of a sensor network through local node interactions. In AFL, nodes start from a random initial coordinate assignment. By applying mass-spring optimization repeatedly, nodes' location estimations can converge to be near their true coordinates. Our work differs from these systems in that they assume nodes with known locations are stationary, whereas our work assumes that nodes are mobile people. In addition, these sensor network location systems assume that nodes with a cluster will not interfere with each other's positioning accuracy. However, in our system, people clustering results in blocked signals and degradation in positioning accuracy.

Hu *et al.* [14] proposed a method for sensor network localization that allows some node mobility. Seeds are nodes with known locations. Non-seed nodes apply a motion model to predict their locations by sensing whether they are entering proximity of or departing from a seed node. Seeds and non-seed nodes can be either mobile or stationary. However, their work does not consider errors in seed nodes' locations. This differs from our work in which node clustering leads to localization errors.

Neighbor information has also been used in network coordinate system at the Internet scale. GNP [15] places nodes with known locations in a network as landmark nodes. Other nodes can compute their approximate coordinates based on network round trip time (RTT) measurements to these landmark nodes. Vivaldi [16] proposed an alternative method without using landmarks. Each node in the network measures RTTs, translated into relative distances, to its neighbors and gradually converges to a virtual coordinate. However, these systems differ from our work in that they are not concerned with high location accuracy.

6 Conclusion and Future Work

This paper targets the problem of human clusters in WiFi-based localization. We have conducted tests to show that a human cluster can block WiFi signals, resulting in degradation of location accuracy. To address this issue, we have designed and implemented *collaborative localization*, which a node with a higher confidence of accuracy can help fine-tune location estimations of neighbor nodes that have a lower confidence. The proposed method consists of the three modules: (1) Neighborhood Detection finds nearby neighbors, (2) Confidence Estimation measures the accuracy of the location estimation, and (3) Collaborative Error Correction uses neighbor nodes' information to reduce the target node's positioning error. Our experimental results have shown that collaborative localization produces 28.2~56% accuracy improvement in stationary human clusters and 16~33.5% accuracy improvement in mobile human clusters.

For future work, we would like to improve the accuracy of our neighborhood detection by using existing Wi-Fi adaptors or exploring alternative proximity sensors. One possible approach is to set WiFi adaptors in an ad-hoc mode for detecting signals strength from neighbor nodes. The advantage of this approach is that it requires no additional hardware. However, the challenge is in accuracy, considering that human body can cause interference to WiFi signals. To address this issue, we are looking for neighborhood detection methods that are not only based on using a single signal strength threshold.

Another future work is to place fixed anchor nodes in the environment where human clusters are likely to occur, e.g., in front of popular exhibits. These anchor nodes, with maximum confidence scores, can help fine-tune any nearby human clusters that border them.

Acknowledgments

This work was partially supported by grants from Taiwan NSC, Quanta Computer, and Intel (#94-2218-E-002-055, #94-2622-E-002-024, #94-2218-E-002-075, and #94-2218-E-002-057).

References

1. Paramvir Bahl and Venkata N. Padmanabhan: RADAR: An in-building RF-based user location and tracking system. IEEE INFOCOM (Mar. 2000) 775-784
2. ITRI, http://www.itri.org.tw
3. Paramvir Bahl, A. Balachandran, and V. N. Padmanabhan: Enhancements to the RADAR user location and tracking system. Technical report of Microsoft Research (Feb. 2000)
4. Ekahau. http://www.ekahau.com
5. V. Seshadri, G. V. Zaruba, and M. Huber: A Bayesian Sampling Approach to In-door Local-ization of Wireless Devices Using Received Signal Strength Indication. IEEE Conference on Pervasive Computing and Communications (PerCom) (Mar. 2005)
6. J. Hightower, and G. Borriello: Particle Filters for Location Estimation in Ubiquitous Computing: A Case Study. International Conference on Ubiquitous Computing (Sept. 2005)
7. D. Schulz, D. Fox, and J. Hightower: People Tracking with Anonymous and ID-Sensors using Rao-Blackwellised Particle Filters. International Joint Conference on Artificial Intelligence (Aug. 2003) 921-926
8. D. Fox, J. Hightower, L. Liao, D. Schulz, and G. Borriello: Bayesian Filtering for Location Estimation. IEEE Pervasive Computing, vol. 2, no. 3 (July-Sept. 2003) 24-33
9. David Graumann, Jeffrey Hightower, Walter Lara, and GaeTano Borriello: Real-world Implementation of the Location Stack: The Universal Location Framework. IEEE Workshop on Mobile Computing Systems & Applications (WMCSA) (Oct. 2003)
10. Youngjune Gwon, Ravi Jain, and Toshiro Kawahara: Robust Indoor Location Estimation of Stationary and Mobile Users. IEEE INFOCOM (Mar. 2004)
11. J. Yie, Q. Yang, L. Ni: Adaptive Temporal Radio Maps for Indoor Location Estimation. International Conference on Pervasive Computing (May 2005)

12. Y.C. Chen, J.R. Chiang, H.H. Chu, Polly Huang, and A. W. Tsui: Sensor-Assisted Wi-Fi Indoor Location System for Adapting to Environmental Dynamics. International Symposium on Modeling, Analysis and Simulation of Wireless and Mobile Systems (Oct. 2005)
13. Masateru Minami, Yasuhiro Fukuju, Kazuki Hirasawa, Shigeaki Yokoyama, Moriyuki Mizumachi, Hiroyuki Morikawa, and Tomonori Aoyama: DOLPHIN: A Practical Approach for Implementing a Fully Distributed Indoor Ultrasonic Positioning System. International Conference on Ubiquitous Computing (UbiCom) (Sep. 2004) 347-365
14. Lingxuan Hu and David Evans: Localization for Mobile Sensor Networks. International Conference on Mobile Computing and Networking (MobiCom) (2004)
15. T. S. Eugene Ng and Hui Zhang: Predicting Internet Network Distance with Coordinates-Based Approaches. IEEE INFOCOM (2002) 170-179
16. Frank Dabek, Russ Cox, Frans Kaashoek, and Robert Morris: Vivaldi: A Decentralized Network Coordinate System. ACM SIGCOMM (2004)
17. Tian He, Chengdu Huang, Brian M. Blum, John A. Stankovic and Tarek Abdelzaher: Range-Free Localization Schemes for Large Scale Sensor Networks. ACM International Conference on Mobile Computing and Networking (MOBICOM) (2003) 81-95
18. Nissanka B. Priyantha, Hari Balakrishnan, Erik Demaine, and Seth Teller: Anchor-Free Distributed Localization in Sensor Networks. ACM International Conference on Embedded Networked Sensor Systems (SenSys) (2003) 340-341

Risks of Using AP Locations Discovered Through War Driving

Minkyong Kim, Jeffrey J. Fielding, and David Kotz

Department of Computer Science
Dartmouth College

Abstract. Many pervasive-computing applications depend on knowledge of user location. Because most current location-sensing techniques work only either indoors or outdoors, researchers have started using 802.11 beacon frames from access points (APs) to provide broader coverage. To use 802.11 beacons, they need to know AP locations. Because the actual locations are often unavailable, they use estimated locations from *war driving*. But these estimated locations may be different from actual locations. In this paper, we analyzed the errors in these estimates and the effect of these errors on other applications that depend on them. We found that the estimated AP locations have a median error of 32 meters. We considered the error in tracking user positions both indoors and outdoors. Using actual AP locations, we could improve the accuracy as much as 70% for indoors and 59% for outdoors. We also analyzed the effect of using estimated AP locations in computing AP coverage range and estimating interference among APs. The coverage range appeared to be shorter and the interference appeared to be more severe than in reality.

1   Introduction

Pervasive computing applications often need to know the location of users. This location information should be available anywhere, both indoors and outdoors. While some location sensing techniques, such as Cricket [11] and Bat [5], provide high accuracy, they are mostly limited to indoor usage. On the other hand, satellite navigation systems like GPS [4] are useful for outdoor navigation, but they do not work well in urban settings due to the "urban canyon" effect.

To address these limits, researchers have started using 802.11 beacon frames from access points (APs) to locate wireless network users. Intel's Place Lab [3, 8] provides software that can track users both indoors and outdoors. Skyhook Wireless [13] provides a similar commercial solution for locating Wi-Fi users. These approaches require knowledge of the (actual or estimated) location of APs. In addition to user-location tracking, researchers also use the location of APs to analyze wireless network characteristics such as the coverage range of APs or interference among APs.

Although we may be able to get the actual location of APs for managed networks, it is almost impossible to get the actual location of unmanaged networks. Thus, researchers [3, 1] recently started using the AP locations estimated through *war driving*. War driving is the process of collecting Wi-Fi beacons by driving or walking through a town, to discover and map the location of APs [7]. Because war driving is easy and

K.P. Fishkin et al. (Eds.): PERVASIVE 2006, LNCS 3968, pp. 67–82, 2006.

can be performed by anybody with a wireless card, a GPS receiver, and war-driving software, it is an effective way of collecting AP location information. The AP locations determined by war driving, however, are estimates rather than actual locations. Thus, it is important to understand the errors in these estimates and the effect of these errors on other applications that depend on these estimated AP locations.

The main goal of this paper is to understand the effect of using AP locations estimated through war driving. We do not want to discourage people from using the estimated AP locations, but rather we want to encourage them to use the data with an appropriate caution. Our focus is on comparing various results using estimated AP locations against those using actual AP locations. We explored the error in estimated AP locations. The median error in estimated AP locations was 32 meters. We considered the error in tracking user positions both indoors and outdoors. Using actual AP locations, we could improve the accuracy of user location estimates as much as 59% outdoors and 70% indoors. We also analyzed the effect of using estimated AP locations in analyzing AP coverage ranges and estimating the inferences among APs. The coverage range appeared to be shorter when estimated AP locations are used and the interference among APs appeared to be more severe.

2 Related Work

Many wireless network users use war-driving data to learn the location of APs for (free) Wi-Fi connectivity. There are several Internet Web sites, including WiFiMaps.com [15], that collect and provide this information. People discover Wi-Fi hotspots through war driving and upload their data to these sites. As the main goal of these Web sites is to discover available Wi-Fi connectivity, it is not important to accurately estimate the location of APs, but this may not be the case for other applications.

Although the accuracy of AP location estimates can be improved with additional hardware, such as directional antennas [12], it is often more time consuming to collect data using extra hardware and this hardware is not commonly available among typical Wi-Fi users. War driving without extra hardware seems to be an easy and convenient way to collect AP locations for larger areas, although its estimates may be inaccurate.

There are many applications that need to know the accurate location of APs. *Localization* is the process of determining the physical location of a user. Localization techniques that use Wi-Fi beacons depend on accurate information about the location of APs. Place Lab [3] uses the AP location estimates from war driving to track a user's location. Other localization techniques [2] assume that the locations of *reference points* are known without specifying methods to discover their locations. Just as in Place Lab, one could use the location estimates from war driving for these approaches. Besides localization, researchers have started using AP location estimates to study AP deployment characteristics such as AP density and interference among APs [1]. Unlike the original motivation for war driving, which is finding Wi-Fi hotspots, these applications are highly affected by the accuracy of AP locations. Thus, it is critical to analyze the accuracy of estimated AP locations and understand their impact on the applications that depend on them. The only previous work that analyzed the accuracy of AP locations estimated through war driving is not comprehensive; it considered the location of only five APs [9]. To the best of our knowledge, ours is the first research study to analyze in a large scale the accuracy and the impact of using AP location estimates.

3 Methodology

As researchers have started using data collected by war driving for applications such as localization, it is important to understand the errors in war-driving data. Given the actual AP locations on our college campus, we performed war driving on the campus and obtained the estimated AP locations.

We believe that the Dartmouth college campus is an ideal place to perform this study. First, Dartmouth has wireless coverage almost everywhere on the campus. Second, all APs on the campus are centrally administrated. Thus, it is relatively straight-forward to obtain information about these APs. Third, information about the location of APs is up-to-date since we have recently replaced all of our APs and recorded detailed location data.

In the following sections, we describe the process of mapping APs on our campus map, war driving on the campus, and the algorithms from Place Lab that we used to estimate AP locations and to track user positions.

3.1 Actual AP Locations

To understand the effect of using AP location estimates, we first need to obtain the actual AP locations to serve as the 'truth'. We were lucky to have access to the actual AP locations on our college campus. Our network administrators keep records of the location of APs on floor plans of campus buildings. Using these floor plans, we determined the precise location of APs on the campus map. These locations serve as the *actual* locations. In this way, we mapped 927 APs. Out of 927, 44 APs are dedicated to air monitoring and the rest are regular APs. The air monitors collect network statistics and work only in a passive mode, not sending out any signals. Except seven APs that support only 802.11g, all APs support both 802.11a and 802.11g. While 100% of the APs on our campus support 802.11g, this ratio is much lower for observed unplanned networks in Pittsburgh: 20% supporting 802.11g and the rest supporting only 802.11b [1].

3.2 War Driving

To understand the effect of using estimated AP locations through war driving, we drove and walked around our campus. We used a Linux laptop and a Cisco *Aironet 350* wireless card, which supports 802.11b. The laptop ran the *Place Lab stumbler 2.0* to collect beacons from APs. We also carried a GPS device, Garmin *etrex*, attached to the laptop.

We drove around the campus with these devices at a speed of 10 miles/hour or less to allow the wireless card enough time to pick up beacons. Our war driving lasted about 80 minutes. Since we could not drive close to many buildings, we decided to augment the war-driving data with *war walking*.

We walked around the main parts of the campus to cover the areas that cars cannot reach. We collected war-walking data for about 200 minutes. Because both war driving and war walking use GPS readings to locate the position of the recorder, we had to stay outdoors. To get signals from as many APs as possible and also not to bias the AP-location estimates towards one direction, we walked *around* each building and tried to stay close to it as long as we had GPS signal reception. Unfortunately, we often encountered obstructions—such as trees, outside structures, and construction vehicles—that prevented us from walking close to buildings.

3.3 Algorithms

Intel's Place Lab project [10] is well-known for using war driving data to locate APs and perform localization by detecting Wi-Fi beacons from APs. We use the software provided by Place Lab to estimate AP and user locations.

To estimate AP locations from war driving and war walking, we looked into three positioning algorithms: centroid, weighted centroid, and particle filters. Given n location measurements, the geometric centroid $\bar{\mathbf{x}}$ is defined as $\bar{\mathbf{x}} = \sum_{i=1}^{n} \mathbf{x}_i/n$ where $\mathbf{x}_i$ is location of the ith measurement. This simple centroid does not consider the signal strength of beacons. The weighted centroid considers signal strength received during the scan. During our war walking and war driving, we observed values between -123 dBm and -25 dBm. These values are linearly mapped to values between 0 and 100 and then used as the weights for the weighted-centroid algorithm. The particle filter [3] is based on Bayes' theory. To estimate an AP's location, it uses a sensor model that assigns probabilities to particles based on the observed signal strength and the distance from the particle to the observer. The default motion model is null since APs do not move.

To estimate user position, we use a particle filter with a sensor model that describes the likelihood of observing a set of APs with their received signal strengths given the particle's distance to each AP. The default motion model moves particles random distances in random directions. Details on particle filters can be found in Hightower and Borriello's paper [6].

4   Understanding War-Driving Data

Our main goal is to understand the effect of using estimated AP locations rather than actual locations on user-location tracking and wireless network characterizations. More specifically, we explore following questions:

- How effective is war driving or war walking in discovering APs?
- How well can we estimate the location of APs by war driving or war walking?
- How well can we track user positions outdoors?
- How well can we track user positions indoors?
- What is the effect of using estimated AP locations on analyzing AP coverage range?
- What is the effect of inaccuracy in AP locations on analyzing AP interference?

4.1   Effectiveness of War Driving

In this section, we consider the effectiveness of war driving or war walking in discovering APs. Excluding 44 air monitors, we know the actual location of 883 APs deployed on our campus. Out of 883 APs, we detected only 334 APs during war driving, and detected an additional 187 APs through war walking. This makes the AP detection rate 38% for war driving and 59% for the combination of war driving and war walking. We also detected 172 APs whose actual locations are unknown. We exclude these APs in our analysis of errors in AP locations since we do not have the ground truth, but later analyze their effect on estimating user locations (see Fig. 7 and 9). Table 1 summarizes the number of APs detected during war driving and war walking.

Figure 1 shows the estimated location of APs on the Dartmouth campus map. We see that the weighted-centroid algorithm estimated APs to be close to the war-driving or war-walking tracks; estimated AP locations are often on the tracks recorded by the GPS device. This tendency is especially strong around the edge of the campus where there are fewer roads. One side effect of this outcome is that APs appear to be close to each other. We later consider the consequences of this in Section 4.6.

Out of 883 APs, we only detected 521 APs during war driving and war walking. Most of the 362 undetected APs are in the outer region of the campus where we did not

Table 1. APs detected during war driving and war walking. Note that the total is smaller than the sum of war driving and war walking because many APs are detected during both.

	APs w/ known location	APs w/ unknown location
Driving	334	56
Walking	384	155
Total	521	172

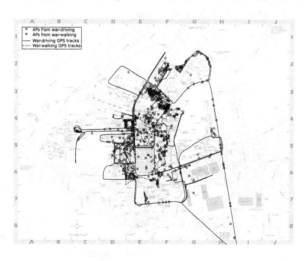

Fig. 1. Estimated AP locations on campus map. 'o' marks denote 521 APs detected during war driving and 'x' marks shows additional APs detected by war walking. Lines show war-driving and war-walking paths recorded by a GPS device.

do war walking (e.g., the west end of the campus). But, some APs are actually in areas that we walked around; these APs are inside large buildings (such as the main library in the center of the campus) and mostly in the basement or on higher floors of buildings.[1] Being outdoors on ground-level apparently prevented us from detecting signals from APs in basements and on upper floors.

One of the important characteristics in understanding AP deployment is the density of APs. The size of our main campus is roughly 1 km^2. Using this size, the density using the actual number of APs is 927/km^2, while those based on the APs discovered by war driving and war driving with walking (*driving-walking*) are 334/km^2 and 521/km^2, respectively. Cheng et al. [3] reported the density of three neighborhoods in the Seattle area. Our density of 927/km^2 is close to those of the downtown Seattle (1030) and Ravenna (1000), while it is higher than that of Kirkland (130). Note that in computing density, we considered only the APs whose locations are known; if we include 172 APs with unknown locations, we get the density of 1099/km^2.

We also present the number of APs detected at each scan by the Place Lab stumbler; the stumbler scanned every two seconds. Figure 2 shows the cumulative fraction of scans as a function of the number of APs for each scan. It includes the result for war driving, war walking, and the two combined. War walking detected more APs than war driving: The averages are 11.5 and 6.1 for war walking and war driving, respectively. Since we did not, or could not, take exactly the same paths for war driving and war walking, it may not be fair to directly compare these two averages, but war walking in general seems to be more effective in detecting beacons than war driving. We expect that this is because war walking is slower and its paths are closer to buildings where APs are located. The average for combined is 10.0 APs per scan; this average is much higher than the average reported by Cheng et al. [3] for three neighborhoods in the Seattle area—2.66, 2.56 and 1.41—although the density of APs in two studies are similar. This is mostly due to the fact that we augmented war-driving data by war walking, while Cheng et al. collected traces only by war driving.

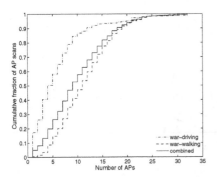

Fig. 2. Number of APs detected per scan

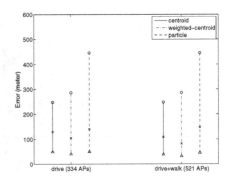

Fig. 3. Error in AP locations. $\triangle$, $\times$, and $\circ$ marks show the value for 50%, 95%, and 100%, respectively

---

[1] The highest building on our campus has six floors above the ground level.

4.2   AP Locations

In this section, we consider the error in AP-location estimates from war driving and war walking using known AP locations on our campus. Figure 3 shows the error in AP locations using three positioning algorithms. We consider two sets of APs: one discovered by war driving only and the other discovered by either war driving or war walking. We see that war walking helped reduce the error for both simple-centroid and weighted-centroid algorithms; we are not sure why this is not the case for the particle filter. For both sets of APs, the weighted centroid outperformed both the simple centroid and the particle filter. Its median error using war-driving data was 40.8 meters, while the error using both war-driving and war-walking data was 31.6 meters. In the remainder of the paper, we only consider the AP location estimates generated by the weighted centroid.

4.3   User Location: Outdoor

To understand the effect of using estimated AP locations to estimate user position, we walked along four, mostly non-overlapping, paths. Together, they cover the central part of the campus. Each walk lasted around 10 minutes, including a one-minute pause at a location. During these four outdoor walks, we detected 8 additional APs. We did not include them in our war-walking AP set because adding the traces from test walks affects the results. Figure 4 shows these four walks on the campus map.

We used Place Lab's particle filter [3] to estimate user position using the beacon data collected during the four walks. We estimated user paths using three sets of the AP locations: actual, war driving only, and war driving and war walking combined.

Figure 5 shows the paths for the four test walks. For each walk, we plotted the GPS track and the estimated paths using the three sets of AP locations. The circles on the GPS track denote the location of the one-minute pauses. When looking at Walk 3, the estimated tracks using AP locations from war driving and driving-walking were particularly inaccurate. This inaccuracy is due to a big open area, which does not contain any APs but is covered by several powerful APs around it. For Walk 4, estimated paths

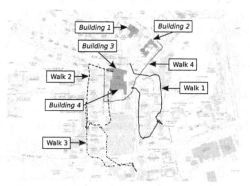

Fig. 4. Test walks on campus map. This figure depicts GPS tracks of four outdoor test walks and the locations of four buildings where indoor test walks were performed.

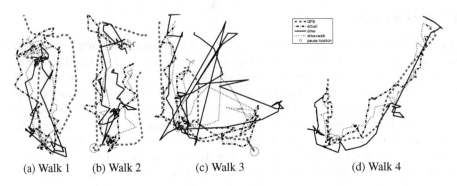

(a) Walk 1   (b) Walk 2   (c) Walk 3   (d) Walk 4

Fig. 5. User location

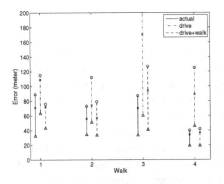 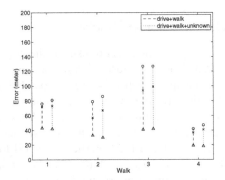

Fig. 6. Error in outdoor user position (△:50%, ×:95%, ○:100%). The 95% and 100% values for Walk 3's drive group are 231 and 250, respectively.

Fig. 7. Error in outdoor user positions with unknown APs (△:50%, ×:95%, ○:100%)

were close to its GPS track because this walk was through an area with dense APs. For all four walks, the estimated paths converged with GPS tracks near the pause locations, presumably because the estimator corrected the user location as it detected beacons from more APs located near the pause location.

Figure 6 shows the error in user location estimates. The GPS tracks again served as the ground truth. The error is the difference between the GPS tracks and the estimated paths, computed every 20 seconds. For each walk, errors with actual, war-driving, and war-driving with war-walking AP locations are shown. The errors using actual AP locations were much smaller than those using the war-driving AP locations. Compared to errors using driving-walking, the errors of the actual set are smaller for Walk 3, and about the same for the other walks. The reason for this closeness is because we walked along similar paths during the war walking. In summary, the median error in four walks using actual AP locations ranged 19–34 m, that for war driving ranged 46–63 m, and that for driving-walking ranged 19–43 m.

Although Figure 6 clearly shows that actual AP locations outperformed war driving, one might wonder whether it is due to the fact that we know the location of a bigger number of APs (883). To factor out this problem, we ignored the actual location of APs

Table 2. Improvement in outdoor user-location estimates by using actual AP locations instead of estimated AP locations. We used a subset of actual locations of APs that were detected during war driving and driving-walking. The median of normalized improvement is depicted.

Walk number	1	2	3	4
Outdoor: drive	33%	31%	17%	59%
Outdoor: drive-walk	13%	5%	28%	14%

that were not detected during war driving and war walking. Thus, we only used the same set of APs that were detected during war driving; we did the same for driving-walking. Table 2 shows the result. Each number is the median of the normalized improvement for every user position: $median(\frac{(e_i - a_i)}{e_i} \times 100\%)$ where e_i and a_i are the errors using estimated and actual AP locations, respectively, for the ith position. We used 334 actual AP locations for war driving, and 521 locations for driving-walking. When we used the actual AP locations, the accuracy improved for both war driving and driving-walking. The median improvement ranged 5%–59%. Having accurate AP locations is important to estimate user position correctly.

During war driving and walking, we discovered 172 APs whose actual locations are unknown. We considered whether using these extra APs reduces the user location error. Figure 7 shows the error for the two sets of APs: drive-walk and drive-walk with unknown APs. Note that all these AP locations are estimates. The result shows that using extra APs did not make much difference; for all four walks, it even increased the 95% error values.

4.4 User Location: Indoor

The main benefit of using Place Lab over a GPS device is that it is usable where a GPS signal is not available. A Place Lab paper by Cheng et al. [3] contains a simple evaluation of indoor accuracy of user positions. They visited nine indoor locations and found that the location error ranges from 9 to 98 meters. In this section, we further explore the accuracy of Place Lab in tracking user positions indoors.

To estimate our position indoors, we marked points on the building's floor plan as we walked. While the latest Place Lab source includes a stumbler using this method, we had trouble getting it to work on our stumbler laptop. In addition, many of the floor plans were oriented at odd angles, which Place Lab's *mapwad* format[2] does not support. We wrote a new stumbler to map the floor plans to the campus map using conversions we derived earlier as we mapped the known AP locations on the campus map.

We chose four buildings, most of whose APs were detected during either war driving or war walking; we in fact walked around each of these four building during war-walking. Figure 4 shows the location of these buildings on the campus map. We walked inside of these four buildings, covering three or more floors within each building. The duration of our indoor walks ranged from 6 to 14 minutes; this duration does not include time that we took to move to the next floor. Table 3 shows the duration and the floors that we walked within each building.

---

[2] A format that includes maps and sets of places [10].

Table 3. Indoor walks. This table shows the floors that we walked within each building.

Building	Duration (minute)	Floors
1	14	Basement, floor 1, 2, 3 and 4
2	9	Basement, floor 1 and 2
3	7	Floor 1, 3 and 4
4	6	Basement, floor 1 and 3

Table 4. Improvement in indoor user-location estimates. We used a subset of actual locations of APs that were detected either during war driving or war walking.

Building number	1	2	3	4
Indoor: drive-walk	14%	53%	17%	70%

During our indoor test walks, we detected an additional 24 APs, many more than the 8 discovered in our outdoor walks. This result is not surprising since we stayed only outdoors during war driving and war walking. We can imagine using our software extension to do war walking indoors to augment the data collected by outdoor war driving and walking. But, indoor war walking may not be possible in other situations since it requires physical access to buildings and digitized floor plans of those buildings.

Figure 8 shows the error in user positions using the actual AP locations and war driving with walking. We could not use the AP locations estimated from war driving only because we did not have enough APs to make reasonable user-location estimates for indoor walks. For example, through war driving, we did not discover any APs in Building 1. The error in user position was computed every 10 seconds.

Compared to outdoor walks, indoor walks had smaller absolute errors. This difference is partly because each indoor walk covered a smaller area than the outdoor walks. The median error using actual AP locations ranged from 7 to 11 meters, while that using estimated AP locations ranged from 15 to 30 meters. On the other hand, the relative difference between using actual and estimated AP locations was bigger than the difference for outdoor walks because we could not do war driving or war walking inside of buildings and the estimated AP locations were often close to war-driving or war-walking paths. Note that Building 1 had some big errors; its maximum error was 91 meters. These large errors were due to the walk in the basement, which is under the ground level without any windows; the other two buildings (2 and 4), in which we also walked in the basement, are half underground with windows.

As we did for the outdoor test walks, we computed the median relative improvement for indoor walks. We used the actual location of the same set of APs that were detected during war driving and walking to compute the user-position errors. We then computed improvements in user position errors using these actual AP locations. Table 4 shows the median relative improvement, which ranged 14–70%. The average indoor improvement for four buildings (38.5%) was greater than that for outdoor walks with driving-walking (15.0%).

We now consider the effect of using the extra 172 APs in estimating indoor user location. Figure 9 shows the error for both driving-walking and driving-walking with

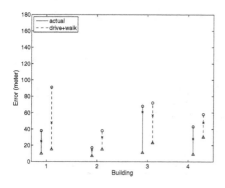
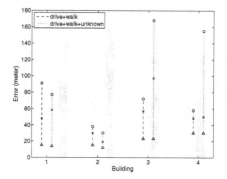

Fig. 8. Error in indoor user location, computed every 10 seconds. ($\triangle$:50%, $\times$:95%, $\circ$:100%).

Fig. 9. Error in indoor user location with unknown APs. ($\triangle$:50%, $\times$:95%, $\circ$:100%).

unknown APs. Using extra APs did not make much difference in median errors; it reduced the 95% error for Building 2, but increased it for the other three buildings. Although there was a much larger worst-case error in two buildings, these cases represent outliers. In summary, for both outdoor and indoors, using extra APs did not make much difference.

For context-aware applications such as a shopping assistant [14], it is important to know whether a user is inside of a building or outdoors. For example, if a user is inside of a grocery store, his context-aware application may pull up the list of items that are running short at home. On the other hand, if a user is passing by a grocery, the application should not pull up the items but just remind the user that he may need to do some grocery shopping.

Figure 10 shows the percentage of estimates for which the particle filter correctly estimated user position to be inside using three different sets of APs: actual location of 883 APs, actual location of 521 APs, and estimated location of 521 APs. (During indoor walks, the user was inside 100% of time.) On average for four buildings, the filter was correct 76% and 71% of time using actual location of 883 APs and 521 APs, respectively, but it was correct only 42% of time using estimated AP locations. Note that using the actual location of 521 APs produced smaller errors than using 883 APs for Building 1; we do not yet have a clear explanation for this result.

4.5 Maximum Signal Coverage

On our campus, we have three models of Aruba APs: 52, 60, and 72. These Aruba APs adjust their power level dynamically and some of them are deployed with special antennas to cover larger areas. Furthermore, signal propagation in a complex environment is difficult to predict. Thus, it is hard to specify the signal coverage range. Instead, we computed it from empirical data gathered while war driving and walking.

For each AP, we computed the distance from the known AP location to the farthest point where each AP was detected during war driving or war walking. Figure 11 shows the cumulative fraction of APs as a function of the maximum signal range. To see the effect of using inaccurate AP locations, we also included the maximum signal range computed from AP locations estimated from war driving and driving-walking. Note

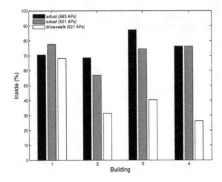

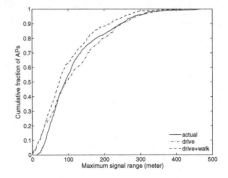

Fig. 10. Inside buildings. This figure shows the percentage of estimates for which the algorithm correctly indicated a user location as inside of each building.

Fig. 11. Maximum signal coverage. The x-axis shows the maximum signal range observed during war driving and war walking. The y-axis shows the cumulative fraction of APs.

that because we used the data collected by war driving and war walking, the recorded maximum range is only an approximation. (Ideally, we should circle around each AP, increasing the radius for each round until we do not hear the signal.) Nonetheless, the median using actual AP locations was exactly equal to the commonly believed range of 300 feet (91.4 m). The maximum observed range of all APs was 470.8 m.

When we used AP locations estimated from war driving or driving-walking, we found more APs with small ranges than when the actual AP locations were used. This results from the tendency of war driving and war walking to estimate APs to be close to where beacons were detected, away from their true locations and closer to roads. The medians were 93.2 and 74.9 meters for war driving and driving-walking, respectively. The maximums were 431.8 and 413.0 meters.

4.6   AP Interference

Although there needs to be some overlap in AP coverage areas to have seamless wireless connectivity, overlaps among too many APs reduce the effective throughput. We computed the interference using AP locations with the 50-meter range used by Akella et al. [1], who focused on characterizing wireless networks that are unplanned and unmanaged based on the assumption that these networks suffer from higher interference than planned-managed networks. Here, we extract the same set of characteristics from our planned-managed campus network.

The data in preceding sections of the paper are based on a campus-wide deployment of 927 APs, as described in Section 3.1. Two months later, we set out to explore interference and the network had grown to 1042 APs, out of which 47 were air monitors. In analyzing interference, we consider only the 995 regular APs.

Using actual AP locations: To analyze interference among APs, Akella et al. presented the degree of each AP, where degree is defined as the number of other APs in interfering range. Figure 12 shows the degrees of 995 APs computed using their actual locations and the 50 m range assumption. Out of 995 APs, 976 APs had 3 or more neighbors.

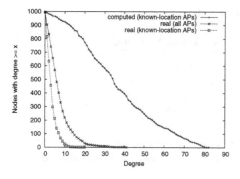

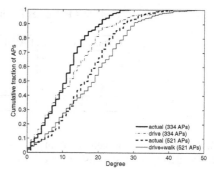

Fig. 12. AP degrees. 'computed' denotes degrees computed with the 50 m interference assumption. Two 'real' lines present degrees observed by APs: one with all APs and the other including only the APs with known locations.

Fig. 13. AP interference. This figure compares the degrees computed using estimated and actual AP locations. For both war driving and driving-walking, the degree using actual locations is smaller than that using estimates.

This ratio of APs with 3 or more neighbors (98%) is actually higher than those for all six cities that Akella et al. reported (approximately 25%–80%). This result suggests that these nodes interfere with at least one other node since only three of the 802.11b channels do not interfere much. The maximum AP degree for our campus was 82. This number is high in the range (20–85) that Akella et al. reported. In short, we found that the computed interference was actually more severe in our planned campus network than the unplanned networks considered by Akella et al.

Figure 12 also includes the real degrees obtained from APs. Each Aruba AP checks periodically which beacons it can detect on every channel and the master switch aggregates this information from APs. Our 995 APs detected 1234 APs, including third-party APs whose locations are unknown. We report two sets of data: one counting only the 995 APs that we know the location of, and the other counting all 1234 APs that our 995 APs detected. The former is included to compare against the computed degree, while the latter presents real observed values. We can see clearly that the real degrees were much smaller than ones computed using the 50-meter interference assumption. The average degree from real data considering all APs is 6.6 and that considering only known-location APs is 2.9. In contrast, the average degree with the 50-meter assumption is 35.0 APs.

The main reason that the computed interference degree is much larger than the real observed one is the fact that our campus wireless network is a planned-managed network and the power levels on APs are adjusted to minimize interference. We expect that the difference will be smaller for unplanned-unmanaged networks [1]. Another reason is that, in reality, obstructions can prevent APs from hearing each other even they are located close to each other.

The interference degree may in fact be even less than the values depicted as 'real' in Figure 12 because multiple channels are used for APs and APs on different channels do not interfere much. The 802.11g APs on our campus are evenly divided into four channels: 1, 4, 8, and 11. We consider the interference degrees observed within each channel, that is, the number of APs whose beacons can be heard on the same channel.

Table 5. AP degrees for different channels of 802.11g

Channel	Number of APs	Average degree	Max degree
1	294	2.3	13
4	229	1.1	8
8	202	1.2	8
11	270	2.6	12

Table 6. Summary. The column 'Actual' shows the values using the actual AP locations. 'D' and 'D+W' denote the results using the estimated location of APs discovered through driving and driving-walking, respectively.

Analysis	Actual	D	D+W
Effectiveness of war driving: War walking was more effective than war driving at detecting APs.			
Percentage of APs detected (%)		38	59
Average number of APs for each scan (war walking only)*		6.1	11.5*
AP location: APs often appear to be closer to roads, or to each other, than in reality.			
Median error in AP location estimates (meter)		40.8	31.6
Outdoor user location: Having accurate AP locations is important to estimate user position correctly.			
Median error over four walks (meter)	19-34	46-63	19-43
Median improvement using the actual AP locations (%)		17-59	5-28
Indoor user location: The improvement obtained using actual AP locations was greater for indoor walks than outdoor walks.			
Median error for four walks (meter)	7-11		15-30
Median improvement using the actual AP locations (%)			14-70
Inside of buildings: Using war driving and walking data poorly estimated whether a user is inside.			
Percentage of correct estimation (%)	76		42
Signal range: Using estimated AP locations, some APs appeared to have shorter signal ranges than when actual locations were used.			
Median signal range (meter)	91.4	93.2	74.9
AP interference: The computed degree using the actual locations (35.0) was overestimated compared to the real interference (2.9). Using the estimated AP locations made the degree even bigger.			
Median degree difference using estimated and actual locations		2	1

Table 5 presents the number of APs on each channel, the average degree, and the maximum degree as observed by the APs. This result includes APs whose locations are unknown. The average degree for the four channels ranges from 1.1 to 2.6.

Using estimated AP locations: We now consider the effect of using estimated AP locations in computing AP degrees. Figure 13 shows the AP interference using four sets of AP locations: actual location of 334 APs, estimated location of those APs detected by war driving, actual location of 521 APs, and estimated location of those APs detected by driving-walking. Not surprisingly, smaller sets (334 APs) have smaller degrees. It is interesting to note that the degree using actual locations is smaller than that using estimated AP locations. This again is because the location of APs are often estimated to be on the path of war driving or war walking, incorrectly placing them closer to one another. We also computed the median of the differences: $median(E_i - A_i)$ where E_i and A_i are the degrees using estimated and actual AP locations, respectively, for AP_i. The median for war driving was 2 and the median for driving-walking was 1.

4.7 Summary

We analyzed the effect of using AP locations estimated by war driving and war walking compared to using actual locations. We present a summary of our findings and necessary cautions.

5 Conclusion

The original purpose for war driving was to discover Wi-Fi hotspots. As researchers have started using war-driving traces for other purposes, it is important to better understand errors in war-driving data and the effect of these errors on applications and network characterizations. We collected war-driving traces on the Dartmouth college campus, estimated AP locations from these traces, and compared the estimated locations against actual AP locations. We also analyzed the impact of using estimated locations rather than actual locations on user-location tracking and AP-deployment characterizations. We found that using accurate AP locations is critical in accurately estimating user positions. We observed that estimated AP locations are often biased towards the war-driving paths, which makes the maximum signal range of APs to appear shorter and the interference among APs to appear more severe than in reality. We also found a danger in making assumptions in analyzing traces; even with a conservative assumption that an AP's interference range is 50 m, we still overestimated interference by 12 times. We hope that our study provides necessary cautions in using AP locations estimated by war driving and helps researchers to take necessary steps to cope with errors in the estimates.

Acknowledgments. We would like to thank Nick DeFrancis for war walking on the Dartmouth campus. This project was supported by Cisco Systems, NSF Award EIA-9802068, and Dartmouth's Center for Mobile Computing.

References

1. A. Akella, G. Judd, S. Seshan, and P. Steenkiste. Self-management in chaotic wireless deployments. In *Proceedings of the 11th Annual International Conference on Mobile Computing and Networking (MobiCom)*, pages 185–199, New York, NY, Aug. 2005. ACM Press.
2. N. Bulusu, J. Heidemann, and D. Estrin. GPS-less low cost outdoor localization for very small devices. *IEEE Personal Communications Magazine*, 7(5):28–34, Oct. 2000.
3. Y.-C. Cheng, Y. Chawathe, A. LaMarca, and J. Krumm. Accuracy characterization for metropolitan-scale Wi-Fi localization. In *Proceedings of the Third International Conference on Mobile Systems, Applications, and Services (MobiSys)*, Seattle, WA, June 2005.

4. I. A. Getting. The global positioning system. *IEEE Spectrum*, 30(12):36–38,43–47, Dec. 1993.
5. A. Harter and A. Hopper. A new location technique for the active office. *IEEE Personal Communications*, 4(5):42–47, Oct. 1997.
6. J. Hightower and G. Borriello. Particle filters for location estimation in ubiquitous computing: A case study. In *Proceedings of International Conference on Ubiquitous Computing (UbiComp)*, pages 88–106, Sept. 2004.
7. Kismet. http://www.kismetwireless.net.
8. A. LaMarca, Y. Chawathe, S. Consolvo, J. Hightower, I. Smith, J. Scott, T. Sohn, J. Howard, J. Hughes, F. Potter, J. Tabert, P. Powledge, G. Borriello, and B. Schilit. Place Lab: Device positioning using radio beacons in the wild. In *Proceedings of the 3rd International Conference on Pervasive Computing (Pervasive)*, pages 116–133, Munich, Germany, May 2005.
9. A. LaMarca, J. Hightower, I. Smith, and S. Consolvo. Self-mapping in 802.11 location systems. In *Proceedings of the Seventh International Conference on Ubiquitous Computing (UbiComp)*, pages 87–104, Tokyo, Japan, Sept. 2005.
10. Place Lab. http://www.placelab.org.
11. N. B. Priyantha, A. Chakraborty, and H. Balakrishnan. The Cricket location-support system. In *Proceedings of the 6th Annual International Conference on Mobile Computing and Networking (MobiCom)*, pages 32–43, Aug. 2000.
12. H. Satoh, S. Ito, and N. Kawaguchi. Position estimation of wireless access point using directional antennas. In *Proceedings of International Workshop on Location- and Context-Awareness (LoCA)*, Oberpfaffenhofen, Germany, May 2005. Springer-Verlag.
13. Skyhook Wireless. http://www.skyhookwireless.com.
14. R. Wasinger, A. Krüger, and O. Jacobs. Integrating intra and extra gestures into a mobile and multimodal shopping assistant. In *Proceedings of the 3rd International Conference on Pervasive Computing (Pervasive)*, pages 297–314, Munich, Germany, May 2005.
15. WiFiMaps.com - Wardriving Maps and Hotspot Locator. http://www.wifimaps.com.

Declarative Support for Sensor Data Cleaning

Shawn R. Jeffery[1,*], Gustavo Alonso[2,**], Michael J. Franklin[1],
Wei Hong[3,*], and Jennifer Widom[4]

[1] UC Berkeley
[2] ETH Zurich
[3] Arched Rock Corporation
[4] Stanford University

Abstract. Pervasive applications rely on data captured from the physical world through sensor devices. Data provided by these devices, however, tend to be unreliable. The data must, therefore, be cleaned before an application can make use of them, leading to additional complexity for application development and deployment. Here we present *Extensible Sensor stream Processing (ESP)*, a framework for building sensor data cleaning infrastructures for use in pervasive applications. ESP is designed as a pipeline using declarative cleaning mechanisms based on spatial and temporal characteristics of sensor data. We demonstrate ESP's effectiveness and ease of use through three real-world scenarios.

1 Introduction

Many pervasive applications rely on data collected from physical sensor devices such as wireless sensor networks and RFID technology. For instance, consider a sensor-enabled library (shown in Fig. 1) that uses RFID readers for detecting tags placed on books and patron's library cards, wireless sensors for monitoring environmental conditions, and various other devices such as motion and pressure sensors. Library monitoring and support applications use readings from these devices to manage inventory and checkouts, adjust temperature, and monitor patron activity. One of the main challenges in this scenario is the unreliability of the data produced by the sensor devices. These "dirty data" exist in two general forms:

- Missed readings: Sensors often employ low cost, low power hardware and wireless communication, which lead to frequently dropped messages. For example, RFID readers often capture only 60-70% of the tags in their vicinity [19]. Wireless sensors also demonstrate similar errors. For instance, in a wireless sensor network experiment at the Intel Research Lab in Berkeley, each sensor delivered, on average, only 42% of the data it was asked to report [24].
- Unreliable readings: Often, individual sensor readings are imprecise or unreliable. For instance, physical devices tend to "fail dirty": the sensor fails but continues to report faulty values. In a sensor network deployment in Sonoma County, CA, for example, 8 out of 33 temperature-sensing motes failed, but continued to report readings that slowly rose to above 100° Celsius [34].

---

* This work was done while the author was at Intel Research Berkeley.
** This work was done while the author was at UC Berkeley as a Stonebraker Fellow.

K.P. Fishkin et al. (Eds.): PERVASIVE 2006, LNCS 3968, pp. 83–100, 2006.

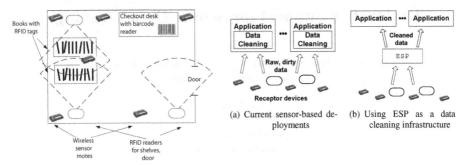

(a) Current sensor-based deployments

(b) Using ESP as a data cleaning infrastructure

Fig. 2. An infrastructural approach to sensor data cleaning

Fig. 1. A sensor-based library

To mitigate the effects of these errors, the data must be appropriately cleaned before use in an application. Of course, existing pervasive applications necessarily deal with these problems to some extent, but they tend to use tedious post-processing and application-specific means to clean sensor data (as shown in Fig. 2(a)). This ad-hoc treatment of unreliable data leads to brittle applications and increased deployment costs.

In contrast, we propose to separate cleaning from application logic by interposing a data cleaning infrastructure between sensor devices and applications (Fig. 2(b)). In such an approach, the cleaning infrastructure translates raw sensor data to cleaned data; applications are unaffected by the unreliable devices over which they are deployed.

In this paper, we present a framework for building cleaning infrastructures to support pervasive applications. *Extensible Sensor stream Processing* (or *ESP*), consists of a programmable pipeline of cleaning stages intended to operate on-the-fly as sensor data are streamed through the system. ESP is designed to be easy to configure and be able to evolve over time.

To provide a simple and flexible means of programming cleaning infrastructures, ESP uses declarative processing and exploits recent advances in relational processing techniques for data streams [4, 9, 12]. Programmers specify cleaning stages in ESP using high-level declarative queries over relational data streams[1]; the system then translates the queries into the appropriate low-level operations necessary to produce their results. Thus, programmers do not have to write low-level device interaction code (e.g., nesC for TinyOS [22]). Additionally, declarative languages provide data independence, such that in many cases cleaning operations do not need to be changed when devices fail, are added, or are upgraded. As an example of a declarative query for data cleaning, consider Query 1 which fills in lost temperature readings from a wireless sensor network using a 5 second moving average over each sensor's readings.

ESP utilizes the temporal and spatial nature of sensor data to drive many of its cleaning processes. Sensor data tend to be correlated in both time and space; the readings observed at one time instant are indicative of the readings observed at the next time instant, as are readings at nearby devices. Thus, we introduce the concepts of *temporal*

---

[1] In ESP, we use CQL [8] as our declarative language as we have a data stream system, TelegraphCQ [12], designed to process CQL. In principle, any declarative language would provide the benefits outlined here.

Query 1. *Example declarative query to interpolate for lost sensor readings. This query runs a 5 second moving average over each sensor's readings.*

```
SELECT node_id, avg(temperature)
FROM sensor_readings_stream [Range '5 sec']
GROUP BY node_id
```

and *spatial granule* to capture these correlations. These granules define a unit of time and space inside which the data are mostly homogeneous. These abstractions can be used to recover lost readings or remove outliers using temporal and spatial aggregation.

The ESP framework segments the cleaning process into five programmable stages, each responsible for a different logical aspect of the data, ranging from operations on individual readings to operations involving complex processing across multiple devices and outside data sources.

Of course, many applications need more advanced processing than that afforded by the declarative approach of ESP. We discuss such advanced processing later in the paper. Nevertheless, as demonstrated in this paper, infrastructures built with ESP's declarative stages are capable of cleaning sensor data in a wide range of deployments.

2   Related Work

Data cleaning is widely recognized as a crucial step for enterprise data management in the context of data warehouses. In this domain, data cleaning occurs separately from any application using the data (e.g., analytic/data mining software). Such traditional data cleaning, however, tends to focus on a small set of well-defined tasks, including transformations, matchings, and duplicate elimination [32, 23]. Extensions to this paradigm include the AJAX tool [21], an extensible, declarative means of specifying cleaning operations in a data warehouse. These techniques focus on offline cleaning for use in data warehouses; the real-time nature of many pervasive applications, however, preclude such approaches. More fundamentally, the nature of the errors in sensor data is not easily corrected by traditional cleaning: such technology typically does not utilize the temporal or spatial aspects of data.

The unreliabilities of sensor data have been widely studied. Work from ETH Zurich recognizes the poor behavior of RFID technology [19]. Work from the Intel Research Lab in Seattle has characterized the performance and errors in RFID technology in order to better guide ubiquitous applications [18, 30]. Other sensor-based applications have encountered similar issues in regard to dirty sensor data [11, 14]. These projects, however, either do not address cleaning or incorporate cleaning logic directly into the application.

Other work has advocated an infrastructural approach to sensor data access and management, but has not directly addressed data cleaning. Several systems provide mechanisms for interacting with wireless sensor networks ([27, 10]). For example, TinyDB provides a declarative means of acquiring data from a sensor network. ALE (Application-Level Events) defines an interface for building RFID middleware [7]. ALE defines concepts similar to our temporal and spatial granules. The Context Toolkit advocates an architectural approach to hiding the details of sensor devices [16].

Various projects have developed techniques for cleaning and error correction for wireless sensor data (e.g., [17, 28]). The BBQ system uses models of sensor data to accurately and efficiently answer wireless sensor network queries with defined confidence intervals [15]. Other work uses regression applied to sensor networks for inference purposes [29]. These approaches usually involve building and maintaining complex models. ESP's declarative approach, in contrast, does not rely on complex models.

Finally, we note that ESP is part of the HiFi project [20]. HiFi is a distributed stream processing system designed to support large-scale sensor-based networks (termed "high fan-in" systems). ESP is intended to clean sensor data streams at the edge of the HiFi network. Previous work discussed some of the preliminary concepts and results presented in this paper [20, 25].

3   ESP's Declarative Sensor Data Cleaning Framework

In this section, we introduce *Extensible Sensor stream Processing* (*ESP*), our declarative pipelined framework for building sensor data cleaning infrastructures.

While building the initial version of HiFi [13], we confronted many of the issues associated with unreliable data produced by sensor devices. Most notably, the system was unable to function correctly using raw RFID data. Our solution was to use a rudimentary pipeline of ad-hoc queries we termed "CSAVA" [20], designed to run throughout HiFi to convert RFID data into application data.

ESP generalizes and extends the CSAVA pipeline with a focus on cleaning sensor data at the edge of the network. ESP enables infrastructures that clean raw physical sensor data by processing multiple sensor streams, exploiting the temporal and spatial aspects of sensor data, to produce a single, improved output stream that can be used directly by pervasive applications. We first define the temporal and spatial abstractions that drive many of ESP's cleaning mechanisms.

3.1   Temporal and Spatial Granules

ESP uses high-level abstractions called *temporal* and *spatial granules* to capture time and space in sensor-based applications. These granules define units of time and space inside which the data are expected to be homogeneous. ESP uses the granule concept to aggregate, sample, and detect outliers. These abstractions exploit the fact that many applications are not interested in individual readings or devices, but with higher-level data in time and space.

Temporal Granules. Although many sensor devices can produce data at frequent intervals, applications are usually concerned with data from a larger time period, or *temporal granule*. For instance, an environmental monitoring application that builds models of micro-climates in a redwood tree needs readings at 5 minute intervals to capture variations in micro-climate [35]. Within a temporal granule, readings are expected to be largely homogeneous.

To support this notion of temporal granules, ESP uses *windowed* processing to group readings. A window defines a finite set of readings (in terms of an interval of time) within a data stream. Within a window, ESP can aggregate multiple readings into one or compare readings to detect outliers.

Spatial Granules. Just as with readings in time, readings from devices physically close to each other are expected to be mostly homogeneous; a spatial granule defines the unit of space in which this homogeneity is expected to hold. Furthermore, a spatial granule is the smallest unit of space in which an application is interested, even though devices may have a finer spatial granularity. Examples of spatial granules include a shelf in a library scenario or a room in a digital home application.

To support spatial granules, ESP organizes sensors into *proximity groups*. A proximity group defines a set of sensors of the same type monitoring the same spatial granule. For instance, a set of motes monitoring the temperature in the same room may be grouped into the same proximity group, as may two RFID readers monitoring the same library shelf. Just as a time window is the unit of processing for a temporal granule, a proximity group is the processing unit for a spatial granule.

In many applications, the size of the temporal and spatial granules are obvious from the nature of the application or environment (e.g., 5 minute intervals in redwood monitoring or rooms in a digital home). In some cases, however, it may be desirable to determine the granule sizes automatically; this is a rich area of on-going work.

3.2 ESP Cleaning Stages

Having described the fundamental abstractions underlying ESP, we now outline ESP's processing stages. Through an analysis of typical sensor-based applications, we distilled a set of logically distinct operations that occur in a large class of applications to clean data produced by many types of sensor devices. Using these observations, ESP organizes sensor stream processing into a cascade of five programmable stages: *Point - Smooth - Merge - Arbitrate - Virtualize*. These stages operate on different aspects of the data, from finest (single readings) to coarsest (readings from multiple sensors and other data sources). Not all stages are necessary for a given deployment.

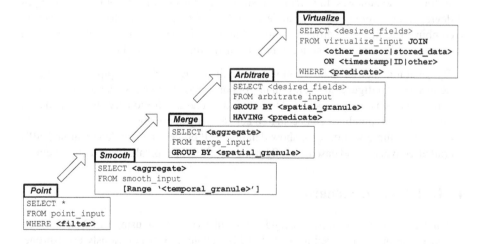

Fig. 3. ESP processing stages with the typical form of the declarative query for each stage. The relevant portion of the query is in boldface.

Stage 1, *Point*: The *Point* stage operates over a single value in a sensor stream. The primary purpose of this stage is to filter individual values (e.g., errant RFID tags or obvious outliers) or to convert fields within an individual tuple. The general form for the *Point* query (as well as all other stages) is shown in Fig. 3. ESP applies the *Point* query to each sensor's readings, filtering all readings that do not match a predicate.

Stage 2, *Smooth*: In *Smooth*, ESP uses the temporal granule defined by the application to correct for missed readings and to detect outliers in a single sensor stream. The *Smooth* query processes its input stream, `smooth_input` (a stream of readings from a single device, provided by ESP), in windows of readings determined by the size of the temporal granule. For each of these windows, *Smooth* runs the specified aggregate function, outputs a processed reading, and then advances the window by one input reading. Note that both *Point* and *Smooth* operations can be pushed down to capable sensor devices (e.g., wireless motes).

Stage 3, *Merge*: Analogous to the temporal processing in the *Smooth* stage, *Merge* uses the application's spatial granule to correct for missed readings and remove outliers spatially. At each time step, *Merge* processes input readings from a single type of device and groups the readings by the specified spatial granule using the `GROUP BY` clause. *Merge* then processes each of these groups using an aggregate function to produce output readings for each spatial granule.

Stage 4, *Arbitrate*: Spatial granules may not map directly to sensor detection fields, leading to possible conflicts between the readings from different proximity groups that are physically close to one another. The *Arbitrate* stage deals with conflicts, such as duplicate readings, between data streams from different spatial granules. The query for *Arbitrate* groups its input stream by spatial granule and then uses the `HAVING` clause to filter readings from spatial granules that do not match a predicate.

Stage 5, *Virtualize*: Finally, some types of data cleaning utilize readings from across different types of sensors or stored data for improved data cleaning. To provide a platform for such techniques, the *Virtualize* stage combines readings from different types of devices and different spatial granules. The *Virtualize* query uses the `JOIN` construct to combine readings from different sources based on timestamps, IDs, or other common attributes. Additional processing can be specified using an optional predicate.

By separating sensor data cleaning into distinct stages, cleaning pipelines are easy to deploy and configure, affording many opportunities to reuse stages from previous deployments with changes localized to individual stages. Additionally, the cleaned data produced by ESP pipelines can be shared across many applications.

In the next three sections, we show detailed ESP processing and demonstrate ESP's overall effectiveness and ease of configuration with three typical sensor deployments.

4   RFID-Based Scenario

The first deployment we address using ESP is a library scenario using RFID technology, similar to the one introduced in Sect. 1. RFID technology is notoriously error-prone: tags that exist are frequently missed while other tags that are not in a reader's normal view are sometimes read. In a library scenario, consider an application that continuously

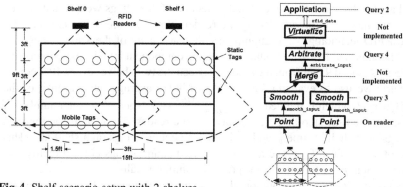

Fig. 4. Shelf scenario setup with 2 shelves, each with an RFID reader and 10 tags statically placed within 6 feet of the antenna (5 tags at 3 feet, 5 tags at 6 feet). Additionally, 5 tags were relocated every 40 seconds

Fig. 5. ESP pipeline for cleaning RFID data

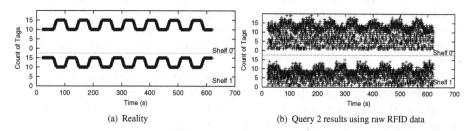

(a) Reality

(b) Query 2 results using raw RFID data

Fig. 6. Query 2 results in reality and over the raw data

monitors the count of books on each shelf using Query 2 (shown below). This query looks at the stream of RFID data in 5-second slices. Within each of these slices, the query groups the readings by the shelf at which the tag was read, and then counts the number of distinct tag IDs at each shelf. Here, the window clause indicates the temporal granule (5 seconds) and the GROUP BY clause denotes the spatial granule (a shelf).

Query 2. *Shelf monitoring query to determine the number of books on each shelf.*

```
SELECT shelf, count(distinct tag_id) as num_books
FROM rfid_data [Range '5 sec']
GROUP BY shelf
```

To study ESP used for cleaning RFID data, we ran an experiment emulating a library scenario. Our experimental setup is depicted in Fig. 4. We used two 915 MHz RFID readers from Alien Technology [6], each responsible for one shelf and thus each forming a proximity group. The readers' sample period was set at 5Hz (i.e., 5 polls per second). Each shelf was stocked with 10 books represented with Alien "I2" tags [5], EPC Class 1 RFID tags designed for long-range detection in a controlled environment. Tags were suspended in the same plane as the reader, spaced 1.5 feet apart from each other, and at two distances from the reader, 3 feet and 6 feet. Tags were oriented such that their antennae were directly facing the reader. Note that this setup is overly favorable to RFID technology as it attempts to alleviate many of the known causes of degraded readings [18, 19]. To introduce a dynamic component into the experiment, we relocated 5 tags placed 9 feet from the reader between the two shelves every 40 seconds.

The metric we use to evaluate our techniques is the average relative error of the results of Query 2, which is defined as $\frac{1}{N} \sum_{i=0}^{N} (\frac{|R_i - T_i|}{T_i})$, where N is total number of time steps, i is the time step at the granularity of the reader (5Hz), R_i is the reported count of tags on a shelf at time i, and T_i is the true count of tags on a shelf at i. This metric denotes how far off, on average, the reported count of tags is from reality. We ran this experiment three times; all runs produced similar results.

The results of our experiment without data cleaning are shown in Fig. 6. Figure 6(a) depicts the trace of the actual count of tags on each shelf over the course of the experiment. Figure 6(b) shows the results of running the application's query over the raw data. If the application were to use the output of the RFID readers directly, the results would be near-meaningless: the average relative error of the output of Query 2 compared to reality for the duration of the experiment was 0.41 (i.e., the count of the number of tags on each shelf was off by almost half, on average). For instance, if an application wants to be notified when the number of books on a shelf drops below 5, then the query using the raw data would report that a shelf has low inventory 2.3 times per second, on average.

We build a ESP pipeline to clean this data. Note that the RFID reader already provides *Point* functionality natively by removing tags that fail a checksum [1]. We use the *Smooth* and *Arbitrate* stages for ESP in this case (as shown in Fig. 5). As there is only one sensor per proximity group here, *Merge* is not needed.

4.1   Stage 2: *Smooth*

At the *Smooth* stage (shown in Query 3), ESP interpolates for lost readings within a temporal granule. ESP runs this query over each reader's data stream. This query begins by breaking the stream into 5-second slices (corresponding to the size of the temporal granule). For each of these slices, *Smooth* groups by tag ID and then counts the number of occurrences for that tag. The output of *Smooth*, then, is a reading for each tag seen at any point within the window and the number of times it was read. After each window is processed, ESP moves the window forward by one input reading. Through this sliding window operation, *Smooth* fills in dropped readings for any tag seen at least once in a 5 second time period.

Query 3. *Interpolating for lost readings in the* Smooth *stage.*

```
SELECT tag_id, count(*)
FROM smooth_input [Range '5 sec']
GROUP BY tag_id
```

The results of Query 2 over the data produced by this stage are shown in Fig. 7(a). The *Smooth* stage is able to eliminate the constant low inventory alerts generated by the query using the raw data.

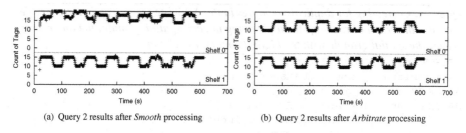

(a) Query 2 results after *Smooth* processing   (b) Query 2 results after *Arbitrate* processing

Fig. 7. Query 2 results after different stages of processing

The count of books per shelf, however, is still fairly inaccurate (an average relative error of 0.24) due to the close proximity of the readers and discrepancies in their performance. As seen in Fig. 7(a), the antenna for shelf 0 read more tags than that of shelf 1, despite being of the same model; the counts reported for shelf 0 were consistently 4 to 5 tags higher than reality. We tried different configurations of antennae and determined that this difference is likely due to known issues with the antenna ports on these particular RFID readers [2]. Processing in the *Smooth* stage has alleviated the issues with dropped readings, but any application using this data will be misled into thinking that shelf 0 has extra books.

4.2 Stage 4: *Arbitrate*

The *Arbitrate* stage (shown in Query 4) corrects for duplicate readings caused by the close proximity of the readers. At each time step, *Arbitrate* determines all tags that were read by multiple spatial granules and the number of times each tag was read by each granule. It then assigns the tag to the spatial granule that read the tag the most. ESP runs *Arbitrate* over the union of the streams produced by Query 3.[2]

The results of running Query 2 over the smoothed and arbitrated data are shown in Fig. 7(b). Observe that ESP de-duplicates the readings as well as corrects for the differing performance of the two antennae to provide a substantially more accurate count of the tags on each shelf. After *Arbitrate* processing, the average relative error of Query 2 is 0.04. This equates to an error of being off by less than one book, on average. The results show that in this scenario, ESP provides a significant reduction in error over the raw RFID data: recall that the original book counts using the raw data were off by almost half compared to reality.

Size of the Temporal Granule. The size of the temporal granule affects the degree to which ESP can effectively clean the data. In order to effectively smooth, the size of the temporal granule (i.e., the window size) must be larger than the longest period of dropped readings in the input. The window size may not be made too large, however, as its size must be balanced with the rate of change of the data values. This tension can be observed in Figure 7(a), where the periods when tags are being relocated are not as accurately captured as the stable periods.

---

[2] Although the *Merge* stage is unused in this case, ESP automatically adds a `spatial_granule` attribute to each stream, corresponding to each proximity group (i.e., each shelf).

Query 4. *Correcting for duplicate readings in the* Arbitrate *stage. The inner query de-termines the count of readings for a given tag in each spatial granule; the outer query selects the spatial granule with the highest count for each tag.*

```
SELECT spatial_granule, tag_id
FROM arbitrate_input ai1 [Range 'NOW']
GROUP BY spatial_granule, tag_id
HAVING count(*) >= ALL (SELECT count(*)
                  FROM arbitrate_input ai2
                  [Range 'NOW']
                  WHERE ai1.tag_id = ai2.tag_id
                  GROUP BY spatial_granule)
```

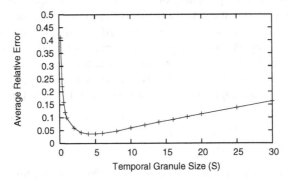

Fig. 8. Average relative error for Query 2 over data produced by ESP using different size temporal granules

To investigate this issue, we compared the relative errors of ESP using different tem-poral granule sizes for the *Smooth* stage. The results are shown in Figure 8. At very small and very large granules, the error is larger than for granules around 5 seconds. Essentially, an effective temporal granule size is bounded at the low end by the reliability of the de-vices and at the high end by the rate of change of the data. In Sect. 7, we discuss our ongoing work exploring dynamic adaptation of the temporal granule.

5   Environment Monitoring Scenario

In the previous section, we demonstrated the ability of an ESP pipeline to clean RFID data streams. Next, we present a use case where ESP hides the unreliabilities of wireless sensor networks.

Wireless sensor networks enable new classes of pervasive applications that monitor environments such as the home and office with high resolution. In order to alleviate the effects of imprecise readings, calibration errors, outliers, and unreliable network com-munication, previous deployments involving sensor networks have had to post-process the readings, primarily by hand, to produce data that can be used by the application [11, 14, 15]. To reduce the complexity associated with sensor network application deploy-ment, applications can use ESP to provide cleaned sensor data. We demonstrate two types of wireless sensor network data cleaning: outlier detection of fail-dirty motes, and temporal and spatial smoothing to correct for dropped messages.

5.1 Outlier Detection

Recall that sensor motes are known to "fail-dirty" and produce outlier readings. ESP can be used to alleviate the effects of these fail-dirty motes. To demonstrate the effectiveness of outlier detection using ESP, we use a 2 day trace from a sensor network deployed in the Intel Research Lab in Berkeley to monitor the lab's environment [24]. We focus on three motes in the same room, assigned to the same proximity group. In this trace, one of the motes fails by reporting increasing temperatures, rising to over 100^oC. We program the *Point* and *Merge* stages of ESP to eliminate the outlier readings. *Smooth* is not used because it cannot correct for extended errors produced by one sensor.[3] *Arbitrate* is not necessary as there is only one spatial granule.

Stage 1: *Point*. The *Point* stage filters any readings beyond its expected range; in this case, ESP filters readings where the temperature is higher than 50^oC (Query 5) .

Query 5. *Simple filtering at the* Point *stage.*

```
SELECT *
FROM point_input
WHERE temperature < 50
```

Stage 3: *Merge*. In this example, the *Merge* stage does outlier detection within a spatial granule by computing the average of the readings from different motes in the same proximity group and then omitting individual readings that are outside of two standard deviations from the mean (shown in Query 6). Note that these techniques are not intended to be statistically complex, but to the contrary, demonstrate the simplicity of ESP programming.

Query 6. *Outlier detection in the* Merge *stage.*

```
SELECT spatial_granule, AVG(temp)
FROM merge_input s [Range '5 min'],
     (SELECT spatial_granule, avg(temp) as avg,
                    stdev(temp) as stdev
     FROM merge_input [Range '5 min']) as a
WHERE a.spatial_granule = s.spatial_granule AND
     a.avg + (2*a.stdev) < s.temp AND
     a.avg - (2*a.stdev) > s.temp
```

Figure 9 shows the outcome of this experiment. The top line represents the outlier mote's readings. The middle line depicts the average of all three motes. If an application were to use the average of the three motes as a representation of the room's temperature,

---

[3] *Smooth* could, however, be used to correct for individual outlier readings in a single mote using the same mechanisms presented here.

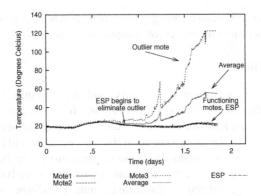

Fig. 9. Outlier Detection using ESP. The "ESP" line tracks the two functional motes' lines

it would see temperatures exceeding 50°C. The bottom lines show the traces of the two functioning motes as well as the output of ESP with outlier detection processing. Observe that ESP is able to detect when the outlier mote begins to deviate from the other motes and then omit its reading from its average calculation.

5.2   Temporal and Spatial Smoothing of Sensor Data

Wireless sensor networks have another serious problem beyond fail-dirty motes: the network frequently drops messages. This problem is especially prevalent when sensor networks are deployed in the real world.

An ESP pipeline for a wireless sensor network can mask the unreliability of a sensor network by both temporally and spatially aggregating to correct for dropped readings. We demonstrate this cleaning through an application responsible for monitoring the temperature of a redwood tree at each elevation range in the tree.

We validated ESP processing on a three and a half day trace of data collected from sensors on a redwood tree in Sonoma County, CA as part of a large-scale sensor network deployment to study micro-climates of redwood trees [34]. 33 motes were placed along the trunk of the tree at varying heights. Data (e.g., temperature and humidity) were sensed at 5 minute intervals and logged to a local storage buffer (collected at the end of the experiment) and also sent over the multi-hop network. We grouped the motes at nearby heights into 2-node, non-overlapping proximity groups (corresponding to the spatial granules in this deployment), where the distance between motes in a proximity group was less than one foot.

Note that the log data is incorrect with respect to the ground truth due to fail-dirty sensors: 8 out of the 33 motes failed dirty. The readings from these motes were removed by hand shortly after data collection, but before we received the data.[4]

As ESP is addressing communication errors in this case, our metric of success is the epoch yield. Epoch yield describes the number of the readings reported to the application as a fraction of the total number of readings the application requested. For the raw data, the epoch yield in this trace was 40% (ideally, the epoch yield should be 100%). In other

---

[4] ESP could employ the techniques shown in Section 5.1 to remove these outliers automatically.

words, the application only received 40% of the data it requested. Additionally, we measure the percent error in the readings. Based on experience collaborating with biologists, an error of less than 1°C is acceptable for trend analysis. Therefore, the goal of ESP in this application should be to increase the epoch yield while minimizing the percent of readings with an error greater than 1°C.

Here, we implement the *Smooth* and *Merge* stages in ESP to temporally and spatially aggregate sensor readings to increase the epoch yield of the sensor deployment.

Stage 2: Smooth. In the *Smooth* stage (not shown), ESP temporally aggregates readings from a single sensor. By running a sliding window average on each sensor stream, lost readings from a single mote are masked within the window. After the *Smooth* stage, the epoch yield is increased to 77%. 99% of these readings were within 1°C of the logged data.

Stage 3: Merge. In the *Merge* stage (not shown), ESP performs spatial aggregation for each spatial granule (again, in the form of a windowed average) to further alleviate the effects of lost readings. The *Merge* stage increases the epoch yield to 92%. This improvement of reporting is at the slight cost of decreasing the percent of readings within 1°C of the logged data to 94%. Thus, with ESP cleaning, biologists can get nearly complete data with a slight decrease in the accuracy.

Through the use of simple outlier detection and temporal and spatial smoothing, in this case an ESP pipeline is able to increase the ability of applications to make sense of the data they are getting from their sensors. Rather than spending time tediously post-processing the data, applications can focus on the high-level logic and not conversion, calibration, and error correction.

6   Digital Home Scenario

In Sects. 4 and 5, we demonstrated how ESP can provide a cleaning infrastructure to correct for a wide variety of problems associated with different physical devices. Next, we demonstrate the ease of configuration of ESP and highlight the use of multiple types of sensors to enhance data cleaning.

Multiple projects are developing sensors and infrastructures to instrument the home to provide both a better living experience for inhabitants as well as a more efficient use of home resources [3, 26]. Such applications use a wide variety of sensor devices providing low-level data (e.g., RFID, sensor motes, pressure sensors). In this section, we show that pipelines defined for other deployments (i.e., pipelines from the previous two sections) can be easily re-tasked to a new environment due to ESP's high-level declarative nature. Furthermore, ESP can serve platform for combining readings from multiple devices to provide a virtual "person detector" sensor. This type of processing is a higher level of cleaning; data from multiple heterogeneous devices, appropriately combined, can provide higher quality data. The output of ESP is a stream of events describing the presence of a person in the room.

We demonstrate the use of ESP in a digital home scenario by outfitting a room with two RFID readers, a small sensor network of three motes, and three X10 motion detectors [36] tasked to determine when someone is in the room (Fig. 10(a)). The room

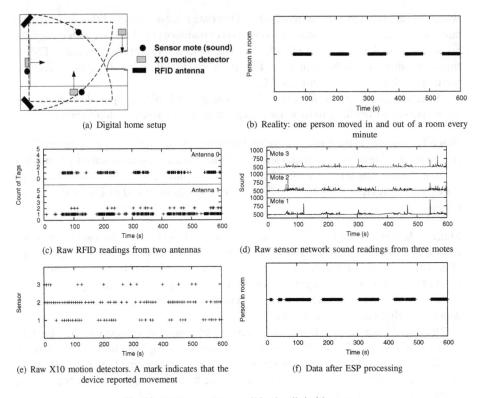

(a) Digital home setup

(b) Reality: one person moved in and out of a room every minute

(c) Raw RFID readings from two antennas

(d) Raw sensor network sound readings from three motes

(e) Raw X10 motion detectors. A mark indicates that the device reported movement

(f) Data after ESP processing

Fig. 10. A "Person Detector" in the digital home

corresponds to one spatial granule for the application; thus, the two RFID readers make up one proximity group, the motes constitute another, and the X10 detectors form a third. During the experiment, one person, outfitted with an RFID tag, moved in and out of the room, while talking, at one minute intervals (Fig. 10(b)).

We present the ESP processing to clean the individual sensor streams and then describe how ESP utilizes these streams to create a person detector.

6.1 Low-Level Sensor Cleaning

Recall the main advantages of ESP's declarative pipelined approach: previously built stages can be reused, changes necessary to tailor processing to each new deployment are isolated to small logical units, and these changes are easy to make and reason about as the stages are expressed as high-level queries. In this deployment, the programming for the ESP pipelines to clean the individual sensor streams (RFID, wireless sensors, and motion detectors) utilize almost exactly the same processing stages as defined in the previous two sections. Changes necessary for this deployment involved slightly modifying queries in a small number of stages. The raw data from these devices are presented in Figs. 10(c)-10(e). We omit the details of this cleaning due to space considerations.

6.2   Stage 5: *Virtualize*

The main new feature of this use case (as compared to the previous scenarios) is the use of the *Virtualize* stage. *Virtualize* allows a deployment to combine readings from multiple different types of devices to perform application-level cleaning. In this case, *Virtualize* turns the set of heterogeneous devices into a "person detector." It uses a voting query that normalizes all sensor input streams to a single vote of whether it has determined that a person is in the room or not (Query 7). The query then adds up the votes and registers that a person is in the room if the sum is higher than a threshold.

Query 7. *"Person Detector" logic at the* Virtualize *stage.*

```
SELECT 'Person-in-room'
FROM (SELECT 1 as cnt
      FROM sensors_input [Range 'NOW']
      WHERE sensors.noise > 525) as sensor_count,
     (SELECT 1 as cnt
      FROM rfid_input [Range 'NOW']
      HAVING count(distinct tag_id) > 1)
      as rfid_count,
     (SELECT 1 as cnt
      FROM motion_input [Range 'NOW']
      WHERE value = 'ON') as motion_count
WHERE sensor_count.cnt +
      rfid_count.cnt +
      motion_count.cnt >= threshold
```

The output of the ESP pipeline is shown in Fig. 10(f). As can be seen, simple and easy to deploy logic is capable of generally approximating reality. ESP is able to correctly indicate that a person is in the room 92% of the time.

Virtualize Configuration. The *Virtualize* query involves many numerical parameters, such as thresholds for sensor noise processing and overall voting. ESP's declarative query approach made this type of setup simple: high-level queries are easy to reason about and adjust until adequate cleaning is achieved. Furthermore, because ESP's cleaning is segmented, any adjustment of *Virtualize* is isolated to a single operation: lower-level cleaning remains the same. Nevertheless, there are many cases where this simple approach for *Virtualize* will not work; we discuss such cases in Sect. 7.

7   Advanced Cleaning

In Sects. 4, 5, and 6, we showed that cleaning infrastructures built using ESP are capable of cleaning data in a wide range of realistic scenarios. Perhaps surprisingly, these significant improvements in data quality were produced by a pipeline of fairly simple declarative queries. Of course, there are many applications and deployments where such a simple approach may not be effective. In this section, we outline some of these cases and discuss extensions to ESP that will enhance its effectiveness in such deployments.

Adaptive Granules. In this paper, we required the application to supply the size of the temporal and spatial granules. In some cases, however, this is not possible: the environment may be too complex for the application to adequately determine appropriate sizes or too dynamic for a single size temporal or spatial granule to work. Thus, it is preferable to have the system determine and adapt the granule size based on the data it observes.

To this end, our on-going work involves modeling unreliable sensor data as a statistical sample of the physical world. With this model in place, we are investigating techniques from sampling theory to help guide data cleaning and granule size adaptations. For instance, ESP can use π-estimators [33] to determine the population of RFID tags in an area or the temperature of a set of sensors *without* seeing all the data. The variance of the estimator can be used to guide granule size decisions.

Soft Sensors. While these deployments were configured using numerical parameters that were easy to derive empirically (e.g., *Virtualize* in Sect. 6), in many cases determining the parameter values may not be so easy. More advanced processing for *Virtualize* can involve machine learning techniques such as those used in soft sensors [31]. To support this type of operation, ESP can be extended to support stages defined by both declarative queries and user-supplied code.

Query-Driven Operations. The cleaning infrastructures presented here have focused on providing "raw" (but cleaned) streams to the applications. In most cases, however, the application poses queries over these streams. Application-level queries are a mechanism for the application to alert the cleaning infrastructure of additional requirements. ESP should be able to incorporate this information to help drive cleaning operations. For instance, query predicates (e.g., `temp > 0`) should be pushed down to the appropriate level in the pipeline.

8   Conclusions

Data produced by physical sensor devices are notoriously dirty: readings are frequently either missed or dropped and individual readings are unreliable. Furthermore, these error characteristics vary from deployment to deployment. This leads to high application deployment costs for both data cleaning and configuration.

To directly address these issues, we developed ESP, a framework for building sensor data cleaning infrastructures in support of pervasive applications. By taking an infrastructural approach to sensor data cleaning, ESP allows applications to use sensor data without incorporating complex cleaning logic. Furthermore, applications using an ESP infrastructure can be write-once, run anywhere: ESP shields the application from changes in the error characteristics of the devices or the underlying environment. Finally, an infrastructure built using ESP allows multiple applications to use the same cleaned data, further reducing deployment costs.

To drive ESP's cleaning mechanisms, we introduce the concepts of temporal and spatial granules. These abstractions capture application-level notions of time and space. ESP utilizes these concepts in a pipeline of programmable processing stages designed to clean sensor data as it streams through the system.

ESP infrastructures are easy to deploy and evolve due to the following properties:

- Declarative: ESP cleaning logic is easy to program through high-level declarative queries. The system can utilize the well-understood techniques of relational query processing to efficiently execute these queries.
- Pipelined: ESP consists of separate, pipelined cleaning stages allowing operations to be independently programmed and reused across deployments.
- Cleaning framework: ESP defines logically distinct cleaning operations designed to directly address the error characteristics of sensor data.

While there are many complex operations that can be used to clean sensor data, we show here that in practice, some applications and deployments do not need such complexity. We validate the ESP platform through three real-world deployments demonstrating that infrastructures built using high-level declarative queries can successfully alleviate both missed and unreliable readings in sensor data. As a result, many pervasive applications were able to use data provided by ESP pipelines as they would any sensor data, but without many of the associated errors.

Sensor-based pervasive application development and deployment today is fraught with complexities stemming from the unreliable nature of devices on which they are built. Cleaning infrastructures built using ESP address these problems leading to reduced application complexity, faster deployment times with lower costs, and better manageability.

Acknowledgments

The authors would like to thank David Liu, Matt Denny, and other members of the Berkeley Database Group for feedback on early drafts, Nathan Burkhart for assisting in some of the experiments, Ryan Aipperspach for supplying insight and equipment in regards to pervasive computing, and the anonymous reviewers for providing many useful comments. This work was funded in part by NSF under ITR grants IIS-0086057 and SI-0122599, and by research funds from Intel and the UC MICRO program. G. Alonso was supported (in part) by the NCCR-MICS, a center supported by the Swiss National Science Foundation under grant number 5005-67322.

References

[1] Alien Technology. Nanoscanner Reader User Guide.
[2] Alien Technology. Personal correspondence.
[3] MIT House_n. http://architecture.mit.edu/house_n/.
[4] D. Abadi, et al.. Aurora: a data stream management system. In *SIGMOD*. 2003.
[5] Alien ALL-9250 I2 RFID tag. http://www.alientechnology.com/products/rfid-tags.
[6] Alien ALR-9780 915 MHz RFID Reader.   http://www.alientechnology.com/products/rfid-readers/alr9780.php.
[7] Application Level Event (ALE) Specification Version 1.0. Http://www.epcglobalinc.org/standards_technology/EPCglobal_ApplicationALE _Specification_v112-2005.pdf.
[8] A. Arasu, et al.. The CQL continuous query language: Semantic foundations and query execution. *VLDB Journal*, (To appear).

[9]   B. Babcock, *et al.*. Models and issues in data stream systems. In *SIGMOD*. 2002.

[10] P. Bonnet, *et al.*. Towards sensor database systems. In *Proc. Mobile Data Management*, volume 1987 of *Lecture Notes in Computer Science*. Springer, Hong Kong, January 2001.

[11] P. Buonadonna, *et al.*. TASK: Sensor Network in a Box. In *EWSN*. 2005.

[12] S. Chandrasekaran, *et al.*. TelegraphCQ: Continuous Dataflow Processing for an Uncertain World. In *CIDR*. 2003.

[13] O. Cooper, *et al.*. HiFi: A Unified Architecture for High Fan-in Systems. In *VLDB*. 2004.

[14] Demand-response. http://dr.me.berkeley.edu/.

[15] A. Deshpande, *et al.*. Model-Driven Data Acquisition in Sensor Networks. In *VLDB Conference*. 2004.

[16] A. K. Dey. *Providing Architectural Support for Building Context-Aware Applications*. Ph.D. thesis, Georgia Institute of Technology, 2000.

[17] E. Elnahrawy *et al.*. Cleaning and querying noisy sensors. In *WSNA '03: Proceedings of the 2nd ACM international conference on Wireless sensor networks and applications*. 2003.

[18] K. P. Fishkin, *et al.*. I Sense a Disturbance in the Force: Unobtrusive Detection of Interactions with RFID-tagged Objects. In *Ubicomp*. 2004.

[19] C. Floerkemeier *et al.*. Issues with RFID usage in ubiquitous computing applications. In *Pervasive Computing: Second International Conference, PERVASIVE 2004*. 2004.

[20] M. J. Franklin, *et al.*. Design Considerations for High Fan-In Systems: The HiFi Approach. In *CIDR*. 2005.

[21] H. Galhardas, *et al.*. Declarative data cleaning: Language, model, and algorithms. In *VLDB*, pp. 371–380. 2001.

[22] D. Gay, *et al.*. The nesC language: A holistic approach to networked embedded systems. In *SIGPLAN*. 2003.

[23] Informatica. http://www.informatica.com/.

[24] Intel Lab Data. http://berkeley.intel-research.net/labdata/.

[25] S. R. Jeffery, *et al.*. A Pipelined Framework for Online Cleaning of Sensor Data Streams. In *ICDE*. 2006.

[26] C. D. Kidd, *et al.*. The Aware Home: A Living Laboratory for Ubiquitous Computing Research. In *Cooperative Buildings*, pp. 191–198. 1999.

[27] S. Madden, *et al.*. The Design of an Acquisitional Query Processor For Sensor Networks. In *SIGMOD*. 2003.

[28] S. Mukhopadhyay, *et al.*. Data aware, low cost error correction for wireless sensor networks. In *WCNC*. 2004.

[29] M. A. Paskin, *et al.*. A robust architecture for distributed inference in sensor networks. In *IPSN*. 2005.

[30] M. Philipose, *et al.*. Mapping and Localization with RFID Technology. Technical Report IRS-TR-03-014, Intel Research, December 2003.

[31] S. Qin. Neural networks for intelligent sensors and control — practical issues and some solutions. In *Neural Networks for Control*. 1996.

[32] E. Rahm *et al.*. Data cleaning: Problems and current approaches. *IEEE Data Eng. Bull.*, 23(4):3–13, 2000.

[33] C.-E. Särndal, *et al.*. *"Model Assisted Survey Sampling"*. Springer-Verlag New York, Inc. (Springer Series in Statistics), 1992.

[34] Sonoma Redwood Sensor Network Deployment. http://www.cs.berkeley.edu/˜get/sonoma/.

[35] G. Tolle, *et al.*. A macroscope in the redwoods. In *SenSys*. 2005.

[36] X10. http://www.x10.com.

Detecting and Interpreting Muscle Activity with Wearable Force Sensors

Paul Lukowicz[1], Friedrich Hanser[1], Christoph Szubski[1,2],
and Wolfgang Schobersberger[2]

[1] Institute for Computer Systems and Networks, UMIT, A-6060 Hall, Austria
csn.umit.at
[2] Research Department for Leisure, Travel and Alpine Medicine,
UMIT, A-6060 Hall, Austria
http://www.umit.at

Abstract. In this paper we present a system for assessing muscle activity by using wearable force sensors placed on the muscle surface. Such sensors are very thin, power efficient and have also been demonstrated as pure textile devices, so that they can be easily integrated in such garments as elastic underwear or tight shorts/shirt. On the example upper-leg muscle we show how good signal quality can be reliably acquired under realistic conditions. We then show how information about general user context can be derived from the muscle activity signal. We first look at the modes of locomotion problem which is a well studied, benchmark-like problem in the community. We then demonstrate the correlation between the signals from our system and user fatigue. We conclude with a discussion of other types of information that can be derived from the muscle activity based on physiological considerations and example data form our experiments.

1 Introduction

Motion monitoring is an important aspect of many pervasive computing applications. For one, user motion is indicative of the general user activity. The most obvious case are the modes of locomotion (sitting, standing, walking, running etc.). In other applications hands motions were analyzed to recognize steps of an assembly procedure [1], interaction with objects, or general gestures. Beyond activity recognition motion analysis plays an important role in a variety of pervasive computing applications related to rehabilitation, nursing, lifestyle monitoring, sports and wellness [2]. As an example, our group is involved in a project devoted to a wearable nordic walking trainer. The aim of the project is to monitor user motions and ensure that the user gets the maximum benefit of the exercise while minimizing risk factors such as joint damage or overextension. In another project we look at assistive system for the elderly where motion patterns are important to understand the users general condition including, for example, assessing the risk of serious falls.

Today the main approaches to motion analysis are visual tracking and body-worn inertial sensors (acceleration, gyroscopes). In the paper we propose a novel

K.P. Fishkin et al. (Eds.): PERVASIVE 2006, LNCS 3968, pp. 101–116, 2006.

method for unobtrusive motion monitoring: the use of wearable force sensors to assess muscle activity. This approach is based on the following ideas:

- Muscle activity is associated with changes of muscle shape. In particular in the limbs, these changes are noticeable on the surface as certain parts of the muscle 'inflate' or 'deflate'.
- Force sensors that react to surface pressure can be manufactured as ultra thin foils or even in textiles using capacitance change between two conductive layers. If integrated in tight garment or elastic bands such sensors can be used to detect muscle shape changes.
- The relationship between muscle activity and different limb motions is well understood. Thus, general activity information can be inferred from muscle shape changes.
- Muscle activity contains information that goes beyond mere motion type. This includes physical effort and fatigue as well as subtle motion characteristics that are of interest to many medical, nursing and sports applications.

1.1   Related Work

Monitoring muscle activity is widely practiced in medicine and sports. The scientific standard technique is called electromyography (EMG, e.g. [3]). It relies on a pair of electrodes placed at specific locations on the surface of the muscle belly (International standards written by Merletti [4]). EMG is a rich and reliable source of information about muscle activity by detecting the electromechanical properties of muscle fibres. However, since the electrical potentials that it measures are very faint, it requires careful electrode placement and excellent contact with the skin. In general, EMG electrodes require glue in order to attach to the skin. In some cases even small needles are used. In addition, complex signal processing is needed to make sense of the signals, so that EMG devices are bulky and expensive. In summary they are not suitable for typical pervasive applications.

The second tool for monitoring muscle activity is the mechanomyographic (MMG) technique. While EMG comprises the sum of the electrical contributions, the MMG signals (using vibration transducer, such as accelerometer or piezoelectric crystal contact sensors) present the mechanical oscillation that is detectable over a contracting muscle by attaching electrodes on the skin overlying the target muscle [5].

Force sensors have been used in pervasive computing for event detection. Examples include force sensors placed in shoes to detect heel strikes [6, 7] and in furniture components to automatically verify the correctness of assembly procedures [8].

Motion monitoring using body-worn sensors is a vast research field. The main two directions are activity recognition oriented work (e.g. [9, 10, 11, 12, 13] and many more) in the classical pervasive computing field and motion characterisation oriented work (e.g. [14, 15, 16, 17, 18] and many more). The latter has its roots in the biomechanics/sports community, however, is increasingly gaining importance in pervasive computing with the advance of applications related to sports, wellness and health.

The approach presented in this paper can benefit activity recognition as well as motion characterisation. In both areas it will do so by enhancing existing systems in two ways:

1. It will provide an additional *source* of information about user motion. Such additional information can be combined with existing approaches to improve system accuracy through sensor fusion. It can also be used as an alternative, wherever existing approaches are inappropriate. Thus, for example, accelerometers and gyroscopes mounted on the leg will register not only leg motion, but also the overall motion of the user system of reference. By contrast, our muscle-activity-based method will only provide information about leg motion.
2. It will provide an additional *type* of information about user motion. This includes such things as physical effort associated with the motion, user fatigue or subtle motion characteristics related to the way the motion is generated by the musculo-skeletal system of the user.

1.2   Paper Contributions

In this paper we focus on showing that

1. under realistic assumptions it is possible to acquire good muscle activity signal with our approach, and
2. information relevant for a range of pervasive applications can be extracted from this signal.

To this end we begin in section 2 by describing the general idea of muscle activity measurement using force sensors. Section 2 also contains the characterisation of our sensors and a description of our system. We then proceed in section 3 to a quantitative experimental evaluation of the influence of sensor attachment and position on signal quality. In doing so we prove that reasonable signal quality can be reliably achieved with a simple, practical attachment scheme such as an adjustable elastic band. In section 4 we give two specific examples how activity information can be derived from such signals. The first example is the well known modes of locomotion problem (walking, fast walking, going downstairs, going upstairs). It demonstrates that our system provides an additional source of information for standard context recognition tasks. In the second example we show the correlation between the signals from our sensors and user leg muscle fatigue. This demonstrates how our sensors can provide information that goes beyond what can be derived from inertial motion sensors. For both examples we provide a physiological explanation of how the information is extracted and quantitative experimental data. We conclude in section 5 with a qualitative discussion of further examples of information that can be derived from muscles signals.

2   The Idea

2.1   Muscles and Muscle Inflation

It is a well known phenomenon that the muscle tends to 'inflate' when put under strain. This phenomenon is used by body builders when 'showing off'. When using inertial sensors to monitor limbs motion it is often a source of errors as sensor mounted on the limbs register muscle shape changes instead or together with the actual limbs motions. Dealing with such errors has been the inspiration for the work presented in this paper. Rather than filter them out as noise we propose to use muscle shape changes as source of information.

Physiological Background. To understand what type of information can be extracted from muscle shape changes some physiological background is needed. From a physiological point of view the muscle inflation can be explained as follows: Muscle is a contractile form of tissue and it consists of a large number of muscle fibres. A muscle contraction occurs when the muscle fibre shorten. The higher the force production during short-term muscle exercises the more fibres are activated and extended which contributes to larger physiological cross sectional area and this means an increased muscle volume during a muscle contraction. When muscles contract during long-term exercises, blood vessels within the muscle become wider (vasodilation) and blood flow is increased more than 20-fold. Repetitive mechanical muscle contractions consume large amounts of energy and therefore require delivery of considerable amounts of oxygen and substrates, as well as the efficient removal of metabolic waste products (e.g., lactate, CO_2, H^+). Long-term physical activities with higher intensities or motion velocities result in accumulation of lactate and other metabolites within the muscle and reduced muscle blood circulation in small arteries and arterioles. This resistance in arteries yields a blocked muscle blood circulation, an increased blood volume within the muscle, and an inflation of muscle volume during sustained and intensive exercises.

2.2   Measurement Idea

From the above physiological considerations the following sources of muscle shape change and the associated interesting information can be identified:

1. Shape change associated with each muscles contraction, with the amount of volume increase given by the load on the muscle, as can be seen in Fig. 1 (left). Since muscle contraction is the driving force behind limbs motion, detecting contractions will provide us with information about limbs movement. Since, in general, each limb is moved by a combination of muscles looking at the activity pattern of the relevant muscles should provide detailed information on the type of motion.
2. Shape change associated with long term exercise as the blood flow in the muscle is increased to provide more oxygen. This can provide information about the intensity of physical activity, as can be seen in Fig. 1 (right).

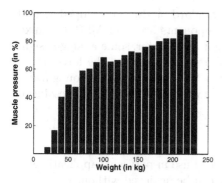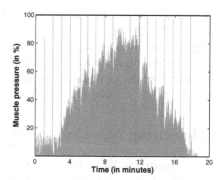

Fig. 1. *Left:* single-leg press with weight increasing in 10kg steps beginning with 20kg (left). The final weight which could be lifted was 230kg. *Right:* Muscle fatigue test using a step mill. Intensity was increased every minute till a maximum point and then decreased again.

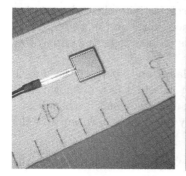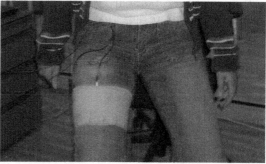

Fig. 2. Left: The force sensor and the elastic band used in our experiments. Right: One of the subjects with the band on the leg doing squats.

3. Shape change associated with muscle fatigue. Such fatigue is an important information on its own.

We propose to detect the shape changes by attaching force sensors integrated in tight fitting garments or elastic bands to the surface of the relevant muscles. The actually employed setup is depicted in Fig. 2.

2.3   Measurement System

The force sensors used in our experiments are so-called force sensitive resistors (FSR). Such sensors consist of thin ($<<$ 1 mm) electrodes that change their electrical resistance when subjected to pressure. Specifically, we have used the FSR-153NS device from Conrad Electronics. It is 0.09 mm thick and has an area of 13×13 mm^2. The measurement range is between 0.1 and 100 N with a corresponding resistance between 2 kΩ and 2 MΩ. The maximum achievable sampling rate is between 100 and 1000 Hz.

For signal acquisition a module from a standard platform developed at ETH Zürich (PadNET [19]) is used. Its main components are a TI MSP 430 mixed signal processor with a built-in analogue digital converter, some analogue signal processing circuits, a voltage regulator and a serial interface. The force sensors are connected to the analogue input of the MSP in a voltage divider configuration with a 47 kΩ resistor. The sensors are sampled with 100 Hz and 12-Bit resolution.

3   Measuring Muscle Activity

For our approach to be viable for a widespread use in pervasive applications we must ensure that acceptable signal quality can be achieved without excessively complex attachment and adjustment procedures. We envision the sensors to be integrated in garment such as pants or in an elastic band that is put on top of clothing. In both cases two issues are critical for signal acquisition:

1. The baseline pressure between the sensor and the muscle. As described in the previous section our system detects muscle activity through variation on mechanical pressure that the muscle surface exerts on the sensor. Thus, obviously, the signal that we will get depends on how tight the garment or the band is put on the muscle.
2. The sensor position; The sensor must be placed on a part of the muscle where a detectable inflation occurs. For each muscle it is well known from human physiology where such a spot is. It can also easily be felt when flexing the muscle. For practical applications the key question is how sensitive the signal quality is to small displacements.

Below we describe the results of a systematic experimental evaluation of the above issues on the example of upper-leg muscles.

3.1   Sensor Attachment

Due to the complexity of garment integration in our initial work we consider the elastic band variant as shown in Fig. 2.

1. The band is wrapped around the upper-leg in such a way that it exerts no perceivable pressure.
2. The band is tightened in increments of two centimeters. After each increment the user bends his knees about 90 degree in a partial squat and the maximum of the signal is noted.
3. Point two is repeated after the signal with bent knees reaches between 15% and 20% of the maximum (as given by sensor range).

The above procedure was performed on 10 subjects, each repeating it three times. We used a commercial elastic bandage which was folded in half wrapped around the upper-leg between two and three times. On all subjects signal in the desired range was achieved by tightening the band between a minimum of 4 cm and a maximum of 16 cm. For all subjects the required amount of tightening was the same in all three attempts.

The results of this experiment mean that an individual value has been established for tightening the band and that it can be put on in a single deterministic step. The search for the right value is matter of a view simple steps not much different from fitting a shoe.

3.2   Sensor Placement

The placement of the sensor on the muscle is performed according to international standards for EMG written by Merletti [4]. To evaluate the effect of sensor displacement on the signal quality we systematically displaced the sensor from the above position in increments of 1 cm and then looked at the signal produced during squats. An example result is shown in Fig. 3. The measurements have revealed two things:

1. The optimal EMG placement spot does not correspond with the best placement for our sensors, although it does produce good signals.
2. Depending on the direction of sensor displacement even a 1 cm move from the original position can lead to a loss of signal. However, within a 4 cm × 4 cm square around the optimal position there are many points with good signal quality.

The above means that for practical applications one would have to work with a sensor array rather then with a single sensors. Since the force sensors are thin and easily integrable this is not a problem. Such 4 × 4 arrays with about the right area have even been demonstrated as purely textile devices. In summary, it can be said that, as long as we can work with an array, sensor placement is not a serious obstacle to achieving good signal quality with realistic setups.

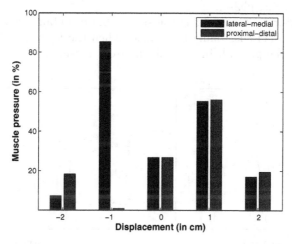

Fig. 3. The effect of sensor displacement on signal quality

4   Interpreting Muscle Activity

The previous section showed that reliable acquisition of muscle activity signals is possible under realistic conditions. Staying with the example of upper-leg muscles this section leverages physiological knowledge to extract from those signals information relevant to a wide range of pervasive applications.

4.1   Modes of Locomotion

The recognition of different modes of locomotion is a standard context problem that has become sort of a benchmark for new approaches. In the following we investigate the problem of distinguishing between level walking with normal stride, level walking with extra long stride, walking downstairs, and walking upstairs.

Physiological Foundations. To monitor motion patterns in level walking, going upstairs and downstairs by using force sensors, muscle activity of the front-leg muscles (m. vastus lateralis) and back-leg muscles (m. biceps femoris) were selected. For the purpose of analysis, steps are usually divided into the swing phase and the stance phase. In the swing phase the leg is brought forward without ground contact. The stance phase begins with the leg being put down and ends with the leg pushing off the ground.

While walking styles differ between people, there are some general considerations valid for the majority of people. Also wherever variations are present they are consistent in the sense that a given person will always display certain muscle activation patterns for a particular mode of locomotion.

1. For all types of walking there can be expected to be little to no muscle signal during the swing phase.
2. Typically, during level walking the stance phase contains two distinct muscle activities: (1) cushioning the impact when the leg is put down and (2) pushing off the ground. In general, the front muscle is more active during

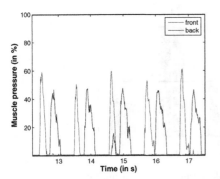 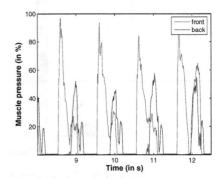

Fig. 4. Example of level walking signals from the front-leg and the back-leg muscle with normal step size (left) and long step size (right)

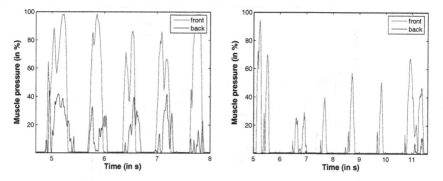

Fig. 5. Example of signals from the front-leg and the back-leg muscle for walking downstairs (left) and upstairs (right)

impact, whereas the back muscle tends to dominate the push-off. While the activity between the impact and the push-off as well as signal ratios will vary between people the presence of a front muscle dominated peak in the beginning and a back muscle dominated one at the end is a very strong indication of level walking, as can be seen in Fig. 4 (left).

3. For faster walking and longer strides we will see a decrease in the delay between the peaks and an increase in the muscle activity amplitudes. This illustrates Fig. 4 (right).

4. The main activity when going downstairs is the cushioning of impact. Except for very wide steps there is nearly no push-off observed. The cushioning involves both front-leg and back-leg muscles working synchronously. While the exact ratio differs from person to person, the front muscle plays a clearly dominant role. This can be seen in Fig. 5 (left).

5. When going upstairs, front-leg muscles are dominantly used at the beginning of the stance phase to lift the body up. There is no similar synchronized front and back muscle activity as considered in going downstairs. This trend was already presented in elderly by using electromyographic measuring method [20]. An example of walking upstairs, can be seen in Fig. 5 (right).

From the above considerations the ratio of front-leg to back-leg muscle activity and the delay between the two (both during the stance phase) can be derived as appropriate features to separate the four modes of locomotion under consideration. The swing phase with a null or near null activity level from both muscles provides an excellent way to segment the signal into individual steps.

Experiment. To verify the above hypothesis 4 subjects were asked to walk around the hall. Part of the distance was to be covered with normal steps and with particularly long steps. At the end of the hall the subject were to walk down and then back up a flight of stairs. For each subject the data was segmented into steps using the swing phases and the two features suggested above were computed for each step segment. The result is shown in Fig. 6. It indicates

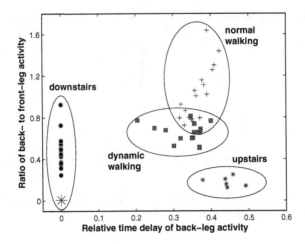

Fig. 6. The separation between the four investigated modes of locomotion using the features described in the text. Asterisk indicates the accumulation of downstairs steps with identical feature values.

excellent separation, even though we have combined data from all four persons in a single plot (8 user independent case).

4.2   Muscle Fatigue

The level of user muscle fatigue is an important piece of information for a variety of applications. Straining the muscles to the point of volitional fatigue may lead to loss of muscular reflexes and may increase the risk for injury as a consequence of proprioceptive deficit in muscle receptors and joint proprioception. Thus detecting fatigue can prevent accidents in areas such as sports, emergency response teams and in elderly, frail persons. In addition, the level of fatigue is also relevant for many classical pervasive applications such as for a context sensitive-tourist guide. A tired user is more interested in the next restaurant then in the nearby hiking trail.

General Considerations. Fatigue is a vague term that can describe a wide range of condition and is often difficult to quantify. In our work we focus on muscle fatigue. As described in section 2.2 sustained, strenuous muscle activity leads to increased production of lactate and other metabolites. This, in turn, leads to an increased blood circulation and with it to an inflation of the muscle. In general terms, it can be said that in medicine the level of production of such metabolites is taken as a measure of muscle fatigue, as it causes the muscle performance to deteriorate.

From the above we can conclude that the amount of muscle inflation can be seen as an objective fatigue indicator. Obviously, with our setup and without detailed large-scale experimental calibrations we can not hope to have any sort of medically accurate fatigue measurement. However, for the majority of applications mentioned above this is not needed. Instead, a rough scale with a small

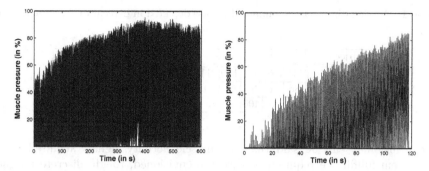

Fig. 7. Two examples of signals acquired from the front-leg muscle during the squats fatigue experiments

number of discrete states between 'fresh', and 'totaly exhausted' is sufficient. To this end the following is required:

1. A definition of 'totally exhausted' must be found that can be applied to all subjects.
2. Between the 'fresh' and the 'totally exhausted' states there must be enough difference in signal intensity to allow reliable, repeatable discrimination between states.
3. The signal must follow a deterministic, repeatable trajectory that agrees with established facts about fatigue. In general terms the relation between the duration of a strenuous activity and the level of fatigue should be vaguely linear with a saturation towards the top as an equilibrium is reached. The slope, level of saturation, and level of linearity are obviously likely to vary between subjects depending on physical condition and individual anatomy.

Experiment. To evaluate the feasibility of assessing fatigue with our system 12 subjects were asked to perform squats for as long as possible with a force sensor attached to the front-leg muscle surface as described in section 3. An example of the resulting signal for two subjects is shown in Fig. 7. An overview of the results for all 12 subjects is given in Table 1. The key results of the experiment are:

1. Only two subjects have managed to reached saturation (steady state). All others gave up before coming that far. This is not surprising since it is well known that only well trained persons can get into the equilibrium state and continue exercise. As a consequence 'totally exhausted' must be defined as either a value corresponding to the steady state or a value at which the user is unable to continue putting strain on the muscle.
2. For all subjects a significant signal difference was registered between fresh and exhausted (between 25 and 85% of the overall sensor range).
3. For all subject the increase of the signal intensity (filtered with a moving average) was close to linear.

Table 1. Muscle fatigue data summary; Increase depicted in percent of the total sensor range

Subject	1	2	3	4	5	6	7	8	9	10	11	12
Period [s]	113	530	600	150	211	80	144	550	441	125	203	188
Increase [%]	85	56	37	61	61	46	51	61	88	53	66	25
Steady state [s]	—	—	400	—	—	—	—	372	—	—	—	—

In conclusion it can be said that the muscle activity signals acquired with our system fullfill the requirements for the envisioned, rough, discrete fatigue detection.

5   Outlook: Further Information

This section presents several additional observations that we made during our experiments. In each case we provide example data and a quantitative physiological explanation. The data presented below is meant as an illustration of the richness of information available from the muscle signals and motivation for further study. Using the respective phenomena in an application would require a detailed experimental study amounting to a publication on its own.

Physical Effort. As described in section 4 without fatigue the amount by which a muscle inflates during action is determined by the load which it has to bear. This is illustrated in Fig. 1. Whereas fatigue is a trend that develops over a longer period of time load-related inflation is a short-term phenomenon directly associated with a certain action. Thus short-term variations in the signal can be interpreted as an indication of the effort that the user puts into a given activity. This could be the weight of an object that the user is lifting, the amount of force put into operating a tool or the load that the user is carrying. Clearly, this is an information that is relevant for a variety of context recognition tasks and can not be extracted from inertial sensors.

Personal Walking Style. It is well known that people have different walking styles. While humans are good at spotting such individual patterns, the actual difference in terms of physical motion is often small and difficult to capture with inertial sensors (although gait-based person recognition has been demonstrated [21]). On the other hand, as shown in Fig. 8, the different styles show very clearly in the muscle activation pattern. Interesting application of walking style evaluation emerge in monitoring rehabilitation progress and in assissitive systems for elderly care. In the latter case changes in the walking pattern might indicate a deterioration of the physical state and an increased risk of falls.

Joint Stress Reduction. An important feature of a personal walking style is illustrated in Fig. 9. It shows the signals from the front-leg and back-leg muscles during walking downstairs. When compared with the signals in Fig. 5 an additional, large peak in the front-leg muscle activity can be seen for each step. This

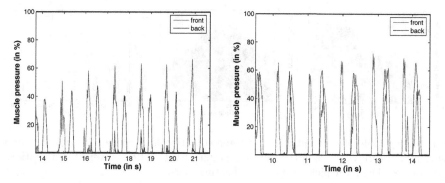

Fig. 8. Example of signals from the front-leg and the back-leg muscle for level walking with long strides

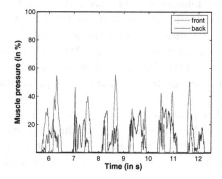

Fig. 9. Example of signals from the front-leg and the back-leg muscle for walking downstairs *in a joint friendly way that manifests itself through the initial peak in the front muscle signal*

peak is an artifact of a downward walking style that cushions step impact in a particularly joint-friendly way [22, 23]. Joint damage is one of the key concerns of many popular recreational sports such as hiking or nordic walking, in particular for overweight people. Thus, the ability to detect joint-friendly walking styles with an unobtrusive setup opens up interesting applications in terms of 'wearable electronic trainer' systems.

Correctness of Exercise Patterns. Like with walking styles in many other physical activities differences that look very subtle when looking at a motion 'from the outside' can have very different muscle 'signatures'. Examples encountered during our fatigue experiments are shown in Fig. 10. In those specific experiments two front-leg muscles (vas. lat. and rec. fem. muscle) were monitored. In the first upper graph on the left the signal amplitude is similar for both muscles and steadily increases for both muscles with the level of fatigue. This indicates user doing the squats in the 'correct way'. In the lower graph on the left we see the data from a user that starts the exercise with a stance and weight distribution that puts all the load of the squats on vas. lat. muscle. It is only after a certain

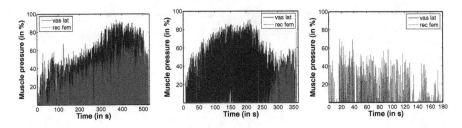

Fig. 10. Example of different muscle fatigue condition for two muscles (vas. lat. and rec. fem. muscle) when doing the squats experiment with different weight distributions and stances. The right picture shows a 'cheating' person.

level of muscle fatigue had been reached that the subject changed his technique to activate the rec. fem. muscle. We then see a decrease in the vas. lat. muscle signal that is nearly perfectly matched by an increase in the signal from the rec. fem. muscle until the muscles share the load almost equally. Finally, the figure on the right shows a person 'cheating'. We see only sporadic signal from the rec. fem. muscle with little sign of fatigue. In this case the user takes the gross of the load from the legs by 'swinging' the squats from the hips and the upper body.

The above is another example of our system providing information that is hard or impossible to get from inertial sensors which currently dominate context recognition and motion analysis. It again underscores the value of our system for sports, recreation- and rehabilitation-based pervasive computing applications.

6   Conclusion

We demonstrated that muscle activity signals can be detected through force sensors attached to the muscle surfaces. We showed that using an array of thin sensors and a conventional elastic band good quality signals can be acquired with an easily usable setup suitable for real world applications. From a physiological understanding of muscle role in walking behavior we proved that modes of locomotion recognition can be implemented by looking at the relation between signals from the front-leg and the back-leg muscles. Furthermore, we have established that long-term muscle inflation detected by our system is suitable as a simple muscle fatigue indicator. Finally, a qualitative discussion of selected interesting data collected during our experiments indicates that our concept can provide a wide range of relevant activity information.

In summary we showed that what others consider a source of noise when working with inertial sensors can be turned into a source of valuable information. Clearly, the results presented in this paper are no more then a starting point towards real life use of force-sensor-based motion analysis and activity recognition. Our group is currently working on more detailed investigation of recognition performance for different tasks. We are also looking into sports applications in which muscle activity information is combined with signals from inertial sensors to produce an even more complete picture of user motion.

References

1. Lukowicz, P., Ward, J.A., Junker, H., Stäger, M., Tröster, G., Atrash, A., Starner, T.: Recognizing workshop activity using body worn microphones and accelerometers. In Ferscha, A., Mattern, F., eds.: Pervasive. Volume 3001 of Lecture Notes in Computer Science., Springer (2004) 18–32

2. Lukowicz, P., Kirstein, T., Tröster, G.: Wearable systems for health care applications. Methods of Information in Medicine **43** (2004) 232–238

3. Moritani, T., Yoshitake, Y.: The use of electromyography in applied physiology. Journal of Electromyography and Kinesiology **8** (1998) 363–381

4. Merletti, R.: Standards for reporting EMG data. Journal of Electromyography and Kinesiology **9** (1999) 3–4

5. Orizio, C., Gobbo, M., Diemont, B., Esposito, F., Veicsteinas, A.: The surface mechanomyogram as a tool to describe the influence of fatigue on biceps brachii motor unit activation strategy. Historical basis and novel evidence. European Journal of Applied Physiology **90** (2003) 326–336

6. Paradiso, J.A., Hsiao, K., Benbasat, A.Y., Teegarden, Z.: Design and implementation of expressive footwear. IBM Systems Journal **39** (2000) 511–529

7. Junker, H., Lukowicz, P., Tröster, G.: Locomotion analysis using a simple feature derived from force sensitive resistors. In: Proc. 2nd International Conference on Biomedical Engineering. (2004)

8. Antifakos, S., Michahelles, F., Schiele, B.: Proactive instructions for furniture assembly. In: Proceedings of the 4th international conference on Ubiquitous Computing. Volume 2498 of Lecture Notes In Computer Science., London, UK, Springer-Verlag (2002) 351–360

9. Kern, N., Schiele, B., Schmidt, A.: Multi-sensor activity context detection for wearable computing. In: Proc. European Symposium on Ambient Intelligence. (2003) 220–232

10. Mantyjarvi, J., Himberg, J., Seppanen, T.: Recognizing human motion with multiple acceleration sensors. In: 2001 IEEE International Conference on Systems, Man and Cybernetics. Volume 2. (2001) 747–752

11. Randell, C., Muller, H.: Context awareness by analysing accelerometer data. In: ISWC. (2000) 175–176

12. Seon-Woo, L., Mase, K.: Recognition of walking behaviors for pedestrian navigation. In: Proc. IEEE International Conference on Control Applications. (2001) 1152–1155

13. Van-Laerhoven, K., Cakmakci, O.: What shall we teach our pants? In: Proc. 4th International Symposium on Wearable Computers. (2000) 77–83

14. Luinge, H.J., Veltink, P.H., Baten, C.T.M.: Estimation of orientation with gyroscopes and accelerometers. In: Proc. First Joint BMES/EMBS Conference. Volume 2. (1999) 844

15. Najafi, B., Aminian, K., Paraschiv-Ionescu, A., Loew, F., Bula, C.J., Robert, P.: Ambulatory system for human motion analysis using a kinematic sensor: monitoring of daily physical activity in the elderly. IEEE Transactions on Biomedical Engineering **50** (2003) 711–723

16. Sekine, M., Tamura, T., Fujimoto, T., Fukui, Y.: Classification of walking pattern using acceleration waveform in elderly people. Engineering in Medicine and Biology Society **2** (2000) 1356–1359
17. Tamura, T., Abe, Y., Sekine, M., Fujimoto, T., Higashi, Y., Sekimoto, M.: Evaluation of gait parameters by the knee accelerations. Engineering in Medicine and Biology **2** (1999) 828
18. van den Bogert, A.J., Read, L., Nigg, B.M.: A method for inverse dynamic analysis using accelerometry. Journal of Biomechanics **29** (1996) 949–954
19. Junker, H., Lukowicz, P., Tröster, G.: Padnet: Wearable physical activity detection network. In: Proceedings of the 7th International Symposium on Wearable Computers. (2003) 244–245
20. James, B., Parker, A.W.: Electromyography of stair locomotion in elderly men and women. Electromyography and Clinical Neurophysiology **29** (1989) 161–168
21. Kale, A., Rajagopalan, A.N., Cuntoor, N., Kruger, V.: Gait-based recognition of humans using continuous HMMs. In: Proceedings of the 5th IEEE International Conference on Automatic Face and Gesture Recognition, Washington, DC, USA, IEEE Computer Society (2002) 336–341
22. Heino-Brechter, J., Powers, C.M.: Patellofemoral joint stress during stair ascent and descent in persons with and without patellofemoral pain. Gait Posture **16** (2002) 115–123
23. Kuster, M., Sakurai, S., Wood, G.A.: Kinematic and kinetic comparison of downhill and level walking. Clinical Biomechanics **10** (1995) 79–84

The Design of a Portable Kit of Wireless Sensors for Naturalistic Data Collection

Emmanuel Munguia Tapia, Stephen S. Intille, Louis Lopez, and Kent Larson

Massachusetts Institute of Technology,
1 Cambridge Center, 4FL,
Cambridge, MA, 02142, USA
{emunguia, intille}@mit.edu

Abstract. In this paper, we introduce MITes, a flexible kit of wireless sensing devices for pervasive computing research in natural settings. The sensors have been optimized for ease of use, ease of installation, affordability, and robustness to environmental conditions in complex spaces such as homes. The kit includes six environmental sensors: movement, movement tuned for object-usage-detection, light, temperature, proximity, and current sensing in electric appliances. The kit also includes five wearable sensors: onbody acceleration, heart rate, ultra-violet radiation exposure, RFID reader wristband, and location beacons. The sensors can be used simultaneously with a single receiver in the same environment. This paper describes our design goals and results of the evaluation of some of the sensors and their performance characteristics. Also described is how the kit is being used for acquisition of data in non-laboratory settings where real-time multi-modal sensor information is acquired simultaneously from several sensors worn on the body and up to several hundred sensors distributed in an environment.

1 Introduction

A barrier that many researchers face when attempting to conduct pervasive computing research is lack of access to affordable, flexible, robust, and easy-to-use tools for the study of behavior and technologies in complex, non-laboratory settings such as homes. Computing trends such as Moore's Law suggest that at some time in the future it will be possible to deploy small and affordable sensors ubiquitously and inconspicuously throughout homes and on the body, perhaps enabling many novel and useful pervasive computing applications. Further, recent work suggests that many sensors placed throughout a home environment (e.g., [1-4]) in combination with a few sensors worn on the body (e.g., [5-7]) may permit a system to automatically and unobtrusively recognize everyday activities and states as diverse as cooking, "making tea," ambulation, posture, "in conversation," vacuuming, and others. The same types of sensors can also be used to study behavior, providing designers and ethnographers with new data gathering tools.

Despite the promise of pervasive sensing, most researchers today who wish to populate environments such as homes with multi-modal sensors are likely to find this

K.P. Fishkin et al. (Eds.): PERVASIVE 2006, LNCS 3968, pp. 117 – 134, 2006.
© Springer-Verlag Berlin Heidelberg 2006

to be a difficult and costly (in time and money) endeavor. Past studies have generally been conducted either in homes that were specially (and laboriously) wired with sensors (e.g., [8, 9]), in homes wired with a small number of sensors for short periods of time, or in controlled laboratory home simulations (e.g., [10, 11]). During prior work installing sensors in homes, we identified a set of design goals for a portable sensing kit that could be easily retrofitted in existing homes and used in longitudinal pervasive computing experiments. We could not find an existing hardware platform that met these goals and therefore designed and built a sensor system optimized for researcher and subject usability. In this paper we introduce MITes: MIT Environmental Sensors, a portable wireless sensor platform that can be used to collect data on people's activities in non-laboratory settings such as homes.

The MITes platform includes six environmental sensor types, five of them being among the most typically needed in ubiquitous and pervasive computing applications [12]: (1) movement using ball, mercury, and reed switches, (2) movement tuned for object-usage detection (using acceleration), (3) light, (4) temperature, (5) proximity, and (6) current consumption. The MITes platform also includes five wearable sensors: (1) accelerometers to acquire body motion information, (2) heart rate, (3) ultra violet radiation exposure, (4) an RFID reader in a wristband form factor, and (5) location beacons. All of these sensors can be used simultaneously, and a single receiver acquires the data, which is sent to a PC or mobile computing device for real-time processing.

Usability criteria for researchers, particularly those interested in sensor-driven pervasive computing research, drove our design decisions. The MITes have been optimized to be easy for researchers and non-technical home occupants to "install," wear, and use. Battery life has been optimized for conducting longitudinal experiments. A *single* power efficient receiver connected to a mobile device can gather data from a variety of sensor types. Device size has been optimized for comfort, flexibility, and ease of attachment to home objects. Finally, the entire system is designed so that components can be affordably manufactured and assembled by researchers, even in low quantities.

This paper describes the design and development of the MITes sensor kit and performance of key components in non-laboratory settings. The hardware and software specifications for MITes can be found online for interested researchers [32].

2 Motivation and Design Goals

Most researchers who have tried to test novel technologies and study the behavior of people in non-laboratory settings have found that testing outside of the lab in complicated environments such as homes is logistically and technically challenging. Testing is particularly difficult when components of the sensing or interface technology must be distributed throughout the environment. For example, recent work by several groups has suggested that very simple and small sensors such as switches [1, 2, 11] and RFID tags or readers [3, 13] non-obtrusively attached to many objects in an environment may enable a computer system to infer contextual information about the home occupant's movement and activities. Developing and testing such systems, however, requires laborious sensor installations and time-consuming maintenance of complex technical infrastructures. It is not surprising, therefore, that most prior work on home sensing has generally been conducted with a single type of sensor tested in a single environment with a single user. Wearable sensor researchers interested in conducting non-laboratory studies with comfortable, multi-modal sensors placed on multiple parts of the body face similar challenges – sensor systems can be difficult to use and maintain in the field for longitudinal studies.

Based on our prior work deploying environmental and wearable sensors in homes, we have identified four usability goals for a portable sensor kit that could be used for non-laboratory pervasive computing studies, particularly for those designed for the home setting. Table 1 lists these general goals as well as the sensor design goals they motivated and the benefit(s) of achieving the usability goals for the researcher and/or the subject in an experiment.

Table 1. Usability design goals that motivated the development of the MITes, listing benefits to the researcher and the subject. More detail on how the sensor design goals were implemented is found in Table 2 and throughout the paper.

Usability Goals (What)	Sensor Design Goals (How)	Benefit to Researcher(R) and Subject (S) (Why)
Ease of installation	• Light weight, and small sensor nodes (portable) • Self-contained single point of contact to body/home • Single receiver to collect data from multiple sensors • Real-time simultaneous data -acquisition from high and low sampling rate sensors • No pre-configuration required or threshold setting • Good indoor Tx/Rx range and easy to detect if in range	• Minimizes installation time (R) • Subjects can install sensors themselves (R/S) • Subjects can re-install sensors if they dislodge, simplifying maintenance for researchers during studies (R/S)
Ease of use	• Real-time simultaneous data acquisition from multiple high and low sampling sensors with single receiver • Each sensor does one thing well • Convenient battery life • Robustness to environmental noise	• Facilitates maintenance (R/S) • Low training overhead (R/S) • Facilitates the addition of new sensors(R) • Reduces failure points (R) • Decreases probability of data loss (RS)
Adequate longitudinal performance in natural settings	• Convenient battery life/low power • Robustness to environmental noise • Self-contained, resistant packaging • Good indoor Tx/Rx range and easy to detect if in range • Performance valuated in a natural setting (Section 5.1)	• Decreases probability of data loss (R/S) • Facilitates design of data collection (R)
Affordable for researchers	• Design with low-cost components • Each sensor does one thing well	• Deployment of hundreds of sensors (R)

These usability goals have driven our design decisions for the MITes. For example, if sensors are used and tested only in a laboratory setting, then installation time is often a minor concern. Previous studies, even those where sensors have been installed in homes of subjects (e.g., [1, 2]) have often relied upon complex installation of switch sensors. A typical switch sensor that must be installed on a cabinet in a volunteer's home has a microprocessor, a reed switch, and a magnet. All three components must be placed on the cabinet in a way that properly activates the reed switch when the cabinet is operated but also in a way that will not be easily knocked off, cause damage to the cabinetry, or create aesthetic concerns that make the subject uncomfortable. Meeting all these concerns can be challenging, and we have found that a single such sensor takes 5-10 minutes to install and test. Installation of 200 sensors, a number that might be desired for some types of pervasive computing research in a moderately sized home, could require 16-32 man-hours of effort. This is a tremendous inconvenience to both the researchers and the subject in an experiment. Minimization of installation time, therefore, was a key MITes design goal. One way this was achieved was by minimizing points of contact for sensors using accelerometers instead of switch sensors. MITes based on accelerometers are self-contained and sufficiently small so that they can be placed on nearly any household object, and installation requires simply throwing a sensor in a drawer or sticking it with putty to a cabinet door. No multi-point alignment is required, and installation is reduced from 5-10 minutes to 5-60 seconds. Installing 200 single-point-of-contact sensors may take a little as 1-2.5 man-hours of effort, a tolerable amount of time for many subjects.

Ease of use is just as important as ease of installation. Ease of use can be facilitated by having devices with robust communication protocols and good communication ranges so that additional complex devices that introduce failure points such as routers are not necessary. Sensors should require infrequent battery replacement, and when battery replacement is required it should be possible for a non-technical subject to perform this task. Further, it should be easy for a researcher or a subject to add and remove sensors with little or no post configuration. Finally, the system must perform well not only in the laboratory but also in natural settings. Devices should also be packaged robustly, since they can be bumped or jostled (especially the wearable ones), and sensors must perform predictably in realistic conditions, with environmental noise and EMI interference from electric household appliances such as vacuum cleaners, microwaves, cordless phones, WLAN, and Bluetooth devices. We later describe how the MITes system design enabled us to achieve these goals.

3 Existing Sensor Kits and Applicability for In-Home Studies

When we began exploring the possibility of non-laboratory ubiquitous computing experiments, we were reluctant to invest time in making a new sensor kit given the number of systems that exist and the growing number of commercial sensor network products. Popular wireless sensor network platforms available to the research community include Motes in all their varieties (MicaDOT [14], Micaz [15], iMotes [16], tMotes [17], etc.), uParts [18] (previously Smart-Its [19]), ECOs [20], BTnodes [21], and Millennial nodes [22], among others.

We considered each of the available options relative to the usability goals in Table 1 and the design goals in Table 2. While each of the systems has its strengths, none met our needs. In this section, we explain why.

Goal 1: Ease of installation. Many of the existing platforms were designed to permit multiple sensors to attach to the same wireless transmitter or transceiver. However, making each transmitter multi-functional and expandable adds size, weight, and complexity to the devices. Many use snap-in sensor boards, often with somewhat bulky battery boards (usually based on AA batteries). The iMote snap-in sensor board and battery board, for instance, more than doubles the original node's size and weight. Moreover, some of these wireless platforms work at relatively low Tx/Rx frequencies, such as 433 and 868Mhz, that result in dangling wire antennas of several centimeters long. These cumbersome antennas make the sensors more difficult to install and greatly increase likelihood of breakage or dislodgement. For instance, although the

MicaDOT [14] (smallest Mote) and µParts [18] sensor nodes are small, the antenna is large relative to the sensor node, increasing the sensor size in practice.

Goal 2: Ease of use. Most wireless sensor network kits have been designed either to demonstrate novel wireless sensor network architectures (e.g., [14, 15, 17]) or for industrial applications (e.g., [23]). In practice, some of the systems use generic but difficult to customize operating systems, as well as network and MAC protocols that require non-trivial configuration difficult to customize for researchers who are not experts in networked sensors. Quite often, the use of mesh network topologies that promise self-configuration and unlimited coverage area result in increased cost, complexity, points of failure (due to their research/prototype stage), and degraded battery life during research data collections. Existing systems are also not optimized for data collection from multi-modal home sensors. Most available sensor network platforms are designed for either event detection from relatively low sampling rate sensors (e.g., Motes , µParts [18], and BTNodes [21]), or data collection from wearable sensors of relatively high sampling rate (e.g., ECOs [20], MIThril [24], iMotes [25]).

There do exist some off-the-shelf sensor technologies that have been extensively tested in non-laboratory settings by researchers in a diverse set of fields. Examples include actigraphs for aggregate measures of onbody acceleration (e.g., [26]), and power monitoring in electric devices (Watt's Up Pro [27]). These devices do not provide real-time data wirelessly since they were designed as data loggers. More importantly, there is no easy way to integrate data from these multiple devices without requiring a subject to wear an unacceptably cumbersome amount of gear. Acquiring real-time, synchronized multi-modal data simultaneously from low and high sampling sensors is difficult with both wearable and in-home sensor systems that can be easily deployed in the field.

Goal 3: Adequate performance in natural settings. Performance parameters such as Tx/Rx ranges, battery life, and effects of environmental noise have not been reported in the literature for most of the existing sensor systems. Thus, it is difficult for a pervasive computing researcher to estimate resource needs and design a data collection study. The Motes have been extensively tested, but the performance data are not clearly presented by the manufacturer and are scattered among many research publications, making it difficult to find. Moreover, most sensor network platforms are either designed for laboratory settings with no robust packaging whatsoever or with bulky packaging for industrial applications.

Goal 4: Affordability. A significant problem with most of the readily available sensor platforms is their high cost to the researcher. Assuming a installation of 200 sensors distributed throughout a home, the market price for a single system would range from $15,600 (Motes [14, 15, 17, 25]) including only generic node with microcontroller and transceiver) to $26,000 including sensors such as 2–axis accelerometers (commercially available of-the-shelf accelerometer sensor board adds $120 per node in least expensive option for the Mica2DOT [14]).

Of existing wireless sensor solutions, the platforms that most closely meet our usability and affordability design goals are the ECO system and µParts. ECOs are small (12x12x4.5mm, no battery), relatively inexpensive (e.g., $57 production price each including a 2-axis accelerometer) sensors designed for the particular task of monitoring motion in infants. However, their extremely small form factor results in a limited wireless range of 10.7m (testing conditions not reported). Furthermore, ECOs do not allow multi-modal data collection, just 2-axis acceleration. µParts on the other hand, are a system of small sensor nodes (10x10mm) designed for settings requiring a high population of relatively low sampling rate sensors. The sensors were designed for low cost applications with a target market price of $36 (including a light, temperature, and a ball switch sensor for motion detection) in quantities of 100. µParts designers made design decisions explicitly to keep the cost of each device down, such as constraining components to a single side of the PCB and placing the battery on the opposite side. A similar strategy has been employed in the design of the MITes. Despite their low cost and small size, results of testing µParts in naturalistic environments have not yet been reported.

In summary, researchers who want to deploy large numbers of sensors simultaneously in settings such as homes have limited options for robust, affordable, and well-characterized sensor solutions optimized for longitudinal, non-laboratory deployments. This observation led to the development of the MITes.

4   Challenges and Achievement of Design Goals

Designing a system that satisfied our usability goals while maintaining a feasible technical design required carefully balancing all aspects of the hardware design. For example, an adequate battery life could be achieved by selecting high-energy capacity batteries; however, this would lead to unacceptably large sensor footprints increasing installation complexity because such batteries are usually bulky. Sufficient battery life could also be achieved by lowering power consumption, however, power consumption depends on many factors such as the node energy consumption, network topology, and medium access control protocol (MAC). Table 2 indicates how we have achieved the usability goals with the design of the MITes system and the benefit of each goal to the researcher and/or the subject in an experiment.

5   System Overview

The MITes consist of 3.2x2.5x0.6cm and 8.1g (including battery) stick-on nodes that sense environmental or onbody information and transmit it wirelessly to one or several reception nodes. The receiver node(s) collect the sensor data and send it to the host computer (PC/handheld/phone) through the USB or RS232 serial ports. Finally C# and Java code is available to save the incoming data or forward it through a UDP connection for processing in real-time on multiple computers. MITes were designed using a generic communications board with an easy-to-replace sensor connector so that multiple sensor nodes (light, temp, etc.) can be obtained by only replacing the onboard sensor and microcode.

The MITes wireless sensor nodes are designed around the nRF24E1 chip by Nordic VLSI. The nRF24E1 integrates a RF transceiver (nRF2401), an 8051 based microcontroller, and miscellaneous peripherals (9-channel ADC, IO ports, etc.). The

Table 2. Sensor design goals (motivated by usability design goals from Table 1) with more detail on how these goals were achieved and the benefit to the researcher and the subject. Some information refers to the mobile and object motion version of MITes only. Some other versions require larger form factors due to external sensor attachments (e.g., a current flow MITes requires a current transformer that wraps around a cable).

Sensor Design Goals (What)	Implementation (How)	Benefit to Researcher (R) and Subject (S) (Why)
Light weight and small form factor	• Low-profile highly integrated chip components, 3cm Microstrip antenna (possible with 2.4GHz), 3.2x2.5x.0.6cm PCB design, 20mm coin cell battery • Total board size of 3.2x2.5x.0.6cm • Total weight (including battery) of 8.1g	• Facilitates installation (R) • Minimizes sensor dislodgement (S) • Improves portability (R) • Comfortably wearable (S) • Sensors fit on most household objects (R/S)
Self-contained and resistant packaging	• Sensors embedded in low-cost water resistant plastic cases	• Facilitates installation (R) • Physically robust (R)
Self-contained, with single point of contact to body/home	• Single, self-contained acceleration sensor to measure object usage • No dangling antennas • Minimize external sensors whenever possible	• Rapid installation (R) • Easy to reattach if dislodged (R/S) • Attach with only a small bit of putty (R/S) • No parts to break/yank (R/S)
Real-time simultaneous data acquisition from multiple high and low sampling sensors with a single receiver	• FDMA in wearable/high sampling rate sensors, and single channel shared by low sampling environmental sensors • Combination of TDMA and FDMA at receiver to collect data from sensors	• Data acquisition from environmental and wearable sensors (R) • Reduced costs – only one system needed (R) • Rapid installation (R) • Real-time applications possible (R/S) • Many wearable sensors can be used without bulky receiver devices or wires (S)
No pre-configuration required or threshold setting	• Simple star network topology • A featherweight MAC protocol with only one parameter that is fixed (num. of retransmissions) (See Section 4.3) • Receiver outputs simple data format via serial port or USB serial for easy programming	• Minimizes installation time (R) • Subjects can install sensors themselves (R/S) • Facilitates first time setup of system (R) • Decreases points of failure (R)
Good indoor Tx/Rx range and easy to detect if in range	• Transceiver with 0dB output power • PCB design that maximizes antenna ground plane • Optimally cut $\lambda/4$ monopole microstrip antenna • Extensive field measurements of outdoors and indoors range (see Section 5.1)	• Reduces cost since a typical home requires few receivers (R) • Facilitates deployment (R) • Facilitate subject mobility (S)
Convenient battery life (mobile MITES > 24 hr; receiver if attached to mobile device >24 hr; other sensors > weeks)	Node • Low power components • Low duty cycles • Embedded intelligence at the sensor node to broadcast information only when necessary Overall System • Simple star topology – no overhead • A Featherweight MAC protocol – no overhead	• Long data collection deployments (R) • Reduce battery replacements (S) • Acceptable weight when worn (S) • Fits in pocket when receiver embedded in mobile device (S)
No dangling antenna	• $\lambda/4$ Microstrip monopole onboard antenna and high Tx/Rx frequency of 2.4GHz	• Facilitates installation (R) • Minimizes sensor dislodgement/breakage (S) • Easy to carry/pack (R) • Comfortable and aesthetical form factor (S)
Robustness to environmental noise	• EMI reduction bead cores • Tantalum capacitors where required • Noise efficient PCB design	• Decreases probability of data loss (R/S) • Decreases probability sensor failure (R/S) • Permits deployment in natural settings when noisy appliances are being used (R/S)
Design with low-cost components	• $3 integrated μC and transceiver (RF24E1), $0.01 microstrip antenna, $0.30 CR2032 coin cell battery	• Easy to add as many sensors as desired (R)
Each sensor does one thing well	• One sensor optimized per task (reducing complexity and cost of individual sensor)	• Reduces learning-curve/implementation complexity (R)

nRF2401 transceiver operates at 2.4GHz and data rates of 250K/1Mbps, maximum output power of 0dBs, and 125 Tx/Rx channels. Its cost is only $6 per unit (or $3 in quantities of 10,000). The MITes sensor board also includes the EEPROM program memory, a 16Mhz crystal, a 1/4 λ microstrip monopole antenna, and a T matching network. The nRF24E1 is run at 16MHz and the transceiver at 250kbps. The MITes receiver nodes include the same circuitry as the sensor nodes plus a RS232 level converter, a USB to serial converter, and a voltage regulator, so that it can be powered from 3.5 to 12V. The receiver node can also measure 2-axis acceleration onboard or 3-axis acceleration with an attached daughter board. The receiver is powered 100% of the time to avoid data loss and consumes an average of 28mA. The receiver battery life is 43.7hrs using three 1.2V 1400mA NiMH batteries in series.

5.1 Receiver Sampling and Implications

MITes sensor nodes operate at one of two sampling rates (SR) – low and high. Low SR nodes are those that either transmit only when changes in their sensor's values are detected or those where data need only be transmitted infrequently (e.g., < 10Hz). High SR nodes are those with SRs higher than 10Hz, and in our system include the onbody accelerometers (200Hz). This distinction is important because all low SR nodes operate on a single channel, whereas high SR nodes have dedicated channels, as explained shortly.

MITes receiver node(s) combine frequency division multiple access (FDMA), and time division multiple access (TDMA) techniques to collect the data from the sensor nodes. FDMA is used to assign each high SR rate sensor node a unique Tx/Rx frequency channel so that they can transmit simultaneously without collisions. Furthermore, a single channel is shared among all low SR sensor nodes. Channel 0 corresponding to 2.4Ghz was selected for this purpose, since it provides the higher reception quality given the hardware design (the antenna's characteristics, T matching network, and PCB layout design) as tested in practice (see Figure 3c). Since the master receiver node(s) can only listen to a single Tx/Rx channel at a time, TDMA is employed at the receiver node to collect the data from all the channels by listening a fixed amount of time to each channel. This is possible due to the fast (200µ) channel switching time of the nRF2401 transceiver. Although this is not the most efficient way to use the available spectrum, it allows us to collect data simultaneously from up to 6 high SR (30Hz) sensors using *a single receiver* simultaneously with and a large number (4095) of low sampling rate nodes.[1] Multiple receivers permit additional high SR sensors to be added. The main advantage of combining FDMA and TDMA is that no anti-collision protocol for high SR sensors is required and a simple retransmission strategy can be used to avoid collisions for many low SR sensors in a power efficient manner, as described later.

The behavior of the master receiver node(s) during data reception is as follows: The receiver node spends a time (t_{listen}) of 5.5 ms at each channel currently assigned to sensors present in the system listening for incoming samples. The t_{listen} time should

---

[1] The limitation on the number of low SR nodes results from a packet length restriction made to balance number of possible sensors with likelihood of collision and battery consumption.

be sufficiently long to allow the reception of samples from the sensor with highest sample rate in the system. In our current configuration, this time is determined by the onbody accelerometers, sampling at 200Hz (5 ms). If no sample is received during t_{listen}, a header sequence is sent to the host computer to indicate a timeout. Once t_{listen} has finished for the current channel, the receiver restarts the t_{listen} timer, checks for incoming PC commands through the RS232 port, and gets the packet received in the previous timeblock from the transmitter (if any) and sends it through the serial port to the host computer. Finally, the receiver changes the reception channel to the next channel in the list and starts reception in it. The process is repeated in the new channel for the maximum number of channels in use. All data is time stamped by the host computer as soon as it is received from the serial port.

The previous design decisions discussed have some practical consequences. For example, our system requires that the list of channels to listen to (low SR shared channel plus one channel per each high SR sensor used) be specified beforehand. Furthermore, the more high SR sensors there are, the lower the effective sampling rate for each channel (due to the TDMA). For example, if there were six accelerometer sensors in our system and the maximum receiver channel switching and sampling rate is 180Hz, the effective SR of the data collected from each would be 33.3Hz (180Hz/6) when only one receiver is used. Another way to think about this is that the channel switching time and t_{listen} introduced by TDMA at the receiver introduce a delay between the sensor samples proportional to the number of channels being listened to. For example, if the receiver listens to two channels, the time between two samples from the first channel would be 11ms ($2 \cdot t_{listen}$) and if listening to three channels, it would be 16.5ms ($3 \cdot t_{listen}$). In practice, we have found the capability to collect data from hundreds of low SR sensors (see plot 1b) and up to 9 3-axis accelerometers (each at 20 Hz) using a single receiver to be sufficient for a variety of research projects. Previous research, for example, has shown that 20Hz is often sufficient for recognizing activities from wearable accelerometers. Adding more accelerometers may provide more value for some applications than increasing the sampling rate of a single accelerometer. Finally, if a higher SR is required, additional receiver nodes can be used.

5.2 Data Format and Implications

The receiver node collects the sensor data received at the transceiver and sends it to the host computer through the serial or USB ports using the following convention that can be easily decoded by end applications. Each serial port packet consists of a sequence of 7 bytes corresponding to the header (2B), channel (1B), and payload (4B) information. The header indicates the beginning of data packet, and is represented by the ASCII characters 'DD', the channel is the Tx frequency used by the sensor node sending the data, and the payload contains the sensor data.

Different node types encode data slightly differently in the payload, to maximize use of the 4 bytes. Adding a new node type simply requires that a new packet type be defined so an end user application can determine the type of data and then decode it. The payload format for the wearable accelerometer high SR MITes consists of the 10 bit values of the X, Y, and Z acceleration packed into 4 bytes. For the low SR nodes, the payload consists of the sensor ID (12 bits), sensor type (4 bits), and sensor data

(16 bits). The system can accommodate up to 16 low SR node types, ten of which are already in use. The sensor data for low SR nodes consists of the sensor value (11 bits), retransmission ID (3 bits), battery low indicator (1 bit), and alive indicator (1 bit). The sensor value is dependent on the node type. For example, the object motion sensor sends the max acceleration (9 bits) and number of continuous activations experienced (2 bits), while the temperature and light sensor only send the sensor value read (11 bits).[2] Even though our current system can only distinguish among 4095 different low SR sensors (IDs) and there are only 16 sensor types allowable we believe these constraints are reasonable given the sensors most typically used in ubiquitous and pervasive computing described in [12], the number of different household objects (3135) found in Open Mind Indoor Common Sense database [31] (a database containing common sense information of everyday objects indoors), and our previous experience installing sensors in real homes.

5.3 Network Topology and Implications

The MITes networking system consists of a star network topology in combination with a simple featherweight MAC protocol. This design decision was made to minimize overall power consumption, reduce cost, and increase usability of the sensors when deployed in practice by pervasive computing researchers.

A star network topology results when all sensing nodes are in the Tx/Rx vicinity of the master reception node(s). The star network topology is the simplest single-hop network topology available and is widely used for its maximum power efficiency. The use of a such a simple topology has become possible in practice due to advances in transceiver electronics and antenna designs that allow Tx/Rx ranges sufficiently large to cover areas of interest such as one-bedroom apartments, as we have confirmed in practice (See Section 5.1).

Since there are only 125 communication channels available in MITes, it is not possible to assign each low SR node its own channel and still be able to receive data from hundreds of sensors. Thus, given that the probability of collision is low (as we will soon discuss) for low SR nodes that primarily broadcast when changes in their sensor values are detected, we selected a simple featherweight MAC protocol to share a single channel among all low SR nodes. The featherweight MAC protocol, also known as automatic transmission [28-30], maximizes the probability that a packet will be received at the master receiver node(s) by retransmitting it several times. In other words, channel noise and collisions are not avoided but overcome by the retransmission of packets.

Simple retransmission of packets can be highly effective in applications with the following characteristics: (1) the sensors sampling rate or data bandwidth is moderate or low, (2) nodes are physically distributed in a single-hop star topology, (3) the data flow is unidirectional from data collection nodes to receiver node(s), (4) small propagation delays in the order of milliseconds are tolerable, and (5) the application can afford the sporadic loss of data packets during periods of high sensor activity. We

---

[2] There is currently one exception to the format described for low SR nodes. The RFID wristband node payload format consists of the lowest 30 bits of the RFID tag ID number read.

believe that these characteristics are mostly true for home deployments with the type of sensors contained in our kit for research studies or activity recognition applications

The advantages of featherweight retransmission are: (1) significant cost savings, since no wireless receiver, carrier detection circuitry, or high precision synchronization clock is required at every sensor node, (2) energy savings, since no time is spent listening for control packets or forwarding data, (3) simple hardware and software implementation, and (4) small network set-up, and maintenance time since almost no time is spent tuning network parameters.

The featherweight protocol retransmits a packet n times, using random delays (on the order of milliseconds) between retransmissions to minimize the probability of multiple collisions due to synchronous firings from objects being manipulated simultaneously. The probability of collision is further minimized by the use of short duration packets (8B), and a high wireless Tx rate of 250kps that minimizes time in air (256µs). Note that a Tx rate of 1Mpbs could have been used for a shorter time in air of 64µs at the expense of a reduced Tx/Rx range (due to a decrease of 9dB at Rx sensitivity). Finally, the unique ID of the sensor node is used as the initialization seed for the software random number generator. The random initial and congestion delays introduce an error in the final timestamp of the data of 1-120 milliseconds (for 6 retransmissions and random delays of 20mS). However, this delay is only present for low SR sensors and is negligible for most activity recognition applications.

Assuming that each packet retransmission is independent, the probability of correctly receiving a packet after n retransmissions can be computed from $P_{Rx} = 1 - (P_{Loss})^n$. The probability of packet loss depends on the probability of channel impairment (environmental noise, shadowing, fading, reflection, refractions, obstacles, etc.) and the probability of packet collision (due to the simultaneous transmission of different sensor nodes). Figure 1a shows a plot of P_{Rx} vs. n (number of retransmissions). For $n=6$ (number of retransmissions used in MITes), P_{Loss} can be as high as 0.3 (30%) and the probability of reception will still be 100%. For a P_{Loss} of 0.6 and 0.7, the probability of reception would be 95 and 88% respectively. Thus, assuming independence between retransmissions, by retransmitting packets channel impairments and collisions can be overcome.

In order to show that the number of collisions is indeed low for activity recognition applications using low SR sensors, we measured the number of collisions over two weeks of real activity sensor data collected in [1] from two subjects, each living alone. During this data collection, 77 and 88 sensor boards (not MITes) equipped with EEPROM memories and external reed switches were installed in two single person apartments. The percentage of collisions was 3.2% (77 sensors) and 0.71% (88 sensors) respectively. These numbers are relatively high because (1) the time resolution of the sensors was ±2 secs after linearly interpolating the timestamps and (2) some of the collisions were caused due to the activation/motion of adjacent sensors. Even if the percentage of collisions is 3.2% in a typical home setting, for the MITes two retransmissions would be enough to increase P_{Rx} to 99.9%.

We also performed a software simulation as in [28] to find the probability of collision when the number of nodes is increased from 1 to 500 and each sensor is assumed to fire randomly over time windows of 10, 5, 1, and 0.5 seconds. The simulation results over 10,000 windows are shown in Figure 1b. The graph shows that even when all the sensors are fired randomly every 5 secs, P_{Rx} is better than 97% for 500 sensors. Even in a worse-case scenario where all 500 sensors are fired every 0.5 seconds (as in a period of extremely high activity with multiple people), P_{Rx} is 0.6 and can be increased to 1 by retransmitting 6 times. The simulation was run using a message length of 256μs (as used by the MITes).

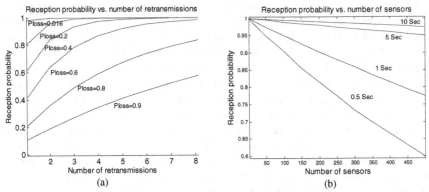

Fig 1. (a) Plot of P_{Rx} vs. number of retransmissions and (b) Plot of P_{Rx} vs. number of sensors in the system

5.4 Multi-modal Sensor Types

Using the design and protocols described above, we have been able to create a system of multi-modal sensors where a single receiver can collect 10 types of data from a home setting. Table 3 presents a summary of the different types of MITes sensors we have built and evaluated as well as well as some of their most important parameters. For battery life computation we assume a 0dB Tx output power, six retransmissions per sensor activation, and a CR2032 battery, if not otherwise noted. The cost listed in Table 3 is the production cost (administration and NRE cost not included) and was calculated assuming a production quantity of 50 and a two-month lead time, as quoted by a U.S company (including PWB tooling, masks, stencils, soldering, and no electrical testing). Finally, an asterisk in the price column indicates that the hand labor cost of soldering the external sensor was not included.

The MITes kit has been designed so that it can be easily expanded to include a few additional node types. Any sensor with RS232, I2C, or SPI output can be easily attached to the nodes with minor firmware modifications. Adding sensors with analog output is also possible, however, external circuitry would be required to condition the signal to the ADC input voltage range of 1.5V. A low SR location tracking node useful for much pervasive computing research, and a high SR audio node that could transmit raw audio would be valuable additions to our kit. These additions could be made in future work without impacting the performance characteristics of the other sensor types. Figure 2 shows some images of existing MITes.

Table 3. Summary of MITes types available and performance parameters

MITES Type	Measures	Sensor	Range	Res	Battery life (days)	Cost ($)
Object usage	Object manipu-lation	Accelerometer. ADXL202	±2g 2-axis	0.005	46, 10Hz	28.43
Mobile	Onbody Acceleration (Acc)	Accelerometer. ADXL202/10	±2g or ±10g 3-axis	0.005	1.5, 200Hz	44.3
Temperature	Temperature	MAX6677	–40C to 125C	±1.5	1309, 1Hz	20.3[*]
Light	Ambient light intensity	Digital TSL235R	0.003-1ku W/cm2 at 320-1050nm	16bit	620, 1Hz	21.0[*]
Current sensing	Current con-sumption	Split-core current transformer	30mA to 28A	10bit	14, 1Hz	75.5[*]
Heart rate	Beats per minute	WearLink Polar chest strap/receiver	30-240 bmp	1	2.5 @1-255bmp 9Vbattery	95.5[*]
Ultraviolet exposure	Onbody UV exposure	UV Photodiode Eryf by Sglux	0-28UV	0.027	2.58, 1Hz	93.5[*]
Location beacons	Rough location with respect to a receiver node	Tx beacon and Rx node counting packets received	2.5, 3.8, 4.8, and 9.4m outdoors 0.7, 3, 4.5, and 6m indoors	-	5, 12Hz	48.5[*]
Proximity	Proximity to area (binary output)	PIR motion KC7783R	Circle with 0-2.6m varying radius (by replacing lid)	1	47.5, 2Hz 9Vbattery	33.1[*]
RFID wrist-band	Acc + RFID tagged objects	ADXL202/10 M1 Mini SkyTek	10cm	-	0.2, 5Hz 4.7 Li-Po.	181[*]

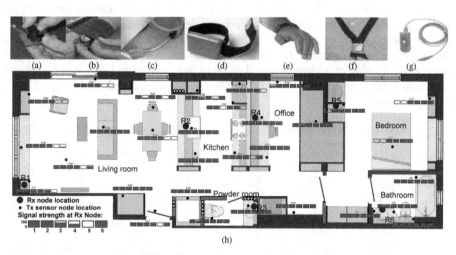

Fig. 2. Images of MITes (left to right): (a,b)mobile, (c)current sensing, (d) UV, (e) RFID, (f) location, (g) USB receiver, and (h) PlaceLab Tx/Rx range at 31 test points

Finally, MITes can be extended to cover areas larger than an individual receiver node's Tx/Rx range by simply adding more receivers. Each receiver must be attached to a PC or small microcomputer (such as the Maxim-Dallas TINI board) that broadcasts the data through a UDP connection to a central computer. The central computer timestamps, stores, and processes the data. Delays introduced by the UDP network communication can be compensated for by time stamping the data at each receiver node and synchronizing the computers. This architecture has been implemented in a live-in laboratory that uses six receivers.

6 Evaluation

As each MITes type is used in ongoing work (see Section 10), researchers are validating their performance in use in natural environments. Here we focus on evaluation of data transmission that applies to *all* the MITes types and demonstrates that the protocols described in Section 4 provide good performance in a real home for both low and high sampling nodes when multiple node types are used simultaneously.

6.1 Wireless Link

The transmission reception line of sight (LOS) range was first measured experimentally outdoors in an open athletic field free of obstructions. The Tx/Rx range was measured by broadcasting 180 [8B] packets per second on channel 0 (2.4GHz), counting the number of intact received packets per second (PPS) at the receiver node (2B CRC error checking), and computing the mean over a 100s window. The plot shown in Figure 3a was generated by changing the distance between the Tx and Rx nodes in increments of 7.6m while keeping the antennas parallel to each other. The plot in Figure 3b was generated by additionally rotating the transmitter antenna randomly by hand trying to cover as many antenna orientations as possible; this plot shows the antenna directionality or robustness to changes in antenna disposition in applications such as wearable computing. The final range was computed as the distance at which the average number of packets received drops to 90%. The experiment was performed on a sunny day with 56% RH, 8.9°C, 0dB Tx output power, and nodes placed 1.2m from the ground.

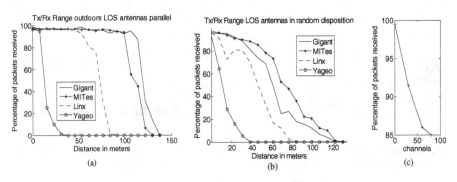

Fig. 3. (a) LOS range outdoors with antennas parallel. (b) LOS range with the Tx antenna in a random disposition. (c) %Packets received(y) vs. Tx/Rx channel(x) 0-81.

Table 4 shows the resulting Tx/Rx ranges for multiple commercially available antennas. Given the size of the microstrip antenna, this compares well with other bulkier or more expensive options.

Table 4. Tx/Rx LOS range outdoors with different antennas on the same MITes

	MITes microstrip ($0.01)	Linx Chip($1.5) ANT2.45CHP	Yageo chip ($3)	Monopole Gigant ($35)
Parallel orient.	106.6 m	60.96 m	15.24 m	114.3 m
Random disp.	38.1 m	15.24 m	7.62 m	30.48 m

A more useful test for many pervasive computing applications than an open field LOS test is a test in a typical home environment. We therefore tested the wireless signal indoors in an instrumented residential home (PlaceLab).[3] The Tx/Rx range was again measured by broadcasting 180 PPS, counting the number of received PPS at the receiver node, and computing the mean over a 100s window. We first measured the percentage of packets received at each of the six receivers roughly located in every room while installing a Tx sensor node at 31 *worse case* locations throughout the apartment. Figure 2h shows the location of the receivers as blue dots and the location of the test points as black dots. The Tx sensor node was installed with random antenna orientation, and varying heights from the floor while all room doors were shut and one person was present in the apartment. Some of these locations consisted of installing the Tx node inside closed drawers and cabinets (places where object motion sensors might be placed). We found that the average percentage of packets received at each receiver R1...R6 was 88.6, 88.4, 93.5, 98.4, 70.9, and 75% respectively. Figure 2h shows the packet reception probability at each receiver with respect to each of the 31 test points as bars. The tests show that it is possible to receive 98.4% of the packets correctly using only one receiver node located at the center of the apartment. In this setting, we can further increase the reception probability at every receiver to 100% by retransmitting each packet two times (see plot 1a). This result strongly suggests that MITes are suitable for simple data collection in natural settings. It is important to note that the range described in the previous experiment results when using a high 16-bit error correction to assure the quality of the packets received.

6.2 MITes Environmental Noise, Number of Wireless Broadcasts, and Installation Time

In order to characterize the MITes performance in the presence of environmental noise, we measured the maximum increment in the percentage of packets dropped while the WLAN was on at the PlaceLab (as a worse case of environmental noise) and when the following devices were also turned on: (a) a vacuum cleaner 3.7% (drop), (b), the microwave 4.3% (drop), and (c) a cordless telephone at 2.4GHz 1.2% (drop). The drop just by turning on the WLAN is 0.006%. To maximize the wireless Tx/Rx performance, we also found the channel with best Tx/Rx reception performance experimentally by measuring the percentage of packets dropped at each channel. The plot is shown in Figure 3c, and the channel with best performance is

---

[3] This is a 16.5x5.2m condominium in a modern building. Interior walls use steel frame construction with drywall. The environment has several kilometers of digital and electrical wiring embedded in the walls, which may provide far more wireless interference than in a typical stand-alone, single family home.

channel 0. This channel was chosen as the shared channel for the low SR sensor nodes in our system.

To provide a more intuitive characterization of the battery life of MITes, we measured the total number of wireless broadcasts supported using a CR2032 coin cell battery. This was measured by programming three MITes sensor nodes to transmit packets continuously until they ran out of battery. The average number of total broadcasts is 20.85 million. Finally, we measured the average installation time per sensor experimentally by asking two subjects to install sensors in their own homes by themselves. Subject one installed 75 sensors in 45min and second subject installed 100 sensors in approximately one hour. These gives an average installation time per sensor of 36 seconds in both experiments.

7   MITes Deployment and Summary of Contributions

Because MITes meet our usability criteria in Table 1, we have been able to deploy them in a variety of research projects both by the authors and others. Of particular interest to medical researchers is that they allow the simultaneous measurement of two or more states. For example, medical researchers are using MITes to study the relationship between physical activity and other states, such as heart rate and use of objects in the home (e.g. television). The mobile MITes are being validated by researchers at Stanford Medical School who are reporting excellent performance relative to the state of the art actigraphs used in that field, and they have been used in projects on detecting convenient times to interrupt, the correction of human balance, feedback systems for rehabilitation, as well as context-awareness and activity recognition. They are being used in two external medical projects where the sensors are worn for days or weeks at a time so medical researchers can study the behavior of people in naturalistic settings, and in both cases the mobile MITes are being used in combination with other node types such as heart rate, current flow, and light. The UV MITes were developed for cancer researchers interested in the relationship between sun exposure and physical activity. The proximity MITes are being installed in an office to study behavior in office spaces and to develop real-time recognition of meeting, visiting, and chatting events and create new architecture design tools. Finally, 125 object usage MITes have been used in four different research studies in the PlaceLab.

In summary, we have designed a sensor kit that is affordable and robust and optimized for longitudinal, non-laboratory deployments. This kit can be used by researchers who want to deploy large numbers of sensors simultaneously in settings such as homes.

A website with MITes hardware and software specifications provides more detail [32]. Researchers interested in using MITes in their own work should contact the authors. In practice, the greatest barrier to using MITes is ordering the MITes hardware, attaching the specialized sensors, and programming the EEPROM, since the devices are not commercial products.

Acknowledgements

This work was supported, in part, by National Science Foundation ITR grant #0313065 and the MIT House_n Consortium.

References

[1] E. Munguia-Tapia, S. S. Intille, and K. Larson, "Activity Recognition in the Home Setting Using Simple and Ubiquitous Sensors," in *Proceedings of PERVASIVE 2004*, vol. LNCS 300, B. Heidelberg, Ed.: Springer-Verlag, 2004, pp. 158-175.

[2] D. Wilson, "Simultaneous Tracking & Activity Recognition (STAR) Using Many Anonymous, Binary Sensors," in *Proc. The 3rd International Conference on Pervasive Computing (Pervasive '05)*. Munich, Germany, 2005, pp. 62-83.

[3] M. Philipose, K. P. Fishkin, M. Perkowitz, D. J. Patterson, D. Hahnel, D. Fox, and H. Kautz, "Inferring Activities from Interactions with Objects," *IEEE Pervasive Computing Magazine*, vol. 3, 4, 2004.

[4] M. Perkowitz, M. Philipose, D. J. Patterson, and K. Fishkin, "Mining Models of Human Activities from the Web," in *Proceedings of The Thirteenth International World Wide Web Conference (WWW '04)*. New York, USA, 2004.

[5] L. Bao and S. S. Intille, "Activity Recognition from User-Annotated Acceleration Data," in *Proceedings of the Second International Conference in Pervasive Computing (PERVASIVE '04)*. Vienna, Austria, 2004, pp. 1-17.

[6] J. H. J. Mantyjarvi, and T. Seppanen., "Recognizing Human Motion with Multiple Acceleration Sensors.," *IEEE International Conference on Systems, Man, and Cybernetics.*, pp. 747-52, 2001.

[7] S.-W. Lee and K. Mase, "Activity and location recognition using wearable sensors," *IEEE Pervasive Computing*, vol. 1, 3, pp. 24-32, 2002.

[8] D. J. Cook, M. Youngblood, E. O. Heierman, K. Gopalratnam, S. Rao, A. Litvin, and F. Khawaja, "MavHome: An Agent-Based Smart Home," in *Proceedings of The First IEEE International Conference on Pervasive Computing and Communications (PerCom'03), PerCom*. Fort Worth,Texas, 2003, pp. 521-524.

[9] M. Mozer, "The Neural Network House: An Environment that Adapts to its Inhabitants," in *Proceedings of the AAAI Spring Symposium on Intelligent Environments*, *Technical Report SS-98-02*. Menlo Park, CA: AAAI Press, 1998, pp. 110-114.

[10] University of Rochester Center for Future Health. "The Smart Medical Home." [cited March 11 2005]. Available from http://www.futurehealth.rochester.edu/smart_home/.

[11] T. Barger, D. Brown, and M. Alwan, "Health Status Monitoring through Analysis of Behavioral Patterns.," in *Proceedings of The 8th National Congress of Italian Association for Artificial Intelligence: Workshop on Ambient Intelligence (AI*IA 2003)*. Polo didattico "L. Fibonacci", University of Pisa, 2003.

[12] M. Beigl, A. Krohn, T. Zimmer, and C. Decker, "Typical Sensors Needed in Ubiquitous and Pervasive Computing," in *Proceedings of the First International Workshop on Networked Sensing Systems (INSS '04)*. Tokyo, Japan, 2004, pp. 153-158.

[13] M. Philipose, K. Fishkin, D. Fox, H. Kautz, D. Patterson, and M. perkowitz, "Guide: Towards Understanding Daily Life via Auto-Identification and Statistical Analysis," in *Proc. The 2nd International Workshop on Ubiquitous Computing for Pervasive Healthcare Applications (Ubi-Health 03)*. Seattle, WA, 2003.

[14] Crossbow Technology Inc. "MICA2DOT Wireless Microsensor Mote." 2005 [cited October 3rd, 2005]. Available from http://www.xbow.com/Products/Product_pdf_files/Wireless_pdf/MICA2DOT_Datasheet.pdf.

[15] Crossbow Technology Inc. "MICAz Wireless Measurement System." 2005 [cited October 3rd, 2005]. Available from http://www.xbow.com/Products/Product_pdf_files/Wireless_pdf/MICAz_Datasheet.pdf.

[16] R. M. Kling, "Intel Mote: An Enhanced Sensor Network Node," in *Proceedings of The International Workshop on Advanced Sensors, Structural Health Monitoring and Smart Structures*. Keio University, Japan, 2003.

[17] Moteiv. "tmote Sky: Ultra Low Power IEEE 802.15.4 Compliant Wireless Sensor Module." 2005 [cited October 3rd, 2005]. Available from http://www.moteiv.com/products/docs/tmote-sky-datasheet.pdf.

[18] M. Beigl, C. Decker, A. Krohn, T. Riedel, and T. Zimmer, "uParts: Low Cost Sensor Networks at Scale," in *Proceedings of The Sevent International Conference on Ubiquitous Computing (UBICOMP '05)*. Tokyo, Japan, 2005.

[19] M. Beigl and H. Gellersen, "Smart-Its: An Embedded Platform for Smart Objects," in *Smart Objects Converence (sOc '03)*. Grenoble, France, 2003, pp. 15-17.

[20] C. Park, J. Liu, and P. H.Chou, "Eco: an Ultra-Compact Low-Power Wireless Sensor Node for Real-Time Motion Monitoring.," in *Proceedings of The Fourth International Conference on Information Processing in Sensor Networks (IPSN '05)*. Sunset Village, UCLA, Los Angeles, CA, 2005, pp. 398--403.

[21] J. Beutel, O. Kasten, F. Mattern, K. Romer, F. Siegemund, and L. Thiele, "Prototyping Wireless Sensor Applications with BTnodes," in *Proceedings of The First European Workshop on Sensor Networks (EWSN '04)*. Zurich, Switzerland, 2004, pp. 323-338.

[22] M. Net. "MeshScape 2.4GHz Modules and Assemblies." 2005 [cited October 3rd, 2005]. Available from http://www.millennialnet.com/products/meshscape24.asp.

[23] Crossbow Technology Inc. "MSP-SYS MSP Mote Developer's System." 2005 [cited October 3rd, 2005]. Available from http://www.xbow.com/Products/Product_pdf_files/Wireless_pdf/MSP-Sys_Datasheet.pdf.

[24] R. DeVaul, M. Sung, J. Gips, and A. Pentland, "MIThril 2003: Applications and Architecture," in *Proceedings of the 7th International Symposium on Wearable Computers (ISWC '03)*. White Plains, NY, 2003.

[25] R. Kling, R. Adler, J. Huang, V. Hummel, and L. Nachman, "The Intel iMote: Using Bluetooth in Sensor Networks," in *Proceedings of The 2nd International Conference on Embedded Networked Sensor Systems*. Baltimore, MD, USA: ACM, 2003, pp. 318.

[26] MTI Actigraph. "GT1M Actigraph." 2005 [cited October 3rd, 2005]. Available from http://mtiactigraph.com/products.aspx.

[27] Electronic Educational Devices. "Watts Up? Pro KWH Meter Review." 2005 [cited October 3rd, 2005]. Available from https://www.doubleed.com/powertear.pdf.

[28] D. G. Fern and S. C. Tietsworth. "Automatic Wireless Communications." *Sensors Magazine*, vol. 16, 9 1999.

[29] M. Feldmeier and J. A. Paradiso, "Giveaway Wireless Sensors for Large-Group Interaction," in *Proceedings of the ACM Conference on Human Factors and Computing Systems (CHI '04)*. Vienna, Austria, 2004, pp. 1291-1292.

[30] J. A. Paradiso, "Wearable Wireless Sensing for Interactive Media," in *First International Workshop on Wearable and Implantable Body Sensor Networks*. Imperial College, London, 2004.

[31] M. J. Kochenderfer and R. Gupta, "Common Sense Data Acquisition for Indoor Mobile Robots," in *Proceedings of the Nineteenth National Conference on Artificial Intelligence (AAAI-04)*. San Jose, California, 2004.

[32] E. Munguia-Tapia and S. S. Intille. "MITes: MIT Environmental Sensors Hardware and Software Specifications." 2006 [cited February 1st, 2006]. Available from http://architecture.mit.edu/ house_n/MITes.

The Smart Tachograph – Individual Accounting of Traffic Costs and Its Implications

Vlad Coroama

ETH Zurich, Institute for Pervasive Computing,
8092 Zurich, Switzerland
coroama@inf.ethz.ch

Abstract. Today, several costs caused by road traffic may either be only roughly approximated, or cannot be clearly assigned to the drivers causing them, or both. They are typically distributed evenly among a large fraction of drivers, which is both unfair and economically inefficient. We have built a prototypical platform, called the "Smart Tachograph", that allows us to measure traffic-related costs on an individual basis, thus supporting a more fine-granular charging of the responsible parties. Sensors observe the manner and circumstances in which a vehicle is driven, while several accounting authorities can evaluate this information and charge motorists on a pay-per-use basis. The Smart Tachograph offers valuable insights for the deployment of future ubiquitous computing services in general: its implementation has obvious requirements in terms of security and privacy; its deployment model is realistic through the strong economic incentives it offers; and its usage directly affects core societal values such as fairness and trust. This paper summarizes our design considerations and discusses the feasibility and wider economic and societal implications of fielding such a system.

1 Introduction

The *Smart Tachograph* is a system that allows an individual, fine-granular analysis and accounting of traffic costs. Nowadays, many of the traffic-related costs are not accounted to their originators, but rather spread across a larger group, mainly due to the impossibility of exact measurements. Ecology-oriented vehicle taxes, for example, typically depend on the vehicle's type, more polluting vehicles having to pay a higher tax. Such taxes fall short of fulfilling their ecological aim, however, since they do not take into account the annual mileage of the vehicle, nor the conditions in which the car is being driven, like ozone levels.

Likewise, today's car insurance schemes typically divide drivers into about two dozen different risk categories, using only a few criteria such as the driver's age, gender, driving experience, place of residence, or car model. While all these parameters are being determined before the insurance goes into effect, the actual behavior of the driver after signing the policy (e.g., a safe driving style) will reflect only slowly on his or her insurance rate, typically over many years. Young people will pay high insurance fees only because, on average, young drivers tend to drive more aggressive and accident-prone. The individual young motorist often has no means of proving himself or herself to be a safe driver, other than several years of accident-free driving.

K.P. Fishkin et al. (Eds.): PERVASIVE 2006, LNCS 3968, pp. 135–152, 2006.

Through the use of ubiquitous computing technology, however, much of the data that has been previously unavailable might now easily be measured. According to the place, time, and manner someone is driving, the economical and ecological costs, as well as the risk of being involved in a traffic accident can be estimated with a high degree of accuracy. The Smart Tachograph is a prototypical system designed to allow a determination of these momentarily costs and risks and subsequently bill drivers in a pay-per-use/pay-per-risk manner. Its aim is to offer valuable insights for the development of future ubiquitous computing services in general by providing a realistic model for analyzing the technical, economical, and societal challenges such applications will pose.

The remainder of the paper is organized as follows: Section 2 presents in larger detail the problems that arise due to the impossibility to measure many traffic costs. Section 3 gives a detailed view of the system. Section 4 presents related work. Section 5 addresses several issues raised by the deployment of a system such as the Smart Tachograph: its economic feasibility and practicability, its privacy implications, its broader societal implications, as well as the influence of system design decisions on these dimensions.

2   Motivation

2.1   Information Asymmetry in Insurance Markets

Various authors argue that the nowadays practiced classification of automobilists into a few classes – typically based on their driving experience, accident history and type of driven car – is not optimal. According to [10], within such a class (of presumably similarly skilled drivers), there is still a large spread of risks, depending on such factors as: the annually driven mileage; the time of day and the season predominantly driven at; weather conditions; the type of route (a certain distance in a crowded city being more accident-prone than the same distance on a highway) or the neighborhood where the car is usually parked. Litman [9] also argues that today's rigid insurance premiums are both economically and ecologically obsolete: "What would be the consequences if gasoline were sold like vehicle insurance? With gasoline sold by the car-year, vehicle owners would make one annual advance payment which allows them to draw gasoline unrestricted at a company's fuel stations. Prices would be based on the average cost of supplying gasoline to similar motorists. Unmetered fuel would cause a spiral of increased fuel consumption, mileage, and overall vehicle costs, including externalities such as accident risk, congestion and pollution." Instead, the insurance should be related to the mileage driven because, all other parameters equal, there is a strong correlation between driven distance and accident risk [9]. Connecting the insurance rate to the annual mileage would be fairer and economically more sensible. Moreover, since a larger fraction of vehicle costs would depend on the driven distance, it would also have a positive environmental side-effect. Oberholzer goes further and builds up a detailed matrix of how much the insurance kilometer should cost depending on two factors: type of road (highway vs country road vs city) and the hour of driving [10].

All these distinctions not being done today, two phenomenons occur. First, inside one of the risk classes of presumably equally-skilled drivers, the ones with a higher annual accident risk (due for example to a higher annual mileage) are being cross-financed by lower risk motorists. Second, as mentioned above, all the parameters determining the insurance rate are measured before the insurance goes into effect. A safe driving style or other safe behavior (like parking only in secure areas) will not be reflected immediately on the insurance rate, but rather slowly. Neither will a low-mileage driver be rewarded with an insurance bonus. The other way around, exhibiting dangerous driving behavior will not influence the insurance rate in any way except when the driver gets involved in an accident. The aggressive driver lacks a direct feedback on how his or her driving style increases the risk of being involved in a traffic accident.

Both these problems are well-known in insurance markets. The cross-financing from low to high risks is called *adverse selection*, while *moral hazard* denotes the tendency to handle an insured good more carelessly after it has been insured. They both ultimately root in the same phenomenon of *information asymmetry*, first described in an influential article by George Akerlof [1]. Information asymmetry denotes the state in which one market side has more information than the other side. In the context of insurances, it describes the insurers' lack of information about the actual behavior of their customers and thus the exact dimension of the risks they insure. Because of this lack of information, the insurer can not reward customers that have a low-risk behavior. Instead, he has to insure an average risk through a larger customer group. This is not only unfair towards the ones having less risk, it is also economically inefficient, since it hinders a market for "high-valued goods" (low risk drivers) to emerge [1].

2.2 Road Pricing

Road Pricing is a tool for regulating the traffic flow through selectively penalizing the driving on specific roads at particular times or under specific conditions. Deploying a road pricing scheme may have several political or societal aims. For overcrowded city centers, it may be deployed for replacing the regulation of traffic through queuing (the "communist" solution) by a free-market mechanism. It may also be used to steer the traffic away from some streets to others (by penalizing the former more) or to other means of transport. Road pricing may further pursue environmental aims, like reducing emissions or noise levels. Finally, it may simply be used to raise money for the maintenance of the road infrastructure. However, as [6] argues, whatever the main reason – financing, improving the environment, or managing traffic and improving accessibility – a road pricing system will have all these effects to a certain extent.

Road pricing has become increasingly popular over the last years, since the two traditional tools for charging drivers, fuel and vehicle tax, are rather coarse and cannot fulfill all of the above mentioned aims. The annual vehicle tax penalizes people for owning dirty cars, but this says nothing about the actual pollution caused by those cars. Since the car's overall pollution is the product of its emissions per distance unit and the car's usage, this flat tax fails short of fulfilling its environmental aim. Fuel tax is better at penalizing people for the consumption of gasoline, but does not look at the other side – how dirty the emissions resulted from that consumption really are or under which circumstances the gasoline has been burned (e.g., ozone levels). Moreover, neither tax can have a traffic management effect [14].

Hence, many places worldwide have started to deploy road pricing systems as a complementary tool to the existing taxes. There is a wide spread in the level of detail that existing road pricing systems take into account. At one end are rather coarse systems, such as the London Congestion Charge. There, motorists are charged once every 24 hours for the permission to drive in the city center [6], regardless of the actual usage during these 24 hours. Even so, the introduction of the Congestion Charge has reduced traffic by 15% and increased speed by 22% in central London [14]. At the other extreme, having a much more detailed usage model, stands the ERPS (Electronic Road Pricing Scheme) from Singapore. There are different taxes for the usage of distinct roads, and they also vary with the hour of driving. Furthermore, every three months, the whole price structure is analyzed and readjusted [6].

Many other cities play with the idea of road pricing systems: Viennese officials think of a city-wide street usage charge of 2 to 8 Euro-Cents per kilometer [12]. A large study has been carried out by the Swiss Center for Technology Assessment to investigate the public's acceptance of a generalized road pricing scheme, envisioned by parts of the government [11]. Britain also thinks of a nationwide, satellite-based road pricing system, no earlier than 2014 though [13].

3   The System

To analyze the implementation requirements and the subsequent economic and societal consequences of such traffic-related cost allocation issues, we have proposed the Smart Tachograph generic platform [4]. The Smart Tachograph uses off-the-shelf ubiquitous computing technologies and a newly developed prototypical software infrastructure to allow for measurement of driving parameters, the transformation of those parameters into costs, and billing these costs to their originators (Fig. 1). The software infrastructure of the prototype runs on a laptop computer that can be placed anywhere in the car. Any number of sensors can be attached to the system. They are depicted above the car in Figure 1. The sensors gather data about the way and the circumstances in which the vehicle is being driven and send this information to the computer. Several accounting authorities (connected from below in the figure) may evaluate this information and charge motorists on a pay-per-use basis. The software platform serves not only as a sink for sensor data and as back-end connection for the accounting entities, but also (not shown in Figure 1) as a front-end interface to the vehicle's driver.

3.1   Sensors

A small plastic box (Fig. 2) has been fitted for our prototype with a collection of sensors. It contains a GPS unit and a sensor board carrying two accelerometers (for longitudinal and cross acceleration), a temperature sensor, and a light sensor. Raw GPS coordinates are not the only information that can be obtained from the GPS unit. The current time is also encoded in the satellite signal and the current speed can be inferred as distance traveled over time. The data gathered by all these sensors is sent via

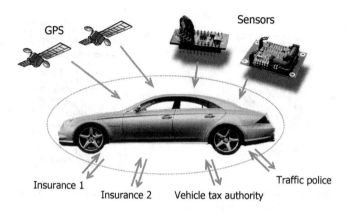

Fig. 1. Top-level view of the Smart Tachograph with the main involved instances

Bluetooth to the computer running the Smart Tachograph software infrastructure. We used a Bluetooth-enabled GPS sensor, while the sensor board sends its data through a BTnode. The BTnode[1] is a small computing device for sensor network applications equipped with Bluetooth communication capabilities.

"Installing" the system is pretty straightforward. The box has to be placed in a spot where the GPS sensor can easily receive the satellite signals, for example underneath the car's windshield. The only other point to be ensured is that the sensor box is placed on an even surface and that it faces in the correct direction. Both conditions are needed for a correct functioning of the accelerometers. The controlling computer can be placed anywhere in the car, since it wirelessly communicates with the sensors.

We have chosen to deploy the mentioned type of sensors for two reasons. First, they all measure data that is potentially relevant to one of the envisioned accounting authorities. Having the raw GPS coordinates, the system can always determine on which street the vehicle is on and the speed limit for that street, using a commercial geospatial database installed on the computer. This information is obviously relevant for a road pricing scheme. But it could also influence the current accident risk, for example if the driven speed significantly exceeds the speed limit. Excessive longitudinal acceleration and especially excessive cross acceleration seem to be equally important indicators for a high accident risk. Finally, the light intensity sensor gives information about light conditions, which could also influence the accident risk. The second reason to include these sensors in the Smart Tachograph prototype was that all of them are already available in a typical medium to high end state-of-the-art car. They have been placed there for other reasons, but could be reused in a real deployment for a system such as the Smart Tachograph. A modern car is equipped with acceleration sensors for the electronic stability programs, with a temperature sensor for signaling the driver a possible slippery road, and with light sensors for automatic headlight activation. Most cars today also come with a GPS system and navigation maps.

Apart from the sensors used in our example, many modern cars come with a variety of other sensors that could be used to determine the insurance rate or road pricing tax

---

[1] See www.btnode.ethz.ch.

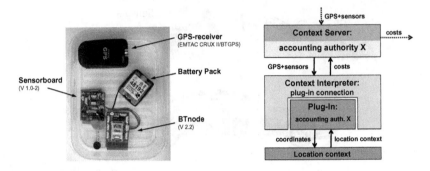

Fig. 2. The plastic box containing the Smart Tachograph's sensors (left) and the plug-in-architecture for the accounting authorities (right)

even more accurately. A distance sensor used in many cars as parking aid could be reused to measure the distance to the car in front. This information, correlated with the type of street and driven speed, is a major determinant for the current risks taken while driving (see section 5.4). If the car is connected to the Internet (e.g., via UMTS), it could also download environmental data that possibly determine its road pricing tax, like ozone levels or the concentration of carbon dioxide in a specific city.

Why haven't we used the car's sensors if they are already there and probably more precise than ours? The practical reason was that we did not have access to the vehicle data bus, since the work has been academic research so far. The aim of the work lies not in the highest possible sensor precision, or in the most realistic approximation, but in creating a proof of concept for a generic traffic accounting platform and to analyze the various implications of deploying such a system. The fact that similar sensors already exist in vehicles only underlines the feasibility of the presented concept.

3.2   Software Infrastructure

The main role of the software infrastructure is to query data from the sensors, and to mediate communication with the accounting places. Due to the flexible software design, adding accounting entities is as easy a task as adding new sensors. At the time being, three different kind of accounting entities have been included in the system (see Figure 1): insurance companies, a vehicle tax authority, and the police. The traffic police has been included in order to show how powerful the paradigm of a smart tachograph is and what far-reaching social consequences it could have. These consequences are discussed in Section 5.

To connect with the accounting authorities, the Smart Tachograph uses a plug-in-architecture as depicted in Figure 2. The system is built on top of Anind Dey's Context Toolkit [5], with every accounting authority represented by a Context Toolkit *server*. This server is registered through the Context Toolkit's publish/subscribe mechanism to receive all events from the GPS unit and the other sensors. The server sends this information to a Context Toolkit *interpreter* that generates the corresponding costs according to the rules defined by a plug-in that has to be loaded when starting the system. The costs are then "consumed" by the accounting authorities, registered in the system as *context handlers*. The plug-ins define how the telemetry data are transformed into costs: they infer the road fee or calculate the accident risk and transform this risk to an insurance rate, for example. To be able to transform the raw GPS coordinates into meaningful location context, the plug-ins also have direct access to the commercial geospatial database installed on the computer. Every predefined period of time (a week or a month would probably be meaningful), the interpreter returns an aggregated sum to the context server, which in turn sends this sum to the accounting authority (over the vehicle's UMTS connectivity or the home WiFi network that can be received from the garage, for example). The fact that the accounting authority does only receive the accumulated sum but not the raw sensor data will be relevant for the privacy and security discussion in section 5.2.

By using the Context Toolkit, adding new sensors or new accounting instances become easy tasks. To add a new sensor, a new *widget* has to be written that encapsulates the proprietary communication with that sensor. Similarly, a new accounting authority is being added by registering it as new *handler*.

From a functional perspective, the Smart Tachograph knows three kind of predefined accounting entities: `compulsory`, `required-select`, and `optional`. In a system configuration file, three corresponding lists have to be filled out. In a realistic setting, these could be for example:

```
compulsory: vehicle-tax-authority; traffic-police
required-select: liability-insurance
optional: own-damage-claim
```

Every item in the "compulsory" list has to be active before the system can be started. An accounting entity is active when its server has been registered in the system as a subscriber for sensor values, and the plug-in has been downloaded from the corresponding authority server. Likewise, for every item in the "required-select" list, one plug-in has to be present. The difference is that the user may choose here between different plug-ins (e.g., from different insurance companies), while for compulsory plug-ins there is no choice. Any number of "optional" plug-ins can be loaded before starting the system, but none is required. In the prototype presented here, the Smart Tachograph software does not start until all mandatory servers have been started. In a real deployment, it is conceivable that the system would be connected to the electronic anti-theft device, so that the car would not start until all the legally required plug-ins are active. Also, in a real deployment, the tasks accomplished for the prototype by the laptop computer would probably be taken over a by a computing on-board-unit.

3.3 Driver Interface

The Smart Tachograph's software further includes a front-end interface to the driver (Fig. 3). The main system window, in the lower right corner, is needed to setup and start the prototype system. Several parameters can be set here. Among them, the driver may choose for all required but selectable items a specific instance. For example, he or she may choose a liability insurance from the existing offers. The driver may further choose any number of optional insurances. To have an up-to-date view of the existing offers, when the user starts the system (read: "enters the car" for a real deployment),

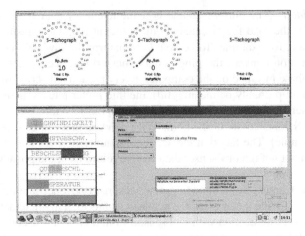

Fig. 3. A typical screenshot of the system's interface

the Smart Tachograph accomplishes the following two steps. First, it connects via the car's wide area communication system to a root-server, retrieving a list of available vehicle insurance companies. Then it connects to the server of each insurance company to retrieve the available insurance schemes. After choosing everything needed, the user starts the Smart Tachograph by clicking the "start" button.

The second window (in the lower left corner) presents the sensor data as a collection of bars. The raw GPS coordinates are translated into the actual street that's been driven on using the geospatial database. Knowing the speed limit for all streets in the administrative region of Zurich, the system displays this information on the second bar from top. It uses this information, together with the actual speed (displayed on the topmost bar), for risk approximation. The lower bars show the data from the other sensors – longitudinal and cross acceleration, temperature, and light intensity. The data from all these sensors, as well as the GPS coordinates, are ascertained and transferred to the computer once every second.

The third type of interface windows (upper part of Figure 3) would probably be the only ones shown in a real deployment while driving. They show the current costs (insurance rate, road tax), which are continuously calculated from the received sensor data. The indicators presenting these aggregations should be perceived by the driver similar to the momentary gas consumption indication built into some cars. It allows the driver to receive instant feedback on how his or her driving habits influence the traffic costs. Traffic fines (window in the upper right corner) can also be issued automatically. They are not expressed as money per kilometer, but as one-time events (i.e., when the speed limit has been exceeded for more than ten seconds in a row).

4   Related Work

Within the ubiquitous and pervasive computing community, there has been little research regarding road pricing or pay-per-risk insurances. There have been, of course, numerous location-awareness projects in the broader domain of traffic, most prominent CoolTown's WebBus [8], but none that we are aware of regarding specifically road pricing or dynamic insurances. Our work has largely benefitted from context awareness research. The Smart Tachograph platform is built on top of Dey's Context Toolkit [5]. Some economists and business analysts [7, 10], aware of the potential of ubiquitous computing technology, have examined the impact of ubiquitous and pervasive computing on insurance markets from an analytical point of view, specifically highlighting the vehicle insurance market. Other related work can be found in publications on road pricing or vehicle insurances.

A good overview on road pricing systems in use today can be found in [6]: the London Congestion Charge, Singapore's ERPS, the systems in Oslo and Trondheim, and California's expressway SR91. All systems but the one in Singapore have a very coarse area model. They either penalize the usage of one road only (the California expressway), or the entrance to a specific area, typically the city center (London, Trondheim, Oslo). In all these examples, the fee is flat for a multi-hour usage permit, typically for 24 hours. Obviously, this only allows a coarse traffic management, keeping some traffic out of the surcharge area, but having much of that traffic redistributed on the borders of the restricted area. Moreover, such a flat system does not acquire a high degree of fairness, since everybody pays the same independent of the actual usage. In Singapore, the model is more complex, every usage being charged and the fees varying from street to street and with the hour of driving. The more jam-prone the street and the less fluent the traffic rolls, the higher the tax gets. Singapore's road pricing has a very fine-granular model, however, it can not include other parameters, such as ozone or carbon dioxide levels. Another drawback of all these systems, as compared to the Smart Tachograph architecture, is that they rely on a heavy infrastructure of active RFID tags, ubiquitous gates with powerful antennas to read those tags, numerous cameras to identify the cheaters, and partially also payment machines and manned stations.

Early discussions in the field of pay-per-risk insurances revolved around considering driven mileage only. [9] made the case for including the driven mileage into the calculation of the insurance rate, also pointing out the positive environmental and traffic safety side-effects, but ignored other criteria. Progressive, a US-insurer, initiated a pilot project (called Autograph) between 1998 and 2000. It took into account the driven distance, and in addition the time of day and the geographic location.[2] More recently, Norwich Union, a UK-based insurer, offers a black box for what they call "pay-as-you-drive" insurance,[3] but disclose only that they take into account the hours of driving, not whether their black box also considers other attributes. Privacy does not seem to be a central issue: "The black box device measures vehicle usage and sends data directly to Norwich Union using similar technology to that used by mobile phones." Progressive also started last year to offer a more sophisticated insurance product, called TripSense.[4] TripSense is based on a black box that has to be installed in the car as well, but their webpage is more detailed about what it will record: "[...] which measures your actual driving habits and allows you to earn discounts on your insurance by showing us how

---

[2] See www.epa.gov/projectxl/progressive/index.htm.

[3] See www.norwichunion.com/pay-as-you-drive/.

[4] See https://tripsense.progressive.com/home.aspx.

much, how fast and what times of day you drive." The driver may analyze the data recorded over several months at his or her PC at home (and see, for example, the per-day number of "aggressive brakes" and of times driving over 75mph) and decide for himself or herself on sending the data to the insurance company or not. If the data is not sent, a no-punishment policy is advertised. This seems to be a more privacy- and customer-friendly approach than Norwich Union's, although in order to gain the price advantage, the customer has to send all data and thus give up privacy here, too. The more important point, however, is that the responsibility lies with the customer. He or she has to decide on sending the data to the insurer, without possibly realizing what the longer-term consequences of such action will be. What will happen at the next contract renewal if the driver has not sent any data to the insurer in the previous period of time? What if the data was sent and points to a risky driving style? Who else will gain access to the data and will "my" data ever be used against me? Progressive states that: "We may retain the information that you send to us indefinitely" and further that "If you are in an accident, you may have a legal obligation to preserve the information on the TripSensor. This information may be sought by opposing parties in a civil lawsuit or by police when investigating the cause of an accident. We may be legally obligated to provide such information in response to a subpoena or as otherwise required by law."

To sum up, neither of the above-mentioned systems have been built with customer privacy at its core. All presented road pricing infrastructures record the places where the vehicle has been (or at least where it entered and exited the fee area) through transponders, while the existing insurance models continuously gather data about the driver's habits and whereabouts and send them to the insurance company. With the Smart Tachograph, we try to provide evidence that highly personalized insurance rates are also feasible without such a massive loss of privacy and control.

Also, we know of no approaches so far that tried to develop an open platform that could be used to calculate and charge a great variety of traffic-related costs. Proprietary black boxes have been the standard solution so far for pay-per-risk insurance prototypes; transponders and a heavy gate infrastructure have been the standard for road pricing schemes; but the two concepts have not been combined before. Summarizing, we believe that the power of our approach lies in its simpleness, flexibility, and open character. Such power, however, can also be misused, as the next section will discuss.

5   Evaluation and Discussion

A technical evaluation of the Smart Tachograph platform would encompass answering questions such as how well the system estimates traffic costs, how robust these estimations are with respect to different driving styles, vehicle types, and environmental conditions, or if the chosen algorithms for calculating risks and costs (that will be presented later in this section) are appropriate and how they could be improved. We have not conducted thorough research in any of these directions. Many issues would require a close collaboration with representatives from the insurance sector or traffic policy makers. We hope to be able to further investigate these directions in the future. The main scope of the system so far has been to build a reasonably realistic prototype in a relevant setting and then to vertically analyze privacy-related, societal, and economical implications of the individual design decisions and of fielding such a system. These conclusions will be presented throughout this section.

5.1 Deployment Experiences

During the development of our prototype, we have been out on the streets for several weeks, testing and tuning the system, gaining experiences about difficult driving situations that challenge the system, and partially solving those problems. We have also been an entire day on a closed circuit, where a professional driver tested the Smart Tachograph under different conditions – from "normal" driving to a driving style that would qualify as very aggressive and highly risky for an average driver.

Any developer of vehicle navigation systems will probably have their own tale of solving the inherent imprecision of GPS measurements in urban areas, which was one of our first practical challenges. As probably many others before, we use a circle around the reported position to search for streets, and a sliding window to minimize the erroneous reporting of another street that is in the vicinity for a short period of time (e.g., at crossroads or when driving on a highway under a bridge). After ascertaining the street the vehicle is being driven on, the next point is to determine the speed limit for that street. This should be trivial in theory – a lookup in the geospatial database that contains, among other attributes, the speed limits for individual streets. In practice, however, this data is not easily available. After extensive research, we found only two providers of street topology data worldwide – Navteq and TeleAtlas.[5] All providers of GPS-based car navigation platforms seem to buy the raw geographical data from one of these two producers. Navteq has no speed limits recorded for Switzerland and the ones from TeleAtlas database were often incorrect. Although this is in part a rather pragmatic problem, that presumably occurs only for some geographical regions, there is also a conceptual issue behind it. Speed limits on individual streets change with quite a rapid pace, so that a CD containing them will be partly outdated from the first day of usage. Speed limits may change due to changes in the street architecture (e.g., a street enlargement may come with an increase in the speed limit), or traffic-policy reasons, but also because of short-termed construction sites. To have an outdated database in a system that could in consequence charge a sum one or two orders of magnitude larger than the true one, is obviously unacceptable. A prerequisite for such a system to work is thus to have an efficient way of propagating speed limit changes to vehicles. Many solutions are conceivable, but they all require quite a massive infrastructural support, which is unavailable today. A centralistic solution could be for example to have a publicly-accessible database where all changes are published. Vehicles would lookup that database on a regular basis, updating their local copy. A distributed way would be to have electronic tags on all speed limiting signs, which could be read by the vehicles.

We also had positive experiences with the used technology. The measurements from the cheap, off-the-shelf acceleration sensors were always exact and we did not experience any failures. Having both the BTnode and the Bluetooth-enabled GPS-sensor

---

[5] See www.navteq.com, and www.teletlas.com, respectively.

wirelessly transmitting data to the laptop computer has also proven to be robust – the communication never failed.

5.2 Privacy and Security Considerations

The architecture of a system that continuously analyzes the driving parameters to ascertain momentary costs on a pay-per-use basis can be realized in three different ways. The first, chosen by some insurance companies and which is also the standard for road pricing schemes (see related work in Section 4), is to send all sensed data to the accounting entity, be it tax authority or insurance company. The data could be sent online (via the car's wide area communication system) or offline, on a regular basis. This solution is the most simple yet most privacy invasive.

A second possible implementation – at least for the insurance part – would be not to disclose the data by default, but store it and reveal it in order to get a retroactive reduction for a safe driving style. The data could be stored either locally in the car's blackbox, or it could be encrypted with the motorist's private key and transferred to the insurance company. To qualify for the reduction, the customer has to reveal the data to the insurer. This is the model chosen by Progressive for its TripSense product. Aside from being a different insurance model than the risk-dependent momentary insurance rate presented here, this solution has several drawbacks. As pointed out in section 4, in order to get the price advantage, the customer has to reveal all data and thus give up privacy in this model, too. Furthermore, the responsibility lies with the customer, and it is unclear what the long-term consequences of both revealing or not revealing the data would be. Finally, it is unclear how this approach could work for a road pricing scheme, being thus rather unsuited for a generic solution for all types of traffic costs.

In the third and chosen model, all data is processed locally and only the total rate is transferred to the accounting authority, as described in section 3.2. The data is processed by a plug-in that has been downloaded from the respective authority (technically a Java-class). Such a client-side personalization insurance scheme [3] guarantees a high-level of privacy, since the accounting authority receives only a monthly sum. Should it be high, there can still be a multitude of reasons – a large amount of safe driving, or a small amount of risky driving under bad weather conditions, to name just two. Past whereabouts and behavior of users are protected, yet they pay their fair share. Moreover, since the sensor data needs not to be cached (the continuously incremented overall sum will suffice), the driver retains full control over his or her data – at least in theory. In practice, however, the sensor data might be stored, e.g., for a possible later legal dispute on the charged amounts. In such a scenario, the data could be used in a lawsuit against the driver, after all.

In terms of mutual safety between insurer and customer, all models have to face several challenges. As more thoroughly analyzed in [3], one issue induced by our client-side personalization model is the driver tampering with the software module downloaded from the accounting authority. However, through the use of a trusted computing platform on the vehicle, this problem could be overcome. The trusted platform would verify the software signed by the accounting authority, deciding upon its authenticity. In all implementation versions, on the other hand, the user could try a man-in-the-middle attack, modifying the message transmitted by the black box to the accounting authority.

By having the black box signing the messages, such an attack can be prevented. By using timestamps in the messages, replay-attacks (i.e., replacing the message with an original but older message) can also be easily avoided. Finally, the vehicle owner could try to tamper with the vehicle sensors. For example, he could cap the acceleration sensors, or cover the rain sensor. This security issue is also common to all implementation models. However, this would not only potentially endanger the driver by disabling some important security functions such as the electronic stability programs, it can also be further avoided by including most of the sensors in a tamper-proof hardware environment (this would hardly work for a rain sensor, though).

The most obvious way an accounting authority could try to cheat would be to charge a different (i.e., higher) sum than the real one. This problem is common to all architectures as well, but in the client-side personalization paradigm the user has the most effective means to verify the claims coming from different accounting authorities. One way would be to run the same software on a client-trusted platform with the same sensorial input. Another possibility would be to have the black box issued by a third party trusted by both sides (e.g., a governmental agency). The black box would receive the billing contract (digitally signed by both parties), verify the signatures, extract the billing formula, and compute the sum in a secured environment.

Although we have not implemented in our first demonstrator any of these security features, it seems that the client-side personalization paradigm does not add crucial security-related issues when compared to a more privacy-invasive approach.

5.3   Economic Feasibility of Pay-Per-Risk Insurances

Among the first issues to suggest themselves when thinking of pay-per-risk insurances is the question of economical feasibility. Is there a market attractive enough for both sellers to offer such insurances and customers to buy them? The mere technological possibility does not imply economical feasibility. There are many examples of products and services that could easily be offered per-use, but due to economical reasons are charged on a flat basis. Ski resorts, for example, could charge skiers for every ride, yet all over the world ski passes are offered almost exclusively as per-day flat charges. Likewise, breakfasts in hotels could also be charged "per-use", yet more often than not they are "all you can eat" (a flat fee). Looking at insurances, the short answer would be that there is a market for pay-per-risk insurances, since at least two companies have started offering these (see section 4 on related work). A more detailed answer would be that it is in the insurer's best interest to identify the good risks, and offer them a more advantageous rate that reflects their actual risk. The insurer would thus be able to gain new market shares in the attractive market of low-risk drivers, while at the same time filtering out the "bad risks" (due to the then increased rate they would have to pay to stay with the insurer) [2, 10]. On customer side, there would probably also be enough interest for such a model. Lower risk customers, who nowadays partially subsidize the higher risk drivers, would presumably welcome a model that could bring them important savings.

Even if individual pay-per-risk insurance schemes still lie a few years in the future, there are some areas more likely than others to be early adopters of such technology on a large scale. All domains where people drive cars that do not belong to them, but are merely borrowed, rented, or co-owned, fall into this category. In such areas, the driver of the car has an explicit or implicit obligation to handle the confided vehicle with care. And the lending or owning part can more easily enforce a black box analyzing the way customers handle the assets. For example, a car rental company has started as early as 2001 to protect its vehicles from overspeeding by charging customers exceeding 70mph with a high fine.[6] Car sharing models, such as the popular Mobility-network in Switzerland,[7] have to pay relatively high insurance rates because of the few accident-prone risky drivers. Eventually (after two or three accidents in a short period of time) these drivers are sorted out, but the damage is done, and through the continuous flow of new members the insurance rates stay high. Car sharing networks would presumably be happy to detect such risky drivers before they cause accidents, by having their driving style analyzed from the very first ride. And the "How am I driving?" sign could soon disappear as well, if companies would start equipping their car fleets with black boxes analyzing (and reporting) the way their drivers behave. Furthermore, in such examples it seems less probable that drivers would try to tamper with the system since the vehicle returns periodically to its owner, who may detect the fraud.

5.4   Measuring the Risk

As a proof of concept of the Smart Tachograph paradigm, we designed two plug-ins, one for road pricing, the other one for a liability insurance. The road pricing plug-in is a simple one, it only differentiates between streets in the city and roads outside the city, and between high-peak and low-peak hours. It charges, depending on these two parameters, a fee between 2 and 8 cents per driven kilometer. Since we have access to comprehensive geospatial data, refining the plug-in to differentiate between individual streets and taking into account more fine-granular time slots would be a trivial (yet laborious) task.

The insurance plug-in is more complex. It takes into account five parameters: type of street, difference between driven speed and speed limit, the two acceleration types (longitudinal and cross acceleration), and the time of day. Converting sensor data into an accident probability and expressing this risk in a monetary way are obviously no trivial tasks. We made the following assumptions: There is a basic per-kilometer risk, that depends on the type of street and on the time of day, as suggested in [10]. The per-kilometer accident risk is lowest on highways, followed by country roads, and is highest in cities. It varies between 2 and 10 cents per kilometer. In a real deployment, this minimum would presumably also depend on the "classical" risk factors such as driver age or experience, which are used today to classify customers into driver categories.

With respect to acceleration, we acknowledge that some thresholds have to exist. At every traffic light stop, every departure, and every curve taken by the driver, there are accelerations involved. Such accelerations within normal limits pose no special danger and have to be allowed without punishment. According to our subjective danger sensation correlated to the measured accelerations, the thresholds for the prototypical plug-in have been set to $2m/s^2$ $(1/5g)$ for the cross accelerations as well as the positive longitudinal acceleration, and to $3.5m/s^2$ for negative longitudinal acceleration (braking).

---

[6] See http://archives.cnn.com/2001/TECH/ptech/06/22/gps.airiq/.

[7] See www.mobility.ch.

After that, we assume that the risk increases exponentially with a low base of 1.5. We further assume that exceeding the speed limit with 10% does not notably increase the risk, and only after that it increases exponentially as well, but with a lower base than in the case of acceleration. This base further depends on the street type, varying between 1.05 for highways and 1.2 within cities. The overall formula for the momentary insurance rate for the experimental system (expressed in cents per kilometer) thus results in

$$R = B_{st,t} * 1.5^{Max(0, \frac{A_c-2}{2})} * 1.5^{Max(0, \frac{Abs(A_{ln})-3.5}{3.5})} * VC_{st}^{Max(0, \frac{V_{driven}}{1.1*V_{limit}}-1)} \tag{1}$$

where R is the resulting momentary insurance rate, B the basic rate depending on street type and time, A_c the cross acceleration, A_{ln} the negative longitudinal acceleration (actually, this is a slightly simplified version of the formula, ignoring the positive acceleration), VC the base for the speeding coefficient, V_{driven} and V_{limit} the driven speed and the speed limit, respectively.

From subsequent discussions with representatives from the vehicle insurance industry, we learned that they have a pretty clear picture of when a driving style becomes dangerous. Vehicle insurance companies have a strong accident research tradition, where they analyzed such data for many years. Until now, they have not been able to transfer this know-how to insurance schemes due to the bulky equipment and high costs involved. It appears that some of our assumptions have been quite exact, while other were rather erroneous. The experts confirmed that a defensive driving style usually remains under $0.2g$ and that the cross acceleration becomes dangerous around $1g$. At $1g$ cross acceleration, our formula results in an insurance fee almost 8 times higher than the basic fee (and then continues to grow exponentially). Choosing an exponential function seems to have been the right decision, details aside. Our formula seems to have over-estimated the velocity component though. Overspeeding is one determinant for accidents, but this depends much more on the actual context than, for example, with accelerations. Often, speed limits are set very conservative or with respect to other criteria (such as noise reduction), thus overspeeding may often have no influence whatsoever on the risk of causing an accident. Another highly relevant parameter to be considered, according to the industry representatives, would be the distance to the car in front, especially when it is correlated to the driven speed.

5.5 Practicability

Requesting customers to sign a complex mathematic formula as the one presented in the previous section as part of an insurance contract seems to be unacceptable, no matter how much a realistic risk estimation it encompasses. Insurance companies know that a good contract (one easily accepted by customers) must comprise two features: simplicity and upper bounds. To keep complexity low, two or no more than three new attributes should be considered. Because of their outstanding importance, these could be cross acceleration and the distance to the car in front. To further reduce the complexity, discrete intervals are preferable over a continuous function. There could be for example three different classes of driving: safe, normal, and dangerous driving. After a journey, the motorist would get different per-kilometer prices for the times he or she exhibited any of these styles.

Not having upper bounds in the insurance tariff could lead in extreme circumstances (when an accident will most likely happen) to a chronic situation in which the insurance rate would get as high as the expected damage costs. This would, of course, undermine the idea of an insurance, making such a practice unacceptable. But even in less extreme situations, customers seem to feel much more at ease if they know what to expect in terms of maximum possible costs, no matter of their behavior.

A common misconception, on the other hand, is that such highly personalized insurance rates, that finally lead to "risk communities of one" (Andreas Schraft, Head Risk Engineer of SwissRe, a reinsurance company, in a recent talk) would undermine the idea of insurances and would thus not be a realistic concept. This often-heard interpretation originates in the (wrong) assumption that an insurance company has to insure the same risk for a large number of people in order to work. As a matter of fact, insurance companies insure unlikely, but high-cost events of individuals with a sum that represents the probability of that event's occurrence times the costs it will produce (plus the insurance's security margin and its profit). Since many individuals are insured with one company, some of these events will occur, most will not, and due to the law of large numbers the company will pay exactly the expected cumulated costs (if it estimated correctly the individual risks). While the company does need a large number of individuals for the system to work, it does not need to insure the same risk for everyone – highly personalized risks will do just fine.

5.6   Societal Issues

"Having everyone paying for his or her individual risk and usage pattern is much fairer than today's pricing scheme!" Is it? There are several examples of costs that could easily be allocated to their originators, yet they are burdened by the society as a whole. One such example are health insurances. Instead of evaluating the individual risk of illness based on age, gender, and health history, many countries have decided to spread those costs throughout the society, willingly cross financing the elderly or the ones with chronical diseases from the young and healthy. However, personal mobility does not seem to have the same societal value as health and does not seem to be in need of redistribution. Today's cross-financing of traffic costs is probably more the consequence of the imperfections stressed out in this paper, than the result of a socio-political master plan. Hence, charging the responsible parties for the caused traffic costs would presumably be seen by many as fairer indeed. Economists have also argued that in the extreme situation where all information asymmetry (and thus adverse selection and moral hazard) could be eliminated, a Pareto-type welfare improvement could appear, thus having all drivers being better off [7].

The ubiquitous presence of a system such as the Smart Tachograph could have other consequences as well. If many vehicles would have such devices installed, then the technical prerequisites would be given that also authorities such as the traffic police can require access to that data. From a technical perspective, this would be an easy game: generating a new plug-in and enforcing it to all vehicles. To illustrate this scenario, we have included a traffic police plug-in into our first prototype. When driving above the speed limit, it issues an audio warning: "You are above the speed limit. Please slow down." If ten seconds later the car is still above the speed limit, an automatic traffic fine is issued. Since there have been some similar examples lately (e.g., airlines forced to give away data on passengers and their flying habits, data that they had initially collected for their frequent flyer programs), this scenario seems not to be that far from reality. We thus think that the Smart Tachograph is a good example to illustrate some of the Pandora boxes that could be opened by ubiquitous computing technology in the near future.

6   Conclusion and Outlook

We have presented the Smart Tachograph, a prototypical platform that facilitates an individual and accurate accounting of generic traffic costs. We have built a prototypical black box containing the sensors used by the system and a software infrastructure supporting a set of basic features. Even if our prototype does not yet address many practical deployment issues (such as guaranteeing mutual security between accounting authority and customer), it already supports various core features of a deployment-ready system. Being a generic platform, it allows different kinds of traffic costs to be measured and billed through it – we included road pricing and insurance rates for illustration. The prototype is easily extensible to include new sensors that may be relevant for measuring some of these costs. It can be extended to include new accounting authorities, too. Where applicable, the infrastructure allows several accounting authorities to compete for the driver's favor. The prototype already includes several insurers. The system automatically downloads and presents their different offers to the driver, who may choose among them.

We have subsequently analyzed several technical, societal, and economic issues that could arise from the deployment of such a system. Such consequences are often outside the focus of typical ubiquitous computing prototypes. Thus, the Smart Tachograph seems to be a good ubiquitous computing case study. It involves a collection of technologies and concepts typical for ubiquitous computing applications, such as sensors and sensor nodes, wireless communication, location and context awareness, and machine-to-machine communication. There is a realistic business model behind it. And, as mentioned, it allows further exploration of many highly-relevant questions regarding economic models, welfare, security, or fairness and trust throughout the society, as well as the specific tradeoffs among these. As a consequence, we have further made the point for a privacy-friendly solution that could at least alleviate some of the potential societal drawbacks, and included this solution in our prototype.

There are several interesting future directions of research. For example, evaluating the system – how well does it ascertain different kind of costs? A more intense dialogue with stakeholders from the insurance industry and government agencies could be enlightening. How robust are these calculations with respect to different driving styles and environmental conditions? A more structured testbed seems necessary in order to answer this question. A study with other categories of stakeholders, mainly with potential customers, also seems imperative. By presenting them different possible implementations of the Smart Tachograph with their specific advantages and drawbacks, a substantial overview of user opinions could result. Finally, including the different mutual security features in the system would imply a large leap towards a realistic system and would more clearly show the related challenges.

Acknowledgements. Christoph Plüss has programmed most of the Smart Tachograph during his master thesis. Dr. Jochen Jagob pointed out information asymmetry, adverse selection, and moral hazard as relevant economic issues. Prof. Friedemann Mattern, Prof. Hans Gellersen, and Dr. Marc Langheinrich have provided many helpful comments on earlier drafts of this paper. The Gottlieb Daimler- and Karl Benz-Foundation, Germany, has generously supported a large part of this work as part of the project "Living in a Smart Environment – Implications of Ubiquitous Computing".

References

1. George Akerlof. The Market for Lemons: Qualitative Uncertainty and the Market Mechanism. *The Quarterly Journal of Economics*, 84(3):488–500, 1970.
2. Vlad Coroama and Norbert Höckl. Pervasive Insurance Markets and their Consequences. *First Int. Workshop on Sustainable Pervasive Computing at Pervasive 2004*, April 2004.
3. Vlad Coroama and Marc Langheinrich. Personalized Vehicle Insurance Rates – A Case for Client-Side Personalization in Ubiquitous Computing. *Workshop on Privacy-Enhanced Personalization. CHI 2006*, April 2005.
4. Vlad Coroama and Marc Langheinrich. The Smart Tachograph. *Video submission abstract. Adjunct Proceedings of UbiComp 2005*, September 2005.
5. Anind Dey. *Providing Architectural Support for Building Context-Aware Applications*. PhD thesis, College of Computing, Georgia Tech, December 2000.
6. Jonas Eliasson and Mattias Lundberg. Road Pricing in Urban Areas. www.transport-pricing.net/download/swedishreport.pdf, January 2003.
7. Lilia Filipova and Peter Welzel. Reducing Asymmetric Information in Insurance Markets: Cars with Black Boxes. In *Proceedings of the 32nd Conference of the European Association for Research in Industrial Economics (EARIE)*, September 2005.
8. Tim Kindberg, John Barton, Jeff Morgan, Gene Becker, Debbie Caswell, Philippe Debaty, Gita Gopal, Marcos Frid, Venky Krishnan, Howard Morris, John Schettino, Bill Serra, and Mirjana Spasojevic. People, Places, Things: Web Presence for the Real World. *Mobile Networks and Applications*, 7:365–376, 2002.
9. Todd Litman. Distance-based vehicle insurance. Victoria Transport Policy Institute, 2003.
10. Matthias Oberholzer. *Strategische Implikationen des Ubiquitous Computing für das Nichtleben-Geschäft im Privatkundensegment der Assekuranz*. PhD thesis, Basel University, Switzerland, 2003.
11. Lucienne Rey. publifocus – Road Pricing. Technical report, TA-Swiss, July 2004.
12. "Der Standard" staff. Wien droht doppelt so viel Autoverkehr. *Der Standard – Austrian daily newspaper*, April 24th-25th, 2004.
13. The Economist staff. Driven to radicalism. *The Economist*, June 11th:33–34, 2005.
14. The Economist staff. Jam yesterday. *The Economist*, June 11th:14, 2005.

Domino: Exploring Mobile Collaborative Software Adaptation

Marek Bell, Malcolm Hall, Matthew Chalmers, Phil Gray, and Barry Brown

Department of Computing Science,
University of Glasgow, Glasgow, UK
{marek, mh, matthew, pdg, barry}@dcs.gla.ac.uk

Abstract. Social Proximity Applications (SPAs) are a promising new area for ubicomp software that exploits the everyday changes in the proximity of mobile users. While a number of applications facilitate simple file sharing between co–present users, this paper explores opportunities for recommending and sharing software between users. We describe an architecture that allows the recommendation of new system components from systems with similar histories of use. Software components and usage histories are exchanged between mobile users who are in proximity with each other. We apply this architecture in a mobile strategy game in which players adapt and upgrade their game using components from other players, progressing through the game through sharing tools and history. More broadly, we discuss the general application of this technique as well as the security and privacy challenges to such an approach.

1 Introduction

Discovering and learning about new software tools and customisations are important parts of using modern computer systems. However, attempts to support the process of software change and adaptation have generally had limited success. Most users still rely on browsing websites, reading magazines or conversing with friends and colleagues, to obtain new software. Most frequently, users generally call upon the experience of others to find more efficient or enjoyable systems and practices [16, 17, 19]. There are key advantages to learning about software from others. One can reduce the time spent learning about software that might not be applicable to one's actual activities and interests. Instead, one can concentrate on what colleagues and friends in similar contexts found to be useful or interesting [8]. Applications, recommended by expert users, are also likely to be worth the time and effort it takes to investigate and learn, and are likely to fit smoothly into the user's current pattern of use. Through this social process, many members of a community of use benefit from others' unique areas of expertise and experience.

One example of this is finding new plug-ins that are both useful and compatible with the current configuration of one's web browser or email tool. Relying on community and expert knowledge aids in avoiding what was called, in a recent ACM Queue article, the 'plug-in hell' of incompatible plug-ins with complex patterns of interdependence and joint use [4]. Such levels of complexity may become more likely

K.P. Fishkin et al. (Eds.): PERVASIVE 2006, LNCS 3968, pp. 153–168, 2006.

in the future if we see more applications such as the 1000 plug-in system that Birsan reports on in [4].

System adaptation and evolution are especially important as the use of computers expands beyond work activities focused on pre-planned tasks, into leisure and domestic life. Indeed, users' modification (or 'modding') of complex software structures is relatively common within at least one leisure area, games—although the skill threshold required for modding is high. Ubicomp applied to leisure and domestic life suggests even more variety and dynamics of peoples' activities, contexts and preferences, making it especially hard for the designer to foresee all possible functions and modules, and their transitions, combinations and uses. Instead of relying on the developer's foresight, incremental adaptation and ongoing evolution under the control of the users may be more appropriate [11, 25].

The Domino architecture actively supports incremental adaptation and ongoing evolution of ubicomp systems. In effect, Domino changes a system's structure on the basis of the patterns of users' activity. It supports each user in finding out about new software modules through a context-specific collaborative filtering algorithm, and it integrates and interconnects new modules by analysing data on past use. Domino allows software modules to be automatically recommended, integrated and run, with user control over adaptation maintained through acceptance of recommendations rather than through manual search, choice and interconnection. One way of looking at Domino is to see it as a means of broadening access to and lowering the skill threshold needed for system adaptation—not just for games, but for many mobile applications. Our overall approach is exemplified by the following scenario. James enjoys dining out and going to the theatre, and he frequently travels into the city centre by bus. On his phone is a Domino-powered application consisting of a restaurant guide, a list of upcoming theatre shows and a map of bus routes. As he walks down the street, his phone discovers another Domino system carried by someone else nearby. The two systems connect and transfer data between each other. Later in the evening, he notices that he has a recommendation on his phone for a module displaying bus time schedules. This module is clearly useful to him and complements his map of bus routes perfectly, and so he accepts the recommendation. Domino installs the module, and James soon makes use of it to plan when to make his journey home. In summary, while James simply went about his day as normal, his phone discovered another Domino system, shared data with it, generated module recommendations, prepared new modules, and presented them for his approval before installing and running them. Most of this adaptation was carried out with minimal explicit user interaction, as James only had to handle the choice of which recommendations, if any, to accept.

In the next sections we summarise related research and then describe the details of our implementation work, set within the Equator IRC (www.equator.ac.uk). We describe Domino's application model, involving a modular architecture, the logging of modules' use and configuration, the transmission of modules between mobile computers and the dynamic integration of new modules into a user's running configuration, and we discuss issues of security and privacy. We report on initial experiments with a prototype application, a strategy game for phones and PDAs. We discuss our ongoing work and issues of generalisation and evaluation of such system models and applications.

2   Related Work

One of the early landmarks in the study of collaboration in software adaptation centred on the Buttons system [18], in which modules were shared via email, and could be activated individually within the Xerox Lisp desktop environment. Users could make small changes to buttons, generally by setting parameters via pop-up menus, but deeper changes and integration of buttons were feasible only for experienced programmers. Instead, MacLean et al. relied on a 'tailoring culture' in which changes were made by experts and then spread among the community. More broadly, this tailoring culture has been supported by tools such as Answer Garden [1], which allowed users to help each other through creating a knowledge base of information about systems and organisation processes. These tools supported the creation of an 'organisational memory' of previously implicit knowledge.

We have also drawn from recent work in ubicomp, in particular recombinant computing and Speakeasy [20]. This relies on three key elements: a small set of fixed domain-independent interfaces that modules can use to initiate communication, mobile code that allows dynamic extension of functionality to meet possibly unforeseen requirements, and 'user-in-the-loop' interaction that accepts that users will be the ultimate arbiters with regard to when and whether an interaction among compatible entities occurs. Speakeasy relies on contextual metadata, in the form of predefined name/value pairs, which are used in describing the semantics of each component to a potential user. Such descriptions also support users' editing of task templates, changing or setting parameters, much as in Buttons. Speakeasy focuses on supporting users in handling a relatively small number of components associated with devices and related services in the local context, filtering on the basis of known locations, owners and other contextual features, but "information filtering was only static—components did not update their contextual information, and the organisation of components was not responsive to the user's current context". Newman et al. also stated that "a more dynamic approach to information filtering, in which the organisation presented to the user is tailored to the user's location, history, and tasks, could prove useful".

Another ubicomp system that supports adaptation is Jigsaw [14], but it may be better described as *adaptable* rather than *adaptive*, to use the distinction of Findlater and McGrenere [12]. A graphical editor allowed a user to choose from a small set of components based on JavaBeans, and configure to form simple data-flows. Like Speakeasy, Jigsaw focused on a relatively constrained set of devices and transformations particular to one location—in this case, a home. When a component had several outputs (or inputs), the user made an explicit choice as to what to interconnect. Users were given little support for knowing what might be a useful component to choose or connection to make, but successful connections between components were confirmed through 'snap-together' motion and audio feedback. Findlater and McGrenere focused on relatively 'shallow' system changes in [12], i.e. on menu items rather than deep system structure, but they offered a useful comparison and overview of the issues surrounding static, adaptable and adaptive interfaces. They carried out an experiment comparing a static interface with an adaptable one, in which a user could manually reorder menu items, and an adaptive interface, in which the system reordered items according to a predictable but simple algorithm based on the user's most frequently and recently used items. Building on the premise that personalisation is needed in the face of the growing size and dynamism of the sets of functions in modern applications, and citing [27], they suggest that "adaptable and adaptive interaction techniques are likely the only scalable approaches to personalisation." Their study found overwhelming support for personalisation, and more of their experimental subjects preferred a manually adaptable menu to an automatically adaptive one. However, they found that users who favoured the adaptive system expressed very strong support for it. This echoes earlier adaptive systems work such as [7], which suggested "collaborative dialogues with the user" might help strengthen adaptive systems. Their suggestion was that the best way to satisfy a wide range of users may be the under-explored area of 'mixed-initiative' interfaces, i.e. combining adaptable and adaptive elements so that the system and the user both control some of the interaction.

Persson et al. [22] created a mobile phone application, DigiDress, which transmits profiles to other users as a digital expression of oneself. It was able to self-replicate and spread among phones using Bluetooth and infrared connections. The application was able to spread through a population of users in a viral manner, similar to epidemic algorithms for replicated database maintenance [9]. Persson et al. stated that this distribution technique was "critical to the success" of the application as such an epidemic spread of the application allowed for an extremely quick uptake.

3 System Overview

The current version of Domino runs on Windows systems (Desktop and PocketPC) that support WiFi. We have tested Domino on various brands of PocketPC devices including HP iPAQ hx2750s with built in WiFi, Qtek S100 phones with a WiFi SD card, and O2 XDA IIs phones with built in WiFi. Domino is also capable of running on desktop machines, and on a wireless or a wired Ethernet connection.

Each instance of the Domino system consists of three distinct parts: handling communication with peers; monitoring, logging and recommending module use; and dynamically installing, loading and executing new modules. We refer to the items that Domino exchanges with peers and dynamically loads and installs as modules. A module consists of a group of .NET classes that are stored in a DLL (Dynamic Link Library) that provides a convenient package for transporting the module from one system to another. Each Domino system continually monitors and logs what combination of modules it is running. When one Domino system discovers another, the two begin exchanging logs of usage history. This exchange allows each system to compare its history with those of others, in order to create recommendations about which new modules a user may be interested in. Recommended modules are then transferred in DLL format between the systems. Recommendations that the user accepts are dynamically installed, loaded and executed by Domino. This constant discovery and installation of new modules at runtime allows a Domino system to adapt and grow continually around a user's usage habits.

Domino systems continually broadcast their existence over their local network connections in order that they may quickly become aware of any nearby peers. We use local network connections, mainly ad hoc, rather than long distance connections such as GPRS and UMTS. Firstly, local connections offer the possibility of filtering relevance by location. That is to say, that those geographically proximate to a user may potentially have software components more relevant to a particular user—in that we spend much of our time in close proximity with friends and work colleagues.

Moreover, WiFi and Bluetooth are currently free to use whilst, for mobile devices, longer-range connections are expensive if large amounts of data are to be exchanged. Furthermore, local WiFi connections offer significant bandwidth and speed, important since Domino needs to transfer large amounts of data. Finally, by using only local connections rather than public phone and WiFi networks, we strengthen privacy, in that no personal data about users is ever sent through a third party. If connections such as 3G improve in the future then it may become prudent to use them, as they would greatly increase the population of available peers from which information can be cultivated—but only with the addition of a privacy system offering a suitable degree of anonymity for users interacting with each other, to mask personal data such as phone numbers.

Awareness of peers is critical to Domino, and having a variety of up-to-date log data from these peers is key to the recommendation system's performance. When connected to a network, be it fixed or wireless, each Domino system repeatedly sends out packets containing an IP address and port number on which it can accept connections from other Domino systems. This allows any other Domino systems on the same network to discover, connect to, and request and receive history data and modules quickly from other peers. In order to maximise opportunities for encounter, peers continually attempt to meet on a certain network, and will consistently switch to one appropriate network. Domino systems running on devices with wireless connectivity actively seek out infrastructure mode networks and connect to them whenever possible. When no networks are available, Domino switches to its own ad hoc network. Since most standard wireless drivers may attempt connections to the nearest network and interrupt the user with a "New Network Found" notification window when such a connection happens, we created a custom wireless driver that allows the system to 'lock on' to a chosen network SSID until explicitly directed to switch to another. These features allow Domino systems to contact each other even when no 802.11 infrastructure mode networks are present, while still permitting users to use infrastructure access points, i.e. hotspots, to connect to the Internet as they normally would. In our trials we found our custom wireless driver code was extremely quick in carrying out the required switching between networks and network modes. Typical times involved with Domino's 802.11 connections are as follows:

- Switching between infrastructure mode and ad hoc mode: 1ms
- Associating with an infrastructure access point: 3s
- Time to acquire IP address via DHCP for infrastructure: 5s
- Time to set IP address for ad hoc: 3s
- Discovering a peer after joining a network: 1s

The DHCP time for infrastructure varies strongly with the quality of signal to the access point and the number of users on the network. When in ad hoc mode we assign static IP addresses, as we found automatic private addressing to be slow and unreliable. It should be noted that the above times are taken from the moment a Domino system makes the decision to switch to another network. In our code we typically make this decision after trying but failing to reconnect to the previous network four times with a period of 250ms between each attempt. Thus, the effective total duration for switching from one infrastructure network to another is typically 9s ±5s.

This 'network discovery followed by service discovery' approach has advantages over IP-based discovery protocols such as ZeroConf, which only provide the latter service. Searching for other networks and discovering new clients continues even while connected and transmitting data over a network. This behaviour results in nearby Domino systems being able to locate each other in most situations. Indeed, unless the network card is required to be exclusively locked to another application, a Domino system is likely to locate another nearby in a matter of seconds.

The UDP packet that each Domino system broadcasts every second holds an IP address, a port number and a unique ID for the device. In order to protect a Domino user's privacy, his or her own username, actual device ID or MAC address are never used as identifiers in any of the data transmitted over the network. Instead, each user can choose one of two types of anonymous ID. Firstly, when Domino is initially run on a system, a random number can be generated and permanently stored on the device to be used as the ID in all subsequent Domino transactions. As the ID is randomly generated the user's anonymity is preserved. The main advantage of this technique is that if two or more sets of data are exchanged with a peer at different times then the receiver, although not able to identify the actual user, will be able to identify that the data comes from the same source and so will subsequently be able to determine more exact recommendation weightings for the entries. For example, if a new set of data is received and shows a moderate similarity to the current Domino user, the likelihood of it being recommended would be high. However, if it was found that previous data had been received from this user in the past, in addition to this new set, the chance of recommendation could be significantly higher.

The alternative ID that can be used is simply a random number generated for each transaction with a peer. Whilst this technique is the most efficient at protecting the originator's identity, it does result in it being impossible to determine if two different data sets came from the same source. However, the recommendation system mainly relies on finding similarities within short windows and, as these windows are commonly far smaller than any set of data transferred in a typical Domino transaction, this method actually has little impact on the quality of the overall recommendations.

When another Domino system receives the UDP packet broadcast by another, it can use the information contained therein to act as a client and create a TCP connection to the advertised IP address and port. Thus, the systems temporarily assume the traditional client/server roles. The most commonly used requests in our systems so far are to list the users for whom one has history data, to send the N most recent history entries for user X, and to send N history entries starting from the Mth most recent entry for user X. These three request types allow a client to identify which histories are available on the server, to begin obtaining the most recent history data and then to continue to gather more data as time allows. As connections can be lost at any time, a request generally consists of a single message, and we parse incoming streams so that we can make use of most of the data received up to the point when the connection was lost. As all connections are threaded and handled separately, each Domino system can act as a server and a client simultaneously. Indeed, this is the typical behaviour for Domino systems, as they will normally discover each other at approximately the same time.

The recommendation subsystem employs a collaborative filtering algorithm based on that of Recer [5] in order to recommend new modules for a Domino system. It also logs all the information required to generate such recommendations, and trades usage data with peer recommenders on other devices. Whenever a module is activated or deactivated, the entire configuration—that is, the set of identifiers of all running modules—is logged to the history database. It is by scanning through this logged history of other users' data and searching for sections that are similar to the current user's current module configuration, i.e. the current 'context', that recommendations can be generated. Matching in this context-specific way distinguishes the collaborative filtering algorithm from most others, which tend to match people on the basis of all the data logged for each user rather than attempting to concentrate on specific windows of history data that are most likely to relevant.

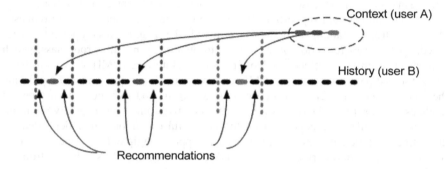

Fig. 1. Recommendations for user A are taken by finding past occurrences of the modules in A's current context, and then finding which other modules were most frequently used at those times

When similar, but not exactly matching, history sections are found, the modules not in the current context are tallied, ranked and delivered as recommendations (Figure 1). New recommendations are generated whenever a module is activated or deactivated, as these changes alter the current context of the user and so may alter the recommendation results—even if no new history data has been created in the interim. Recommendations are also generated when new history data is received from another Domino system, as this is likely to provide novel module recommendations.

Each Domino system can carry not only its own user's history but also the histories of many other users. The recommendation system periodically analyses the similarity between the owner's history and all other cached histories. It identifies the most similar histories in terms of overlap in module usage, and stores the IDs associated with their owners. As the more similar users are likely to provide the most relevant recommendations, similar users' histories are the last to be thrown out when storage space is low and the first to be requested from other devices when they meet. The similarity comparisons are carried out as an average of matches per history entry since a basic overlap would unfairly favour longer histories.

4   The Spread of Modules and Data

The transfer of history data and modules when Domino clients meet leads to controlled diffusion that is inspired by the epidemic algorithms of Demers et al. [9]. Popular modules are quickly spread throughout the community, while modules that fulfil more specific needs spread more slowly but are likely eventually to locate a receptive audience because of history-based context matching and the use of 'wanted lists' to find required modules.

Once a module recommendation is received, it is the role of the adaptation component to seek and obtain this new module and, subject to user acceptance, dynamically load it into the running configuration. Due to the inherent unreliability of ad hoc connections, it cannot be guaranteed that the Domino system that was the source of the recommendation will still be available to service a subsequent module transfer request. This is one of the reasons why Domino maintains a 'wanted module list'.

Each Domino system supports FTP, for receiving modules and servicing requests. Once the DLL containing a module is received, the adaptation component is triggered. First, it uses reflection over the DLL to obtain the module's root class, which implements a simple interface, the Domino Module Interface (DMI). As well as basic start, stop and pause methods, the DMI contains methods for querying and modifying the module's dependencies and dependants, and a method to expose what types of modules it can support. During development, the programmer must specify the minimal set of modules it is dependent on for successful execution. Since dependencies are defined as type name strings, modules can support multiple dependencies according to the class or interface types its DMI-implementing class inherits from or implements.

Due to the generic nature of the system model, when a module is received there is no predetermined place for it in the system. In the simplest case, the new module can query the Domino system's running modules to find ones that satisfy its dependencies, by analysing their classes and the interfaces they implement. However, a problem arises when multiple satisfactory modules are found. For example, if there are two map viewers running (i.e. two instances of the same map viewer class), each of which could support a new map layer module, which viewer should the new module be connected to? To resolve such ambiguities, we make a second use of the history data and the recommendation algorithm. By using the new recommended module as the 'context', we can obtain a ranked list of modules previously used in conjunction with it, to determine which is the most likely target. For example, imagine the case where a new 'pollution' layer module is to be added to a system that has two existing map viewers running, one with a *traffic* layer and the other with a *restaurant* layer. By using this technique it becomes possible to determine that the *traffic* and *pollution* layers are used in conjunction more often than the *pollution* and *restaurant* layer. Thus, Domino would connect the new *pollution* layer to the viewer that has the *traffic* layer, where it is likely to be of most value. Alternatively, when starting up a new module, one or more of its dependencies may not be matched. If the required module is available on the system, then a new instance of it can be started up-generating a new check for dependencies and so forth. However, if the required module is not available on the system, the adaptation process for the new module is suspended, and the module is added to the wanted list. The user is informed, and can either drop the recommendation or wait until the wanted module is discovered.

5 Security

Security is a serious problem for any system that uses mobile code which moves between different devices, and it has been an important focus of our own and others' research, e.g. [2], [21], [23], [24]. One particular threat is so called 'sleeper viruses' that act as valid and useful modules for a period of time, become accepted in a community, and then after an incubation period 'turn bad' and start to act as damaging viruses.

Currently, one of the most widely used techniques for deciding which applications to trust is that of signing, in which a trusted authority analyses each possible application or module, and decides whether it is harmful or not. Those that are determined to be non-harmful are signed with a secure key that end-clients know they can trust. In theory this can inhibit harmful applications from spreading to many machines, however most implementations permit a user to decide to force an unsigned module or application to run, allowing dangerous code to spread regardless of its lack of authorisation.

Whilst employing signing for Domino would provide an almost complete solution to security concerns, there are severe disadvantages that have, so far, stopped us from implementing it. Firstly, one of Domino's main strengths is that it allows for an extremely open community where anyone can contribute a new module or amend an existing one. In an environment where each module had to be signed a large number of users would decline to create new modules, as those modules would then have to go through the signing process. As this would be likely to involve some cost (in terms of money or time for developers) this would further deter potential developers from contributing to the community. Furthermore, forcing each module to go through a central location where it was signed would negate the strength of the epidemic spreading Domino supports. There would be little or no reason to provide epidemic spreading if one source had access to every possible module in the community and could therefore, in theory, simply distribute them all from one central location.

A second possible solution is to create a sandbox environment for both the entire Domino environment running on a device and for each individual module within that environment. Indeed, as Domino is coded in the .NET language it already runs through the CLR (Common Language Runtime)—basically a virtual machine. It is extremely easy, and fully supported in the .NET API, to restrict any .NET application from having access to a part of or the entirety of the rest of the operating system. Furthermore, as every Domino module must adhere to an interface it would be a simple matter to get them to communicate through a mediator rather than directly with one another. Such a mediator could ensure that one module did not have the opportunity to damage another.

Another possible solution is to use a permission–based model, in a manner similar to the Java language and to most modern operating systems. For example, if a Domino module wanted to access a file on the local device, it would first have to ask permission from the user who could deny, accept once or accept forever the module's request. Whilst this method is employed by many languages that run on virtual machines, it would be likely to be too intrusive to users in a Domino environment. Previously, this method has usually been used where the number of new modules or applications is relatively low, and so the user is required to intervene on an infrequent basis. In a typical Domino system there can be an extremely large number of modules running at any one time, and requiring the user to intervene for each one could prove too time-consuming. Furthermore, as one of the advantages of Domino is that it allows users to quickly obtain expert tools, it is unlikely that the user would have the required in-depth knowledge of each particular module to make the correct decisions about when to trust them. Methods of automating the process of determining which applications should be permitted to run or have access to a particular part of the operating system may aid the user in this process. For example, *Deeds* [10] attempts to analyse code and roughly categorise it before comparing it to the access levels given to code that previously fell into the same category. Such a technique could make permissions a viable option in the Domino architecture, by removing many of the constant interruptions that might otherwise be presented to the user.

A third potential solution relies on the same epidemic algorithms as the spread of the modules themselves, spreading information about malicious modules during any contact with peers. For example, if one user found a malicious module they could, after removing it, add it to a list of known bad modules. From then on, the list would be transmitted to any Domino peers that were encountered. A Domino client which had received this information could then refuse to accept the module if it ever encountered that module. Similarly, a client that was running the module and received information that it was malicious could quickly remove the module even if it had not yet done any damage. As the information about malicious modules would be constantly spread rather than having to be recommended, and as clients would be able to remove the module before it done any damage, the spread of the information that the module was malicious would be faster than the spread of the module itself. In this way, viral outbreaks of malicious modules could generally be prevented. However, this solution is not perfect as, although it would stop a large viral outbreak in the community, it would not stop damage to a particular client who received the module before receiving the information that it was malicious. More advanced implementations could make use of the Internet to broadcast information about malicious modules, 'overtaking' their spread through peer-to-peer contact. In so-called 'honeypot' implementations, this has been shown to be particularly effective at stopping the spread of conventional computer viruses [13].

Apart from these technical approaches to countering viruses, it is possible for a user to view a module's history of use: on which device it originated, on which other devices it was used prior to its arrival, and in what contexts it was used along the way with regard to other modules. This helps users to decide for themselves whether the history is typical of a trustworthy module. Alternatively this history information could be fed into an algorithm such as that in [6] or [26], to give a calculated level of trust. Although this technique may not be sufficient in itself, we advocate its use as an additional protection method to be used in conjunction with other measures.

As stated, security is a serious issue and, whilst we are researching these and other possible solutions, we have not yet settled on a single robust solution that we fully trust. For this reason, we have so far avoided creating 'mission critical' applications based on the Domino architecture and have instead, for the time being, concentrated implementing Domino into game systems. While this does not avoid problems of viruses and malware (since 'bad' modules could destroy a user's game, or be used as a way of cheating) it does provide an environment for experimenting with module recommendation and broader security issues, limiting the potential damage to users' devices.

6 A Prototype Application: Castles

To test the Domino architecture we developed a mobile strategy game, Castles. Games have wide social and financial impact, and form an interesting application area in themselves, but we chose a game because one can design a game to explore specific technical issues raised by wider research, and adapt it with ongoing findings relatively easily. Additionally, players find new ways to stretch one's designs, assumptions and concepts, and are often keen to participate in tests of one's systems. Games offer an example of an application area in which users are already often involved in radical re-engineering of systems, i.e. in modding. Our work is influenced by *Treasure* [3], which was a mobile game used to explore the exposure of system infrastructure in a 'seamful' way, so that users might appropriate variations in the infrastructure. Similarly, Castles is a seamful design in that it selectively exposes software structure to users, so that they can be aware of software modules and appropriate them for their own contextually relevant patterns of use.

The majority of the Castles game is played in a solo building mode, in which the player chooses which buildings to construct and how many resources to use for each one. Each type of building is a Domino module. The goal of this stage is for the player to create a building infrastructure that efficiently constructs and maintains the player's army units. For example, a player may wish to have many 'Knight' units being produced. However, to achieve this, the player must first ensure that he or she has constructed suitable buildings to produce enough food, iron, stone and wood to build and continually supply a Knights' 'School'. When the game starts, there are over thirty types of building and eleven types of army units available to the player, allowing for extremely varied combinations of buildings supporting distinct types of army. For example, one player may wish to have an army consisting mainly of mounted units whilst another may try a strategy of having a large number of ranged units such as archers. In addition to buildings, there are 'building adapters', which are Domino modules able to alter the output level of buildings. Adapters may have different effects based on which building they are applied to. For example, the 'scythe' adapter has no effect if applied to the Knight School but doubles output levels when applied to a wheat field. In order to mimic the way that plug-ins and components for many software systems continually appear over time, new buildings, adapters and units are introduced throughout the game, as upgrades and extensions that spread among players while they interact with each other.

When two players' devices are within wireless range, one may choose to attack another. Behind the scenes, Domino also initiates its history-sharing and module-sharing processes. When a battle commences, both players select from their army the troops to enter into battle. Players receive updates as the battle proceeds, and at any time can choose to retreat or concede defeat. At the same time, players can talk about the game, or the modules they have recently collected, or modules they have used and either found useful or discarded.

With such a high number of buildings, adapters and units, there is significant variation in the types of society (module configurations) that a player may create. Selecting which buildings to construct next or where to apply building adapters can be a confusing or daunting task. However, Domino helps by finding out about new modules as they become available, recommending which modules to create next, and loading and integrating new modules that the player accepts. When new buildings and units are available to be run but not yet instantiated, we notify the user of the new additions by highlighting them in the menu of available buildings. The three buildings that the system most recommends the user construct next are shown when the user clicks the R (recommendation) button (Figure 2). Thus, the user has quick access to guidance from the Domino system about how to proceed.

 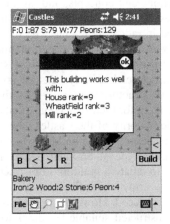

Fig. 2. Recommendations show when user clicks the R button

Fig. 3. Details showing why a recommendation was made

If the user desires, he or she can get additional information about recommendations, such as its dependencies or the modules most frequently used in conjunction with it in the past in similar contexts. This information, obtained in a pop-up dialog by clicking the recommendation information button in the build panel, can help the player understand more fully how the module might be used (Figure 3). Thus, a new module is smoothly integrated into the player's system without requiring substantial module management, or indeed any knowledge of the low-level transfer or installation process. Simply, the user sees the new options and recommendations, and can make use of that information without having to search manually for or install the new modules. On the other hand, Domino does not go too far in automatically loading and running modules. It presents them in a way that lets the user see them as he or she plays, find out something of their past use, and show this information to others when meeting and talking with other players. Overall, Domino complements the conversation and discussion among players about new and interesting modules, and eases the introduction of new modules into each individual system and into the community.

7   Initial Experience and Ongoing Work

Having run a pilot study we now offer some initial evidence from the system's use during that study. We set up the game so that four players sat in different rooms, out-with wireless network range of each other. We periodically moved the players between rooms, so that they passed by each other, and met up in pairs. This meant that users spent most of the time alone but periodically met up to start battles and to talk about the game and its modules, much as they might if they were walking with their phones during a normal day.

Each player started with the same base set of buildings, adapters and units available, as well as two extra buildings, two extra adapters and one extra unit. Thus, each player started with a substantial core set of items (33 buildings, 10 building adapters and 11 units) plus 5 items that were unique to him or her. For example, amongst the additional items given to one player was the catapult factory. As anticipated, when players met for battle, their Domino systems exchanged usage information and transferred modules between phones so as to be able to satisfy recommendations. Thus, the catapult factory and catapult unit began with one player, but were transferred, installed and run by two of the three other players during the game. Several players who had been performing poorly because of, for instance, a combination of buildings that was not efficient for constructing large armies, felt more confident and seemed to improve their strategies after encountering other players. They started constructing more useful buildings by following the recommendations. In each of these cases, this did not appear to stem from players' conversation, but directly from the information provided by the system. After the first meeting with another player, the system had gathered its first history data from another player to compare against, and thus it was the first time the player saw recommendations. When the player began to construct a new building, he or she always saw at least one recommendation for which building to construct next—and followed it.

Each Domino system's interactions with others were mainly hidden from the users. When devices came into wireless range of one another they exchanged history data and modules, but this was not explicitly shown to the users. Rather, the information was stored and displayed to users when they were constructing new buildings. For example, in one game we introduced diverse building adapters to each system after approximately ten minutes of play, when the users were still isolated from one another. Player A was given an 'advanced toolkit' adapter with the deliberately generic description "A set of tools which workers can use to do their jobs more efficiently". Later, when players A and B were in the same room, they went into battle. When B returned to solo play and continued constructing buildings, the new toolkit adapter appeared in his available adapter list and, when he selected it, the game suggested that he use it with the Iron Mine building. Player A had discovered that the toolkit worked quite efficiently in conjunction with the iron mine and had mainly used it on that building. This example is typical of Domino helping to disambiguate how or where modules can be used based not only on general or objective fit, but with specific patterns of use in play. In the toolkit example, the toolkit may be applied to any building at all and does provide an improvement in output regardless of the building's type. However, the toolkit provides most benefit (the highest output multiplier) when used with quarries rather than any other building type. Although B had no way of knowing this from the description provided with the module, the history of use from other players allowed a recommendation about where the adapter might provide the most benefit, and B subsequently used this to add it to one of his quarries.

Overall, our initial experience is promising. Domino's epidemic style of propagation of modules seems to be well suited to mobile applications where users may potentially encounter others away from high-bandwidth and freely (or cheaply) accessible networks, quickly and automatically exchange log data and modules, and possibly engage in more sustained direct interaction with each other. We are preparing for a larger user trial involving non-computer scientists in a less controlled environment than the one used for our pilot. We have begun to instrument the code so as to create detailed logs of GUI activity and module handling, to feed into tools for analysis and visualisation of patterns of use.

We are working on making Domino show the benefits in removing a running module from a system, rather than only adding new ones. Users can manually remove modules, to reduce the system becoming bloated or confusing, but at the moment Domino does not assist users in this process. Analysing logs of user activity can help with these issues, if we record the detail of modules' use and removal. Normal, continuing use could involve periodically recording a small positive weight for each module in the current configuration. However, if users consistently install one module and then manually remove another soon after, this may indicate that the former is an upgraded version of the latter or otherwise replaces the latter's functionality. This recorded pattern of use might then be interpreted by the system so as to record a substantial negative weight for the removed module in the history database, to help lower it in the rankings of modules while the new module builds up its use. If a user does not have the apparently older or superseded module, then he or she will be less likely to receive recommendations for it. If a user does have the module, the system may be able to recommend the new module as well as the removal of the old one.

A different area of our ongoing work relates to the way that the concepts and techniques behind Domino have application to less mobile settings. We are exploring applications in software development, and plug-ins for IDEs (integrated development environments) and web browsers such as Firefox. As pointed out in [4], many such systems are large and yet rather chaotic, and a Domino-like system might assist users.

In IDEs, mail tools and in mobile systems, we suggest that Findlater and McGrenere' comments about involving the user should be borne in mind. There may well be applications that would demand or involve automatic changes to an interactive system without a user's permission, but we have not been able to come up with very many examples of them. Instead, we see the techniques explored in Domino as a means to combine adaptable and adaptive elements, so that the system and the user both control some of the interaction. Unlike most other systems that we are aware of, we also suggest that collective records and patterns of use can be a productive resource for individuals adapting their adaptive systems.

8 Conclusion

In this paper we introduced the Domino architecture, and its approach to dynamic adaptation to support users' needs, interests and activities. Domino identifies relationships between code modules beyond those specified in code by programmers prior to system deployment, such as classes, interfaces and dependencies between them. It uses those relationships, but it also takes advantage of code modules' patterns of use and combination after they have been released into a user community. The Castles game demonstrated Domino's components and mechanisms, exemplifying its means of peer-to-peer communication, recommendation based on patterns of module use, and adaptation based on both module dependencies and history data. The openness and dynamism of Domino's system architecture is applicable to a variety of systems, but is especially appropriate for mobile systems because of their variety and unpredictability of patterns of use, their frequent disconnection from fixed networks, and their relatively limited amount of memory. As people visit new places, obtain new information and interact with new peers, they are likely to be interested in new software, and novel methods of interacting with and combining modules.

In our ongoing work, we continue to evaluate and refine Domino's effectiveness in Castles as well as in other seamful designs. Building larger and longer-lived applications will provide us with an opportunity to evaluate system robustness and performance, as well as user interest and acceptance. We foresee a strong need to tightly interweave the technical and interactional evaluation of the system, as Domino operates in a way that is simultaneously highly technological and thoroughly social. Again, we perceive this as appropriate to the area of ubiquitous computing, where technology is seen not as standing apart from everyday life, but rather as deeply interwoven with and affected by everyday life. In the long run, we hope to better understand how patterns of user activity, often considered to be an issue more for HCI than software engineering, may be used to adapt and improve the fundamental structures and mechanisms of technological systems.

Acknowledgements

This research was funded by the UK EPSRC (GR/N15986/01). We wish to thank all the trial participants for their involvement in the pilot, and also colleagues working on Castles and related projects such as Louise Barkhuus, Julie Maitland, Alistair Morrison, Jose Rojas, Scott Sherwood and Paul Tennent.

References

1. Ackerman, M. S. and Malone, T. W., Answer Garden: A Tool for Growing Organisational Memory, *Proc. ACM Conf. on Office Information Systems*, 1990, 31-33
2. Ametller, J., Robles, S. & Ortega-Ruiz, J. A. Self-Protected Mobile Agents. *Proc. Joint Conference on Autonomous Agents and Multiagent Systems (Volume 1)*. July 2004.
3. Barkhuus, L. et al., Picking Pockets on the Lawn: The Development of Tactics and Strategies in a Mobile Game *Proc. Ubicomp* 2005, 358-374.
4. Birsan, D. On Plug-ins and Extensible Architectures. ACM Queue 3(2) March 2005

5. Chalmers, M., et al., The Order of Things: Activity-Centred Information Access. *Proc. WWW 1998.* 359-367.
6. Chen, F. and Yeager, W., Poblano: A Distributed Trust Model for Peer-to-Peer Networks, *JXTA Security White Paper*, 2001.
7. Crow, D., Smith, B., The role of built-in knowledge in adaptive interface systems. *Proc. ACM IUI 1993*, 97-104
8. Cypher, A., EAGER: programming repetitive tasks by example, *ACM CHI 1991*, 33-39.
9. Demers A. et al, Epidemic algorithms for replicated database maintenance, *Proc. 6th ACM Symposium on Principles of Distributed Computing* (PODC), 1987, 1-12
10. Edjlali, G., Acharya, A. & Chaudhary, V. History-based Access Control for Mobile Code. *Proc. ACM Computer and Communications Security 1998*, 38-48.
11. Edwards, W.K., Grinter, R. At Home with Ubiquitous Computing: Seven Challenges. *Proc. Ubicomp 2001*, Springer LNCS, 256-272
12. Findlater, L, McGrenere, J. A comparison of static, adaptive and adaptable menus. *Proc. ACM CHI 2004*, 89-96.
13. Goldenberg, J., Shavitt, Y., Shir, E. & Solomon, S. Distributive immunization of networks against viruses using the 'honey-pot' architecture. *Nature Physics, 1(3),* December 2005, 184-188.
14. Humble, J. et al., Playing with the Bits: User-configuration of Ubiquitous Domestic Environments, *Proc. UbiComp 2003*, Springer LNCS, 256-263.
15. Khelil, A, Becker, C. et al. An Epidemic Model for Information Diffusion in MANETs, *Proc. ACM MSWiM*, 2002
16. Mackay, W. Patterns of Sharing Customizable Software. *Proc. ACM CSCW 1990*, 209-221.
17. Mackay, W. Triggers and barriers to customizing software. *Proc. ACM CHI 1991*, 153-160
18. MacLean, A., et al. User-Tailorable Systems: Pressing the Issues with Buttons. *Proc. ACM CHI 1990*, 175-182.
19. Nardi, B.A. and Miller, J. Twinkling Lights and Nested Loops: Distributed Problem Solving and Spreadsheet Development, *CSCW and Groupware*, Academic Press, 1991, 29-52
20. Newman, M., et al. Designing for Serendipity: Supporting End-User Configurations of Ubiquitous Computing Environments, *Proc. ACM DIS 2002*, 147-156.
21. Page, J., Zaslavsky, A. & Indrawan, M. A buddy model of security for mobile agent communities operating in pervasive scenarios. *Proc. Australasian Information Security, Data Mining and Web Intelligence, and Software Internationalisation—Volume 32.* CRPIT 2004.
22. Persson, P. et al., DigiDress: A Field Trial of an Expressive Social Proximity Application. *Proc. Ubicomp 2005*, 195-212.
23. Pfitzmann, A., Pfitzmann, B. & Waidner, M. Trusting Mobile User Devices and Security Modules. *Computer,* February 1997, 30(2), 61-68.
24. Ravi, S. et al., Security as a new dimension in embedded system design. *Proc. Design Automation,* June 2004
25. Rodden, T., Benford, S. The evolution of buildings and implications for the design of ubiquitous domestic environments. *Proc. ACM CHI 2003*, 9-16.
26. Saeb, M., Hamza, M. & Soliman, A. Protecting Mobile Agents against Malicious Host Attacks Using Threat Diagnostic AND/OR Tree. *Proc. sOc 2003*
27. Weld, D. et al. Automatically personalizing user interfaces. *Proc IJCAI 2003*, Morgan Kaufmann, 1613-1619

Keep Your Eyes on the Road and Your Finger on the Trigger - Designing for Mixed Focus of Attention in a Mobile Game for Brief Encounters

Liselott Brunnberg and Oskar Juhlin

Mobility studio, the Interactive Institute, P.O. Box 24081, 104 50, Stockholm, Sweden
{liselott.brunnberg, oskar.juhlin}@tii.se
http://www.tii.se/mobility

Abstract. In this paper we present an initial user feedback study of the Road Rager prototype. Road Rager is a mixed reality game, designed to enable passengers in different cars to play against each other during an encounter in traffic. We are concerned with how to design a game which balances the player's focus of attention between traffic and the computer interfaces, to provide a game which is comprehensive, interesting and challenging during a very limited lifetime. The study shows that a tangible user interface enables the player to handle the interaction in the game while watching for cars in the vicinity. Further, the users found multiplayer gaming during brief encounters exciting. However, the study also showed that minimalism is critical to the design. The gestures should preferably be indexical rather than symbolic, and elaborate forms of identification as a condition for manipulative success should be avoided. Finally, tangible user interfaces also allow a type of gaming where players only focus on the computers' interface, which suppresses the experience of combining traffic interaction with computer interaction.

1 Introduction

In recent years, a number of studies have focused on the exploration of tangible user interfaces to create augmented reality games [5, 16, 18, 19, 21, 23, 24]. These studies are concerned with the possibilities for graspable user interfaces to create experiences that mix real life with virtual life. We suggest that this form of interaction is especially suited to multiplayer gaming, which only occurs during brief social encounters in mobile situations. Therefore, we have designed a game prototype, called "the Road Rager", which includes a tangible user interface. Gaming is enabled by wireless ad hoc networking technology between car passengers as they convene within a limited range.

The choice of a tangible user interface was motivated by the high relative speed of the players, which makes an encounter very brief. Occasionally, such an encounter last no longer than a couple of seconds. We wanted to generate a user interface that can be handled and experienced while watching for cars in the vicinity during this limited time. Screen-centric interaction risks causing the player to focus on the computer, rather than look out the windows, and thus spoils the specific benefits of a mixed reality game. Consequently, a key challenge concerns the possibility to enable

K.P. Fishkin et al. (Eds.): PERVASIVE 2006, LNCS 3968, pp. 169–186, 2006.

and balance the player's engagement between computer and traffic, when the time available for identification and interaction with the opponent is very restricted. In this paper we present an initial user feed back study of the game. The game was tested by a total of twelve children in three different cars, during three sessions, circling around a route to generate encounters.

Travelling along a road conveys a continuous flow of impressions and new situations where changing scenes, the sense of motion and contingent encounters provide a very special experience [1]. It can be seen as a sequential experience, resembling a dramatic play of space and motion, i.e. the highway experience. Still, passengers look for other opportunities to pass the time. They might read, talk or play mobile games. But mobile games, and car embedded entertainment systems, are often portable versions of classic computer games where the focus is on a screen [2]. Thus, gaming becomes a complete alternative to the highway experience. This form of traditional computer game obscures the highway experience, rather than exploiting the journey for fun, exploration, play and creativity. The possibility of incorporating different aspects of mobility to create immersive experiences is therefore still a promise not yet realised [3]. Our hypothesis is that a game could be particularly engaging if it included the vivid and dynamic mobile context. Contingent traffic encounters such as rapid frontal meetings, protracted overtaking or gatherings, e.g. traffic jams or queues at red lights constitute an essential part of the experience of travelling along a road [4]. These meetings can be used to create fun and compelling mobile games and can add to the gaming experience [5].

The purpose of the study is twofold. First, we will investigate the general experience of a concept, which draws on brief social encounters in a game. Here, our initial user feedback study shows positive reactions towards the idea. Second, we will investigate how to afford interaction in use-contexts where the lifetime of the mixed reality is very limited. We will, in the following, discuss how the interaction could be supported by the design of the user interface, the tasks and the reward structures. Our study shows that the challenge of the use-context itself is so difficult that minimalism is critical. Furthermore, the study suggests that neither support nor rewards for real world focus are needed for the players to maintain a visual focus of attention on the traffic. Instead a blended experience between traffic and the computer occurs very much because the players accept and like the experience that playing in the same space allows.

The research is of interest for the design of pervasive and mobile mixed reality applications that include tangible user interfaces. Tangible user interfaces (TUI) were originally developed to close a "gap" between parallel, but related, activities in a real and a virtual world [6]. The problem of providing a proper mixture of virtuality and reality in mixed reality applications has been raised by Trevisan, Gemo et al [7]. They argue that the multiple sources of information available, and the two worlds of interaction, demand that the users make "choices about what to attend to and when." They suggest that we move beyond the first design agenda of creating a seamless, invisible fit where things are blended together, to see mixed reality as consisting of discrete elements between which users alternate. The issue is to design the boundaries to allow alternation but preclude improper mixture. This study contributes a better understanding of how to design such boundaries in situations with very limited "lifetimes" [8].

Enabling interaction in temporally restricted situations is an emergent issue when mobile technologies become embedded into "truly mobile" use contexts where people interact with objects and co-located people as they move [9, 10].

2 Related Work

This paper is related to research in the area of *proximity based games, augmented reality* and *tangible interfaces*. A number of academic research projects make use of proximity between players as a resource in a computer generated game, e.g. Treasure [11], Pirates! [12], PacMan Must Die and Earth Defenders [13]. This possibility is also exploited by the industry, e.g. the commercially available Botfighters from It's Alive [14]. These games are played via the interface of a mobile device using traditional graphical user interfaces, with buttons and stylus as interaction mechanisms. Thus, the players have to choose between looking at their surroundings and engaging in the game. "Can you see me now?" and Bystander [15] are mixed reality games where online participants compete or collaborate with mobile participants on the street. Both games are played via a traditional screen-based GUI. The participants can also collaborate by communicating via a real-time audio channel while moving through the city streets. In this way the participants themselves have the means to co-focus on the game and the physical world.

There are several projects that propose the use of augmented reality (AR) to enhance existing games [16]. Augmented reality is generally defined as "any mixture of real and virtual environments", but often specifically refers to "see through" displays [17]. ARQuake [18] and Human Pacman [19] are examples that allow the user to walk around within an outdoor game-space. ARQuake seeks to map the traditional game Quake onto a physical arena. Human Pacman integrated fantasy features of traditional computer entertainment with physical and social aspects. The games superimpose graphics directly upon the real world using a see-through head-mounted display. The accuracy of the overlaying is a critical problem [20]. Calibration errors and lags in the system easily contribute to a mismatch between the two worlds, especially when the viewpoint or the object is moving. This problem would be even more apparent in a dynamic and mobile situation such as travelling in a car, and especially in an application where both the viewpoint and the object are moving in relation to each other. Furthermore, a user study of the Human Pacman system revealed that a majority of the players found the system too bulky and cumbersome.

Tangible User Interfaces (TUI) allow more embodied interaction with the computer. Ping Pong Plus was designed by Hiroshi Ishii et al already in 1999 as a form of "digitally-augmented cooperative play." Table tennis has been augmented with an interactive surface, which incorporates sensing, sound and projection technologies. The players can focus either on real objects, such as the ball, or look at the augmented effects when it hits the table [21]. There are a number of projects exploring the field of tangible interfaces and games [22, 23, 24]. However, these games are stationary, and are dependent on a pre-set infrastructure, such as projectors or tabletops.

3 The Road Rager

The game is developed for a PDA equipped with WLAN capability. Gaming activity is accomplished through peer-to-peer wireless ad hoc networking, allowing connection between the devices without any further infrastructure. It is aware of the player's aiming direction by means of a digital compass, and the geographical position through a GPS-receiver. A Basic stamp II microcontroller controls LEDs and external buttons on the tangible interface (figure 1).

Fig. 1. Clutcher, PDA and Bluetooth GPS

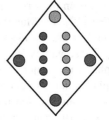

Fig. 2. LEDs on top of Clutcher

The devices automatically initiate a game-event when two players are in close proximity, i.e. within approximately 100 to 200 meters of each other, depending on the surrounding environment. When the game begins the player takes on the role of a character with magic powers. The player's goal is to acquire power in preparation for the yearly witchcraft convention. Power is measured in stars and frogs, which are gained or lost when duelling with other players. A duel is automatically launched when two players are within wireless range. The event ends when one player becomes enchanted, or if they move out of range. If a player charms her opponent, the objects she possesses are traded for more powerful ones, e.g. frogs are exchanged for stars. If the connection is broken they receive stars or frogs dependent on their results up to that point.

It is important to account for traffic safety when designing a game for use in a moving vehicle. This game is therefore intended for passengers in the back seat who are not engaged in the manoeuvring of the car. Still, the game could affect driving if badly designed. Therefore, we have tried to minimize the player's urge to request assistance of the driver. More specifically, there is no support in the game for predicting or making the traffic encounter happen more frequently by changed travel routes or driving styles. Further, it is essential that the player should feel comfortable with the embodied interaction provided by the game, even though they are buckled-up and remain so. However, the discussion in this particular paper is concerned with how the players experience the game per se.

3.1 Game Interaction

The concept depends on the players' possibilities to look out the windows of the car, and spot the opponents, in conjunction with playing a computer game. Since the time for interaction is limited, these activities have to be tightly integrated. Therefore, we chose a tangible interface. The assumption is that the players can concentrate on spotting each other and act instantly without withdrawing their visual attention from the traffic.

The tangible interface, called the *Clutcher*, is equipped with fourteen LEDs and a button. Four of the LEDs, hereafter referred to as "locator LEDs", are placed in each corner (figure 2) to inform the player of the direction of the opponent. Ten smaller LEDs are placed in two rows. They are sequentially turned on and off to indicate the amount of magic power the player possesses. One of the rows indicates the player's own power and the other that of the opponent. The button is for changing virtual tools (see section 3.2).

We have chosen to use the screen of a PDA as an interface to provide additional information to further stimulate the imagination of the player, and to provide the player with feedback on the results of the duels. The information is not critical for the gameplay during an encounter, but is intended to be observed and experienced in between game-events.

3.2 Balancing the Focus of Attention Through Design

The Road Rager concept is specifically designed to enable what we refer to as a *blended* focus of attention. Blended attention occurs when the players engage in gameplay and interact with the computer in various ways, e.g. to make gestures or listen to sounds, at the same time as they are looking out of the windscreen. We have provided for blended attention through the specific design of the user interface as well as the choice of game characteristics such as tasks and the rewards for fulfilling them.

According to Trevisan, Gemo et al [7] designers can influence what users look at and interact with by controlling attention through the design of the synchronization and integration of the user interface. Synchronisation refers to the ways in which an event controlled by the system is temporally unfolded. The system can present media, demand input or request a task either simultaneously or in a sequence. Integration refers to choices of what types of interaction will occur, e.g. how the user will receive feedback and how the media are distributed to output devices. Furthermore, integration refers to where the media is presented vis-a-vis the user's attention, i.e. in the central or peripheral context of the focus of attention.

The users' attention can also be influenced through the design of game characteristics such as the way the game is *explored* or how it should be *manipulated* [25]. Exploration refers to the players' experience of moving and travelling within the game. In this case, the players' view from the windscreen becomes integrated with that experience, and especially the ways in which they look at surrounding vehicles to *identify* contestants. Manipulation refers to tasks provided in the game, where players actively change the state of "*temporal, spatial, causal and functional relations and properties.*" According to Eskelinen, a game can do without interesting narratives or other forms of exploration, but it must always have manipulative challenges to be a game. Finally, a specific focus of attention can be afforded by the reward structure in a game.

Three tools (the *Magic Wand*, the *Sludge Thrower* and the *Electro Squeezer)* were designed, which in various ways combine user interfaces, tasks and rewards, in order to investigate the possibilities of enabling and experiencing blended attention.

Fig. 3. Casting spells   **Fig. 4.** Throwing sludge   **Fig. 5.** Triggering electric shocks

The *Magic Wand* (figure 3) strongly requires that the player be engaged in blended attention to be successful. The player has one chance to cast a spell, while very close to the opponent, to get a high score. Therefore the player needs to know exactly who she is contending with. The identification is made possible by the "locator LEDs" on the Clutcher (see figure 1), which give clues as to the direction of the opponent. When the adversary is located, i.e. when she has decided who in that direction she is contesting with, the player visually focuses on that car and makes the gesture when they are very close. It is the most rewarding of the tools if the player identifies the opponent and waits until they are close, which is approximately 20 meters, to cast the spell, to further favour visual identification. If the spell is cast directly after peer connection the gain is only minimal.

The tool affords a sequential order of tasks to be successful. The player must first identify the opponent and then wait until the other car is really close before engaging in manipulation. The user interface is designed to allow a visual focus on the traffic both during identification and manipulation. The player can simultaneously look at traffic and the LEDs on Clutcher as a form of sight, when trying to identify the opponent. The player can continue to look at traffic, while making gestures in a circular pattern to cast a spell, when engaging in game manipulation. Further, sounds are played while the Clutcher is moved, and when the spell is properly cast.

The *Electro Squeezer* is designed with minimal demands on the player to blend attention, and identify the opponent, in order to be successful (figure 5). It only requires that she recognize that a contestant is within wireless range, which is conveyed by a specific sound, before starting to manipulate. There are no limits as to how many times the player can score but the rewards are small. It sends out fictive electric shocks and plays a specific sound if the Clutcher is squeezed. Thus, there are no demands for either simultaneous or sequential ordering of tasks.

The *Sludge Thrower* (figure 4) is designed to require interaction with traffic to a degree somewhere in between that of the previous tools. It enables the player to throw virtual sludge at the opponent and score points if it hits. Similarly to the Magic Wand, the process requires that identification and manipulation be carried out sequentially. The design to support identification is also the same. However, the tools have different manipulative tasks. The Sludge Thrower only requires that the Clutcher be aimed towards the contestant to be successful. Further, the integration of modes of interaction is similar to that of the Magic Wand. The player can throw magic sludge, in the same way as if throwing a smaller real object, to score points. The gesture recognition registers when the player moves the Clutcher forward and downward. The player will hear a sound indicating that something is flying through the air for approximately two seconds and then a sound indicating hit or miss. This interaction could be done simultaneously with looking out of the windows. There are no limits as to how many times the player can score.

4 Method and Setting

Road Rager is intended for chance encounters on the road against unacquainted players. These meetings may take place anywhere along the road network. However, in order to ensure encounters with other players as well as to be able to observe the gameplay, the field trial was restricted to a preset circular route where the subjects used the prototype during a limited period of time. Each lap took about ten minutes. Fourteen children tested the game. Half of them were eight years old and half of them were ten years old. The two age groups played the game separately for approximately thirty minutes. Three cars drove simultaneously along the route with two to three children in each car. Each vehicle was equipped with a game device and the children within a car took turns playing the game. Before the test, all the participants received an explanation of the game and practiced the techniques of the tools. One or two researchers, sitting in the front seats, rode along in the car during the test. This set-up created a number of events where the Road Rager concept was experienced.

The activities were video recorded, and a loosely structured interview was carried out after the gameplay, in order to pursue an analysis of the test subjects' visible behaviors and to increase our understanding of their experiences. Video recorders are increasingly used to collect data during HCI evaluations [26]. However, as of yet there are no common standards for transcribing video recordings similar to the code schemes in conversation analysis [27]. Consequently, we have developed a coding scheme that accounts for the details of the children's activities of relevance for this study. Unfortunately, because of certain technical problems, the test cases turn out to be fewer than originally intended, which resulted in recorded material from a total of seven players. These video recordings have been transcribed and coded. We studied facial expressions, general appearance, visual focus of attention, handling of device and spontaneous comments during the game session. Careful analysis of visible behavior increases the possibility of understanding their appreciation and skills.

The test situation was unrealistic in certain ways. The children encountered the same cars several times since the route was circled during the test session. The children soon learnt what they where searching for, which otherwise would be unlikely. However, it also made it possible for us to study the difference in gameplay between acquainted and unacquainted encounters. The game is constructed to promote different strategies. This is hard to test during such a short period of time, and would instead require that the players played the game for an extended period of time. The same applies when studying the experience and fun of the gameplay in the long run. Regardless, this test provides input of importance for future design both concerning the experience of the gameplay and the design of user interfaces for short lived mixed reality applications.

5 Analysis

We are concerned with how players direct their attention between the visually available traffic situation and the device, in actual gaming, as well as how the gameplay is experienced. First, we will analyse how the focus of attention is pursued for each of the tools. Second, we will analyse the focus of attention during other phases of gaming, such as when the player are out of wireless range and during peer connect. The players' comments in the excerpt and the interviews are translated from Swedish.

By player we mean the child who is in control of the Clutcher, and by partner we mean another child riding in the back seat of the same car. The opponent is the child participating in the test who is riding in an encountered car. Finally, a game-event is defined as the period during which two devices are connected during a meeting.

5.1 Differences Between Tools

The way the players directed their attention varied between the three tools. For each tool we have structured the material accordingly. First, we discuss whether the players understood how the tool was supposed to be used. Second, we analyse the players' focus of attention during gameplay. Finally, we present the players' experience of using the tool.

Casting magic spells. The Magic Wand is designed to require a high degree of visual focus on traffic, in conjunction with a focus on the computer interface. It was difficult for the players to meet these demands as discussed with reference to the following two excerpts:

Table 1. (P=player, F=partner, R=Researcher)

Time	Sound	Hand movement	Visual focus	Comments
10:22	Magic Wand		F looks out P looks at device	
10:26	Connect		F looks out P looks at device	P: aaa
10:27		P lifts the device	P looks out F looks at device	F: aaa
10:28		P moves the Clutcher in a circle	P and F look out through the windscreen	
10:29	Spell			
10:30		F points at a passing car they meet in opposite lane	P looks down at the screen. F looks out through the left window. P quickly glances at F's hand then back to screen	F: there!
10:31			P and F look at screen	P: where?

In the excerpt above the player already has the Magic Wand activated when the game-event begins (10:26). Both the player and the partner quickly look down at the screen when they hear the connect sound. They both look out through the windscreen and the player immediately makes the gesture to cast a spell (10:28). Then he directly focuses on the screen. Not even his partner's pointing towards the opponent drags his attention away from the computer (10:30). He seems confused, which is further supported by his comment "where?" while he is looking at the display and refuses to look where his partner is pointing. Thus, the player casts the spell almost immediately after the connection sound is heard with very limited attempts to identify the opponent. He doesn't perform the tasks of identification and manipulation in a sequence as intended in the design, but rather almost juxtaposes them. However, during manipulation the player simultaneously maintains visual focus out through the windscreen while interacting with the computer, i.e. listening to the audio feedback and interacting with gestures. Thus, here the player blends his focus of attention.

Table 2. (P=player, F1 and F2 =partners , R=Researcher)

Time	Sound	Hand movement	Visual focus	Comments
05:51	Connect		P looks at PDA screen	
05:52	Spell + hit	P moves the Clutcher in a circle	P looks at the PDA screen	P: help!
05:55			F1 looks down at the PDA screen	F2: was it someone who hit us?
05:58	Electro Squeezer hit		P and F1 look at the PDA screen	F1: try and take this one

The excerpt in table 2 presents another type of gameplay when the Magic Wand is used. The player has the tool activated before they come into wireless range, as in the previous example. When the connect sound is heard (05:51) the player looks at the screen on the PDA and immediately makes the gesture to cast a spell (05:52). As in the previous case, the player goes straight into manipulation, casting the spell immediately after the connection sound is heard. They display limited attempts to identify the opponent and no delay for the cars to come close enough to get a high score. Then both the player and the partner look at the PDA screen (05:55). One of the partners asks whether they got hit (05.55) and they then get into a discussion on what tool to use next (05.58). However, in contrast to the other case, the player pays no visual attention to the traffic when engaged in manipulation, and solely focuses on the computer screen. Thus the player displays what we term *device centric attention*. This type of gaming did not fit with our intention to require visual focus on the traffic.

There could be several explanations to the juxtaposition of identification and manipulation as well the device centric attention. It seems like the players understood the concept of the wand in general and how it depended on identifying the opponent and delaying the casting of the spell until they were really close. This general understanding of the concept is visible in other parts of the field test. On one occasion a partner says: "I think we see them ... be prepared...I think we should take the Sludge Thrower, it has better distance than the Magic Wand." Thus, we need to look at other possible explanations. The demand for interaction could be set too high given the brief duration of gameplay. Or they could just have become too excited to wait until the contestant was identified and was close enough. However, the concept of a Magic Wand cannot be ruled out altogether since its proper use is difficult to evaluate during such a short field test.

It is not surprising that the players commented in the interviews that they did not like the Magic Wand. Some children had thought that the Magic Wand was going to be the most fun and useful tool before the test. Erik said they had thought the wand would be the best tool "...because you died immediately." However, they soon changed their minds because, as Bill says, "...it didn't turn out that way. You earned more by choosing a less effective tool."

Throwing sludge. The Sludge Thrower provides information on the direction to the opponent and requires that a gesture be made in that direction to be successful. Thus, it provides valuable information on where to look for the adversary, but does not require that they know exactly where in that direction the car is in order to score.

The majority of the children quickly got the idea of how to handle the Sludge Thrower. Most of them practiced throwing sludge when there were no opponents around. There were two ways of using of the tool where the players balanced their focus of attention in different ways. First we will look at gameplay where the player successfully engages in interaction with blended attention.

Table 3. (P=player, F=partner, R=Researcher)

Time	Sound	Hand movement	Visual focus	Comments
23:17	Connect		P and F look at the screen	F: now
23:22		P casts an unsuccessful magic spell	P looks at the screen. F looks out thought the windows and searches actively for opponent.	F: I think they are behind us
23:25		P casts a magic spell	P first looks at the LEDs and then glances out through the windows for a second	
23:27	Sludge Throwe r	P changes tool to Sludge Thrower, F points towards the left side-window	P looks at the screen, F looks out thought the windows and searches actively for the opponent.	F: wait! here ...
23:31		P holds up the Clutcher aims towards the left side-window	P first looks at the LEDs and then out through the windows for the opponent	
23:34	sludge + miss	P throws sludge	P looks at the LEDs and then out again	
23:36		F points towards a blue car parked in the opposite lane		F: there was Troll-pelle!
23:37	sludge	P throws sludge in direction F is pointing	P and F look in the direction toward the opponent.	
23:39	Sludge-hit		P and F look down at the screen.	P: yes! R: did you get him? P: yes I got him!

During the game-event the player changes tool to the Sludge Thrower (23:27) He holds up the Clutcher towards the windscreen. He looks at the LEDs and then out in the direction designated (23:31). After another quick glance at the LEDs he throws sludge in the indicated direction (23:34). He looks out in that direction as the device plays a sound indicating that it is flying through the air. Thus, identification and manipulation are smoothly performed in sequence two times. Furthermore, the player holds the Clutcher in his line of sight. The player shifts visual focus between it and the traffic. This could be considered blended attention where traffic is in visual focus.

The excerpt in table 1 also displays a collaborative approach to blended attention. The partner is actively searching for the opponent (23:27). He identifies a suspected car and points it out to the player (23:36). The player then throws sludge in that direction (23:39). Thus, the partner makes the identification for the player.

There was also a type of Sludge Thrower use in which visual attention was solely on screen, like that previously discussed. We will, in the following, discuss such a case, even though detailed transcriptions have been excluded for brevity. In this case, both the player and the partner look down at the screen on the PDA when the sound indicating peer connection is heard.

The player holds the Clutcher in her lap. She soon changes her visual focus to the LEDs and throws sludge in the direction indicated by the green light. They meet the opponent driving in the opposite direction and the locator LEDs switch in response and indicate that the adversary is now located behind them. They observe the locator LEDs and turn the Clutcher backwards so that the green LED lights up. Once more she makes a gesture to throw sludge with her eyes steady on the Clutcher. Neither the player, nor the partner, even once look out through the windows during this game-event, but identify the direction to the opponent player simply by looking at the locator LEDs. Still, as in the previous case, their interaction follows a sequence of identification and then manipulation.

To sum up, the Sludge Thrower was both used in a way where the players blended their attention and in way with *device centric attention*. This was similar to the way the Magic Wand was used. However, the Sludge Thrower provided a more interesting gaming experience than the Magic Wand, since the gameplay was often successful and conducted sequentially between identification and manipulation in the way that was intended in the design of this tool. The Sludge Thrower also provided a better experience according to the interviews. Several of the players thought that the Sludge Thrower was the most fun tool to use, even though it was considered somewhat difficult. A player said: "I think the Sludge Thrower is easiest to shoot with…but it is harder to hit with it". Another player preferred the gesture per se.

We suggest that the difference in success and experience between the Sludge Thrower and the Magic Wand can be understood with reference to the classical semiotic notion of indexical and symbolic signs. The gesture in the Sludge Thrower, i.e. the required movement of the Clutcher forward and downward, can be interpreted as an indexical sign [28], in the sense that it gets its meaning from the local context. Throwing implies that something in the context gets something thrown at it. In this case, the availability of an adversary in the direction of the gesture supports an interpretation of the gesture as a throw. The spell, on the other hand, is a symbolic sign, which means that it gets its meaning from a social convention. In brief interaction, such as in a traffic encounter, the indexical throw gesture is more intuitive and easier to understand than the more abstract gesture of a circle referring to a spell. When time is brief, and players are excited, it is possible that this minimal difference is of importance.

Triggering electric shocks. The Electro Squeezer requires no visual attention on the traffic for successful scoring. The player only has to pay attention to the sound indicating that an opponent is within wireless range. Then he can directly start to score points by pressing the Clutcher. Consequently, all the children quickly understood the concept.

Again, we identified two types of focus of attention during gameplay. We will start by discussing the type of gaming where the players blend their focus of attention. For brevity, we do not provide the transcriptions.

Just before the event the player and partner discuss what tool to use. The connect sound is heard. They look at the screen and the player selects the Electro Squeezer. The partner says "Push! Squeeze! You don't have to aim." He looks out of the windows in search of an opponent, while holding up the Clutcher in the line of sight. The player squeezes the Clutcher while looking out. He suddenly says "there!" and then glances down on the PDA screen. He lifts his gaze and smiles, as he continues to squeeze the tool. Both the player and the partner looked at a car, in the opposite lane. The player keeps on squeezing while holding up the Clutcher, aiming it towards the passing car. The partner waves towards the car (see figure 6). In this event, the player engages in what we have referred to as blended attention even though it is not required to score, i.e. he looks out through the windows while simultaneously interacting with the computer.

Fig. 6. Blended attention

Fig. 7. Device centric attention

We also observed a type of gaming where the players' attention was centred on the devices. In the following event, the player and partner immediately look down at the screen as the connect sound is heard (see figure 7). The player holds the Clutcher in her lap and they both look at the LEDs, while she persistently squeezes the tool. After a while the player exclaims "aaa! there is only one left." The player observes the power LEDs, which present the scores in the current exchange, taking no notice of the surrounding traffic.

Thus, the players used the Electro Squeezer in the same two ways as when interacting with the previous tools. The difference is that in this case, the visual focus on traffic, as displayed by the boys above, was not required to score points. We suggest that it occurred since the players found the visual presence of the contestants interesting and fun. In the interviews, the boys discuss the experience of meeting someone physically in a multiplayer game. The best part of the game, according to them, was:

Bill: ...the feeling...
Erik: when you met someone...
Bill: ...you become sort of ... it gets exciting somehow

Some children preferred this tool because they didn't have to aim. The interviews reveal that they considered this to be especially good when something blocked their view of the opponent. Still, for other children this tool was not considered as fun as the Sludge Thrower, because it was only about squeezing.

5.2 Additional Game Interaction

The interaction discussed in the previous section covers events where players are engaged in multiplayer gaming. However, there are other parts of the Road Rager game, where the player does not interact with contestants. First, multiplayer gaming is preceded by a momentary boundary phase (peer discovery) occurring when two cars come within wireless range and the devices discover each other. Second, it is directly followed by a short phase where network contact is dropped (peer loss). Finally, Road Rager is in single player mode during a longer phase where the devices are out of wireless range and the player is waiting for the next game-event. In the following we will discuss how the players focussed their attention in these situations.

Peer discovery. The peer discovery phase, presented through a distinctive sound, is brief and marks the transition from single-player mode to multi-player mode. The sound was supposed to give the player a quick "non-visual" notification to facilitate the immediate possibility of searching for the opponent. All the children understood the significance of this sound. However, instead of looking out the windows or at the locator LEDs in order to locate the opponent, the children most often watched the screen immediately after the connection-sound was heard. This includes both the player and the partners in the car. There are two feedbacks available on the screen that could have been of interest for the players at this moment. First, the screen provides additional visual confirmation that an opponent is in the vicinity, i.e. that the devices are connected, namely a big red square with the text "[*name of the adversary character*] is in your vicinity". Second, it provides graphic information about the opponent's character, consisting of a picture, a name text and the items in his possession, i.e. stars and frogs.

Peer loss. Disconnection of the wireless network was also signalled with a distinctive sound. The result of the game-event was then presented on the screen. This information attracted their attention. All the children immediately looked down at the screen in order to view the result of the game-event. Here the gameplay unfolded in accordance with the design intention.

Out of wireless range. The game prototype provided no manipulative challenges when network connection was lost. Still, the children engaged in various related activities. First, they tried out and practiced the different tools available. They experimented with the gestures and listened to the sounds they generated. Second, they looked for contestants. The children maintained a visual focus out through the windows of the car, searching for opponents, during most of the time between the game-events. Interestingly, this search for opponents was also eagerly pursued by the players who mainly displayed device-centric attention during the game-events. This identification work was done by looking for cars with children inside or for colours they thought the opponents' cars had. Looking for cars with specific colours was an activity appreciated by the children and was animatedly discussed. It was also something that was mentioned as a possible improvement during the interviews. A map was suggested where they would be able to see where the other car was and its colour.

Third, some players used the Clutcher to "scan" their surrounding by holding it up and sweeping it back and forth, treating it as a kind of "directional radar" able to sense the proximity of opponents. Additionally, if the player occasionally forgot to perform this activity some partners commented on it as being necessary in order to discover the opponents. This was something that the children themselves had come up with, and it indicates that they conceived of there being a fictitious connection between the game and the surrounding physical world. Finally, they settled on the tool to use in the next encounter.

6 Discussion

Our user study provides initial feedback on how to design for interaction when the boundaries in a mixed reality world are very short-lived and when people move quickly around. The study is a starting point for understanding the possibilities of designing for this context as well as the requirements for doing so.

The interviews and the observations of the players during gameplay made it clear that these temporary encounters created a thrilling gaming experience, even for the partners in the cars. Several children mentioned that the feeling when someone was in the vicinity, and the search for the opponent, was fun and thrilling.

We have gained insights into how the users balanced their focus of attention between the traffic and the gaming device. We identified a type of gaming, which was observable in the use of all the three tools, where the visual focus of attention was directed solely towards the screen or the tangible interface, and never out towards traffic. This was a successful form of interaction, in terms of scoring, for the Sludge Thrower and the Electro Squeezer, but a failure when using the Magic Wand. Thus, for those tools, where identification was not necessary, the players occasionally did not engage with the traffic, and even when it was required they still did not do so. In that sense, it was also a failure for the design intention to require players to identify the opponent and thus engage in looking at the traffic in those situations. On the other hand, both the Sludge Thrower and the Electro Squeezer were also used in a way where the players blended their visual focus of attention on traffic with engagement with the computer.

The Magic Wand provided for a sequential unfolding of the tasks of identification and manipulation, which was not applied by the players. Instead they went straight into manipulation as soon as the connection sound was heard. Perhaps the pressing situation in those brief encounters pushed the player to go directly to action. We cannot conclude that demands for sequential unfolding of tasks should be completely ruled out in future designs. In game design, the easiest solution is not always the best. However, it is clear that this type of sequence of tasks, which requires a delay for more exact positioning, should not be a general design principle. Further, the Magic Wand, which was designed to require identification, and thus visual focus on traffic, generated the least amount of attention out of the windows. Possibly, this tool is too complex and demanding for the limited time available for gameplay in such brief encounters.

The Sludge Thrower provides a both fun and imaginative experience, and we observed frequent occurrences of blended attention. Here, the sequential unfolding of tasks was smoother. Even though it is only slightly different than the Magic Wand, the difference seems to be crucial. First, the Sludge Thrower requires weaker positioning and gives the players many chances to score. Second, the Sludge Thrower recognised an indexical gesture while the Magic Wand recognised a symbolic gesture with a more abstract meaning. Thus, the Sludge Thrower provided a tighter blend in the manipulation, but was more forgiving in terms of identification.

When using the Electro Squeezer the focus of attention was very much on the surrounding traffic, although it wasn't required to score points. Still the players enjoyed it. We suggest that the experience of being able to see the contestant makes a very simple gameplay more exciting. Thus, the success of the Electro Squeezer supports the general design concept of drawing on meetings to make a game which is both comprehensive and challenging in an interesting way.

In general, it is difficult to enable gameplay when the lifetime of the game-event was so short. There is just too little time to engage in extensive identification before getting into manipulation. There is, of course, a possibility of developing other means to enable strong identification in future research. See-through displays are one alternative, or the use of interfaces on the device in the other car. The remote device could in some way announce that a player was sitting in a particular car.

However, our study also showed that the weak approach to identification was appealing to the children. On several occasions, the players successfully blended their visual orientation on traffic, with a focus on the computer interface. And they enjoyed identifying who they were playing against, even though it wasn't necessary for scoring. Weak identification, in this sense, adds to the exploration of the game landscape.

Furthermore, indexical gestures, such as throwing, make interaction more intuitive. Other examples for future design could be scooping, patting or hugging. These gestures are less complex than esoteric symbolic gestures of various kinds.

Finally, the users on many occasions looked at the screen for additional information than the audio feedback e.g. directly following peer discovery. Although, we thought of the graphical information as rudimentary, and not interesting in itself, it got lots of attention. In future research, it would be interesting to study whether a user interface with even less graphical information would engender more blended interaction.

To sum up, minimalism is critical for success when designing for brief lifetime in mixed reality applications. The features and tasks of the game have to be cut down to the minimum. Even such a meagre task as supported by the Magic Wand was too complicated. Of course, games should not be designed to be easy, but to provide interesting challenges. However, in this case, the challenges of the use context themselves are so difficult that the designer as a first priority should focus on making the concepts achievable. Then, social situations such as traffic encounters, could become new use contexts for mobile multiplayer games.

7 Conclusions

We have in this paper been concerned with how to combine and balance a player's focus of attention between traffic and a computer, while at the same time providing a game which is comprehensive, interesting and challenging. It seems possible to exploit contingent traffic encounters to create a both compelling and fun game experience. We observed two types of gaming concerning focus of attention. First, a type where the players focused their visual attention solely on the gaming device. Second, a type where they blended their focus on the mobile devices with a visual focus of attention on the traffic.

The study also suggests that neither support nor rewards were needed for the players to maintain a visual focus of attention on the traffic. Instead a blended experience occurs very much because the players accept and like the imaginative activity that playing in the same space allows. Exploration of the physical game space was a highly popular activity, and the experience of seeing the contestant made a very simple gameplay exciting. Often the players enjoyed identifying who they were playing against, even though it wasn't necessary for scoring. Consequently, weak identification in the design added to the exploration of the game landscape.

The approach taken in this project is to establish a mixed reality by the use of tangible user interfaces rather than see-through displays. See-through displays strongly influence the user to see the world as a mixed reality, whereas the approach in Road Rager rather depends on the user actively engaging in the creation of such an experience. Therefore it is not so surprising that we find both a type of focus where people mix their attention between traffic and the computer's interfaces, as well as a form of attention where the users did not engage in creating this experience. Still, it is possible to argue, based on this study, that TUIs could be an alternative if used in contexts and for applications where players find it interesting enough to actively contribute in mixing realities. As discussed, the children often interacted with Road Rager in ways in which the traffic, with people and cars, and the mobile technology with its user faces, came to create a coherent reality.

In conclusion, this study suggests that the possibility of enabling interaction within such a temporally restricted mobile situation, and the positive experience shown by the users, motivates further research into support for interaction in brief encounters. We have specifically addressed short encounters where people sit in the back seats of cars. But it is possible to imagine other brief encounters where people quickly move in and out of range, e.g. public transportation, elevators, and ski lifts. Encounters in such circumstances could provide a specific experience if the design of the services accounts for this rather particular use context.

Acknowledgements

We would like to acknowledge the Swedish Foundation for Strategic Research, which funded this research through the Mobile Life research programme. We would also like to thank Mattias Östergren for the development of the MongerLib library. We would also like to thank Mattias Esbjörnsson, Daniel Normark and Alberto Frigo for helping us out at the field trial, and Barry Brown as well as anonymous reviewers for valuable comments. Finally we would like to thank Matthew Chalmers for shepherding this paper to its final state.

References

1. Appleyard, D., Lynch, K., et al.: The View from the Road. MIT press (1964)
2. Kuivakari, S.: Mobile Gaming: a Journey Back in Time. Computer Games & Digital Textualities, Copenhagen, Denmark (2001)
3. Brunnberg, L., and Juhlin, O.: Movement and Spatiality in a Gaming Situation - Boosting Mobile Computer Games with the Highway Experience. Proceedings of Interact'2003, - IFIP TC 13 International Conference on Human-Computer Interaction, Zürich Switzerland, IOS Press (2003) 407-414
4. Juhlin, O.: Traffic Behaviour as Social Interaction – Implications for the Design of Artificial Drivers. In Glimell and Juhlin (eds.), Social Production of Technology: On everyday life with things, BAS Publisher, Göteborg, Sweden (2001)
5. Brunnberg, L: The Road Rager - Making Use of Traffic Encounters in a Mobile Multiplayer Game. Proceedings of MUM'04, Conference on Mobile and Ubiquitous Multimedia, College Park U.S.A, ACM Press (2004) 33 - 40
6. Ishii, H. and Ullmer, B.: Tangible Bits: Towards Seamless Interfaces between People, Bits and Atoms. Proceedings of CHI'97, Conference on Human factors in computing systems, Atlanta, USA (1997) 234-241
7. Trevisan, D. G., Gemo, M., et al.: Focus-Based Design of Mixed Reality Systems. Proceedings of the 3rd annual conference on Task models and diagrams, Prague, Czech Republic (2004) 59-66
8. Koleva, B., Benford S. and Greenhalgh, C.: The Properties of Mixed Reality Boundaries. Proceedings of the Sixth European Conference on Computer-Supported Cooperative Work, Copenhagen, Denmark (1999) 119-137
9. Sherry, J. and Salvador, T.: Running and Grimacing: the Struggle for Balance in Mobile Work. B. Brown, N. Green and R. Harper (eds.) Wireless World: Social Interactional Aspects of the Mobile Age, Springer Verlag (2002) 108-120
10. Juhlin, O. and Östergren, M. Time to Meet Face to Face and Screen to Screen. Forthcoming in Traffic Encounters, (Diss.) (2006)
11. Barkhuus, L., Chalmers, M. et al.: Picking Pockets on the Lawn: The Development of Tactics and Strategies in a Mobile Game. Proceedings Ubicomp'05 - The Seventh International Conference on Ubiquitous Computing, Tokyo, LNCS 3660 (2005) 358-374
12. Björk, S., Falk, J. et al.: Pirates! - Using the Physical World as a Game Board, Proceedings of Interact'2001, Conference on Human-Computer Interaction, Tokyo, Japan (2001) 423-430
13. Sanneblad, J. and Holmquist, L.E.: Designing Collaborative Games on Handheld Computers. Proceedings of SIGGRAPH'03 Sketches & applications, International Conference on Computer Graphics and Interactive Techniques, San Diego USA (2003)
14. Botfighters. http://www.botfighters.com/ Last visited Sept. 30 (2005)
15. Flintham, M., Benford, B., et al.: Where On-line Meets On-The-Streets: Experiences with Mobile Mixed Reality Games. Proceedings of CHI'03, Conference on Human factors in computing systems, Ft. Lauderdale, Florida, USA (2003) 569 - 576
16. Nilsen, T., Linton, S. and Looser, J.: Motivations for Augmented Reality Gaming. New Zealand Game Developers Conference NZGDC'04, Dunedin, New Zealand (2004)
17. Milgram, P. and Colquhoun, H.: A Taxonomy of Real and Virtual Worlds Display Integration in Mixed Reality-Merging Real and Virtual Worlds. Berlin:Springer Verlag (1999) 1-16
18. Thomas, B., Close, B., et al.: ARQuake: An Outdoor/Indoor Augmented Reality First Person Application. In 4th Int'l Symposium on Wearable Computers, Atlanta, Ga, (2000) 139

19. Cheok, A.D., Fong, S.W., et al.: Human Pacman: A Mobile Entertainment System with Ubiquitous Computing and Tangible Interaction over a Wide Outdoor Area. Proceedings of Mobile HCI'03 - the 5th International Symposium on Human-Computer Interaction with Mobile Devices and Services, Udine, Italy, Springer Verlag (2003) 209 - 223

20. Azuma, R.T.: A Survey of Augmented Reality. Presence: Teleoperators and Virtual Environments 6, 4 August (1997) 355 – 385

21. Ishii, H., Wisneski, C., et al.: PingPongPlus: Design of an Athletic-Tangible Interface for Computer-Supported Cooperative Play. Proceedings of CHI'99, Conference on Human factors in computing systems, Pittsburgh, Pennsylvania, USA (1999) 394- 401

22. Mueller, F., Agamanolis, S. and Picard, R.: Exertion Interfaces: Sports Over a Distance for Social Bonding and Fun. Proceedings of CHI'03, Conference on Human factors in computing systems Ft. Lauderdale, Florida, USA (2003) 561-568

23. Magerkurth, C., Memisoglu, M. and Engelke, T.: Towards the Next Generation of Tabletop Gaming Experiences. Proceedings of GI'04, Conference on Graphics Interface, London, Ont., Canada (2004) 73-80

24. Mandryk, R.L., Maranan, D. S. and Inkpen, K. M.: False Prophets: Exploring Hybrid Board/Video Games. In Extended Abstracts of CHI'02, Conference on Human Factors in Computing Systems, Minneapolis, Minnesota USA (2002) 640-641

25. Eskelinen, M.: The Gaming Situation. In Game Studies – The International Journal of Computer Game Research, Issue 1 (2001)

26. Hindmarsh, J., Heath, C., et al.: Creating Assemblies: Aboard the Ghost Ship. Proceedings of CSCW, Conference on Computer Supported Cooperative Work, New Orleans, USA (2002) 156-165

27. Heath, C. and Hindmarsh, J.: Analysing Interaction: Video, Ethnography and Situated Conduct. In May, T. (ed.) Qualitative Research in Action, London, Sage (2002) 99-121

28. Fiske, J.: Kommunikationsteorier – En introduktion, Stockholm, Wahlström & Widstrand, (1982)

Unobtrusive Multimodal Biometrics for Ensuring Privacy and Information Security with Personal Devices

Elena Vildjiounaite, Satu-Marja Mäkelä, Mikko Lindholm, Reima Riihimäki,
Vesa Kyllönen, Jani Mäntyjärvi, and Heikki Ailisto

Technical Research Centre of Finland,
Kaitoväylä 1, Oulu, Finland
{FirstName.LastName}@vtt.fi
http://www.vtt.fi

Abstract. The need for authenticating users of ubiquitous mobile devices is becoming ever more critical with the increasing value of information stored in the
devices and of services accessed via them. Passwords and conventional biometrics such as fingerprint recognition offer fairly reliable solutions to this problem, but these methods require explicit user authentication and are used mainly
when a mobile device is being switched on. Furthermore, conventional biometrics are sometimes perceived as privacy threats. This paper presents an unobtrusive method of user authentication for mobile devices in the form of recognition
of the walking style (gait) and voice of the user while carrying and using the
device. While speaker recognition in noisy conditions performs poorly, combined speaker and accelerometer-based gait recognition performs significantly
better. In tentative tests with 31 users the Equal Error Rate varied between 2%
and 12% depending on noise conditions, typically less than half of the Equal
Error Rates of individual modalities.

1 Introduction

There are more than a billion users of mobile devices, mainly mobile phones, in the
world, and in that sense pervasive computing is here already. The security and privacy
issues related to ever-present mobile devices are becoming crucial, since not only the
devices themselves but the information stored in them (names and addresses, short
messages, images and future plans stored in a user calendar) has a significant monetary and personal value. Furthermore, the services which can be accessed via mobile
devices (e.g., emote transactions such as banking and m-commerce) represent a significant value. Thus, the risk of a mobile device ending up in the wrong hands presents a significant and unfortunately very common threat to information security and
user privacy. UK statistics, for example, show that "a mobile phone [is] stolen approximately every three minutes" [1]. Passwords, PIN codes or conventional biometrics such as fingerprint recognition could be used for user identification in mobile
devices, but the existing security mechanisms are seldom used [2]. The reasons are at
least twofold. First, both passwords and conventional biometrics require explicit user
action, which is annoying in frequent use. Second, some users perceive conventional

K.P. Fishkin et al. (Eds.): PERVASIVE 2006, LNCS 3968, pp. 187–201, 2006.

biometrics as a threat to their privacy. This may be a reflection of more general concerns related to the threats to civil liberties associated with biometrics [3].

Thus there is a clear need for an unobtrusive, implicit security mechanism for personal devices. This paper presents a novel method for creating such a mechanism by verifying the identity of the user of a portable device while he or she is walking and talking with it. User authentication by voice and walking style is very natural and unobtrusive, since users carry personal devices while moving from one place to another, and since many devices such as mobile phones and PDAs have an audio input.

Speaker recognition is a widely researched area with many commercial applications available. One latest tutorial on text-independent speaker verification can be found in [4]. Speaker recognition systems are difficult to compare, however, for many reasons; one of them is that methods are not tested on the same databases. The National Institute of Technology (NIST) has arranged annual text-independent speaker recognition evaluations since 1996 with a large database containing conversational telephone speech [5] and one of the top results shows the Equal Error Rate (EER, for a definition see Section 2) for different methods to be in the range 0.2 -0.7% [6]. The usability of systems, however, is limited due to the vulnerability of speech to the background noise which is present in real-life situations. Recent publications show that the performance of a baseline system deteriorates from EER = 0.7% on clean speech to EER = 28.08% in the presence of white noise with a Signal-to-Noise Ratio (SNR) of 0 dB [7], and that a Speaker Identification rate of 97.7 %, achieved under conditions of car noise with SNR 30 dB, can drop to 21% under conditions of SNR 5 dB [8]. Thus active research is going on how to increase noise robustness. This can be done on three levels: acoustic, parametric and modelling, i.e. a degraded speech signal can be enhanced, the features can be designed to be more robust for noise and pattern recognition can be noise robust [7-9]. The performance improvement achievable with noise-robust methods is in general greater when the noise conditions are worse. In reference [7] the use of a noise-robust method for 0 dB white noise reduced the EER from 28.08% to 11.68%, while for white noise of 18 dB, where the initial EER was 1.36%, the use of a noise-robust method improved the EER to 1.06%.

Video-based gait recognition has been studied for more than a decade [10-13] for the purpose of surveillance, e.g. recognising a criminal from a security camera video. Gait is known to differ between individuals and to be fairly stable [14], whereas deliberate imitation of another person's gait is difficult. The performance of gait biometrics is generally poorer than that of fingerprint biometrics, however, and the method is still in its infancy [15].

Although it is well-known that differences in walking styles between individuals present problems for accelerometer-based activity recognition [16], and that accelerometers can be used for detecting whether two mobile devices are being carried by the same person [17], accelerometer-based gait recognition has not been suggested for securing personal devices, their communication capability or the data contained in them. Instead, various other biometric modalities have been proposed and used for this purpose, including signature [18], voice [19-20] and fingerprints, which have been employed in a commercial PDA device [21]. All these approaches - except speaker recognition - require explicit actions for user authentication, e.g. the giving of a fingerprint or writing on a touch screen.

Apart from speaker recognition, face recognition could serve as unobtrusive form of user authentication. Face recognition systems do not work reliably under arbitrary lighting conditions, however, and often require user cooperation in positioning the face correctly with respect to the camera position. Moreover, frequent face recognition can be a threat to privacy (due to requirement for frequent image capturing), in a similar way to that described by Bohn et al. [22] with respect to video recording. A multimodal (face and voice) user identification system has been implemented on an iPAQ handheld computer [23] and has shown good performance with a database of 35 persons in a low-noise environment. The system performed face recognition under different lighting conditions, but was tested only on frontal images of people. Hazen et al. [23] acknowledge that rotation of faces presents additional challenges compared with recognition of frontal images, but they expect that users will cooperate with the system during the identification process and will generally be looking at the handheld computer screen while using it, which is not always the case with mobile phones.

We present a combination (fusion) of accelerometer-based gait recognition and speaker recognition as an unobtrusive and only marginally privacy-threatening means of verifying the identity of the user of a mobile device. Recognising users by gait is natural when they carry mobile devices with them while moving. Recognising a speaker is also natural when people talk to each other via a mobile device or in its close proximity. Since more and more mobile devices nowadays offer speech recognition functionality, people can also talk directly to their mobile devices and don't perceive speaker recognition as a major threat to their privacy. On the other hand, mobile devices are often used under very noisy conditions, where speaker recognition alone does not work reliably. Lee et al. found that the measured SNR inside a car can vary between plus 15 and minus 10 dB [24], and corresponding situations could be found in places where there was heavy traffic passing by or other machinery in the vicinity. Similarly, the performance of accelerometer-based gait recognition is insufficient (or not yet sufficient, since the method is very new) for serving as the main means of device protection. Performance of gait recognition depends on the position of accelerometer sensor. The first experiments with acceleration-based gait recognition have been presented in an earlier paper [25], where the users were carrying an accelerometer module at their waist, in the middle of their back. The EER achieved in these experiments with a correlation method was about 7%. Unfortunately, the performance of gait recognition decreases when users carry the accelerometer module in a more natural place, such as in a hip or breast pocket or in the hand.

While the performance of speaker recognition under noisy conditions and that of gait recognition is fairly low, the performance of combined recognition is significantly better. The fusion of two modalities in biometrics normally improves performance compared with each modality alone [26]. This depends on the fusion method used, however, and on the performance of each modality (if one of modalities is significantly worse than the other one, the performance of the multimodal system can be poorer than that of the better modality). Several top-choice fusion methods [27] usually show similar improvements in performance. Among these, we selected the Weighted Sum as being the simplest method and one that is suitable for mobile devices with limited computational power.

The two main contributions of this paper are 1) introducing the idea of using unobtrusive multimodal biometrics for ensuring the legitimacy of the user of smart personal objects such as mobile phones and suitcases, and 2) demonstrating the feasibility and performance of the method by means of experiments. Thorough investigation of acceleration sensor-based gait recognition methods, speaker recognition methods and fusion methods is beyond the scope of this paper.

The paper is organized as follows. The short overview of the system and the experiments, together with an introduction to the authentication and performance evaluation methods used, is presented in Section 2. The gait and speaker recognition methods are presented in Section 3, together with the fusion method. The experimental set-up is described in Section 4 and the recognition performance of the gait and voice modalities and the fusion performance are given in Section 5. The results are discussed in Section 6 and finally, the conclusions are made in Section 7.

2   Overview of the Unobtrusive User Authentication Method and Its Evaluation

Many personal mobile devices such as mobile phones have an audio input which can be used for speaker recognition. Acceleration sensors are fairly inexpensive, and embedding them into personal devices and smart artefacts has been proposed for the purpose of user activity recognition [28]. Thus asynchronous user verification from audio and accelerometer signals should be possible in a personal device. To evaluate the feasibility of the idea, we performed off-line experiments with 31 persons whose accelerometer signal was recorded while they were walking and carrying the accelerometer module in three positions, and whose speech samples were recorded and contaminated with different noises under three sets of SNR conditions. A summary of the method is presented in Figure 1.

User authentication in biometric applications is normally performed as follows: first, biometric data for training the system is collected, and the system is trained. After that the system is ready for user authentication, i.e. comparison of a new biometric sample (voice, gait or multimodal biometrics) with the stored model. If the similarity score exceeds the acceptance threshold set during the training phase, the user is accepted, otherwise the user is rejected. The case of a new biometric sample from user A being compared with a model for user A is called client access, and the case of a new sample from user A being compared with a model for user B is called impostor access. The system performance is evaluated in terms of two types of possible error, False Rejection Rate and False Acceptance Rate, calculated according to the formulae (1) and (2):

$$FRR = \frac{N\_reject\_clients}{N\_clients} \tag{1}$$

$$FAR = \frac{N\_accept\_imp}{N\_imp} \tag{2}$$

where $N\_clients$ is a total number of client accesses and $N\_reject\_clients$ is the number of rejected clients. Similar, N_imp is a total number of impostor accesses and N_accept_imp is the number of accepted impostors. A trade-off between these two

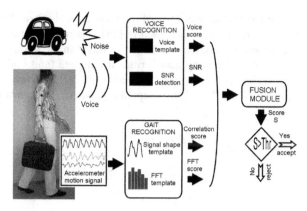

Fig. 1. Overview of the proposed method for unobtrusive authentication

types of error is achieved by varying the acceptance threshold, so that as error of one type decreases, error of the other type increases. Thus a common way of evaluating the performance of a biometric system is to estimate the point where FAR and FRR are approximately equal. This is called the Equal Error Rate (EER).

Since there are always variations in biometric samples taken on different days, one common practice in performance evaluation is to collect training data on one day, and data for testing some time later. Usually all test samples for users are compared with their own models (created from training data) to estimate the False Rejection Rate and with the models for all other users to estimate the False Acceptance Rate.

3   Methods for Unobtrusive Biometrics

3.1   Gait Recognition

Acceleration signal-based gait recognition is performed by processing the 3-D signal from the accelerometer module carried by the user. Training and test data for gait recognition were collected in two sessions at a one month interval (see Section 4).

The data for both the training and testing phases were first preprocessed, i.e. normalized to a range -1 and 1, low-pass filtered and decimated by a factor of 2 in order to reduce the number of samples. After that, we calculated two similarity scores by comparing the test data from the accelerometer module in a certain placement with the training data for the same placement: a correlation score and a FFT (Fast Fourier Transform) score. The two methods complement each other, as the correlation score represents the similarity between the shapes of the signals in the time domain while the FFT score represents the similarity in the frequency domain.

The correlation score was calculated by dividing the 3-D accelerometer signal into separate steps by searching for local minima and maxima in the acceleration data and calculating the mean points of a data block of four steps. Since the right and left steps were not symmetrical, they were treated separately as "a" steps and "b" steps, see Fig. 2. No attempt was made, however, to identify whether the "a" and "b" steps are right or left steps. The steps belonging to the same group were normalized in length and amplitude and then averaged over 60% of the most typical steps. (More details of the correlation-based recognition are provided in [25], where the method was applied to data from an accelerometer module carried at the waist, in the middle of the back). The averaged steps from the training data formed a template (gait code) comprising the shape of three accelerometer signals (vertical, right-left and forward-backward acceleration) for the "a_tr" and "b_tr" steps separately, where "tr" stands for training.

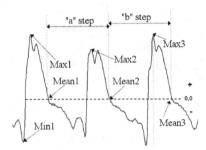

Fig. 2. The acceleration signal in a forward - backward direction, steps "a" and "b" are marked

Similarly, at the authentication phase, several averaged "a_test" and "b_test" steps from the test data are taken to form a test sample for comparison with the templates by cross correlation. The resulting similarity score is calculated according to formula (3), where C stands for correlation:

$$\text{Cor}=\text{Max}((C(\text{a\_tr, a\_test})+C(\text{b\_tr, b\_test})), (C(\text{a\_tr, b\_test})+C(\text{b\_tr, a\_test}))) \quad (3)$$

Since it is feasible to presume that different individual gait patterns would be distinguishable in the frequency domain, we used for the recognition of gait patterns also FFT coefficients, calculated in a 256-sample window with a 100 sample overlap. The 128 FFT coefficients of each training file were clustered with K-means algorithm into eight clusters. The FFT gait score for fusion was produced by finding the minimum distance of the test data FTT coefficients from the trained clusters.

3.2 Speaker Recognition

Our speech database contained five utterances from each speaker, each utterance being an eight-digit string. The first four utterances, acquired during the first data collection session, were used for training the speaker recognition system, and the fifth, acquired during the second data collection session, was used for testing. We used a very small amount of data for training the system because users are usually unwilling to invest effort in system training.

Speaker recognition was text-independent and was performed using the widely known MASV (Munich Automatic Speaker Verification) environment [29]. MASV uses a Gaussian Mixture Models (GMM) classifier and allows changes to be made in many of the input parameters, including the number of GMM components and the feature set based on Mel Frequency Cepstrum Coefficients (MFCC). The GMM in the verifier was used with 32 components and the feature vector contained 39 components (12 MFCCs and log energy together with their first and second derivatives). The world model was generated from a small subset of the training samples.

3.3 Fusion of Gait and Speaker Recognition Classifiers

The gait-based and voice-based similarity scores were fused by the Weighted Sum method, which is a very popular fusion method in multimodal biometrics [26-27] and has the advantage of being very fast and simple. The Weighted Sum method requires normalizing of the scores for each modality to the range [0, 1] and in our case combines the normalized scores according to the formula (4):

$$Score = Ws_K * S_{SPEECH} + Wg_{COR} * Sg_{COR} + Wg_{FFT} * Sg_{FFT} \qquad (4)$$

where S_{SPEECH}, Sg_{COR} and Sg_{FFT} are the similarity scores produced by speaker recognition and gait recognition by the correlation and FFT methods, respectively; and Ws_K, Wg_{COR} and Wg_{FFT} are the weights of these modalities. The weight denotes how much we trust in that modality, and the common way of assigning weights is according to the performances of the modalities, see formula (5) for our case.

Our experiments were carried out with the different types and levels of noise commonly used in speaker recognition research. The performance of speaker recognition differs significantly between low-noise and noisy environments, and it also depends on the type of noise. Since there are many kinds of noise in real life, it is not realistic to distinguish all of them in real applications. It is possible to estimate the Signal-to-Noise Ratio (SNR) of speech samples in various ways, however. One common way is to find the speech pauses with a VAD (voice activity detector) and use this information to estimate the SNR of the speech signal. Consequently, we had three sets of weights, one for each noise level: the first set of weights for clean speech and for four speech samples contaminated with low-level noise: car, city, white and pink noise with SNR 20dB, a second set for medium-noise speech samples (SNR 10 dB) and a third set for high-noise speech samples (0dB). In each set weights were calculated according to the formula (5):

$$Ws_K = \frac{EERg_{COR} + EERg_{FFT}}{EERs_K + EERg_{COR} + EERg_{FFT}}$$

$$Wg_{COR} = \frac{EERs_K + EERg_{FFT}}{EERs_K + EERg_{COR} + EERg_{FFT}} \qquad (5)$$

$$Wg_{FFT} = \frac{EERs_K + EERg_{COR}}{EERs_K + EERg_{COR} + EERg_{FFT}}$$

where Ws_K is the weight for the speaker recognition system at noise level K (K is either 20dB or 10dB or 0dB), Wg_{COR} and Wg_{FFT} are weights for gait recognition by the correlation and FFT methods, respectively, $EERs_K$ is the average EER for speech samples with noise level K and $EERg_{COR}$ and $EERg_{FFT}$ are Equal Error Rates for gait recognition by the correlation and FFT methods, respectively, averaged over three different positions of accelerometer module.

4 Experimental Set-Up

In order to evaluate the feasibility of the proposed unobtrusive method for verifying the users of personal devices, we collected voice samples and gait acceleration data from 31 test subjects (19 males and 12 females) in two sessions. Thus the tests were performed with both voice and gait samples belonging to the same real person.

4.1 Gait Modality Set-Up

Gait data was collected in the form of a three-dimensional acceleration signal from an accelerometer module carried by test subjects while walking. We collected two sets of data, training and test data, at a one month interval between sessions. During each session the subjects were asked to walk along the corridor (about 20 metres) at their normal walking speed and then the same distance "in a hurry" (at a fast walking speed), then after a short break, the same distance slowly with each of the three placements of the accelerometer module as shown in Figure 3.

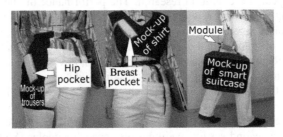

Fig. 3. Gait data collection: subjects carried the accelerometer module in their hip pocket, breast pocket and hand

The accelerometer attachment system was designed in such a way that the positioning of the module mimicked two common places where people often carry things: the breast pocket of a shirt and the hip pocket of trousers. A third common way to carry things is in the hand, and thus the third position of the accelerometer module included in our experiments was attached to a handle of a suitcase.

Since not all of our 31 test subjects had both chest and hip pockets in their clothes, we made mock-ups of "clothes with pockets" from pieces of cloth, which the subjects put on over their normal clothes (black pieces of cloth in Fig. 3) and fixed with strips of elastic. Consequently, the position of the pocket in which the user carried the accelerometer module (see white pieces of cloth in Fig. 3) was affected somewhat by shifting of these pieces of cloth. Although the accelerometer module was not moving freely inside the pocket itself, the shifting of the cloth led to some differences in its positioning during data collection in the training and test phases. We believe that this resembles real life situations in the sense that mobile devices are not firmly attached to people, but usually do not flap very much, either.

Data acquisition was performed using a three-dimensional accelerometer module (composed of two perpendicularly positioned Analog Devices ADXL202JQ accelerometers) and a laptop computer equipped with a National Instruments DAQ 1200 card. The accelerometer signals were recorded at a sampling frequency of 256 Hz, but the data were decimated by a factor of two after collection.

4.2 Voice Modality Set-Up

The speech samples were collected by computer in a quiet environment from the same people as for the gait data. Each speech sample was an eight-digit string. Each subject spoke the required four utterances (used as training data) in the first session and one utterance (used as test data) in the second session. The data for both sessions were collected in wave format at a sampling frequency of 8000 Hz. The speech samples were normalised and contaminated with white, pink, city and car noise at three SNR conditions, 20, 10 and 0 dB. The pink and white noise was artificially generated and the city and car noise samples were taken from the NTT-AT Ambient Noise Database [29].

5 Experimental Results

The system performance was evaluated in terms of Equal Error Rate; see Section 2 for the definition.

5.1 Performance of Gait Modality

The performance of gait recognition as assessed by the correlation and FFT methods separately is presented in Table 1. Gait recognition appeared to be highly dependent on the subject. First of all, as in biometrics generally, two users can have very similar biometric samples while others are easily distinguishable. Second, some persons show a fairly stable walking pattern (very similar signal shape and frequency at all three walking speeds) while for others a distinct speed difference was observed between the two sessions, due either to mood changes or to the fact that asking people to walk "normally" is rather artificial. Interestingly enough, we had one pregnant lady in our test group, and her walking pattern did not change much over the interval of one month despite a significant change in body weight. Some errors were caused by changes in shoes, but this was also person-dependent.

Table 1. Equal Error Rates of gait recognition by the correlation and FFT methods with different placements of accelerometer module

Method	Placement of accelerometer module		
	In hand	In breast pocket	In hip pocket
Correlation	17.2%	14.8%	14.1%
FFT	14.3%	13.7%	16.8%

5.2 Performance of Voice Modality at Different Noise Levels

Since the speaker recognition system was trained with a fairly small amount of data, its performance was not as good as the top results achieved in speaker recognition [6], although comparison with state-of-the-art experiments is difficult because the databases are different. In our tests the EER for clean speech was 2.93% and the performance under noisy conditions was as shown in Table 2.

Table 2. Equal Error Rate for speaker recognition under different noise conditions

SNR	Noise			
	Car	City	White	Pink
20 dB	3.12%	2.82%	21.18%	9.05%
10 dB	12.06%	2.92%	31.25%	25.82%
0 dB	27.75%	12.06%	41.61%	43.09%

5.3 Performance of Gait and Voice Fusion

The performance of the combined gait recognition and speaker recognition classifiers is presented in Table 3 and graphically in Figure 4.

Table 3. Equal Error Rate for fusion

Noise/ Device position	In hand	In breast pocket	In hip pocket
clean speech	2.83%	2.19%	2.83%
car noise 20dB	3.19%	2.83%	3.96%
city noise 20dB	2.15%	1.97%	2.25%
white noise 20dB	10.7%	11.8%	9.18%
pink noise 20dB	5.18%	4.38%	4.91%
car noise 10dB	6.08%	4.43%	4.91%
city noise 10dB	5.21%	3.87%	3.32%
white noise 10dB	9.58%	9.34%	9.76%
pink noise 10dB	8.91%	6.57%	8.63%
car noise 0dB	8.55%	8.44%	9.23%
city noise 0dB	5.94%	4.91%	6.93%
white noise 0dB	9.63%	9.90%	11.6%
pink noise 0dB	9.14%	10.6%	11.8%

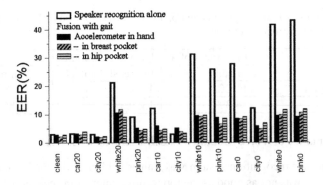

Fig. 4. Performance of the combined gait and speaker recognition classifiers at different noises by comparison with speaker recognition alone

6 Discussion

Since mobile devices currently provide only means for explicit user authentication, this authentication normally takes place once, when the device is being switched on, and after that the device will operate for a long time without protecting user privacy. If it is lost or stolen, a lot of private information (user calendar, address book, photos and financial data) can become available to an outsider. The networking capabilities of a mobile device can be also used freely until the owner discovers the loss of the device and finds a means to inform the network provider. In order to reduce the risks to the owner's security and privacy, mobile devices should check frequently and unobtrusively who is actually carrying and using them. Speaker recognition is well suited for this purpose but is difficult under noisy conditions. Since the risk of a mobile devices being stolen is highest in noisy environments (in city streets, on public transport or in shopping areas), the method for unobtrusive user authentication should work at high noise levels. Since people often move about on foot (at least for short distances) in places where the chances of losing a mobile device are high, a fusion of audio processing with such unobtrusive biometrics as gait recognition is a natural option for trying to protect personal devices in noisy environments.

It is envisaged that a multimodal biometric user verification system in a personal device would function as follows. When the device, such as a mobile phone, is first taken into use it would enter a *learning mode* for a suitable time period, say two days. During this time the system would not only form the voice and gait templates, but also analyze the stability of the behavioral biometrics with respect to the user in question. PIN code or password-based user authentication would be used during the learning period. If the stability of the gait and voice biometrics was adequate, the system would enter a *biometric authentication mode*, a step that would require confirmation from the user. In this mode the system would asynchronously verify the user's identity every time he or she walked while carrying the phone or talked into it. The system would be in a *safe state* for a certain period of time after verification. If new verification failed, the system would use other means to verify the user, e.g. wireless communication with another user's personal device, or asking for the PIN code prior to use. Some actions such as m-commerce or the use of toll services could be defined as always requiring a PIN code or as requiring both biometric verification and a PIN code.

Gait biometrics is a behavioural biometrics, and gait can be affected by injuries, drunkenness, the carrying of a heavy load or tiredness, or indeed by soft ground or the wearing of high-heeled shoes. Further experiments are needed to study how these factors affect the usability of gait recognition. In order to allow for behavioural changes to affect gait recognition, we have chosen a fairly long time period (one month) between the collecting of the training and test data. The test results nevertheless suggest that gait stability depends primarily on walking speed, the slow walking pattern being the least stable and a fast walking pattern being slightly more stable than normal walking. Secondly, its success is person-dependent: some (female) test subjects were easily recognised even in shoes with much higher heels than at the first data collection session, while some test subjects were not recognised despite wearing the same shoes. Stability of gait appeared to be higher in the male test subjects. There were also cases in which male test subjects were misrecognised as females and vice versa. Some of the recognition errors were due to the fact that for some persons "normal walking" was almost twice as fast on one day as on another, but these errors should be evened out after a longer training period.

Although the use of gait biometrics alone might be insufficient for user authentication, our experiments have shown that its use as a complementary modality to speaker recognition does not reduce performance under low noise conditions (where speaker recognition alone performs well), while under high noise conditions performance is improved significantly. For white and pink noise with SNR=0 dB the EER for speaker recognition exceeded 40%, while the combined gait and voice system achieved EER 9.1-11.8% depending on the placement of the accelerometer module.

Comparison of our results with results obtained using noise-robust audio processing methods shows that fusion with gait achieves a similar or better EER. For example, in the work of Yoma et al. [7] EER for white noise at 0 dB was reduced from 28.08% to 11.68% by employing such processing methods, while our system achieved a similar final performance despite having a worse starting point (EER about 40% due to using a fairly small number of voice samples for training). Pink and white noises represent artificial forms of noise commonly used in speaker recognition research. A frequently encountered urban noise type is a car noise. The EER for speaker recognition in the presence of car noise with SNR=0 dB in our system was 27.8% and that reported by Yoma et al. [7] was 24%, but while the latter were able to reduce the EER to 11.9% by using noise-robust audio processing methods, our approach involving fusion with gait reduced it to 8-9%.

Further experiments are needed to study the feasibility of fusing noise-robust speaker recognition with gait recognition, e.g. to assess the system performance and complexity in this case. Implementation of the best-performing noise-robust methods in mobile devices may well be too resource-consuming, but we would expect the fusion of noise-robust speaker verification with gait to improve performance under noisy conditions because the two modalities are fairly uncorrelated [27], although this hypothesis would need confirmation in future tests.

Only a fairly small tilting of the accelerometer module was allowed in the current tests, whereas in normal usage mobile devices are held in various orientations and additional tilting occurs. Tilting a device during walking introduces variations into the accelerometer signal shapes that may decrease the performance of the correlation-based method. Mäntyjärvi et al. [31] have successfully employed a tilt compensation procedure for the user-dependent and user-independent recognition of gestures performed while holding a handheld device. This method could potentially improve gait recognition in more realistic use cases.

Further experiments will also be needed for the designing of application settings for real-life use, e.g. the system's acceptance threshold could be context-dependent: fairly low in a trustable environment (e.g. in the home) and higher in public places. Another form of context-dependence would be a higher trust in gait recognition in the case of long-term level walking and less trust in the case of a few steps. Further experiments should be conducted with other placements of the accelerometer module and with cross-recognition between diverse placements and walking speeds.

7 Conclusions

Frequent unobtrusive authentication of users of mobile devices is needed because they are currently not well protected in a working state, having only an explicit authentication procedure, and users are not willing to perform explicit authentication very frequently. Thus mobile devices are often lost or stolen in a state in which they can be used without any authentication. This presents high risks with regard to information security and privacy. The unobtrusive method for the protection of mobile devices proposed here is based on combined recognition of the user's voice and walking style (gait). The use of these two biometric modalities in mobile device is very natural because users frequently walk while carrying their devices and talk into them or in close proximity to them. In addition, these two biometric modalities are not perceived as privacy-threatening in the same way as conventional biometrics (e.g. fingerprint recognition) or the continuous image processing required for frequent face recognition.

An embedded audio input would allow mobile devices to perform speaker recognition frequently and unobtrusively, as a background task, while the user is speaking. This would protect mobile devices in an "on" state, but would be vulnerable to background noise, especially if the noise level were high. Since there is a fairly high risk of mobile devices being lost or stolen in noisy urban environments such as streets, public transport or shopping areas, the combination of speaker recognition with another unobtrusive biometrics, gait, should be beneficial for protecting user privacy.

The unobtrusive multimodal biometric method for frequent authentication of users of mobile devices proposed in this paper was tested in off-line experiments on the database of 31 persons, which contained their voice recordings at different noise levels and their gait data with three placements of the accelerometer module: in the hand, in the breast pocket and in the hip pocket. The experimental results show that in most cases performance was significantly improved compare to performances of individual modalities. Under high noise conditions (white and pink noise with a Signal-to-Noise Ratio of 0 dB), where Equal Error Rates for speaker recognition exceed 40%, multimodal authentication achieved EER of 9%-12% depending on the position of the accelerometer module. In cases of low noise level, where voice modality alone performed well enough (EER 2-3%), the performance of the combined voice and gait modalities was similar to this (in fact, slightly better in most cases). These results suggest the feasibility of using the proposed method for protecting personal devices such as mobile phones, PDAs and smart suitcases. In a future of truly pervasive computing, when small and inexpensive hardware can be embedded in various objects, this method could also be used for protecting smart cards, smart wallets and other valuable personal items.

References

1. http://news.bbc.co.uk/1/hi/uk/1748258.stm
2. Miller, A., PDA security concerns, Network Security, 2004 (7, July): p. 8-10
3. Johnson, M., Biometrics and the Threat to Civil Liberties, IEEE Computer, 2004, 37(4), p. 90-92

4. Bimbot F, Bonastre J-F., Fredoulle C., Gravier G., Magrin-Chagnolleay I., Meignier S., Merlin T., Ortega-Garcia J., Petrovska-Delacretaz D and Reynolds D. A., A tutorial on text-independent Speaker Verfication. Eurasip Jasp 2004:4 (2004) pp. 430-451

5. Przybocki M.,Martin A., NIST's Assessment of Text Independent Speaker Recognition Performance, The Advent of Biometircs on the Internet, A COST 275 Workshop in Rome, Italy, Nov. 7-8 2002

6. Campbell, J. P., Reynolds, D. A., Dunn, R. B., Fusing High- and Low-Level Features for Speaker Recognition, In Proc. Eurospeech in Geneva, Switzerland, ISCA, pp. 2665-2668.

7. Yoma, N.B.; Villar, M.; Speaker verification in noise using a stochastic version of the weighted Viterbi algorithm Speech and Audio Processing, IEEE Transactions on Volume 10, Issue 3, March 2002 Page(s):158 - 166

8. Hu Guangrui; Wei Xiaodong; Improved robust speaker identification in noise using auditory propertiesIntelligent Multimedia, Video and Speech Processing, 2001. Proceedings of 2001 International Symposium on 2-4 May 2001 Page(s):17 – 19

9. Drygajlo, A.; El-Maliki, M.; Speaker verification in noisy environments with combined spectral subtraction and missing feature theory, ICASSP '98. Proceedings of the 1998 IEEE International Conference on Volume 1, 12-15 May 1998 Page(s):121 - 124 vol.1

10. Niyogi, S.A., Adelson, E.H. Analyzing and recognizing walking gures in XYT. in Conference of Computer Vision and Pattern Recognition. 1994. Seattle,WA.

11. BenAbdelkader, C., Cutler, R., Nanda, H., Davis, L.S. EigenGait: Motion-based Recognition of People using Image Self-similarity. in Intl Conf. on Audio and Video-based Person Authentication (AVBPA). 2001.

12. Nixon, M., Carter, J., Shutler, J., Grant, M., New Advances in Automatic Gait Recognition, Information Security Technical Report, 2002. 7(4): p. 23-35.

13. Wang, L., Tan, T., Hu, W., Ning, H., Automatic gait recognition based on statistical shape analysis, IEEE Trans. Image Processing, 2003, 12(9): p. 120-1131.

14. Bianchi, L., Angelini,D., Lacquaniti, F., Individual characteristics of human walking mechanics. Eur.J.Physiol, 1998, 436: p. 343 –356.8

15. 15 Bolle, R.M., Connell, J.H., Pankanti, S., Ratha, N.K., Senior, A.W., Guide to Biometrics. 2004, New York: Springer. 365.

16. Heinz, E., Kunze, K., Sulistyo, S., Junker, H., Lukowicz, P., Tröster, G., Experimental Evaluation of Variations in Primary Features Used for Accelerometric Context Recognition, Proceedings of Europian Symposium on Ambient Intelligence (EUSAI 2003), pp. 252-263

17. J. Lester, Hannaford, B., Borriello, G., "Are You with Me?" – Using Accelerometers to Determine if Two Devices are Carried by the Same Person," presented at 2nd Int. Conf. on Pervasive Computing, Linz, Austria, 2004

18. Rragami, L., Gifford, M., Edwards, N., DSV - Questions remain..., Biometric Technology Today, 2003. 11(11): p. 7.

19. Sang, L., Wu, Z., Yang, Y. Speaker recognition system in multi-channel environment. in IEEE International Conference on Systems, Man and Cybernetics, System Security and Assurance. 2003. Washington, DC: IEEE Press.

20. Ailisto, H., Haataja, V., Kyllönen, V., Lindholm, M. Wearable Context Aware Terminal for Maintenance Personnel. in Ambient Intelligence, First European Symposium, EUSAI 2003. 2003. Veldhoven, The Netherlands: Springer.

21. Mainguet, J.-F., Biometrics for large-scale consumer products, in International Conference on Artificial Intelligence IC-AI 2003. 2003.

22. Bohn, J., Coroama, V., Langheinrich, M., Mattern, F., Rohs, M., (2005) Social, Economic, and Ethical Implications of Ambient Intelligence and Ubiquitous Computing, In: W. Weber, J. Rabaey, E. Aarts (Eds.): Ambient Intelligence. Springer-Verlag, pp. 5-29
23. Hazen, T., Weinstein, E., Kabir, R., Park A., Heisele, B., Multi-Modal Face and Speaker Identification on a Handheld Device, In Proceedings of the Workshop on Multimodal User Authentication, pp. 113-120, Santa Barbara, California, December, 2003
24. Lee B, Hasegawa-Johnson M, Goudeseune C, Kamdar S, Borys S, Liu M, Huang T., "AVICAR: Audio-Visual Speech Corpus in a Car Environment", INTERSPEECH2004-ICSLP Jeju Island, Korea, October 2004
25. Ailisto, H.; Lindholm, M.; Mäntyjärvi, J.; Vildjiounaite, E.; Mäkelä, S.-M., Identifying people from gait pattern with accelerometers, SPIE, Vol. 5779, Biometric Technology for Human Identification II, Anil K. Jain & Nalini K. Ratha (Eds.), pp. 7 - 14
26. Jain, A., Ross, A., Multibiometric Systems, Communications of the ACM, Special Issue on Multimodal Interfaces , Vol. 47, No. 1, pp. 34-40, January 2004.
27. State-of-the-Art Report on Multimodal Biometric Fusion, http://www.biosec.org/index. php
28. Gellersen, H.-W., Schmidt, A., Beigl, M., Multi-sensor context-awareness in mobile devices and smart artifacts, Mobile Networks and Applications, 7, 341-351, 2002
29. http://www.bas.uni-muenchen.de/Bas/SV/
30. NTT-AT Ambient Noise Database: http://www.ntt-at.com/products_e/noise-DB/
31. Mäntyjärvi, J., Kallio, S., Korpipää, P., Kela, J., Plomp, J., Gesture Interaction for Small Handheld Devices to Support Multimedia Applications, In Journal of Mobile Multimedia, Rinton Press, Vol.1(2), pp. 92 – 112, 2005.

LoKey: Leveraging the SMS Network in Decentralized, End-to-End Trust Establishment

Anthony J. Nicholson[1], Ian E. Smith[2], Jeff Hughes[3], and Brian D. Noble[1]

[1] University of Michigan
{tonynich, bnoble}@eecs.umich.edu
[2] Intel Research, Seattle
ian.e.smith@intel.com
[3] University of Washington
jeffdh@cs.washington.edu

Abstract. People increasingly depend on the digital world to communicate with one another, but such communication is rarely secure. Users typically have no common administrative control to provide mutual authentication, and sales of certified public keys to individuals have made few inroads. The only remaining mechanism is key exchange. Because they are not authenticated, users must verify the exchanged keys through some out-of-band mechanism. Unfortunately, users appear willing to accept any key at face value, leaving communication vulnerable. This paper describes *LoKey*, a system that leverages the Short Message Service (SMS) to verify keys on users' behalf. SMS messages are small, expensive, and slow, but they utilize a closed network, between devices— phones—that are nearly ubiquitous and authenticate with the network operator. Our evaluation shows LoKey can establish and verify a shared key in approximately 30 seconds, provided only that one correspondent knows the other's phone number. By verifying keys asynchronously, two example applications—an instant messaging client and a secure email service—can provide assurances of message privacy, integrity, and source authentication while requiring only that users know the phone number of their correspondent.

1 Introduction

People increasingly depend on the Internet for daily interactions with others. We send email instead of letters, send digital pictures rather than prints, and pay bills online rather than write and mail checks.

The financial sector of our digital lives has at least a modicum of protection and security. Businesses have certified public keys [1], and use SSL [2] to provide reasonable authentication of a service to its users. Of course, such services are still vulnerable to phishing [3], DNS spoofing [4], and users' apparent willingness to accept any certificate presented as valid, no matter how problematic [5].

Unfortunately, person-to-person communication remains largely vulnerable. Secure email has made few inroads, and many messaging systems provide no security model at all. There are several structural reasons for this. Family members,

K.P. Fishkin et al. (Eds.): PERVASIVE 2006, LNCS 3968, pp. 202–219, 2006.

friends, and colleagues often have no central point of administrative control, making mutual authentication based on third-party services, such as Kerberos [6], impossible. Furthermore, individuals have little conscious incentive to purchase their own certified public keys.

The only remaining model is key exchange. The essential weakness of this model is that exchanged keys are *unauthenticated*—the users have no idea if the key they have is the correct key, or if some attacker has replaced it with one of their own choosing.

To confirm the veracity of a key, users are expected to verify it using some out-of-band mechanism. For example, they can call one another on the phone, and compare their *key fingerprints*. Typically, such fingerprints are long sequences of digits. In practice, users rarely verify keys out of band and tend to accept whatever keys are presented to them [7], though there has been work on more user-friendly verification techniques [8, 9, 10].

The unique properties of pervasive and mobile computing devices exacerbate this problem. Users would clearly like the devices they carry with them to communicate securely with the ever-changing and expanding set of users and devices encountered in their everyday travels.

Rather than rely on users to manually verify potentially compromised keys, we have constructed a system, called *LoKey*, that exploits the Short Message Service [11] to verify keys on users' behalf. There are several advantages to SMS. It utilizes a closed network, making internal attacks more difficult. The end user devices—phones—are authenticated by network operators, nearly always connected, and rarely out of their users' possession. These facts together allow us to construct an out-of-band channel between two corresponding users' machines; if a key can be verified by such a channel, it can be used with high confidence.

LoKey removes the need for users to trust any party beyond the person they want to communicate with and their phone service provider—no certificate authorities, public key infrastructures, or third-party intermediaries. Instead, it leverages the security properties of a network of limited usefulness (the SMS network) to secure traffic on the insecure, but vastly more powerful, Internet.

However, there are also challenges in using SMS—messages must be small, cannot use the full symbol space, have very high latency, and are expensive to transmit. Furthermore, the SMS service must be used judiciously, else the phone's battery will be expended too quickly.

This paper describes LoKey's approach to meeting these challenges, while still establishing a valid key. First, we establish a secure association between each user's phone and their computing devices. Thereafter, a user can establish a secure relationship with another knowing only the correspondent's mobile phone number—something users are already accustomed to doing. The calling user initiates key establishment with the correspondent via SMS, the two exchange keys via the Internet, and confirm the veracity of those keys via SMS.

The established key can either be used directly as a symmetric key between two users, or used as a session key to provide an authenticated channel. Such channels can be used to distribute public keys, group keys, et cetera, in a reliable and authenticated way. LoKey is a general framework for trust establishment that is agnostic to the specific key technologies in use.

In addition to describing our system, we also present two sample applications that use LoKey. The first is an instant messaging client, that establishes a secure session key when a new correspondent is added for the first time. The second is a plug-in for the Mozilla Thunderbird email client. This tool lets email users swap their public keys in an authenticated way, in order to send and receive encrypted email.

Two users can exchange and verify a key in just over 30 seconds; this time is dominated by SMS message latency. While this is too expensive for on-demand, synchronous communication, it is acceptable for asynchronous or one-time tasks, such as signing a piece of email before it is sent for delivery or adding a user to a list of correspondents for future use. Half of this cost is incurred to initiate key establishment via an SMS message, rather than over the IP Internet. This is an expensive feature, but an important one for mobile clients, as it prevents DNS-based attacks.

2   Background: Why Key Establishment Is Hard

Key establishment is trivial when all users belong to one administrative domain. For example, all employees in a department trust their system administrator implicitly. This allows Kerberos-style authentication [6] between employees who have a common trusted entity (the sysadmin), but is obviously impractical for establishing trust across the global Internet.

The Diffie-Hellman key establishment protocol [12] lets two users with no previous relationship establish a key in a way that is secure against eavesdroppers. Alice and Bob each generate a random integer (a and b) and exchange (g^a mod n) and (g^b mod n), where g and n are public protocol parameters. The key is (g^{ab} mod n). Alice can calculate this, knowing a and having received (g^b mod n) from Bob, because (g^b mod n)$^a = g^{ab}$ mod n. Bob can do likewise because (g^b mod n)$^a = g^{ab}$ mod n. But an eavesdropper cannot calculate the key feasibly, because deriving a and b from $\{(g^a$ mod $n), (g^b$ mod $n), g, n\}$ is intractable [13].

Unfortunately, the protocol is vulnerable to active attacks. If Mal can remove and insert messages as shown in Fig. 1, she can force Alice and Bob to unwittingly establish keys with her instead of each other. As long as Mal tunnels all traffic between Alice and Bob, they cannot detect the attack. SSL [2] and the Station-to-Station protocol [14] both solve this problem by requiring users to have certified public keys. In this model, all users must trust a small number of certification authorities (CAs) [1], whose public keys are broadly distributed and well-known. Alice and Bob then sign all their key establishment messages to each other, and can detect if a message originated from someone else.

But how do users get these key certificates? This places an unreasonable burden on users to find a secure side-channel with the CA, such as physically visiting a key signing kiosk. There is little incentive for users to do this. For example, most merchants authenticate individuals by their credit cards. Many

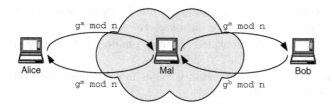

Fig. 1. Vulnerability of Diffie-Hellman to man-in-the-middle attacks

institutions also self-sign their certificates, acting as their own CA. This leads to a balkanization of the world into islands of trust. While there has been work toward bridging this gap [15], each trust domain must still somehow establish trust with each other or with a hierarchical set of CAs. SSL is also vulnerable to "DNS hijacking" attacks [16]. While users are informed the host key has changed when such an attack occurs, too often they are conditioned to just click "OK" on every security alert message [5].

At the other end of the spectrum lies the decentralized PGP "web-of-trust" model. Users sign the keys of others whom they trust, or keys that they receive over a secure side-channel. When Alice receives Bob's public key for the first time, she accepts it as valid if someone she already trusts has signed it, attesting to its integrity. In order to sign someone's key, one needs to receive or verify the key out-of-band to preclude man-in-the-middle (MiM) substitution attacks. In practice, users rarely verify keys out of band and tend to accept whatever keys are presented to them [7]. Unfortunately, these signature chains are only as strong as their weakest link. Furthermore, two users cannot communicate unless they have at least one trusted user in common.

The end result is the situation we have today, where each time we converse with a new correspondent, we are presented with a key fingerprint that we have no intention of verifying. While much work has focused on making key verification easier [7, 8, 9, 10], in general such techniques have not yet made the transition to practice. Meanwhile, most users just click "OK", accept any certificate or key which is presented to them, and go about their business [5, 7].

3   Design

The crucial point of the previous section is that Diffie-Hellman exchanges are sufficiently secure to establish pairwise trust between users, provided that the man-in-the-middle problem could be solved. This is possible if there was a trusted out-of-band channel Alice and Bob were willing to use to verify that their keys match. We argue that one such out-of-band channel already exists: the Short Message Service (SMS) network used to send text messages between mobile phones. This network has the following nice properties:

– It is a closed network. To complete a MiM attack, one must remove messages which are in transit. This requires access to phone company resources or the ability to masquerade as a network tower.

- Phone companies have a strong economic incentive to secure their network, to avoid customers defecting *en masse* to competitors.
- Users are universally identified by their phone number, a paradigm people already understand.
- SMS messaging is already standard on most phones, and all signs point toward increasing adoption [17].

We are not claiming attacks against the SMS network are not possible, but rather argue the bar is much higher than what is required for similar attacks against Internet traffic. A MiM attack against the SMS network would require coordinating radio eavesdropping with intrusion into at least one phone network.

Unfortunately, the SMS network has limitations. Each message holds at most 160 bytes. Delivery time is slow and variable, and typically has a per-message charge. Performing the entire key establishment over SMS would take dozens of messages, last prohibitively long and run up users' bills.

LoKey leverages the strengths of both the Internet and the SMS network to establish a secret key between two users without requiring they start from any shared secret, use certified keys, or both trust any other entity—in an efficient and user-friendly way. After establishing a secret key using standard Diffie-Hellman key exchange, Alice and Bob each calculate a cryptographic hash of their key, and send this hash to their mobile phone. The phones swap these hashes via SMS messages, and then download the other party's hash to its user's computer. LoKey then checks if the hashes match—if so, Alice and Bob know with a high degree of confidence that their key is genuine.

Cryptographic hash functions are ideal for verifying keys because they map an arbitrary-length key to a small, fixed number of bytes [18]. Given this hash, it is infeasible to discover the key from whence it came, or to construct another key which will hash to the same value. We use SHA-256 [19], which outputs a 32 byte hash. The hash can be exposed to eavesdroppers because it gives them no advantage toward reconstructing the secret key.

Key verification may take several seconds, due to SMS delivery latency. Users may be unwilling to incur this overhead every time. LoKey can either cache secret keys or, preferably, leverage public key cryptography to make this a one-time cost. After establishing and verifying a secret key, LoKey swaps Alice and Bob's public keys under the cover of the secret key. They can then generate a session key using any number of protocols which rely on certified keys [14].

The user can secure the communication channel between her phone and her computer in several ways, since she controls both devices. We assume the phone and computer communicate via Bluetooth. Her phone remains in her pocket, and the entire process is user-transparent, apart from the one-time task of pairing her phone and computer [20]. To pair two devices, the user chooses a variable-length PIN and manually inputs it on both devices. The devices then negotiate a secret key, using the shared secret of the PIN to thwart MiM attacks. Recent work [21] demonstrated vulnerabilities in this pairing process, but only against PINs less than 8 digits long. Since the standard supports up to 128-bit PINs, this is not a blanket indictment of the pairing protocol but rather an implementation issue.

3.1   Threat Model

We assume the attacker Mal is an active attacker who can remove, insert, and modify messages in flight anywhere in the Internet. She may even completely control one or both users' access points to the Internet. With regard to the SMS network, we assume that Mal can eavesdrop on all text messages sent and received by both Alice and Bob, but that she cannot remove or modify SMS messages.

We also assume Mal cannot eavesdrop on the Bluetooth channel between the user's computer and phone. As we argue above, the pairing protocol is secure, given sufficiently-long PINs.

It must be noted that in current GSM technology, phones authenticate themselves to the network tower, but the converse is not true [22]. An attacker could therefore masquerade as a GSM tower, trick the user's phone into associating with it, and then act as the man-in-the-middle between the user and a legitimate phone company tower. The attacker could then modify key hashes as appropriate to conceal his presence. This requires specialized hardware, but is not beyond the capacity of organized crime, law enforcement, and national governments.

Emerging standards (specifically, 3GPP) will preclude this sort of attack. For the time being, users can leverage their mobility to re-confirm hashes from multiple locations via multiple network towers. Our previous work [23] establishes an insecure key between two users over the Internet, like LoKey, but then exchanges key hashes also over the Internet. In lieu of an out-of-band channel (such as the SMS network), this system repeatedly rebroadcasts key hashes over the different access points the two users encounter in the course of their ordinary, daily travels. Our initial results show such mobility ensures, with high probability, that multiple path-diverse routes between the two users will be generated, requiring an attacker to control an unreasonably large portion of the Internet in order to conceal his presence. We argue that adding such capabilities to LoKey would similarly thwart such "dummy tower" attacks. We have not implemented this in our prototype, however.

3.2   Protocol Design

Figures 2 and 3 illustrate our protocol for establishing a secret key between two users. It is a two-phase process. First, the two users perform standard Diffie-Hellman key establishment over the Internet. Second, the key is verified via the SMS network.

Consider an example scenario where a user Bob wants to establish a key with another user, Alice:

Insecure Key Establishment (Fig. 2):

1. Bob's laptop sends a key establishment request message to his phone, via Bluetooth. This request contains both Bob's IP address and Alice's mobile phone number.

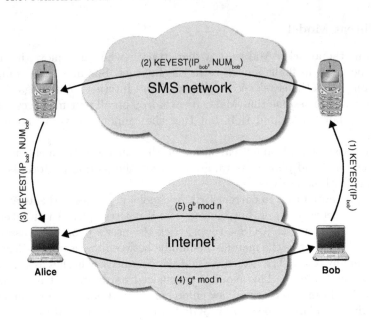

Fig. 2. Phase 1: Initiation and insecure key establishment

2. Bob's phone encapsulates the request in an SMS message payload, and sends it to Alice's phone via the SMS network.
3. Alice's phone receives the request, and forwards it to Alice's laptop.
4. Alice initiates Diffie-Hellman key establishment, by calculating a pseudorandom integer a and sending the integer $(g^a \bmod n)$ to Bob over the Internet. Bob generates his pseudorandom parameter b, and calculates the key: $K_B = (g^a \bmod n)^b = g^{ab} \bmod n$.
5. Bob sends Alice $(g^b \bmod n)$, and she also calculates the key: $K_A = (g^b \bmod n)^a = g^{ab} \bmod n$.

Note: if there was a man-in-the-middle attack, then $K_A \neq K_B$. Otherwise, they are the same. The next phase of the protocol determines which case it is.

Key Verification via SMS (Fig. 3):

6. Both Alice and Bob calculate the SHA-256 cryptographic hash of their key. They then send the hash, and the other party's mobile phone number, to their phone via the secured Bluetooth link.
7. Alice's phone sends SHA-256(K_A) to Bob's phone in an SMS message. Bob's phone likewise sends SHA-256(K_B) to Alice's phone.
8. Once each phone receives the other's text message, it downloads the hash and the sender's phone number to its paired computer. Both Alice and Bob check if SHA-256(K_A) = SHA-256(K_B). If not, then the key establishment failed and LoKey discards the key. If they match, Alice and Bob know with high confidence that $K_A = K_B$.

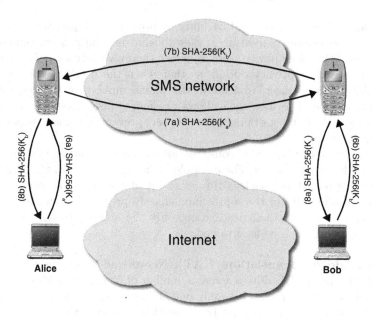

Fig. 3. Phase 2: Key verification via SMS

A lightweight version of the protocol omits steps 1-3 in cases where Bob already knows Alice's IP address. In that case, he can initiate Diffie-Hellman establishment directly. This saves the overhead of one SMS message delivery latency (step 2 of the above protocol).

3.3 Discussion

Usability and Privacy. To establish a key with another user, all we need to know is their mobile phone number. This is attractive since users are already accustomed to identifying people by their phone numbers. While remembering a phone number is more difficult than remembering an email address (numbers rather than names and words) we argue it is not unreasonable. Phone numbers are also easy to communicate out-of-band since they are short strings of digits, and people are already accustomed to doing so.

LoKey fails if someone else has the user's phone, because we will establish a key with the attacker and his laptop, rather than the user we intended. We argue that the window of opportunity between when a phone is lost and its owner cancels service or recovers it will be short—at most, on the order of one day. Since users typically pay per usage, there is a strong incentive for them to quickly stop unauthorized use.

LoKey raises some privacy concerns, however. In the above example, Alice may not want to disclose her IP address to Bob. Automatically initiating Diffie-Hellman key establishment in response to Bob's SMS message does just that. While an IP address doesn't provide GPS-level information, it can reveal a user's presence on a certain university campus, or at least in a certain city. We resolve this tension between privacy and usability by providing the user with the phone number of the person requesting key establishment. Since users opinions on privacy vary [24], we empower users to decide their own privacy policies. LoKey users can activate a privacy option, so that when the user's phone receives a key establishment request, it displays the phone number of the requester on the mobile phone. The user then allows or denies the request via her mobile phone keypad. A whitelist of pre-approved users prevents common requests from annoying the user.

For even more privacy, users could use an anonymous routing system to hide their IP address from others. For example, a *tor* (http://tor.eff.org/) uses onion routing to redirect packets through a set of overlay peers, each of whom only know the identity of the source immediately preceding it in the sequence. Once packets arrive at their destination, only the identity of the most recent node in the overlay can be ascertained.

Network Address Translation (NAT). Network address translators (NATs) multiplex one public IP address across a number of private IP addresses. This is often used by wireless routers to share one DSL or cable modem, causing problems in establishing point-to-point IP connections. To solve this, we leverage the well-known technique of "hole-punching" [25, 26]. Each host maintains a connection with a well-known rendezvous server (RS), which determines the host's globally-visible IP address and port pair. When requesting key establishment via SMS, a host which is behind a NAT sends both its local IP address (behind the NAT) and the globally visible IP address and port. When Alice then establishes a TCP connection to Bob (to initiate Diffie-Hellman key establishment) on his global IP and port, the existing outbound TCP connections to the RS are broken, and Alice and Bob are connected directly. Full details can be found in the literature [25, 26].

Clearly, the channel between the RS and the user must be authenticated or Mal can trick users into connecting to the wrong user. An active attacker could pose as a rendezvous server and connect Alice to a third-party, Charlie, rather than the principal (Bob) with whom she intended to exchange keys. Charlie can then perform a man-in-the-middle attack by tunneling traffic between Alice and Bob, as described above in Sect. 2. One solution is to use LoKey to establish a secret key between Alice and the RS, then use this shared secret to authenticate all subsequent traffic between Alice and the rendezvous server.

Multiple User Devices. Users have multiple computing devices. If all of these are connected to the Internet then IP discovery is not a trivial one-to-one mapping. When your phone receives a key establishment request from a friend, and you have both your PDA and your laptop with you, which device should handle the key establishment? Should your 3G phone handle the entire process itself?

In our current implementation, we elide this issue by having users choose which device to associate with when they start the LoKey process on their mobile phone. Since a user owns and controls all her devices, she can establish a shared secret which allows them all to communicate confidentially. Ongoing work is focused on extending LoKey to forward keys established and verified by one of the user's devices to all of the others. For example, if Alice's PDA was her only device in contact with her mobile phone when Bob tried to establish a secret key, it would handle the key establishment and then transmit the key to her laptop, desktop, et cetera, the next time they were reachable via the network.

4 Implementation

We developed a working prototype of LoKey, consisting of two main components: a *service daemon*, running on the user's computer, and an *SMS bridge*, running on the user's phone. The computer and phone communicate via Bluetooth.

4.1 Service Daemon (SD)

The SD is a user-level service on the user's computer, listening in the background for incoming data on one of three connections: (1) a well-known, local TCP port number to which user applications connect to request services from the SD, (2) an externally-visible socket on another well-known LoKey port, to which SDs running on other users' computers connect, and (3) the computer's Bluetooth stack creates a pseudo-device which behaves like a normal RS-232 serial port. The SD listens on that port for incoming data from the user's mobile phone.

We developed the SD in C++, using the OpenSSL crypto library for Diffie-Hellman establishment to leverage its optimized implementation. The SD has been ported to both Windows XP and Linux.

4.2 SMS Bridge

We implemented the SMS bridge process as a Python script, running on a Nokia 6600 mobile phone. The 6600 runs the Symbian operating system with the Nokia Python runtime library. When the script starts, it presents the user with a list of Bluetooth devices in the area. The user chooses her computer from the list, and pairs the phone with the computer if she has not done so previously. The script now retreats into the background—the user can make calls and use all other phone features, even while key verification messages are passing back and forth.

The SMS bridge consists of two threads of execution. An upstream thread listens on the Bluetooth serial port for data from the user's computer. These messages consist of a phone number and a payload. The upstream thread parses requests from the computer and sends the payload to the specified number as an SMS message. A downstream thread waits for a text message to arrive in the phone inbox. If it is a LoKey message rather than a text generated by a human, it removes the message from the inbox and sends the payload and the sender's phone number to the user's computer. LoKey messages are identified by a special control code to prevent users from accidentally deleting them while manually sending SMS messages.

4.3   Application Services

Regardless of how useful LoKey may be, if application programmers cannot easily use its services, it will be abandoned. This is why we pushed the complexity of interacting with mobile phones and other users down into the service daemon. Applications merely request one of the following two services by sending a request over the local LoKey socket and waiting for a response. We implemented this interface as a socket rather than using IPC or named pipes to both maximize portability and increase ease of use, since the Berkeley socket interface is a common, simple abstraction that most programmers already understand.

Secret Session Key Establishment

```
key = est_and_verify_key( remote_phone )
```

An application sends the SD a message containing the phone number of the user with which they want to establish a secret key. The SD then performs key establishment as described in Sect. 3.2. Once the key has been established but before it has been verified, the SD returns the key to the calling application. Once the key has subsequently been verified or disproved, the SD returns an appropriate success code. If the hashes matched, the application can now establish a secure connection to its peer in confidence, using any symmetric cryptographic cipher of its choosing.

Authenticated Public Key Exchange

```
remote_PK = auth_pk_swap( remote_phone )
```

Since establishing and verifying a secret key can take tens of seconds, users will want to make this a one-time cost. Caching the key accomplishes this, but at the cost of exposing the pairwise key if one user's computer is stolen or compromised. A better solution is to use the secret key LoKey provides as a one-time session key, and leverage public key cryptography to swap both users' public keys in a completely authenticated fashion. They can subsequently establish a session key entirely over the Internet via any number of well-known methods [14] that require certified keys (since both public keys are completely trusted). Our prototype uses Gnu Privacy Guard (GPG), a PGP-style system, to manage public keys locally.

Applications send a phone number to the SD, which first establishes and verifies a secret key. Alice and Bob then swap copies of their public keys, encrypted by the secret key. The keys are ASCII-armored for transport, which adds a standard PGP header to the key. This is critical for verification, since an attacker cannot just send an arbitrary message of the correct length to a user, and trick her into importing a bogus public key. If the data sent was not encrypted by the secret LoKey key it will decrypt to gibberish, without the correct PGP header formats. Thus, users only accept keys which originate from each other.

5 Example Applications

Along with our LoKey prototype, we developed two examples to illustrate how applications can leverage LoKey to enhance user security and usability.

5.1 Instant Messaging: Jabber

Jabber is an open-standard Internet chat protocol, also known as XMPP. We used the xmpppy open-source Python library to write a Jabber client. LoKey-Jabber is an ordinary IM client, with one exception: each time the user adds a new contact to her "buddy list", LoKeyJabber establishes and verifies a key with that buddy. We do this immediately rather than on demand, because it may take several seconds due to SMS latency.

When Alice first imports Bob into her buddy list, she specifies both his chat handle and his mobile phone number. His name first shows in the buddy list as red, indicating Alice has no key with him. LoKeyJabber immediately starts the key establishment process. Meanwhile, Alice and Bob are free to communicate without a key, if they wish. Once the key has been established over the Internet, but before it has been confirmed via SMS, the SD returns the key to LoKeyJabber. Bob's name now turns yellow, because LoKeyJabber has a key with him which may or may not be trustworthy. Our implementation uses AES (Rijndael) [27] symmetric encryption, with 128-bit keys, to secure chat messages. Meanwhile, the SD verifies key integrity via hash exchange. This may take on the order of 20 seconds or more. During this time, Alice and Bob can communicate *provisionally* using the unverified key, if what they need to say is not particularly confidential. Once the key has been confirmed, each party's SD returns the result to their LoKeyJabber. Bob's name turns green and Alice knows she can communicate with him in full confidence. Confirmed keys are cached, so key establishment is a one-time cost.

5.2 Email Client: Mozilla Thunderbird

One arena in which public key cryptography has made some inroads is email. Basic encryption/decryption is standard in many email clients. As we have observed, the problem is distributing everyone's public key over the insecure, unauthenticated Internet. EnigMail, a third-party plug-in to the Mozilla Thunderbird email client, is a graphical front-end to PGP. When users compose messages, they choose a user's public key from a provided list, and EnigMail encrypts the message with that key. Likewise, EnigMail automatically decrypts received messages with the user's private PGP key.

We extended EnigMail to add an option to swap public keys with a user, given their phone number. Assume Alice wants to swap keys with Bob. First, Alice's Thunderbird requests authenticated public key exchange with Bob. If the SD returns success, then Bob's public key is now on Alice's PGP keyring, and Alice's public key is on Bob's keyring. If Alice now composes an email to Bob, she will see his public key on the list of possible recipients, since EnigMail also uses the PGP keyring.

6   Evaluation

In evaluating our implementation of LoKey, we sought to answer three questions:

1. What is the user-perceptible time overhead imposed by using LoKey for authentication?
2. What are the reasons for this overhead? Are we limited by SMS network latency, or some artifact of our design?
3. Since these are mobile, battery-powered devices, is LoKey's power consumption acceptable?

Our test setup consisted of two x86 laptops running Windows XP. Each had a 866 MHz CPU and 256 MB of RAM. The laptops were both connected to the same campus 802.11 wireless network. We created a GMail email address, PGP public key, and Jabber chat handle for two imaginary users (Alice LoKey and Bob LoKey). We paired a Nokia 6600 mobile phone with each laptop and ran the experiments inside an office to simulate the GSM network conditions users would commonly experience. Our GSM signal strength was good, typically at the high end of the scale. Note that SMS delivery latency will vary on different networks.

6.1   Application-Level Metrics

All numbers in this section are from the initiator—the user who started the chat or the public key exchange—because the time delay is longest for that user.

To test the overhead a user would see in using the LoKeyJabber chat client, we added Bob to Alice's buddy list 20 times. This triggered chat key establishment and verification. Table 1 shows the delay in seconds, averaged across all 20 runs. LoKey requires just over 30 seconds to establish and verify a key.

Similarly, we used our email client plug-in to swap Alice and Bob's public keys 20 times. As Table 2 shows, the time required for key establishment is

Table 1. LoKeyJabber chat key establishment. Values in seconds.

	Key establishment
mean	36.05
median	36.41
stdev	6.17

Table 2. Public-key exchange plug-in for Mozilla Thunderbird. Values in seconds.

	Total	Key establishment	Public key exchange
mean	34.17	29.61	4.30
median	34.45	30.06	4.07
stdev	2.01	1.90	0.54

comparable to that shown in the chat client test. An additional 4 seconds is required, on average, to securely exchange public keys under the cover of the new secret key. This overhead is primarily the result of communication overhead between LoKey and the user-level Gnu Privacy Guard client, incurred when importing a new user's key into a local keyring.

6.2 Infrastructure-Level Delays

We instrumented the Service Daemon and collected internal profiling information during all of the 40 test runs described above. Tables 3 and 4 show the breakdown of time spent in each phase of the key exchange and public key exchange protocols. As expected, SMS delivery delays comprise the overwhelming majority of overhead. One does see a small communication delay in key establishment for exchanging the Diffie-Hellman key material over the Internet. Even across a true WAN this delay is unlikely to be more than a few seconds. As discussed above, importing the exchanged public keys into the local GPG keyring incurs overhead of several seconds. All these local delays are still dwarfed by SMS network delays, however.

Table 3. Secret key establishment. Values in seconds.

	Total	Request key exchange	Diffie-Hellman exchange	Verify hashes
mean	35.84	17.83	0.14	17.87
median	36.33	18.02	0.11	18.53
stdev	6.22	2.55	0.48	3.99

Table 4. Secure public key exchange. Values in seconds.

	Total	Request key exchange	Diffie-Hellman exchange	Verify hashes	Public key exchange
mean	33.27	14.04	0.14	14.31	3.44
median	33.52	13.96	0.08	14.52	3.50
stdev	1.91	0.77	0.29	1.80	0.53

6.3 Power

Since both sending SMS messages and communicating with the user's computer via Bluetooth can be power-intensive for mobile phones, we sought to quantify the effect LoKey would have on battery life. To examine power drained during active operation, we started from fully charged batteries and performed secret key establishment from Alice to Bob 100 times. After the 100 runs, neither phone had dropped off the highest battery setting, meaning that at least 87.5% of the battery remained. We did not run until the batteries drained because these are live, expensive SMS messages.

We believe that because the standby battery life of the phone is at most 10 days, users are unlikely to establish brand-new relationships with hundreds of users before recharging the phone at least once. Users' phone plans also typically budget only several hundred messages per month.

We also considered standby power consumption, because LoKey requires that the Bluetooth interface on the user's phone is always enabled, expending power while waiting for a connection. Bluetooth radios draw on the order of 0.3 mA while quiescent [28]. The Nokia 6600 battery is rated at 850 mAh (milli-amp hours) when fully charged. According to the 6600 user manual, the phone should last 150-240 hours in standby mode. Thus, the standby mode current draw of the phone must be in the range of $(850\ mAh)/(150\ h)$ to $(850\ mAh)/(240\ h)$, or 5.7 mA - 3.5 mA. We therefore expect LoKey will reduce standby time by at most 10%, by one day (from 10 to 9 days) in the worst case.

7   Related Work

Thompson describes a system whereby banks push secret PINs to users via text messages [29]. While the risk is small, one cannot consider the SMS network secure from eavesdropping. That is one reason we exchange cryptographic hashes. Claessens [30] uses SMS messages as a sort of receipt for online transactions. Both require that users read the message and manually perform some action, while LoKey is automatic.

Maher [31] first suggested using a short hash of a long key to ease key verification. This approach has been adopted by many others [32, 33], but all still require a good deal of user intervention—one must either connect the devices physically, read and verify hashes on two different screens, or manually input a code on several devices. Users seem resistant to all of these tasks.

These limitations have sparked work on helping users more easily verify fingerprints [8, 9, 7]. Unfortunately, few or none of these techniques have yet made the transition into everyday use. Perrig and Song [10] generate images from fingerprints, exploiting the fact that humans recall images much better than strings of letters and numbers. Similarly, Madhavapeddy et al. [34] suggested the voice channel of mobile phones could be used to verify keys through user to user communication. While we could modify LoKey to verify hashes in any of these ways, this would require user intervention, where our solution is automatic.

Stajano and Anderson introduced the "Duckling" [35]—a small device which performs actions on behalf of its "mother" device. This is similar to the role users' mobile phones play in LoKey. They are bound to the user's computer, and are trusted completely because the user controls both. Other work in the ad-hoc networking space has shown how capitalizing on such side channels when they arise can enhance security [36, 37].

8   Conclusion

As users are more mobile, they interact with a varied set of people and devices. Since the Internet is insecure and unauthenticated, we need to use data encryption to ensure confidentiality of our communications. Current methods for establishing end-to-end trust put too much burden on users, and demand trust in either a centralized authority or strangers on key signature trails.

We introduced LoKey, a decentralized, automatic system for generating end-to-end trust between users. LoKey uses standard Diffie-Hellman key establishment, and defeats the man-in-the-middle by leveraging the mobile phones that users already carry. By exchanging key hashes over the SMS network, LoKey detects after the fact if a MiM attack occurred. We provide users with a simple API for establishing secret keys and exchanging public keys in an authenticated fashion.

We developed two proof-of-concept applications to showcase our implementation. Evaluation of our prototype shows one-time delays of approximately 30 seconds to establish a secure communication channel with a remote user. By either caching the generated secret key or leveraging public key cryptography, this cost can be eliminated for future communications between the two users.

Acknowledgements

We would like to thank our shepherd Nigel Davies, and the anonymous reviewers, for their insightful comments and feedback that greatly improved the quality of our paper. We also gratefully acknowledge the helpful feedback of James Mickens and Sam Shah.

References

1. CCITT, Draft Recommendation X.509: The Directory-Authentication Framework. Consultation Committee, International Telecommunications Union, Geneva (1989)
2. Freier, A., Karlton, P., Kocher, P.: Secure Socket Layer 3.0. Internet Draft (1996)
3. Warner, B.: Billions of "phishing" scam emails sent monthly. Reuters News Service (2004)
4. Bellovin, S.M.: Using the Domain Name System for system break-ins. In: Proceedings of the 5th USENIX Security Symposium. (1995)
5. Xia, H., Brustoloni, J.C.: Hardening web browsers against man-in-the-middle and eavesdropping attacks. In: Proceedings of the 14th International World Wide Web Conference (WWW '05). (2005)
6. Neuman, B., Ts'o, T.: Kerberos: An authentication service for computer networks. IEEE Communications Magazine **32** (1994) 33–38
7. Whitten, A., Tygar, J.D.: Why Johnny can't encrypt: A usability evaluation of PGP 5.0. In: Proceedings of the 8th USENIX Security Symposium. (1999)
8. Dohrmann, S., Ellison, C.: Public-key Support for Collaborative Groups. In: Proceedings of the First Annual PKI Research Workshop. (2002)

9. Garfinkel, S., Margrave, D., Schiller, J., Nordlander, E., Miller, R.: How to make secure email easier to use. In: Proceedings of the Conference on Human Factors in Computing Systems (CHI). (2005)
10. Perrig, A., Song, D.: Hash Visualization: A New Technique to Improve Real-World Security. In: Proceedings of the International Workshop on Cryptographic Techniques and E-Commerce (CryptEC). (1999)
11. Peersman, C., Cvetkovic, S.: The global system for mobile communications: Short Message Service. IEEE Personal Communications **7** (2000) 15–23
12. Diffie, W., Hellman, M.: New directions in cryptography. IEEE Transactions on Information Theory **6** (1976) 644–654
13. Maurer, U.: Towards the equivalence of breaking the Diffie-Hellman protocol and computing discrete logarithms. In: Proceedings of the 14th Annual International Cryptology Conference (CRYPTO '94). (1994)
14. Diffie, W., Oorschot, P., Wiener, M.: Authentication and Authenticated Key Exchanges. Designs, Codes, and Cryptography **2** (1992) 107–125
15. Kaminsky, M., Savvides, G., Mazieres, D., Kaashoek, M.: Decentralized User Authentication in a Global File System. In: Proceedings of the 19th ACM Symposium on Operating Systems Principles. (2003)
16. Burkholder, P.: SSL Man-in-the-middle Attacks. The SANS Institute (2002)
17. Xu, H., Teo, H., Wang, H.: Foundations of SMS Commerce Success: Lessions from SMS Messaging and Co-opetition. In: Proceedings of the 36th Hawaii International Conference on System Sciences (HICSS). (2003)
18. Naor, M., Yung, M.: Universal one-way hash functions and their crytographic applications. In: Proceedings of the 21st ACM Symposium on the Theory of Computing (STOC '89). (1989)
19. National Institute of Standards and Technology (NIST): Secure Hash Standard (SHS). National Technical Information Service (2002)
20. Bluetooth SIG: Specification of the Bluetooth System, http://www.bluetooth.org/spec/ (2005)
21. Shaked, Y., Wool, A.: Cracking the Bluetooth PIN. In: Proceedings of the Third International Conference on Mobile Systems, Applications, and Services (MobiSys '05). (2005)
22. Anderson, R.: Security Engineering. Wiley (2001)
23. Nicholson, A.J., Han, J., Watson, D., Noble, B.D.: Exploiting Mobility for Key Establishment. In: Proceedings of the Seventh IEEE Workshop on Mobile Computing Systems and Applications (WMCSA '06). (2006)
24. Smith, I., Consolvo, S., Abowd, G.: Social Disclosure of Place: From Location Technology to Communication Practice. In: Proceedings of the Third International Conference on Pervasive Computing. (2005)
25. Biggadike, A., Ferullo, D., Wilson, G., Perrig, A.: NATBLASTER: Establishing TCP Connections Between Hosts Behind NATs. In: Proceedings of the SIGCOMM Asia Workshop. (2005)
26. Ford, B., Srisuresh, P., Kegel, D.: Peer-to-Peer Communication Across Network Address Translators. In: Proceedings of the USENIX Annual Technical Conference. (2005)
27. Daemen, J., Rijmen, V.: AES Proposal: Rijndael. NIST (2000)
28. Fischer, K.: Bluetooth Wireless Technology. In: Proceedings of the IEEE EMC Wireless Workshop. (2000)
29. Thompson, K.: A Security Review of the ASB Bank Netcode Authentication System (2004) http://www.crypt.gen.nz/papers/asb_netcode.html.

30. Claessens, J., Preneel, B., Vandewalle, J.: Combining World Wide Web and Wireless Security. In: Proceedings of IFIP Network Security. (2001)
31. Maher, D.: Secure communication method and apparatus. U.S. Patent Number 5,450,493 (1995)
32. Gehrmann, C., Mitchell, C., Nyberg, K.: Manual Authentication for Wireless Devices. RSA Cryptobytes **7** (2004)
33. Hoepman, J.H.: The Ephemeral Pairing Problem. In: Proceedings of the 8th International Conference on Financial Cryptography. (2004)
34. Madhavapeddy, A., Sharp, R., Scott, D., Tse, A.: Audio Networking: The Forgotten Wireless Technology. IEEE Pervasive Computing **4** (2005)
35. Stajano, F., Anderson, R.: The Resurrecting Duckling. In: Proceedings of the 7th International Workshop on Security Protocols. (1999)
36. Balfanz, D., Smetters, D., Stewart, P., Wong, H.C.: Talking to Strangers: Authentication in Ad-Hoc Wireless Networks. In: Proceedings of the Network and Distributed System Security Symposium (NDSS '02), San Diego, California, USA (2002)
37. Capkun, S., Hubaux, J.P., Buttyan, L.: Mobility Helps Security in Ad Hoc Networks. In: Proceedings of the Fourth ACM International Symposium on Mobile Ad Hoc Networking and Computing (MobiHoc '03), Annapolis, Maryland, USA (2003)

Scalability in a Secure Distributed Proof System

Kazuhiro Minami and David Kotz

Department of Computer Science, Dartmouth College,
Hanover, NH, USA 03755
{minami, dfk}@cs.dartmouth.edu

Abstract. A logic-based language is often adopted in systems for pervasive computing, because it provides a convenient way to define rules that change the behavior of the systems dynamically. Those systems might define rules that refer to the users' context information to provide context-aware services. For example, a smart-home application could define rules referring to the location of a user to control the light of a house automatically. In general, the context information is maintained in different administrative domains, and it is, therefore, desirable to construct a proof in a distributed way while preserving each domain's confidentiality policies. In this paper, we introduce such a system, a secure distributed proof system for context-sensitive authorization and show that our novel caching and revocation mechanism improves the performance of the system, which depends on public key cryptographic operations to protect confidential information in rules and facts. Our revocation mechanism maintains dependencies among facts and recursively revokes across multiple hosts all the cached facts that depend on a fact that has become invalid. Our initial experimental results show that our caching mechanism, which maintains both positive and negative facts, significantly reduces the latency for handling a logical query.

1 Introduction

One of the major goals of pervasive computing is to meet a user's continuously changing requirements without taking explicit input from the users. Therefore, a system in pervasive computing needs to consider the user's context and change its behavior dynamically based on a set of rules. Many systems [7, 10, 19, 22] in pervasive computing apply a logic-based language to express those rules, since it also makes it possible to define a context model where a contextual fact is expressed with a boolean predicate. Besides defining triggering actions [22] of pervasive applications (e.g., a smart meeting room), a logical language provides a way to infer high-level context information [13, 19], such as a user's activity, from raw sensor data. One promising application of the logic-based approach is a context-sensitive authorization system [1, 2, 6, 8, 11, 18, 24] that considers a requester's context as well as his identity to make a granting decision; the system derives the granting decision (true or false) with a set of rules encoding policies and facts encoding context information.

Those logic-based systems assume a central server that maintains global knowledge of all the context information. However, in many realistic applications of pervasive computing, sources of context information are inherently distributed among many administrative domains that have different security policies. For example, imagine a large

K.P. Fishkin et al. (Eds.): PERVASIVE 2006, LNCS 3968, pp. 220–237, 2006.

office building where there are sensors managed by the city, the building owner, the companies leasing space, and the individual employees. An active-map application that displays the current location of an employee in that building might need to access multiple indoor location tracking systems in different organizations.

To achieve such information sharing among organizations, we must address two trust issues. First, each administrative domain (organization) defines confidentiality policies to protect information in that domain. It is necessary for an administrator of a location tracking system to protect users' location privacy [5, 18], for example. Therefore, a requester must satisfy the confidentiality policies of an information provider to access the requested information. Second, each administrative domain defines integrity policies that specify whether to trust information from other domains in terms of the integrity (correctness) of that information. Because context information is computed from raw sensor data, it inherently involves uncertainty. It is, therefore, important for each domain to choose reliable sources of information to derive correct context information. We assume that these trust relationships are defined by *principals*, each of which represents a specific user or organization, and that each host is associated with one principal (e.g., the owner of a PDA, or the manager of a server).

Our previous work on a secure context-sensitive authorization system [16, 17] enables mutually untrusted principals, which have partial knowledge about rules and context information, to evaluate a logical query without a universally trusted principal or a centralized knowledge base. The core of the approach is to decompose a proof for making an authorization decision into a set of sub-proofs produced on multiple different hosts, while preserving the confidentiality and integrity policies of the principals operating those hosts. Our scheme relies on public-key operations to enforce security policies of the principals, and those public-key operations might cause long latency during the process of making an authorization decision. However, we had not previously reported the performance of the system.

In this paper, we present the design and implementation of a novel caching and revocation scheme that significantly improves the performance of the original system. Our current target application is an emergency-response system [12] that provides an information dissemination infrastructure for responders in a disastrous incident. Since the responders who belong to different state or local agencies share information across the agencies on a need-to-know basis, we adopt context-sensitive authorization policies that consider a responder's location and medical condition to grant access to information about the incident. Our system should, therefore, scale to support tens of different administrative domains, meeting three key goals:

Speed: the average latency for handling a query should be comparable to that of a local query in a centralized system; we, therefore, aggressively cache query results from remote hosts to avoid issuing remote queries.

Freshness: a query result must be derived only from context information that satisfies a timeliness condition; all the context information in the proof must be generated within a given interval between the current time and a recent past time.

Fault tolerance: a query result, if produced, must be guaranteed to be correct under the presence of host failures or adversaries that intercept messages between hosts.

To achieve those goals, our caching mechanism enables each host to maintain both positive and negative query results to avoid issuing remote queries. To ensure the freshness of cached results, we develop an efficient capability-based technique for revoking cached query results. Unlike existing revocation methods [26] in which only an issuer of a certificate can revoke it, our scheme must allow multiple hosts to revoke a given cached result because the result might depend on (contextual) facts maintained by different hosts. Every principal that handles a query returns a query result with a randomly generated capability so that it can revoke the result by sending that capability to the receiver of the result. Each host maintains dependencies among cached facts, and the revocation process is recursively iterated across multiple hosts until all the cached facts that depend on the fact that has initially become invalid are revoked. Each host maintains the freshness of each cached result by exchanging messages that update the timestamp associated with the result and discards obsolete results periodically.

To demonstrate the effectiveness of our caching scheme, we measured the performance of our system with and without our caching mechanism. The results show that our caching mechanism significantly improved the amortized cost for handling queries, and the performance with the caching mechanism was comparable to that of a centralized system where all the rules and facts are stored in its local knowledge base. We also measured the latency for revoking a query result to show how our scheme can meet the timeliness condition on cached results.

The rest of the paper is organized as follows. We introduce our secure context-sensitive authorization system in Section 2, and cover the design of our caching and revocation mechanism in Section 3. Next, we describe a mechanism for keeping cached information updated in Section 4. We show the results of our experiments in Section 5 and discuss some limitations of our scheme in Section 6. We cover related work in Section 7 and conclude in Section 8.

2   Overview of a Secure Context-Sensitive Authorization System

In this section, we provide an overview of our secure context-sensitive authorization system [16, 17]. The system consists of multiple identical servers, which collaborate peer-to-peer to construct a proof for an authorization query in a distributed way. We first describe the structure of each host and then show how a set of servers, each of which only maintains partial knowledge about policies and (contextual) facts, make an authorization decision in a distributed environment.

2.1   Structure of the Authorization Server

Figure 1 shows the structure of an authorization server that consists of a knowledge base and an inference engine. The knowledge base stores both authorization policies and facts including context information. The context server publishes context events and updates facts in the knowledge base dynamically. The inference engine receives an authorization (or a logical) query from a remote server, such as a resource server, that receives a user's request and returns a proof that derives the fact in the query by retrieving information in the knowledge base. If the engine cannot construct a proof, it returns

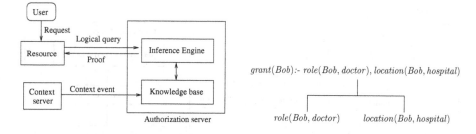

Fig. 1. Structure of an authorization server

Fig. 2. Sample proof tree

a proof that contains a false value. In an open environment of pervasive computing, each server could belong to a different administrative domain.

Rules and facts in a knowledge base are represented as a set of Horn clauses in Prolog. For example, a medical database may define an authorization policy that requires a requester P to hold a role membership "doctor" and to be physically located at the "hospital" as follows.

$$grant(P) :\text{-} role(P, doctor), location(P, hospital)$$

The atoms $role(P, doctor)$ and $location(P, hospital)$ on the right side of the clause are the conditions that must be satisfied to derive the granting decision $grant(P)$ on the left. If a user Bob issues a request to read a medical database, the proof tree in Figure 2 could be constructed based on the above rule. The root node in the tree represents the rule and the two leaf nodes represent the facts respectively. Notice that variable P in the rule is replaced with a constant Bob. A user's location, which is expressed with the $location$ predicate, is a dynamic fact; i.e., the second variable of the predicate $location$ should be updated dynamically as Bob changes his location.

2.2 Proof Decomposition in Distributed Query Processing

Multiple servers in different administrative domains handle an authorization query in a peer-to-peer way, since there need not be any single server that maintains all the rules and context information; a server must issue a remote query to another server when it does not have necessary information in its local knowledge base. However, the principals running those servers must preserve their confidentiality and integrity policies. The key idea for this goal is that when a principal who issues a query trusts a principal who handles a query in terms of the integrity of the query result, the handler principal does not disclose all the information in the proof. It might be sufficient to return a proof that simply states the fact in the query is true, and a proof thus is decomposed into multiple sub-proofs produced by different hosts.

Figure 3 describes such collaboration between a querier and a handler hosts. Suppose that host A run by principal Alice, who owns a projector, receives an authorization query $?grant(Dave, projector)$ that asks whether Dave is granted access to that projector. Since Alice's authorization policy in her knowledge base refers to a requester's location (i.e., $location(P, room112)$), Alice issues a query $?location(Dave, room112)$

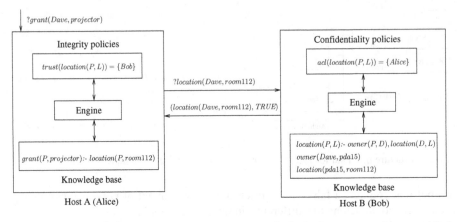

Fig. 3. Remote query between two principals. Alice is a principal who owns a projector, and Bob is a principal who runs a location server.

to host B run by Bob. Alice chooses Bob, because Bob satisfies Alice's integrity policies for queries of the type $location(P, L)$ (i.e., $trust(location(P, L)) = \{Bob\}$). Each principal decides to which principal a query should be sent by looking up his integrity policies. Bob processes the query from Alice, because Alice satisfies Bob's confidentiality policies for queries of the type $location(P, L)$ as defined in Bob's policy $acl(location(P, L)) = \{Alice\}$. Bob derives that Dave is in *room112* from the location of his device using the facts $location(pda15, room112)$ and $owner(Bob, pda15)$. However, he only needs to return a proof that contains a single root node that states that $location(Dave, room112)$ is true, because Alice believes Bob's statement about people's location (i.e., $location(P, L)$) according to her integrity policies. The proof of the query is thus decomposed into two subproofs maintained by Alice and Bob. In general, Bob could return a proof tree that contains multiple nodes. If Alice only trusts Bob's rule that derives Bob's location instead of Bob's fact, he would need to submit a larger proof tree to satisfy Alice's integrity policies.

2.3 Enforcement of Confidentiality Policies

Each principal who participates in constructing a proof enforces his confidentiality policies by encrypting a query result with a receiver principal's public key. A principal who returns a query result is allowed to choose a receiver principal from a list of upstream principals in a proof tree; a query is appended with a list of upstream principals that could receive the query result. Therefore, it is possible to obtain an answer for a query even when a querier principal does not satisfy the handler principal's confidentiality policies. Figure 4 shows the collaboration among principals p_0, p_1, p_2, and p_3. When principal p_0 issues an authorization query q_0 to principal p_1, p_1 issues a subsequent query q_1, which causes principal p_2's queries q_2 and q_3. Since a receiver principal of a proof might not be a principal who issues a query, a reply for a query is a tuple $(p_i, (pf)_{K_i})$ where p_i is an identity of a receiver principal and $(pf)_{K_i}$ is an encrypted proof with the receiver's public key. We assume that, in this example, each principal

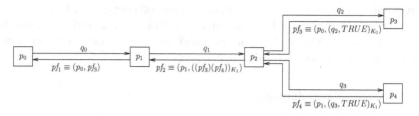

Fig. 4. Enforcement of confidentiality policies. The first item in a proof tuple is a receiver principal, and the second item is a proof tree encrypted with the receiver's public key.

who issues a query trusts the integrity of the principal who receives that query in terms of the correctness of whether the fact in the query is true or not. For example, p_0's integrity policies contains a policy $trust(q_0) = \{p_1\}$.

Suppose that query q_1's result (i.e., true or false) depends on the results of queries q_2 and q_3, which are handled by principals p_3 and p_4 respectively and that p_3 and p_4 choose principal p_0 and p_1 as a receiver respectively since p_2 does not satisfy their confidentiality policies. Because principal p_2 cannot decrypt the results from principals p_3 and p_4, p_2 encrypts those results with the public key of principal p_1[1], which p_2 chose as a receiver. A principal p_2 forwards the encrypted results from p_3 and p_4 because the query result of q_1 is the conjunction of those results. Principal p_1 decrypts the encrypted result from p_2 and obtains the encrypted results originally sent from principals p_3 and p_4. Since p_1 is a receiver of the proof from p_4, p_1 decrypts the proof that contains a true value. Since a query result for q_0 depends on the encrypted proof from p_3, principal p_1 forwards it in the same way. The principal p_0 finally decrypts it and obtains an answer for query q_0. Notice that principal p_0 is not aware of the fact that the query result is originally produced by principal p_3.

Each proof must be signed with a sender principal's public key so that a principal who receives a proof that contains sub-proofs produced multiple principals can check its integrity. Our system applies public-key operations only to a randomly generated symmetric key to reduce the performance overhead and use the symmetric key to encrypt and decrypt a proof; that is, a proof consists of a new symmetric key encrypted with a receiver's public key and a proof encrypted with that symmetric key. In addition to the public-key encryption, the querier and handler principals use another shared symmetric key to protect other data fields (e.g., a receiver identity) in a proof and a query from eavesdroppers. We assume that the two principals share the symmetric key via a protocol using public-key operations when the querier and handler principal authenticate with each other for the first time.

3   Caching and Revocation Mechanism

In this section, we describe a caching and revocation mechanism that improves the performance of our system. Our caching mechanism supports both positive and negative

---

[1] This recursive encryption is necessary to prevent an attack by malicious upstream principals of the message flow. The malicious colluding principals could read principal p_2's query result illegally by modifying the list of upstream principals given to p_2 along with a query q_1.

query results and avoids issuing remote queries, which otherwise cause long latency due to cryptographic operations and the transmission of data over a network. Our capability-based revocation mechanism allows any principal who contributes to producing a proof to revoke the cached result derived from that proof.

3.1 Capability-Based Revocation

A proof for a query contains (context) information provided by multiple different principals, and the derived fact from the proof must be revoked if any information in the proof becomes invalid; that is, there might be multiple principals that are eligible to revoke a given cached fact. We, therefore, developed a revocation mechanism based on capabilities [23] so that all the principals involved in constructing a proof may revoke the derived result from the proof.

Each node in a proof tree is associated with a capability (a large random number). The capability is created by a principal who provides the information (i.e., a fact or a rule) in the node. Since a principal who publishes a proof encrypts the query result and capability together with a receiver principal's public key, the capability is a shared secret between the publisher and the receiver of the proof node. Therefore, the principal who sent the proof can later revoke the fact or rule in the proof by sending the capability to the receiver principal. The sender principal of the revocation message does not need to authenticate itself to the receiver principal who maintains the cached information.

Figure 5 describes our revocation scheme in a distributed environment. A principal p_0 issues a query $?location(Bob, hospital)$, and a principal p_1 returns a proof that consists of a rule node produced by p_1 and two leaf nodes produced by p_2 and p_3 respectively. A principal p_0 caches the fact $location(Bob, hospital)$ derived from the received proof. Since principals p_1, p_2, and p_3 contribute to constructing the proof tree, they all should be eligible to revoke p_0's cached fact. Therefore, each principal p_i for $i = 1, 2, 3$ includes a capability c_i into his produced node so that p_i can revoke the proof later. A principal p_0 who caches the fact $location(Bob, hospital)$ associates it with the capabilities c_1, c_2, and c_3 obtained from the proof. Since principal p_3 chose p_0, not p_1, as a receiver of his proof pf_3, p_3 revokes his proof by sending a capability

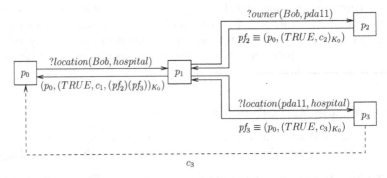

Fig. 5. Capability-based revocation. The dashed line represents a revocation message sent by principal p_3.

c_3 directly to principal p_0. Receiving that revocation message, a principal p_0 removes the cached fact associated with the capability c_3. Principals p_1 and p_2 could revoke the same cached fact in the same way. Our capability-based revocation does not involve any public-key operations, which are computationally expensive, because a revocation message can be directly sent to a principal who maintains a cached fact. When our system constructs a proof tree responding to an authorization query, public-key encryptions are necessary to prevent intermediate principals between a sender and a receiver principal from reading the sender's query result. Furthermore, a revocation message does not need to be signed by a sender principal, because it is not necessary for a sender to authenticate himself to a receiver principal of the revocation message. When we extend the revocation scheme to support negative caching, however, we do require encryption (see Section 3.4).

3.2 Structural Overview

Our revocation mechanism is based on a publisher-subscriber model; that is, a querier principal subscribes to a handler principal who handles his query, and the handler principal sends a revocation message when the query result becomes invalid. This process might occur recursively until all the cached facts that depend on the invalidated fact are revoked across the network. Figure 6 shows the structure of our caching and revocation mechanism and the message flow among the components when a cached fact is revoked. Each server consists of two components (an inference engine and a revocation handler) and four data structures (a subscribers list, a dependencies list, a subscription list, and a knowledge base). The inference engine is responsible for constructing a proof and caching query results obtained from other principals with the knowledge base and the subscription list. The engine also maintains information on other principals who issue a query to the engine with the subscribers and dependencies list so that the engine can revoke cached results in remote hosts. When principal p_1 receives a query q_0 from

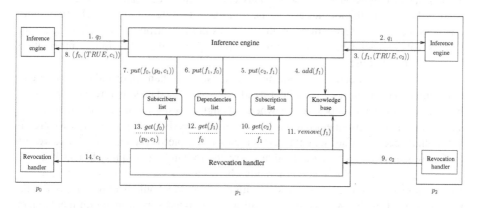

Fig. 6. Structure of a caching and revocation mechanism. We omit the data structures from the servers of p_0 and p_2 for brevity. The number at the beginning of each message represents the sequence of the entire revocation process. The return value of a message is shown under a dotted line in the messages 10, 12, and 13.

principal p_0, p_1's inference engine constructs a proof tree for a fact f_0, which is unified with q_0, and issues a subsequent query q_1 to principal p_2, and p_2 returns a proof tree whose root node contains the unified fact f_1 and the pair of a query result $TRUE$ and a capability c_2. Note that facts f_0 and f_1 are identical to queries q_0 and q_1 respectively if those queries do not contain any variables. Principal p_1 stores f_1 as a fact into its knowledge base and also puts a key-value pair (c_2, f_1) into the subscription list (a hash table). Notice that we use the same knowledge base to store cached results as well as local rules and facts. After constructing a proof tree for f_0, the engine stores the pair (f_1, f_0), which represents f_0's dependency on f_1, and a nested tuple $(f_0, (p_0, c_1))$ into the dependencies and subscribers list respectively. The nested tuple $(f_0, (p_0, c_1))$ expresses an if-then rule stating that a capability c_1 must be sent to principal p_0 if fact f_0 becomes invalid. The inference engine finishes handling query q_0 by returning a proof tree whose root node contains fact f_0 and the pair of a query result $TRUE$ and a capability c_1.

The revocation process occurs when principal p_2 sends a revocation message that contains a capability c_2. Principal p_1's revocation handler receives the message, obtains a fact to be revoked with capability c_2 from the subscription list, and removes fact f_1 from the knowledge base. Next, the revocation handler obtains fact f_0, which depends on f_1, from the dependencies list and then accesses the subscribers list to obtain a capability c_1 for revoking principal p_0's cached fact f_0, and sends c_1 to p_0's revocation handler. The same process is repeated on p_0's server.

If a capability is a shared secret that is only used once, a capability does not need to be encrypted as we explain in this section. In Section 3.4 below, though, we add support for caching negative results and in that case we do need an encrypted channel for this message.

3.3   Synchronization Mechanism

There is a race condition to be resolved between the inference engine and the revocation handler, because both modules access the four data structures in Figure 6. For example, it is possible that the revocation handler accesses the subscription list with a capability c that revokes a fact f before the inference engine writes the subscription information (i.e., (c, f)) to that list.

However, we cannot use a coarse mutual exclusion mechanism that allows the thread of the inference engine to block other threads' access to the data structure while processing a query, since a deadlock occurs when the engine issues a remote query that causes a closed cycle of subsequent queries by remote servers. For example, if a downstream server that receives a subsequent query issues a remote query back to the server of the inference engine, a new thread that is created to handle that query blocks because the inference engine on that server already obtains a lock on the data structures, which the new thread needs to access. Thus, the inference engine would wait for a reply for the remote query forever. We, therefore, built a fine-grained synchronization mechanism that ensures that the engine that receives a proof-tree node with capability c updates the data structures before the revocation handler that receives a capability c accesses them.

3.4   Negative Caching

Our system also supports caching negative facts (i.e., facts that are false), because a principal cannot return a negative result when he does not find any matched fact for the query in the local knowledge base; another principal might have a fact that matches with the query. To make a negative decision locally, a principal must cache a negative result after the attempt to obtain the queried fact from remote principals fails.

To support negative caching, each principal maintains the same set of data structures in Figure 6; that is, each server maintains another knowledge base that stores negative facts. The semantics of a negative revocation is different from that of positive caching; that is, when a cached negative fact is revoked, that fact can be cached as a positive fact. (On the other hand, to revoke a positive fact does not necessary mean that the revoked fact is no longer true; there might be another proof that derives the fact. Note that if a host that maintains a positive fact has first-hand knowledge about the validity of that fact without checking with other hosts, that host could convert the revoked positive fact into a negative cached fact.)

When a negative fact is revoked, we must find an entry (c, f) in the negative subscription list, where c is a capability and f is the revoked fact, and move it to the subscription list for positive cached facts. However, we cannot use the same capability c for the entry in the positive list, because it might cause inconsistency about the subscription information between the sender and receiver of a revocation message in the case where the revocation message is lost. For example, suppose that we use the same capability for a switched positive cached fact. When a principal who sends another principal a revocation message for a negative cached fact, the sender principal moves the corresponding subscription information from the subscribers list of negative facts to that of positive facts. However, if the receiver principal does not receive the message because of a network failure, the receiver principal continues to maintain the negative cached fact, which is supposed to be revoked. When the sender principal later sends a revocation message that revokes the switched positive cached fact, the receiver principal revokes the negative cached fact instead. Thus, the inconsistency about the cached information occurs.

Therefore, a revocation message for a negative cached result needs to contain a new capability to revoke the switched positive cached result. Since the new capability must be a shared secret between a sender and a receiver of the revocation message, we need to encrypt the message with a shared key between those two parties. However, to establish a symmetric secure channel for all the pairs of two principals that participate in our system requires n^2 symmetric keys, where n is the number of participating principals. To avoid this key-management problem, our system encrypts a revocation message with the same randomly generated symmetric key that is used to encrypt the proof node that contains the cached result as we describe in Section 2.3; that is, each server records the capabilities in a received proof with a symmetric key that is used to decrypt that proof. Suppose that the proof contains a node with a capability c_n and was encrypted with a symmetric key K when the server receives it. A server stores a (c_n, K) pair in a hash table to handle a revocation message $(c_n, (c_n, c_p)_K)$ where c_n is a capability that revokes a current negative result, c_p is a capability that revokes the switched positive result in the future, and K is the symmetric key associated with c_n. When a server receives this message, it first obtains a symmetric key K corresponding to the capability c_n in the message from the hash table, and decrypts $(c_n, c_p)_K$ with that key. If the first element of the decrypted tuple is same as the capability in the first field of the revocation message, the server considers that revocation message valid and revokes the corresponding fact. We continue to use the key K if we later revoke the fact that corresponds to the capability c_p. In a way, the symmetric key K is a real capability and the capability c_n is an indirect reference to K.

4   Timeliness of Cached Information

Our system must ensure that all the cached facts meet a given timeliness condition; all the timestamps associated with cached facts must be within a given interval between the current time and a recent past time. To simply keep the latest messages does not guarantee the freshness of the cached facts because some hosts might crash or an adversary might intercept revocation messages so a server would make an incorrect decision based on obsolete cached information.

We, therefore, develop a mechanism that ensures the freshness of cached positive and negative facts obtained from remote servers. The updater thread on each server periodically sends each subscriber in a subscribers list a message that updates the timestamp of a cached fact by sending the capability with a new timestamp. We assume that all the server clocks are approximately synchronized. Since the server sends the same capability to refresh the same cached fact repeatedly, the updater thread encrypts the message with the same symmetric key that would be used to send a revocation message for revoking that cached fact. The watcher thread on another server receives that message and updates the timestamp of the fact in a subscription list. The watcher thread must synchronize with the inference engine using the same synchronization method we describe in Section 3.3. If the watcher thread finds any subscription with an old timestamp (possibly because an adversary intercepts revocation messages), it discards that subscription and initiates the revocation process described in Section 3.2.

5   Experiments and Evaluation

We set out to measure the performance of our system. Since many context-aware applications, such as an emergency-response system in which responders continuously access information on an incident over a duration of a few hours to several days, need to keep track of a user's privileges continuously, our focus is to show that our caching mechanism significantly improves amortized performance of our system.

We used a 27 node cluster connected with a Gigabit Ethernet. Each node had two 2.8GHz Intel XEONs and 4GB RAM, and runs RedHat Linux 9 and Sun Microsystem's Java runtime (v1.5.0-hotspot). Our system has approximately 12,000 lines of Java code, extending a Prolog engine XProlog [25]. We used the Java Cryptographic Extension (JCE) framework to implement RSA and Triple-DES (TDES) cryptographic operations. We used a 1024-bit public key whose public exponent is fixed to 65537 in our experiments. The RSA signing operation uses MD5 [21] to compute the hash value of a message. We used Outer-CBC TDES in EDE mode [9] to perform symmetric key operations. The length of our DES keys was 192 bits, and the padding operation in TDES operations conforms to RFC 1423 [20].

5.1 Analysis of Performance Overhead

We first show the latency of the system with two hosts that did not use the caching mechanism. One host maintains a rule $a0(P) \leftarrow a00(P)$, and the other host maintains a fact $a00(bob)$. When the former host receives a query $?a0(bob)$, it issues a remote query $?a00(bob)$ to the other host. We measured the wall-clock latency for handling a query and also the latency of each cryptographic operation in that process. The measurement is iterated one hundred times, and we report the average of the measurements. Table 1 shows the results.

As we see in Table 1, public-key operations consumed most of the processing time. On host 0, RSA decryption on DES keys from host 1 takes 53% of the local processing time. TDES decryption on a proof also takes another 22% of the time. On host 1, RSA encryption on DES keys takes 22% of the local processing time, and signing the proof with a RSA public key takes another 17%. These results indicate that our caching scheme should improve the performance because a successful cache hit avoids all of these public key operations.

Table 1. Average latency of processing a query with two hosts without caching capability. The latency is measured in milliseconds. The *ratio* columns shows the ratio of the latency of each primitive operations compared with the total local processing time.

	host 0		host 1	
	latency	ratio	latency	ratio
Total latency	138.1		85.2	
Issue remote queries	87.9		0.0	
Local computation	50.2	1.00	85.2	1.00
TDES decryption on a received query	0.0	0.00	2.2	0.03
TDES encryption on a returning proof	0.0	0.00	10.9	0.12
TDES decryption on a received proof	10.9	0.22	0.0	0.00
TDES encryption on an issued query	1.2	0.02	0.0	0.00
RSA decryption on DES keys	26.6	0.53	0.0	0.00
RSA encryption on DES keys	0.0	0.00	18.7	0.22
Create a RSA signature for a proof	0.0	0.00	14.4	0.17
Verify a RSA signature for a proof	2.2	0.04	0.0	0.00

5.2 Latency for Handling Queries

We next measured the latency of handling a query with different size proof trees to evaluate the scalability of our caching scheme. We performed our experiments with 27 servers run by different principals; those servers could correspond to 27 different agencies in the emergency-response system. Our test program generated authorization, confidentiality, and integrity policies of those principals such that our system constructs a proof tree of a given size (i.e., the number of nodes in the proof tree) for the given query. Each query takes the form of $?grant(P, R)$ where P is a principal and R is a resource. The body of each rule takes the form of $a_0(c_0), \ldots, a_{n-1}(c_{n-1})$ where a_i for $i = 0$ to $n - 1$ is a predicate symbol and c_i for $i = 0$ to $n - 1$ is a constant. The size of the domain of predicate symbols is 1,000, and the size of the domain of constants is 20. There are possibly 20,000 different atoms in authorization policies that our test program generates, and it is, therefore, unlikely that a cache hit occurs when a query is evaluated for the first time. Those policies are independent of any particular application in a sense that the test program chose the topology of a proof tree randomly. However, we conducted our experiment up to a proof tree with 50 nodes, which we believe is significantly larger than that in most applications, and, therefore, our results should provide guidelines about the worst-case latency of those applications. We prepared the facts and rules to allow ten different proof trees of the same size, and in the experiment a given host issued a sequence of ten different queries of that size.

Our latency measurements also include the performance overhead for handling revocation messages. While measuring latency for handling queries 100 times, our test driver program updates all the facts in the knowledge bases dynamically. We assumed the extreme case that all the facts in each proof tree are dynamic contextual facts, and updated every fact 20 times per second during the experiments. We believe that this update frequency is much faster than most context-aware applications need.

Figure 7(a) compares query-handling latency under five different conditions; each data point is an average of 100 runs. In the *No caching, with RSA* case, each server did not cache any results obtained from other servers and used public-key operations for encrypting DES keys and signing proof trees. *No caching, with TDES* is same as the first case, except that every pair of the principals shared a secret DES key and used it to attach a message authentication code (MAC) using Keyed-Hashing for Message Authentication (HMAC-MD5) hashing algorithm [4, 14] to authenticate an encrypted proof. We included this case to show that to use symmetric key operations instead of public-key operations (assuming that all the pair of the principals share a secret key) does not solve the problem of the long latency for handling a query. In the *Cold caching* case, every server cached results from other servers and all the latency data including that of the initial round of queries were used to compute average latency. In the *Warm caching* case, every server cached results from other servers and we used only the latency data after the first round of ten different queries to compute average latency. In the *Local processing* case, all the rules and facts were stored in a single server. Therefore, there was no remote query involved, and no encryption.

The two cases without caching show significantly longer latency than the other three cases, although using MD5 and DES operations rather than RSA reduced the latency 15 – 50%. The latency grew longer than 500 ms when a proof tree contained more than ten nodes. Figure 7(b) shows the same latency results for the other three cases, omitting the case of no caching. The latency of the cold caching case is 5 to 20 times longer than that of the warm caching, because the initial queries require the whole process of constructing a proof tree as in the case of no caching. The latency of the warm caching case were 2 to 15 times higher than that of the local processing case. The reason for the longer latency is a cache miss due to a revocation of a positive cached fact. However, the latency of the warm caching case was 3 to 23 times faster than the cold caching case, and thus we could improve the performance by prefetching query results in advance.

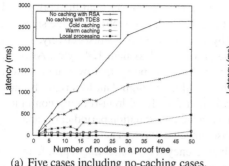 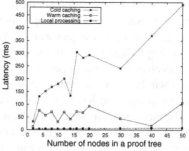

(a) Five cases including no-caching cases.   (b) Three cases without no-caching cases.

Fig. 7. Latency for handling queries

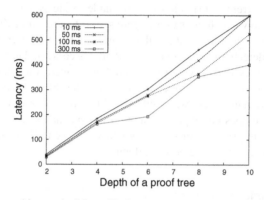

Fig. 8. Latency for revoking cached facts. Each curve represents a different period between fact updates in the knowledge bases, in milliseconds.

5.3 Latency for Revoking Cached Facts

We measured the latency for revoking cached facts with another experiment. We used linear proof trees of various depths to measure the latency between the moment the test driver sent an event that updates a fact in the knowledge base and the moment that the test driver received the notification of a revoked cached fact from the root server that handles queries from the test driver. We conducted the same experiment 100 times and report the average of the measurements. Figure 8 shows the latency for revoking cached facts with four different frequencies for updating the knowledge bases. The results show that the latency increased linearly as the depth of a proof tree grows. The latency slightly increased as the period for publishing an event decreases. The system handled 100 events per second with the latency less than 600 ms and a proof tree of depth 10.

6   Discussion

Although, in Section 5, we conducted the experiments in a cluster with low-latency connections, our implementation, to some extent, simulates a low-latency network by encoding a proof as a set of Java objects, which is much larger than the corresponding string representation. For example, in the experiment in Section 5.1, the sizes of a query object and a proof object were 723 bytes and 34184 bytes respectively, and the corresponding strings for the query and the proof were less than 124 bytes. Also, our caching mechanism could improve the performance of the system even more drastically in a wireless environment with low bandwidth and high data-loss ratio, because to handle a query with local cache is a common case for a long-running continuous query. The mechanism in Section 4 refreshes cached information periodically, and thus prevents false positive decisions due to a disconnected wireless network.

To process an authorization query involves latency for constructing a proof, and the authorization decision is thus derived from the proof that might contain dynamic facts previously published at different times. Since an authorization decision is made based on information collected in the past, our system might grant a request that should have been denied if the current information was available to the system. This limitation in our system might allow a malicious user to gain access to a resource illegally by changing his context from a legitimate state (that grants his access) to an illegitimate state before the system detects the change of the the user's context. Therefore, our system should provide a policy maker with a way to define explicit timeliness constraints on authorization decisions; that is, a policy maker should be able to specify a time T such that all the information in a proof was published within time T prior to the current time. Although our system does not explicitly support this mechanism, the experimental results in Section 5.3 imply that our system would work even if T were as small as six hundreds milliseconds for a large proof of depth 10.

7   Related Work

In this section, we cover systems that support caching mechanisms for an inference engine. See our technical report [15] for a comprehensive survey on distributed authorization.

We developed our caching and revocation mechanisms based on our previous research on the secure context-sensitive authorization system [17]. We measured the performance of our original scheme in detail, which is not included in our previous paper.

Ranganathan [19] proposes to use a first-order logic to model a user's context and reason about it. To reason with context information stored in multiple hosts, each context provider on those hosts provides an interface that handles a query from a remote host. However, their scheme does not support any caching mechanism across the hosts. Bauer [3] developed a distributed proving system that constructs a proof that grants access to a resource in a distributed way; a principal who constructs a proof could delegate a task of building a sub-proof to another principal rather than collecting all the certificates that are necessary to construct a whole proof. Bauer's scheme is similar to ours in a sense that a proof is produced by multiple principals in a distributed environment. However, the algorithm does not address the issue of protecting confidential information in certificates, which are used to construct a proof. Although their system caches both positive and negative facts, there is no detail about mechanisms for revoking cached information. Katsiri [13] built a prototype of a dual-layer knowledge base based on a first-order logic. The higher Deductive Abstract layer caches abstract context information derived from low-level knowledge in the lower to make the system scalable. The system consists of a single server and does not support a revocation mechanism in a distributed environment.

8   Summary

We describe a novel caching and revocation mechanism that improves the performance of a secure context-sensitive authorization system. Our major contribution is to show that we could build a secure distributed proof system whose amortized performance scales to a large proof that spans across tens of servers. Our capability-based revocation mechanism combines an event-based push mechanism with a query-based pull mechanism where each server publishes a revocation message over a network recursively by maintaining dependencies among local and remote cached facts. Our revocation mechanism supports both positive and negative caching and is capable of converting a revoked negative fact into a valid positive cached fact to reduce the number of cache misses, while ensuring the secrecy of a new capability without having n^2 secret keys among n principals. We also incorporate a mechanism that ensures the freshness of cached information under the presence of an adversary that is capable of intercepting revocation messages.

Our experimental results show that the performance overhead of public-key operations involved in the process of a remote query were large and that our caching mechanism significantly reduced the amortized latency for handling a query. Therefore, our system is suitable to a context-aware application in which a user's privileges must be continuously monitored. Since our experiments were conducted with a wide range of parameters, the results should serve as guidelines about the worse-case performance of many systems in pervasive computing.

Although we describe our system in the context of a logic-based authorization system, we believe our scheme is general enough to support various kinds of rule-based policies in pervasive computing.

Acknowledgments

This research program is a part of the Institute for Security Technology Studies, supported under Award number 2000-DT-CX-K001 from the U.S. Department of Homeland Security, Science and Technology Directorate. This work is also part of the Center for Mobile Computing at Dartmouth College, and has been supported by IBM, Cisco Systems, NSF grant EIA-98-02068, and DARPA Award number F30602-98-2-0107. Points of view in this document are those of the authors and do not necessarily represent the official position of the U.S. Department of Homeland Security or its Science and Technology Directorate, or any of the other sponsors.

References

1. Jalal Al-Muhtadi, Anand Ranganathan, Roy Campbell, and Dennis Mickunas. Cerberus: a context-aware security scheme for smart spaces. In *Proceedings of the First IEEE International Conference on Pervasive Computing and Communications*, pages 489–496. IEEE Computer Society, March 2003.

2. Jean Bacon, Ken Moody, and Walt Yao. A model of OASIS role-based access control and its support for active security. *Proceedings of the Sixth ACM Symposium on Access Control Models and Technologies*, 5(4):492–540, 2002.

3. Lujo Bauer, Scott Garriss, and Michael K. Reiter. Distributed proving in access-control systems. In *Proceedings of the 2005 IEEE Symposium on Security and Privacy*, pages 81–95, Washington, DC, USA, 2005. IEEE Computer Society.

4. Mihir Bellare, Ran Canetti, and Hugo Krawczyk. Keying hash functions for message authentication. In *Proceedings of the 16th Annual International Cryptology Conference on Advances in Cryptology*, pages 1–15, London, UK, 1996. Springer-Verlag.

5. Alastair R. Beresford and Frank Stajano. Location Privacy in Pervasive Computing. *IEEE Pervasive Computing*, 2(1):46–55, January-March 2003.

6. Patrick Brezillon. Context-based security policies: A new modeling approach. In *Second IEEE Annual Conference on Pervasive Computing and Communications Workshops*, pages 154–158. IEEE Computer Society, March 2004.

7. Harry Chen, Tim Finin, and Anupam Joshi. An Ontology for Context-Aware Pervasive Computing Environments. *Special Issue on Ontologies for Distributed Systems, Knowledge Engineering Review*, 18(3):197–207, May 2004.

8. Michael J. Covington, Wende Long, Srividhya Srinivasan, Anind K. Dey, Mustaque Ahamad, and Gregory D. Abowd. Securing context-aware applications using environment roles. In *Proceedings of the Sixth ACM Symposium on Access Control Models and Technologies*, pages 10–20. ACM Press, 2001.

9. Data Encryption Standard (DES), October 1999. `http://csrc.nist.gov/publications/fips/fips46-3/fips46-3.pdf`.

10. Karen Henricksen and Jadwiga Indulska. A software engineering framework for context-aware pervasive computing. In *Proceedings of the Second IEEE International Conference on Pervasive Computing and Communications (PerCom'04)*, pages 77–86, Washington, DC, USA, 2004. IEEE Computer Society.

11. R. J. Hulsebosch, A. H. Salden, M. S. Bargh, P. W. G. Ebben, and J. Reitsma. Context Sensitive Access Control. In *Proceedings of the 10th ACM Symposium on Access Control Models and Technologies*, pages 111–119, Baltimore, MD, June 2005.

12. National incident management system, March 2004. `http://www.fema.gov/pdf/nims/nims_doc_full.pdf`.

13. Eleftheria Katsiri and Alan Mycroft. Knowledge representation and scalable abstract reasoning for sentient computing using first-order logic. In *Proceedings of Challenges and Novel Applications for Automatic Reasoning (CADE-19)*, pages 73–87, July 2003.

14. Hugo Krawczyk, Mihir Bellare, and Ran Canetti. Hmac: Keyed-hashing for message authentication. Internet RFC 2693, February 1997. `http://www-cse.ucsd.edu/users/mihir/papers/rfc2104.txt`.

15. Kazuhiro Minami. Secure context-sensitive authorization. Technical Report TR2006-571, Dept. of Computer Science, Dartmouth College, February 2006.

16. Kazuhiro Minami and David Kotz. Secure context-sensitive authorization. In *Proceedings of the Third IEEE International Conference on Pervasive Computing and Communications (PerCom)*, pages 257–268, Kauai, Hawaii, March 2005.

17. Kazuhiro Minami and David Kotz. Secure context-sensitive authorization. *Journal of Pervasive and Mobile Computing*, 1(1):123–156, March 2005.

18. Ginger Myles, Adrian Friday, and Nigel Davies. Preserving privacy in environments with location-based applications. *IEEE Pervasive Computing*, 2(1):56–64, January-March 2003.

19. Anand Ranganathan and Roy H. Campbell. An infrastructure for context-awareness based on first order logic. *Personal Ubiquitous Computing*, 7(6):353–364, 2003.

20. RFC 1423 - Privacy Enhancement for Internet Electronic Mail: Part III: Algorithms, Modes, and Identifiers, February 1993. `http://www.faqs.org/rfcs/rfc1423.html`.

21. Ronald L. Rivest.   The MD5 message-digest algorithm, April 1992.   `http://www.ietf.org/rfc/rfc1321.txt`.

22. Bill N. Schilit, Norman Adams, and Roy Want.   Context-aware computing applications. In *Proceedings of IEEE Workshop on Mobile Computing Systems and Applications*, pages 85–90, Santa Cruz, California, December 1994. IEEE Computer Society Press.

23. Andrew S. Tanenbaum, Robbert van Renesse, Hans van Staveren, Gregory J. Sharp, and Sape J. Mullender. Experiences with the amoeba distributed operating system. *Communications of the ACM*, 33(12):46–63, 1990.

24. Anand Tripathi, Tanvir Ahmed, Devdatta Kulkarni, Richa Kumar, and Komal Kashiramka. Context-based secure resource access in pervasive computing environments. In *Proceedings of the Second IEEE Annual Conference on Pervasive Computing and Communications Workshops*, pages 159–163. IEEE Computer Society, March 2004.

25. Jean Vaucher. XProlog.java: the successor to Winikoff's WProlog, Feb 2003. `http://www.iro.umontreal.ca/~vaucher/XProlog/AA_README`.

26. Peifang Zheng. Tradeoffs in certificate revocation schemes. *ACM SIGCOMM Computer Communication Review*, 33(2):103–112, 2003.

Secure Mobile Computing Via Public Terminals

Richard Sharp[1], James Scott[1], and Alastair R. Beresford[2]

[1] Intel Research,
15 JJ Thomson Avenue, Cambridge CB3 0FD, UK
[2] Computer Laboratory, University of Cambridge, 15 JJ Thomson Avenue,
Cambridge CB3 0FD, UK
richard.sharp@intel.com,
james.w.scott@intel.com,
alastair.beresford@cl.cam.ac.uk

Abstract. The rich interaction capabilities of public terminals can make them more convenient to use than small personal devices, such as smart phones. However, the use of public terminals to handle personal data may compromise privacy. We present a system that enables users to access their applications and data securely using a combination of public terminals and a more trusted, personal device. Our system (i) provides users with capabilities to censor the public terminal display, so that it does not show private data; (ii) filters input events coming from the public terminal, so that maliciously injected keyboard/pointer events do not compromise privacy; and (iii) enables users to view personal information and perform data-entry via their personal device. A key feature of our system is that it works with unmodified applications. A prototype implementation of the system has been publicly released for Linux and Windows. The results arising from a pilot usability study based on this implementation are presented.

1 Introduction

It is often convenient to access personal data and applications from public terminals (e.g. viewing documents in a hotel business center, or checking email in an Internet cafe). However, it is also dangerous: public terminals are an easy target for criminals intent on harvesting passwords and other confidential information from legitimate users.

This is not just a theoretical threat. The Anti-Phishing Working Group (APWG) report that the use of *crimeware* (e.g. software-based keyloggers) has recently *"surged markedly"*, with the number of new crimeware applications discovered doubling from April to June 2005 [2]. As well as software-based vulnerabilities, the public terminal hardware itself can be compromised. Tiny, inexpensive devices embedded in keyboards or PS2/USB cables [8] can log millions of key strokes to flash memory. Attackers can easily install such devices on public terminals, leave them for a while and return later to collect users' private data and authentication information. In addition, attackers can often obtain user credentials from public terminals without installing any malicious software

K.P. Fishkin et al. (Eds.): PERVASIVE 2006, LNCS 3968, pp. 238–253, 2006.

or hardware at all. For example, persistent data stored in browser caches some-times includes usernames/passwords [20] and legitimate *Desktop Search* packages installed on shared terminals enable attackers to browse the private documents and emails of previous users [23]. Of course, when terminals are located in busy public places, attackers can also *shoulder-surf*: stand behind a user in order to read the content of the display and watch them type on the keyboard [25].

In the field of mobile computing research, a great deal of effort has been ex-pended in developing architectures and interaction techniques that exploit shared public terminals. For example, the Internet Suspend Resume [9] project aims to provide users with the ability to *"logically suspend a machine at one Internet site, then travel to some other site and resume . . . work there on another machine"*; the authors of the Virtual Network Computing thin-client technology [18] were motivated by creating a world where *"users can access their personal . . . desktops on whatever computing infrastructure happens to be available—including, for ex-ample, public web-browsing terminals in airports"*; and interaction techniques such as *Situated Mobility* [15], *Parasitic Computing* [12] and *Opportunistic An-nexing* [16] rely on small mobile devices co-opting computing resources already present in the environment in order to facilitate interaction with their users (e.g. taking over a public display and data-entry device). If mobile computing research is to achieve its goal of providing anytime, anywhere access to personal information via shared public terminals, it is clear that the security and privacy problems highlighted above must be addressed.

In this paper we present a framework that allows users to access their appli-cations and data securely using a combination of public terminals and a trusted personal device such as, for example, a smart phone or a PDA[1]. Our system en-ables users to enjoy the rich interaction capabilities of large situated displays and keyboards, whilst performing security-critical operations via their smart phone. For example, passwords are typed via the smart phone's keypad, thwarting key-loggers running on the public terminal. Similarly, secure information is displayed only on the smart phone's screen preventing both screengrabbing attacks per-petrated by software running on the public terminal[2]. Using the smart phone for private display and data-entry also helps protect against shoulder-surfing. A major benefit of our approach is that we do not require applications to be re-written; our system is specifically designed to work with existing Windows, Linux and MacOS applications.

The key contributions of this work are: (*i*) A general system architecture suit-able for the scenario above (Section 2), (*ii*) A *threat model* formalising the attacks against users of public terminals, and a set of *security principles* addressing these

---

[1] Although a variety of small personal devices with displays and keypads are adequate for our purposes, for the sake of brevity, the remainder of this paper will refer to the trusted personal device as a smart phone. In Section 2 we will justify our belief that smart phones are indeed more trusted than public terminals.

[2] Packages such as *PC SpyCam 2.0* combine key logging and screen grabbing to build a complete picture of what a user did with a computer. Programs such as this can often be configured to take screenshots in response to specific actions (e.g. when a user opens their email package).

threats (Section 3), (*iii*) a *GPL implementation* of the architecture (Section 4), which is equally applicable to both the *Remote Access Model* [18] where the user's thin-client server is located on a remote machine accessible via the Internet; and the *Personal Server Model* [26], where the user's applications run locally on their personal device, and (*iv*) a *pilot usability study* showing the feasibility of our approach (Section 5). We also survey related research (Section 6) and present conclusions and directions for future work (Section 7).

2   System Overview

Our system is based on thin-client technology. When a mobile session is initiated, the smart phone and the public terminal connect concurrently to a user's thin-client server as shown in Figure 1. On connection, the public terminal's display shows the user's entire desktop; the phone's (smaller) display shows a scrollable portion of this screen. As well as performing data-entry via the public terminal, the user can also type via the keypad (or virtual keypad) on their smart phone.

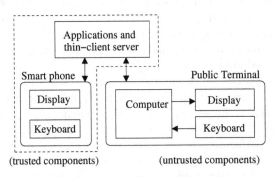

Fig. 1. Using our system to access private information via a public terminal

When performing operations that are not security critical the user interacts with the public terminal in the usual fashion, via its own display and keyboard. However, when a user performs a security critical operation (e.g. entering a credit card number) they can use their smart phone to activate a variety of security features. The security features currently supported include (*i*) applying image processing filters to censor content on the public display; (*ii*) controlling the way in which (untrusted) mouse and keyboard events arising from the public terminal are interpreted; and (*iii*) entering security-critical data, such as passwords, via the (trusted) smart phone's keypad.

The security provided by our system is based on the premise that a user's smart phone is inherently more trustworthy than a public terminal (e.g. it is less likely that crimeware will be running on a user's smart phone than on a public terminal). There are a number of reasons why this assumption is justified: (*i*) whereas it is easy for hackers to gain physical access to a public terminal (in order to install crimeware, for example), it is much harder to gain physical access to a users' phone; (*ii*) users install applications on their phones relatively infrequently, and often only inside sandboxes such as Java MIDP which do not permit general keylogging/screengrabbing, thus limiting the risk of trojan-based crimeware [3]; and (*iii*) the developers of phone-based operating systems often go to great lengths to prevent installed applications from performing silent network communication—this makes it difficult for crimeware to transmit information (such as keylogs etc.) back to hackers without alerting the user. (We note that, in previous work, other security researchers have made similar arguments, claiming that personal devices offer a greater degree of security than general purpose PCs [3]).

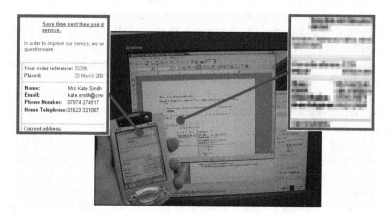

Fig. 2. Our prototype in use. Content on the public terminal is censored (right inset); the area around the mouse pointer appears uncensored on the private display (left inset). In this case, pixellation is used for censoring the public display, but other filters are also provided.

Figure 2 shows a picture of our system in the case where a user has opted to censor the content on the public display. When content on the public display is censored, the area of the screen surrounding the mouse pointer[4] is automatically displayed *uncensored* on the smart phone's private display. As the user moves the mouse pointer, the uncensored smart phone's display scrolls accordingly. Although one cannot use the censored public display to read the text of the private document, it still provides a great deal of contextual information—for example, the positions of windows, scroll bars, icons etc. Users can thus perform *macroscopic operations* (e.g. dragging or scrolling windows) via the censored public display, whilst performing *microscopic operations* (e.g. selecting options from a menu or reading a private email) via their smart phone's private display.

---

[3] Legitimate applications which incorporate crimeware functionality.

[4] We assume that the public terminal provides some kind of pointing device: e.g. it is a touchscreen, or a mouse or tracker-ball is available.

3   Security Model

Following standard security engineering practice we start by presenting our *threat model* and *security policy model* [1]. The threat model characterises attackers' motivation and capabilities; the security policy model provides an abstract, architecturally-independent description of the security properties of our system.

3.1   Threat Model

Attackers' motivation is to steal private and confidential information, often with a view to committing identity theft and fraud. Attackers are capable of mounting both *passive monitoring attacks* and *active injection attacks* against the public terminal. Passive monitoring attacks include recording everything shown on the public terminal's display, typed on the public terminal's keyboard and transmitted over the network. Active injection attacks include injecting malicious data packets into the network and also injecting fake User Interface (UI) events (e.g. keypresses and mouse clicks) into the public terminal.

For an example of an attack based on injecting fake UI events, consider the following. An attacker installs crimeware on the public terminal that waits until the user opens their email client. At this point the crimeware generates click events, selecting each email in turn. When the emails are displayed on the screen (as a result of the injected click events) the attacker performs a screen grab, thus obtaining users' private information.

We assume that users' smart phones are not compromised and that attackers therefore have no means of either recording or injecting phone-based keyboard, screen or UI events. However attackers can nonetheless monitor and inject network packets travelling to and originating from the phone.

3.2   Security Policy Model

We address the threat model presented above by adopting the following four security principles:

1. *The connections between the smart phone and the application server must be authenticated and encrypted.* This protects against network monitoring and injection attacks[5].
2. *Users must be able to enter text via their (trusted) phone at all times in the interaction.* This protects against keylogging attacks since information entered via the phone cannot be recorded by keyloggers running on the public terminal.
3. *Users must have control over what is shown on the public display* (e.g. show everything, remove all text, turn off entirely). This protects against malicious screengrabbing software running on the public terminal.

---

[5] In the case where it is more probable that the network is compromised than the public terminal itself, one may also consider authenticating and encrypting the connection between the public terminal and the application server.

4. *Users must have control over how events originating from the public terminal are interpreted.* For example, users may tell applications to ignore all key-presses from the public terminal, allowing only keypresses originating from their phone; similarly, users may instruct applications to ignore all mouse clicks originating from the public terminal. This protects against User Interface injection attacks.

4   Technical Details

Our system is based on the well-known, open-source VNC thin-client software [18]. Figure 3 presents a diagrammatic view of our system's architecture, showing the dataflow of control messages and UI events between the thin-client server, public terminal and smart phone. (Although we start by assuming that the thin-client server is running on a separate machine, Section 4.3 shows that this general architecture is also applicable to the Personal Server Model [26] where the user's applications run locally on their smart phone.) Like VNC, we use the Remote Frame-Buffer (RFB) protocol [24] to send pixel data from the server to remote displays and to send mouse and keyboard events from remote input devices back to the server. However, we have modified both VNC server and client software in order to enforce our Security Policy Model (above). Our source code is freely available for download [22].

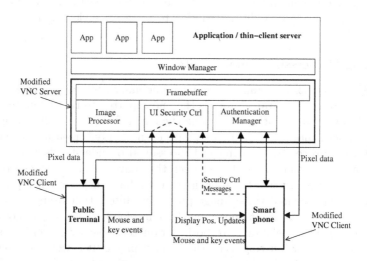

Fig. 3. Dataflow of control messages and UI events through the thin-client server, public terminal and smart phone

As shown in Figure 3, the VNC server is augmented with 3 extra components: the *Image Processor*, *Authentication Manager* and *UI Security Controller*. These components are described below.

Image Processor: This component is responsible for removing private content from the public display, censoring the image transmitted to the public terminal as requested by the user. We have currently implemented three censoring algorithms: *uniform blur*, *pixellation* and *text removal*. (Our image processing algorithms are discussed in more detail in Section 4.1.)

Authentication Manager: In accordance with our Security Policy Model, all data transmitted between the thin-client server and the smart phone is tunnelled over the standard SSH protocol [27]. SSH already contains provision for two-way client/server authentication. The public terminal is authenticated by means of a one-time password displayed on the smart phone's screen. The authentication manager relies on SSH's standard authentication primitives to determine which of the connections to the thin-client server originates from the trusted smart phone and which originates from the public terminal, configuring the UI Security Controller and Image Processor components accordingly.

UI Security Controller: The UI Security Controller filters mouse and keyboard events generated by the public terminal in order to protect against UI injection attacks; (this functionality will be discussed in detail in Section 4.2). The UI Security Controller also processes *Security Control Messages* generated in response to a user activating or deactivating a particular security feature via their smart phone. As shown in Figure 3, the UI Security Controller forwards mouse movement events originating from the public terminal to the smart phone. These display position updates are interpreted by the smart phone as an instruction to move its uncensored display window to a new screen location, as described in Section 2.

4.1   Image Processing Components

The Image Processor maintains a second framebuffer containing a censored version of the screen. This framebuffer is the one exported to the public terminal's display. To avoid constantly recensoring the entire framebuffer, the Image Processor is hooked into VNC's screen update events; only screen areas that have changed are reprocessed. The Image Processor also understands VNC's *Copy-Rect* events [24]—when areas of the screen that have already been censored are copied or moved (e.g. when the user drags a window) they are not reprocessed.

We have implemented three image processing filters that users can activate or deactivate via their smart phone: pixellation, blurring and text removal. The pixellation and blurring filters are both parameterisable—the user can set the level of pixellation or blurring using their smart phone. It is worth noting, however, that whatever level of blurring or pixellation is used, attackers may be able to use sophisticated *image restoration* software to reconstruct some of the censored information. To protect against this eventuality, in the case where a user wants to hide text from attackers, we implemented a text removal filter. This component explicitly detects areas of text, replacing them with filled rectangles.

The text removal filter is based around a 5-stage image processing pipeline: (*i*) transformation to a 1-bit (binary) image by means of adaptive threshold-

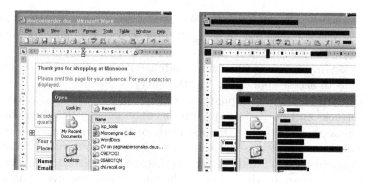

Fig. 4. The text detection and removal filter. *left*: a portion of the uncensored public terminal screen; *right*: the same portion after text removal has been activated.

ing; (*ii*) building a tree of contours using edge detection on the 1-bit image; (*iii*) marking possible text by contour analysis; (*iv*) applying heuristics to remove false positives; and (*v*) blanking out regions which are believed to contain text. The full technical details of the image processing are beyond the scope of this paper; interested readers may wish to examine the source code for more information [22]. Our approach is similar to recent work on general text and information extraction from images and video [7].

We tested our text removal filter on a variety of Windows applications, including Word, Excel, Internet Explorer, Adobe Reader and Visual Studio; a typical example is shown in Figure 4. In general we found that text removal was near 100% effective. However, performance dropped to a 92% success rate on Adobe Reader due to its heavily anti-aliased fonts. Most of the detection failures on Adobe Reader only revealed single characters, although in one case an entire word went undetected. We measured the speed of the algorithm on an Intel Pentium 4 (3.2 GHz) machine, by executing the algorithm on a variety of typical Windows screenshots (at a resolution of 1280x1024). The average processing speed was 102 fps (*s.d.* 4 fps).

In future work we intend to improve the text removal filter to handle anti-aliased text better. Nonetheless, our current implementation demonstrates that text removal through image processing is a viable method for censoring a public display, in terms of both accuracy and execution time.

4.2   Dealing with Untrusted Mouse/Keyboard Events

To protect against UI injection attacks (as described in Section 3.1) untrusted mouse and keyboard events originating from the public terminal are filtered by the UI Security Controller. In this section we describe the various filtering policies supported. Users can activate or deactivate mouse/keyboard filtering policies at any time using their smart phone.

We currently support 3 different policies for dealing with keyboard events from the public terminal: ignore all keyboard events entirely, allow all keyboard events from the public terminal and only allow alphanumeric/cursor keypress events. This latter policy deserves further explanation—we argue that it provides a convenient tradeoff between allowing the user to perform many common tasks (e.g. editing a document) whilst making it more difficult for an attacker to mount dangerous key-injection attacks (which often rely on using Alt- or Ctrl- key combinations to access application functionality).

Of course, only allowing alphanumeric key events does not preclude key-injection attacks entirely—some applications may allow critical functions to be accessed via alphanumeric key presses; furthermore, when a user clicks on the "File" menu in a Windows application, for example, alphanumeric and cursor keys can be used to select and execute critical functions (such as "Open New", "Exit" etc.). However, filtering all but alphanumeric keypress events nonetheless makes it *more difficult* to execute key-injection attacks, offering users a sweet-spot on the security-usability spectrum.

Pointer events from the public terminal (mouse, touchscreen, tracker ball etc.) are also filtered by the UI Security Controller. We provide two mouse filtering modes: one which allows all mouse events from the public terminal to pass through unmodified (in the case where the user is not concerned about mouse event-injection attacks); and one which allows only *mouse movement events* from the public terminal, but filters all click events. The second of these policies is based on the principle that it is difficult to mount a dangerous UI-injection attack by inserting mouse movements alone. Of course, it is also difficult for the user to perform any legitimate actions without clicking, so to address this we map one (or more) of the smart phone's buttons to click events; in essence these buttons on the smart phone take the place of the regular mouse buttons. This mode of operation gives the user the best of both worlds—they can use the public terminal mouse (or touchscreen or trackerball etc.) to point at arbitrary screen areas; however, click events are generated by the phone and thus trusted.

One *can* envisage scenarios in which dangerous mouse event injection attacks may be executed entirely via faking mouse movement events. However, just as filtering all but alphanumeric keypress events makes key-injection attacks harder, our model of removing clicks from the public terminal's event stream makes mouse-injection attacks harder. Again, we feel that this mode of operation finds a sweet-spot on the security-usability spectrum.

4.3   Adapting Our Architecture to the Personal Server Model

Figure 3 shows three distinct devices all communicating over the network: the user's thin-client server (which may, for example, be located in their office, at home or in an ISP data-center), the user's smart phone and the public terminal. This is the *Remote Access Model* as envisaged, for example, by the creators of the X Window System [21], VNC [18] and the Internet Suspend/Resume project [9]. However, our architecture is equally applicable to the *Personal Server Model* [26], in which users' personal data and applications are not accessed over the Internet, but instead reside locally on their personal mobile device—in our case, on their smart phone.

We can map our architecture onto a Personal Server Model by assuming that the user's smart phone runs not only our thin-client viewer, but also the thin-client server, window manager and applications. Whilst the architecture as presented in Figure 3 remains broadly the same, adopting the Personal Server Model results in two significant differences to the system as a whole. Firstly, the job of the Authentication Manager becomes simpler—the trusted client is the one connecting via the loopback interface (since both trusted client and thin-client server now reside on the smart phone). Secondly, there is no longer any need for Internet connectivity. The smart phone (containing all applications and personal data) can simply connect *directly* to the public terminal via a communication technology of choice (e.g. Bluetooth, WiFi or even a USB cable).

We observe that modern smart phones are already powerful enough to support a thin-client server and general purpose applications. The Motorola E680, for example, contains a 500 MHz Intel XScale Processor. As the trend of increasing computational power on mobile devices continues we believe that smart phones running both applications and thin-client servers have the potential to form the basis of a powerful mobile computing platform.

5   Pilot Usability Study

We performed a pilot usability study that primarily aimed to address one key question: can novice users interact with their personal applications and data via our system, even when all the security measures are activated? We chose to focus particularly on this question because it is one of the most fundamental; after all, if participants find the combination of a smart phone display and censored public display too difficult to interact with, our architecture offers little value.

We simulated a scenario in which participants accessed emails and documents using a combination of a large censored display and a small, mobile uncensored display. We used a 19-inch flat panel monitor and a mouse/keyboard to simulate the public terminal, and an iPaq to simulate the participant's smart phone. We installed our system (as described in Section 4) on the public terminal and iPaq and configured it as shown in Figure 2: as participants moved the mouse, the pointer moved across the censored public display and the iPaq's display scrolled to show the uncensored screen area surrounding the pointer. As described in Section 4.2, buttons on the mouse were disabled—to click participants used one of the four buttons on the iPaq's physical keypad. The keyboard on the public terminal was also disabled. The study was performed using the Mozilla web-browser and OpenOffice Writer applications running over the Gnome Desktop on Linux. We used a pixellation filter to censor content on the public display (see Section 4.1). The level of pixellation was sufficient to render all text used in the study completely illegible.

8 participants took part in the study: 4 male, 4 female. The average age was 29 (*s.d.* 5.7; min 25, max 39). Participants were an educated, mostly professional group; 4 participants worked in computing, 4 came from non-technical backgrounds. All used computers on a regular basis and all owned mobile phones. No

participants reported any difficulties with vision or motor skills; all were right handed.

Participants performed two tasks. *Task A* involved using the Mozilla web-browser to access a Gmail account containing 8 emails. Participants were presented with the Gmail Inbox page and asked four comprehension-style questions (e.g. "What did people buy Bob for his birthday?"). To answer the questions participants had to navigate the Gmail interface and read the content of emails—some of the emails were in the Inbox and some were in the Sent Mail folder. *Task B* involved using OpenOffice Writer, a word processing package similar to Microsoft Word. Participants were presented with the OpenOffice Writer application and asked to open 3 documents in turn: an order receipt from a large UK-based clothing company (1 page long), a personal CV (3 pages long) and a product order form for educational materials (2 pages long). The process of opening a document involved selecting *File→Open* from the menu bar or clicking on the Open File Toolbar Icon, and then navigating a File Browser Dialog Window. For each document, participants were asked two comprehension-style questions, requiring them to find specific pieces of information. Since the documents were too large to fit on the public terminal, participants had to scroll the OpenOffice Writer window down in order to find the answers to some of these questions.

Before starting the tasks participants were allowed to practice using the system for as long as they liked. In this familiarisation phase, participants were given the free reign of the Gnome Desktop to play with. (All participants finished practicing within five minutes.) To avoid ordering effects half the participants performed Task A first, and half performed Task B first. We used the *think-aloud protocol* [10] and conducted the studies under quiet, office conditions with only the participant and one researcher present. During the study, we recorded the time taken for the participant to complete each task; afterwards we performed structured interviews in order collect qualitative data regarding the participant's experiences of the system.

Our key result was that all participants were able to complete the tasks without prompting and in a reasonable time. Task A was completed in an average of 82 seconds (*s.d.* 16s; min 56s, max 195s); Task B was completed in an average of 196 seconds (*s.d.* 42s; min 124s, max 252s). Participants answered all comprehension questions correctly. This gives an unequivocally positive answer to our initial question: novice users can interact with applications and data via our system, even with all the security measures activated (i.e. disabled public keyboard, disabled mouse buttons and censored public display).

We were interested in finding out whether participants felt that the censored public display was useful, or whether they preferred to rely on the iPaq's screen alone. All participants claimed that they found the censored public display useful for Task B, where they used it to scroll through different pages of documents and navigate File Dialog windows. One participant commented *"I couldn't use ... [the censored public display] to read anything, so I used it more as a map I suppose. Without it I would have found it hard to find scroll bars, menus and open files.".* However, for Task A, only four of the participants claimed that the censored public display was useful. For example, one participant observed *"in the GMail task I only used the big screen a little bit to find the back button on the browser; everything else I just did through the [iPaq's] little screen.".* We believe that the reason participants relied less on the public display in Task A was that this task did not require participants to scroll or navigate between multiple windows; it is for these kinds of actions that the *"map"* provided by the censored public terminal is particularly useful.

Six participants commented that they initially found it confusing to click with the iPaq buttons rather than with the mouse buttons. A typical response was *"at first I kept clicking with the mouse button, which didn't do anything, but as it went on I started to get the hang of clicking with the other [iPaq] button. It's not difficult though, you just get used to it."* The fact that participants consistently made comments about confusion relating to clicking with the iPaq buttons suggests that users would probably prefer to leave the mouse buttons enabled whenever possible. At present we feel that leaving mouse buttons enabled would not present a great security threat; of all the attacks highlighted in our threat model (see Section 3.1), mouse injection attacks are probably the most unlikely in practice. One participant made an interesting suggestion: *"when you accidentally click with the mouse button the system could maybe beep to remind you to click with the iPaq button."* The idea of incorporating automatic, interactive help features into the system that assist the user in this kind of way is something we would like to explore in future work.

We see this study as providing promising initial results. However, we recognise that there are many other important questions that we have not yet addressed. For example, would users be able to understand *when* they should activate/deactivate security measures (e.g. when to type on their smart phone, when to censor content on the public display)? Are users sufficiently concerned about security to use our system at all when using a public terminal? These are questions that we intend to address in further studies. However, as a precursor to studying the second question, we note that a number of participants explicitly mentioned that they were concerned about shoulder-surfing when accessing personal information in public spaces. For example, *"Being able to blur the [public] screen is really useful. I don't want people to see what I'm reading—I'm really scared of people looking over my shoulder."*

6   Related Work

We have already highlighted how our research relates to number of other projects including VNC [18], The X Window System [21], Internet Suspend/Resume [9] and the Personal Server [26]. In this section we further explore the relationship between our work and the research of others.

A number of researchers have proposed blurring electronic information in order to provide privacy. However, these projects have tended to focus on protecting users' privacy in always-on video used to support distributed workgroups

[5, 28]. In contrast we focus on general purpose access to applications and data, addressing not just privacy concerns (e.g. screen blurring) but also other ways in which public terminals may be attacked in order to violate privacy, including keylogging and UI-injection attacks.

Berger *et al.* developed an email application which blurred sensitive words on a projected display; selecting blurred words caused them to appear (uncensored) on a private wrist-watch display [4]. A calendaring application with similar functionality was also proposed. The concept of blurring words on a public screen, whilst allowing them to be displayed on a personal private display is similar to ours. However, our work extends this in two ways: firstly we present a security model and architecture that enables users to access *existing*, unmodified applications securely via public terminals; secondly, as well as *displaying* private content, we also deal with secure mouse and keyboard *input* (to avoid logging and UI-injection attacks), issues not considered by Berger *et al.*

Ross *et al.* developed a web-proxy which split an HTML page into secure content and insecure content according to a user-specified, programmable policy [19]. The secure content was then displayed on a WAP browser running on a mobile device whilst insecure content was displayed on a public display. Again, the idea of splitting content between personal/public devices in this way is similar to ours. The relationship of our work to Ross' is similar to the relationship of our work to Berger's research: (*i*) our framework is immediately applicable to *all* applications (not just web browsing); and (*ii*) as well as dealing with displaying sensitive information on public displays, we also consider secure *input* to applications.

Our thin-client architecture for securing mobile computing systems is similar to that of Oprea *et al.* [14]. The major difference between this project and our work is that Oprea does not provide mechanisms for obfuscating the content on the untrusted display whilst viewing portions of it in unobfuscated form on a trusted personal device. Indeed Oprea states that *"it turned out that the performance of the RFB protocol and VNC software on our PDA was too poor to make this approach work efficiently"* [14]. In contrast we have shown that it is possible to implement this interaction technique efficiently on top of VNC/RFB[6] and, further, that novice users can cope with dual displays without significant difficulty.

The idea of simultaneously using multiple displays to access applications and data has been explored extensively by the research community [11, 17]. Our work adopts these ideas, simultaneously using users' smart phone display and public terminals to enable secure access to personal information via situated displays and input devices.

Many researchers have explored users' privacy concerns surrounding accessing information via public displays [13]. Our system addresses these concerns, enabling users to access documents and applications via situated displays while allowing them to view sensitive information privately via their personal phone display.

---

[6] At least for the personal-server model where applications run on the mobile device, (see Section 4.3) or remotely when a low-latency network connection is available.

7   Conclusions and Future Work

In this paper we have presented a thin-client architecture capable of supporting secure, mobile access to unmodified applications. Our system allows users to benefit from the rich interaction capabilities of large situated displays, whilst relying on a trusted personal device to protect them against the inherent insecurity of shared, public terminals.

The implementation described in this paper gives users full control over which security policies to apply in which contexts (e.g. when to type on the phone keypad rather than the public keyboard, when to censor content on the public display etc.). This is fine for experts, but further studies are required to determine whether non-technical users can successfully select the right policies to apply in order to protect their privacy. In future work we would like to explore whether automated *activity inference* methods may benefit novice users, automatically suggesting suitable security settings in different contexts. Another possibility is to explore ways that enable service providers (such as banks, for example) to specify a particular security policy, removing some of the control from users. In this scenario, web services could be explicitly written to enforce a pre-determined split between a general purpose PC and a trusted, personal device (e.g. credit card numbers and account transfers are *always* performed via an interface on the personal device, whereas statements may be browsed on the public terminal).

While this paper discusses a thin-client implementation of our Security Policy Model (Section 3.2), other implementations are also possible. For example, we may choose to implement a system which works at the window-manager level, enabling users to (say) select which windows to censor on the public display and which to leave uncensored. Similarly, we could implement a system for secure web-browsing on public terminals which works at the HTML-level, using an HTTP proxy to censor parts of the web page (c.f. [6]) and to migrate secure input fields and hyperlinks to the personal device.

Our thin-client approach has the advantage of working with existing applications, with the disadvantage of having a coarser granularity of privacy controls than the other solutions above. However, we can also achieve the "best of both worlds"—by exposing an API from the UI Security Controller, applications themselves can specify detailed secur ity policies for particular areas of the display. Thus, the user is afforded always-present basic privacy controls at the framebuffer layer, while also enjoying the usability advantages of precise privacy-control support in whatever suitably enabled applications they may have.

Acknowledgements

The authors would like to thank Tim Kindberg, Claudio Pinhanez and Ian Smith for insightful comments on a draft of this paper.

References

1. Ross Anderson, Frank Stajano, and Jong-Hyeon Lee. Security policies. In *Advances in Computers vol 55*. Academic Press, 2001.
2. Anti-Phishing Working Group (APWG). Phishing activity trends report, June 2005. http://antiphishing.org/.
3. Dirk Balfanz and Ed Felton. Hand-held computers can be better smart cards. In *Proceedings of USENIX Security*, 1999.
4. S. Berger, R. Kjeldsen, C. Narayanaswami, C. Pinhanez, M. Podlaseck, and M. Raghunath. Using symbiotic displays to view sensitive information in public. In *Proceedings of PERCOM*. IEEE, 2005.
5. Michael Boyle, Christopher Edwards, and Saul Greenberg. The effects of filtered video on awareness and privacy. In *Proceedings of ACM CSCW*, 2000.
6. Richard Han, Veronique Perret, and Mahmoud Naghshineh. WebSplitter: a unified XML framework for multi-device collaborative web browsing. In *Proceedings of CSCW 2000*. ACM, 2000.
7. Keechul Jung, Kwang In Kim, and Anil K. Jain. Text information extraction in images and video: a survey. *Pattern Recognition*, 37:977–997, 2004.
8. Amecisco KeyLogger product range. http://www.keylogger.com/.
9. M. Kozuch and M. Satyanarayanan. Internet suspend/resume. In *Proceedings of the WMCSA 2002*, June 2002.
10. C. Lewis and J. Rieman. Task-centered user interface design—a practical introduction, 1993. University of Colorado, Boulder. (This shareware book is available at ftp.cs.colorado.edu).
11. Brad A. Myers. Using handhelds and PCs together. *Communications of the ACM*, 44(11):34–41, 2001.
12. Chandra Narayanaswami, M. T. Raghunath, Noboru Kamijoh, and Tadonobu Inoue. What would you do with 100 MIPS on your wrist? Technical Report RC 22057 (98634), IBM Research, January 2001.
13. Kenton O'Hara, Mark Perry, and Elizabeth Churchill. *Public and Situated Displays: Social and Interactional Aspects of Shared Display Technologies*. Kluwer Academic Publishers, Norwell, MA, USA, 2004.
14. Alina Oprea, Dirk Balfanz, Glenn Durfee, and Diana Smetters. Securing a remote terminal application with a mobile trusted device. In *Proceedings of ACSA 2004*. Available from http://www.acsa-admin.org/.
15. Trevor Pering and Michael Kozuch. Situated mobility: Using situated displays to support mobile activities. In *Public and Situated Displays: Social and Interactional Aspects of Shared Display Technologies*. Kluwer, 2003.
16. Jeffrey S. Pierce and Heather Mahaney. Opportunistic annexing for handheld devices: Opportunities and challenges. In *Proceedings of HCIC 2004*, 2004.
17. Mandayam Raghunath, Chandra Narayanaswami, and Claudio Pinhanez. Fostering a symbiotic handheld environment. *Computer*, 36(9):56–65, 2003.
18. Tristan Richardson, Quentin Stafford-Fraser, Kenneth R. Wood, and Andy Hopper. Virtual network computing. *IEEE Internet Computing*, 2(1):33–38, 1998.
19. Steven J. Ross, Jason L. Hill, Michael Y. Chen, Anthony D. Joseph, David E. Culler, and Eric A. Brewer. A composable framework for secure multi-modal access to Internet services from post-PC devices. *Mob. Netw. Appl.*, 7(5), 2002.
20. Ken Salchow. Sorting through the hype of ubiquitous secure remote access and SSL VPNs. SecurityDocs white paper. http://www.securitydocs.com/library/3103.

21. Robert W. Scheifler and Jim Gettys. The X window system. *ACM Trans. Graph.*, 5(2):79–109, 1986.
22. Richard Sharp, James Scott, and Alastair Beresford.   Resources and code accompanying this paper. `http://www.cambridge.intel-research.net/securemobilecomputing/`.
23. Tom Spring.   Google Desktop Search: Security Threat?   Today@PCWorld. `http://blogs.pcworld.com/staffblog/archives/000264.html`.
24. T. Richardson, RealVNC Ltd.   The RFB Protocol, 2005.   `http://www.realvnc.com/docs/rfbproto.pdf`.
25. Desney S. Tan and Mary Czerwinski. Information Voyeurism: Social impact of physically large displays on information privacy. In *Extended Abstracts of CHI 2003*. ACM, 2003.
26. Roy Want, Trevor Pering, Gunner Danneels, Muthu Kumar, Murali Sundar, and John Light. The personal server: Changing the way we think about ubiquitous computing. In *Proceedings of UbiComp 2002*. Springer-Verlag, 2002.
27. T. Ylonen. SSH transport layer protocol. RFC 3667.
28. Qiang Alex Zhao and John T. Stasko. The awareness-privacy tradeoff in video supported informal awareness: A study of image-filtering based techniques. Technical Report 98-16, Georgia Institute of Technology, 1998.

iCAP: Interactive Prototyping of Context-Aware Applications

Anind K. Dey[1], Timothy Sohn[2], Sara Streng[3], and Justin Kodama[4]

[1] Human-Computer Interaction Institute, Carnegie Mellon University, Pittsburgh, PA, USA
anind@cs.cmu.edu
[2] Computer Science and Engineering, University of California, San Diego, La Jolla, CA, USA
tsohn@cs.ucsd.edu
[3] Institute for Informatics, University of Munich, Munich, Germany
sara.streng@gmx.de
[4] Palm, Inc., Sunnyvale, CA, USA
justin.kodama@palm.com

Abstract. Although numerous context-aware applications have been developed and there have been technological advances for acquiring contextual information, it is still difficult to develop and prototype interesting context-aware applications. This is largely due to the lack of programming support available to both programmers and end-users. This lack of support closes off the context-aware application design space to a larger group of users. We present iCAP, a system that allows end-users to visually design a wide variety of context-aware applications, including those based on if-then rules, temporal and spatial relationships and environment personalization. iCAP allows users to quickly prototype and test their applications without writing any code. We describe the study we conducted to understand end-users' mental models of context-aware applications, how this impacted the design of our system and several applications that demonstrate iCAP's richness and ease of use. We also describe a user study performed with 20 end-users, who were able to use iCAP to specify *every* application that they envisioned, illustrating iCAP's expressiveness and usability.

1 Introduction

In the past several years, there has been an increased effort and interest in building and deploying context-aware applications. Users' environments contain context information that can be sensed by an application, including location, identity, activity, and the state of nearby people. Context-aware computing involves sensing this context to implicitly provide appropriate information and services. Many groups have developed infrastructures and toolkits to support this next era of ubiquitous computing, however few have focused on empowering end-users in building context-aware applications [5,7,11]. Currently, developing a context-aware application requires developers and end-users alike to either build their application from scratch (involving laborious direct interaction with hardware sensors and devices), or to use an enabling toolkit. While low-level toolkits provide much-needed support for acquiring context [2,3,4,8], large amounts of code must still be written to develop simple sensor-rich applications.

K.P. Fishkin et al. (Eds.): PERVASIVE 2006, LNCS 3968, pp. 254–271, 2006.
© Springer-Verlag Berlin Heidelberg 2006

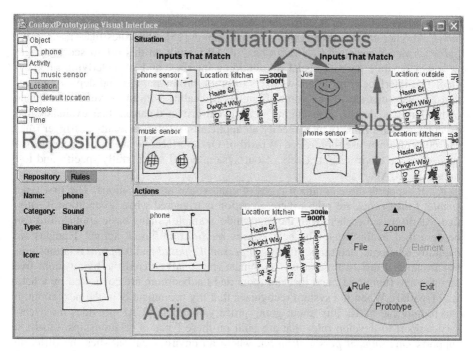

Fig. 1. The iCAP user interface has two main areas: a tabbed window on the left that acts as a repository for user-defined objects, activities, locations, people, time and rules and the situation area on the right where these components can be dragged to construct a rule. The rule shown uses 2 situation sheets, where one (on the right) is split into 2 slots. The rule being prototyped is: *If* the phone rings in the kitchen and music is on in an adjacent room or if Joe is outside and the phone rings in the kitchen *then* turn up the phone volume in the kitchen.

This inhibits the design of interesting applications, especially for end-users, who end up having little control over how these applications behave. End-users with little technical expertise should be able to exercise control over context-aware systems and rapidly prototype applications. They have more intimate knowledge about their activities and environments than a hired programmer and they need the ability to create and modify applications as those activities and environments change. Without such ability, context-aware applications acting implicitly could significantly annoy users as they fail to meet users' needs.

To address these issues we built the interactive Context-aware Application Prototyper (iCAP), a system aimed at lowering barriers for end-users to build interesting context-aware applications for their instrumented environment, *without requiring them to write any code*. In particular, iCAP allows a user to describe a *situation* and associate an *action* with it. It is a visual, rule-based system that supports prototyping of 3 common types of context-aware behaviors: simple if-then rules, relationship-based actions and environment personalization. In supporting prototyping without writing code, iCAP allows end-users to exert control over sensing systems and dictate application behavior.

The most common context-aware applications are described naturally as a collection of rule-based conditions. A museum tour guide is a common example [1]:*"when a user stands in front of a particular exhibit, show them content related to that exhibit.*" Another canonical example is a smart home [15], with rules like "*turn on the lights whenever someone is in the room.*" iCAP is built on this rule-based paradigm with two separate parts: a visual rule building interface and an underlying rules engine. The interface (Fig. 1) allows users to build, prototype, test and deploy applications. It also separates users from difficulties in dealing with low-level sensor inputs or toolkit-level details. The engine is an event-driven database that evaluates and executes a user's rules (which specify an application). Context inputs to trigger rules can come from a user-controlled Wizard-of-Oz interface, or from an instrumented context-aware environment. Users of our system could successfully specify and test rules using iCAP.

iCAP supports three common types of context-aware applications. The first type, *simple if-then rules*, are rules where an action is triggered when a condition is satisfied. As discussed earlier (with the tour guide example), many basic applications can be described in this way. The next type is *relationship-based actions*. Humans are naturally relational, and think in terms of *personal, spatial* and *temporal* relationships. For instance, I am aware that my roommate (personal) entered the living room five minutes ago (temporal), and that my room and his bedroom are connected by a hallway (spatial). When the system recognizes that my roommate is in the next room, it can prompt me to ask him about going grocery shopping. iCAP provides the necessary support to develop rules that are built on these types of relationships. Lastly, it supports *environment personalization*, where an environment satisfies the differing preferences of its occupants. For instance, one user may enjoy bright lights and rock music, while another prefers dim lights with classical music. To satisfy both users, the environment must account for their preferences and adjust itself accordingly.

The next section describes a formative study we conducted with target end-users to understand their conceptual models of context-aware applications. We then present the iCAP interface through the building of an example context-aware behavior. We then describe how the design of iCAP was guided by our findings. We show that iCAP supports users' conceptual models through a user study we conducted, where *every* user successfully specified *every* application that they envisioned. We also demonstrate that iCAP can cover an important design space in context-aware computing. We then survey previous research in the areas of context-aware computing and rule-based systems, providing further motivation for our work. We conclude with a discussion of the limitations of iCAP and future directions for this research.

2 User Conceptual Models of Context-Awareness

To guide the design of an end-user prototyping environment for context-aware applications, we conducted 90-minute interviews with 20 subjects (9 female, 11 male) with ages ranging from 19 to 52. All participants were experienced with computers but had no experience with programming. Our goal for this study was to gain an understanding of users' conceptual models of context-awareness: how they want to build context-aware applications and the types of applications they want to create.

To provide some context for the interview, participants were provided with a description of a smart home, a concept that most were already familiar with. This generic smart home had sensors that could sense a large variety of environment state and user activities and could execute services on behalf of users. We intentionally were vague about sample applications and did not discuss any means for specifying them, so as not to bias our study results. Then participants were asked to create their first context-aware application. Specifically, they were asked to describe how, when and where they would want music to play in their smart home. This included both how they listen to music now and hypothetical situations in their smart home. The music scenario was chosen because it is easy to understand and is unconstrained, allowing for creativity and flexibility in specifying application behavior. The last part of the study was more freeform with subjects creating their own scenarios and applications that they found useful and desirable in their home. Here our goal was to collect a large set of user-specified scenarios to better understand users' needs, and descriptions of those scenarios to understand how they naturally conceptualize them.

2.1 Study Results

We collected a total of 371 application descriptions from our subjects, including those from the music scenario. Scenario domains were widespread and included temperature and lighting control, cooking, bathing and watching television or controlling entertainment devices. There was quite a bit of overlap among subjects. From these scenarios and descriptions, we uncovered some interesting findings.

First, *every subject* described their applications in terms of *if-then rules*, using the form "*"if I ..."* or *"when I ..."* am in a particular situation, perform this action'. Fewer than 5% of the rules created used declarative statements instead, for example, "*The nightlight in the bathroom should dim at night*" or "*During parties, usually play hip hop, going out music.*" The uniformity of this result across users was surprising. Almost one-quarter (23.5%) of all rules involved explicit Boolean logic (*e.g.* use of 'and' or 'or' statements). An example is "*If it is nighttime **and** my roommate's door is closed with the light off, turn the television off*".

Second, subjects specified a wide variety of rules, but *most rules* (78.7%) fell into the *simple if-then category*. The remaining rules were divided among the temporal, spatial and personal relationship rules evenly (7, 7, and 6.5% respectively). Less than 1% of rules focused on environmental personalization. However, environment personalization depends on knowing the preferences of the environment's occupants and 14% of specified rules required knowing some user preference. For example, "*When my alarm clock goes off, turn the volume up louder than normal. But when I wake up, turn it down to normal,*" requires knowledge of what normal is for this person.

Third, the rules that subjects wanted to create were *less complex* than we expected. We broke down each rule into a set of constituent elements, trying to determine the kinds of language used in describing them. After analyzing all the rules, we came up with six categories: Activity, object, location, time, person and state. The rules used an average of 2.5 (SD=0.71) instances of these categories. While this varied across users from a low of 2.0 to a high of 2.9, the results were fairly uniform. An example rule is "*When I'm cleaning, whether it's the dishes, vacuuming, or other cleaning activity, play music and have it follow me where I go,*" and it consists of 3 activities and 1 variable location. Another example is "*When I open my pajama drawer, then turn on the hot water in the shower*," consisting of 2 objects. In general, the older the subject, the more complex the rules were.

We found that 56.4% of all rules involved objects (*e.g.* radio) or the state of objects (*e.g.* radio on/off or volume). In decreasing order of importance were activities (19.1%), locations (12.8%), time (7.6%) and people other than the subject (4%). We were surprised that subjects focused so much on objects, expecting that they would describe rules more in terms of the activities they were performing or wanted to have performed for them. Similar to other work, though, subjects did not mention sensors or sensing [23], only the devices they would normally interact with in their home.

Finally, we learned how subjects naturally conceptualized context-aware applications, along three different dimensions (situation, action, and preference). First, all the rules specified by our subjects had the system detecting a situation of interest. But, there was variation on whether the system was detecting a subject's state or the state of the house. An example using subject's state is "*When I'm cleaning, ... play music.*" An example using house state is "*When the water [on the stove] starts to boil, turn off the heat.*" Rules that involved detecting the subject's state were far more common (70.9% vs. 29.1%). Second, on the action side, subjects viewed the smart home in two different ways: as a piece of technology that they command to perform a context-aware behavior; and, as something that can assist them in performing their own tasks. An example of the former is "*If I leave the house, turn off the lights*", while an example of the latter is "*When close friends are over, they know a lot of my music, so I'd like to expose them to some new quirky stuff*". Similar to the results of Truong *et al.* [23], viewing the house as something to command was far more common, covering all but 7 of the 371 rules. Third, subjects greatly preferred (86% vs. 14%) to state specific behaviors rather than to state preferences about what they would like their home to do. A command example is, "*When the water on the stove starts to boil, turn off the heat.*" A preference example is "*It would be good if music was playing that was based on what I was cooking. Like salsa music for Mexican food.*"

Our findings from this study guided the design of iCAP, our end-user visual prototyping system for context-aware applications. Our interface was designed to support the ways in which users overwhelmingly preferred to specify rules (describe a subject's situation and command the house to act on that state, describing specific behaviors rather than preferences). In the next section, we describe the iCAP interface through an example application.

3 iCAP Interface

One can imagine a buddy alert application where a user, John, wants to be notified when his friends are in a location adjacent to his. His rule would be:

IF I am in location1 AND my friend is in an adjacent location (location2)
THEN beep my cell phone

The user first creates the people and artifacts involved in the rule and adds them to the repository (top left of Fig. 1). For each person, the user sketches an icon or selectsan image that will be associated with that person, and specifies that it is part of a "friends" group (Fig.2a). He then creates a new output, the "cell phone" and specifies

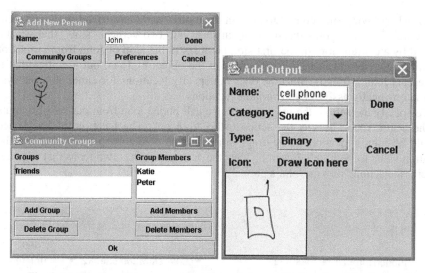

Fig. 2. (a) Creation of person and his personal groups (b) Creation of "cell phone"

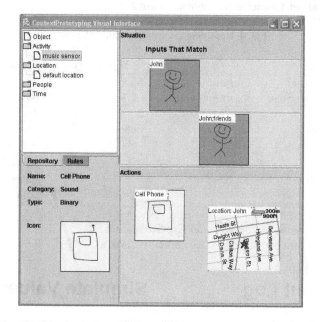

Fig. 3. Rule layout for the example rule

the category of the output (sound), the type of output (binary: ON/OFF, for simplicity), and a sketch/image of the output (Fig. 2b). It is now ready to use in designing rules by simply dragging the appropriate icon onto the rule sheets.

The user selects "New Rule" and the system creates one visual area, or *sheet*, on top, in beige, for entering the situation (IF) and another sheet on bottom, in green, for the action (THEN) (Fig. 3). The example situation has two conditions that are specified by laying out icons: "John is in location1" and "any friend of John's is in location2". The user splits the single input sheet into two vertical "slots" that will be related by a conjunction. In the first slot, he drags in the icon of John from our set of inputs. In the second slot, he again drags in the object of John, but specifies that it represents John's friends. Since he does not specify locations for either slot, the system automatically assigns them variable locations.

To specify the action, the user drags in the cell phone icon from our set of outputs to the action sheet, he sets the action to be "turn on". The location of this device should be John's location, so he drags in a Location object (map icon), and sets the location value to be John's location. Thus the action sheet has two icons that together specify the action "turn on John's phone".

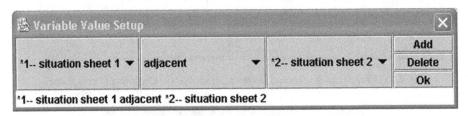

Fig. 4. Resolving the variable value relations

Name	Sensors	Current Value	Possible Value
office thermometer	thermometer	55.4	55.4
bedroom thermometer	thermometer	60.8	60.8
bedroom lights	light intensity	9	9
office presence	IDENTITY	peter	peter
bedroom presence	IDENTITY	katie	katie ▼
			peter
			katie
			john

-- office thermometer => thermometer @ office state: 55.4
-- bedroom presence => IDENTITY @ bedroom state: katie

Event Log   Simulate Values

Fig. 5. Prototyping mode where users can simulate values and see event changes throughout the system in the event log

Finally, the rule is saved and the user is shown a drop down menu to resolve any relations between the variable location values (Fig. 4). He specifies an adjacency relationship, indicating "John's location should be adjacent to his friend's location." iCAP uses information provided by the user or known by the underlying context infrastructure to determine what locations are adjacent to each other. The rule is saved and appears in the rule panel on the left. He can test his buddy alert application by selecting the prototype mode from a pie menu (see Fig. 1). This launches another window where he can either control (simulate) the relevant context inputs or connect to an existing context infrastructure, and see if his rule behaves as expected (Fig. 5).

4 The iCAP System

As almost all of the applications in our study were specified as rules (if <situation> then <action>), iCAP supports the building and execution of context-aware rules and has two main components: a visual rule-building interface and a rules engine that stores the built rules and evaluates them when the rule is being run. The iCAP interface (Fig. 1) provides a simple way for users to design and prototype context-aware applications. The user only needs to deal with defining necessary elements (objects, activities, location, people, time) and use them to visually create situations and associated actions, or if-then rules. No coding is involved, which is a tremendous benefit for non-programmers allowing them to easily explore context-aware computing.

We chose a visual prototyping system because visual programming languages have proven effective in taking advantage of user's spatial reasoning skills [22]. Our study showed that the average user-specified rule has low complexity, so a visual environment seems quite appropriate, supporting both simplicity and familiarity. We iterated on the design of the user interface multiple times, starting with paper prototypes through to the final interface which we present here. At each stage, we obtained feedback from local experts and test subjects. The interface has one window with two main areas (Fig. 1), a tabbed window on the left that is the repository for the user-defined elements and rules, while on the right, a rules area where these components can be dragged to construct a conditional rule. The rules area is split into two areas, one (top) for situations (IF) and one (bottom) for actions (THEN). We built iCAP on top of SATIN, a toolkit for building sketching-based applications [9].

After a number of rules have been defined, the entire rule set can be tested using the iCAP rules engine. The engine can either be set to simulate the context-aware environment, or be used in conjunction with a real context-aware environment via the Context Toolkit [4], an open-source toolkit for enabling programmers to build context-aware applications. Users can interact with the engine in simulation to change the value of defined inputs and evaluate the behavior of the rules being tested. In simulation mode, outputs are visually updated onscreen, whereas with a real environment, real outputs in the physical environment are controlled. With the engine, users can quickly design and test their applications, without having to create an entire infrastructure for collecting or simulating context and without writing any code.

4.1 iCAP Interaction

Interaction with iCAP has three steps. First, users create elements relevant to their rules (if they do not already exist in the repository). Second, these elements are dragged and composed to create rules. Finally, the entire rule set can either be simulated or connected to a live context sensing infrastructure in the prototyping mode.

Creating Elements. There are five categories of elements in the repository: objects, activities, locations, people and time. These categories (and their order in the repository) come directly from the analysis of the rules from our study (the sixth category found in our study, object state, was combined into the object category). iCAP contains a repository of elements that is populated either automatically by the real sensor-enhanced environment that iCAP is connected to, or manually by the user (or a combination). When the user creates an element, it is associated with a user-sketched graphical icon and added to the repository. Objects have, by default, a binary (on/off) mode and, optionally, a gradient mode (range from 1-10) for objects with different levels (*e.g.* volume, lighting). An example object is the phone in Fig. 1. In addition, objects have a content field used to simulate output modalities. For example, with a music player we could set the content field to "Beethoven Symphony", which would output that string when turned on, to simulate the playing of a classical music piece. iCAP treats activities like objects. Activities either have a binary mode or a gradient mode. Activity objects detect user or home activities and can only be dragged onto the situation sheet.

People and location elements are created similarly to objects. These objects are essential for relationship and personalization rules. By default, there always exists an "I" people object, since users preferred to write rules about their own state and activity. People objects are created with a name and optional fields (Fig. 2a) for preferences as well as community groups. The system recognizes 3 predefined preferences for a person: lighting, sound, temperature, and uses them to configure objects for environment personalization. Custom preferences such as a music category can be defined with preference being 'classical music'. People objects can also be created with community groups such as 'friends' or 'family', allowing the creation of general rule structures such as "*if a family member...*" or "*if a roommate....*"

Location elements specify that a condition or action must take place in a particular location. They simply require a name upon creation. Optionally, a user can indicate what locations are connected together, allowing the creation of rules that take advantage of these spatial adjacencies. In addition, the user can specify whether environment personalization should be turned on for this location, and, if so, the location will attempt to satisfy the preferences of its occupants using the objects in its vicinity.

Time elements allow users to indicate that a situation or an action must occur at a specific day/time. By default, elements correspond to the current time and day.

Constructing Rules: Simple if-then rules, Relationship-based Action and Environment Personalization. Subjects in our study had strong tendencies to build rules that were command-oriented and specific, making it much easier to support rule construction. After users create necessary elements, they can use them to define rules. iCAP supports the construction of simple if-then rules, spatial, temporal and personal relationship-based actions and environment personalization. As *simple if-then* rules were quite common in our study, iCAP focuses on making these easy to build. Users build these rules by dragging and dropping elements onto the situation and action sheets for each rule. After dragging each icon, the users specify conditions (*e.g.* <, <=, >, >=, =, != and combinations for ranges) governing the behavior of the input.

Our study showed that rules that use simple Boolean logic were quite common so to support these rules, we implemented Pane and Myers' match form scheme [16].

Their matching layout uses the vertical dimension with a label "objects that match" to represent the AND operator and the horizontal dimension for the OR operator. They showed that this layout provides a simple, intuitive way to fully express Boolean logic, for non-programmers, including both children and adults. By default, a rule contains a vertical and a horizontal split to make Boolean logic rule creation more efficient. Fig. 1 illustrates this, describing a rule that turns up the phone volume in the kitchen if the phone rings in the kitchen (top left) AND music is on in an adjacent room (bottom left) OR if Joe is outside (top right) AND the phone rings in the kitchen (bottom right). Users can subdivide the situation sheet more complex logic is needed.

Rules that leverage *spatial relationships* or adjacencies (*e.g.* the next room) are supported during location creation, when users are able to specify what locations are adjacent to the newly created location. When two or more locations are placed on the interface, users can specify the relationship between them (if any). Relative *temporal relationships* such as "before" and "after" are also supported for creating rules. By default, each situation sheet is labeled with "Inputs That Match". A user can click on this label and change it to "Time Ordering", with the first column representing the first event, the second representing an event happening after the first one, and so on. The situation would then be satisfied if these events happened in the desired order. Objects can be set to keep track of a certain time period of activity (*e.g.,* 5 minutes before) or a relative event ordering (*e.g.,* after the next person who walks in). These temporal relationships further exhibit the power of iCAP in building conditional rules.

Personal relationships and *environment personalization* are tightly integrated together. Personal relationships are supported through the use of community groups. Examples of community groups include family, friends and co-workers, allowing rules to be created about any of these groups or the individuals in these groups. We support personalization by allowing individuals to set preferences and community groups. By setting a flag for a location, a user can indicate whether the environment should take these preferences into account and change itself when users are in that location. When a person enters a room (with a set flag), the location analyzes the preferences of each person present and tries to satisfy them. We support combinations of personal relationships and personalization, for example, in combining the preferences of all my family members. Preference aggregation to a single result is performed by following a set of heuristics. Because environment personalization was rare in our study, we only support a few common heuristics (*e.g.,* oldest person wins and person who has been in the room the longest wins) and others can only be added by writing code. In future versions, we will allow end-users to visually create these.

Ambiguity and Conflict Resolution. iCAP allows users to initially create rules that are ambiguous or conflict with each other. A small fraction of the rules from our study used terms like "anyone" and "anywhere". When users do not specify the name of a person or a location or provide a time, these values default to wildcards that will match any value. If when the user saves her rule, there are multiple wildcards, the system prompts the user to disambiguate them. For example, a spatial relationship rule that performs an action when I am in an undefined location and my friend is in an undefined location, could be disambiguated by setting the 2 undefined locations to be equal or adjacent (or their complements). Also, when rules are saved, the rules engine checks other saved rules for this user to determine whether any of the rules could potentially conflict and highlights these rules for the user to resolve the conflicts or ignore them. If 2 rules conflict at runtime, iCAP, by default, executes the rule that was most recently updated.

4.2 Rules Engine

The rules engine sits between the visual interface and a real or simulated context-aware infrastructure. Rules are represented in the engine as a situation and an associated action, with each represented as a Boolean tree. Non-leaf nodes represent Boolean operators (*e.g.,* AND, OR) and leaf nodes contain comparisons (*e.g.,* John is in the bedroom or temperature > 15°) or actions (*e.g.,* call Anne's pager). The rules engine supports all general comparison operations (*e.g.,* =, >, <), as well as relative temporal, spatial and personal relationships for evaluating rules, as described earlier.

Evaluating the Rules. Evaluation of rules is based on context input received from either a Wizard-of-Oz interface (Fig. 5) and/or a real context environment. Since a real context sensing environment may not be available, we provide three different modes for rule evaluation. The first is a pure simulation interface giving the user control over all inputs through the Wizard-of-Oz interface. This mode allows users to use inputs that may not exist in their environment. The second mode is a real environment only mode. In this mode, all sensors and devices developed in the visual interface are bound to real objects through the context-sensing environment. The sensors (and interpretations of those sensors) and devices that are available in the physical environment are made available for use in iCAP. If a sensor or device made by the visual interface cannot be mapped to an appropriate object in the real environment it is discarded along with any rules that depend upon it. The last mode is a combination of the first two. We call it a "map all possible" mode, where the system maps all possible objects to the real environment, and for those that cannot be mapped, they are allowed to be simulated in the simulator.

Integration with the Context Toolkit. The engine provides an interface to the Context Toolkit (CTK) [4], to support the automatic population of the iCAP repository, passing of events from the real environment to the rules engine, and to support the rules engine in executing actions in the real environment. Leaf nodes in our Boolean trees act as queries to a discovery service in the CTK, enabling them to bind to real-world sensors and actuators in a user's smart environment.

If either of the two modes that rely on a real context environment are active, the rules engine will attempt to bind sensors and devices to the Context Toolkit. For sensors and actions, the engine will construct a description query using each element's location, name and type (Boolean/gradient). This description query is given to the CTK's discovery system to locate any components in the environment that can provide the requested information. If an appropriate component is found, it will be the sole provider for the sensor (or service for the action) in the rules engine. iCAP is able to send events to and receive events from a real context infrastructure, making it a real tool ready for deployment.

There does need to be a common naming scheme between objects in iCAP and in the Context Toolkit. We anticipate additional features in iCAP that would show all available components and services in the CTK and allow the user to choose from these when composing rules. Our main goal here is to demonstrate that iCAP can send events to and receive events from a real context infrastructure, making it a real tool ready for deployment.

5   Validation

In the preceding sections, we motivated and described the design of iCAP. Although its iterative design was guided by our findings from our formative study, we still need to determine how usable it is and whether it supports the conceptual models we discovered. Here, we validate iCAP by answering the following questions:

- Can users use iCAP to easily and accurately build context-aware rules?
- Does iCAP support the conceptual models that we elicited in our formative study?
- Does iCAP support the construction of an appropriate range of rules?

We address the first two questions through an initial user study we conducted on iCAP. We address the third question through an analysis of the set of rules provided by our subjects in our formative study, by showing how iCAP covers an important design space from the literature and by showing how iCAP enables end-users to build canonical applications taken from the literature.

5.1   User Study

Although the design of iCAP was guided by our findings from our formative study and we followed an iterative design process, we still need to determine how usable it is and whether it supports the conceptual models we discovered. To do this, we conducted a study of 20 non-programmers (age range from 23-67, 10 males, 10 females) using iCAP to perform a set of open-ended tasks and fixed tasks. As with our formative study, we described the concept of a smart home, which all subjects were familiar with. We asked each subject to write down succinct descriptions of 3 different applications they would find desirable and useful. Subjects were presented with iCAP and a short tutorial and asked to create and test their 3 applications. We were most interested in seeing whether iCAP allowed users to specify rules in ways natural to them. The applications our subjects came up with spanned a wide range of domains, overlapping the results from the previous study, but including new ones like reminders to take medicine, notifying users when a baby woke up, and routing phone calls to a user's location (landline phone vs. cell phone). Users were asked to implement their open-ended rules as close to their written specification as possible.

In the second part of our study, users created a set of 7 rules we specified to test general usability. These rules were taken from the set of user-specified rules from our formative study and included 3 straightforward if-then rules with varying complexity (using 2, 3, and 4 elements respectively), 1 if-then rule that required users to resolve ambiguity in a person's identity, 1 spatial relationship rule that required users to resolve ambiguity in location, 1 personal and 1 temporal relationship rule.

In both study parts, users had no trouble creating rules, or the elements for each of their rules. All users were able to complete all rules in a reasonable amount of time, including the time to create the necessary elements for each rule and test the rule, using Wizard-of-Oz testing, verifying that the correct action was taken when they manually set the appropriate contextual conditions. From our own experiences, the time end-users took to complete each rule is less than it would take a programmer using the Context Toolkit to create an application that supports it (Table 1). More importantly, each rule was implemented by an end-user who, without iCAP, would not have been able to do so.

Table 1. Average rule completion time (and standard deviation), in minutes

Type	Rule	Time
If-Then	If I'm sleeping, turn the stereo off. (complexity level is 2)	3.05 (0.67)
If-Then	If I'm in the living room after 10pm, dim the living room lights. (complexity level is 3)	3.36 (0.74)
If-Then	When I walk into the kitchen and turn on the stove, turn on the television with the volume low. (complexity level is 4)	3.58 (0.71)
If-Then	If anyone is sleeping at noon, turn on his/her alarm clock (person identity ambiguity)	3.17 (0.48)
Spatial	If I am in a room next to Karen, page me. (spatial ambiguity)	2.86 (0.54)
Personal	If my roommates are not home, turn my favorite music on high.	3.72 (0.83)
Temporal	When I go from the kitchen to the bedroom, turn the lights on in the bedroom.	3.54 (1.23)

Users were able to specify elements, specify preferences (*e.g.* my favorite music) and create community groups (*e.g.* roommates), although the latter two were slightly more time consuming. A few users objected to the amount of time element creation took and suggested that this be done automatically. (Note that iCAP can populate the element repository automatically using the Context Toolkit to collect components from a smart space, however, we wanted to study how users created these elements on their own.) Users did not have any difficulty creating rules that involved resolving ambiguity (*e.g. if anyone is sleeping, turn on his alarm clock*). In each case, they simply created their rules with ambiguity in them, and resolved that ambiguity when iCAP prompted them to. All users were able to use the Pane and Myers matching scheme [16] to correctly define 'AND' and 'OR' relationships. While spontaneously thinking aloud, several users referred to the label on the sheet and said "it says inputs that match, so that means everything on this sheet is an AND relationship". Because iCAP automatically divides the situation area into 4 quadrants for creating Boolean relationships, actually specifying Boolean rules was quite simple for them. However, some users had trouble with the overloaded column operator. In most cases, columns support ANDing two expressions together, but when used in temporal rules, they represent an ordering of events. This overloading confused a few users who had trouble remembering where to click to achieve a temporal event ordering. Finally, users were able to successfully test their rules using the Wizard-of-Oz prototyping interface. For each rule, they verified that the correct action was executed when they manually set the appropriate contextual conditions.

During the first phase of our study, iCAP readily supported users in implementing *every one of the applications* they had described. There was always a simple and direct mapping from the written rule to the visual specification in iCAP. We attribute this to the fact that this group of users shared the same predominant mental models with those in our formative study. The majority of the rules specified were simple if-then with only a few relationship-based rules, and consisted of about 3 elements each. In their descriptions, users focused on home objects and their own activities, and not sensors. For example, one wrote *"when I close the kitchen door, lock the door and turn off the kitchen light,"* readily specified visually with door, location (kitchen) and people (I) objects for the situation and door, light, and location objects for the action.

During the second phase of the study, users were again able to specify *every rule asked of them* using iCAP. Table 1 summarizes the types of rules and average times (with standard deviation) required to specify them.

Summary. Our evaluation of iCAP showed that it was both usable and supported users' conceptual models. Users were successful in building rules specified by users and by us. These rules spanned the range of simple if-then rules, environment person-alization and personal, spatial and temporal relationship-based actions. In the first, open-ended phase of the study, users often constructed rules quite different than those envisioned by us, and were always successful in specifying them in iCAP. While users had some issues with iCAP, all indicated that they would use it if hardware to outfit a smart home were readily available. One user said iCAP was "exactly what I imagined a visual programming interface would be like to develop these applica-tions." Another user described it as "easy to use" and "fun and exciting to be able to easily build applications for my home."

5.2   Context-Aware Design Space

As further validation for iCAP, we show that iCAP facilitates the building of a wide variety of context-aware applications, supporting almost all the rules obtained in our formative study, an important design space in context-aware computing and canonical applications taken from the literature. We analyzed each of the 371 rules from our formative study, and found that iCAP could *support all but 12* of them. Three rules involved actions to be repeated based on time intervals that we did not support (*e.g. "Remind me to feed my bird every 3 days"*). Five rules involved too much ambiguity to create them, either in the specification of what the action is (*e.g. "When close friends are over, they know a lot of my music, so I'd like to expose them to some new quirky stuff"*) or in which action to perform (*e.g. "If not in my room with friends over, then turn the music off or turn it down"*). Four rules were limited by iCAP's ability to express complex concepts (*e.g. "It would be good if music was playing that was based on what I was cooking. Like salsa music for Mexican food."*). Overall, iCAP can sup-port the vast majority of context-aware behaviors that users want to build, including all the behaviors from the first part of the iCAP user study.

iCAP also supports the 4 application categories defined by Schilit in his seminal work on context-awareness: Context-triggered actions, automatic contextual recon-figuration, contextual information and commands, and proximate selection [21].

Allowing users to visually create applications with *context-triggered actions* (if-then rules specifying how a context-aware system should adapt) has been the basis of our work in iCAP and we have described several examples. An example of *automatic contextual reconfiguration* taken from [21] is reconfiguration to share an object/ resource among people. iCAP supports this through environment personalization where, for example, a room's lighting devices are adjusted to meet the preferences of its occupants. An example of *contextual information and commands* is Schilit's location browser that presents information relevant to a user's location. We support this in an application that delivers a list of people in adjacent rooms to a user's cell phone and updates this when the user enters a new location. We built a *proximate selection* (*i.e.* local objects are emphasized or made easier to choose) application that displays available output devices in the user's current location on fixed displays in the room.

Finally, we have used iCAP to build a variety of canonical context-aware applications taken from the literature including tour guides [1], reminder systems [12], and environment controllers [15]. Tour guides can be built by creating a collection of rules that present user-defined content when someone enters a particular location, similar to Schilit's contextual information and command category. Content delivery can be customized based upon a user's profile or preference, *e.g.*, to display information about the building information to a user interested in architecture. A reminder system can be built in much the same way, by creating a number of rules that deliver content, a reminder, when the user is in a particular situation. For example, *"when I am in a room adjacent to Katie, remind me to give her the book I borrowed from her"*. Finally, iCAP supports home automation systems or environment controllers applications through rules that control heating and lighting conditions and environment personalization when occupants of a space have differing preferences.

6 Related Work

Context-Aware Computing. Since Weiser's vision of ubiquitous computing [24] more than a decade ago, many groups have explored the domain of context-aware applications. Architectures and applications such as stick-e notes [17] and GeoNotes [6] focused on allowing end-users to contextually share data with each other by placing virtual objects in a context-aware environment. However, many of these types of applications were being written from scratch with a high development cost [18]. One must interface to an external sensing system, gather the appropriate sensor data, develop a rule-based engine, and execute the desired actions. With these architectures, there is little support for rapidly prototyping applications. While existing infrastructures that enable programmers to build context-aware applications, such as JCAF, SOLAR, Context Toolkit and Context Fabric [2,3,4,8], support many of these steps, they do not provide any interface for allowing end-users to use them.

Various commercial home automation products like X10 ActiveHome and Vantage QLink, are readily available, however these mainly provide interfaces to directly control the hardware in a home. QLink provides a text-based configuration interface for end-users but it does not support the use of context and it requires in depth knowledge of the hardware deployed which most end-users would not have. In essence, existing systems do not provide support for context-aware application prototyping by end-users, thus demonstrating a need for a system like iCAP.

Visual Rule-Based Systems. We chose to make iCAP a visual environment for users to prototype context-aware applications for reasons of simplicity and intuitiveness. Visual programming languages have proven effective in taking advantage of user's spatial reasoning skills [22]. This programming style is not only simple and effective for many types of users, but is especially intuitive for end-users. When applied to a new domain like context-aware computing, visual programming provides tools needed to allow creative end-users to easily build novel applications. Although a text environment could have been used, Pane and Myers [16] found that in rule generation tasks, users generated more accurate Boolean rules using their graphical technique than textual methods. We have applied this technique to the context-aware domain. While text-based interfaces provide increased expressiveness, we focus on a graphical interface here to increase end-users' ease of use in creating applications. Our formative study showed that users think about context-aware applications in terms of rules, and indeed most context-aware applications can be *and are* described this way, so we chose to make iCAP a rule-based system despite well-known drawbacks of rules: limited expressiveness, may be easily broken, hard to detect and deal with rules that have conflicting actions. In addition to the work of Pane and Myers described above, Mackay, *et al.* showed in the Information Lens project that people with little computer experience could create and use rules effectively to filter email [14].

In earlier work, we presented a Cappella, a programming by demonstration interface for end-users to build context-aware applications [5]. While it addresses a similar problem space as iCAP, it is intended for building applications that are difficult for a user to express directly. We were inspired by the CAMP system, a magnetic poetry system for allowing end-users to construct capture-and-access applications. Similar to iCAP, the CAMP interface was grounded in a study of users' conceptual models about the application domain. However the variety and complexity of rules we found in our study does not match well to the restricted vocabulary used by CAMP. Agentsheets capitalizes on the idea of visual rule-based programming by allowing end-users to establish relationships among different autonomous agents [19]. Although it could be expanded to support context-aware applications, it still required a high level of expertise to use [20], and supports limited sensing and actuation. In contrast, we aim to provide even novices with the ability to build context-aware applications. The Alfred system uses recordable speech-based macros to support users in building applications for a smart environment [7]. However, Alfred focuses on rules based on explicit user interaction (pressing a button, speaking a phrase), and unlike iCAP, does not support conditions based on contextual cues. The Jigsaw Editor addresses novice users by supporting end-user reconfiguration of home devices using a novel jigsaw puzzle metaphor [11]. However, the creators recognize the limits of a constrained metaphor and state that they "do not seek the richness of programming expression allowed by iCAP" [11]. Our goal is to support the building of expressive applications by novice users, trading off some learnability for this expressiveness. Mobile Bristol and Topiary demonstrate the value of supporting designers in building location-aware systems [10,13], however they do not provide support for applications or rules without interfaces.

Summary. There is a need for a context-aware prototyping environment that enables end-users to build rule-based context-aware applications. By building upon work in visual rule-based systems, we address this by providing an effective prototyping tool, empowering end-users to build interesting context-aware applications that cover an important design space in context-aware computing.

7 Conclusions and Future Work

In this paper, we presented iCAP, a visual prototyping system for context-aware applications. iCAP is a visual rule-based environment that supports end-users in prototyping context-aware applications without writing any code. iCAP provides two main benefits: opening up the design space of context-aware application design to a larger group of users than just programmers, and giving control of what should happen in a context-aware environment to the people it most affects, the end-users.

iCAP supports users in designing and implementing a context-aware application, testing it under simulated and real conditions and revising it, as needed. In particular, it supports the creation of if-then (or situation-action) rules that are triggered by contextual cues, the building of spatial, temporal and personal relationship-based rules, and the building of environment personalization systems.

iCAP's design was based on a formative study of 20 end-users that demonstrated the appropriateness of rules as a mental model for end-user construction of context-aware applications. After constructing and iterating on iCAP, we validated its usefulness in two ways. First we ran a user study with 20 end-users who successfully used iCAP to create *every* application they envisioned or were asked to create by us, in less time than it would take to program them. Our subjects told us that iCAP was a powerful system they would like to use in the future. We then showed that it could be used to build almost all the applications from the formative study, canonical context-aware applications and ones that covered Schilit's design space.

Most systems designed for end-users have more constrained functionality than systems designed for programmers. While we have used iCAP to build a wide variety of context-aware applications, it is not as expressive as existing programming systems for building applications [2,3,4,8]. To make it more expressive, we need to support more sophisticated Boolean logic, the ability to activate and deactivate rules based on contextual cues and support for ambiguous context. In addition, we would like to extend iCAP to support context-based retrieval systems that tag captured information with contextual cues to aid future retrieval [12]. iCAP can already capture contextual cues, so we would need to add the ability to store those cues persistently and attach them to user-provided content and provide a mechanism for querying the cues and content. We would like to increase the expressiveness of iCAP while, at the same time, maintaining its ease of use and increasing its learnability to improve users' performance in creating rules. One approach we will explore is to provide support for both visual and textual specification of rules. Finally, we will deploy iCAP in a real environment to understand how users will use it in practice, dealing with rules that evolve over time, conflicting rules and more complex rules.

References

1. Abowd, G.D. *et al.* Cyberguide: A mobile context-aware tour guide. *ACM Wireless Networks* 3(5). pp. 421-433, 1997.
2. Bardram, J.. The Java Context-Awareness Framework (JCAF) – A service infrastructure and programming framework for context-aware applications. *Pervasive 2004*, 98–115.
3. Chen, G. and Kotz, D. Solar: An open platform for context-aware mobile applications. *Pervasive 2002.* 41-47.
4. Dey, A.K., Salber, D. and Abowd, G.D.. A conceptual framework and a toolkit for supporting the rapid prototyping of context-aware applications. *Human-Computer Interaction Journal,* 16(2-4), 97-166, 2001.
5. Dey, A.K. *et al.* a Cappella: Programming by demonstration of context-aware applications. *CHI 2004.* 33-40.
6. Espinoza, F. *et al.* Geonotes: Social and navigational aspects of location-based information systems. *UBICOMP 2001.* 2-17.
7. Gajos, K., Fox, H. and Shrobe, H. End user empowerment in human centered pervasive computing. *Pervasive 2002.* 134-140.
8. Hong, J.I. and Landay, J.A. An infrastructure approach to context-aware computing. *Human-Computer Interaction Journal,* 16(2-4). 287-303, 2001.
9. Hong, J.I. and Landay, J.A. SATIN: A toolkit for informal ink-based applications. *CHI 2000,* 63-71.
10. Hull, R., Clayton, B. and Melamed, T. Rapid authoring of mediascapes. *Ubicomp 2004,* 125-142.
11. Humble, J. *et al.* 'Playing with your bits': user composition of ubiquitous domestic environments. *UBICOMP 2003,* 256-263.
12. Lamming, M. and Flynn, M. Forget-me-not: Intimate computing in support of human memory. *International Symposium on Next Generation Human Interfaces 1994.* 125-128.
13. Li, Y., Hong, J.I. and Landay, J.A. Topiary: Tool for prototyping location-enhanced applications. *UIST 2004,* 217-226.
14. Mackay, W.E. *et al.* How do experienced Information Lens users use rules? *CHI '89.* 211-216.
15. Mozer, M.C. The neural network house: An environment that adapts to its inhabitants. *AAAI Spring Symposium on Intelligent Environments.* 110-114, 1998.
16. Pane, J.F. and Myers, B.A. Tabular and textual methods for selecting objects from a group. *IEEE International Symposium on Visual Languages 2000.* 157-164.
17. Pascoe, J. The Stick-e Note Architecture: Extending the interface beyond the user. *Intelligent User Interfaces 1997,* 261-264.
18. Pascoe, J., Ryan, N. and Morse, D. Issues in developing context-aware computing. *HUC 1999.* 208-221.
19. Repenning, A. and Citrin, W. Agentsheets: Applying grid-based spatial reasoning to human-computer interaction. *IEEE Symposium on Visual Languages 1983.* 77-82.
20. Scerri, P. and Reed, N. The EASE actor development environment. *Swedish AI Society 2000.*
21. Schilit, B., Adams, N. and Want, R. Context-aware computing applications. *Workshop on Mobile Computing Systems and Applications,* 1994.
22. Shu, N.C. Visual Programming: Perspectives and Approaches. *IBM Systems Journal,* Vol. 28. 525-547, 1989.
23. Truong, K.N., Huang, E.M. and Abowd, G.D.. CAMP: A magnetic poetry interface for end-user programming of capture applications for the home. *Ubicomp 2004,* 143-160.
24. Weiser, M. Computer for the 21st century. *Scientific American,* 265(3). 94-104, 1991.

iCam: Precise at-a-Distance Interaction in the Physical Environment

Shwetak N. Patel[1], Jun Rekimoto[2], and Gregory D. Abowd[1]

[1] College of Computing & GVU Center,
Georgia Institute of Technology,
801 Atlantic Drive, Atlanta GA 30332-0280, USA
{shwetak, abowd}@cc.gatech.edu
[2] Interaction Laboratory,
Sony Computer Science Laboratories, Inc.,
3-14-13 Higashigotanda,
Shinagawa-ku, Tokyo 141-0022, Japan
rekimoto@csl.sony.co.jp

Abstract. Precise indoor localization is quickly becoming a reality, but application demonstrations to date have been limited to use of only a single piece of location information attached to an individual sensing device. The localized device is often held by an individual, allowing applications, often unreliably, to make high-level predictions of user intent based solely on that single piece of location information. In this paper, we demonstrate how effective integration of sensing and laser-assisted interaction results in a handheld device, the iCam, which simultaneously calculates its own location as well as the location of another object in the environment. We describe how iCam is built and demonstrate how location-aware at-a-distance interaction simplifies certain location-aware activities.

1 Introduction and Motivation

We have seen great progress in our research community towards the goal of practical, precise indoor localization. A variety of techniques, including those that introduce new infrastructure (e.g. ultrasound [20, 2], camera tracking [28], ultra-wideband [24]) and those that leverage existing infrastructure (e.g. 802.11 [3, 12], GSM [18], Bluetooth [14]) show that we are not far off from having everyday devices that know where they are in the physical world.

Location-aware applications are limited, however, when using only knowledge of a single object's location. This location information is usually that of the device itself, and applications assume that the device is in the possession of an individual. In that case, device location relates to the owner, and services provided are dependent on the owner's assumed location. This technique is unsatisfactory for applications, such as the canonical mobile tour guide, in which focus of attention, not just location, may be the desired trigger for delivering information (*e.g.*, for what object is the tourist wanting further information) [1, 8].

One augmented reality solution is to gain precise location and orientation information of the individual and project information about the world in the field of view of

K.P. Fishkin et al. (Eds.): PERVASIVE 2006, LNCS 3968, pp. 272–287, 2006.
© Springer-Verlag Berlin Heidelberg 2006

that individual. However, it can be difficult to place content in the environment, that is, to create the link between physical location and virtual information. Another solution is to tag the environment with glyphs and recognize those tags, usually through some form of computer vision or active tagging approach. Tagging is not always feasible or aesthetically desirable, though this solution does allow for objects to be moved in the environment and does not require precise localization.

In this paper, we provide another alternative: augmenting a precisely located device with a laser-based range finder so that it can also accurately determine the location of an object at-a-distance. We describe the iCam handheld device as a demonstration of this concept (shown in Figure 1). iCam integrates a commercially available indoor

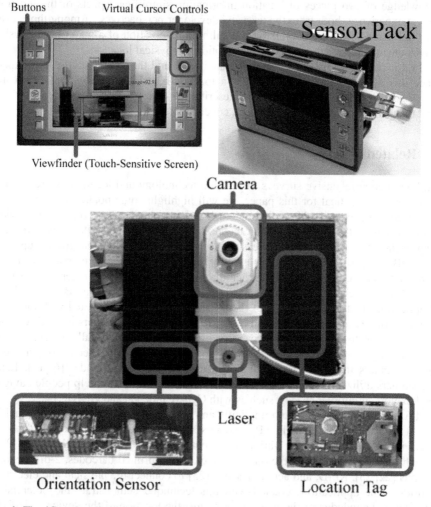

Fig. 1. The iCam handheld. The back of the device (shown on the bottom) houses the laser pointer and the camera in addition to the collection of sensors inside the housing.

ultra-wideband positioning system [24] with a magnetic compass, an accelerometer, a camera, and a laser pointer. This portable handheld device tracks its own location and orientation to within 7 cm and 1.5 degrees of rotation. By using the laser pointer, a user can point to any object or surface in the physical environment and iCam calculates that object's absolute 3D location to 20 cm accuracy from a distance of up to 5 meters for our prototype. With this capability, we demonstrate how one can use iCam to place information at any arbitrary location in the environment and how it can greatly simplify both the authoring of location-triggered content as well as calibration. The same iCam handheld features a camera which allows users to view any digital content through an augmented viewfinder.

The important contribution of this paper is a demonstration of how simultaneous knowledge of two pieces of location information simplifies aspects of the location-aware experience, both from the user and developer perspectives. Among those tasks that are made easier are overall system calibration, creation of a map of the physical environment, and attaching virtual information to physical locations.

In this paper, we first describe the related work and then illustrate the user experience this system enables. We present a location-based tour guide application that leverages iCam's unique capabilities, describe the detailed implementation of iCam, and then finish up with future work and conclusions.

2   Related Work

Although comprehensive surveys of location technology and location-aware applications are not practical for this paper, we will highlight some notable examples. Researchers have extensively studied indoor location technologies. Hightower provides an overview of the various location technologies and techniques [9]. The two basic approaches are to build the entire sensing infrastructure from the ground up (*e.g.*, ActiveBadge [26], Cricket[20] , and Active Bat[2]) or to leverage existing infrastructure that can yield localization, either through triangulation or fingerprinting (*e.g.*, 802.11 work such as RADAR[3] and Place Lab[12], GSM [18], and Bluetooth [14]). Applications that leverage some of these location technologies started with the original location research at Olivetti and Xerox PARC, where researchers used office tasks as motivation to create experiences such as Audio Aura, auto call forwarding, and desktop migration [16, 26]. Location information has also been used to trigger events and reminders in applications like Forget-me-not and CybreMinder [6, 11]. Later, researchers utilized location-awareness in tourist applications to help people navigate and explore unfamiliar spaces, such as with CyberGuide [1] and GUIDE [4].

Location has been used both implicitly and explicitly to attempt to describe and interact with the physical world. Researchers have explored selection of physical objects in an environment for various augmented reality tasks (*e.g.*, NaviCam [23]), which includes ways to tag the physical world using printed barcodes, 2-dimensional glyphs [22, 23], RFID, and active beacons [25] to connect the physical and electronic worlds. The applications created with this technique demonstrate the potential of leveraging knowledge of the world beyond just the location of the device or individual. However, the current solutions that use static labels (such as barcodes or 2-dimensional glyphs) are limited in distance due to the camera resolution and perception techniques used to decipher the glyphs. Static labels are also not practical to deploy in highly interactive spaces because of the difficulty inherent to placing labels on every object.

Previous research projects have also explored laser pointer interaction, both for interaction at-a-distance with large displays [5, 10, 15, 17] and for the selection tasks of physically tagged objects [19, 21]. A popular laser pointer interaction scheme is to use a camera focused on a region of a wall or object in which a laser spot may appear. Simple computer vision techniques locate the red laser dot and follow it around the interaction region. Such a scheme is appealing for meetings or presentations, during which one can interact with a display from a distance by simply pointing at it with an ordinary laser pointer. Two-way laser pointing techniques have been proposed using active tags placed in the environment, but these are subject to the same scalability limitations as static tags mentioned previously.

The XWand system demonstrates how individuals can use laser pointing techniques with a collection of other sensors to support selection of and interaction with devices through a special-purpose device [28]. Although this camera-based tracking solution provides very flexible ways to point and select objects within the environment, it requires significant overhead in terms of camera infrastructure. An extension of XWand, called the World Cursor, removes the vision requirement by using the XWand to steer a remotely controlled laser pointer around a room [27]. The remotely controlled laser pointer has a model of where it is pointing in 3D-space and has sufficient geometric information to know where its red laser dot is pointing. The drawback of this is that it is limited to objects that are within the line-of-sight of the steerable laser. For example, it would be difficult to interact with the sides of an object placed against the wall. iCam's mobility addresses some of these problems.

The drawback of these approaches is the time-consuming setup, calibration, and the difficulty of adding or editing digital content. Most systems assume a model of the space and attributes of the objects that are preprogrammed. Although iCam requires a 3D model of the space, we provide a very quick and easy means to define that model.

3   Demonstrating the iCam Experience

3.1   The iCam Experience

iCam supports two basic modes of interaction. The first is a simple seeking or gathering of information from the physical and virtual space. The second is defining the geometry of the physical space and the digital content that may appear within it. This includes the calibration of the infrastructure, the mapping and defining of the physical space, and the authoring and attaching of virtual content.

A laser pointer mounted on the handheld produces a bright red dot that iCam uses to target objects or places of interest. For example, a user can point the visible laser dot at a light switch or trace the outline of a door by moving the dot around the doorframe (see Figure 2). Additionally, users can interact with the space between the handheld device and the position where the dot lands by moving a virtual cursor on the viewfinder up and down the beam produced by the laser pointer. This movement of the cursor allows interaction within the free space where there may not be physical artifacts for the dot to actually land on. If the user is interested in scanning the space for information, iCam can be used similarly to a video camera (such as when recording a video of a scene) to find the relevant information in the area.

3.1.1 Seeking Information

For seeking information, iCam is used much like a video camera in that the user can scan the space and see augmentations of digital content, such as textual information or pictures, over the live view of the physical space (see Figure 6). A user can also interact with the physical space by, for example, actuating a light switch by pointing at it and pressing a virtual button on the handheld. More complicated widgets may also be available in the space. In the light switch example, the physical switch could be augmented with additional control options (*e.g.*, timing, mood lighting, or dimming capabilities) that appear over the physical switch when the user points at it. The user can then use the virtual cursor in the augmented view to interact with the virtual switch.

iCam also supports zooming to obtain different levels of detail in the scene. If the user is interested in viewing the available virtual content for a space, he can use the zoom out feature to view a large amount of available content quickly and to reduce the amount of movement for scanning the space. Likewise, zooming into a scene can reveal more detailed information. Zooming also enables long distance interaction. If the laser dot is not easily viewable, the user can zoom in and use the virtual cursor to do fine-grained movements from a distance.

3.1.2 Defining the Physical Space and Placing Content

iCam provides an easy method for defining the physical layout of a space (see Figure 2). Users can trace parts of the physical space, similar to outlining with a pen, by using the laser dot as the visual feedback. The viewfinder provides feedback of the trail or "ink" left behind with the trace, which allows users to view exactly what was marked. The accuracy of the system allows users to provide detailed selections of the areas of interest. This selection method allows a person to produce a geometric model quickly by tracing the outlines of the walls, doors, and windows of a room.

We provide a very simple content addition mechanism called *beaming*. Beaming involves the attachment of authored content, such as a note, anywhere in the physical space. Users can create content using the iCam interface or import it from another computer system. After producing the content, the user can either beam it to where the laser dot lies or place the authored content in free space by moving the virtual cursor displayed in the viewfinder along the laser beam.

3.2 Tour Guide Application

To demonstrate the use and capabilities of the iCam system, we revisit the canonical tour guide example. Although this is a popular application in many location-aware systems, an often unaddressed but important task for these applications is creating the digital representation of the physical space. Especially for precise indoor solutions, some level of a geometric model of the space is a necessary component. Thus, we focus on a tour guide application that provides an easy way to create the tour itself.

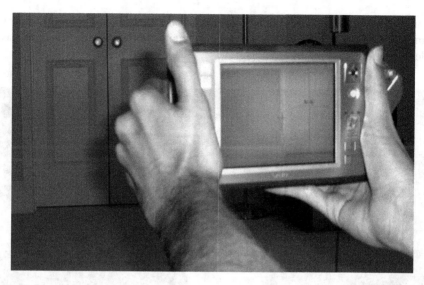

Fig. 2. Example of a user tracing the door frame to create a map of the space. Notice the virtual ink left behind through the viewfinder for visual feedback.

Our system provides a very easy way to define the map of the physical space by using a special "learning" or mapping mode. A user can walk around the space and add annotations to physical objects. The tour creator would create the content on the iCam and beam it to the appropriate physical artifact by pointing at it. Arrows can also be placed in the environment to suggest where to go next from each exhibit. In this case, the tour creator would find an appropriate location and draw a line where an arrow should appear. The creator can also make free hand annotations by using iCam as a pen to mark and produce callouts. Additionally, a user can take a snapshot of the current view, use a stylus to draw directly on the display, and then place the annotation back into the environment. This is desirable since it may be difficult to control the laser for certain strokes, especially from very far distances.

Figures 3-6 show the use of a simple content creation interface with iCam. The interface consists of a blank note on which the user can place any combination of pictures, text, free-hand writing, or short audio clips. The user selects the type of content he wants to add from the toolbar and places it on the note. He can insert pictures by looking through a list of image files on the device, enter text by using the handheld's virtual keyboard, add free-hand writing by directly writing on the screen with a finger or stylus, or add an audio note by speaking into the onboard microphone. He may also import pre-authored content from a remote computer and attach it to the notes created with iCam.

During a tour, the iCam displays the annotations and virtual content through the viewfinder while it is pointed toward the relevant parts of the physical space. Every user will see the same content from every vantage point, similar to how it would look if it were a physical artifact in the space. A user can view all the available annotations in an area by scanning the space with the viewfinder and using the zooming capabilities. Knowing the user intent and focus is an important feature in a mobile tour guide and here it is made explicit without needing to infer based solely location.

Fig. 3. The user scans the physical environment to find a place to add new content

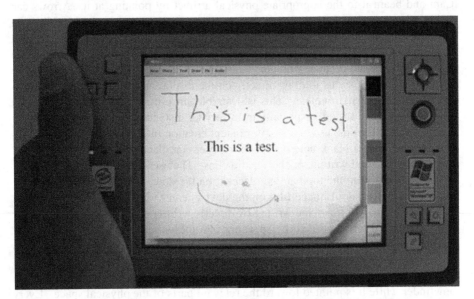

Fig. 4. The user authors the content using the iCam's notes interface

Fig. 5. The user beams the created note to the desired location on the bookshelf. Note the red laser pointer on the green book.

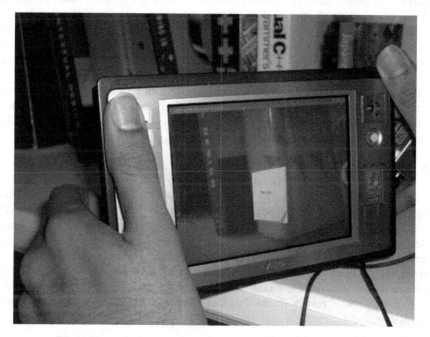

Fig. 6. The user views the same note from a different vantage point

4   iCam Implementation Details

iCam is a handheld device (shown in Figure 1) that can accurately locate its position and determine its absolute orientation when it is indoors. It can also determine the 3D position of any object to which points with its onboard laser pointer. iCam is built using a Sony Vaio Type-U handheld instrumented with a variety of onboard sensors. The device can localize its position in 3D space to within 7 cm of accuracy, determine its orientation (azimuth, tilt, and roll) within 1.5 degrees, and determine the 3D location of other objects and surfaces within 20 cm in all directions.[1] It accomplishes this by integrating a modified version of a commercially available, ultra-wideband location system (from Ubisense [24]), a 3-axis magnetic compass, a 2-axis accelerometer, and a laser pointer tracked by the handheld's camera. The net location update rate is 15 Hz, which is enough for most interactive applications.

4.1 3D Position

The handheld determines its location using the Ubisense ultra-wideband location system installed in the environment. We chose to use the Ubisense system because of its commercial availability and its ability to handle large spaces with mild to moderate occlusions. The handheld device is instrumented with an active tag that constantly emits its identity at very high frequency bands (5.8-7.2 GHz). Sensors placed in the environment detect these signals and triangulate the tag's location based on the signal's time and angle of arrival. The advertised average accuracy of the system is 10-15 cm. However, after modifying the tag's antenna (replacing it with a copper cube antenna with larger surface area) and strategically placing 6 sensors in the space, we obtained average accuracies of 7 cm in all directions. The accuracy was measured by averaging differences between iCam's calculated positions from actual known locations which were measured using a standard tape measure. We instrumented a 10 m x 15 m space using six ultra-wideband sensors. We placed more sensors in the areas where there were more occlusions and thus a greater potential for multi-path reflections (e.g., around desks, structural supports, etc).

4.2 3D Orientation

The iCam system accomplishes absolute orientation with an Aichi Mi AMI201 3-axis magnetic compass and an Analog Devices ADXL series 2-axis accelerometer. The compass determines the handheld's azimuth or bearing angle and the accelerometer determines the tilt and roll angles. Because magnetic compasses are only accurate when held parallel to the ground (perpendicular to the gravitation axis), the accelerometer and the third magnetic axis provide a means to compensate for the tilt and roll angles and keep the compass electronically gimbaled regardless of level. This allows the user to move freely with the handheld and still obtain very accurate bearing information.

---

[1] The 20 cm is an average estimate for the error in our instrumented space of 10 m x 15 m and interacting at distances of up to 5 meters. This value would increase for much larger spaces because of potential angular errors. It is also affect by the resolution of the camera, as we later describe.

A common problem indoors is the magnetic interference produced by some consumer electronic devices such as televisions and computers. The iCam mitigates this problem by constantly monitoring the magnetic values in all directions and dynamically subtracts out any abnormal readings. Since it is difficult to calibrate out all time-varying interferences, especially small changes, we only focus on significant magnetic deviations. iCam accomplishes its dynamic calibration by comparing the current magnetic values with that of the initial calibration data and the history of readings up to that point. The initial calibration is done in an area that is known to have minimal or no magnetic interference. The device also stores the recent component values from the compass (sampled at 15 Hz). iCam detects magnetic disturbances by comparing the magnitude value from the calibration sequence to the current magnitude. Any significant magnetic interference in the environment will cause a magnetic spike in all three directional components of the compass, thus greatly increasing its net magnitude. When this phenomenon occurs, iCam replaces the current magnetic values with the most recent unaffected value. This dead reckoning approach works well for short-lived magnetic disturbances.

4.3 3D Range-Finding

By coupling the handheld's position and orientation with its distance from an object, it is possible to determine the 3D position of that object. We do this by using the camera to track the red dot produced by the onboard laser pointer. We chose the laser tracking approach over ultrasound for two reasons. First, we already had plans to use a laser pointer for visual feedback, so it was natural to leverage its capability. Second, ultrasound is not collimated enough to aim precisely at a small surface.

The laser diode is mounted at a known fixed position parallel to the camera (see Figure 7). The onboard camera has a resolution of 640x480 pixels and horizontal field of view of approximately 50° and vertical field of view of approximately 40°. The iCam projects a laser beam onto an object or surface in the field of view of the camera. The onboard camera captures the dot from the laser along with the rest of the scene and a simple algorithm runs over the image looking for the brightest pixels. We then calculate the range to the object based on where along the vertical axis of the image this laser dot falls. The closer the dot is to the center of the image, the further away the object is. The distance is calculated using the angle, ϕ, between the camera's central focal point and the position of the dot in the camera's view (see Figure 7).

The equation used for this distance is:

$$D = \frac{h}{\tan \phi},$$

$$\phi = C * P$$

where h is the distance between the camera and laser diode centers, and ϕ is the number of pixels from the laser dot to the center of focus (P) multiplied by the radians per pixel constant (C). The radians per pixel constant (C) is an approximation that we derived in the lab through a series of calibration sequences with known distances D. The values are then averaged to determine the final approximation for C. Another reason for the approximation is the curvature of the lens with respect to the focal plane. Depending on which part of the image is used, the radian per pixel value (C) changes slightly. However, this change is very slight, and the approximation works well for our system.

Since the laser dot only appears on the vertical axis near the center of the image, we limit the detection algorithm to only that region. This helps prevent false positives from other bright light sources that may appear in the image. This approach works reasonably well indoors with about 20 cm accuracy for distances between 1 and 5 meters. The accuracy and range are limited by the resolution of the image. In our simple setup, we spread 240 pixels vertically across the 20-degree half field of view, because the laser is parallel to the optical axis of the camera. By using 3 sub-pixel analysis we are able to obtain 20 cm accuracy. Mounting the laser horizontally instead of vertically to the camera would improve the accuracy due to the slight increase in horizontal resolution (320 pixels vs 240 pixels). This produces an increase to about 16 cm for the 1-5 m range. The 20 cm accuracy currently requires 3 sub-pixel analysis and increasing that to 10 sub-pixels would provide about 7 cm accuracy for the 240 pixel vertical resolution case. In addition, an optical zoom capability would also greatly improve accuracy and give the user more precise control for interacting with distant objects. However, this requires manual operation of the lens and optical system by the user.

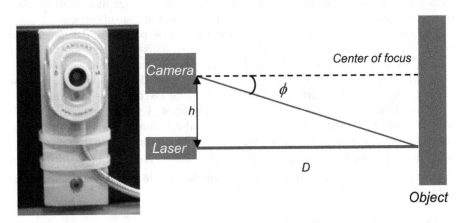

Fig. 7. Left: Camera and laser diode mounted parallel to each other behind the iCam handheld. Right: Diagram showing the components of the distance equation stated previously.

4.4 Calibration

The system requires two calibration steps: the orientation sensors on the handheld and for the location system in the environment.[2] To calibrate the orientation sensors,

---

[2] The ranging system does not need to be calibrate by the end user because the needed values are determined during construction and do not change in different environments.

iCam prompts the user to hold the handheld level to the ground and then fully rotate it around all three axes.

Surveying and calibrating the Ubisense location sensors is typically a fairly time-consuming and tedious task. Since the sensors are mounted at an elevated position, it is difficult to measure absolute positions accurately between multiple sensors. Often, to find the proper setup it requires testing several different configurations. Thus, the overall process can be a very long task, involving the following steps:

1) placing the sensors in the environment;
2) surveying the location of the sensors (both relative to the space and each other); and
3) calibrating each of the sensors to known points in the environment

By leveraging the capabilities of iCam, we can accelerate these steps and greatly ease the overall setup burden.

The Ubisense calibration software requires two pieces of information: the location of the wall-mounted location sensors and mobile sensor readings from known points in space. To survey the locations of the wall-mounted sensors, we initially pick one pair that can be seen by iCam from the same location. Keeping the iCam in the same location in the room, we measure the (X, Y, Z) locations of these two Ubisense sensors using the iCam's range-finding and orientation capabilities. The laser pointer provides visual feedback to assist in aiming. In addition, all the Ubisense sensors have a square marking on the foreside which serves as a consistent reference point for aiming. Then we pick a new wall-mounted sensor and move iCam to a location where this sensor and one of the previous pair are both visible. We measure the (X, Y, Z) locations of these two from the new vantage point and proceed in the same pair-wise fashion around the room until each wall-mounted sensor has been paired and measured with a previously measured one. In the end, we resolve the relative translations between all the pairs into 3D coordinates in a common coordinate system. For this procedure, we can assume that all the coordinate frames are parallel in orientation, since the wall-mounted Ubisense sensors are effectively omni-directional when laid out.

While carrying out these surveying measurements, we also record readings on the mobile Ubisense sensor mounted on iCam. After resolving all the 3D measurements into one coordinate system, these measurements serve as the mobile sensor readings for the other half of the Ubisense calibration input (step 3 from above). Additional readings can also be recorded afterwards to improve position accuracy.

4.5 Overall System Architecture

Figure 8 shows the overall system architecture. The position sensors in the environment are connected through ethernet to a PC. The location software runs on that PC and transmits all resulting location information back to the iCam handheld device via 802.11b. The handheld computes its orientation and its range to other objects locally and then wirelessly transmits these values back to the PC. The handheld's application is written in Java and parts of the user interface (viewfinder and 3D overlays) are created using the OpenGL GL4Java extension. The geometric model and attributes of the physical and virtual space are stored on the PC, but are cached locally on the

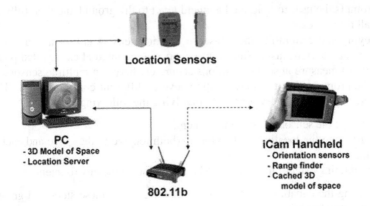

Location Sensors

PC
- 3D Model of Space
- Location Server

802.11b

iCam Handheld
- Orientation sensors
- Range finder
- Cached 3D
  model of space

Fig. 8. Overall system architecture of the iCam system

handheld during startup to speed up interaction. As the user modifies aspects of the space, the system updates the locally stored model and notifies the PC of the appropriate changes.

5 Conclusions and Future Work

We have presented a handheld device called iCam that precisely determines its own location and orientation as well as the position of objects and surfaces in the physical environment. In addition to localizing itself and other objects, iCam serves as an interaction device for augmented reality applications. iCam offers several advantages over other similar devices. It provides accurate position information of both the handheld itself and a point in space indicated by a laser pointer. It uses a practical infrastructure of commercially available equipment to achieve this dual localization. iCam's simple mechanism for interaction between the physical and virtual space facilitates an easy way to map the physical space. Finally, iCam simplifies the calibration of the location infrastructure by making it easier and faster. We have not previously seen a single device that can simultaneously and affordably accommodate calibration and content placement while also serving as a primary end user interaction device.

iCam's ability to localize objects accurately from a distance greatly simplifies the mapping process by allowing the users to define exactly what they intend *in situ*. We have demonstrated this by explaining how iCam would be used to place content for a location-aware tour guide, but this is certainly just the first step in exploring its capabilities. A system like iCam enables many other augmented reality applications that leverage the user's explicit intent and actions with the physical space. One can imagine other practical applications that take advantage of these capabilities. For example, suppose someone is moving into a new space and is trying to decide where to place furniture. He has hired a moving company to handle the actual moving of the furniture, but the person is unable to be there when the actual moving takes place. To ensure that the movers place the furniture where the person needs it to be, the user can use iCam to mark spaces around the room where he would like the furniture placed (*e.g.*, trace a box around the south side of the room and attach a note with the text "black bookcases goes here"). When the movers come to the space, they can then use iCam to view where he has designated the furniture to be placed.

The tour guide and the last example fall into the larger class of groupware of applications that support asynchronous, collocated collaboration. Inventory location for customers (*e.g.*, helping someone find a book in a bookstore or a bottle of wine at a store) is another example. For individuals with mobility challenges, the precise, at-a-distance interaction can effectively extend their reach. These individuals, for example, could use iCam to indicate to caregivers where to find or place certain items around their home.

Authoring of location-aware content can also be generalized to the description of behaviors that are associated to locations. Imagine developing a remote control that can point to a device and then control it. The "programmer" of the remote would need to indicate what physical space is occupied by the device, so that when a user points to that space subsequent control commands are sent to the correct logical device. This suggests a model of "programming the environment" in a very literal sense, and we see promise for this kind of use of location-enhanced, at-a-distance interaction that can extend other recent work in programming simplifications for Ubicomp [7, 13].

These applications require simultaneous knowledge of the user interface's own location and orientation as well as the position of objects and surfaces in the physical environment. Our iCam device enables exploration of this kind of sophisticated location-aware experience, both from the user and developer perspectives. Among those tasks that are made easier are overall system calibration, creation of a map of the physical environment, and attaching virtual information to physical locations.

Acknowledgements

The authors thank all the members of the Ubicomp Research Group, and in particular Julie Kientz, Khai Truong, Gillian Hayes, Giovanni Iachello, and Jay Summet, as well as members of the Interaction Lab at the Sony Computer Science Laboratory in Japan. We also thank John Krumm from Microsoft Research for his help shepherding the final draft of this paper. This work is sponsored in part by the National Science Foundation (Grant No. 0513111).

References

1. Abowd, G. D., Atkeson, C.G., Hong, J., Long S., Kooper, R., and Pinkerton, M. Cyberguide: A Mobile Context-Aware Tour Guide. *ACM Wireless Networks*. Volume 3, pp 421-433. 1997.
2. Active Bat. The BAT Ultrasonic Location System. http://www.uk.research.att.com/bat/. 2006.
3. Bahl, P. and Padmanabhan, V. RADAR: An In-Building RF-Based User Location and Tracking System. In the proceedings of *IEEE Infocom 2000*. Los Alamitos. pp. 775-784. 2000.

4. Cheverst, K., Davies, N., Mitchell, K., Friday, A., and Efstratiou, C. Developing a Context-aware Electronic Tourist Guide: Some Issues and Experiences. In the proceedings of *Conference on Human Factors in Computing Systems (CHI) 2000*. Netherlands. pp 17-24. April 2000.

5. Cooperstock, J. R., Fels, S.S., Buxton, W. and Smith, K.C. Reactive Environments: Throwing Away Your Keyboard and Mouse. *Communications of the ACM*. Volume 40, pp 65-73. 1997.

6. Dey, A.K. and Abowd, G.D. CybreMinder: A Context-Aware System for Supporting Reminders. In the proceedings of *The 2nd International Symposium on Handheld and Ubiquitous Computing (HUC2K)*. Bristol, UK. pp. 172-186. September 2000.

7. Dey, A.K., Hamid, R., Beckmann, C., Li, I., and Hsu, D. aCAPpella: Programming by Demonstration of Context-Aware Applications. In the proceedings of *Conference on Human Factors in Computing Systems (CHI)* 2004. pp. 33-40. April 2004

8. Dow, S., Lee, J., Oezbek, C., MacIntyre, B., Bolter, J.D., and Gandy, M. Exploring Spatial Narratives and Mixed Reality Experiences in Oakland Cemetery. In the proceedings of *ACM SIGCHI Conference on Advances in Computer Entertainment (ACE 2005)*. Valencia, Spain. June 2005.

9. Hightower, J. and Borriello, G. A Survey and Taxonomy of Location Systems for Ubiquitous Computing, University of Washington Tech Report CSC-01-08-03. 2001.

10. Kirstein, C. and Mueller, H. Interaction with a Projection Screen using a Camera-tracked Laser Pointer. In the proceedings of *The International Conference on Multimedia Modeling*. Lausanne, Switzerland. 1998

11. Lamming, M. and Flynn, M. Forget-me-not: Intimate Computing in Support of Human Memory. In the proceedings of *The Symposium on Next Generation Human Interfaces*. Tokyo, Japan. 1994.

12. LaMarca, A., Chawathe, Y., Consolvo, S., Hightower, J., Smith, I., Scott, I., Sohn, T., Howard, J., Hughes, J., Potter, F., Tabert, J., Powledge, R., Borriello, G., and Schilit, B. Place Lab: Device Positioning Using Radio Beacons in the Wild. In the proceedings of *Pervasive 2005*, Munich, Germany. pp. 116 – 133. 2005.

13. Li, Y., Hong, J. I., and Landay, J. A. 2004. Topiary: a tool for prototyping location-enhanced applications. In the proceedings of *The ACM Symposium on User interface Software and Technology (UIST 2004)*. Santa Fe, NM. pp 217-226. October 2004.

14. Madhavapeddy, A. and Tse, T. Study of Bluetooth Propagation Using Accurate Indoor Location Mapping. *The Seventh International Conference on Ubiquitous Computing (UbiComp 2005)*. Tokyo, Japan. pp 105-122. September 2005.

15. Myers, B. A., Bhatnagar, R., Nichols, J., Peck, C.H., Kong, D., Miller, R., and Long, A.C., Interacting at a Distance: Measuring the Performance of Laser Pointers and Other Devices. In the proceedings of *Conference on Human Factors in Computing Systems (CHI 2002)*. Minneapolis, Minnesota. 2002.

16. Mynatt, E.D., Back, M., Want, R., Baer, M., and Ellis, J.B. Designing Audio Aura. In the proceedings of *Conference on Human Factors in Computing Systems (CHI 1998)*. pp. 566-573. April 1998.

17. Olsen, D. R. and Nielsen, T. Laser Pointer Interaction. In the proceedings of *Conference on Human Factors in Computing Systems (CHI 2001)*. Seattle, Washington. 2001.

18. Otsason, V., Varshavsky, A., LaMarca A., and de Lara, E. Accurate GSM Indoor Localization. In the proceedings of *The Seventh International Conference on Ubiquitous Computing (UbiComp 2005)*. Tokyo, Japan. September 2005.

19. Patel, S. N. and Abowd, G.D. A 2-way Laser-assisted Selection Scheme for Handhelds in a Physical Environment. *The Fifth International Conference on Ubiquitous Computing (UbiComp 2003)*. Seattle, WA. pp 200 – 207. 2003.

20. Priyantha, N. B., Chakraborty, A., and Balakrishnan, H. The Cricket Location-Support System. In the proceedings of *The International Conference on Mobile Computing and Networking (Mobicom 2000)*. Boston, MA. August 2000.
21. Ringwald, M. Spontaneous Interaction with Everyday Devices Using a PDA. Workshop on Supporting Spontaneous Interaction in Ubiquitous Computing Settings. Ubicomp 2002. Goeteborg, Sweden. 2002
22. Rekimoto J. and Ayatsuka Y. CyberCode: Designing Augmented Reality Environments with Visual Tags. In the proceedings of *Designing Augmented Reality Environments (DARE 2000)*. Elsinore, Denmark. pp 1 – 10. 2000.
23. Rekimoto, J and Katashi, N. The World through the Computer: Computer Augmented Interaction with Real World Environments. In the proceedings of the *ACM Symposium on User Interface Software and Technology (UIST 1995)*. Pittsburgh, PA. pp 29-36. 1995.
24. Ubisense. http://www.ubisense.net. 2005.
25. Want, R., Fishkin, K., Gujar, A., and Harrison, B. Bridging physical and virtual worlds with electronic tags. In the proceedings of *Conference on Human Factors in Computing Systems (CHI 2001)*, Pittsburgh, PA. 1999.
26. Want, R., Hopper, A., Falcao, V., and Gibbons, J. The active badge location system. *ACM Transactions on Information Systems*. Volume 10. pp. 91-102. January 1992.
27. Wilson, A. and Pham, H. Pointing in Intelligent Environments with the WorldCursor. In the proceedings of *Interact 2003*, Zurich, Switzerland. September 2003.
28. Wilson, A. and Shafer, S. XWand: UI for intelligent spaces. In the proceedings of *Conference on Human Factors in Computing Systems (CHI 2003)*. Ft. Lauderdale, Florida. pp 545 – 552. April 2003.

Gesture Signature for Ambient Intelligence Applications: A Feasibility Study

Elisabetta Farella[1], Sile O'Modhrain[2], Luca Benini[1], and Bruno Riccó[1]

[1] DEIS University of Bologna, v.le Risorgimento 2,
40136 Bologna, Italy
[2] Sonic Arts Research Centre,
Queens University, Belfast, Ireland

Abstract. This work investigates the feasibility of a personal verification system using gestures as biometric signatures. Gestures are captured by low-power, low-cost tri-axial accelerometers integrated into an expansion pack for palmtop computers. The objective of our study is to understand whether the mobile system can recognize its owner by how she/he performs a particular gesture, acting as a gesture signature. The signature can be used for obtaining access to the mobile device, but the handheld device can also act as an intelligent key to provide access to services in an ambient intelligence scenario. Sample gestures are analyzed and classified using supervised and unsupervised dimensionality reduction techniques. Results on a set of benchmark gestures performed by several individuals are encouraging.

1 Introduction

Is it possible to use gesture as an integral part of a personal identification - authentication system? Is there something in how we perform movements which is unique and personal? If we think about handwriting, it is evident that each of us has a different calligraphic identity. Is it possible that there also exists for each of us a calligraphy of gestures? The present work investigates the feasibility of a personal verification system using gestures as biometric signatures, given a constrained scenario. We imagine a user holding her/his Personal Digital Assistant (PDA) or her/his mobile phone and unlocking or locking it through a simple gesture, a kind of gesture signature, which gives the device the ability to recognize its owner. In this example the mobile device is the target: the user wants to interact with the mobile device and access private data, such as their address book, personal notes, files and programs. The PDA can also act as a bridge to allow an individual to be identified in a more general ambient intelligence scenario. Imagine arriving home and being recognized by your house using a personal gesture signature. By performing a simple gesture, all the services you pre-programmed in your house are delivered to you, e.g. your personal mail is read to you or your favourite music is turned on.

Having selected as our target a mobile scenario, some constraints are immediately apparent [1]. Vision and optical systems for motion tracking are not

K.P. Fishkin et al. (Eds.): PERVASIVE 2006, LNCS 3968, pp. 288–304, 2006.

suitable in this context because such systems are either fixed and thereby cumbersome or they require the user to stop moving in order for an entire gesture to be captured. However inertial sensors, due to their small form factor, low-cost and power consumption characteristics appear to provide a viable alternative solution since they are suitable for integration into mobile systems such as PDAs and mobile phones [2]. Moreover gestures enable interactions with a device that do not necessarily require visual support or support from other input devices such as pens, keyboards and joysticks. The use of gesture as an input modality for mobile systems has been considered in many studies [5][15] as a suitable alternative solution to the mentioned usual interfaces. This current work takes a step forward, by exploring the challenge of exploiting inertial sensors embedded in mobile devices for personal identification and authentication. The recognition of a gesture signature is targeted, focusing only on the gesture chosen by the user as her/his personal gesture to authenticate her/himself in the system.

Our analysis was carried out using a prototype of the Mesh platform [1], an expansion pack for palmtop computers integrating 3-axes accelerometers. The prototype is a handheld box equipped with inertial sensors, able to collect accelerations along three orthogonal axes. Results and observations from analysis based on gestures collected from a sample of individuals are presented. Feature extraction from data is implemented using two well known reduction techniques, namely Principal Component Analysis [18] and Locally Linear Embeddings [19]. We demonstrate that results are sufficiently robust to proceed with this line of investigation (e.g. with refining the analysis, increasing the data set and using additional sensors).

Gestures collected in the form of accelerations through low-power, low-cost inertial sensors can be used to authenticate people within a small group, such as to distinguish among members of a family or colleagues who are members of the same group at a workplace. In the following sections we describe prior related work in this area and position our work in the context of biometrics and interaction techniques for mobile devices. Moreover, we describe the chosen dimensionality reduction techniques applied to the data collected from a sample of users. Finally, the results of the feasibility experiments will be presented and discussed.

2   Background

2.1   Interaction Techniques for Mobile Devices

Mobile devices (PDAs, mobile phones, etc.) present unique and specific challenges in terms of interaction design and usability [1]. Designing interfaces for mobile computers is complicated in a mobile setting where the users attention is not fixed on the computer, but on real-world tasks. A limited amount of screen area is available in such devices and the users visual attention is often focused on negotiating their surroundings rather than on the interface [3]. Alternative interaction techniques for mobile devices, which do not use standard pens and touch panels, are based on use of embedded sensors [5]. In particular, inertial sensors are used to exploit changes in position and orientation of the PDA or the mobile phone as input [4]. Tilt and motion based interfaces enable single-handed operation. Interaction is thus minimally disruptive and demanding of cognitive and visual attention. Over the course of a day, a mobile device is picked up many times and typical natural gestures, which regularly occur when using a mobile phone or MP3 player can become an integral part of interaction with the device.

2.2 Gesture-Based Biometrics

The use of inertial sensors in building alternative gestural interfaces has been extensively explored. Because of their reduced size and weight, however, they are also suitable for applications such as signature capture [26] and gesture recognition [14] [6], where detecting movements can be of great help. More innovative is the suggestion that movements collected through inertial sensors can be used for biometric purposes. A biometric is a physiological or behavioural feature that can be used to identify people [16]. In physical biometrics, biological features (e.g. fingerprints, hand geometry, retina or facial characteristics) are examined in order to identify an individual. Behavioural recognition examines the mannerisms of an individual, including signatures, handwriting, voice and keystroke patterns and so on (references can be found in [27]). More generally, techniques for authentication can be based on one of several possible attributes:

- Something you are (a biometric)
- Something you know (a password or PIN)
- Something you have (a key, token card, etc)

Gestures have been used as authentication techniques based on "something you know", that is the gestures or the sequence of movements performed is chosen by the user as he/she might choose a password or a code number. In [7] personal identification is proposed using hand gesture patterns expressing a code number, captured by a CCD camera. A sensor-based authentication mechanism for mobile devices has been presented in [8]. This work explores the problem of verifying a user identity when accessing the public infrastructure, e.g. when he wants to annex his device to I/O resources encountered in the local environment. The recognition mechanism is based on a sequence of shake and pause actions detected by inertial sensors integrated into the mobile device. The sequence is sent to the public infrastructure by the user's mobile device after a discovery procedure has identified the presence of the device.

The aim of our work is somewhat different: using gestures and arm movements as biometrics. In fact, we do not simply want to distinguish among gestures, but to investigate the feasibility of a system, appropriately trained, to distinguish/identify the gesturer from the gesture made. As a consequence, gestures are treated as a behavioural biometric ("something you are"). Thus, the question we pose is whether people can be identified by the way they move. In this area literature is scarce. In [9], simple filters are used to extract features from a gesture captured in the form of still frames, with the purpose of introducing a biometric measure based on hand gestures. Unfortunately, a complete description of this work is not publicly available. In work by Gupta [10] the same work is cited and the authors further state that the algorithm applied could not perform recognition accurately enough to use gestures as biometrics.

Encouraging results come from gait recognition, a relatively new area of study, receiving growing interest, within the realms of computer vision [11]. Gait recognition is the process of identifying an individual by the way in which she/he walks. Early psychological studies into gait by Murray [12], suggested that gait was a unique personal characteristic, with clear cadence and was cyclic in nature. Johansson [13] carried out studies by attaching moving lights onto the principal joints of a group of participants who were than asked to walk across a darkened room. He then showed movies of these "light-point walkers" to a second group of observers. The observers could recognize the biological patterns of gait from the moving light displays, even when some of the markers were removed, once again indicating gait as a potential biometric. Even if conducted in the field of computer vision, these studies suggest that the way we move is personal. Thus it is worth investigating whether it is possible to use data collected with sensors other than cameras.

3   Apparatus and Analysis

Biometric systems typically involve several stages of processing. Data derived from behavioural or physiological characteristics are converted into templates, which are used for subsequent matching and decision-making processes. The work flow in our case is described in Figure 1.

The first decision was the choice of the data acquisition device and consequently the nature of data was determined. We chose the Mesh platform (described later) equipped with inertial sensors. Thus, data collected are accelerations along three orthogonal axes. As a second step, data must be collected from the user and submitted to the system. As it is impossible to collect all the possible samples, a selection of a given amount and kind of sample, considered meaningful and representative for the purposes of the investigation, must be made. A set of four different gestures was selected. For each gesture, a number of examples were collected for each person in the sample group. Data collected were then windowed and grouped in matrices. Rescaling was applied to prepare data for dimensionality reduction. Two different unsupervised dimensionality reduction techniques were applied (PCA and LLE), as described in section 3.4. Being an exploratory study we performed two kinds of analysis. A first qualitative analysis consisted in using data from the initial dimensionality reduction phase to obtain a graphical representation of relationships among gestures performed by different people. Original data are variable, high-dimensional and complex to analyze. As will be described later, PCA and LLE are feature extraction techniques that can be used for dimensionality reduction, to eliminate data redundancy and extract representative vectors from a large amount of data. Reducing data to the first two or three feature vectors, it is possible to plot them and qualitatively identify data clusters, evaluate distances among data representing the same

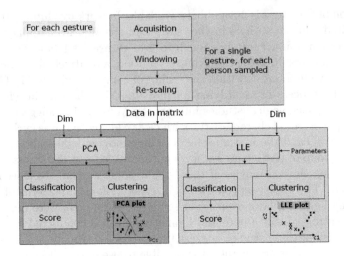

Fig. 1. Steps of the feasibility analysis

gesture performed by different people plotted in a bi-dimensional graphical space. A plot provides a fast but only a qualitative idea with respect to the separation of gestures performed by different individuals. Therefore, a second quantitative evaluation phase was necessary to validate the analysis. For the purpose, we applied a k-Nearest Neighbor method to obtain scores indicating how much a given gesture was distant from another gesture of the same type performed by the same person.

3.1   Acquisition Device

A prototype of the Mesh platform (Figure 2.a) was used to acquire gesture samples. Mesh [24] is an expansion pack for IPAQ handheld computers featuring vibrotactile output and input in the form of motion sensing. The prototype is equipped with a 3-axes accelerometer and can be connected to other devices through the serial port. The accelerometers are two biaxial sensors (ADXL202E), each mounted along and in line with the principal axes of the box prototype, i.e. orthogonally to each other. Thus, gestures are collected as three arrays of samples representing the accelerations referred to axes x, y, z of the box (see Figure 2.a).

The frequency response of the device extends to DC, allowing the acceleration due to gravity to be monitored. Their bandwidth stretches to 100 Hz, yielding sufficient temporal resolution to capture data to drive gesture recognition algorithms. For the work described here, the data is gathered from the sensors at 100Hz, and transmitted over an RS232 serial link to the Personal Computer (PC), where data analysis was performed using Matlab software. The data rate is sufficient for the purpose of this work because human movement frequency is predominantly in the range from 0 to 30Hz.

a.   b.

Fig. 2. a. Acquisition device (Mesh platform) and b. The four gestures chosen

3.2 Data Collection

Two groups of tests were performed, using the apparatus already described. The first was under more controlled conditions than the second. Indeed, the first test involved collecting gestures from a participant who was imitating the gesture performed by a second person. The aim was to obtain intra-personal consistent data, reducing the variability in gesture duration and shape. For the second test no guidance was provided, thus the gestures which resulted were more realistic and hence affected by more variability.

First group of tests. This set of tests involved collecting four different gestures of the type described in figure 2.b from a small group of people. In particular we collected the right arm opening and closing horizontally (gesture 1), the rotation of the wrist (gesture 2), a gesture similar to answering a phone (gesture 3) and a gesture consisting of touching the left shoulder (gesture 4).

Each of the 4 gestures was collected 20 times. The first ten times people were asked to repeat the gesture as consistently as possible, especially with respect to the duration of the gesture. Visual feedback about gesture duration was provided by a clock visible on the PC desktop. People were also asked to pay attention to the inclination of the box during the movement, especially when the direction of movement changed. We obtained a relatively high degree of intra-personal consistency and repeatability among gestures. For the second part of this test we modified the procedure slightly, asking people to imitate a gesture performed by a second person, hereafter called the "target". In practice, *the target* is performing the role of the device owner, and the other participants are trying to imitate his gestures in order to access his personal device. The *target* performed the gesture in synchrony with the people trying to imitate it. In this way the duration of the gestures was the same and each person had immediate visual feedback about the gesture while performing it.

The second group of tests. The second group of tests focused only on gestures 1 and 2 from the initial group of four gestures. A group of 10 people, none of whom had participated in the first test, were asked to perform the gestures and less help was provided to guarantee intra-repeatability of the gesture. This time the gesture was shown only once and the person proposing the gesture did not perform it in synchrony with the participants. Thus, each gesture was repeated by each participant only ten times. We expected that the gestures collected in this second tests would result in less intra-repeatable, but also more personal.

Qualitative results. A major problem in conducting experiments is supporting users for gesture repeatability. In our case we distinguish between performing recognition of a person by the way she/he generally moves and targeting a specific gesture chosen and performed by that person as her/his "gesture signature". From this perspective the same problem can be encountered in other behavioural biometric studies, such as signature recognition. Signature recognition is different from handwriting recognition, mainly for repeatability of data [25]. Handwriting has more intra-personal variability than signatures do. While performing signatures people try to be more consistent with some prototype. They have a real or mental image to imitate each time. Handwriting is generally more variable in time. In this sense our work is aimed at finding a "gesture signature", not a "gesture-writing style". Unfortunately a gesture does not have the same feedback as a signature, which is still visible while and after being performed. This suggests that a way of providing feedback must be found also for gestures: the gesture signature must be experienced while and after it has been performed. Further, it must be easy to remember in order to increase its repeatability.

Instructions given to users about how to perform the gestures were both verbal and visual: in the first test the gesture was explained and simultaneously demonstrated. In the second test, less external support was provided. The gestures were performed only once by *the target*. Despite the invitation to carefully observe and imitate him, people performed the gestures clearly in their own way, especially in the second group of tests, as evidenced by their different physical characteristics and postures and by the different speed of gestures and orientation of the box during the trajectory path (e.g. uncertainty in the initial position of the device). Moreover people did not pay attention to the instruction to repeat each gesture with the same duration. This affected especially gesture 1, which is wider and which therefore takes longer to perform. Moreover since it is wider it is more difficult to control and repeat in the same way. We can also observe that the gestures chosen have different characteristics. The first one is more dependent on physical characteristics, such as the length of the arm of the person performing the gesture. Moreover, this gesture was also reported to be uncomfortable to perform, because it draws attention to the user from passers-by. The

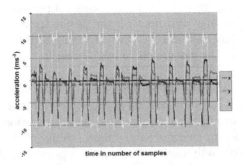

Fig. 3. Accelerations vs time collected along the 3 axes of right-wrist rotation for one person

second gesture is smaller, easy to repeat and was performed with approximately the same duration by many users. The waveform resulting from the acquisition of the three acceleration data streams over time is thus a periodic wave (Figure 3). This gesture is more intra-personally consistent but at the same time we expected more extra-personal similarities, because it is less dependent on individual body characteristics. The last two gestures can be said to provide physical reference to the body. It is expected that allowing the body to act as a frame of reference in this way will improve repeatability, because the gesture is spatially defined having a starting and final position on two precise points of the body.

3.3   Data Pre-processing: Creation of a Biometric Sample

The data collected from a single participant were arranged into a 10 column matrix by gesture. Since people did not perform each of the ten gestures at the same speed, the resulting columns were of different lengths. Variability in data duration was greater in the second group of tests. Thus, to process data with Matlab functions some columns were truncated and others padded. This was done by finding an average duration value (ADV) for each participant and then padding data where a column length did not reach the ADV or cutting extrasamples where a columns length exceeded it. In our opinion this operation is not critical since the differences between columns belonging to the same person and their ADV is in general not significant (e.g. 20-40 samples for a whole duration of 300-400 samples at a sampling rate of 100Hz). A single column vector $\bar{g}$ is shown in Figure 4. The number of samples is averaged to a given ADV' related to the participant and to the length of the gesture performed. Samples s_i $(i = 1 \ldots ADV')$ are related to the temporal window WIN_j with $j = 1 \ldots 10$. Accelerations a_x, a_y, a_z along the three axes are consecutively filled in the column vector. The matrix containing 10 gestures from a single participant is matrix $\Gamma^{P\varphi}$, where $P\varphi$ is an identifier for a given participant ($\varphi = 1 \ldots N$, where N=number of participants) represented in Figure 4.

The differences between individuals, as represented by their ADV, are far more significant (e.g. 100-200 samples), especially for the second group of tests. Thus many possible solutions can be found to adjust data in preparation for applying dimensionality reduction techniques. One strategy could be to compare only people whose gestures have the same ADV or an ADV that is not significantly different. Otherwise a duration value corresponding to the maximum, the minimum or an average duration value among different users could be fixed and user's data padded. In this case, different choices can be made for the value to use for filling the columns. In our case the value chosen to complete the columns was the data value corresponding to the rest position. This choice was verified as the option that would minimally influence the data processing and thus have less impact on the analysis. In conclusion, we identified subgroups of P participants having for a given gesture similar ADVs, (i.e. a difference in length smaller then 10%). In Figure 4 we identified as ADV" the average of the ADVs related to the group of participants selected. Each column vector $\Gamma'^{P\varphi}$

$$\bar{g} = \begin{bmatrix} a_x(s_1) \\ \dots \\ a_x(s_{ADV'}) \\ a_y(s_1) \\ \dots \\ a_y(s_{ADV'}) \\ a_z(s_1) \\ \dots \\ a_z(s_{ADV'}) \end{bmatrix}_{WINj}$$

$$\Gamma^{P\varphi} = \begin{bmatrix} \bar{g}_{WIN1} & \bar{g}_{WIN2} & \cdots & \bar{g}_{WIN10} \end{bmatrix} =$$

$$\begin{bmatrix} a_x(s_1)_{WIN1} & a_x(s_1)_{WIN2} & \cdots & a_x(s_1)_{WIN10} \\ \dots & \dots & \dots & \dots \\ a_x(s_{ADV'})_{WIN1} & a_x(s_{ADV'})_{WIN2} \cdots & a_x(s_{ADV'})_{WIN10} \\ a_y(s_1)_{WIN1} & a_y(s_1)_{WIN2} & \cdots & a_y(s_1)_{WIN10} \\ \dots & \dots & \dots & \dots \\ a_y(s_{ADV'})_{WIN1} & a_y(s_{ADV'})_{WIN2} \cdots & a_y(s_{ADV'})_{WIN10} \\ a_z(s_1)_{WIN1} & a_z(s_1)_{WIN2} & \cdots & a_z(s_1)_{WIN10} \\ \dots & \dots & \dots & \dots \\ a_z(s_{ADV'})_{WIN1} & a_z(s_{ADV'})_{WIN2} \cdots & a_z(s_{ADV'})_{WIN10} \end{bmatrix}$$

$$G = \begin{bmatrix} \Gamma'^{P1} & \Gamma'^{P2} & \cdots & \Gamma'^{PP} \end{bmatrix}_{ADV''}$$

Fig. 4. General structure of the column vector $\bar{g}$ for a single gesture, of the matrix $\Gamma^{P\varphi}$ and of the biometric dataset G

corresponds to $\Gamma^{P\varphi}$ padded to ADV" instead of ADV' (with $\varphi = 1 \dots P$). The biometric dataset created is G, which consists of a $[3 \times ADV'', P \times 10]$ matrix where ten consecutive columns correspond to a single user.

3.4 Dimensionality Reduction: PCA and LLE

Because this is an early stage of this investigation it may be valuable to perform exploratory data analysis to gain insight into the nature or structure of the data. Unsupervised methods are good for this purpose, because they provide a form of data-dependent "smart pre-processing" or "smart feature extraction". The discovery of distinct subclasses - clusters or groups of patterns whose members are more similar to each other than they are to other patterns - or of major departures from expected characteristics is an important input when designing the classifier. Dimensionality reduction is a useful operation for data clustering and pattern recognition. High-dimensional data can contain a lot of redundancies and correlations hiding important relationships among data. The purpose of dimensionality reduction techniques, which can be based on both linear and nonlinear methods, is to ease the analysis of data, eliminating redundancies and reducing the amount of data to be processed.

Here, we will briefly describe Principal Component Analysis (PCA) [18] and Locally Linear Embedding (LLE) [19] [23]. In this work, we apply both methods to the exploratory analysis and visualization of data sets. Both methods are unsupervised procedures for mapping high-dimensional data to a lower-dimensional space. We chose PCA because it is a powerful linear method, widely and traditionally used in many different application fields. LLE is an example of a nonlinear approach that, even if perhaps less tried, has demonstrated robustness and has produced a number of interesting results as shown in other fields [23] [21].

Principal Component Analysis. Principal Component Analysis [18] is a linear method for dimensionality reduction that projects the data into the subspace with a minimum reconstruction error. PCA is a useful statistical technique that has found application in fields such as face recognition and image compression, and it is a common technique for finding patterns in data of high dimensionality. Data processed with the PCA technique are expressed in such a way that their similarities and differences are highlighted. Since patterns can be hard to find in data of high dimensionality, where the luxury of graphical representation is not available, PCA is a powerful tool for analyzing such data. PCA is often used also for compressing data, since it helps to reduce the number of dimensions, without much loss of information. Basically PCA transforms input data so that they are expressed in terms of the patterns between them, where the patterns are the lines that most closely describe the relationships between the data. The result of this simple algebraic technique may be seen from several points of view, either as a variance preserving projection, or a minimal reconstruction error projection, or as a distance preserving projection.

Locally Linear Embedding. Though widely used for its simplicity, PCA is limited by its underlying assumption that the data lies in a linear subspace. Recently, several algorithms for nonlinear dimensionality reduction (i.e. [17]) have been proposed that overcome this limitation of PCA. Like PCA, these algorithms are simple to implement, but they compute nonlinear embeddings of high dimensional data. So far, these algorithms have mainly been applied to data sets of images and video, where they have revealed low dimensional manifolds not detected by purely linear methods. One of these algorithms is Locally Linear Embedding.

LLE is a recent method for data analysis, an unsupervised learning algorithm that computes low dimensionality, neighborhoods preserving embeddings of high dimensional data [23] [21]. LLE attempts to discover nonlinear structure in high dimensional data by exploiting the local symmetries of linear reconstructions. Notably, LLE maps its inputs into a single global coordinate system of lower dimensionality, and its optimizations, though capable of generating highly nonlinear embeddings, do not involve local minima. Because LLE is a new method, it is not yet well known. Thus, it is worth describing it briefly.

As an input, the LLE algorithm requires N points, for example corresponding to N samples of gestures from the same person. We define D as the dimensionality of the original sample and d the embedding dimensionality after applying LLE. In our case for example D is $3 \times ADV$, while d is 2. Each point is a X_i, where $i \in [1, N]$, $X_i \in R^D$. As an output, it gives N points, again the N gestures, re-mapped in a new vector space with lower dimensionality. Thus, each output point is an Y_i, $Y_i \in R^d$, where $i \in [1, N]$, and $d \prec\prec D$. The output is such that geometrical proprieties of the input set of points are locally best preserved. The algorithm consists of three steps:

- Step 1. For each X_i find its K nearest neighbors $X_{i1}...X_{iK}$.
- Step 2. Measure the reconstruction error resulting from the approximation of each X_i by its nearest neighbors and compute reconstruction weights W_{ij} minimizing this error.

– Step 3. Compute low-dimensional embeddings best preserving the local geometry represented by the reconstruction weights.

In Step 1 the Euclidean distances are used to determine a neighborhood around each X_i, though other definitions of "closeness" are possible as well. Step 2 assumes that the manifold is well-sampled, i.e., there are enough data, each data point and its nearest neighbors lie on or close to a locally linear patch of the manifold. Hence, we can approximate each sample X_i by a linear combination of its neighbors. This is equivalent to approximating the nonlinear manifold in the vicinity of X_i by the linear hyperplane passing through $X_{i1}...X_{iK}$. To do so, we need to minimize the reconstruction error. In Step 3 the low-dimensional embeddings are found which best preserve the high-dimensional neighborhood geometry represented by the weights W_{ij}.

Unsupervised clustering techniques provide a first step analysis in order to evaluate separation of data. Afterward, we applied to the processed data a basic classification algorithm, the *k-nearest neighbor classifier*, described below. This additional investigation is carried out in order to provide a quantified evaluation of the results coming from PCA and LLE dimensionality reduction. Their application to gesture data will be described in detail in Section 4.

4   Analysis of Results After Feature Extraction

To summarize, tasks accomplished to this point are shown in the upper part of the Figure 1. As already stated, for each kind of gesture and for each person, data are acquired, segmented and re-scaled. Data are then grouped into a matrix, referred to in the following paragraph as X, where each column vector is $3 \times ADV$ in length, since each column contains time samples of the acceleration along three orthogonal axes. Subgroups of ten consecutive columns represents a given gesture performed by the same person. The PCA script receives as input the matrix A and the parameter d, which is the number of principal components requested (Figure 6 left side). In practice we reduced data dimensionality to $d = 2$ (or 3). Thus, as output, we obtain a matrix B still containing $P \times 10$ columns, but each column is only d samples in length (in our case two or three). In B data are still organized so that subgroups of ten consecutive columns represents a gesture belonging to a given user, with a reduced dimensionality w.r.t. the original input matrix A. Thus, associating a different symbol with each ten columns, it is possible to plot data belonging to the same user with the same symbol. Each point in the plot represents a gesture mapped in the space defined by the first two principal components ($d = 2$). Results are satisfying, as can be seen in Figure 5 a and b. Here clusters are easily distinguished. In the plots we outlined the separation in clusters of data belonging to different people dividing the plane with approximate lines. The plot represents only gestures 1 and 2, but similar results were also observed for gestures 3 and 4 when a similar process was used for the LLE method (Figure 6 right side). Again, the LLE script used [19] receives as input matrix A. Moreover, two parameters are requested: d the embedding

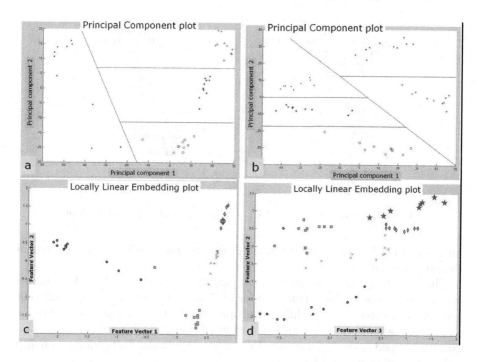

Fig. 5. a) and b) PCA applied to gesture 1 and 2 respectively. In **a** data are collected from 4 different people; the input matrix is 750x40. In **b** data are collected from a further 5 different people. The input matrix is 540x50. In **c** and **d** LLE is applied to gesture 1 (with the same input data as plot **a**; $K = 12$) and 2 (the same input data as plot **b**; $K = 13$) respectively.

dimensionality and K the number of nearest neighbors. While d was fixed at 2, we tested different values of nearest neighbors K. In [22] it is observed that the results of LLE do not depend considerably on the choice of the number of nearest neighbors. However several criteria are indicated to help the choice of K. One of them is based on the fact that the algorithm can only be expected to recover embeddings whose dimensionality, d, is strictly less than the number of neighbors, K, and some margin between d and K is desirable to improve the algorithm's robustness. For us the choice of a value for K around 5 or lower means that we are using as neighbors almost always gestures from the same person, with the result that data would seem falsely divided. In fact our matrices have ten by ten gestures from different people. If we chose a too large value for K (e.g around 20) we thereby loose the advantage of the algorithm in terms of showing local properties and thus enhancing differences among data. The algorithm, in fact, is based on the assumption that a data point and its nearest neighbors can be modeled as locally linear; the more the manifold is curved, the more choosing K too large will violate this assumption. That is why we preferred a value for K between 11 and 15. Low variability of results is experienced while choosing one of the value in this range. We can conclude that results are stable over a middle

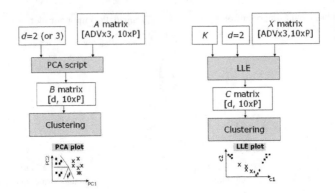

Fig. 6. Data processed by PCA (leftside) and LLE (rightside) scripts

range of values but do break down as K becomes too small or large (i.e. out of the proposed range).

The LLE script provides as output a matrix C, which has $P \times 10$ columns and d rows. The same technique used for PCA is applied to C, therefore different symbols are associated with different people. The LLE plots shown in Figure 5 c and d are again examples relating to gestures 1 and 2. Each symbol represents a gesture mapped in the 2-dimensional space ($d = 2$) obtained after dimensionality reduction performed by LLE.

As already mentioned, the analysis was limited by the different duration of gestures among people, so that it was impossible to compare all the people with a unique matrix without affecting the original data (either truncating or padding the columns of the matrix. The second gesture was more difficult to cluster, again, with both techniques. But the general result is satisfying, since this gesture is really simple and easily repeatable, thus easy to fake. Gesture 3 obtained very good separation. Gesture 4 has lower scores because during the sample acquisition process, we observed that people often performed the gesture incorrectly, thereby explaining the high variability in the intra-personal data collected. To reduce variability in such cases a possible solution is to augment the number of training samples.

An attempt was made to relate physical attributes of the participants (height, length of limb, etc.) to the results obtained from PCA and LLE. We tried to understand whether physical similarities could explain the overlapping clusters, but without success. People corresponding to overlapped results are different in weight, height and gender. This fact probably confirms that physical characteristics cannot explain the way we move, if they are not integrated with behavioral information.

4.1   Classification: KNN

In order to provide a quantitative evaluation of the qualitative results from PCA and LLE presented in the previous section, we applied a supervised technique called k-nearest neighbor, briefly described below. To allow for direct comparison of the following analysis with the preceding graphical qualitative analysis, we further decided to evaluate data in a bi or tri dimensional space. In future work we will explore the possibility of using higher dimensions to obtain better scores.

Evaluation through k-nearest-neighbor classifier. The k-nearest neighbor classifier (kNN) labels an unknown object or point (e.g. a gesture sample) with the label of the majority of the k nearest neighbors [20]. A neighbor is deemed nearest if it has the smallest distance, in the Euclidean sense, in feature space, which is in our case the space obtained after applying PCA or LLE. For $k = 1$, this is the label of its closest neighbor in the learning set. Thus, using a training matrix containing a set of samples for which the label is known, it is possible to classify each new sample, with an unknown label, into one of the groups in the training matrix, calculating its distance in the training space.

The discrimination function implemented by this classifier will in general be an irregular, piece-wise linear function since it is influenced by each object available in the learning set. A disadvantage of this method is its large computing power requirement, since for classifying an object its distance w.r.t. all the objects in the learning set has to be calculated.

Workflow. We applied the k-nearest neighbor classifier with $k = 1$ both on the results coming from the PCA analysis and the LLE technique with different values of K. The following are the steps in both cases:

1. Load a matrix having gestures as columns (subgroup of ten column for each participant).
2. Perform dimensionality reduction with PCA or LLE. In the case where PCA is used, the output matrix is the set of gestures projected in the plane defined by the first three Principal Components. In the case of LLE the output matrix is the set of gestures projected in a two-dimensional space after having been processed with the LLE algorithm with a given value of K (ranging between 5 and 30).
3. Apply the kNN classifier. The algorithm requires as input a reference matrix, containing the training samples for which the classification is known, and one or more samples for which the classification is unknown. Each unclassified sample is assigned to a given group using the nearest neighbor method. In our case the different groups correspond to the different participants in the study. The training matrix is derived from the matrix obtained after feature extraction at step 2 extracting one column. This column, corresponding to a gesture, becomes the sample to be classified with the kNN method. If the gesture is 'near', in the meaning of kNN, to the other nine gestures performed by the same person, it will be classified as belonging to the right group. One by one, all columns are extracted from the matrix obtained at step 2, each becoming the sample to classify.
4. The result of the processing is registered in a vector, which is compared with another vector containing the expected results to obtain the percentage of matching. Thus the percentage says how well samples, processed with PCA or LLE, are grouped in clusters and therefore how well gestures performed by a given person are separated from the same gestures performed by another.

Table 1. kNN scores for first and second set of experiments

NofPeople	% PCA	Best % LLE	gest
3	0.8333	1	1
3	0.8667	0.9333	1
4	1	0.95	1
3	0.9667	0.8	2
3	0.9667	1	2
4	0.8	0.7	2
3	1	0.8	3
3	0.9333	0.9667	3
4	0.8667	0.875	3
3	1	1	4
3	0.7333	0.7333	4
4	0.6333	0.675	4

a) I set of tests

NofPeople	% PCA	Best % LLE	gesture
5	0.84	0.74	2
5	0.8	0.88	2
5	0.98	0.96	2
3	0.9667	0.9667	1
4	0.9750	0.975	1
2	1	1	1
3	0.9667	0.9667	1
5	0.98	0.96	2
5	0.98	...	2
4	0.9750	0.975	2

b) II set of tests

Score and comments. Tables 1.a and 1.b summarize the results coming from the application of KNN. The first column indicates the number of users which is related to the number of gestures stored in the matrix processed (10 multiplied by the number of users). The percentage of matching indicated in the second column of the table refers to the data described in three-dimensional vectors, that is gestures re-mapped along the first three principal components. The third column refers to the best score for data processed with LLE, using different values for K ranging from 10 to 30. The last column indicates the gesture to which analysis is referred. The percentages both for LLE and PCA are in the majority of cases satisfying, but the number of people in each group is low.

The Table 1.a is also organized in groups of three rows. The information is organized as in Table 1.b. Each row describes the percentage of correct classifications after applying LLE or PCA and kNN techniques. The groups of three rows are dedicated to each kind of gesture; the difference among them is related to the data processed. The first row refers to the first ten gestures collected from people, the second row refers to the second ten gestures collected asking people to imitate a target gesture, the third row refers to the same data as in the second row but adding also the ten gestures from the person being copied. It can be seen that the PCA technique provides better scores compared to LLE. In general very good results are obtained except for gesture 4. Note that the plot shown in Figures 5 a and b refers to a 2D space (defined by the first two principal components), while the vectors to which the kNN has been applied are mapped in the 3D space defined by the first three principal components. This improves in some cases the separation of data.

5   Conclusion

The present work investigated the feasibility of using gestures as biometrics, asking whether it is possible to distinguish someone by the way she/he performs gestures. The study was restricted to four hand gestures performed by holding a box with motion sensors embedded in it and collecting acceleration data along three orthogonal axes. Gestures can be considered as behavioral biometrics, and we therefore expected a less defined separation of data between individuals than is found in the case of physical biometrics. In this respect our results shows that percentage of matching is high even with a simple linear cluster method like PCA. Use of a non linear method does not yield significantly better results and has the additional shortcoming of adding the value of a tuning parameter. However, both PCA and LLE lead to a high percentage of matches, around 95% or higher in the majority of cases, thus both techniques can be considered valuable for our purpose. Nevertheless, many improvements to these procedures are possible, e.g. integrating in the acquisition device other kinds of sensors (gyroscopes, bend sensors) into the data acquisition apparatus, analyzing data in higher dimensional spaces and applying more powerful techniques for data pre-processing and feature extraction.

In conclusion, this study shows that for small groups of people (e.g in families or members of small work groups), it is possible to distinguish one person from another by the way gestures are performed. Thus, a system using this result can potentially be useful in Ambient Intelligence applications for context-aware services and application profiling. Moreover, this biometric technique in combination with other biometrics can enforce security policy to log-in to distributed systems or to control access to restricted areas and protected physical environments.

References

1. I. Oakley, J. Angesleva, S. Hughes, S. O'Modhrain: Tilt and Fill:Scrolling with Vibrotactile Display. Proc. of EuroHaptics 2003 (2003)
2. http://www.samsung.com/AboutSAMSUNG/index.htm
3. Pirhonen, A., S.A. Brewster, and C. Holguin.: Gestural and Audio Metaphors as a Means of Control for Mobile Devices. ACM CHI'02 Minneapolis (2002)
4. K. Hinckley, J. Pierce, M. Sinclair, E. Horvitz: Sensing Techniques for Mobile Interaction. ACM WIST (2000).
5. Harrison, B., et al.: Squeeze Me, Hold Me, Tilt Me! An Exploration of Manipulative User Interfaces. CHI'98 (1998)
6. S.Strachan, R.Murray-Smith, I.Oakley, J.Angesleva: Dynamic Primitives for Gestural Interaction. Mobile HCI (2004)
7. Kobayashi T., Sugiyama K.: Hand Image Recognition for Code Numbers. ICITA2002 (2002)
8. Patel, S.N., Pierce, J. and Abowd, G.D.: A Gesture-based Authentication Scheme for Untrusted Public Terminals. Proc. of UIST 2004 (2004)
9. http://www.cnse.caltech.edu/Research01/optics.shtml
10. D. Gupta: Computer Gesture Recognition: Using the Constellation Method. Caltech Undergraduate Research Journal (2001)
11. R. Collins, R. Gross, J.o Shi: Silhouette-based Human Identification from Body Shape and Gait. 5th Intl Conference on Automatic Face and Gesture Recognition (2002)
12. M.P. Murray:Gait as a total pattern of movement. American journal of Physical medicine Vol.46 (1967) 290-333

13. G. Johansson: Visual perception of biological motion and a model for its analysism. Perception and Psychophysics (1973)
14. J.K. Perng, B. Fisher, S. Hollar, K. S. J. Pister: Acceleration Sensing Glove (ASG). IEEE Symposium on Wearable Computers (1999)178–180
15. Strachan, S. Murray-Smith,R.:Muscle Tremor as an Input Mechanism. Proc. of UIST 2004 (2004) Santa Fe
16. http://www.biometricsinfo.org/biometrics.htm
17. J.B. Tenenbaum, V. de Silva, and J.C. Langford: A global geometric framework for nonlinear dimensionality reduction. Science vol. 290 (200) 2319-2323
18. I.T. Jolliffe: Principal Component Analysis. Springer-Verlag New York (1986)
19. http://www.cs.toronto.edu/ŕoweis/lle/
20. L. Devroye, L. GyorfiA: Probabilistic Theory of Pattern Recognition. Springer (1996)
21. S.T. Roweis and L.K. Saul.: Nonlinear Dimensionality Reduction by Locally Linear Embedding. Science. Vol. 290 (2000) 2323-2326
22. L.Saul and S.Roweis. Think Globally: Fit Locally: Unsupervised Learning of Nonlinear Manifolds. Tech. Report MS CIS-02-18. University of Pennsylvania (2002)
23. L.K. Saul and S.T. Roweis. Think Globally: Fit Locally: Unsupervised Learning of Low Dimensional Manifolds. J. Mach. Learn. Res. Vol. 4 (2003) 119-155
24. Hughes, S. Oakley, I and O'Modhrain, S.: MESH: Supporting Mobile Multi-modal Interfaces. Proc. of ACM UIST'04 (2004)
25. V. Boultreau, N. Vincent, R. Sabourin, H. Emptoz: Handwriting and Signature : One or Two Personality Identifiers?. International Conference on Pattern Recognition (ICPR'98)(1998)63-84.
26. W.Bang, W. Chang, K. Kang, E.C. Potanin, A.D. Kim: Self-contained spatial input device for wearable computers. Proc. of Seventh IEEE International Symposium on Wearable Computers (2003) 26- 34
27. S. Pankanti, R. Bolle and A.K. Jain: Special issue of IEEE Computer on Biometrics. Vol.33, I. 2 (2003)

Exploring the Effects of Target Location Size and Position System Accuracy on Location Based Applications[*]

Cliff Randell[1], Erik Geelhoed[2], Alan Dix[3], and Henk Muller[1]

[1] Department of Computer Science, University of Bristol, UK
[2] Hewlett-Packard Laboratories, Bristol, UK
[3] Computing Department, Lancaster University, UK
{cliff, henkm}@cs.bris.ac.uk,
erik_geelhoed@hp.com,
alan@hcibook.com

Abstract. We describe an examination of various physical and human factors which influence the effectiveness of location-based applications. By varying both the target location size and position system accuracy, and hence the ease of use of an application, we are able to identify physical constraints which apply as well as quantifying performance and evaluating human factors. A movement analysis is proposed which allows us to formulate a set of equations that relate the time to find the target to the target location size, distance and positioning system accuracy. We validate our work using a game based application, digital hopscotch, in which the location size and the accuracy of the positioning system are varied. A further set of tests is performed outdoors using a GPS-based application. We show that the results from these experiments concur with the results from our equations. This work may be usefully embedded in software packages that allow designers to build location-based applications.

1   Introduction

Location-based applications for mobile computing have become of increasing interest to the research community, and are entering daily usage by the general public. Examples of this range from GPS-based navigation systems for vehicles and pedestrians, 'where's my nearest' applications for mobile phones and, increasingly, Geographic Information Systems (GIS) which associate information with geographic co-ordinates. Emerging applications include gaming and location-based entertainment. In this paper we explore physical aspects which affect the performance of applications, in particular the parameters of the location or target, and also the specification of the position sensing system. As part of this continuing research we are seeking to contribute to methods for the objective evaluation of such systems.

[*] Funding for this work is received from the U.K. Engineering and Physical Sciences Research Council, Grant No. 15986, as part of the Equator IRC.

K.P. Fishkin et al. (Eds.): PERVASIVE 2006, LNCS 3968, pp. 305–320, 2006.

The class of applications which particularly interests us are those in which digital information is associated with a real location. Examples of this type of application include museum guides where background information is provided about nearby exhibits [1, 2]; tourist guides again providing context related information to users [3, 4]; and mediascapes where sound and images are presented at particular locations to provide a multimedia experience [5, 6].

The information is accessed by a user who employs a position sensing system, such as GPS or ultrasonics, to determine coincidence between the user and the location. Confusion can be caused by the words 'position' and 'location' being used as synonyms (examples of dictionary definitions of position are "a strategic point" and of location "a particular place"). We define a location as a place, or target area, with an assigned label. We define a position as a point in space with specified 3D coordinates and a known error distribution. Our definitions are consistent with Hightower and Borriello's descriptions of 'physical position' and 'symbolic location' [7]. Examples of location are thus a known area such as Cambridge (within the City Boundary), or MacDonalds (inside the restaurant building); and examples of position are 51deg 32.78min N, 2deg 15.35min W, altitude 102m, with a standard deviation of 5m; or x=15.45m, y=6.28m, z=-7.14m relative to a known fixed origin with a 30cm standard deviation. We have used standard deviation as this does not assume a particular error distribution.

We assume that the user of a location-based system has to travel a variable distance to reach a location where the digital information is revealed. The performance of such a location-based application often depends on the accuracy of the position sensing system. A GPS-based city tourist system that correctly identifies which part of a street the user is on is considered acceptable, however a similar system based on mobile phone cell recognition would be of little use.

In this paper we use an ultrasonic positioning system indoors to facilitate a simple game of hopscotch with a PDA interface, and then apply our findings to a similar outdoor application using GPS. By varying the target location size, and for the indoor case, the positioning accuracy, we have collected suitable data to enable us to propose a relationship between location size, positioning accuracy and application effectiveness. The baseline tests were carried out in such a way as to be able to enable to consider the results according to gender, age and relative difficulty of the task (i.e. getting easier or harder).

While much work has already been undertaken examining similar issues for desktop computing, little has been done to objectively assess the relative performance of positioning systems for location-based applications. We believe that a games based approach has the potential to contribute to this line of research.

We first outline theories relating to target acquisition, then describe in detail our indoor location test scenario based on the children's hopscotch game, and then report on our findings with the outdoor GPS-based application. Finally we discuss the results and make our conclusions.

2   Theory

In this section we discuss two possible approaches to analysis of the effects of location size and positioning system characteristics. The first is a physical analysis of the human movements in a location-based application and the second is the well established Fitts' Law, commonly used for pointing analysis though also applicable to target acquisition.

2.1   Movement Analysis

The time taken to acquire a target has two major components. First the time taken to move from the current position to the boundary of the new target area and, secondly, the time required to carry out the search necessary to trigger the application. The search is needed as error in the positioning system may result in false readings which do not trigger the application even though the user has arrived at the physical target area. The search time will also be affected by the update rate of the positioning system as the more often the reading is updated, the sooner a match will be obtained. The overall time can thus be expressed as:

$$T_a = (d - r)/v + 1/(fp) \tag{1}$$

where T_a is the overall time; d is the distance to the centre of the target location, r the radius of the target - and hence $(d-r)$ is the distance to the boundary; v is the average velocity of the user; f is the update rate of the positioning system; and p is the probability of a trigger point being found. This probability can be expressed as the area of the target location divided by the area of uncertainty of the positioning system:

$$p = \pi r^2/(\pi(k\sigma)^2) \tag{2}$$

where k is a constant representing the error distribution and σ is the standard deviation of the positioning system. Note that the term $\pi(k\sigma)^2$ can be refined if the error distribution is known.

Taking equations 1 and 2 together we have:

$$T_a = (d - r)/v + k^2\sigma^2/(fr^2) \tag{3}$$

These equations form the basis of our hypothesis, however we require an alternative approach to test the usefulness of our thinking. We have chosen Fitts' Law as a potentially suitable comparator.

2.2   Fitts' Law

Extensive research has already been carried out into the acquisition of targets, particularly for desktop computer systems, and has resulted in many variations of Fitts' Law [8]. This law states that the time taken to acquire a target is a function of the distance to, and size of, the target. Mathematically this can be expressed as:

$$T = a + b\,log_2(D/S + c) \tag{4}$$

where T = time to move the hand to a target, D = distance between hand and target, S = size (width) of target, and a,b & c are constants, with a or c usually equal to one. $Log_2(D/S + c)$ is known as the Index of Difficulty (IOD).

Fitts' Law is a powerful tool for predicting the performance of a *pointing* based application, usually involving a mouse and screen interface. The objective of Fitts' Law is analogous in the real world to the physical acquisition of a target location by a moving subject. However additional factors need to be considered. The speed with which a mouse pointer traverses a display screen is assumed not to have a first order effect while the speed of a moving subject is patently relevant to the time needed to move to a location in the real world. The accuracy of the positioning of a mouse pointer can also be determined to the nearest pixel, whereas in the real world we are subject to the vagaries of physical position measurement. We would thus expect that for a location-based application, the time taken to acquire a target will also depend on the speed of the user and the characteristics of the position measurement system.

In the following section we test the applicability of both equation 3 and Fitts' Law to a real indoor application, and discuss the validity of our results.

3   Indoor Test Scenario

The elements which we require to test our hypotheses include a measured position, a target location, a distance to be traversed, and the performance of test subjects measured in time. These requirements can be fulfilled by creating a PDA based game requiring the player to move between a number of bases, or targets. For the results to be meaningful it is necessary for some form of unpredictability to be incorporated to prevent the player second guessing the system.

3.1   Position Sensing

There are many indoor position sensing technologies available for research purposes [7]. For our experiments we require a system which will provide coverage over a limited area with an accuracy predicted to be greater than that needed for the chosen application. GPS accuracy, while suitable for navigation at street level, has proved problematic at smaller scales [9]. The accuracies provided by systems integrating ultrasonics or magnetic sensing with inertial techniques [10,11] far exceed our anticipated needs, and do not provide coverage over a large enough area.

For our requirements we have used the Bristol ultrasonic positioning system with a reference RF signal and a measured standard deviation(σ) of 5.7cm [12]. This system relies on a synchronising RF pulse followed by a number of timed ultrasonic signals transmitted from known positions in the infrastructure. A receiver decodes these signals and provides a position to a wearable or handheld computer.

3.2   Digital Hopscotch

The children's game of 'hopscotch' comes close to meeting our requirements and has inspired our design. In this game the player moves across a grid, or pattern of bases, in a predetermined sequence. There are many variations of this game, however for our purposes we wish to create uniform, but still unpredictable, paths for the players to follow. A pattern of eight circles, or bases, whose size for detection purposes can be varied for each game, can be used to provide six equally long paths which can be chosen at random (see Figure 1). The positions of the bases and path are chosen to ensure that the distance from each base to the next on the path is identical. For example, paths [*start-1-3-4-6-end*], [*start-1-3-5-6-end*] and [*start-2-4-3-5-end*] are all the same length. The size of the base circle is set within the application software, with its centre being indicated by a marker on the floor (see Figure 2). We do not require the player to 'hop' as the PDA and positioning system introduce sufficient handicaps!

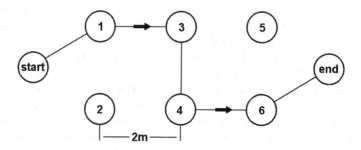

Fig. 1. Layout and typical path

Fig. 2. iPAQ, with ultrasonic sensor, and hopscotch layout

The player is guided along the chosen path by a PDA with a position sensor attached. The PDA displays the number of the base to be located (see Figure 2). Success at reaching each base is determined using the positioning system. The accuracy of the system can be degraded with the addition of random, but statistically limited, error values. After each base is found the number of the next base in the path is displayed on the PDA. By timing each player from start to finish, and combining this with the varying location size, we expect to be able to identify relationships between the variables.

Twenty volunteers, 10 females and 10 males took part in the baseline experiment. In the age range 18-24 years there was one female; in the 25-34 years range there were five females and four males; there were three females and three males between 35 and 44 years and one female and three males were over 45 years.

Based on pilot studies we defined five experimental conditions. In the first condition each target had a diameter of 200 centimetres, for the second condition this was set at 100 centimetres, for the third at 50 centimetres, the fourth at 25 centimetres and for the last, and hardest, the detection size was 12.5 centimetres. Individual experimental sessions were short, no longer than ten minutes, and as a consequence, although subjects had to complete five experimental conditions, this did not result in experimental fatigue.

There were two orders of presenting the experimental conditions: the first from large to small (starting with the 200 cm size, followed by the 100 cm size and subsequently the 50, 25 and 12.5 cm sizes); the second order of presentation was the reverse, from small to large. Half of the subjects (five females and five males) followed the first order of presentation, from large to small, whereas the other half followed the second order of presentation from small to large.

To detect differences, between genders, order of presentation of experimental conditions, age and most importantly between experimental conditions, we carried out several flavours of the analysis of variance (ANOVA). To investigate similarities between the conditions, i.e. to examine if subjects who were fast (or slow) in one condition were also fast (or slow) in the other conditions, we used the product moment correlation coefficient.

The statistic associated with ANOVA is the F-ratio (F) with two accompanying sets of degrees of freedom (df) and the product moment correlation coefficient (r). Both statistics provide an indication of how much the results could have come about by chance alone. This is denoted by the probability (p) value and, in general, a result is called statistically significant if the p-value is 0.05 or smaller.

Further tests were carried out with random subjects using limited noise values added to the sensed positions to degrade the accuracy of the position sensing system. These tests enabled us to examine the effect of positioning system accuracy on the game's effectiveness.

3.3   Baseline Test Procedure

Each test consisted of five movements between bases two metres apart, commencing at a 'start' base and ending at a 'finish' base. The tests were repeated consecutively five times with the base target area either increasing from test to test, or decreasing. The smallest base diameter was 0.125m and the largest 2.0m. A factor of two was used to increase/decrease the difficulty between tests. Thus each participant provided 25 results. Participants were given a single familiarisation test before readings were recorded.

The bases were designated by bright orange plinths 30cm dia by 25cm high with the relevant marking on top. The participants carried an iPAQ PDA with an ultrasonic receiver attached (see Figure 2). They were told that there was a trigger point somewhere above the top of the plinth where the PDA receiver had to be held, and that height was not a factor. The PDA would confirm that the target had been reached by displaying the number of next target. A researcher stands by to resolve any misunderstandings, and to encourage the player to continue searching where the base circle is small relative to the positioning accuracy, and thus hard to find.

User Behaviour and Analysis. The time taken by each subject to complete the course was analysed using ANOVA. There were no differences between the performances of females and males nor did age have an effect. The order of presentation of the experimental conditions (large to small or small to large) also did not result in significant differences. We therefore collapsed all these factors and further statistical results are shown across the group as a whole. We compared each condition with the other conditions and all paired comparisons resulted in highly significant F-ratios (all p-values were well below 0.01, see Table 1. Thus we can conclude that each of the five conditions is significantly different from the other. The means and standard deviations for each condition are given in Figure 3.

Oddly enough there were no significant correlations between conditions. Thus if a volunteer was fast in one condition then this did not automatically mean that

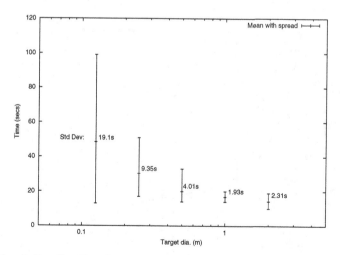

Fig. 3. Baseline Results - Mean Times, Spread and Standard Deviation

Table 1. Paired comparisons between conditions

Size	100 cm	50 cm	25 cm	12.5 cm
200cm	$F(1,19) = 24.48$ $p < 0.001$	$F(1,19) = 42.12$ $p < 0.001$	$F(1,19) = 51.66$ $p < 0.001$	$F(1,19) = 33.25$ $p < 0.001$
100cm		$F(1,19) = 11.14$ $p = 0.003$	$F(1,19) = 42.05$ $p < 0.001$	$F(1,19) = 31.25$ $p < 0.001$
50cm			$F(1,19) = 18.26$ $p < 0.001$	$F(1,19) = 28.95$ $p < 0.001$
25cm				$F(1,19) = 23.83$ $p < 0.001$

this subject was also fast in the next condition (and vice versa), although for the first order of presenting the experimental conditions, where subjects started with the easiest conditions there was one significant correlation between the 200 cm and 100 cm, i.e. the first two conditions, r = 0.76, df = 9, p =0 .01 . In the 200cm and 100cm conditions, the dominant time appears to be walking between the bases, so the correlation is probably walking speed. For the smaller targets there is an acquisition time as well (walking then searching). So for the different conditions, significantly different (in the day-to-day sense) mechanisms dominate the times.

Movement Analysis. Applying Equation 3 to our hopscotch game, with an estimated walking speed of 0.5m/s and the positioning system updating at 1Hz, we see the resulting curve combined with our actual resulting times in Figure 4. It was necessary to estimate the walking speed due to the stop/start nature of the exercise prohibiting normal walking speeds being reached. Actual walking speed measurements were later used for the outdoor GPS application. We used

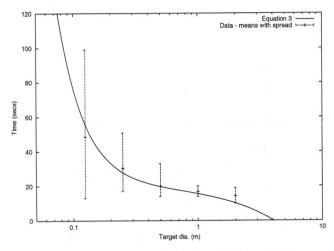

Fig. 4. Movement Analysis with Data Points

a value of $k=3$ which would represent a 99.7 per cent value for a normal error distribution (3σ). Figure 4 indicates a close relationship between our observed data and the hypothetical curve. We carried out a regression analysis on this data and a correlation coefficient of 0.94 was obtained. This indicates a good match between the recorded data and the hypothesis.

The figure illustrates an anomaly with the target location at 2m diameter. This is probably due to the uncertainty of the start point - with a location diameter of 2m there is likely to be a significant error due to the variability in the position of the start point. With smaller locations the participants ensured that they were actually at the centre of the location - the game thus became haphazard with 2m diameter targets.

Correspondence with Fitts' law. To confirm the consistency of our data with Fitts' Law we should obtain a straight line result when our resulting times per game are plotted against the IOD (Index of Difficulty). See Figure 5. The x-axis is the Index of Difficulty $log_2(D/S + 1)$ where D is the distance to the target (in our case 2m) and S is the (variable) size of the target. The results used are the means of the data collected for each target size and are shown where the size S is taken to be the diameter of the target. We observe that for the case where the target diameter is 12.5 cm - the highest IOD in each case - then the results clearly do not correspond with Fitts' Law. We believe that this is because a boundary condition is being approached. Except in special cases, it is not possible to achieve a target which is smaller than the resolution of the position detection system. There are further boundary conditions which we discovered in our preliminary tests - these are where our target locations overlap, and ultimately where our target size is greater than, or equal to, the size of our world (or playing area). Excluding the 12.5 cm case from our analysis we carried out a regression analysis and achieved a correlation coefficient with Fitts' Law of 0.58 - a poor match.

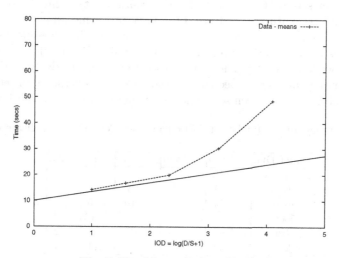

Fig. 5. Fitts' Law - Index of Difficulty

We also note that Fitts' Law was devised for systems where the target is visible. It is important to realise that the target in our tests is actually *virtual*. The target location is not displayed in the real world, it exists in our application's memory and is only represented by our hopscotch bases. It is easier to understand Fitts' Law if one considers the control task of hand-eye coordination. This is an interaction - one moves the mouse (or other pointer), the eyes see the movement, you correct and repeat until the target is reached. Our hopscotch game does not consist of a series of successive movements to acquire each target. Fitts' Law thus appears not to be appropriate in this case but nevertheless provides an interesting counterpoint to our movement analysis.

3.4   Accuracy Tests

The baseline tests investigated the effect of changing target sizes, in this section we further explore theories by carrying out indoor tests varying both positioning accuracy and target size. Again using the hopscotch layout we have carried out 64 tests with 20 participants of mixed age and gender. In these tests the participants were able to select the level of difficulty. This was varied using the target size as well as the accuracy of the positioning system. The accuracy was varied by adding random error values to the detected x:y coordinates (already with an inherent 5.7cm standard deviation). These values were scaled to achieve proximity to preset standard deviations. It is not possible to precisely achieve standard deviation figures as the values generated are random and within an unknown timeframe - the length of the game. The error distribution is also likely to be different to the distribution for the ultrasonic positioning system and hence a different value for k is predictable. The number of tests for each condition are shown in Table 2 with the number of unsuccessful, or timed out, tests shown in brackets.

Table 2 shows that none of the participants were able to complete the test with the target set to 10cm, and with the accuracy set to 2m the test could only be completed with a target size of 2m. With a time limit of 45 seconds for each movement between bases *no* participant was able to complete a test where the system accuracy approached the target size. By the time 45 seconds had elapsed we found that participants ceased to search effectively as they had either lost interest or they suspected that the task was impossible. In retrospect the time limit could have been set higher to further explore the condition where

Table 2. Accuracy Tests: Number of Participants per Condition. () indicate timeout.

Target Dia.	10cm	20cm	50cm	1m	2m
Accuracyσ					
10cm	(5)	3	3	1	2
20cm	(1)	2	10	5	1
50cm	-	(1)	4	13	2
1m	-	(1)	(3)	1	2
2m	(1)	(1)	(1)	(1)	1

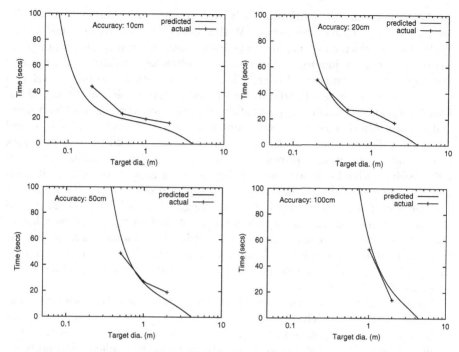

Fig. 6. Effect of Positioning System Accuracy

the target becomes relatively small; perhaps more active encouragement of the participants would have facilitated this. The self selection allowed the participants to choose settings which resulted in a satisfactory game and this is reflected in the distribution of conditions attempted.

The mean results are shown graphically for each accuracy setting in Figure 6, along with the predicted curves using a value of $k=1.5$. We applied regression theory to these curves firstly to assist in determining a suitable value for k, and secondly to evaluate the match of the data to Equation 3. The resulting values were 0.81, 0.65, 0.74 and 0.93 for increasing position error values, indicating fair to good matches.

The curves in Figure 6 indicate that, as a rule of thumb for this application, target locations should have a diameter of at least the size of 2 x standard deviation of the positioning system and at most a quarter of the distance between locations. (Note that in this application we have a generated a *normal* error distribution which may not be typical of such systems). These indoor test applications, however, are not typical and we thus carried out tests outdoors with a standard GPS receiver to provide additional support for the use of Equation 3.

4   Testing Outdoors

Due to the worldwide availability of GPS the majority of location-based applications are found outdoors. As outlined in the introduction, a wide range of location dependent digital information is becoming available ranging from tourist information to situated mediascapes. With this in mind we have designed a GPS application in which a user explores a pedestrianised city centre, surrounding the Bristol Millennium Square, and discovers soundtracks associated with the city and its features. Composer, Roger Mills, and artist, Annie Lovejoy, developed the conceptual mapping of audio content based on the physical attributes of the area. The goal was to reflect aspects of the city; pieces portraying multiculturism and history. Adhoc interviews were conducted in streets, cabs and shops, and a musical collaboration was also included. The user is guided from landmark to landmark using images shown on a PDA connected to a shoulder mounted GPS receiver. Five landmarks were chosen along a 250m trail with each landmark visible from the previous one and displayed in sequence on the PDA. For example see Figure 7. The soundtracks are triggered at each location using GPS data at 1Hz. As with the hopscotch game in our indoor trials, the user has to search for the media at each landmark. Once it has been found an image showing the next landmark is displayed. Again the users were shadowed by a researcher to resolve any misunderstandings, and to encourage continued searching where small target areas were used.

The times and paths between leaving each landmark and triggering the next sound file are recorded. The accuracy of the GPS receiver was determined from a 24 hour test in a fixed position with buildings, trees and a dummy head providing some occlusion of the satellite signals so as to simulate the application conditions. Tests were carried out using target location sizes with diameters of 2m, 4m, 10m, 20m, 40m and 100m. The tests carried out at 2m diameter resulted in the application timing out after three minutes searching and this condition was thus removed from our analyses. The remaining data was normalised by starting measurements at a distance of 80m from each target. The walking speed was

Fig. 7. iPAQ showing the next landmark

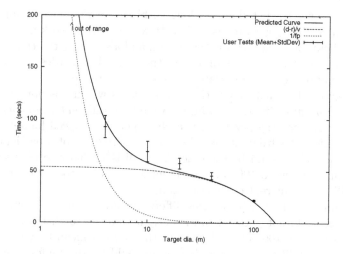

Fig. 8. Actual Task Times with Predicted Curve

determined by sampling along the route at points inbetween the landmarks where the users would not be carrying out any search.

Five sets of tests were thus initially carried out at 4m, 10m, 20m, 40m and 100m target diameter and analysed with our movement analysis equations. We plotted the results against Equation 3, and this is shown in Figure 8. A value of $k=3$ was used again with the GPS error distribution being similar to the indoor positioning system distribution. The dotted curves show the two main elements of the equation - the walking time to reach the target's boundary tapering off as the target radius approaches the distance to be travelled; and the search time ranging from infinity where the target is too small to be detected, to near zero where the target size is less than or equal to the area of uncertainty of the positioning system. Regression analysis was again applied yielding a correlation coefficient of 0.92 indicating a good fit.

The initial tests showed that for a target diameter equal to, or over 40m, the significant component was walking speed. At 5m diameter the uncertainty of the positioning system caused the search to become onerous for the users. Further experiments were thus limited to the 10m and 20m target diameter. A total of 19 subjects of mixed age and gender took part in the experiments: 10 subjects in the 20 metre diameter target size condition and nine in the 10 metre diameter target size. ANOVA resulted in a significant (between subjects) effect for target size, $F(1,17) = 5.49$, $p = 0.033$. There was no (within subjects) effect for targets and no significant interaction.

5   Discussion and Future Work

In the baseline tests we have carried out a study which indicates that a movement analysis is a useful method for the predicting the performance of a location-based application where a target is to be acquired. The correspondence of the data-points to the predicted curve along with regression analysis supported our theories where the target area is varied. However further work is required particularly where the target area is very small, and also where the times are short. We also did not investigate conditions at the target boundaries. A probabilistic approach may be more appropriate in these circumstances.

There were other elements of the baseline tests which are worthy of further discussion. The five different conditions were very different from each other in two respects. Firstly the p-values for each target size showed highly significant statistical differences from all the other sizes. There was not a particular reason to expect that this would be the case. After all the difference between 100 cm and 200 cm, or between 100 cm and 50 cm do not seem too different to expect such significantly different completion times.

The second way in which the sizes differed behaviourally was somewhat puzzling. Subjects did not perform consistently across the conditions, i.e. someone could be fast in the 100 cm condition but this did not mean they were also fast in the 50 cm condition. One possible cause could be the uniform distribution of the error introduced by the positioning system as this would not favour any particular subject. However, observing the subjects it seems that they adopted a particular strategy to deal with finding the target in a (possibly) varying world and carried on with this strategy, e.g. holding the handheld computer at a certain height, moving it about in a circular fashion to detect the target. For those ten subjects that started with the easier targets, however, there was a significant correlation between the first two easy conditions, i.e. those that were fast (or slow) in the 200 cm condition were also fast (or slow) in the 100 cm condition.

The accuracy tests in which both target size and positioning system accuracy were varied, also supported Equation 3, however there is a greater spread of data. This points to the limited sample we have gathered and again the probabilistic nature of this experiment. Equation 3 is not an absolute measure, it actually relates the probability distribution of the time required to complete the test to the probability distribution of the positioning system. Further examination of this aspect could be worthwhile but is beyond the scope of this paper. In particular, a comparison of the application of different measures of accuracy may be worthwhile. The adoption of, say, a 95% confidence level may be more appropriate than the use of standard deviation, and could make it possible to replace the error distribution factor k with a constant value.

The results from the GPS-based application illustrate the intuitively evident in a useful graphical form. Figure 8 appears to confirm the validity of our hypotheses, and is consistent with the authors' experiences of GPS-based systems. We can use this curve by applying, for example, 20% bounds to the optimum time. This then indicates that the preferred values of target location diameter, for our application, are between 6m and 25m .

It was evident that users adopted differing search strategies (with variable results) and an observational study could be productive into the effectiveness of these strategies. We have also assumed that users are aware of digital information being associated with known, visible, points. However if the points of association are not known, or not visible, to the user then it is likely that a systematic search strategy would be adopted e.g. 'lawnmowing'. The choice of search strategy, and relative merits of such strategies as applied to location-based applications, is a logical continuation of this research.

6 Conclusion

The approach which we have employed, demonstrates that it is possible to analyse the human aspects together with the design parameters associated with a location-based application. This gives a greater understanding of the factors which influence performance, and hence designers can usefully employ this approach to inform the design of future applications. The model that we have derived can be included in authoring packages for locative systems that are emerging at present [13, 14, 15]. These packages are designed to allow content designers to quickly deploy location-based applications. By incorporating our model, an authoring package could usefully warn designers when they create target zones that are too small, and thus hard to find, or too close to each other, causing ambiguous triggering of associated media.

We have thus presented a practical approach to reasoning about the relation between the time to complete a location-based task, a targeted location size and the accuracy of the sensed position. A formula has been proposed to describe this relationship, and shown by experiment that, for both an indoor gaming application and for an outdoor GPS application, there is a close correspondence between the formula and our measurements.

References

1. S. Hsi. The electronic guidebook: A study of user experiences using mobile web content in a museum setting. In *Proceedings of IEEE International Workshop on Mobile and Wireless Technologies in Education, WMTE 2002*, pages 48–54, August 2002.
2. B. Brown, I. MacColl, M. Chalmers, A. Galani, C. Randell, and A. Steed. Lessons from the lighthouse: Collaboration in a shared mixed reality system. In *Proceedings of CHI '2003*. ACM Press, April 2003.
3. S. Long, D. Aust, G. Abowd, and C. Atkenson. Cyberguide: Prototyping context-aware mobile applications. In *CHI 96*, pages 293–294, April 1996.
4. Keith Cheverst, Nigel Davies, Keith Mitchell, Adrian Friday, and Christos Efstratiou. Developing a context-aware electronic tourist guide: some issues and experiences. In *CHI '00: Proceedings of the SIGCHI conference on Human factors in computing systems*, pages 17–24, New York, NY, USA, 2000. ACM Press.
5. R. Hull, J. Reid, and E. Geelhoed. Delivering compelling experiences through wearable computing. *IEEE Pervasive Computing*, 1(4):56–61, 2003.
6. Josephine Reid, Richard Hull, Kirsten Cater, and Constance Fleuriot. Magic moments in situated mediascapes. In *ACM SIGCHI International Conference on Advances in Computer Entertainment Technology ACE 2005*. ACM, June 2005.
7. J. Hightower and G. Borriello. Location systems for ubiquitous computing. *Computer*, pages 57–66, August 2001.

8. P.M. Fitts. The information capacity of the human motor system in controlling the amplitude of movement. *Journal of Experimental Psychology*, 47:381–391, 1954.

9. Steve Benford, Mike Fraser, Gail Reynard, Boriana Koleva, and Adam Drozd. Staging and evaluating public performances as an approach to CVE research. In *Proceedings of the 4th international conference on Collaborative virtual environments*, pages 80–87. ACM Press, 2002.

10. Polhemus Incorporated. Fastrak product literature. http://www.polhemus.com/.

11. InterSense Incorporated. Intersense product literature. http://www.isense.com/.

12. C. Randell and H. Muller. Low cost indoor positioning system. In *UbiComp 2001: International Conference on Ubiquitous Computing*, pages 42–48, September 2001.

13. R. Hull, B. Clayton, and T. Melamed. Rapid authoring of mediascapes. *Lecture Notes in Computer Science*, 3205:125–142, October 2004.

14. Yang Li, Jason I. Hong, and James A. Landay. Topiary: a tool for prototyping location-enhanced applications. In *UIST '04: Proceedings of the 17th ACM Symposium on User Interface Software and Technology*, pages 217–226, New York, NY, USA, 2004. ACM Press.

15. C. Greenhalgh, S. Izadi, J. Mathrick, J. Humble, and I. Taylor. Ect: A toolkit to support rapid construction of ubicomp environments. In *In Ubicomp 2004, Conference on Ubiquitous Computing (Workshop on System Support for Ubiquitous Computing UbiSys04)*, September 2004.

Displays in the Wild: Understanding the Dynamics and Evolution of a Display Ecology

Elaine M. Huang[1], Elizabeth D. Mynatt[1], and Jay P. Trimble[2]

[1] College of Computing & GVU Center,
Georgia Institute of Technology,
Atlanta, GA, USA 30332-0280, USA
{elaine, mynatt}@cc.gatech.edu
[2] NASA Ames Research Center,
Moffett Field, CA, 94035, USA
jay.p.trimble@nasa.gov

Abstract. Large interactive display systems are becoming increasingly pervasive, but most have been studied in isolation, rather than in the context of other technologies in the environment. We present an in-depth field evaluation of large interactive displays within a multi-display work environment used in the NASA Mars Exploration Rover (MER) missions, a complex and authentic use setting. We uncover how the role of such displays evolves in the context of other displays as tasks and collaboration practices change, as well as how tasks migrate among different displays over time. Finally, we present suggestions for how to evaluate the success of large interactive displays and multi-display environments in collaborative work environments based on our findings.

1 Introduction

In January of 2004, the National Aeronautics and Space Administration (NASA) landed two unmanned vehicles on the surface of Mars for the purposes of collecting scientific information regarding the terrain, composition, and atmosphere of the planet. The Mars Exploration Rover (MER) mission has continued for the past 20 months, with the two rovers, Spirit and Opportunity, continuing to transmit data to Earth as they traverse the surface.

The actions of the rovers as well as the data that they collect are guided by mission scientists and engineers, and the mission is based at NASA Jet Propulsion Labs (JPL) in California. To coordinate their activities, scientists and engineers employ a variety of tools for collaboration and information sharing. In the group workspaces designed specifically for the MER Missions, shared displays, including large projection screens, large interactive plasma displays, and shared workstations with multiple monitor setups, are ubiquitous. Together, these surfaces form a "display ecology," in which the uses of individual displays influence the roles of others, despite not having been designed as a unified, seamless system. Of particular interest to us is the MERBoard [16], an example of an emerging class of pervasive computing technologies comprised of interactive large multi-user display systems. Although many such systems have been designed, deployed, and studied in a variety of settings

K.P. Fishkin et al. (Eds.): PERVASIVE 2006, LNCS 3968, pp. 321–336, 2006.

in recent years, the NASA MERBoard system, designed at NASA Ames Research Center and deployed specifically to support MER Mission science tasks, is unique in its complexity and the extent of its deployment in authentic work settings.

Unlike many other large interactive display systems, MERBoards were deployed to support specific, time-dependent work tasks of real users (Figure 1). MERBoards were integrated into a fast-paced, round-the-clock and often hectic work schedule to support necessary tasks; this is in contrast to many systems that have been deployed primarily in research or test environments as supplemental support for collaboration, rather than a primary medium for accomplishing work tasks. Additionally, many MERBoards were deployed in parallel, with 18 of the displays in use at JPL during the initial months of the mission, whereas other research prototypes have often been single instances of the technology or deployed in small numbers. Finally, unlike many other large display groupware systems, MERBoard has been integrated into a work environment that contains many display alternatives, including several other large display options. All of these factors led us to investigate not only how users interacted with the MERBoard, but also address the greater issue of the role of interactive large display groupware within highly dynamic, complex display ecologies.

Fig. 1. MERBoards, projectors, laptops, and workstations in the work environment

In this paper, we present the results and analysis of a year-long field study of the MERBoard and the MER mission display environment in which we uncover an ebb and flow of large display use as collaborative tasks and practices evolve over time. Our findings suggest that:

- Large interactive displays are valuable as interactive support for exploratory tasks for which procedures are ill-defined; as tasks become proceduralized, these displays can be useful sources of ambient information.
- Tasks migrate among displays within a display ecology as tasks and collaboration styles change; this migration is deeply influenced by the other displays in the environment and their respective affordances.

- Evaluation should be based on how well and flexibly the entire ecology of displays supports work tasks, rather than a simple measure of use or disuse of individual displays or applications within the environment.

In the following sections of this paper, we present background information on the MER missions, MERBoard, MER display ecology, and related research. We then present our findings regarding the adoption evolution of use of several MERBoard functionalities within the context of the display ecology. We follow this with a discussion of the implications of our findings for design and evaluation of large interactive display systems and multi-display environments.

2 Background on MER Missions

The gathering of scientific information on the MER missions has entailed highly dynamic procedures, especially during the "nominal mission"- the initial three months following the rover landings. Working on a 25-hour cycle (the length of a "Sol", or Martian day), teams of scientists and engineers would receive, process, and analyze downlink data from the rovers and Martian satellites, decide the next course of action for the rovers as well as what data should be collected next based on this information, convert these decisions into sequences of instructions for the rovers, and send this information to the rovers via the data uplink. Each of the steps in this cycle was highly collaborative, and required significant coordination between groups of collaborators working on various steps of the cycle, as well as among group members working together on a single task.

Scientists and engineers generally had distinct responsibilities, although there was considerable collaboration between them. The mission science teams were composed of five theme groups: Atmospheric Science, Geology, Minerology and Geochemistry, Soil and Rock Physical Properties, and Long Term Planning. These groups were responsible for the scientific aspects of the mission, such as analyzing the data gathered by the rovers, deciding what further data goals and exploration should be pursued, and determining at a relatively high level what course of action the rovers should take. In contrast, engineers were responsible for the more tactical aspects of the mission, including determining the rovers' exact sequences of action, controlling the instruments on board the rovers, sending the information to rovers, and collecting the downlink data.

In addition to the distinct responsibilities of the scientists and the engineers, there were also several other differences between the two groups that affected collaboration. For example, the engineering teams consisted primarily of NASA staff and contractors who were resident at JPL; many of them had collaborated previously on other missions. In contrast, while some of the scientists were also NASA employees, the majority came from other institutions all over the country and were working together for the first time. Furthermore, from the standpoint of the engineers, the tasks in which they engaged bore resemblance to their tasks for previous NASA missions. For the scientists, the tasks that they engaged in were highly novel and bore considerably less resemblance to the scientific activities of other NASA missions. For these reasons, work relationships in the science teams were more dynamic and practices less established and proceduralized than those of the engineering teams.

This was particularly true in the nominal mission, thus affecting the ways in which collaborative technologies were used and adopted.

During the nominal mission, all scientists working on the mission were resident at JPL, with all of the science theme groups for each mission collocated within large science assessment rooms. Within these rooms, each theme group had its own area, each with a MERBoard, several workstations, and two projection screens. Additionally, there was a MERBoard and a pair of projection screens in the front of the room used for presentations and meetings. At any given time during the nominal mission, several dozen scientists were present in the space; this number decreased steadily after the end of the nominal mission. Engineers worked in teams in several other smaller spaces at JPL, including Mission Control and Sequencing areas. These rooms had different configurations of displays, with at least one MERBoard and one projector; some had multiple of each.

Table 1. Summary of the MERBoard functionalities focused upon in this study

Functionality	Intended Users	Tool Summary
SolTree Tool	Scientists	Tool for building graphical tree structures to represent possible next actions for the rovers. Plans were visualized as nodes, paths, and branches with annotations to keep track of information associated with each plan. Plans, also called "SolTrees," could be saved, and later modified.
Whiteboard	Scientists, engineers	Tool for authoring documents and images with stylus for freehand drawing and writing, graphical tool palette, or a keyboard as input. Content on personal machines could be put into a shared directory and accessed on MERBoard. Whiteboard content could be saved and retrieved. A tabbing mechanism permitted switching between multiple boards.
Mars Clock	Scientists, engineers	Full-screen, persistent clock that displayed the current Earth time at JPL, Mars time for the Spirit rover, and Mars time for the Opportunity rover.
Schedules	Scientists, engineers	MERBoard could be used to access and display CIP (Collaborative Information Portal) and other schedules, which showed the daily schedule of deadlines, meetings, and events.

During the extended mission that followed the nominal mission, some scientists returned to their home institutions and began to work remotely; science activities were distributed across JPL and other laboratories, while the engineering tasks continued to take place at JPL. As the mission was further extended, science collaborations became increasingly distributed.

Prior to the start of the mission, many of the scientists and engineers participated in a set of mission simulation exercises called the FIDO (Field Integration Design and Operation) trials. During the exercises, the teams engaged in simulated mission activities, on a compressed time cycle. They were also trained on and exposed to the tools and systems that they would be using during the actual mission, including the MERBoard.

3 Related Research

Our evaluation of the MER mission display ecology was designed to complement an earlier observation-based evaluation of the MERBoard conducted by the designers of the system [15]. This study examined the knowledge and data management practices surrounding document creation and use on the MERBoard, whereas our study sought to focus more generally on users' perspectives of the tasks, tools, and collaborative practices over time, as well as the interplay among the many situated displays in the ecology.

Several other interactive multi-user display systems and multi-display environments have been designed for the purposes of supporting work tasks or collaborative work. Like MERBoard, systems such as BlueBoard [12] and Tivoli [11] offer whiteboard-type tools for collaborating on shared artifacts. Designer's Outpost [10] offers scaffolding tools for the purpose of supporting preliminary website design. Tools such as MessyBoard [3] and the Notification Collage [5] support synchronous and asynchronous communication for collaboration. A prototype ubicomp environment from Alias included a system of diverse networked displays, including interactive Powerwall and Chameleon displays and an immersive Vision Dome for supporting collaboration in a design environment [4]. Projects like CoLab [14], ARIS [2] and iRoom [9] focus on the architecture, system design, and interaction techniques of multi-display environments with a focus on how users can interact across the displays. These systems and environments have been evaluated primarily in laboratory studies, used only in research settings (often the home laboratories of the researchers), or in limited-term experimental trials. While the evaluations of these systems have yielded valuable findings regarding the value and use of large interactive displays for supporting group work [6], we still lack a deep understanding of what role these systems play in natural work environments over time. A recent workshop on multi-display environments (both single-user and collaborative) [7] included position papers that identified common types of multi-display environments [13], as well as technical design considerations for such environments [8]. We believe our work builds upon the existing research by providing an in-depth examination of how one of these systems is used in context and in real use. Our findings can help better inform the design of such systems and tools by uncovering the evolving use of multi-display environments over time by users who were not involved in the design of the system, and whose work tasks are so critical that they will only use a tool if it provides a clear benefit in helping them accomplish these tasks.

4 Study Description

This study was designed as a summative inquiry into the overall value of the MERBoard and other display technologies used in the mission, as well as a reflection upon how the roles and perception of these tools changed over time. The study was designed to complement earlier field studies conducted by the designers of the MERBoard, which focused primarily on MERBoard interaction in the early months of the mission, following their initial deployment [15]. The primary motivation for conducting an evaluation retrospectively, after much of the collocated collaboration had ended, was to understand the overall impact that the displays had on the mission and work activities as a whole; understanding the users' perception of the system on the mission in general allowed us to make design recommendations that are currently being used to influence the design of new iterations of the tool for other NASA workgroups and future missions.

We conducted semi-structured interviews with sixteen scientists and engineers on the MER Mission project, as well as initial background interviews with six NASA researchers involved in the original design and deployment of the NASA MERBoard. Two of the scientist interviews, as well as all of the designer interviews took place onsite at NASA laboratories, while the remaining interviews with scientists and engineers were conducted over the telephone. All interviews lasted between 30 and 60 minutes. Interviews with scientists and engineers took place between twelve and sixteen months after the start of the mission, and were conducted by a researcher who had not been involved in the original design or deployment of the MERBoards, and was otherwise unaffiliated with NASA. To arrive at these findings, we performed inductive analysis upon our interview data using open coding [1] to identify patterns and trends. The descriptions of practices and MERBoard uses and opinions on the system we describe were triangulated among multiple study participants, unless we specify that a particular use or reaction to the MERBoard was only reported by a single user.

5   The Evolving Uses of MERBoard over Time

In this section, we present an overview of the use of the MERBoard within the context of the display ecology. Because the functionalities that we examined each displayed some unique uses and patterns of evolution, we break the presentation down by the individual applications, and describe the overarching themes and general implications in the sections that follow.

5.1   SolTree

The SolTree Tool is frequently mentioned by MERBoard designers and MER Scientists as the most utilized tool available on the MERBoard early in the mission. Used regularly during approximately the first 70 Sols of the MER missions for planning activities primarily by the Long Term Planning (LTP) theme group, SolTree can be considered the closest to a "killer app" provided by MERBoard.

This design of a structured scaffolding tool on a shared display surface entails several assumptions; it assumes that the task that it supports will be done by a group of people, rather than an individual. It also assumes that this collaboration will be synchronous and co-located in such a way that a shared visual surface will be beneficial to the collaboration. Additionally, the design of this tool assumes everyday or near-everyday use during the mission, since it was intended to support planning on a Sol by Sol basis. We found that these assumptions did not hold throughout; the nature and timing of the Sol planning task evolved over the course of the mission, as did the type of collaboration used to accomplish the task. The evolution of task and practice eventually caused Sol planning to migrate off of the MERBoard entirely, as the scaffolding provided by the tool and the shared visual surface offered by the large display ceased to fit the task in the later part of the mission. For this reason, SolTree unexpectedly proved to be most effective as a "ramp-up" tool, rather than the steady-state support tool for daily use for which it was intended.

Display size and group size: The process of SolTree planning in the MERBoard involved a small group of collaborators, generally between three and a dozen people. It is clear from the scientists' comments that the number of people involved in SolTree planning decreased during the course of the mission. LTP scientists agreed that the MERBoard's physical size was well-suited to the size of the groups involved in these activities early in the mission.

The actual authoring process varied between instances; in some cases, the group would convene around the board, either sitting or standing, while a single person "drove" the display, building the tree based on input from the group (Figure 2). As the mission progressed, an individual would often draft a plan alone using SolTree, and then collect other planning scientists around the MERBoard for feedback and editing. The role of the display changed from that of a shared authoring surface that allowed many people to take part in the authoring and decision-making process, to a visual display space for presenting a nearly-finished artifact to the workgroup.

Migration to projection screen for large meetings: Although MERBoard was well-suited for the planning task early in the mission, images of SolTrees were often exported as images or transcribed into PowerPoint for the purposes of displaying them on the projectors during meetings when the plans were being presented to larger workgroup. The size and resolution of MERBoard simply was not sufficient to make MERBoard a valuable presentation tool for this type of viewing. The migration to projection was difficult, however. Scientists complained of the overhead necessary to convert the SolTree into a format that could be shown on a projector; there was no simple way to integrate a plan created on the MERBoard into a presentation.

Tool structure supports early collaborative work: Most of the LTP scientists appreciated SolTree's ability to keep track of all of the possible branches and options,

Fig. 2. Scientists collaborating on a plan using SolTree

especially in the earlier parts of the mission. Others praised the fact that SolTree imposed a structure on brainstorming options; it required planners to think down each linear path and consider and annotate all of the possibilities. One user of the tool said that it "forced explicit logic" and required the scientists to consider all possible ramifications. Another scientist emphasized the importance of the tool soon after the rovers landed because the tool "offered scaffolding" for a process that was still new to the scientists and not yet routinized.

Persistence and evolution of plans: Though the general perception of the SolTree tool among scientists is that it was provided as a way to interactively author plans for Rover activities, their descriptions of use illustrate a broader value of the tool as a persistent information display for community awareness. SolTrees were often left open on the LTP theme group's MERBoard even after the planners had completed their planning for the day, simply as a way of maintaining awareness of the planned activities and options, and also as an informal way of making that information available. One scientist described it as a service to others so that they would "absorb it." The SolTrees were often left visible until someone needed the display for another purpose.

The persistence of the artifact also created continuity from day-to-day between the various LTP leads, particularly as the mission progressed and the planning process stabilized. The SolTrees were not only a data product; they were input for the following day's planning and a way of getting an incoming LTP lead up to speed on the previous day's plans. SolTree authoring was sometimes described as an "evolution", with an existing tree repeatedly being pruned, added to, or otherwise edited based on new data, rather than being created anew in each planning session.

Tasks migrate to other displays as collaboration changes: The planning process evolved during the course of the mission, shifting gradually from unfamiliar and exploratory to familiar and proceduralized. As mission goals solidified, planning became more tactical, and scientists generally confined their planning to the consideration of a few potential options rather than a full-blown exploration of all possible next steps. They were better able to anticipate these steps and their implications and the decision making process became increasingly streamlined.

The method of visualizing these plans evolved as well. Scientists described how the tree-shaped plans with their many-branched possibilities gave way to linear path-shaped plans that often spanned multiple Sols. Because they were considering fewer possibilities, the need to specify all of the possibilities in detail decreased. The "inflexibility" of the tool that forced scientists to specify all of the details of the plans became unnecessary overhead. Additionally, the planning process became predictable enough that scientists no longer needed to create them together; it was sufficient for an individual to create the plan on his own and get it approved by the group later. As a result of this evolution of the task, the group use of the SolTree tool on MERBoard for planning eventually gave way to the individual use of PowerPoint on laptops for creating "Sol Paths." In the transition from MERBoard to PowerPoint, some scientists took the intermediary step of using the freeform whiteboard drawing tool to create plans; this supported the collaborative building of trees, while freeing them from the tight scaffolding of the SolTree tool.

5.2 Whiteboard and Image Display on MERBoard

In contrast to the SolTree tool, the MERBoard whiteboard application was not designed to support a specific task, but rather to provide flexible, *ad hoc* support for collaborative tasks. Even so, the design of the tool reflects some of the same assumptions as the design of the SolTree, namely that the use of authoring tools on a shared display surface would be useful for synchronous, collocated collaboration. The fact that the application was not designed to support any specific tasks suggests that it could be useful for any collaborative tasks that might involve shared authoring of artifacts throughout the course of the mission. As we discovered, however, the tasks for which this use of a shared authoring surface were largely exploratory in nature, and thus clustered primarily in the pre-mission work and early in the mission. The whiteboard evolved from a freeform support tool that helped collaborators with tasks for which procedures were not well-defined to a passive information display, as collaborative tasks became more highly proceduralized and moved off of the shared display space. As with SolTree, the interactive uses of the whiteboard proved to be most valuable for exploratory work, in which the MERBoard served as a ramp-up tool while procedures were not yet routinized.

Flexible support for exploratory tasks: During the pre-mission FIDO tests, scientists and engineers used the whiteboard heavily as a support tool while learning how to operate the rovers. In this case, MERBoard served as a learning tool; it was used by the scientists for creating documentation as the training progressed. MERBoard was a good fit because there was no established procedure for creating documentation within the workgroup, and the whiteboard functionality imposed no structure on the note-taking or resulting product. Additionally, this was the type of task for which having a persistently visible representation of collective knowledge was of value. The whiteboard functionality of MERBoard was also used for brainstorming activities during these tests; MERBoard allowed scientists to do freeform sketches with a group, and save and share the designs. The tool's flexibility was valuable for these types of unstructured preliminary planning activities.

During the actual mission, use of the whiteboard was less frequent and decreased over time. As procedures for accomplishing tasks became routinized and streamlined the exploratory aspects of the whiteboard became less necessary. Scientists' practices and procedures became routinized and the need for *ad hoc* support decreased.

Support for transient information and transitional procedures: Early discussions with designers of the MERBoard seemed to suggest that designers were disappointed with the uptake of the whiteboard during the actual mission, and that few documents were created using it. Discussions with several of the scientists suggest, however, that while interaction with the whiteboard may not have been frequent, many scientists perceived the tool to be valuable to work processes during the mission, with one scientist even calling the tool "imperative" to his work activities.

People rarely chose to save the artifacts that they produced, preferring instead to transcribe them into PowerPoint after the collaboration was finished. It seems possible then that part of the reason the whiteboard was perceived by some as not valuable was because the products created on it were highly transient. Unlike the plans created using SolTree, artifacts created on the whiteboard were not often displayed at the larger meetings, perhaps because of their transient, informal content. As a result, informal presentation of this information was done directly on the MERBoard for small groups of collaborators, and did not migrate onto the projection screens. As described in the SolTree section, the need for the whiteboard arose again during the transitional phase of planning when the group still needed to collaborate synchronously on Sol planning, but no longer needed the tight scaffolding of the SolTree tool.

Lack of use for routinized tasks: In contrast to how the scientists used the whiteboard, the engineers we spoke to made almost no use of it for collaboration. In contrast to the science activities, the engineering activities were more structured and proceduralized in large part because they bore significant similarity to activities from previous missions. The sequencing team, whose job was to create very precise, low-level sequences of instructions to transmit to the rovers, had tools with which they were already familiar that had been designed for the purposes of creating sequences. A lead tactical engineer on the mission spoke of the importance of tools that explicitly supported his tasks, stating that he dealt with "very specific bits of hex code going to very specific places" and that a freeform tool like the MERBoard whiteboard simply would not offer the level of detail that he required. Although he and his team worked collaboratively on sequencing tasks, their procedures and tools were well-defined, and the whiteboard's freeform support offered no benefit to their collaboration.

The unexpected value of passive image display: While most scientists claim to have interacted little with the whiteboard, many were positive and enthusiastic towards it because one team member frequently used it to display images taken from Mars orbiters, maps, and panorama cameras, with graphical overlays or line drawings that he had created on his laptop (Figure 3). Often, these images were displayed for days at a time, attracting interest and prompting discussion, or even retrieved later in the mission for reference.

The scientist liked that he could "release" information into the environment, rather than displaying it from his personal machine. The large display naturally drew people's attention; the size and dynamic nature of the board made it "easy to notice changes" when new material was present. The scientist regarded the information sharing as a type of "asynchronous collaboration"; for him it was a way of keeping others informed of his activities, prompting new ideas, and letting his images and ideas "enter the public consciousness" with no effort on anyone else's part. He saw MERBoard as an "easily changed posterboard" through which he could convey ideas and be guaranteed that they would receive attention.

Other scientists who wanted to share information preferred to use projectors, not because they felt that MERBoard was inferior for viewing ambient information, but because it was easier to plug a laptop into a projector than post content to the MERBoard. For this reason, projectors were also used to display images in the environment that might otherwise have been displayed on MERBoard.

Although actual paper printouts of terrain data were also used during the mission, printing images was expensive and few had access to use the poster printer. One scientist said that the use of some paper images was eventually "superceded" by the annotated maps that had been posted on the MERBoard.

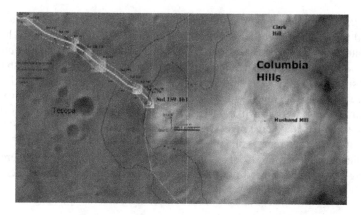

Fig. 3. An image created by a scientist and displayed on the whiteboard

Although the images were admired and drew interest, scientists stated that there was no conflict or awkwardness about appropriating a MERBoard that was currently showing an image. The author of the images said that people understood that the images were "like screensavers" – non-urgent and displayed as objects of interest, and that it was thus acceptable to hide the image using the whiteboard tabbing functionality in order to use the board for other purposes. There was a "sense that it was public space" and that anything left there was "fair game," as opposed to owned content.

5.3 The Mars Clock

Decreasing interaction leads to ambient information display: The Mars clock was a particularly interesting example because of how the ambient display use of MERBoard emerged as the mission tasks and collaboration styles changed. As the mission progressed, the Mars clock became the single most dominant use of the MERBoards used by the scientists. One scientist described the phenomenon as: "When people stopped using the MERBoard, the clock became a useful thing to have up." This statement suggests that it may not have been the case that the clock was perceived a crucial functionality of the MERBoard, but rather that as the other functionalities of MERBoard ceased to be as applicable in everyday work activities, the clock was useful default content for the tool.

While scientists generally described the Mars clock as extremely useful, many of them felt the need to "admit" this appreciation of the clock, as they were aware it was not the use that took the fullest technological advantage of a sophisticated and expensive system. Even so, they expressed a preference for keeping the clock ambient in the environment; clocks on their personal machines would take up valuable personal workspace and would be likely to be covered up by other more pressing applications.

Although the use of the clock was entirely passive, the value of this ambient information as a group resource is clear. Even in the later phases of the mission when some of the MERBoards were being used almost solely to display the Mars time, the administrators of the system were flown in to fix them when they crashed.

Social difficulties stemming from uncertainty of use and ownership: Some scientists suggested that people might have wanted to use the MERBoard, but were hesitant to appropriate the board for fear of depriving other group members of the clock. The scientist who frequently posted images using the whiteboard believed that people were considerably more hesitant to hide the clock to interact with the MERBoard than they were to hide the images that he had displayed; once the clock was on the MERBoard, people were less likely to use it than if it had one of his images displayed on it. The scientists may have perceived the clock as being crucial to others' work and were hesitant to interact with the display for their own benefit if it meant inconveniencing the group at large. It also suggests that images were perceived as interesting but non-urgent and non-task-critical, whereas the clock was perceived as potentially in use at any time.

5.4 CIP and Other Schedules

Structured ambient information: Another use of the MERBoard frequently mentioned by mission scientists and engineers was for the passive display of schedule information. Some of the MERBoards in the science assessment area were used for schedule display nearly as much as they were for clock display. An individual's CIP (Collaborative Information Portal) schedule would be posted on the group's MERBoard and then displayed ambiently throughout the day for the entire group's use. These schedules kept group members aware of important events such as satellite passes and meeting times with very little effort. Interestingly, although this use of the MERBoard was as passive as the display of the Mars clock, the general attitude towards the display of the CIP schedule was somewhat more positive. The schedule information was more inherently group relevant, and therefore may have been perceived as supporting collaboration or coordination to a greater extent than the Mars clock, and therefore more in keeping with the original intent of the shared display.

Low-overhead authoring: The sequencing work done by engineers was highly collocated and required tight time coordination, which made awareness of the schedules crucial. The tactical uplink lead engineer used text on the whiteboard tool of MERBoard rather than the official CIP schedule to type schedules directly onto the MERBoard, including times, events, and primary milestones such as the activity plan approval and sequence walkthroughs. Schedules were generated daily, either created from scratch or modified from the previous day's schedule. Additionally, schedules were modified as necessary throughout the day by the tactical uplink lead engineer in the event that a particular activity "slipped."

The visibility of the MERBoard was extremely important for the display of the sequencing schedules not only because it provided the shared awareness, but also because the schedule did not reside elsewhere, either physically or virtually. The tactical uplink lead emphasized this point by saying that the version of the schedule on the MERBoard served as the "official memory of the activity." If anything needed to change, he would announce it verbally and make the change official by editing the text schedule the MERBoard; thus the MERBoard was the only persistent source of schedule information for this team.

The flexibility and low overhead of using this tool was what made it successful for schedule authoring, editing, and display. The tactical uplink lead admitted that the reason he chose to use the whiteboard for this purpose was because he had never bothered to figure out how to use the CIP schedules that the scientists used. He could not afford to spend "8 hours learning how to do a task." The straightforwardness of the whiteboard tool for text entry and display made it the fitting choice for this task throughout the mission.

6 Implications for Multi-display Environment Design

In looking at the use of the NASA MERBoard over time, several patterns emerge across the various applications. These patterns demonstrate the evolving role of the system in the context of a dynamic work environment, and a complex ecology of displays. The evolution of the role of the MERBoard was clearly tied to several factors:

- *Changes in the collaboration style over time* – MERBoard's value for collaboration was that it supported synchronous sharing of artifacts; multiple users could engage in viewing, authoring and discussing material simultaneously. The fact that procedures became familiar and routinized meant that responsibilities could be divided up among workgroup members and tackled individually, thus reducing the need for a shared work surface for synchronous collaboration.
- *Changes in the tasks of the scientists over time* – MERBoard's value for interaction was primarily as a ramp-up tool that allowed users to conduct exploratory work, especially when procedures or tasks were unfamiliar, and scientists benefited most from doing them together to see and learn how the problems should be addressed. As the mission progressed and mission goals became more focused, tasks required less exploratory work and less time and effort for decision making; groups ceased to need the support for shared exploration and discussion afforded by MERBoard.
- *Other displays and applications available in the environment* – MERBoards were one of many display technologies available to the scientists; the fact that they had other means of displaying information that also could be used for sharing, such as laptops and shared workstations for very small collaborations, and projection screens for large meetings, allowed tasks to migrate off of the MERBoard as necessary. Had MERBoard been the primary or only large display technology available to the scientists, the migration of tasks would have been different.

These three factors together shaped the use of the MERBoard during the mission and the pre-mission training. Taking these factors into account in evaluating the ebb and flow of MERBoard use during the mission and pre-mission, we identified some implications for display ecologies and large interactive displays for supporting group work:

- The transition from interactive use to ambient display – Designers of large displays should expect that the interactive use of large displays may not be constant over time, but that users may continue to find value in the ambient display capabilities of the systems. For this reason, applications and functionalities should not be designed only with interactive use in mind; attention should also be paid to how applications might be designed for passive use, what kinds of content might provide value while the displays are not being used interactively, and how that content can be easily shown on the display. In the case of the MERBoard, ambient use of the whiteboard for image display was valued, but not many users chose to post content. Low-overhead methods of information display might have helped to encourage this use, thus making the tool more valuable to the group. The Mars clock and schedule were both valuable to the group as ambient information; designers might also consider what other types of passive information would be of value for presentation in the environment.

- *The dynamic use of multi-display environments* – Large interactive displays in multi-display environments are by nature group-owned and flexibly appropriable; constant, steady use need not be a goal that determines the success of such systems. Rather their value should be considered in terms of the ease and level of support for task and collaborations that benefit from the use of a shared interactive surface. Multi-display environments should therefore be designed to be flexible and dynamic, perhaps allowing them to be easily reconfigurable, and designing for the fluid easy migration of tasks among the various display surfaces.

- *Support for undefined tasks and proceduralization* – Systems such as MERBoard support exploratory tasks and tasks that do not have a set procedure, becoming less necessary when work becomes streamlined and routinized over time. Designing for continuity by making data products easily accessible and movable between the various displays will help make transitions in work processes smoother, and help ensure that artifacts continue to be valuable as work progresses.

7 Implications for the Evaluation of Large Displays

From our in-depth study of the MERBoard within the context of a display ecology, we garnered several important lessons about evaluating the use of such systems. First, the "success" of a large interactive display within a display ecology cannot be measured by whether a steady state of use is reached. Because people appropriate these tools as necessary when tasks and collaborations require them, there may be a natural ebb and flow of use that does not correspond to success or failure, but rather to the dynamic nature of collaborative work processes. Success is therefore better evaluated by examining the ease and extent of support that such displays provide when tasks call for a shared visual display or interactive work surface.

Similarly, the notion of a "killer application" is one that needs to be reconceived in the context of shared displays in these environments. In the case of the MERBoard, because of changing tasks and collaboration styles, no application was used constantly throughout the mission. However, the SolTree clearly was a tool that got people to use the system, and functioned as a killer app in the sense that it was crucial to their work tasks for a period of time. During much of the time that the scientists were using SolTree for planning, planning methods such as the building of individual trees using PowerPoint would not have been sufficient because they needed the shared visual surface, as well as the shared exploration and decision making process.

For these types of systems, killer apps may be better conceived as applications that support a particular task well enough to allow users to understand the value of the tool for the task.

Another important lesson regarding the value of large displays in work environments came from our observation of the interplay between interactive use and ambient information display. In the realm of large interactive display research, a decrease in interactivity is often viewed as a failure of the system to support workgroup practices. We observed a migration from interactive use to ambient information display, and through our interviews discovered how valuable this ambient information was. We therefore believe that success should be evaluated by looking both at interactivity as well as the value of the display in passive uses.

Finally, in the greater context of a display ecology, it is misleading to evaluate the isolated use of a single system; the existence of other displays in the environment means that it is important to understand how the ecology functions as a whole, not just how individual displays are used. Our findings lead us to suggest that the ebb and flow of use of a large display groupware system may not be an indication of problematic design or failure of the system to support collaboration sufficiently, but rather an indication that the need for such technologies in collaboration are dynamic rather than static. Just as researchers working together to write a paper may initially spend many hours brainstorming together using a whiteboard, the fact that they may later spend more time writing sections individually at their personal machines should not be regarded as a failing of the whiteboard to maintain collaboration; instead the nature of the collaboration changes, making other technologies more appropriate for the time being. In evaluating displays in such multi-display environments, we believe it is better to examine how well and fluidly the ecology as a whole supports the work tasks than to assume that disuse of a tool is a failure of the technology to support the task.

8 Conclusions

Evaluated within the context of a display ecology over an extended period of time, the NASA MERBoard can be considered somewhat successful in how it supported those tasks for which a shared work surface and shared visual display offered benefit. Its interactive and passive uses were important, and even crucial to the users at different points in the mission. The fact that it was used less for interactive purposes over time reflects the changing tasks and collaboration styles of the workgroup more than flawed design. MERBoard still presented several challenges to its users that decreased the overall flexibility and effectiveness of the display ecology as a whole. Users could not migrate content easily from SolTree into a form usable with a projector, creating additional overhead. Similarly, the work required to migrate content from a laptop onto the MERBoard may have decreased the use of MERBoard as an ambient display tool for sharing ideas and artifacts. The findings of our study and our design recommendations are currently being incorporated into new iterations of MERBoard's design that will be deployed at other NASA sites or to support future NASA missions.

References

1. Bernard, H. R. (2000) Social Science Research Methods: Qualitative and Quantitative Approaches. Thousand Oaks, CA: Sage Publications.
2. Biehl, J.T., Bailey, B.P. ARIS: An Interface for Application Relocation in an Interactive Space. Proceedings of ACM GI 2004, 107–116.
3. Fass, A., Forlizzi, J., Pausch, R. MessyDesk and MessyBoard: Two Designs Inspired by the Goal of Improving Human Memory. Proceedings of ACM DIS 2002, 303–311.
4. Fitzmaurice, G. W., Khan, A., Buxton, W., Kurtenbach, G., Balakrishnan, R., Sentient Data Access via a Diverse Society of Devices. ACM Queue 1(8), 2003.
5. Greenberg, S., Rounding, M. The Notification Collage: Posting Information to Public and Personal Displays. Proceedings of ACM CHI 2001, 514–521.
6. Huang, E.M., Russell, D.M., Sue, A.E. IM Here: Public Instant Messaging on Large, Shared Displays for Workgroup Interactions. Proceedings of ACM CHI 2004, 279–286.
7. Hutchings, D.R., Stasko, J., Czerwinski, M. Distributed Display Environments. Workshop call in Extended Abstracts of ACM CHI 2005, 2117–2118.
8. Inkpen, K.M., Mandryk, R.L. Multi-Display Environments for Co-Located Collaboration. Position paper for CHI 2005 Distributed Display Environments workshop.
9. Johanson, B., Fox, A., Winograd, T. The Interactive Workspaces Project: Experiences with Ubiquitous Computing Rooms. IEEE Pervasive Computing Magazine 1(2), 2002, 71–78.
10. Klemmer, S.R., Newman, M.W., Farrell, R., Bilezikjian, M., Landay, J. The Designers' Outpost: A Tangible Interface for Collaborative Web Site Design. Proceedings of UIST 2001, 1–10.
11. Pedersen, E.R., McCall, K., Moran, T.P., Halasz, F.G. Tivoli: an Electronic Whiteboard for Informal Workgroup Meetings. Proceedings of CHI 1993, 391–398.
12. Russell, D.M., Gossweiler, R. On the Design of Person and Communal Large Information Scale Appliances. Proceedings of UbiComp 2001, 354–361.
13. Shen, C., Ryall, K., Everitt, K. Facets of Distributed Display Environments. Position paper for the CHI 2005 Distributed Display Environments workshop.
14. Stefik, M., Foster, G., Bobrow, D.G., Kahn, K., Lanning, S., Suchman, L. Beyond the Chalkboard: Computer Support for Collaboration and Problem Solving in Meetings. Communications of the ACM, 30(1), 1997, 32–47.
15. Tollinger, I., McCurdy, M., Vera, A.H., Tollinger, P. Collaborative Knowledge Management Supporting Mars Mission Scientists. Proceedings of ACM CSCW 2004, 29–38.
16. Trimble, J., Wales, R., Gossweiler, R. NASA's MERBoard: An Interactive Collaborative Workspace Platform. In Public and Situated Displays (2003), O'Hara, K., Perry, M., Churchill, E., Russell, D., (eds.), 18-44.

Modeling Human Behavior from Simple Sensors in the Home

Ryan Aipperspach, Elliot Cohen, and John Canny

Berkeley Institute of Design,
University of California, Berkeley,
Berkeley, CA 94720-1776, USA
{ryanaip, jfc}@cs.berkeley.edu, emcohen3@berkeley.edu

Abstract. Pervasive sensors in the home have a variety of applications including energy minimization, activity monitoring for elders, and tutors for household tasks such as cooking. Many of the common sensors today are binary, e.g. IR motion sensors, door close sensors, and floor pressure pads. Predicting user behavior is one of the key enablers for applications. While we consider smart home data here, the general problem is one of predicting discrete human actions. Drawing on Activity Theory, the language as action principle, and speech understanding research, we argue that smoothed n-grams are very appropriate for this task. We built such a model and applied it to data gathered from 3 smart home installations. The data showed a classic Zipf or power-law distribution, similar to speech and language. We found that the predictive accuracy of the n-gram model ranges from 51% to 39%, which is significantly above the baseline for the deployments of 16, 76 and 70 sensors. While we cannot directly compare this result with other work (lack of shared data), by examination of high entropy zones in the datasets (e.g. the kitchen triangle) we argue that accuracies around 50% are best possible for this task.

1 Introduction

A number of research groups [8],[17],[9] and corporations [2],[4] have begun to study the role of computing in the digital home. There is not yet a consensus on the form that technology in digital homes should take or the purpose it should serve. Several groups, however, are considering the impact that small, inexpensive sensors might have on the home environment [1],[9]. Sensors can be used to support tasks such as activity recognition [9], health monitoring [13], and energy management [8]. In each of these cases, sensor data is used to determine the state of the home, making it possible to construct a more adaptive environment that responds to the needs of its inhabitants. There are several kinds of sensor analysis tasks including sensor fusion, interpretation, and prediction. We are most interested in the prediction task because it involves modeling of human behavior. Prediction from smart home data has been explored by several groups, especially for lighting and heating control [8]. Additionally, predictive

K.P. Fishkin et al. (Eds.): PERVASIVE 2006, LNCS 3968, pp. 337–348, 2006.

behavior modeling can be used to build tutors for cooking or other everyday tasks. Behavior models can typically be used to recognize *anomalous* behavior as well such as deviations from routine, or skipped steps in Activities of Daily Living (ADL) for elders with onset dementia [21].

In this paper we present a very efficient behavior model for predicting future sensor outputs (and the user's location) from previous data. The method is scalable, works with a variety of sensor types, and is independent of the physical layout of the sensors. It can be trained in an *unsupervised* manner without requiring a configuration process or a room model. Setup consists solely of installing the sensors, putting them in training mode for a few weeks, and then starting prediction. The system continues to adapt its model from that time on. For us, it is also important to study models that are plausible from the perspective of our current understanding of human behavior.

We begin the paper by motivating the model we chose, introducing the "language as action" principle. The model itself is based on smoothed n-grams commonly used in language modeling. Then we explain the method in detail. We next describe the smart home datasets we used, which came from MIT and Georgia Tech. Then we present the results from running the model on the smart home datasets. This section includes analysis of the n-gram statistics, showing the classic power law or Zipf distribution commonly seen in speech and language data. We also discuss the limits to this kind of predictive model given the presence of high-entropy regions, like the "kitchen triangle". Finally, we discuss the implications of our results and future work.

2 Background

There has been a remarkable parallel evolution of a principle of language as action. It was articulated first by the psychologist and educational theorist Lev Vygotsky [18] who along with Piaget remain as the two dominant figures in human learning research. Vygotsky also articulated various "genetic principles" governing human behavior. The principles imply that human behavior evolves at both a social and an individual scale. We found interesting support for Vygotsky's genetic principle in our smart home data, as we will discuss in the results section. The principle of language as action is deeply embedded in the work of certain literary theorists, most notably Kenneth Burke [3] one of the most influential theorists of the mid-20th century. And most recently it has been fundamental to the work of the psychologist James Wertsch [19]. The crux of these theories are that language and human action are really the same thing. They are both "mediational means" or tools by which we achieve our ends. They exhibit structure and satisfy "grammars" (Burke's terminology). While the structure exists at many levels, there are strong similarities even at the most simple level – here we model smart home sensor data with language models that are normally used for words in a large corpus of text. We further show that the sensor outputs show the same fundamental statistics as texts (Zipf statistics). This is a far from obvious outcome – Zipf distributions are very "unnatural" in a statistical sense, say if one assumes that behavior is a result of a rational deliberation process. They are however a universal trait of evolution (where they were first studied). In particular, they can arise from the evolution of behaviors – even simple behaviors such as walking around the house. Because of this deep connection, and because language and speech technology is one of the most heavily studied areas of human-machine interaction, we draw our behavior model directly from language modeling. For the latter, the state-of-the-art is a smoothed Markov or n-gram model (not to be confused with Hidden-Markov Models which are used for other tasks in speech processing) [5]. N-gram models are used in virtually every speech understanding system, and increasingly in information retrieval as well.

For the purposes of this paper, when we we refer to sensors we are explicitly considering simple "on/off" sensors such as motion detectors, status-reporting light switches, and appliance usage sensors. We consider these types of sensors for several reasons. First, we agree with the idea of "tape on and forget" [17] sensors that can be easily installed by end users with a minimal amount of configuration. We believe that systems using such sensors will be adopted more quickly than systems using complex sensors that require specialized installation. Simple sensors may also be seen as less invasive than complex sensors like cameras or microphones [17]. Additionally, simple sensors should be easier to integrate into the environment, an important consideration in light of the fact that some subjects describe their homes as seeming "dirty" when visible sensors are installed [1].

As an example of the specific need for local sensor event prediction, we consider the University of Colorado, Boulder, *Adaptive House*, which used sensors to automate lighting control. The *Adaptive House* faced the problem that lights only turned on after an inhabitant's motion in a room was detected, causing a perceptible lag in system responsiveness [8]. This problem was solved through the creation of a customized neural network designed to predict the state of the system two seconds into the future. While effective, the *Adaptive House* was customized to a specific home environment and prediction task, lacking the generality and scalability needed to satisfy the design goals of simplicity and ease in installation.

The MavHome project also focuses on creating intelligent homes through the use of prediction [10],[14]. However, information about data perplexity and running time is not available, making it difficult to compare our results directly.

3   Methods

We used the following five design goals in designing our prediction system[1]:

- **Probabilistic prediction.** The use of probabilistic methods makes it possible to associate a degree of confidence with each prediction and to consider a range of likely events, enabling the system to deal with the noise and ambiguity inherent in sensor data.

---

[1] These design goals are based on those presented by Tapia et al. for activity recognition [17].

- **Model-based vs instance-based learning.** The incremental construction of models from training data makes it possible to build a predictor without the need to save all examples as raw data.
- **Sensor location and type independence.** Systems should operate effectively "even when the algorithm is never explicitly told the location and type of a particular sensor" [17], minimizing installation times and lowering barriers to adoption.
- **Real-time performance.** Any practical prediction algorithm must be able to make predictions in real-time.
- **Online learning.** Any system designed for long-term use must be able to adapt its model to support changes in inhabitant behavior over time.

In addition to these design goals, we found motivation in the similarity between streams of sensor data and language described previously. Language modeling algorithms often assume that languages are ergodic, having the property that the probability of any state can be estimated from a long enough history independent of earlier conditions [15]. One measure of this local structure is perplexity which, roughly speaking, is a measure of the number of words that might follow a particular word given its history. In the English language, perplexity can range from 20 for specialized subsets of the language to 247 for general American English [11]. The sensor data used in this project has perplexity ranging from 4 to 21, suggesting that predictive algorithms which work well in language modeling should work as well or better in short-term sensor event prediction. We chose to begin exploring this direction by using n-gram language models, mapping directly between sensor events in our system and words in language models. As we will discuss later, the actual distribution of sensor data supports the standard assumptions made by n-gram models.

The goal of language modeling is to calculate the probability of a word w_i given its history – that is, to compute $P(w_i|w_1, \ldots, w_{i-1})$. If a language is ergodic, then this probability can be estimated by $\widehat{P}(w_i|w_{i-n+1}, \ldots, w_{i-1})$, for a sufficiently large n. An n-gram language model can be used to calculate the maximum likelihood estimate of $\widehat{P}$ by counting word sequences in a set of training text:

$$\widehat{P}(w_i|w_{i-n+1}, \ldots, w_{i-1}) = \frac{C(w_{i-n+1}, \ldots, w_i)}{C(w_{i-n+1}, \ldots, w_{i-1})}, \tag{1}$$

where $C(\cdot)$ is the count of a given word sequence in the training text. The Hidden Markov Model Toolkit (HTK)'s language modeling tools [22] provide tools for collecting n-gram statistics. We based our system on these tools, augmenting them with code to make predictions based on such models. HTK provides several optimizations in collecting n-gram statistics, including a smoothing method incorporating *back off* and *Good-Turing* discounting as described in [6].

In any set of training data, it is unlikely that all possible sequences will be observed. However, it is unreasonable to assume that unobserved sequences are impossible. This dilemma can be overcome by "discounting" the probability of all observed sequences by some small amount and distributing the extra probability among the unobserved sequences. When using back off, the extra probability is distributed based on the likelihood of shorter sequences – An unobserved sequence $(w_{i-n+1}, w_{i-n+2}, \ldots, w_i)$ will receive higher weight if the shorter sequence $(w_{i-n+2}, \ldots, w_i)$ is common. In HTK, back off is implemented by calculating the probability $\widehat{P}(w_i|w_{i-n+1}, \ldots, w_{i-1})$ using the equation

$$\widehat{P}(w_i|w_{i-n+1}, \ldots, w_{i-1}) = \begin{cases} \alpha \cdot \widehat{P}(w_i|w_{i-n+2}, \ldots, w_{i-1}) & : count = 0 \\ d_C \cdot \frac{C(w_{i-n+1}, \ldots, w_i)}{C(w_{i-n+1}, \ldots, w_{i-1})} & : 1 \leq count \leq k \\ \frac{C(w_{i-n+1}, \ldots, w_i)}{C(w_{i-n+1}, \ldots, w_{i-1})} & : count > k. \end{cases} \quad (2)$$

where α is the fraction of the discounted probability given to the unobserved sequence, d_C is the factor that discounts probability from observed sequences and *count* is the number of examples of the given sequence in the training data. For a full description of the implementation of smoothing in HTK, see [22].

The use of n-gram models fits the design requirements described above:

- **Probabilistic classification.** The counts used in n-gram models provide a probabilistic prediction of sensor events.
- **Model-based vs instance-based learning.** N-grams build a predictive model in the form of gram counts, and original data can be discarded as global statistics are accumulated.
- **Sensor location and type independence.** N-grams do not require any knowledge of the specific sensors being used or their location in the home. Since they consider common sequences in the data, they learn the structure of the data without requiring difficult or tedious system setup (although "good" sensor placement will still improve system performance).
- **Real-time performance.** The authors of [17] suggest that temporal models such as dynamic belief networks (DBNs) may not scale well to environments with hundreds of sensors. N-grams take advantage of temporal information through the use of simple and fast counting methods, allowing them to easily deal with large sets of data. Their empirical performance on sensor data will be discussed later.
- **Online learning.** The gram counts collected by n-gram models can be continually updated, allowing the system to adapt to changing patterns in user's routines.

4   Data Set

We are aware of few projects that have considered sensor data collected from non-laboratory home environments. While it is possible to generate data sets through simulation [14], it is important to validate algorithms on real data collected in complex, noisy environments [17]. We developed and tested our system primarily using data from the Georgia Institute of Technology *Aware Home* project [12], and we conducted additional tests using data from the Massachusetts Institute of Technology *House_n* project [17].

The Georgia Tech data set is a one year database of sensor events collected as part of the digital family portrait project [13]. In the project, the home of a single elderly resident was equipped with 16 in-floor pressure sensors that were triggered whenever someone walked over them. Since the sensors detect pressure in the floor, they can be completely invisible, making them good candidates for deployment in actual homes [1]. The layout of the residence and the sensors is shown in figure 1. Most of the time, the single resident was the only person in the home.

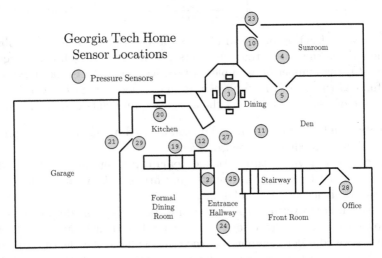

Fig. 1. Georgia Tech Floor Plan and Sensor Layout

The data was provided to us as a list of *(sensor, timestamp)* tuples. Because some sensors would repeatedly fire as the resident walked across them, we collapsed repeat firings into a single event. Additionally, we inserted PAUSE events into the data whenever the time between two sensor events was greater than some time t_{pause}, which was an input parameter. These pause events were inserted in order to model the difference between dwell spots (a sensor followed by a pause event) and paths through the home (a sequence of sensors without a pause event).

We also tested our system on data from the MIT *House_n* project [17]. The data set consists of two week segments of sensor data collected from two different single resident apartments. In the study, the apartments were instrumented with 76 and 70 "state-change" sensors, respectively. The sensors reported the status of numerous aspects of the homes, including doors being open or closed, appliances being in use or idle, and lights being on or off. The smaller amount of training data and the larger number and variety of sensors makes the *House_n* data set an interesting means of exploring the versatility of our algorithm.

Each data set was transformed into an ordered sequence of sensor labels and PAUSE events, and our goal was thus to predict the next sensor to be triggered given the sequence of sensors that were triggered recently.

5   Results

5.1   Data Analysis

The distribution of n-gram sequences in the Georgia Tech data set, shown in figure 2, is similar to a the Zipf distribution often seen in language. Zipf, or power law distributions are described by the relation $N_r \sim 1/r^a$, where r is the rank index of a particular sequence and N_r is the number of occurrences of that sequence. On a log-log plot, such distributions appear as a straight line, which can be seen in the right side of figure 2. Zipf distributions are indicative of "genetic processes", such as those described by Vygotsky [18]. In particular, evolutionary development of "populations" of species in biological genera [20], of city sizes [16], and, in this case, of behaviors has been shown to manifest a Zipf distribution.

Looking more closely at the data, table 1 shows the five most common 6-grams in the Georgia Tech data set (with a sensor timeout, t_{pause}, of 5 minutes). The sequences seem to follow common pathways through the home. Additionally, they reflect a local structure that supports the ergodicity assumption behind n-gram language models. E.g., the local "inner sequence" $27, 3, 11, 5$ is visible in

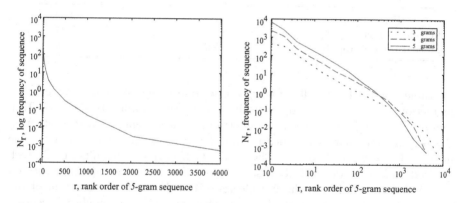

Fig. 2. Distribution of n-gram occurrence counts in the Georgia Tech data set on both linear (left) and logarithmic axes (right). r is the rank ordering of sequences, from most to least common, and N_r is the relative frequency of each sequence. The linear curve on the logarithmic axes is characteristic of a power law (Zipf) distribution.

Table 1. Most common 6-grams in the Georgia Tech data set

Sequence						Percent of Total Observations
20,	19,	20,	19,	20,	19	2.26%
19,	20,	19,	20,	19,	20	2.17%
20,	12,	27,	3,	11,	5	1.72%
12,	20,	12,	27,	3,	11	1.56%
11,	5,	4,	PAUSE,	4,	5	1.26%

each of the last three sequences and is itself one of the most common 4-grams. This mapping between language and human behavior, evidenced through the Zipf distribution of movement sequences and the "local structure" of those sequences, supports the application of language modeling techniques to the modeling of human behavior.

5.2   Model Performance

We first tested our system on the Georgia Tech data set, with and without the back off and smoothing optimizations as implemented in the HTK language modeling tools [22]. The optimizations had a significant impact on performance, as shown in table 2. The results are also significantly above baseline – completely random guessing would result in an expected accuracy of 6.25%[2].

Table 2. Effect of Back Off and Smoothing on the Georgia Tech Data Set. (The "top 2" and "top 3" results consider cases where any one of the top two or three most likely predictions is correct.)

	n-grams with Back Off & Smoothing	Simple n-grams
Percent correct	51%	38%
Percent correct (top 2)	67%	50%
Percent correct (top 3)	72%	62%

Table 3 shows the results of using the n-gram model to compute single-step predictions with back off and smoothing on the three data sets. The "G. Tech Limited" column includes the results of training the system on 2,000 events from the Georgia Tech data set, which is equivalent to the amount of data available in the MIT *House_n* data sets. The similarity between the results in "G. Tech Limited" and the two MIT data sets suggests that the lower performance on the MIT data relative to the full Georgia Tech data set is a function of the amount of training data available rather than of the larger number of sensors in the MIT installations. The n-gram model may be capable of accommodating the increased number and variety of sensors in the MIT data sets, but we cannot confirm this fact without the availability of more training data.

5.3   Discussion of Results

When interpreting the predictive results of the n-gram model, it is important to consider the nature of the paths that residents take through the home. In many

---

[2] Note that it would be possible to make a somewhat smarter guess by picking a neighboring sensor rather than a random sensor, but this would violate the design requirement of sensor location independence since it would require knowledge about the layout of sensors within the home (and thus a more complicated system configuration process).

Table 3. N-gram model results

	G. Tech	G. Tech Limited	MIT 1	MIT 2
n-gram size	5	3	3	3
Percent correct	51%	44%	39%	43%
Percent correct (top 2)	68%	63%	47%	48%
Percent correct (top 3)	72%	68%	49%	49%
Perplexity	3.65	5.69	16.8	17.2
Number of sensors	16	16	76	70

cases, the high entropy in the data may impose a limit on the ability to make predictions of future movement at the sensor level. If in a given situation there are a number of sensors that are equally likely to be the next sensor, then we cannot do better than make a random choice between them. As an example, we consider the Georgia Tech data set.

Many of the most common paths in the Georgia Tech data set occur within the "kitchen triangle" (sensors 12, 19, and 20 – see figure 3), which suggest the process of preparing a meal and moving between the sink, the stove, and the refrigerator. In fact, the top four n-grams shown in table 1 all include various movements among the kitchen sensors as a subsequence. This means that, given that the resident has triggered one of the three kitchen sensors, it is likely that her next movement will be to one of the other two. Choosing between these two sensors would suggest a maximum accuracy of 50%, which is approximately what the n-gram-based model achieves.

This level of accuracy is also useful for many possible applications. In energy management and lighting control systems, any increase in predictive performance will have an impact on system efficiency. Typical systems (e.g., [8]) make use of a *cost function* that penalizes the system both for wasting energy (e.g., turning on lights or heating when no one is around) and for inconveniencing residents (e.g., not turning on lights when someone enters a room). Depending on the balance

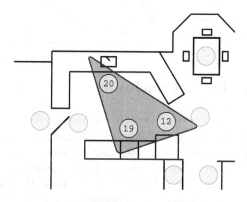

Fig. 3. "Kitchen triangle"

between these two penalties, a system can choose how cautious to be in reducing energy costs. For example, if a resident with a lighting control system begins to move around her home, a system with low predictive performance may turn on most of the lights in the house until the resident stops moving while a system with perfect performance could turn on only the lights along the resident's predicted path. Systems with performance between these two extremes can turn on lights along several of the most highly predicted paths (for example, using the top 2 or top 3 sensors as predicted in table 3), with incremental increases in predictive performance enabling them to move toward more optimal operation.

5.4   Performance

One key advantage of n-gram models is their speed. Because they are implemented primarily through counting, n-grams require very little processing time, especially when compared to complex methods such as dynamic Bayesian networks (DBNs). In our implementation, it took 48 seconds to construct a model of the one year Georgia Tech data set, which consisted of 134,000 data points. (All results are for a 1.6 GHz Pentium M system with 512 MB of RAM running Windows XP.) Prediction times for the three data sets are shown in table 4. Based on the observed per-sensor prediction time of 0.01 ms for 10-gram models, the system should be able to support a deployment of 1,000 sensors while making predictions at a frequency of 100 Hz.

Table 4. Average Time Per Prediction

	Georgia Tech	MIT Apartment 1	MIT Apartment 2
2-grams	0.0216 ms	0.129 ms	0.122 ms
5-grams	0.0610 ms	0.385 ms	0.356 ms
10-grams	0.174 ms	0.857 ms	0.813 ms
15-grams	0.345 ms	1.37 ms	1.34 ms
Number of Sensors	16	76	70
Prediction Time per Sensor (10-grams)	0.01 ms	0.01 ms	0.01 ms

6   Future Work and Conclusion

As suggested by the close ties between human activity and language, predictive models used in language modeling can be applied successfully to behavior modeling. N-grams provide a fast and accurate method for making single-step predictions on home sensor data, and we have argued that they achieve close to the best possible accuracy achievable on the task. However, n-gram models do not take into account higher level information such as task, activity or goal. Systems which integrate such high level information with low level analysis have been shown to be effective [7] in modeling human activity. We plan to explore building a similar hierarchical system on top of our existing framework.

The level of performance necessary in predictive systems will ultimately depend on the types of applications in which they are deployed. Additionally, measures of performance will include more than just accuracy and should be based on the actual impact predictions have on system behavior and their utility to household residents. Such systems must also take into account issues such cost of deployment, privacy, and error recovery methods. We plan to move quickly toward the implementation of applications in actual homes in order to assess the types of prediction errors that are the most problematic and to determine what level of performance is expected by users.

Acknowledgments

We would like to thank Leon Barrett for his help with an earlier iteration of this project. We would also like to thank James Rowan from Georgia Tech and Emmanuel Munguia Tapia from MIT for providing us with their data sets, without which this project would have been impossible.

References

1. J. Beaudin, S. Intille, and E. Tapia, "Lessons Learned Using Ubiquitous Sensors for Data Collection in Real Homes," in *Proceedings of the ACM Conference on Human Factors in Computing Systems* (CHI 2004).
2. B. Brumitt et al., "EasyLiving: Technologies for Intelligent Environments", in *Handheld and Ubiquitous Computing*, September 2000.
3. Kenneth Burke, *Language as Symbolic Action,* University of California Press, 1966.
4. Intel Corporation, "Digital Home, Technology and Research at Intel," http://www.cc.gatech.edu/fce/ecl/projects/dfp/index.html
5. Frederick Jelinek, *Statistical Methods for Speech Recognition*, Cambridge, Massachusetts: MIT Press, 1997, p. 58.
6. S.M. Katz, "Estimation of Probabilities from Sparse Data for the Language Model Component of a Speech Recogniser," in *IEEE Transactions on Acoustic, Speech and Signal Processing*, 1987, vol. 35 no. 3. pp. 400-401.
7. L. Liao, D. Fox, and H. Kautz, "Learning and Inferring Transportation Routines," in *Proceedings of AAAI-04*, 2004.
8. M. Mozer, "Lessons from and Adaptive House", in *Smart Environments: Technologies, protocols, and applications*, D. Cook and R. Das Eds. Hoboken, NJ: J. Wiley and Sons, 2005, pp. 273-294.
9. M. Philipose, et al., "Inferring Activities from Interactions with Objects," in *Proceedings of the Conference on Pervasive Computing*, October 2004, pp. 50-57.
10. S. Rao and D. J. Cook, "Identifying Tasks and Predicting Actions in Smart Homes using Unlabeled Data", in *Proceedings of the Machine Learning Workshop on The Continuum from Labeled to Unlabeled Data*, 2003.
11. S. Roukos, "Language Representation," in *Survey of the State of the Art in Human Language Technology*, R.A. Cole et al., Eds. Center for Spoken Language Understanding CSLU, Carnegie Mellon University, 1995.

12. J. Rowan, Digital Family Portrait project, `http://www.cc.gatech.edu/fce/ecl/projects/dfp/index.html`.

13. J. Rowan and E.D. Mynatt, "Digital family portraits: Providing peace of mind for extended family members," in *Proceedings of the ACM Conference on Human Factors in Computing Systems* (CHI 2001), Seattle, Washington: ACM Press, 2001, pp. 333-340.

14. A. Roy, et al., "Location Aware Resource Management in Smart Homes", in *Proceedings of the Conference on Pervasive Computing*, 2003.

15. C.E. Shannon, "A Mathematical Theory of Communication," in *The Bell System Technical Journal*, vol. 27, 1948. pp. 379-423.

16. H.A. Simon, "On a class of skew distribution functions," in *Biometrika*, vol. 42, 1955. pp. 425-440.

17. E. Tapia, S. Intille, and K. Larson, "Activity recognition in the home setting using simple and ubiquitous sensors," in *Proceedings of PERVASIVE 2004*, vol. LNCS 3001, A. Ferscha and F. Mattern, Eds. Berlin Heidelberg: Springer-Verlag, 2004, pp. 158-175.

18. L. S. Vygotsky, *Mind in Society: The development of higher psychological processes.* Edited by Michael Cole, Vera John-Steiner, Sylvia Scribner and Ellen Souberman, Harvard University Press, 1978.

19. J. Wertsch, *Mind As Action*, Oxford University Press, 1998.

20. J. C. Willis and G. U. Yule, "Some statistics of evolution and geographical distribution in plants and animals, and their significance," in *Nature*, vol. 109, 1922. pp. 177-179.

21. D.H. Wilson and C. Atkeson, "Simultaneous Tracking and Activity Recognition (STAR) Using Many Anonymous, Binary Sensors," in *Proceedings of PERVASIVE 2005*, Munich, Germany, May 2005.

22. S. Young, et al., *The HTK Book*, Microsoft Corporation and Cambridge University, 3.2.1 edition, 2002.

Using a Live-In Laboratory for Ubiquitous Computing Research

Stephen S. Intille, Kent Larson, Emmanuel Munguia Tapia,
Jennifer S. Beaudin, Pallavi Kaushik, Jason Nawyn, and Randy Rockinson

House_n, Massachusetts Institute of Technology,
1 Cambridge Center, 4FL,
Cambridge, MA, 02142, USA
{intille, kll}@mit.edu

Abstract. Ubiquitous computing researchers are increasingly turning to sensor-enabled "living laboratories" for the study of people and technologies in settings more natural than a typical laboratory. We describe the design and operation of the PlaceLab, a new live-in laboratory for the study of ubiquitous technologies in home settings. Volunteer research participants individually live in the PlaceLab for days or weeks at a time, treating it as a temporary home. Meanwhile, sensing devices integrated into the fabric of the architecture record a detailed description of their activities. The facility generates sensor and observational datasets that can be used for research in ubiquitous computing and other fields where domestic contexts impact behavior. We describe some of our experiences constructing and operating the living laboratory, and we detail a recently generated sample dataset, available online to researchers.

1 Introduction

Technologies that can automatically detect and respond to context may permit the development of useful, novel, and user-friendly computational devices for the home setting [1]. In order to fully realize such *context-aware* user interface technologies at least three key challenges must be overcome:

1. **Need for comprehensive sensing:** Testing promising context detection algorithms that use multiple (and sometimes multi-modal) sensors in a real home is logistically difficult and costly in early stages of research. Therefore, results are often published on small test datasets acquired from "simulations" of home activity done in a laboratory setting. Even those tests done in actual homes are usually conducted for a short time with only a small portion of the environment instrumented.
2. **Need for labeled training datasets:** Some of the most robust and promising context detection algorithms for the home setting use statistical models that must be trained on example datasets – often *annotated* datasets. Datasets for people performing common domestic activities, particularly those that may take hours or days, are difficult to obtain. Accurate labels for the activity and contexts of such datasets are often dependent on participant recall or diary recordings, both of which have been demonstrated to be error-prone [2, 3].

K.P. Fishkin et al. (Eds.): PERVASIVE 2006, LNCS 3968, pp. 349–365, 2006.

3. **Need for complex, naturalistic environments:** Researchers developing context-aware applications for the home must ultimately evaluate how typical users will react to a prototype technology in a representative setting. Users will be multi-tasking, experiencing interruptions, dealing with tens of objects, interacting with other people, and engaging in other complex behaviors that are difficult to simulate in the lab. Researchers need observational tools that help them study how people are reacting to novel technology in the complex home setting.

These challenges, among others, have led to a growing interest in so-called "living laboratories" for ubiquitous computing research, which are naturalistic environments instrumented with sensing and observational technologies and used for experimental evaluation (e.g., [4, 5]. Researchers thinking of developing living laboratory facilities must pick a target along two dimensions: richness of physical sensor infrastructure and behavioral realism. Ideally one would have access to many real home environments that have an extensive physical sensor infrastructure. However, the cost of more extensive sensing may limit how long data can be collected and the complex ad hoc setup may inhibit how natural the behavior observed actually is. Living laboratories require a compromise, therefore, such as having someone move temporarily into a home that is not their own. Nevertheless, the environments may be valuable when attempting to bridge the gap between traditional laboratory experimentation and small-number-of-subject studies in multiple, real homes. Living laboratories can also play an important role in iterative hypothesis generation and testing (see Fig. 1).

Fig. 1. Living laboratories may help researchers bridge from laboratory testing to larger studies in real homes using portable ubiquitous computing technologies

We have developed a new live-in, apartment-scale research facility called the PlaceLab, which opened in July of 2004 in an urban neighborhood in Cambridge, Massachusetts. Volunteer research participants individually live in the PlaceLab for days or weeks, treating it as a temporary home. Meanwhile, a detailed description of their activities is recorded by sensing devices integrated into the fabric of the architecture. The PlaceLab was designed from the outset to support the collection of rich, multi-modal sensor datasets of domestic activity, which are intended to be shared among researchers in different organizations and fields, including researchers working on context-aware ubiquitous computing technology, preventive healthcare, energy conservation, and education.

In the remainder of this paper, we describe the PlaceLab facility and some of the challenges we have faced in the design, development, and early phases of operation. We aim to provide some guidance for researchers currently operating or considering the construction of residential living laboratories. We conclude by inviting other researchers interested in using our living laboratory data to study example data we have made available online and to contact the authors to learn more about how to take advantage of this resource (and more extensive datasets) in their own work. As much as is administratively possible, we would like the PlaceLab to be a community resource.

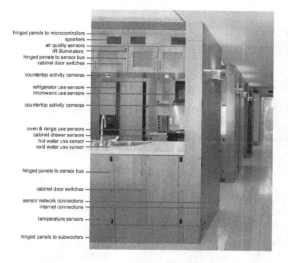

Fig. 2. Sensors are located throughout the cabinetry in a consistent way in every room of the apartment. Some sensor locations are indicated here (left). All of the observational sensing is built directly into the cabinetry. Although the sensors are ubiquitous, they become part of the design aesthetic (small black windows). Pilot volunteers have expressed that they are easy to forget. The cabinetry has been designed with channels for the sensor bus, making it easy to distribute sensors throughout the environment. The channels hinge open, allowing easy access for maintenance and sensor additions/upgrades (right). Adding a sensor simply requires adding a splitter in a channel (circled) and plugging in the device.

2   PlaceLab Overview

Fig. 2 shows the interior of the PlaceLab facility. The 1000 sq. ft. apartment consists of a living room, dining area, kitchen, small office, bedroom, full bath and half bath. Fig. 3 shows a floor plan. The interior of the PlaceLab consists of 15 prefabricated and recon-figurable cabinetry components. Each contains a micro controller, an addressable speaker system, and a network of up to 30 sensors that capture a complete record of audio-visual activity, including information about objects manipulated, environmental conditions, and use of appliances. *All* wired sensors are discreetly integrated into the cabinetry, appliances, and furnishings and fixtures. The wireless sensors utilized are small (4.5 x 4.0 x 1.75 cm) and can be placed inconspicuously on any objects of interest.

New sensors can be easily added to this network as required. The exact list of portable sensors used varies slightly from study to study, depending upon the principal goals at that time. As of December 2005, the sensors were as follows. Eighty small, wired switches detect on-off and open-closed events, such as the opening of the refrigerator, the shutting of the linen closet, or the lighting of a stovetop burner. Interior conditions of the apartment are captured using distributed temperature (34), humidity (10), light (5), and barometric pressure (1) sensors. The PlaceLab also features electrical current sensors (37), water flow (11) and gas flow (2) sensors. Wireless object movement sensors can be easily taped onto any non-wired objects. Currently 125 of

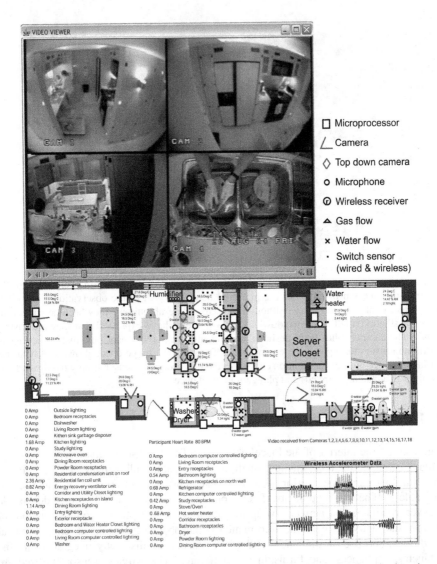

Fig. 3. A data visualization tool for the PlaceLab and a floor plan indicating the location of most sensors described in the text. Data from two wireless 3-axis accelerometers outputting data at 67 Hz is also represented. The display shows the 4 views that were automatically selected from the 18 possible video streams, using computer vision processing. An annotation tool allows researchers to click on a particular sensor and then see the rest of the data (including video and audio) at the time of that sensor's activation – this may simplify data analysis or searching for particular events of interest in multiple days of data.

such sensors are installed on objects such as chairs, tables, appliances, brooms, remote controls, large containers, and other objects people may manipulate [6]. Participants in the PlaceLab can wear up to three wireless 3-axis, 0-10 G accelerometers that measure limb motion. A wireless heart rate monitor (using a standard Polar chest strap) can also be worn. Five receivers spread throughout the apartment collect all wireless object motion, accelerometer, and heart rate data sent via the MITes wireless sensors [6]. Nine infrared cameras, 9 color cameras, and 18 microphones are distributed throughout the apartment in cabinet components and above working surfaces, such as the office desk and kitchen counters. Eighteen computers use image-processing algorithms to select the 4 video streams and 1 audio stream that may best capture an occupant's behavior, based on motion and the camera layout in the environment. Two other computers synchronize the audio-visual data streams with the other sensor data and save all data to a single portable disk drive. Fig. 3 shows the location of the sensors. More technical details of the PlaceLab's sensor infrastructure are described in the Appendix.

3   Living Labs: Complementing Existing Tools and Methods

A key motivation for the creation of the PlaceLab arose from our prior work developing context-detection algorithms in traditional laboratory settings. Controlled laboratory studies allowed dense sensor installation useful for the study of behavior and development of new context-aware algorithms, but simulated rooms or short stays severely constrained behavior variability. In response, we developed portable tools that can be installed in real homes, but practical limitations dictate that only a subset of a full laboratory system can be deployed at once. We thought that we needed a resource to bridge the (large) gap from studies in the lab to studies in real homes.

A common criticism of living laboratories such as the PlaceLab is that requiring people to move temporarily out of their own homes will reduce the complexity and variability of the home environment and may have a corresponding effect on the participant's behavior. We agree. However, just because behavior may be altered in some ways does not mean that we will not observe complex and important activity. Despite some limitations, a live-in lab still allows for more natural behavioral observation and data collection on everyday activities such as cooking, socializing, sleeping, cleaning, working from home, and relaxing than can be obtained from short laboratory visits. Our preliminary experiences using the PlaceLab suggest this to be true. Activities that present challenges for context detection algorithms – multi-tasking, interruption, task-switching, use of objects, context-dependent variation of behavior over time, and interaction with other people – have all been observed in the PlaceLab.

The PlaceLab does take a behaviorist approach with respect to activity recognition and annotation. Some activities or participant states of mind may not be possible to adequately annotate retrospectively by an independent observer or even the participants themselves. It can be difficult, for example, for a PlaceLab researcher to later determine if someone was "deep in thought" or simply closing his or her eyes and resting for a moment. The PlaceLab infrastructure, however, does permit researchers to employ novel self-report strategies that can help the researcher understand some of this behavior, such as context-triggered experience sampling [7]. Standard subject self-report with paper or electronic surveys can also be used.

As long as one is cognizant of the limitations of living laboratories, they can be used to complement other tools being used to study behavior in the home. Table 1 in [8] describes how living labs could be used to compliment surveys and interviews, experience sampling, direct observation, and in-home portable kits.

4 PlaceLab Design Goals

The PlaceLab was designed with "ubiquity" of sensing technology as the primary goal. Most living labs built to date consist of relatively typical homes where ubiquitous computing technologies are included, but not in a truly ubiquitous way. Typically a portion of the environment is wired with a few sensors of interest to the researchers who constructed the facility. Often different parts of the home have completely different technologies and each data type is not synchronized. In practice, individual researchers tend to tweak the highly specialized sensor subsystems as needed for specific projects (e.g. changing lighting and camera views for computer vision, installing directional microphones pointed at specific locations). The benefit of this type of approach is that specialized systems can be rapidly prototyped and tested for use on focused tasks (e.g., memory aids in the kitchen while cooking [9], testing gait recognition [10]).

We have deliberately chosen a different strategy. Each sensor subsystem is ubiquitous and consistent throughout the environment, and all data sources are synchronized and recorded in a common format. Our goal was to invest time up front to create a facility that would eventually allow researchers to spend less time custom tuning sensor subsystems in specific locations and more time studying what might be called the "whole house" problem – how can sensor fusion be used to create useful ubiquitous computing systems, and how can user interfaces that respond to multi-tasking, interruption, etc. be created and evaluated?

Another key design decision was to focus on quantity and ubiquity of sensing rather than quality of any particular sensor. In part, this decision was justified based upon our belief that many context detection tasks are simpler to solve with many distributed sensors and sensor fusion rather than a smaller number of more generalized sensors that require complex interpretation at the sensor itself. Distributed sensors may improve redundancy as well, allowing higher-level reasoning about activity structure to be more easily encoded in useful representations. For example, promising results have recently been obtained for recognizing activities in the home using RFID gloves and contact switches superseding the capabilities of most vision systems (e.g., [11-13]). If deemed necessary, the PlaceLab does allow any particular sensor to be easily replaced with a higher quality version, supporting multiple strategies of investigation simultaneously.

Our third key design decision was to create a system that would provide a single, unified, synchronized living laboratory dataset in a format that could be easily provided to other researchers and reused in multiple projects. In that spirit, we later describe an introductory dataset that we have placed online.

5 Running a PlaceLab Study

To our knowledge, the PlaceLab is the first living laboratory in which multi-day studies are run such that researchers and volunteers have no (or extremely limited) face-to-face interaction during the data collection period. This is quite unlike some prior instrumented homes inhabited by the researchers themselves (e.g., [14]) . Since opening in July 2004, three pilot PlaceLab studies and three technology evaluation studies of about 10 days each had been run by December 2005. In addition, our research team has conducted numerous short, informal test sessions. The sensor infrastructure operates and saves some data types continuously, even when an official study is not ongoing, which is useful for monitoring system status and conducting environmental condition quality studies (e.g., our partner TIAX is studying topics such as changes in dust mite populations relative to indoor humidity and load balancing among power consuming devices during power outages).

Participants

The PlaceLab is optimized for studies that would benefit from multi-day or multi-week observation of single individuals living alone or a couple. (In 2003, 26% of U.S. households consisted of a person living alone [15]). Participants for the initial studies were recruited via electronic mailing lists, posters, and word-of-mouth. Advertisements contained lines such as, "Teach Researchers about Your Everyday Life ... help us design better technologies and homes ...". Participants for studies were selected by questionnaires and interviews and ranged in age from 35 to 60 years. Each was compensated about $25 US per day for participation. The participants expressed that the primary reason they were participating was a belief that this research could yield long-term social and scientific benefits. A database of interested volunteers has since been created to support future work, including not only individuals but also couples interested in participating together.

There is nothing inherent in the facility that prevents data collection and experimentation on multiple people. By default the facility saves a single audio and video stream, but by simply adding an additional computer and disk space one could save additional streams. Even with the current settings, studies that investigate activity recognition algorithms for detecting activity when the home is occupied by more than one individual could be done.

Study Design

To date, three types of study designs have been employed in the PlaceLab. Our initial three pilot studies were primarily observational, where data was collected on the everyday activities of the participants for activity recognition training. Participants additionally completed surveys about their behavior for comparisons between subject report and observations using PlaceLab sensors. Two studies were designed to evaluate novel ubiquitous computing technology that used a house-wide sensor system. In one, a context-sensitive reminder strategy was compared against a traditional time-based reminder strategy. This study represented a more controlled, albeit exploratory, within-subject design where a participant was asked to follow an experimental regiment and results were compared between conditions. The second study examined participant initiated use of a sensor-driven technology for motivating behavior change in the course of everyday routines. The participant returned for two separate stays in the PlaceLab and therefore some comparison of behavior before and after introduction of the technology into the environment was made possible. Results from these and other studies will be submitted to the appropriate scientific venues as analysis is completed; at that time some anonymized datasets (including sensor activation data) will be available as well.

Participant Procedures

In each study, care is taken to ensure that participants maintain ultimate control over their data and that they recognize their right to withdraw from the study at any time for any reason. PlaceLab volunteers are informed of all the sensor locations in the apartment and how the recorded data will be used. Recordings from the PlaceLab are never observed in real-time, so the participants may choose to omit segments of audio, video, and/or sensor readings before releasing their data. Participants are asked to have visitors sign informed consent forms.

In post-stay interviews, participants expressed that they quickly acclimated to the PlaceLab and that, despite the ubiquitous sensing, it is a pleasant, comfortable space. For example, one participant offered as evidence of her quick acclimation the fact that she fell asleep on the couch at night watching TV, an activity she thought she would only do in a familiar environment. At first, she was embarrassed to have this behavior captured on video, and she logged that the data from that time should be deleted. However, by the end of her stay, she decided the only data she needed to remove was some audio during personal phone calls. Furthermore, this participant made the PlaceLab more comfortable and personal during her stay by gradually bringing in items from home, including her bedspread, placemats, flower vases, coffee mug and coffee maker, and, eventually, even her own coffee table. All PlaceLab subjects to date have expressed an interest in returning for another study; we believe this is a good sign that the facility and the experimental procedures in place establish a high level of comfort despite the ubiquitous sensing.

The behavior of our initial participants raises some issues that must be considered in future work as the PlaceLab is used for longer stays. For example, when wireless object motion sensors [6] are used in the PlaceLab and participants bring new objects, procedures must be established whereby the participants or the researchers add sensors to the new objects. Based upon the topics being studied at the time, procedures must be established to deal with visits from non-study participants and labeling the activities of multiple people.

6 Example Data

Our vision is that datasets from living laboratories such as the PlaceLab can serve as general purpose resources for the ubiquitous computing community. These datasets may become more useful over time as they are annotated in increasing detail by researchers. For instance, initially an unannotated dataset may be used by researchers interested in unsupervised learning and context-detection; only sensor activations and rudimentary labeling may be required. Researchers studying supervised learning algorithms may then invest time annotating the data using a set of activity tags organized into an activity hierarchy. Next a user interface designer may use the sensor data and the detailed annotation to qualitatively study the data, searching for specific events of interest that may support or inspire novel user interface ideas for the home setting. Later a discourse researcher may code speech utterances, further enriching the dataset. Meanwhile, the facility can be used to run new studies and generate new datasets where the sensor technology is improved and extended.

There are some serious challenges to achieving this vision. Some researchers may decide the data does not perfectly suit their needs, perhaps missing a key sensor. Other researchers may feel the participants who have been used in prior experiments are not representative of their target user group. Others may find that the activity herarchies used by past researchers do not map well onto their own needs.

Our experience, however, suggests that ubiquitous computing researchers – especially those developing algorithms that use sensor data – are intensely interested in high-quality datasets with observational and sensor data from homes. In response to our needs and those of others, we have invested over two years of planning and development in the creation of a living laboratory that can generate rich, sharable datasets. The grand challenge is whether we can operate this living laboratory so that it has value for the larger UbiComp community.

During the last several months, we have been stress testing and improving the PlaceLab infrastructure. To facilitate research community involvement, we have created an example PlaceLab test dataset that includes four hours of fully-annotated intensive home activity. We have put this 4.1 GB dataset with usage instructions online at http://architecture.mit.edu/house_n/data/PlaceLab/PlaceLab.htm. In the remainder of this section, we briefly describe this resource.

6.1 "Intensive Activity" Test Data Set

The *intensive activity* sample dataset was recorded with a member of our research team who was familiar with the PlaceLab but not a creator of the core technical infrastructure. The researcher wore two 3-axis mobile accelerometers in known orientations (one on the upper left thigh and the other on right wrist) and a wireless heart rate monitor (using a Polar chest strap). The researcher was asked to perform a set of common household activities anytime during a 4-hour period. These activities consisted of doing laundry, preparing a meal, baking, and performing light cleaning tasks. The researcher volunteer determined the sequencing, multitasking, pacing, and execution of the tasks and integrated additional home activities, such as making phone calls, watching TV, using the computer, grooming, and eating. Our intent was to have a short test dataset that showed a variety of activity types and activated as many sensors as possible, but in a natural way.

At the conclusion of the test period, each hour of the data was manually annotated using a hierarchy of 89 activity, body posture, and room/context types we have developed for PlaceLab data. Some of these are listed in Table 1. Trained (undergraduate) annotators required about 2 hours of effort for each hour of video annotated using professional annotation software (ProcoderDV). Initial annotation sets analyzed using Cohen's Kappa (a standard technique for determining inter-rater reliability) revealed some variation in labeling outcome. Body postures with extended state (e.g., standing, sitting, walking) received higher agreement between annotators than fast-action body postures (e.g., sitting down action, turning/pivoting). Activities that involved single appliances (e.g., ironing, vacuuming, using telephone) received the highest agreement between annotators. Based on these results, we are revising our annotation training procedures and the label hierarchy. We are also including "background" activities (e.g., "cooking" can continue even as someone makes a bed, if pots are on the stove). Our experiences annotating early PlaceLab datasets have also led us to develop custom annotation tools that help annotators label this unique type of dataset. Since an annotation session may last only a few hours, but a "background" activity can last much longer (e.g. an extended episode of "cooking" or "cleaning"), we have found that annotators need tools that help ensure they do not forget to mark start or end times of longer events. Using the sensors activations themselves can also help annotators spot check work (e.g., if one clicks on the microwave sensors, a tool that helps quickly check for "cooking" labels is of great value). We will provide our latest tools along with each dataset and we invite members of the community developing annotation tools to contribute as well.

Table 1. Activities manually annotated in the intensive activity test dataset and one waking hour (10/16/04, 7-8 PM) of PlaceLab Participant 3, with number of bouts, total percentage time, and mean time in seconds

Activities (out of 89) observed by annotator for an hour of intensive activity dataset
Activity: Prep. food bkgrnd (1, 85%, 3068s), Wash laundry bkgrnd, (1, 26%, 953s), Use computer (3, 14%, 171s), Hand-wash dishes (6, 11%, 65s), Meal prep. misc. (6, 8%, 49s), Make bed (1, 8%, 270s), Mix/stir (9, 7%, 29s), Laundry misc. (1, 4%, 155s), Dry dishes (2, 3%, 49s), Clean a surface (1, 3%, 96s), Retrieve ingred./cookware (7, 3%, 13s), Fold laundry (2, 2%, 27s), Measure (2, 0.9%, 15s), Put away dishes (2, 0.7%, 12s), Clean misc. (1, 0.7%, 24s), Dishwash misc. (1, 0.6%, 19s), Combine/add (1, 0.5%, 17s), Listen to music/radio (1, 0.2%, 7s), Put things away (2, 0.2%, 3s), Dispose garbage (1, 0.05%, 1s), Wash laundry (1, 0.04%, 1s), Drink (1, 0.04%, 1s)
Posture/mobility: Stand still (state) (40, 50%, 45s), Walk (45, 25%, 20s), Sit (state) (4, 15%, 132s), Walk w/ load (6, 3%, 20s), Bend (15, 3%, 7s), Kneel (3, 2%, 23s), Stand up (action) (15, 0.8%, 1s), Sit up (action) (3, 0.3%, 3s), Sit down (action) (4, 0.2%, 1s), Turn/pivot (1, 0.09%, 3s)
Location: Kitchen (13, 50%, 137s), Bedroom (6, 19%, 116s), Office (3, 14%, 177s), Out of view (6, 8%, 49s), Hallway (29, 5%, 6s), Dining area (6, 3%, 16s), Living room (1, 0.3%, 11s)
Activities (out of 89) observed by annotator for an hour during Participant 3's stay
Activity: Meal prep. misc. (2, 17%, 314s), Watch TV/movies (1,14%, 487s), Prep. food bkgrnd (1, 14%, 487), Read paper/book/magazine (1, 8%, 273s), Info/leisure misc. (3, 7%, 88), Mix/stir (2, 5%, 88), Toileting (1, 4%, 153s), Use phone (1, 4%, 139s), Put things away (4, 4%, 31s), Combine/add (6, 3%, 20s), Retrieve ingred./cookware (6, 1%, 7s), Wash hands (1, 0.8%, 28s), Clean a surface (1, 0.6%, 19s), Groom/hygiene misc. (1, 0.5%, 19s), Undress (1, 0.4%, 13s), Drink (2, 0.2%, 4s), Put away laundry (1, 0.2%, 7s), Wash ingred. (1, 0.1%, 5s),Dispose garbage (1, 0.1%, 4s), Enter house (1, 0.06%, 2s)
Posture/mobility: Sit (state) (6, 31%, 188s), Stand still (state) (56, 30%, 18s), Walk (23, 11%, 16s), Turn/pivot (50, 6%, 4s),Bend (13, 4%,11s), Sit down (action) (6,0.5%,3s), Stand up (action)(5, 0.2%,1s)
Location: Living room (3, 26%, 318s), Kitchen (5, 26%, 185s), OutOfView (3, 19%, 234s), Dining area (7, 19%, 95s), Bathroom (1, 4%, 159s), Office (1, 4%, 132s), Hallway (8, 2%, 7s)

Table 1 is not intended as a comprehensive summary of activity, only a representation of the diversity of activities that may be observed. Researchers interested in particular topics are able to search the PlaceLab dataset for activities or times of interest. Currently most searching must be done based on one-to-one sensor activations (e.g. playing back video and audio and sensor activations just before and after the refrigerator was opened). However, as algorithms for automatic detection of activities are employed on datasets, those computationally inferred labels can and will be added to the set of annotations, ideally reducing annotation time for certain types of data analysis tasks. Researchers who are attempting to do activity recognition studies with in-home sensor systems lack access to datasets with well-annotated activities. Further, some PlaceLab studies result in other types of data than activity performed being collected, such as subject self report and subject responses to interviews with researchers pre and post study.

We are currently using PlaceLab annotations to validate the PlaceLab and wireless sensor infrastructure itself. For example, one hour of the test set has been annotated with all instances of interaction with objects or furnishings that (according to multiple annotators) should have produced a sensor activation. Fifty sensors (cabinets, appliances) were identified that should have fired. In practice, 42 sensor firings were recorded (84%). Three errors were due to a broken oven switch, one was due to a sticky cabinet door that does not close all the way, and four resulted from TINI board latency and very fast cabinet open/close events (see the Appendix for a discussion about sensor latency and how we have reduced it). The wired infrastructure of the PlaceLab is also being used to fully characterize the performance of the wireless sensors [6], which are intended for *in situ* ubiquitous computing research in the actual homes of volunteers. The cost of maintaining the PlaceLab sensor infrastructure over time is something we plan to monitor. The greatest barrier to using PlaceLab data is simply the manpower required to annotate datasets in detailed ways. We can currently generate far more data than we can annotate and analyze and therefore hope others in the community can participate in the effort.

6.2 Data from PlaceLab Volunteers

The intensive activity test set is designed to introduce other ubiquitous computing researchers to PlaceLab data. However, our ultimate goal is to have researchers productively using data from our volunteer subjects. The bottom of Table 1 lists activities observed during one waking hour of PlaceLab Participant 3. Clearly, even in this single hour, a variety of complex activity is observed. This same hour contains (as tabulated by one of our researchers) the following activities: learning behavior (using a new appliance), planning behavior (making lists), searching behavior (looking in cabinets), gesturing (purposeful and not), communication impacting behavior (talking on phone and pacing), and use of a large and diverse set of household objects. This high density of "interesting" activities in a single hour suggests that they will be quite common throughout typical PlaceLab datasets with multiple day or week stays. Although techniques such as ethnography could be used to learn more about such activities, those methods do not provide multi-modal datasets synchronized with specific examples.

Our experiences running PlaceLab studies and examining our preliminary datasets suggest that living laboratories can generate rich, multi-modal sensor datasets of activity in the home setting unlike those that can be acquired using other methods. Our group will be using the PlaceLab for studies on the development and evaluation of context detection and context-aware technologies. However, we believe that the facility can be used as a shared resource and that the data it generates will become more useful as more researchers use it in their own work. We will continue to improve the facility, our experimental methods, and the quality of the datasets we produce.

7 Conclusion

The technical and administrative complexity of building and operating this kind of residential living laboratory is great, and we therefore expect the number of living laboratories available to ubiquitous computing researchers to be small. However, our pilot testing has already created datasets that we could not have obtained in any other way. These datasets are a detailed record of home behavior synchronized with sensor data that simplifies the annotation of and searching for items of interest and can be used for context-detection algorithm development and evaluation. We believe that living laboratories can provide valuable datasets for the ubiquitous computing research community, and in that spirit we have described our facility and the type of data it can generate. We are making example data available to the community with the hope that researchers will report how they might use the data in their own work and what additional information would be beneficial. The PlaceLab is not intended to replace other ethnographic research tools and sensor data collection methods, but rather to fill a gap. Living laboratories may become increasingly important as researchers begin to migrate ubiquitous computing technologies from the traditional laboratory into actual homes.

Acknowledgements

This work was supported, in part, by National Science Foundation ITR grant #0313065. The PlaceLab is a joint initiative between the MIT House_n Consortium and TIAX, LLC. The authors would like to thank Kenan Sahin, Tyson Lawrence, and other employees of TIAX for their support on PlaceLab development and operation, the anonymous reviewers for thoughtful comments, and the PlaceLab participants for sharing their everyday life activities.

References

[1] G. D. Abowd and E. D. Mynatt, "Charting past, present, and future research in ubiquitous computing," *ACM Transactions on Computer-Human Interaction*, vol. 7, pp. 29-58, 2000.

[2] A. A. Stone, S. Shiffman, J. E. Schwartz, J. E. Broderick, and M. R. Hufford, "Patient non-compliance with paper diaries," *BMJ*, vol. 324, pp. 1193-4, 2002.

[3] A. A. Gorin and A. A. Stone, "Recall biases and cognitive errors in retrospective self reports: A call for momentary assessments," in *Handbook of Health Psychology*, A. Baum, T. Revenson, and J. Singer, Eds. Mahwah, NJ: Erlbaum, 2001, pp. 405-413.

[4] C. D. Kidd, R. J. Orr, G. D. Abowd, C. G. Atkeson, I. A. Essa, B. MacIntyre, E. Mynatt, T. E. Starner, and W. Newstetter, "The Aware Home: A living laboratory for ubiquitous computing research," in *Proceedings of the Second International Workshop on Cooperative Buildings - CoBuild'99*, 1999.

[5] K. Matsouoka, "Smart house understanding human behaviors: Who did what, where, and when," *Proceedings of the 8th World Multi-Conference on Systems, Cybernetics, and Informatics*, vol. 3, pp. 181-185, 2004.

[6] E. Munguia Tapia, S. S. Intille, L. Lopez, and K. Larson, "The design of a portable kit of wireless sensors for naturalistic data collection," in *Proceedings of PERVASIVE 2006*. Berlin: Springer-Verlag, 2006.

[7] S. S. Intille, J. Rondoni, C. Kukla, I. Anacona, and L. Bao, "A context-aware experience sampling tool," in *Proceedings of CHI '03 Extended Abstracts on Human Factors in Computing Systems*. New York, NY: ACM Press, 2003, pp. 972-973.

[8] S. S. Intille, K. Larson, J. S. Beaudin, J. Nawyn, E. Munguia Tapia, and P. Kaushik, "A living laboratory for the design and evaluation of ubiquitous computing interfaces," in *Extended Abstracts of the 2005 Conference on Human Factors in Computing Systems*. New York, NY: ACM Press, 2005, pp. 1941 - 1944.

[9] Q. Tran, G. Calcaterra, and E. Mynatt, "Cook's Collage: memory aid display for cooking," in *Proceedings of HOIT 2005*, 2005.

[10] S. L. Dockstader, M. J. Berg, and A. M. Tekalp, "Stochastic kinematic modeling and feature extraction for gait analysis," *IEEE Transactions on Image Processing*, vol. 12, pp. 962-976, 2003.

[11] D. H. Wilson and C. Atkeson, "Simultaneous Tracking & Activity Recognition (STAR) Using Many Anonymous, Binary Sensors," in *Proceedings of PERVASIVE 2005*. Berlin Heidelberg: Springer-Verlag, 2005.

[12] E. Munguia Tapia, S. S. Intille, and K. Larson, "Activity recognition in the home setting using simple and ubiquitous sensors," in *Proceedings of PERVASIVE 2004*, vol. LNCS 3001, F. Mattern, Ed. Berlin: Springer-Verlag, 2004, pp. 158-175.

[13] M. Philipose, K. P. Fishkin, M. Perkowitz, D. J. Patterson, D. Fox, H. Kautz, and D. Hähnel, "Inferring activities from interactions with objects," *IEEE Pervasive Computing*, vol. 3, pp. 50-57, 2004.

[14] M. C. Mozer, "An intelligent environment must be adaptive," *IEEE Intelligent Systems*, pp. 11-13, 1999.

[15] J. Fields, "America's Families and Living Arrangements: 2003," U.S. Census Bureau, Washington, DC, Current Population Reports, P20-553 November 2004.

Appendix: PlaceLab Infrastructure

In this section additional details of the PlaceLab's technical infrastructure are described.

Initial Fit-Out and Wiring

Prior to the installation of the custom-designed PlaceLab cabinetry, an extensive home-run wiring infrastructure was embedded behind the drywall by professional installers. Coaxial and CAT6 cables run from patch panels in the server closet directly to each of the cabinets, where gangs of coaxial and RJ45 outlets are installed in the drywall. The heads of the cabinets cover these outlets, providing researchers with easy access to hidden, robust commercial plug connections (Fig. 4a). Over a mile of coaxial and CAT6 cable run in the wall cavities. Although the coaxial wiring is insulated and the CAT6 wiring is twisted pair, we were concerned that electrical interference might compromise the PlaceLab systems. In practice, this has not been a problem.

To accommodate unanticipated wiring needs, plastic conduit (1 inch diameter, the largest possible given other wiring bundles) was run from the server room to each of the cabinet locations (Fig. 4b). We have already used the conduit on multiple occasions to add special sensors (e.g. wireless receivers). A cable television and Internet network was also installed for the resident, which operates independently of the research systems.

Cabinet Wiring and Sensors

Within the head of each of the 15 cabinets is a Dallas Semiconductor TINI networked microcontroller (DSTINIS400 with 2MB SRAM for data and 2MB of flash ROM for application storage and DSTINIM400 evaluation socket). This board runs (TINI OS and TINI SDK 1.12), a Java virtual machine with an API for 1-wire sensor operation. The 1-wire sensor network driven by the TINI board was chosen as an affordable, extensible, and robust architecture allowing data from many sensors (typically 30) in a single cabinet unit to be sent via TCP/IP to control computers aggregating and time stamping data. The 1-wire network uses a single wire (plus ground) to accomplish both communication and power transmission at speeds of 16kbps and 142 kbps.

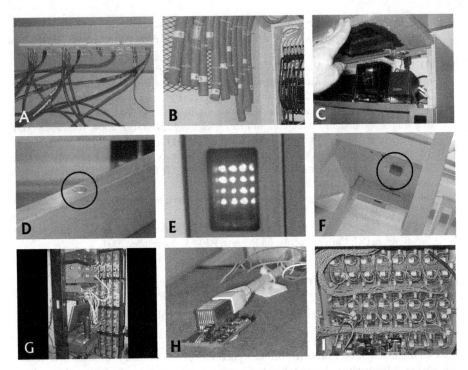

Fig. 4. A) Professionally-installed coaxial and CAT6 wires terminate in gangs of outlets inside the heads of cabinets; B) Some of the 30 conduits running to all cabinetry; C) The head (shown), foot, and side channels of all cabinets open for sensor maintenance and upgrades; D) Every sensor was installed with attention to detail so that sensors would be robust and inconspicuous; switch sensors are embedded in the wood; E) The black acrylic covers many sensor types; here an infrared emitter is shown (invisible to the naked eye); emitters are scattered throughout the cabinetry; F) Wireless movement detection sensors can be placed on objects of interest, here on a chair; G) All data are sent to the server closet where 20 PCs process and synchronize all data streams; H) Custom boards were developed for some sensor types so that they can be rapidly plugged into the 1-wire network in each cabinet with a single RJ45 connection; each sensor has a unique ID; I) 37 current sensors near the circuit breaker monitor each of the circuits in the apartment

The head, sides, and foot of each cabinet, which are locked when participants live in the PlaceLab, can hinge open to reveal the sensor infrastructure, making it easy to add new sensors when needed (Fig. 4c). The 1-wire network typically uses a RJ11 connector and modular telephone cable, however after experiencing problems with noise in a prototype cabinet, we modified all sensors to use high-quality RJ45 connectors and CAT6 cable. CAT6 cable in convenient, short lengths can also be readily obtained. A single CAT6 cable runs from the TINI board throughout the cabinet, splitting once at each sensor. CAT6 splitters are not manufactured commercially and so our group produced approximately 400 of such splitters. Further, we were adding so many sensors to the network that a small circuit needed to be designed to simplify sensor installation. This board allowed up to two reed magnet contact switches to be attached to the 1-wire network by simply plugging in a CAT6 cable. Each 1-wire device has its unique ID, however, an additional ID was burned into the EEPROM memory of sensors using ADCs (DS2438) such as light, humidity, current and flow to differentiate among them (to avoid requiring control code to have a look-up table matching IDs with sensor types, which is problematic to maintain when sensors are moved/replaced). Similar circuits were also designed for light sensors, humidity sensors, barometric pressure sensors, flow sensors, and current sensors (Fig. 4h). Commercial 1-wire temperature sensors were purchased and hand-wired to connect directly to RJ45 wires. In some cases, short wires run from the circuit boards in the cabinetry channels to the actual sensors. For example, reed switches and magnets were carefully installed in 80 cabinets and appliances so that they were not visible and would be protected from damage during heavy use (Fig. 4d).

To minimize cabling that needed to be run in the cabinet side channels, the same CAT6 cable used for 1-wire communication in the cabinet is used to provide 5V and 12V power. When a sensor needs power, a splitter can be used and a hand-made CAT6-to-power-connector cable. This is how 85 custom-made IR illuminator boards are powered, which provide some illumination to each room even in total darkness for the IR cameras (Fig. 4e). Java code on the TINI board repetitively polls each of the sensors and reports their state back to a control computer. Overall, we have found the distributed TINI boards and 1-wire networks to be a reliable and affordable way to gather input from the wired digital and analog sensors in the apartment.

The 18 video cameras are located in the heads of cabinets or above counter surfaces and can be easily moved between studies to any part of the apartment (Fig. 4c). The IR cameras are behind visible light filter acrylic. The color cameras are behind clear acrylic that appears black from the living spaces because each camera is housed in an encasement that blocks/absorbs light. The cameras feed directly to the coaxial outlets.

Nineteen of the cabinets are outfitted to provide localized audio input and output. Small electret microphones flush-mounted in the cabinet side rails have been distributed throughout the apartment to provide complete coverage, including both washrooms. At each cabinet, a pre-amplifier boosts the signal to line-level to prevent electromagnetic crossover from adjacent 1-wire cabling. Input is run over the coaxial cables to distributing amplifiers in the server room.

Audio output is provided by commercial multimedia speaker systems that include two satellite speakers mounted behind acrylic grills in the head of each cabinet. A subwoofer is located at the foot of the cabinet. A custom RJ-45 to 3.5mm stereo headphone jack adapter allows audio to be carried over the structured cabling from the server room, where the specific output locations are selected by a matrix switcher.

Server "Closet" and Synchronization of Data

Inaccessible to PlaceLab volunteers is a 40 sq. ft. closet in the office that has been converted to the server room. This space is designed for sound attenuation and is cooled by an air conditioning unit. All data are processed by a bank of 20 2GHz PCs with running Windows XP. A key challenge has been to synchronize all data sources.

Each of the 18 video streams and 19 audio streams feed into a Kramer 1x3 video and audio amplifier/splitter and then into a particular computer. Each of the AV streams also feed into a Kramer Electronics 32x32 AV matrix switcher. Eighteen of the computers run Java code that digitizes incoming video and runs image differencing software –

computing degree of motion. Another computer that integrates reports across the 18 cameras and, using heuristics about camera placement, selects the 4 views most likely to be informative at that moment. The computer routes the 4 best views using the matrix switcher into a video multiplexer in quad mode, to generate an image such as that in Fig. 3. That image stream is sent to a control computer that digitizes and saves the video in Indeo 5.0 AVI format, with a special timestamp file.[1] The timestamp corresponds to the master PlaceLab time on the primary data archiving computer and allows for synching with other data sources later even though the video capture frame rate tends to vary with scene complexity. One of the 19 microphones is also selected, based upon the location of microphones and the primary area of motion. In practice, the microphones are extremely sensitive, and activity is generally audible as long as a microphone is on the side of the apartment near the person. The designated microphone output is switched via the matrix switcher into the computer saving the video. Video and audio are therefore automatically synchronized. The PlaceLab is currently optimized to record one participant, but actually does a reasonable job capturing activity from two. Even a single microphone can capture audio from different spaces in the apartment, and the selected microphone input switches between spaces. The infrastructure is flexible, however, so that recording of an additional audio stream (or even *all* audio streams) could easily be done with the addition of more disk space.

The data archiving computer receives data from all the TINI microcontrollers in the cabinets and immediately timestamps it and saves it to a large external disk in a logical file structure, by sensor type, day, and hour. The video and audio is saved to this same disk, in 1-hour segments with the added frame synchronization information. All data from TINI boards is synchronized once it arrives via the network at the archiving computer. In practice, the 1-wire network and TINI board introduces a latency of up to 3 seconds for many switch sensors, discussed later in this section.

Six of the computers, in addition to processing video, process data from the wireless MITes receivers, which are connected by cable home runs to the serial port. These machines filter each individual receiver data stream and remove duplicate events recorded by multiple receivers. Real-time limb motion data are saved, as well as data from object motion detectors (hundreds possible) and a wireless HR monitor.

In summary, the PlaceLab saves video (best 4 streams at 320 by 240 pixel resolution each) and audio (16kHz, 8-bit, mono stream from microphone close to activity) synchronized with 358 streams of other data. In a typical 24-hour period, approximately 24 GB of data are generated and conveniently saved onto a large portable disk drive that is picked up by a researcher at the conclusion of a multi-day study.

Latency
Although all PlaceLab data are synchronized, we have experienced latency in the 1-wire sensors. This results from our decision to use Java code on TINI microprocessors, which turns out to be slow (up to 200 ms) when querying an analog sensor. Consequently, the

---

[1] As researchers outside of our group began to look at the test datasets, we realized that reliance on a particular video codec was problematic both when attempting to keep data synchronized and when others tried to view/use it. Newer PlaceLab datasets save static images at a high sampling rate with short synchronized audio to simplify the sharing and annotation of data.

Java code cannot continuously poll analog sensors without introducing latency for digital switches. Until recently, the software was setup to continually poll switch sensors and only poll most analog sensors (current flow, water flow, temperature) once per minute. We have recently removed this limitation by replacing most of the TINI boards with direct 1-wire connections to the PCs in the control closet. In new datasets, latency of these sensors has been reduced to less than 100 ms.

Maintenance

The PlaceLab is a true live-in laboratory, and ideally during studies there is little or no contact between researchers and participants. There is no researcher at the site when a study is being run, and to protect the data from being compromised, we decided to physically disconnect the sensor infrastructure from the Internet during times when the unit is occupied.

In practice, it has become necessary to relax this design decision to allow for some system monitoring during a study in case a key piece of equipment malfunctions. We have therefore added a single special-purpose serial cable that connects the researcher infrastructure to a computer on the residential network (but in the server closet). That computer, the sentinel, sends an hourly report on PlaceLab systems to the researchers running a study. Each sensor in the PlaceLab, including wireless sensors, sends an "alive" ping to the archiving computer at least once per hour. The sentinel emails reports indicating whether all systems are functional as well as any anomalous values that might be cause for concern. It does not report any information about the participant's actual activity.

The sentinel has proved invaluable both for debugging PlaceLab systems as well as for protecting the system from damage. For example, a recent storm when the PlaceLab was not occupied resulted in the air conditioning unit that cools the server closet malfunctioning. Our team identified the problem within a few hours and shutdown the PlaceLab systems when a temperature of 90+ degrees was reported for the server closet. The PlaceLab can recover from power failures and runs continuously.

The Diet-Aware Dining Table: Observing Dietary Behaviors over a Tabletop Surface

Keng-hao Chang[1], Shih-yen Liu[2], Hao-hua Chu[1,3], Jane Yung-jen Hsu[1,3],
Cheryl Chen[4], Tung-yun Lin[3], Chieh-yu Chen[1], and Polly Huang[5]

[1] Department of Computer Science and Information Engineering
[2] Department of Information Management
[3] Graduate Institute of Networking and Multimedia
[4] School and Graduate Institute of Nursing
[5] Department of Electrical Engineering,
National Taiwan University
r93018@csie.ntu.edu.tw, b90701219@ntu.edu.tw,
{hchu, yjhsu}@csie.ntu.edu.tw, cheryl.chen@ha.mc.ntu.edu.tw,
{r94944009, r94054}@csie.ntu.edu.tw, phuang@cc.ee.ntu.edu.tw

Abstract. We are what we eat. Our everyday food choices affect our long-term and short-term health. In the traditional health care, professionals assess and weigh each individual's dietary intake using intensive labor at high cost. In this paper, we design and implement a diet-aware dining table that can track what and how much we eat. To enable automated food tracking, the dining table is augmented with two layers of weighing and RFID sensor surfaces. We devise a weight-RFID matching algorithm to detect and distinguish how people eat. To validate our diet-aware dining table, we have performed experiments, including live dining scenarios (afternoon tea and Chinese-style dinner), multiple dining participants, and concurrent activities chosen randomly. Our experimental results have shown encouraging recognition accuracy, around 80%. We believe monitoring the dietary behaviors of individuals potentially contribute to diet-aware healthcare.

1 Introduction

Our dietary habits affect our health in many ways. Research [12] has confirmed that dietary habits are important factors for healthy living and have profound impacts on many chronic illnesses. The vast majority of the population has chronic illnesses [4] such as heart disease, diabetes, hypertension, dyslipidemia, and obesity. A recent Surgeon General Report indicated that approximately 300,000 U.S. deaths are associated with obesity and overweight each year. The total cost attributed to overweight and obesity amounts to $117 billion in 2000. Proper dietary intake and related interventions are effective in ameliorating symptoms and improving health [5][12][13].

Nutritious dietary is one of the most accessible means for people to prevent illness and to promote well-being [5]. Unlike traditional healthcare in which professionals assess and weigh one's dietary intake and then develop a plan for behavioral changes, ubiquitous healthcare technologies provide an opportunity for individuals effortlessly to quantify and acknowledge their dietary [5][6] intake. For example, at home patients

K.P. Fishkin et al. (Eds.): PERVASIVE 2006, LNCS 3968, pp. 366–382, 2006.
© Springer-Verlag Berlin Heidelberg 2006

face the cumbersome need to record everything they eat, a task which can take a minimum of 15-20 minutes per day [2]. Ubiquitous computing technologies provide a means for individuals to proactively monitor their intake and act upon it, leading to better food selection and more sensible eating.

This paper proposes a diet-aware dining table that automatically tracks what and how much each individual eats over the course of a meal. This is in accord with the *vision of disappearing computers* [15], where computing hardware (HW) & software (SW) are hidden into everyday object (i.e., dining table) and remain *invisible* to human users. There are *no* digital access devices (such as cell phones, PDAs, or PCs) needed in order for human users to interact with this digital dietary service. In comparison, traditional dietary tracking software requires human users to recall the amount of food consumed, and then manually enter the data. This is less precise due to mistakes in visual measurement and imperfect memory. More importantly, the traditional method requires explicit human effort to operate digital devices.

We have augmented a dining table with two layers of *sensor surfaces* underneath – the *RFID (Radio Frequency Identification) surface* and the *weighing surface*. By combining the RFID and weighing surfaces, our system can trace the complete *food movement path* from its tabletop container source to other containers, and eventually to the individual. To validate our diet-aware dining table, we have performed experiments, including live dining scenarios (afternoon tea and Chinese-style dinner), multiple dining participants, and concurrent activities chosen randomly. Our experimental results have shown encouraging recognition accuracy around 80%, which is as good as the 80% accuracy of the traditional dietary assessment methods [3].

Fig. 1. Typical Chinese dining table setting

Our diet-aware dining table supports multiple people sharing a meal on the same dining table. Fig. 1 shows a typical meal setting for a Chinese family – the family members sit around a circular table with the main dishes placed in the center. Individual rice bowls and plates are arranged on the table periphery. Participants first use shared utensils to transfer food servings from the main dishes to their personal plates or rice bowls, and then eat from there. In this dining scenario, multiple table participants are *continuously* and *concurrently* engaging in food transferring and eating motions. This creates *multiple, concurrent person-object interactions* (objects are tabletop objects such as plates, bowls, etc.) from which a single table surface needs to observe, track, and then infer high level interaction semantics. This is the *main technical challenge* addressed in this paper – how to design a sensor-embedded tabletop surface to track food consumption from each of many table participants.

The remainder of this paper is organized as follows. Section 2 states the design choices, assumptions, and limitations. Section 3 presents our design and implementation. Section 4 describes the experimental set-up and results. Section 5 describes the related work. Finally, Section 6 draws our conclusion and future work.

2 Design Choices, Assumptions, and Limitations

Although the ultimate design objective is to create a *restriction-free,* automated dietary-tracking system that can achieve both *high accuracy* and *precision*, this is a grand challenge requiring extensive future research efforts [9]. We acknowledge this fact, and consider our dietary-tracking system as an early effort to address this problem. Since our work is not yet a perfect solution, we need to state our assumptions, present our design rational, and discuss our design limitations.

2.1 Why RFID and Weighing Surfaces?

Our diet-aware dining table tracks tabletop interactions such as transferring food among containers and eating food by an individual. To correctly infer individuals' dietary behaviors from their tabletop interactions, our system needs to track how much (weight) and what food items are involved in these interactions. To observe these interactions, a weighing surface and a RFID surface are embedded into an ordinary dining table. Assume that food items are correctly labeled by the RFID tags on food containers, the surface can then be used to identify these RFID-tagged containers. Furthermore, the RFID surface can obtain nutritional information such as calorie count by looking up a food label database indexed by RFID code.

This assumption raises a question as to who would perform the work of inputting the food information for the RFID tags into the database. Three possible scenarios apply: (1) prepared foods (e.g., microwave-ready) are purchased from supermarkets are heated and then placed on the dining table with their original containers and packages containing RFID tags. This is applicable to people who subscribe to a weight-loss dietary program; (2) when the food containers (dishes) are first placed on the dining table, the table explicitly asks users for the food contents through a natural, easy-to-input UI, such as speech interface; and (3) when food is prepared in the kitchen, the cooking person can input the food's content as the food is placed in a serving container.

The weighing surface is used to measure (1) the amount of food transferred across different tabletop containers, as servings of food are transferred between different tabletop containers, and (2) the amount of food consumed by an individual, as personal plates lose weight. More details on how the weight measurements are used to detect food transfer and food consumption events are described in Section 3.

2.2 Complex and Concurrent Interactions Involving Multiple Tabletop Objects

In a typical family meal setting, there are multiple people dining together on a dining table, and table needs to track multiple, concurrent person-object interactions. In an afternoon tea scenario, if one person is pouring tea to a cup while another one is eating cake, it is impossible to use a single weighing surface to distinguish the amount of tea weight transfer to the cup vs. the amount of cake weight lost through a person's consumption. This scenario is shown in Fig. 2-(a). This is also called the *single-cell-concurrent-interactions* problem where it is impossible to distinguish multiple, concurrent person-object interactions over a single surface using the weight information from only one sensor[1]. To address this problem, our solution is to divide the tabletop surface into multiple cells, shown in Fig. 2-(b). When the size of each cell is small enough, it is likely that each tabletop object occupies a different cell. Therefore, our solution uses multiple weighing sensors at different cells to distinguish the weight-change of the tea cup from the weight-change of the cake plate. This idea is generalized as follows: the larger the size of each weighing cell relative to the average size of objects, the higher the likelihood that multiple, concurrent person-object interactions can occur within the same cell, therefore the higher the probability of single-cell-concurrent interactions. To reduce this probability, we divide the weighing surface into cells of an appropriate size that just fit the average size of tabletop food containers, such as plates, bowls, etc.

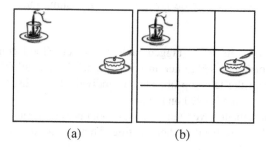

(a)   (b)

Fig. 2. Surface structure [This illustrates that a multi-cells surface (b) can track multiple person-object interactions whereas a single-cell surface (a) cannot]

Where *single-cell-concurrent-interactions problem* still occurs, we introduce *common sense semantics* to discern the amount of weight-changes in these concurrent interactions. Consider the situation where a cup and a plate are placed at the same cell X at the same time. When a user pours tea from a tea pot to a cup (leading to weight increase at cell X), we can correctly infer the tea is transferred to a cup rather than to a plate by using common sense in normal dining behavior.

Also, relying only on a weighing surface (i.e., without RFID surface) is insufficient to identify tabletop objects. Distinguishing a tabletop object by its weight is difficult, given that the weights of food containers change over the course of a meal as people

---

[1] In the Lancaster's approach [14], the scale is made up of four weighing sensors at four corners of a table.

transfer food servings. Therefore, we augment the weighing surface with a passive RFID surface to help identify tabletop objects. Each cell contains a RFID antenna that can read the unique IDs from RFID-tagged objects on that cell.

2.3 Intelligent Surface vs. Intelligent Containers

Early in our design, we faced a fundamental design choice between embedding intelligence into the table or into the food containers. One advantage for choosing the intelligent food containers is that they do not have the *single-cell-concurrent-interactions problem*, because each food container can weight itself and detect its own weight-change events. However, the intelligent containers approach also has many disadvantages. First, it may result in high cost since every food container must have a weight scale and wireless networking module. Second, the smart food containers require battery installments and replacements, whereas the dining table is a piece of stationary furniture that can be plugged into a wall socket. The third disadvantage is that people may buy prepared food items from restaurants that have their own disposable packages and RFID tags. It is inconvenient to have people transfer the food into the intelligent containers every time, in contrast to the convenience of putting tagged packages directly on the intelligent table.

2.4 Assumptions

From the above discussion on design choices, our assumptions for our system in this paper are:

- The dining table, its RFID-tagged tabletop objects (food containers), and table participants form a closed rather an open system. That is, all food transfers can occur only among the tabletop objects and individual mouths. External objects and food sources are not allowed on the table.
- All dining participant have their personal containers (personal plates and cups) that are usually placed in front of their seating. They are used to identify each individual user.
- Food containers must be tagged with RFID tags. We assume that weight, nutrition, and ingredients of the food, as well, as, the weight and owners of food containers are known a-priori.
- Tabletop objects are placed within each individual cell. No cross-cell objects are allowed.
- Dining participants avoid leaning their hands and elbows on the table.

3 Design and Implementation

Our system is consisted of HW & SW components. The HW component is made up of the RFID and weighing sensors embedded underneath the table surface shown in Fig. 3. The SW component is made up a rule-based system that aggregates, interprets, and infers tabletop dietary behaviors shown in Fig. 4. The HW component is described first, followed by the SW component.

Fig. 3. Embedded RFID and weighing table surfaces

3.1 Hardware Design and Implementation

Our current table prototype has a dining surface of 90x90 cm^2, which is about the size of a small dining table. To detect multiple, concurrent person-object interactions on the tabletop surface, the tabletop surface is divided into a matrix of 3x3 cells, each with the size of 30x30 cm^2, about the average size of food containers. Each cell contains a weighing sensor and a passive RFID antenna as shown in Fig. 3. The RFID reader is the i-scan MR100 made by Feig. The RFID antennas are connected to the RFID reader through a multiplexer. Each RFID antenna is positioned underneath the table surface such that it has an average, effective read rage of 3 cm above the table surface. The weighing sensor is attached to a weight indicator with a resolution of 0.5 $gram$ which can output weight readings through a serial port at a frequency of 8 samples per second.

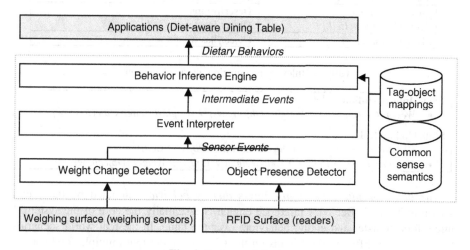

Fig. 4. System architecture

3.2 Software Design and Implementation

We have come up with a rule-based approach that applies our multi-cells weighing and RFID surfaces to detect multiple, concurrent person-object interactions. The system and inference rules are implemented in JESS rule engine [8].

The system architecture is based on a bottom-up event-triggered approach shown in Fig. 4. High level dietary behaviors, such as *pour-tea* and *eat-cake*, can be inferred by interpreting sensor *Cell-Weight* events and *RFID-Presence* events. We describe each software component as follows.

The *weight change detector* performs the following two tasks: (1) it aggregates weight samples collected from each of the 9 weighing sensors; (2) it reports *Cell-Weight* events when the weight has changed by filtering out noises in the stream of weight samples. The *object presence detector* performs similar tasks: (1) it continuously checks for presence and absence of RFID-tagged tabletop objects within each of the 9 RFID reader cells, and reports *RFID-Presence* events as long as the change happens.

The *event interpreter* interprets *intermediate events* shown in Table 1. The event interpreter builds internal states using sensor events from the weight change detector and the object presence detector, and then interprets *Weight-Change* events. Table 2 shows the rules to interpret events. For example, the *Weight-Change(Object$_i$, Δw)* event represents that the *Object$_i$*'s weight is changed by Δw, where *Object$_i$* $\in$ *{object on the table}* and *Cell$_j$* $\in$ *{cell$_{[1-9]}$}*.

Table 1. Intermediate events, sensor events, and internal states

Intermediate Events	Descriptions
Weight-Change(Object$_i$, Δw)	*Object$_i$*'s weight is changed by Δw.
Sensor Events	**Descriptions**
RFID-Presence(Object$_i$, Cell$_j$)	*Cell$_j$* detects the presence of *Object$_i$*.
Cell-Weight(w, Cell$_j$)	*Cell$_j$* measures weight *w*.
Internal State	**Descriptions**
Location(Object$_i$, Cell$_j$)	*Object$_i$* locates on *Cell$_j$*.
Weight(Object$_i$, w)	*Object$_i$* has weight *w*.

Table 2. Rules for recognizing intermediate events

Event Interpretation Rules
- *Weight(Object$_i$, w$_1$)* $\cap$ *Weight'(Object$_i$, w$_2$)* $\rightarrow$ *Weight-Change(Object$_i$, w$_2$-w$_1$)*

State Update Rules
- *RFID-Presence(Objecti1, Cellj)* $\rightarrow$ *Location(Objecti1, Cellj)*
- *Location(Objecti, Cellj)* $\cap$ *Cell-Weight(w, Cellj)* $\rightarrow$ *Weight'(Objecti, w)*

The *behavior inference engine* infers *dietary behaviors* initiated by the user *u* shown in Table 3. Behavior inference engine is essentially the core of the system. It infers food transfer and eating behaviors over the table. In the real world scenarios, there are often different food items on the table, meaning that multiple food sources can be transferred to the same personal container. For example, the weight-increase to a cup may be contributed by pouring of coke, juice, or tea from different bottles and pots. Moreover, given that there are multiple food transfer interactions happening concurrently, how does the system identify and differentiate the food being transferred from which food source container to which user's personal container?

3.2.1 Weight Matching Algorithm

To track a food movement path from the food's source containers to personal containers, we design a *weight matching algorithm*. The basic idea is to match a weight-decrease from one container to a complementary weight-increase from another container. This matching process can be thought as *a hop of food transfer* from the source food container in the center of the table, to the personal containers on the table periphery. This weight matching model is realized by maintaining a queue of recent *Weight-Change* events. When a new *Weight-Change* event is detected, our model applies a matching function to find a complementary *Weight-Change* event(s) in the waiting queue. A good match is found when the difference between the weight-decrease and the weight-increase pairs is smaller than a chosen *weight matching threshold* value (ε). This weight matching model is coded as rules in Table 3. For example, *Transfer(u, w, type)* means that a serving of cake with a weight w has been transferred from the share-plate containing food of *type* to the user u's personal plate, where *type* is obtained from RFID mappings. This behavior event can be inferred by first observing a weight decrease Δw_1 (<0) in the share-plate, followed by a matching weight increase Δw_2 on the user u's *Object$_{i2}$*. A match is found when $|\Delta w_1 + \Delta w_2| < \varepsilon$. The *tag-object mappings* provide two relations: *Contains(Object, type)* shows *Object* contains food of the type (*type*), such as cake or tea, and *Owner(Object, u)* means the owner (u) of the *Object*. In addition, *Eat* is inferred if there is a weight-decrease in any personal container.

Table 3. Inference rules for dietary behaviors

Dietary behaviors	Behavior Inference Rules
Transfer(u, w, type)	*Weight-Change(Object$_{i1}$, Δw_1)* $\cap$ *($\Delta w_1 < 0$)* $\cap$ *Weight- Change (Object$_{i2}$, Δw_2)* $\cap$ *($\Delta w_2 > 0$)* $\cap$ *Contains(Object$_{i1}$, type)* $\cap$ *Owner(Object$_{i2}$, u)* $\cap$ *($|\Delta w_1 + \Delta w_2| < \varepsilon$)* $\rightarrow$ *Transfer (u, Δw_2, type)*
Eat(u, w, type)	*Weight-Change(Object$_{i1}$, Δw)* $\cap$ *($\Delta w < 0$)* $\cap$ *Contains(Object$_i$, type)* $\cap$ *Owner(Object$_i$, u)* $\rightarrow$ *Eat(u, $-\Delta w$, type)*

In real world scenarios, there are special, complex interactions that require matching among three or more events. For examples, a person may pour tea from a tea pot to two cups within one continuous motion, or another person may transfer soup from a soup bowl to a personal bowl through multiple scoops. These two examples can be mapped to (1) the amount of one weight decrease matches with the sum of multiple weight increases, or (2) the amount of one weight increase matches with the sum of multiple weight decreases. To address this issue, the weight matching algorithm is extended to match more than two weight transfer events.

3.2.2 Common Sense Semantics

Although dividing the table into cells can reduce the probability of multiple objects on one cell, the situation mentioned in Section 2.2 may still happen. To address this situation, we add *common sense semantics* to extend the inference routines that can disambiguate the multi-objects on one cell problem. For example, if there are one *cup* and one *plate* on the same cell, and the user pours tea from the *pot* to the *cup*; the *Weight-Change* event of *{cup, plate}* will be reported by the *Event Interpreter*.

According to the common sense, tea should be poured into the cup rather than the plate. Therefore, the *behavior inference engine* matches the weight-decrease of the *pot* to weight-increase of *{cup, plate}* and generates *Transfer(pot, cup, w)* behavior.

4 Experimental Set-Up and Results

We have conducted several experiments to evaluate the accuracy of our dietary tracking table under different dining scenarios. The evaluation metric, *weight accuracy,* measures how well the system can correctly recognize the amount of weight from different food items consumed by the dining participants. It is determined by how well the system can correctly recognize the high-level dietary behaviors: specifically the food *transfer* event and *eat* event. Therefore, the intermediate evaluation metric, *behavior accuracy,* is listed as well. Note that both behaviors are associated with attributes defined in Table 3. The *transfer* event has three attributes (source object, destination object, weight), whereas the *eat* event also has three attributes (user, source object, weight). Correct event recognition is defined as the event's attributes, except the weight attribute, are correctly identified. Since the weight measurements have inherent sensor errors, they are evaluated separately. Specifically, the behavior accuracy is the number of behaviors recognized divided by the number of behaviors conducted by participants. The weight accuracy is the sum of measured weight divided by the sum of actual weight corresponding to dietary behaviors.

The experiments involve three participants. The first two participants are graduate students from our research team who are familiar with our system. The third participant is a graduate student from our department, who is not familiar with our system.

Dining Scenarios (# participants, predefined vs. random activity sequences)
We have designed four different dining scenarios. The varying parameters are (1) the number of dining participants and (2) whether dietary behaviors are *predefined* or *random*. As the number of dining participants increases, we expect that they will generate higher number of non-overlapping and concurrent events. Predefined activities mean that the dining participants repeat some pre-arranged sequences of dietary steps which we expect in normal dietary behaviors. The predefined activities may include both sequential and concurrent activities. The exact activity sequences depend on the dining settings described in later subsections. Random activities mean that the dining participants are more or less free to follow their natural eating behaviors within the assumptions of our system defined in Section 2.4.

Dining Settings (afternoon tea vs. dinner)
There are two dining settings: an *afternoon tea* setting and a Chinese-style *dinner* setting. The dinner setting is more complex than the afternoon tea setting since it involves a larger number of food containers. We describe these two settings in more details as follows. In the afternoon-tea scenario, participant(s) enjoyed an afternoon tea with a cake, a pot of tea, sugar, and milk. The objects (food containers) on the intelligent table are shown in Fig. 5-(a), including a tea pot, a cake plate, a sugar jar, a milk creamer, personal cake plates, and tea cups. The personal cake plates and tea cups are placed on the cells in front of each participant. The cake plate is placed on one center cell. The tea pot, the sugar jar, and the milk creamer are placed together on

another center cell. Possible high-level dietary behaviors are *transferring-cake (to a personal plate), pouring-tea (to a personal cup), eating-cake (from a personal plate),* and *drinking-tea (from a personal cup).* In the dinner scenario, three dining participants enjoyed a sumptuous dinner with three shared dishes, one shared soup bowl, and a shared rice bowl. The objects (food containers) on the table are shown in Fig. 6-(a), including these shared plates & bowls, as well as personal bowls located on cells in front of each of three participants. Possible high-level dietary behaviors are *transferring-food (to a personal bowl)* and *eating-food (from a personal bowl).* Note that given the weight and type of the food items consumed, it is relatively straight-forward to compute the calorie count by looking up a nutritional table for these food items.

(a)   (b)

Fig. 5. Afternoon tea scenario showing the placements of table objects and participants

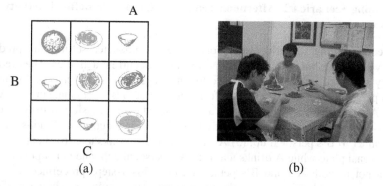

(a)   (b)

Fig. 6. Chinese-style dinner scenario showing the placements of table objects and participants

We describe the result for each of four dining scenarios as follows. A summary of their experiment results are shown in Table 4.

4.1 Dining Scenario #1: Afternoon Tea – Single User – Predefined Activity Sequence

The first dining scenario involves the afternoon tea setting, single user, and predefined activity sequence. The predefined activity sequence is consisted of the following steps: (1) cut a piece of cake and transfer it to the personal plate; (2) pour tea from the tea pot to the personal cup; (3) add milk to the personal cup from the creamer; (4) eat the piece of cake from the personal plate; (5) drink tea from the personal cup; and (6) add sugar to the personal cup from the sugar jar. This 6-steps sequence is repeated twice during the experiment. The results are shown in Table 4. Based on our measurements, the dietary behavior's recognition accuracy (i.e., transfer & eat events) is 100%. This result is expected, given that the predefined activity sequence has been anticipated and tested extensively during our prototyping. In addition, this scenario involves only a single user with no concurrent interactions.

Table 4. Experimental results for 4 dining scenarios & their recognition accuracy

Scenarios			Event Statistics		Results	
Dining Scenarios	# of users	Activity Sequence	Time Duration (seconds)	# of Dietary Behavior	Dietary Behavior Recognition Accuracy	Dietary Weight Recognition Accuracy
#1 Afternoon tea	1	Predefined	73	12	100%	-
#2 Afternoon tea	2	Predefined	162	24	100%	-
#3 Afternoon tea	2	Random	913	78	79.49%	-
#4 Chinese style dinner	3	Random	1811	162	83.33%	82.62%

4.2 Dining Scenario #2: Afternoon Tea – Two Users – Predefined Activity Sequence

The second dining scenario also involves the afternoon tea setting and predefined activity sequence, but with two users performing concurrent activities. The predefined activity sequence is consisted of the following steps: (1) A cuts cake and transfers it to A's personal plate; (2) B pours tea from the tea pot to B's personal cup; (3) A pours tea to A's personal cup while B cuts a piece of cake and transfers it to B's personal plate; (4) A adds sugar from the sugar jar to A's personal cup while B adds milk from the creamer to B's personal up; (5) A eats cake and B drinks tea; (6) B eats cake from B's personal plate while A drinks tea from A's personal cup; and (7) A pours tea from the tea pot to both A's and B's personal cups. This 7-steps predefined activity sequence is repeated twice during the experiment. The results are shown in Table 4. Based on our measurements, the dietary behavior recognition accuracy is 100%. This result shows that our table is accurate in recognizing concurrent activities from multiple participants.

4.3 Dining Scenario #3: Afternoon Tea – Two Users – Random Activities

The third dining scenario involves the afternoon tea setting and two users, but with random dietary activities. Random activities mean that the table participants are more or less free to perform any impromptu dietary behaviors for 913 seconds over the table within the bound of our assumptions described in Section 2.4. The results are shown in Table 4. Based on our measurements, the recognition accuracy is 79.49%. Table 5 shows the recognition accuracy for each of the two dietary behaviors. The eat events have better recognition accuracy than the transfer events, because they can be directly deduced by personal container's *Weight-Change* event.

To determine the causes for the misses in activity recognition, we videotaped the afternoon tea scenario. By analyzing the video in combination with the system event logs, we derive four main *leading causes* shown in Table 6. They are described as follows.

Table 5. The accuracy of activity recognition under afternoon tea scenario

Dietary Behavior	# of Actual Events	Recognition Accuracy
Transfer event	41	70.73%
Eat event	37	89.19%

(c1) *Event interference within the weighing cell's weight stabilization time*: for activities such as putting down an object on the table, it takes about 1.5 seconds for our weighing sensor to output a stable weight value. If two events occur on the same cell and their time interval is less than the weighing cell's stabilization time, our system cannot differentiate these two *Weight-Change* events. Instead, our system will incorrectly recognize them as a single *Weight-Change* event. Consider the case where user A puts down the tea pot at cell X while user B immediately (within 1.5 seconds) grabs a sugar cube from the sugar jar on the same cell X. There are actually two *Weight-Change* events of amount (Δw_1) and of amount $(-\Delta w_2)$. However, due to two events interfering with each other within the weight stabilization time, our system can only detect one erroneous *Weight-Change* event of amount $|\Delta w_1 - \Delta w_2|$.

Table 6. Causes of miss recognition in afternoon tea scenario #3. There are 78 activities analyzed from the video log. The number of misses counts both false positives and false negatives.

Causes of misses	# of misses of transfer events	# of misses of eat events	Total
(c1) Event interference within the weighing cell's weight stabilization time	6	2	8
(c2) Weight matching threshold	2	0	2
(c3) (c3) Slow RFID sample rate	3	0	3
(c4) Noise from weighing cell	1	2	3
Total of misses	12	4	16

(c2) *Weight matching threshold*: the current threshold value is set to be four grams to filter out noises in the weight readings from weighing cells. However, in some cases, such as transferring one cube of sugar, this threshold value may still be too large. As a result, it may lead to false weight matching involving unrelated weight transfers of similar amounts. Consider the example that user A is removing a cube of sugar from the sugar jar. This results in a *Weight-Change* of approximately four grams in the sugar jar. At the same time, user B is transferring food weighted approximately eight grams. Eight grams is twice as much as four grams, but they are still within the weight matching threshold. Therefore, this leads to false weight matching. To address this issue, we may change the weight matching threshold to be a percentage of transferred weight rather than an absolute value of four grams.

(c3) *Slow RFID sample rate*: we have found cases when a user picks up a cup and quickly puts it down. This interval is less than the amount of time the RFID reader performs one round of reading over nine antennas. Therefore, a *Weight-Change* event is generated without any corresponding RFID-Presence event. This leads to false inference.

(c4) *Noises from weighing cells*: although we ask users not to touch the table, some still do during the experiment out of personal habits. This leads to erroneous generation of *Weight-Change* events.

4.4 Dining Scenario #4: Chinese-Style Dinner – Three Users – Random Activities

The fourth dining scenario involves the Chinese-style dinner setting, three users, and random dietary activities for 1811 seconds. Similar to the third scenario, three participants perform impromptu dietary behaviors within the bound of our assumptions described in Section 2.4. The results are shown in Table 4. Based on our measurements, the recognition accuracy is 83.33%. Note that increasing number of table participants only slightly increases the activity rate. The reason is that as the number of table participants increases, out of politeness they try to go the dishes less frequently to avoid *in-the-air conflicts* over the dishes.

Table 7 shows the recognition accuracy (for the transfer and eat events) and weight accuracy for each of dietary behaviors. The weight accuracy is computed as the ratio between the *measured* and the *actual* weight transferred or consumed during dietary behaviors. Both the recognition and weight accuracy for the food transferring behaviors are between 80~85%, except for dish A, which is fluid-covered food. The reason for lower accuracy on transferring fluid-covered food is that juices from the fluid-covered food can easily drip from the chopsticks during food transfer (from a very lousy chopstick user). The juice dripping leads to erroneous generation of *Weight-Change* events with both positive and negative values, causing mismatches in the weight matching algorithm. Furthermore, the weight accuracy of transferring dish A is low at 68.42%, because these transfer recognition misses can accumulate to a large weight sum. Similar to the afternoon tea scenario, the eat events have better recognition accuracy because they can be directly deduced from the personal container's *Weight-Change* event.

Table 7. The accuracy of the Chinese-style dinner scenario #4

Dietary Behavior	# of times	Recognition Accuracy	Weight Accuracy
Transfer dish A events	19	73.68%	68.42%
Transfer dish B events	29	79.31%	78.75%
Transfer dish C events	23	82.61%	79.19%
Transfer rice events	12	83.33%	81.88%
Transfer soup events	19	84.21%	80.16%
Eat events	60	88.33%	91.23%
Overall	162	83.33%	82.62%

To determine the causes for the misses in activity recognition, we videotaped the Chinese-style dinner scenario and analyzed the video in combination with the system event logs. We derive five main *leading causes* shown in Table 8. They are described as follows.

(c1) *Segmented Weight-Change events*: during a lousy food transfer where a user drops a part of food back into the container or on the table, the weight matching algorithm fails because of the difference between weight change values of the container and the personal plate.

(c2) *Eating before transferring food on personal containers*: this occurs when a user picks up a serving of food from a shared plate. However, before the user completes the transfer to his/her personal plate, he/she eats a bite of food. This violates one of our assumptions in Section 3.4 that eating must come from food in the personal plates. In this case, weight matching method fails to recognize the food transfer event due to the disappearing weight on the intermediate bite. Although the users are told about this restriction, some of them still do it out of personal habits.

(c3) *Weight matching ambiguity*: weight matching ambiguity occurs when two unrelated *Weight-Change* events of similar weight values are mismatched by our system.

(c4) *Noises from weighing cells*: the same as (c3) in afternoon tea scenario.

(c5) *Slow RFID sample rate*: the same as (c4) in afternoon tea scenario.

Table 8. Causes of miss recognition in Chinese-style dinner scenario #4. There are 162 activities analyzed from the video log. The number of misses counts both false positives and false negatives.

Causes of misses	# of misses of transfer events	# of misses of eat events	Total
(c1) Segmented weight-change events	5	0	5
(c2) Eating before transferring food on personal containers	5	5	10
(c3) Weight matching ambiguity	7	0	7
(c4) Noises from weighing cells	3	2	5
(c5) (c3) Slow RFID sample rate	3	0	3
Total of misses	23	7	30

5 Related Work

The related work is organized into the following three categories: traditional dietary assessment methods, ubiquitous dietary tracking systems, and intelligent (tabletop) surfaces. The traditional dietary assessment methods consist of keeping food records, using twenty-four-hour recall, and filling food frequencies questionnaires [16]. In the food record method, food quantities can be either accurately weighed or estimated by household measures before a meal. The twenty-four-hour recall method asks a user to recall the amount of food intakes within the past 24 hours. Food Frequencies Questionnaires (FFQ) list popular food items and ask a user how often and how much these food items are consumed within a defined period, e.g., a week or a month. All traditional assessment methods fail to capture actual energy intakes precisely [3]. Most methods underreport actual energy intake by at least 20 percent. Some of the errors are inevitable because human beings tend to misreport their food intakes. In other words, underreporting errors can be higher (30 percent or more) for certain groups of users. In comparison, our method can achieve 80% plus accuracy, which is as good as the accuracy from these traditional assessment methods.

For the dietary-tracking systems, Mankoff et al. [9] has designed a low-cost tracking system based on scanning shopping receipts to estimate what food items people buy and consume. By analyzing the nutritional values of the purchased food items, their system detects missing nutrients and recommends healthier food items to achieve a better nutritional balance. However, their system does not perform individual dietary tracking. The purchased food items in a family setting may be consumed by different household members in different quantities. The household purchased food items can be considered healthy, but the dietary consumption of individual household member can be nutritionally unbalanced due to personal dietary preferences and habits.

Dietary tracking at the individual level has been proposed by Amft et al. [1]. Their approach is to place a microphone around a person's inner ear to detect chewing sound from the mouth. Since different types of foods (e.g., potato chips, apples, pasta, etc.) can give different chewing sound, their system can infer what a person is currently eating in his/her mouth. However, different food sources that vary in nutritional contents give out similar chewing sound, e.g., similar sound from drinking water vs. beer. Rather than tracking food intake from chewing sound, this work takes a different approach. It creates a smart dining table, enabling the table to track food transfers among containers and into the individuals' mouths.

The 3rd category of related work is about intelligent surfaces that can infer tabletop human-surface interactions. The closest system to our work is the load sensing table [14] from Lancaster University. They utilized four weighing cells installed at four corners of a rectangular table to acquire the positional information of tabletop objects, and infer interaction events such as adding, removing an object from the surface, or knocking an object over. They demonstrated success with these interaction events. However, their main limitation is recognizing *complex, concurrent interactions involving multiple objects*. For example, their positioning algorithm fails if two or more objects are moved concurrently on the tabletop surface. In comparison, this paper expects such complex, concurrent interactions to be relatively common in family dining scenario; therefore, they are the paper's target.

Other related but less relevant works apply load sensing to derive context information. Smart floor [11] demonstrated that by applying pressure sensors underneath the floors, it is possible to identity users and to track their locations. The posture chair by Selena [10] deployed two matrices of pressure sensors (called *pressure cells*) in a chair to recognize the posture of children, and then infer their affective interest level. To our knowledge, no work that attempts to address complex, concurrent person-object interactions from a load sensing surface. This paper is believed to be the first to augment the load sensing surface with a RFID surface to enable tracking of multiple, concurrent person-object interactions over a tabletop surface.

6 Conclusion and Future Work

We are what we eat. This paper describes the design and implementation of our diet-aware dining table. We have augmented an ordinary dining table with two layers of sensor surfaces underneath the table – the RFID surface and the weighing surface. Given certain assumptions, the diet-aware dining table automatically tracks what and how much each individual eats from the dining table over the course of a meal. We have performed several experiments, including live dining scenarios (afternoon tea and Chinese-style dinner), multiple dining participants, and random concurrent activity sequences. Our experimental results have shown reasonable recognition accuracy of around 80%, which is at least as good as the accuracy of the traditional dietary assessment methods.

Our future work will further improve the recognition accuracy, address some of the main causes of inaccuracy from our experimental results, and relax some of the assumptions and restrictions. Note that some of the restrictions can be solved by making simple design changes. For examples, the current prototype does not allow hands or elbows on the table. To relax this restriction, we can add a slightly protruding frame around the edge of table, so that users can rest their elbows on the frame without affecting our system. We also believe in multi-sensor approach. For example, by deploying a video camera above the table, it is possible to observe events that cannot be detected by RFID and weighing surfaces. Since this table can track tabletop person-food interactions in real time, we hope to build *just-in-time persuasive feedbacks* to encourage better healthy dining behaviors. For examples, users under a dietary program could benefit from weekly warnings of unhealthy food. Patients who cannot consume high amount of sugar (diabetes patients) or water (patients with heart problems) could receive just-in-time notifications when they are over their recommended daily consumption.

Acknowledgments

This work was partially supported by grants from Taiwan NSC, Quanta Computer, and Intel (#94-2218-E-002-055, #94-2622-E-002-024, #94-2218-E-002-075).

References

[1] Amft, M. Stäger, P. Lukowicz, G. Tröster, "Analysis of Chewing Sounds for Dietary Monitoring", In Proceedings of Ubicomp 2005, M. Beigl, S. Intille, J. Rekimoto, H. Tokuda (Eds). Lecture Notes in Computer Science, Vol 3660, ISBN 3-540-28760-4; Springer Verlag, Tokyo, Japn, September 2005

[2] J. Beidler et al. The PNA project. In Proceedings of the sixth annual CCSC northeastern conference on The journal of computing in small colleges, pp. 276–284. The Consortium for Computing in Small Colleges, 2001.

[3] Dietary Assessment, http://encyclopedias.families.com/dietary-assessment-516-518-efc

[4] Dishman, E. Inventing wellness systems for aging in place. Computer, May 2004, 34-41

[5] S. Hankinson et al., editors. Healthy Women, Healthy Lives: A Guide to Preventing Disease. A Harvard Medical School book. Simon & Schuster Inc., 2001.

[6]   INSIGHT 19. Beliefs and attitudes of americans toward their diet. USDA Center for Nutrition Policy and Promotion, June 2000.

[7]   INSIGHT 20. Consumption of food group servings: People's perceptions vs. reality. USDA Center for Nutrition Policy and Promotion, October 2000.

[8]   JESS. http://herzberg.ca.sandia.gov/jess/

[9]   J. Mankoff, G. Hsieh, H. C. Hung, S. Lee, E. Nitao, "Using Low-Cost Sensing to Support Nutritional Awareness", In Proceedings of Ubicomp 2002, G. Boriello and L.E. Holmquist (Eds). Lecture Notes in Computer Science, Vol 2498, ISBN 3-540-44267-7; Springer Verlag, Gothenburg, Sweden, September 2002

[10] S. Mota and R. W. Picard (2003), "Automated Posture Analysis for Detecting Learner's Interest Level." Workshop on Computer Vision and Pattern Recognition for Human-Computer Interaction, CVPR HCI, June, 2003.

[11] R. J. Orr and G. D. Abowd. The Smart Floor: A Mechanism for Natural User Identification and Tracking. GVU Technical Report GIT-GVU-00-02, 2000.

[12] Rosenberg, I. H. (1996). Nutrition research: an investment in the nation's health. Nutrition Review, 54, s5-s6.

[13] R. Weinsier and C. Krumdieck. Dairy foods and bone health: examination of the evidence. American Journal of Clinical Nutrition, 72(3):681–689, September 2000.

[14] Schmidt, M. Strohbach, K. Van Laerhoven, A. Friday and H.-W. Gellersen. "Context Acquisition based on Load Sensing". In Proceedings of Ubicomp 2002, G. Boriello and L.E. Holmquist (Eds). Lecture Notes in Computer Science, Vol 2498, ISBN 3-540-44267-7; Springer Verlag, Gothenburg, Sweden, September 2002

[15] Mark Weiser, John S. Brown, The Coming Age of Calm Technology, 1996.

[16] Thompson FE, Byers T. (1994) Dietary assessment resource manual. J Nutr. 124:2245S-2318S

[17] United States Department of Agriculture. USDA Nutrient Database for Standard Reference. http://www.nal.usda.gov/fnic/foodcomp/Data/

Lessons for the Future: Experiences with the Installation and Use of Today's Domestic Sensors and Technologies

Mark Stringer, Geraldine Fitzpatrick, and Eric Harris

Department of Informatics, University of Sussex, Brighton, East Sussex, BN1 9QH
{M.Stringer, geraldin, erich}@sussex.ac.uk

Abstract. Domestic environments are receiving increasing attention as sites of deployment for pervasive technologies, as evidenced by the growing number of studies of homes and maturing technologies in prototype aware/smart homes. The challenge now is to move technologies out of purpose built homes into everyday environments in ways that will fit with existing buildings and the people who live in them. However, there are many aspects of this future vision that people live with right now in the form of sensors and technologies already in the home. We describe findings from three studies – in-home interviews, a questionnaire about home sensors, and interviews with commercial smart home installers – that explore current experiences with sensors and technologies in the home. These lead us to reflect on the implicit assumptions in, and future design directions for, pervasive research for the home.

1 Introduction

The home is gaining increasing attention as a possible site for deployment of pervasive computing technologies [6]. Prototype 'aware/smart homes' such as the Georgia Tech Aware Home [1] and MIT PlaceLab [14] demonstrate the possibilities for sensor and network technologies in home environments. In parallel to, and preceding, this work, there has also been considerable interest in the home as a site of study in its own right, both to understand how the home is experienced and made home, and to identify opportunities for design. O'Brien, for example, has looked at the role of different technologies and how they modulate the social life of the home [17]. Crabtree et al. explored the flow of information through a home, highlighting activity centres with a view to how these could be supported by technology [5]. An implicit notion in much of this work is that there is a gap between the vision of some possible future with an aware/smart home making use of various sensors and complex infrastructures and technologies, and the reality of lived-in homes today with their everyday technologies and patterns of social life that are far removed from this vision (as evidenced by the need to build purpose built homes as demonstrators).

Our recent studies of some everyday homes within a UK context, however, show that many aspects of this vision are already a part of many homes. The contribution of this paper is to explore some of the current experiences of living with sensors and technologies and draw out implications for how we might approach future pervasive technologies if they are also to become part of our existing homes.

K.P. Fishkin et al. (Eds.): PERVASIVE 2006, LNCS 3968, pp. 383–399, 2006.

The studies reported in this paper are part of a larger project concerned with the design, prototyping, and in-situ evaluation of pervasive technologies in domestic settings. Because our approach is to try to design for real homes and involve users as participants in the design process, we undertook a set of initial in-home studies to serve as a baseline understanding of each particular home and family so that we could better tailor our co-design sessions with them. These studies gave rise to findings that, while not overly surprising in hindsight, lead us to reflect more closely on the implicit assumptions and directions in current pervasive technology research. One finding was the ways in which "everyday" sensors in the home are often broken or require various workarounds to be used. Another was the multiple factors beyond just functionality that determine what technologies are in the home and the ways in which these too are often problematic or not well understood. This led us to triangulate our findings through a survey about everyday sensors and through interviews with smart home installers to explore experiences with more advanced technological arrangements in the home.

In this paper we first review some of the background work around studies of domestic environments and pervasive technologies for domestic settings; we then describe three studies we have undertaken exploring current experiences of technology in the home. Finally we discuss our findings and their implications for future efforts to design applications of pervasive computing for domestic settings.

2 Background

Since Weiser [27] first articulated a future of ubiquitous and pervasive computing, domestic settings have been receiving increasing attention from researchers as an application domain.

Sociological strands of work, especially through ethnographic studies, have sought to understand the current nature of the home and, having gained that understanding, to suggest sites and artifacts within the home that might be possible targets for technical augmentation in the manner envisioned by Weiser. For example, ethnographies of the domestic environment have found a strong focus on the flow of information, coordination of activities and presence of routines in the home [5,10,17]. Information-based artifacts that support coordination and routines have been highlighted as candidates for technological enhancement. These artifacts include calendars, family noticeboards, wall-planners [5]; and shopping lists and the kinds of notes that are attached with magnets on a fridge [23,24]. Other work has highlighted the importance of everyday technologies in supporting the maintenance of routines, such as using episode length of children's videos as a timing device [20]. These and other similar studies make evident the practical accomplishment of home life and provide important points of sensitization when thinking about designing for the home. The studies we present here are somewhat different as we are not so much concerned with issues of how people live in their home but more pragmatically concerned with technology and sensor issues and relationships with technologies. This is similar to Edwards and Grinter [6] but whereas they studied advanced home networks looking at skilled computer people as early adopters, we are primarily concerned with 'everyday' households and their technology experiences.

In parallel, there have been technological strands of work to implement aspects of the pervasive vision for home environments. With recent technological advances, we are now seeing relatively stable prototype developments and some initial in-home deployments. For example, sensor networks are being developed in conjunction with sophisticated inferencing processes to make higher-order sense of continuous sensor data [22]. Component applications are being developed such as SMS messaging displays in the home [23]. One way in which these advances have been both explored and realized has been through the development of purpose-built prototype 'aware/smart' homes, such as the Georgia Tech Aware Home, created as a "living laboratory" with various technologies including location sensing technologies, large-screen projected displays and camera-based eye-tracking [1]; and the MIT "The PlaceLab" at MIT that has its Home-n augmented with over a hundred sensors, including sensors of temperature, humidity, light, barometric pressure, electric current and water flow, "where the routine activities and interactions of everyday home life can be observed, recorded for later analysis, and experimentally manipulated" [14]. These developments have resulted in important advances in understanding and technical sophistication but they tend to do so at a loss of the authenticity of everyday settings and avoid the issues of integration into existing environments.

Other research has sought to deploy technologies into existing homes, as with Beckmann et al's sensor installation kit [2]. Others have used in-home deployments as a form of technology probe to elicit interesting responses to new technologies which may act as inspiration for future design [13]. More provocative installations of technology such as a weight-sensitive 'drift table' have been undertaken by Gaver et al. as part of their curious home project [7]. These implementations in 'everyday' homes complement purpose-built installations by starting to point to issues entailed in realizing the pervasive vision with current housing stock, as noted by [9,19]. There are also increasing efforts to develop toolkits that minimize the time and effort to build pervasive applications [8] and that facilitate engaging household inhabitants more directly in thinking about the applications they want to live with [19,25]. This provided a starting point for our work, where we wanted to explore novel pervasive applications for and with people that would fit into their existing homes and that we could quickly prototype and deploy through use of toolkits. However as suggested by Rodden and Benford [19], and Grinter and Edwards [6], we still have much to learn about the practical realities of engaging in such implementations. The studies to be reported here suggest further that we also still have much to learn from experiences with existing sensors and technologies as well that will help inform the more pragmatic design and deployment of technologies in the home.

3   Overview of Studies

As stated previously, given the substantial and maturing amount of work both in understanding domestic life and in developing technologies, it is timely to think more seriously about how to move from purpose-built homes to augmenting everyday domestic environments. While the potential vision points to homes that could be very different to experiences today, the path to there will be incremental from the base of today's homes and currently available technologies. Below we report on three studies as part of understanding this current base and focus on the experiences that people have with sensors and technologies in the home. The first study consisted of in-home interviews and tours with "average" middle class UK participants in their homes. We then sought to triangulate some of the findings from this study through an online survey of sensors in the home and through interviews with professionals who install current "state of the art" technologies into the homes of the wealthy.

3.1 Study 1: In-Home Interviews and Tours

The initial intention of the in-home interviews and tours was to have a baseline understanding of the participants and their homes in order to inform future co-design work with them, enabled by available toolkits for prototyping and deployment. We recruited 12 people from 7 UK households to participate in this study (see Table 1 for an overview of the households). All the interviewees were "middle class" by English standards – they were professionals or worked in clerical professions in support of professionals and had a university education.

Table 1. Profile of participant households (Pseudonyms used)

Household	Occupants (Ages)	Adult professions	Type of home
1.(Chloe & Jack)	Parents mid 30's, children 6 and 8	Teacher, director of technology company	Detached, brick, early 1900s
2. (Emily & Thomas)	Couple late 20's	Admin assistant, software developer	2-bedroom terraced house
3. (Megan & James)	Couple, late 50's	Admin assistant, Teacher	Detached, late 19th century
4. (Charlotte & Joshua)	Couple, mid-30's, children 5, 10, 12	Human Rights consultant, homemaker	Detached, early 1900s
5. (Sophie & Daniel)	Couple, mid 60's	Retired Astronomer, homemaker	Detached, early 1900s
6. (Lauren & Harry)	Couple, late 30's, children 8, 10, 14	Director of technology company, homemaker	Detached, early 1900s
7. (Lucy & Sam)	Couple in 60's	Retired telephone engineer, homemaker	New detached, brick bungalow

A study session with each household consisted of an in-home tour and interview with one or two of the adult family members. Each session lasted approximately 90 minutes and was conducted by two researchers and captured on video. A study protocol was developed focusing especially on the current relationship of participants to the technology in their homes. Participants were asked to give the interviewer a tour of the house and discuss the technology in each room. The participants were asked how each piece of technology came to be there, what it was used for, and if there were any problems or issues with it. If the technology had been bought by the participants they were asked where they bought it and what criteria were used to decide on the purchase. As interviews were informed by previous ethnographic work on the home, questions were also asked about areas of the home and activities and artifacts that had been identified as potential candidates for digital augmentation, e.g., as in [5, 10, 20]. Analysis of the videos was conducted through transcription, repeated viewing and identification of recurring themes and issues.

Findings: In-Home Technologies. As expected, we saw many of the same things that others have noted in studies of home settings. For example the fridge and other notice boards were commonly used as spaces in which information was displayed and through which family life was coordinated [5]. All of the households also owned a diverse array of technologies: every house had at least one computer, at least one mobile phone, and at least one TV, DVD system, and audio system; two homes had burglar alarms; six had broadband internet connections (although one of those had never worked); three had wireless connectivity; and every home had a thermostat and a smoke detector. What caught our attention however was the extent to which sensors and technologies – similar to the component sensors and technologies that would go to make up new pervasive installations in the home – already made up the home, the stories around those technologies, and the issues that people experienced living with these. For the purposes of this paper, we will focus on the following: technology choices, gendered relationships to technology, information requirements, general technology experiences, and sensor experiences.

Technology Choices: How technology gets into the home. In purpose-built aware/smart homes, technology configurations are pre-determined as part of some configurable package, largely by the researcher in an academic context or the provider/installer in a commercial context, albeit modified by consumer choice. In the 'everyday' homes we looked at, there were much more diverse and complex reasons for how technologies arrived there. People received technologies as (possibly unwanted) gifts from relatives and they felt a social obligation to keep them or at least bring them out for display when those relatives visited (as did Chloe & Jack with a face spa and sewing machine). Parents gave their financially struggling children hand-me-down technology (as was the case with Megan & James' television). Children gave their less-technology-savvy parents hand-me-down mobile phones or computers (as with Chloe and Jack). Of course people also bought new technology but when they did, performance and technical features were not necessarily the primary reasons for purchase. Form and aesthetics also played a factor (as also found when we talked to smart home installers (detailed below)). *"Has it got the couple of features I know I want? Does it look nice [...]I get fed-up with everything else because you could spend months choosing."* [Megan, House 3]

People made trade-offs between functionality and aesthetics. In house 7, Lucy said she was unhappy with the interface to her microwave because it was difficult to use but when asked how she'd come to choose it, it was for aesthetic reasons because it would be the same shade of white as her conventional oven.

If the form and aesthetics aren't right the technology may never be used as was the case with the radio Lauren asked her husband to buy: *"I asked my husband for a christmas present, I wanted a little radio that could sit on the bench when I'm getting dinner and cooking and stuff. And when I opened it this is what I got. I said, this is nothing like what I asked for! And his rationale was that this was just too good a deal to overlook. But I asked for something very small, so consequently it never gets used, hence the dust."* [Lauren, House 6]

Technology choices were also often driven by a strong sense of values. Many of the interviewees saw their choice of technology as a fundamental expression of their beliefs but wanted the technology to fit in with, rather than transform, those beliefs.

"I want to live in a yurt with internet access"[Emily, House 2]

For the 'yurt' couple, Emily and Thomas, almost all their technology choices were influenced by their desire to live an ecologically responsible lifestyle, and they spent considerable time researching products on internet sites that specialized in selling technologies for ecological living. These products included energy-saving thermostatic air-mixing taps, electricity generating solar panels and a fibre-optic "light-pipe". Interestingly, picking up on our 'not-working and not-used' theme, the solar panels had never been installed and were languishing in the spare bedroom and the light pipe, although it was installed, was missing a part and not working.

The very choice of these technologies serves to explicitly convey to visitors in the home what values are held there or what impressions they want to project. *"I printed that out [tide tables] because I wanted people to think that we're the kind of family that goes boating. We're not."[Joshua, House 4]*

Gendered Relationships with Technology. Some of the examples above also point to issues of different relationships to technologies within the home, often playing out on gendered lines. In almost all of the households, women played a key role in deciding what technology was purchased for the home and where and how it was placed. As has been seen in other studies [10], the women also played a large part in the construction and maintenance of domestic routines, handling mail, doing the filing, and managing the family diary/calendar. Calendar management/display has frequently been discussed as one possible application of ubiquitous computing [5]. It is therefore perhaps interesting to note that in many homes the family calendar was either "in the head" of the woman of the house or in a small personal diary, that was carried by the woman in her handbag. For one woman, this control was also explicitly associated with a particular location in the house:

"This is my chair and no-one else is allowed to sit here. And that's my work basket, the radio and I always have you can see, the Ikea catalogue [laughs] and my crossword. I sit here and I can see the cooker and I can hear the front door and I can answer the phone and I'm near the back door and I can see the sink. My poor husband has nothing like this, but then he doesn't do anything like that. I organise the house I run the house, I do all the paperwork."[Megan, House 3]

We saw other examples of men similarly exerting control over other domains in the home. In two houses there was some kind of restriction by the husband on the wife's use of central heating controls. In house 7 Lucy was 'forbidden' from touching the central heating controls: *"I don't touch that [central heating control], it's more than my life's worth"[Lucy, House 7]* In house 2, Thomas had stuck a cardboard flap over the button which altered the thermostat temperature *"...because Emily is always tempted to just put the temperature up when she wants the central heating to come on and that flap is to sort of remind her not to."[Thomas, House 2]*

Information Requirements. An emphasis of many studies and applications is the flow of information around the home and information for coordination, as noted above [5]. Interestingly, amongst our interviewees there were no problems or dissatisfaction with the current (mainly paper) solutions that they used to manage information although one user did express frustration with an electronic calendaring system which he was forced to use as part of working from home. Participants did mention other kinds of information, more to do with values or curiosity than with functionality, that they would like technology to provide. Emily and Thomas (House 2), who were very keen on environmental issues, said they would like to know how windy and sunny it was on their roof. Megan (House 3) said that she would like to know more about the history of her Victorian-period house and the people who had lived in it. She also wanted to know was in the guttering of her three-storey house. Lucy and Sam (House 7) who live in a nearly-new home wished that they had all the documentation (guarantees, instruction manuals, etc) that came with the pre-fitted appliances and a circuit diagram of the burglar alarm.

General Technology Experiences. A recurring theme across the households was the number of technologies that did not work properly and the inadequate or incorrect strategies people had for fixing their non-working technologies.

Networking was a case in point. In house 3 the ADSL broadband internet connection had not worked in the six-months since it was installed. The participants were unable to give any real explanation for why it didn't work, and their only strategy for getting the broadband to work was to buy a new laptop and hope that it would mysteriously work better than with existing computers in the house. Another interviewee [Jack, House 1] was having problems with his second attempt at wireless networking. His first wireless router had "just packed up for no apparent reason" and because he felt that his second was becoming unreliable, he was intending to buy a third wireless networking box. He seemed to be unaware of two of the three main problems that might be affecting his wireless connectivity – using WEP data encryption and interference from other wireless networks in surrounding houses – and seemed to think that the solution would be to buy a "stronger" base station.

Further, many homes had a large number of *technologies that were not used* and were either left to languish in a cupboard or put into a 'back room' to be dealt with at some later time. Some were unwanted gifts. Some were obsolete but the owners did not feel able to throw them out. Some were devices they wanted to use but were unable to get working properly. In house 1 a video camera was bought to take video during a tropical holiday but it didn't work in the humid conditions and as a result was never used again. Other technologies were missing a part (an extraction hood in house 1, in house 2 a fibre optic "light tunnel"). Yet others were ones that householders thought they wanted but in hindsight didn't, pointing to potential problems in asking people what they want from future pervasive applications.

While there was no scarcity of technology in evidence, there was often a serious *lack of understanding of, and know-how about, the technology.* Only one couple {House 7] had attended computer courses but found that it still didn't help them solve problems such as getting their webcam to work. Lack of know-how seemed to be a strong contributing factor to why various pieces of technology remained broken or unused. Sometimes family members traded knowledge e.g., in how to program the video recorder in exchange for some other household task, as also found by Rode [20]. Sometimes the *presence* of know-how was problematic as when Charlotte and Joshua's (House 4) daughters knew more than they did. Their 12 year old daughter had set up her own website but wanted to take it down because they felt its content was unwise. However, they could only do so with the help of their 10-year-old daughter. We also found cases where the know-how required to fix a problem was not present in the household. In these cases, external help was often sought, but with mixed success. Some accessed informal networks of friends and work colleagues. Others sought help from an advertised PC Repair/Support services. In one case however, this was a fragile solution in the face of subsequent changes:

"I got a man in and he set up all the networking, and that was fine until this laptop got filled up with shareware and other junk and I had to re-install it and now the networking doesn't work."[Joshua, House 4]

Sensor Experiences – Work Arounds. All of the households had at least one sensor-based technology, e.g., thermostat, burglar alarm, smoke detector. Three of the seven homes had problems with these, despite them being commonplace and "mature" technologies. Three households stated that they thought their thermostat was not triggered at the correct temperature, for example: *"That's the underfloor heating, but it only works if you turn it up to 35 degrees centigrade – that's not the temperature that it gets to in here, that's the temperature that the mice enjoy under the floorboards."[Joshua, House 4]*

Burglar alarms also proved problematic. One couple, who did use their burglar alarm extensively, referred to the burglar alarm being falsely triggered during power cuts. Another couple no longer used their burglar alarm after the alarm went off falsely when there was a power cut. It was also difficult to use even if they had wanted to because the control panel had been installed in an under-the-stairs cupboard with no lighting: *"It's a bit difficult to turn that thing on and then get out of the door with two kids in 30 seconds."[Chloe, House 1]*

These pointed to issues people had with not understanding and/or not trusting the ways in which their sensors worked, as well as the practical realities of location and timing and false alarms that render them less useful. Given that the future of pervasive computing within home is often oriented around numerous sensing technologies acting in concert [1, 14], it is a serious concern that a substantial number of the "everyday" sensors that are found in homes today either do not work properly or, equally importantly, are not regarded by their users as working properly.

In Summary. While it is not possible to generalize from these few households, to the whole of the United Kingdom, let alone to other countries, the findings from these in-home studies do provide some evidence of use and experience of a wide variety of existing sensors and technologies and raise interesting questions around the issues of the multiplicity of ways technologies get into a home, gendered relationships with technology, the different types of information we could be supporting in the home, and the everyday troubles with commodity technologies and sensors and the technical know-how and models needed to make them work. The findings around current sensor-based technologies in particular led us to undertake the following study.

3.2   Study 2: Household Sensor Questionnaire

The lack of understanding of current sensor technologies and the number of supposedly mature sensors that didn't work well led us to question whether or not these were common experiences or particular to our household sample. To explore this we developed an on-line questionnaire that asked about sensors that are commonly found in the domestic environment: respondents were asked if they had a thermostat, smoke detector or burglar alarm and, if they did, whether it worked properly. They were asked to detail any problems they had and also to give details of occasions when smoke detectors or burglar alarms had produced false alarm situations. Subjects were recruited via an email to acquaintances and colleagues who were also asked to pass it on.. 101 people responded to the questionnaire, 48 men and 53 women with an average age of 38 (age range of 21-70). 43% of the respondents were tenants in rented accommodation and 57% were home owners.

Findings: Domestic Sensors. 77% of the respondents had a thermostat in their house. 14% of these reported that their thermostat didn't work properly. Location of the thermostat was a common cause of complaint: *"Temperature always different in different rooms too near the boiler. In a well heated room. Need to make sure boiler door is closed."* Some respondents also complained that the control of the thermostat had a large range of temperature in which it was not responsive: *"The thermostat is just wrong and also has a huge temperature range (10 degrees or so) where it doesn't turn on or off."*

94% of all the respondents reported that they had a smoke alarm in their house, of which 82% reported that their smoke alarm worked properly. However, when asked if their smoke alarm had ever gone off when there wasn't a fire, 71% of respondents who had a smoke alarm (including those who said it worked properly) said it had. In many cases the detailed explanation of when the smoke alarm was triggered falsely indicated that this was a regular occurrence. *"Alarm continually going off when cooking"*, *"The toaster causes them to go off."*, *"They go off when the room is too hot regardless of there being no smoke."*

29% of respondents had burglar alarms. Of these, 79% said that their burglar alarms worked correctly. However, when asked if their burglar alarm had gone off falsely, 62% of respondents with an alarm said that it had: *"Mistakes entering code"*, *"Detector went of when intruder not present"*, *"It briefly goes off when power is restored after a power cut"*.

Hence, while not universal, these results suggest that alarm-based sensors were often experienced as problematic but that this was not necessarily *perceived* as problematic (as with 82% saying that the smoke alarm worked properly yet 71% had had issues with false alarms).

In summary. The findings from both the in-home interviews and the follow-up sensor questionnaire suggest that users' knowledge of and interaction with everyday sensors, which they regard as unproblematic, is in fact complexly nuanced and not well-understood. There is some evidence in these results to suggest that "false alarms" may play an important role in reassuring the user that a sensor is working: *"The smoke alarm is positioned on the ceiling in the hallway just outside the kitchen. So any smoke coming out of the kitchen goes straight up to the alarm. We just wave a tea towel in front of it to clear the smoke and stops. It's quite good in that we know it is working!"* This phenomena has been observed in the use of sensors and alarms in non-domestic settings [18] but has not been thoroughly discussed with regard to domestic settings.

In working with sensors for more novel outdoor pervasive experiences, Rogers and Muller [21] conclude that sensor performance is too poor to be relied on in "real-world" applications. But neither the field of ubiquitous computing, nor today's home owners, have given up on the use of sensors. In order to design sensor-based applications for the future we need to accept and understand the limitations of current sensors technologies, the lived experience of users with these technologies and the strategies which they adopt to deal with this sensor performance.

3.3 Study 3: Smart Home Installer Interviews

Apart from 'everyday' issues with sensors, our in-home studies also highlighted how much technology people already had in their homes, albeit relatively simple 'stand-alone systems or devices. This led us to think about other homes at the higher end of the market and their experiences with more complex infrastructures and technological arrangements. These were of interest because they represent 'state of the art' commercialization of aware/smart home technologies. As highlighted by Edwards and Grinter [6] the history of technology adoption may in some ways be a useful guide to the way in which technology is adopted in the future. As was the case with television, the technologies that wealthy people can afford to have professionally installed one day may well be the technologies that the rest of us will be able to buy as an of-the-shelf solution the next.

Participants and Methods. Ideally, we would want to interview the householders themselves about their 'smart home' installations. However, the demographics of the people who are in this category make it difficult to access them as participants – on the characterization of the people who do the installations, they are normally very wealthy people with high pressured jobs, often involving travel, who would not prioritize time for study participation. Instead, we chose to conduct interviews with representatives of companies that install "smart home" technologies as a way of gaining indirect access to a diverse range of customer experiences, albeit filtered through the company interviewees.

We interviewed two people who worked in customer-facing technical roles at two different companies, referred to here as Smith Ltd and Jones Ltd. Jones Ltd is a company with approximately 20 members of staff. It began as an audio equipment stall at record collectors' fair 30 years ago and now offers integrated home entertainment and automation systems solutions. Smith Ltd is a similar company, with 3 full-time staff members. It has been in business for approximately 5 years and was formed by two programmer/engineers who had previously run a company providing technical support services to industry. An example of a recent installation they delivered into a 16th century house was of a video/music server which could be accessed from any room in the house, networked plasma and projection screens, a complex lighting control system, in room web-cams and CCTV monitoring of the grounds.

Interviews with the company representatives lasted approximately 2 hours. The interviewees were asked to discuss the requirements of a typical customer, perceived trends in the industry, which features were popular or unpopular and the common causes of support calls. As part of this we encouraged them to tell us specific stories of customer experiences. Again an interview protocol was developed and used as background preparation while leaving the actual conduct of the interview free to follow leads as they emerged. A content analysis was conducted on the interview notes to identify common themes.

Findings: Smart Home Installers. In both companies, interviewees described very similar pictures of the customers they served, the systems they installed and the experiences reported back to them from customers via their service centres or representatives. One very important difference from the 'everyday homes' just discussed is that most 'smart home' installations begin with an empty shell of the house, or with discussions with the architect before the house is even built. In this way, these homes are similar to the research-based aware homes. None of the everyday houses that we visited, even the one that was newly built, had acquired their technology as the result of one monolithic installation.

Technology Choices: What was or was not in demand. How people choose to prioritize and allocate their money in designing these installations is an important indicator of the technologies they at least think they want to live with (though as we have seen with everyday homes this may not in fact work out to be the case). Both companies reported that one of the most commonly requested 'smart home' components were motion-sensitive lights in hallways to allow night-time navigation to the bathroom. Other components that were popular included an "Occupancy Simulation" – turning the lights on and off in a pattern that might deter burglars – and a bedside switch which allows all the lights in the house to be turned off at once.

Television and entertainment systems, particularly distributed or networked solutions, were also high on people's purchase lists: *"People are really into telly."[Smith Ltd].* A feature which allows the user to pause a TV show in the living room and resume watching it from another room (typically the bedroom) was a popular request, as was waterproof TVs fitted in bathrooms.

There were also a number of technologies that the installers noted little demand for or that fell low on people's priority lists. Interestingly, these tended to be the ones with more advanced or automated features. In the category of 'technologies which might seem like a good idea and which customers thought they wanted', Smith Ltd cited voice activation as a technology that they no longer recommended. This is because they found that when they did install them, people did not use them in practice: *"Voice recognition stuff, kind of works, it's fun for about five minutes, but it drives you up the wall after two days."[Smith Ltd]*

Other seemingly archetypal home automation features moved from high to low priority, even for the most wealthy of customers, when they discovered how much they cost. *"People like the idea of automatically opening and closing curtains until they find out that it costs about £1600 per large window."[Smith Ltd]*

While talking to these people, we also asked them about their opinion about potential for user-configurable solutions. This is because there has been a current research trend towards the production of toolkits that would allow the user to reconfigure aspects of their digital infrastructure and conduct some forms of end-user programming [8, 4]. Neither company felt that there was a strong demand for this: *"They can't even plug the right cable into the right socket at the back of their DVD recorder to get the best signal for their plasma screens. Reconfiguration will probably happen but only in the IT-savvy/early adopter community."[Smith Ltd]*

Both companies reported a strong gender divide in attitude and approach to the technologies chosen and installed. Men were largely drawn to the technology and wanted it on display but women were much more concerned with the aesthetics of the installations and that they fitted in with the interior décor: *"Boys want all the toys – wives want*

*everything to be out of the way and have the minimum number of remote controls."
[Smith Ltd]* "This installation has a wall-mounted display and in-ceiling speakers. The woman was wearing the trousers, she wanted nothing on display."[Jones Ltd]. Smith Ltd reported that, as a consequence, as much as 50% of the cost of many installations was spent on cabinet-making and carpentry to ensure that the technology was aesthetically concealed.

Complex systems, complex infrastructures and controls. The complexity of the installations also entail a number of practical implications. The first is around networking infrastructure – complex integrated solutions require complex infrastructures to support them. However these infrastructures tend to be hard-wired rather than wireless because of practical concerns with current wireless solutions including insufficient data rates for the transport of high quality video. As such, one of the most important services that smart home installation companies provide is designing the layout of cables around the home and laying the cable around the home. Thus installations, once designed and installed, remain relatively inflexible.

These more complex systems also require more complex interactions to manage and control them relative to the more stand-alone technologies of the 'everyday' homes reported earlier. A typical home cinema system installed by Smith or Jones Ltd involves at the very least a control for the projection screen, the screen projector, the DVD player, and also possibly for the lights, the curtains and the sound. The options offered by the companies include: individual controls for each of the boxes (the problems with which have well-documented [16]); a single remote control from which all of the commands can be sent by infra-red as a macro; and, the most expensive option, an LCD panel to control all the devices via RF to a controlling system.

None of these solutions is perfect. The use of individual remote controls means that the user has to identify several remote controls and press the right button while pointing at the right device: *"The [infra red] remote doesn't know what state appliances are in when it sends the signal. If a remote has to send out a whole string of commands the user has to stand there while all the commands are sent."[Smith Ltd].* The interfaces for the LCD displays are only programmable using proprietary applications and a large amount of systems programming to the proprietary API is required to interface a new appliance.

It is no surprise then that one of the most reported causes of support calls to the companies' service centres were problems with remote controls. The most common problem was that the battery had gone flat but this was often only able to be diagnosed after a time-consuming support call, or even a visit.

There were several hints in the discussion of these smart home controls being a source of dispute, especially where one person, often the woman, found it difficult to perform everyday tasks: *"Hubby [the husband] gets all the kit installed and then he goes off on a business trip and the wife's left alone, sitting on the sofa with all the remotes and she can't put the telly on or turn off the lights."[Jones Ltd]*

In Summary. The reported everyday experiences of living with more advanced sensor and technology arrangements as found in current 'smart homes' suggest similar issues to everyday homes, e.g., in the gendered relationships around technologies and how people make choices about technologies, but also issues that point to more pragmatic concerns when we move beyond simple standalone technologies, e.g., around networking infrastructures, control mechanisms and they models they have for understanding them.

4 Discussion

While the full realization of the aware/smart home is still some way off as the norm for everyday household living (if that is even the sort of home we want to live in, a discussion for another time), there are many aspects of this vision that people 'live' with right now. We argue that understanding these current experiences can provide valuable lessons and insights for the types of issues and troubles people might have with even more sophisticated and complex sensor and technical networks in the home of the future and provide more sobering and realistic filters for shaping future design directions. The lessons reported here provide empirical evidence that at times elaborate upon, and at other times question, lessons drawn out for designers of pervasive technologies for the home in other work: Edwards and Grinter [6] present them as seven conceptual challenges, covering a range of technical, social and pragmatic concerns; Beckmann et al [2] draw out five principles for end user sensor installation, based on in-home deployments of sensor kits in 15 existing homes.

The studies we describe here challenge several implicit assumptions about homes of the future which tend to be embodied in prototype aware homes. Homes of the future tend to be "new builds" where they are constructed from the ground up and fitted with all their technology in a short space of time. In existing homes, technology is acquired in a piecemeal way, as postulated by Edwards and Grinter [6] and evidenced by the findings of our studies.

Where people make purchase decisions about technology, functionality is only one of many considerations, as identified by the themes of "balance installation usability with domestic concerns" [2] and "design for domestic use" [6]. As we saw in both everyday and smart homes, technologies need to fit in: to the power structure; to the physical space; to the values; and to the aesthetics of the home. In this arena, technology choices are often contended along gender lines and can be highly value-laden. For example, the management of the home and its routines was often the domain of the woman; applications which interfere with this power structure or make it more difficult to do the things that she already does are unlikely to find favour. Other aspects of running the home – control of the heating – might be a male domain. This has implications for the types of technologies we develop and the importance of understanding the power structures and values within the home.

Ultimately people will need to be persuaded to purchase these new technologies for the home; seeing where people allocate their spending power and their effort and attention now is instructive for directing attention to what applications might be more acceptable. In the smart homes especially, people were prioritizing safety (in sensor-based lighting choices) and entertainment/leisure (in high-end home entertainment system choices). In neither smart homes nor everyday homes did we see evidence of demand for many, what might be called "typical", smart home features, such as curtain openers, voice control and kitchen automation. Such automation, where deployed, was often experienced initially as a novelty then as annoying. This has implications for what we think people will want or what they say they want compared to what they will actually find useful, fun or are happy to live with.

However our studies also highlight an extra level of complexity in the way technologies are acquired. Not only are people incrementally evolving their own homes with new technology purchases, but in some houses technologies are as likely (or even more likely) to be hand-me-downs, second-hand purchases, or gifts, wanted or unwanted. Some commentators have claimed that the practice of gift giving is in crisis, citing a tension between the need of gift-givers to continue giving and the need of gift-receivers to demonstrate aesthetic control over their domestic environment [12]. While how technology comes into the home needs to be recognized, as per the "accidentally smart home" challenge [6] and it needs to co-exist with older-generation technology (see also the "impromptu interoperability" challenge [6]), there is a further challenge to acknowledge, perhaps encourage, these alternative routes of entry into the home. This has implications for how we think in the future about the introduction of new technologies into the home and opens up opportunities to support new forms of technology gift giving or sharing.

Another factor associated with future smart home research is that they tend to be constructed and used in environments where advanced technical expertise is always at hand. In everyday homes this is not the case and even "unproblematic" technologies like ADSL broadband and wireless networking are still causing huge problems and may go unused for months because the people do not feel that they have access to proper technical support. Edwards and Grinter [6] phrase this understanding as a challenge to make technologies reliable but even if technologies are "reliable" in the sense intended, our studies suggest that they may still be unusable without access to ongoing technical know-how. Design for reliability may be part of the solution, but it may be that pervasive computing has to recognize and incorporate into its design, the social capital of providing technical support and know-how of friends and family, as well as providing access to a wider community of support. It may be that, as with personal computing, pervasive computing in the home will have to go through a "hobbyist phase". Given the large amounts of money that several of our participants were prepared to spend (e.g., to buy a new laptop to fix a broadband connection, to buy a new PC to fix a troublesome CD Re-Writer) it seems that seeking to understand how best to provide domestic users with access to the required know-how may be a fruitful area of research.

One suggestion for making technologies easier to understand has been for the 'pervasive' designer to "make appropriate use of user conceptual models for familiar technologies" [2] but this implies that correct and agreed mental models exist and can be identified. Our findings suggest that often people do not have such well-developed conceptual models in the first place, as evidenced by the limited understanding of how sensors worked, nor do they have the skills and know-how as evidenced by the inadequate strategies people had for problem solving.

Another suggestion had been to support system inferencing in the presence of ambiguity [6]. The findings here, both of everyday homes and the smart homes, suggest that the reverse is also required: users need to be supported to make inferences in the face of system uncertainty as they seek to trouble shoot problems. Even something as simple as turning a device on or off can become much more difficult with the smart homes, pointing to a need for intuitive easy to use controls and reflective support for trouble shooting (which as discussed is not straightforward the more complex the installation gets).

Future aware home research can also tend to work with particular assumptions about the kinds of information would be useful in a domestic setting, e.g., activity monitoring [14] or coordination information [5]. When participants in our study were asked about information they wanted in their home, they responded with a diversity of answers which reflect the crucial role which the home has in embodying far more than work-like values. For example, "I'd like to know how windy it is on my roof," embodies a desire to express strong beliefs about care for the environment and the use of renewable sources of energy (such as wind power). "I want to know the history of this house, who used to live here," reflects a curiosity and interest in knowing more about (very) local history. Such answers suggest whole new application areas for pervasive information somewhere between utilitarian [1,22] and ludic [7] ones.

A further assumption in much aware home work is that hundreds of sensors can be embedded and networked together in the home, passively and unobtrusively go about their sensing, and, where needed (as in aging in place scenarios), their output can be remotely monitored and interpreted [14]. Yet the studies here suggest that the stand alone 'mature' sensors that we have in home today generate a large number of false alarms and instances of problematic behaviour. At the same time, the people who live with these sensors have developed ways of understanding and interpreting (albeit incorrectly at times) the behaviour of the sensors in response to local conditions, to the point where 'problems' are routine and workarounds are well understood. While reasonable for single simple sensors, this has serious implications if we consider hundreds of sensors possibly not working or sending out false alarms, and where the interpretation of 'routine' problems is removed from the local context and local strategies for addressing them.

5   Conclusion

Significant technical advances are being made that mean that the vision of pervasive computing in the home is closer to becoming a reality. In this paper we have reported on three complementary studies that explore people's current experiences with technologies already in homes in a UK context. These are interesting because the technologies and sensors in everyday homes and in the higher-end 'smart homes' share many of the same sensor and technology components, albeit in much simpler configurations, that will be used to realize these future visions. Our findings around the ways technologies are brought into the home and the everyday experiences and troubles with technologies and sensors suggest that the design issues to be addressed to realize the vision will be much more about the human, social, cultural and marketing issues than the technical issues. They also point to the future work we need to work with people better understand what applications we should be looking at building for the home.

Acknowledgements

Thanks to Beyond the Invisible (http://www.beyondTheInvisible.co.uk) and Cornflake (http://www.cornflake.co.uk). Thanks to all those who took part in our studies.

Thanks also to Eva Hornecker, Manuela Jungmann, Dagmar Kern and Paul Marshall and the reviewers for their considered comments and suggestions for improvement. This work was funded by the UK EPSRC through the Equator IRC Project (EPSRC GR/N15986/01).

References

1. Abowd, G., Bobick, A., Essa I., Mynatt, E., and Rogers, W.: The aware home: Developing technologies for successful aging. In: Proc AAAI Workshop Automation as a Care Giver. Alberta, Canada (July 2002) 185 - 192

2. Beckmann, C., Consolvo, S. and LaMarca, A..: Some assembly required: Supporting end-user sensor installation in domestic ubiquitous computing environments: Proc Ubicomp 2004. Nottingham, UK. Springer-Verlag. (September 2004) 107-124

3. Blackwell, A.F. and Hague, R.: AutoHAN: An Architecture for Program-ming the Home. In Proc IEEE Symposia on Human-Centric Computing Languages and Environments, (2001) 150-157

4. Brand, S.: How Buildings Learn. Viking Penguin. New York. ISBN 0-14-013996-6 (1994)

5. Crabtree A, Rodden T, Hemmings T and Benford, S.: Finding a Place for UbiComp in the Home. Proc Ubicomp 2003, Seatle WA, Springer-Verlag, (2003) 208-226

6. Edwards, W. K., Grinter, R. E.: At home with ubiquitous computing: seven challenges. Proc Ubicomp 2001: Ubiquitous Computing International Conference; Atlanta, GA. Springer Verlag, (2001) 256-272

7. Gaver, W. W., Bowers, J., Boucher, A., Gellerson, H., Pennington, S., Schmidt, A., Steed, A., Villars, N., and Walker, B.: The drift table: designing for ludic engagement. In CHI '04 Extended Abstracts. ACM Press, Vienna, Austria, (April 2004). 885-900

8. Greenhalgh C, Izadi S., Mathrick J., Humble J. and I. Taylor.: ECT: A Toolkit to Support Rapid Construction of Ubicomp Environments. In Proc Ubicomp 2004, , Nottingham, UK, (2004), 207-234

9. Grinter R. E., Edwards W. K., Newman M., Ducheneaut N.: The work to make the home network work. In Proc ECSCW'05. Paris, Springer-Verlag. (2005) 97-119

10. Harper, R., Evergeti, V., Hamill, L., and Strain, J.: Paper-mail in the 21st century: an analysis of the future of paper-mail and implications for the design of electronic alternatives. presented at the Oikos 2001 workshop, Denmark: http://www.surrey.ac.uk/dwrc/Publications/okios.pdf (2001). (last accessed 3rd October 3, 2005)

11. Hindus, D., Mainwaring, S., Hagstrom, A. E., Leduc, N., and Bayley, O.: Casablanca: Designing social communication devices for the home. In Proc CHI'01. ACM Press. (2001) 209-216

12. Hurdley, R.: Objecting relations: the problem of the gift, discussed on BBC Radio 4, http://www.bbc.co.uk/radio4/factual/thinkingallowed_20050330.shtml, 30th March 2005 (last accessed 9th February 2006)

13. Hutchinson, H., Mackay, W., Westerlund, B., Bederson, B. B., Druin, A., Plai-sant, C., Beaudouin-Lafon, M., Conversy, S., Evans, H., Hansen, H., Roussel, N., and Eiderbäck, B.: Technology probes: inspiring design for and with families. In Proc CHI'03. Florida, USA, ACM Press, New York, NY, (2003) 17-24

14. Intille, S. S., Larson, K., Beaudin, J. S., Nawyn, J., Tapia, E. M., and Kaushik, P.: A living laboratory for the design and evaluation of ubiquitous computing technologies. CHI '05 Extended Abstracts, Portland, OR. ACM Press, (2005) 1941-1944

15. LaMarca, A., Chawathe, Y., Consolvo, S., Hightower, J., Smith, I., Scott, J., Sohn, T., Howard, J., Hughes, J., Potter, F., Tabert, J., Powledge, P., Borriello, G. and Schilit, B.: Place Lab: Device Positioning Using Radio Beacons in the Wild. In Pervasive 2005, Munich, Germany, LNCS Vol. 3468, Springer-Verlag, (2005) 421 - 486

16. Norman, Donald. A.: Home Theater: Not Ready for Prime Time, IEEE Computer, Vol. 35, Number 6, (2002) 100-102.

17. O'Brien, J., Rodden, T., Rouncefield, M., and Hughes, J.: At home with the technology: an ethnographic study of a set-top-box trial. ACM Trans on Computer Human Interactions. Vol. 6, No. 3. (1999), 282-308

18. Randell, R.: Accountability in an alarming environment. In Proc CSCW'04, Chicago, Illinois, USA. ACM Press, New York, NY, (2004) 125-131

19. Rodden, T., Crabtree, A., Hemmings, T., Koleva, B., Humble, J., Åkesson, K., and Hansson, P.: Between the dazzle of a new building and its eventual corpse: assembling the ubiquitous home. In Proc DIS'04. Cambridge, MA, USA. ACM Press, New York, NY, (2004) 71-80

20. Rode, J.A., Toye, E.F. and Blackwell, A.F.: The Domestic Economy: a Broader Unit of Analysis for End User Programming. Proc CHI' 2005, ACM Press, (2005) 1757 - 1760

21. Rogers, Y. and Muller, H.: A framework for designing sensor-based interactions to promote exploration and reflection. International Journal of Human-Computer Studies, (2005). 64 (1), 1-15

22. Schilit B, LaMarca A, Borriello G, Griswold W, McDonald D, Lazowska E, Balachandran A, Hong J and Iverson V.: Challenge: Ubiquitous Location-Aware Computing and the Place Lab Ini-tiative. In Proc ACM Int Workshop on Wireless Mobile Applications & Services on WLAN (WMASH 2003), San Diego, CA. (2003) 29-35

23. Swan, L. and Taylor, A. S.: Notes on fridge surfaces. In CHI '05 Extended Abstracts, Portland, OR, USA. ACM Press, New York, NY, (2005) 1813-1816

24. Taylor, A. S., and Swan, L.: List making in the home. Proc CSCW '04. Chicago, IL, ACM Press, (2004) 542-545

25. Truong, K. N., Huang, E. M. and Abowd, G. D.: CAMP: A Magnetic Poetry Interface for End-User Programming. Proc. Ubicomp 2004, Springer-Verlag (2004), 143-160

26. Venkatesh, A., E. Kruse, and E. C. F. Shih.: The Networked Home: An Analysis of Current Developments and Future Trends, Cognition, Technology and Work, vol. 5, no. 1, (2003) 23-32

27. Weiser, M.: The computer for the 21st century. Scientific American, 265(3): (1991) 66-75

28. Woodruff, A., and Scott Mainwaring.: Everyday Practices in Great Rooms. Ubicomp. Workshop on "Situating Ubiquitous Computing in Everyday Life; Bridging the Social and Technical Divide", Tokyo, Japan (2005)

Author Index

Lecture Notes in Computer Science

For information about Vols. 1–3852

please contact your bookseller or Springer

Vol. 3904: M. Baldoni, U. Endriss, A. Omicini, P. Torroni (Eds.), Declarative Agent Languages and Technologies III. XII, 245 pages. 2006. (Sublibrary LNAI).

Vol. 3903: K. Chen, R. Deng, X. Lai, J. Zhou (Eds.), Information Security Practice and Experience. XIV, 392 pages. 2006.

Vol. 3901: P.M. Hill (Ed.), Logic Based Program Synthesis and Transformation. X, 179 pages. 2006.

Vol. 3899: S. Frintrop, VOCUS: A Visual Attention System for Object Detection and Goal-Directed Search. XIV, 216 pages. 2006. (Sublibrary LNAI).

Vol. 3898: K. Tuyls, P.J. 't Hoen, K. Verbeeck, S. Sen (Eds.), Learning and Adaption in Multi-Agent Systems. X, 217 pages. 2006. (Sublibrary LNAI).

Vol. 3897: B. Preneel, S. Tavares (Eds.), Selected Areas in Cryptography. XI, 371 pages. 2006.

Vol. 3896: Y. Ioannidis, M.H. Scholl, J.W. Schmidt, F. Matthes, M. Hatzopoulos, K. Boehm, A. Kemper, T. Grust, C. Boehm (Eds.), Advances in Database Technology - EDBT 2006. XIV, 1208 pages. 2006.

Vol. 3895: O. Goldreich, A.L. Rosenberg, A.L. Selman (Eds.), Theoretical Computer Science. XII, 399 pages. 2006.

Vol. 3894: W. Grass, B. Sick, K. Waldschmidt (Eds.), Architecture of Computing Systems - ARCS 2006. XII, 496 pages. 2006.

Vol. 3893: L. Atzori, D.D. Giusto, R. Leonardi, F. Pereira (Eds.), Visual Content Processing and Representation. IX, 224 pages. 2006.

Vol. 3891: J.S. Sichman, L. Antunes (Eds.), Multi-Agent-Based Simulation VI. X, 191 pages. 2006. (Sublibrary LNAI).

Vol. 3890: S.G. Thompson, R. Ghanea-Hercock (Eds.), Defence Applications of Multi-Agent Systems. XII, 141 pages. 2006. (Sublibrary LNAI).

Vol. 3889: J. Rosca, D. Erdogmus, J.C. Príncipe, S. Haykin (Eds.), Independent Component Analysis and Blind Signal Separation. XXI, 980 pages. 2006.

Vol. 3888: D. Draheim, G. Weber (Eds.), Trends in Enterprise Application Architecture. IX, 145 pages. 2006.

Vol. 3887: J.R. Correa, A. Hevia, M. Kiwi (Eds.), LATIN 2006: Theoretical Informatics. XVI, 814 pages. 2006.

Vol. 3886: E.G. Bremer, J. Hakenberg, E.-H.(S.) Han, D. Berrar, W. Dubitzky (Eds.), Knowledge Discovery in Life Science Literature. XIV, 147 pages. 2006. (Sublibrary LNBI).

Vol. 3885: V. Torra, Y. Narukawa, A. Valls, J. Domingo-Ferrer (Eds.), Modeling Decisions for Artificial Intelligence. XII, 374 pages. 2006. (Sublibrary LNAI).

Vol. 3884: B. Durand, W. Thomas (Eds.), STACS 2006. XIV, 714 pages. 2006.

Vol. 3882: M.L. Lee, K.-L. Tan, V. Wuwongse (Eds.), Database Systems for Advanced Applications. XIX, 923 pages. 2006.

Vol. 3881: S. Gibet, N. Courty, J.-F. Kamp (Eds.), Gesture in Human-Computer Interaction and Simulation. XIII, 344 pages. 2006. (Sublibrary LNAI).

Vol. 3880: A. Rashid, M. Aksit (Eds.), Transactions on Aspect-Oriented Software Development I. IX, 335 pages. 2006.

Vol. 3879: T. Erlebach, G. Persinao (Eds.), Approximation and Online Algorithms. X, 349 pages. 2006.

Vol. 3878: A. Gelbukh (Ed.), Computational Linguistics and Intelligent Text Processing. XVII, 589 pages. 2006.

Vol. 3877: M. Detyniecki, J.M. Jose, A. Nürnberger, C. J. '. van Rijsbergen (Eds.), Adaptive Multimedia Retrieval: User, Context, and Feedback. XI, 279 pages. 2006.

Vol. 3876: S. Halevi, T. Rabin (Eds.), Theory of Cryptography. XI, 617 pages. 2006.

Vol. 3875: S. Ur, E. Bin, Y. Wolfsthal (Eds.), Hardware and Software, Verification and Testing. X, 265 pages. 2006.

Vol. 3874: R. Missaoui, J. Schmidt (Eds.), Formal Concept Analysis. X, 309 pages. 2006. (Sublibrary LNAI).

Vol. 3873: L. Maicher, J. Park (Eds.), Charting the Topic Maps Research and Applications Landscape. VIII, 281 pages. 2006. (Sublibrary LNAI).

Vol. 3872: H. Bunke, A. L. Spitz (Eds.), Document Analysis Systems VII. XIII, 630 pages. 2006.

Vol. 3871: E.-G. Talbi, P. Liardet, P. Collet, E. Lutton, M. Schoenauer (Eds.), Artificial Evolution. XI, 310 pages. 2006.

Vol. 3870: S. Spaccapietra, P. Atzeni, W.W. Chu, T. Catarci, K.P. Sycara (Eds.), Journal on Data Semantics V. XIII, 237 pages. 2006.

Vol. 3869: S. Renals, S. Bengio (Eds.), Machine Learning for Multimodal Interaction. XIII, 490 pages. 2006.

Vol. 3868: K. Römer, H. Karl, F. Mattern (Eds.), Wireless Sensor Networks. XI, 342 pages. 2006.

Vol. 3866: T. Dimitrakos, F. Martinelli, P.Y.A. Ryan, S. Schneider (Eds.), Formal Aspects in Security and Trust. X, 259 pages. 2006.

Vol. 3865: W. Shen, K.-M. Chao, Z. Lin, J.-P.A. Barthès, A. James (Eds.), Computer Supported Cooperative Work in Design II. XII, 659 pages. 2006.

Vol. 3863: M. Kohlhase (Ed.), Mathematical Knowledge Management. XI, 405 pages. 2006. (Sublibrary LNAI).

Vol. 3862: R.H. Bordini, M. Dastani, J. Dix, A.E.F. Seghrouchni (Eds.), Programming Multi-Agent Systems. XIV, 267 pages. 2006. (Sublibrary LNAI).

Vol. 3861: J. Dix, S.J. Hegner (Eds.), Foundations of Information and Knowledge Systems. X, 331 pages. 2006.

Vol. 3860: D. Pointcheval (Ed.), Topics in Cryptology – CT-RSA 2006. XI, 365 pages. 2006.

Vol. 3858: A. Valdes, D. Zamboni (Eds.), Recent Advances in Intrusion Detection. X, 351 pages. 2006.

Vol. 3857: M.P.C. Fossorier, H. Imai, S. Lin, A. Poli (Eds.), Applied Algebra, Algebraic Algorithms and Error-Correcting Codes. XI, 350 pages. 2006.

Vol. 3855: E. A. Emerson, K.S. Namjoshi (Eds.), Verification, Model Checking, and Abstract Interpretation. XI, 443 pages. 2005.

Vol. 3854: I. Stavrakakis, M. Smirnov (Eds.), Autonomic Communication. XIII, 303 pages. 2006.

Vol. 3853: A.J. Ijspeert, T. Masuzawa, S. Kusumoto (Eds.), Biologically Inspired Approaches to Advanced Information Technology. XIV, 388 pages. 2006.